Handbook of Applied Econometrics

D1379634

Blackwell Handbooks in Economics

Handbook of International Macroeconomics
Edited by Frederick van der Ploeg

Handbook of Environmental Economics
Edited by Daniel W. Bromley

Handbook of the Economics of Innovation and Technological Change
Edited by Paul Stoneman

Handbook of Applied Econometrics: Macroeconomics
Edited by M. Hashem Pesaran and M.R. Wickens

Handbook of Applied Econometrics

Volume I: Macroeconomics

Edited by
M. Hashem Pesaran and Michael R. Wickens

BLACKWELL
Publishers

Copyright © Blackwell Publishers Ltd, 1995, 1999

First published 1995
Reprinted 1998
First published in paperback 1999

Blackwell Publishers Ltd
108 Cowley Road
Oxford OX4 1JF
UK

Blackwell Publishers Inc.
350 Main Street
Malden, Massachusetts 02148
USA

British Library Cataloguing in Publication Data

A CIP catalogue record for this book is available from the British Library.

Library of Congress Cataloging-in-Publication Data

Handbook of applied econometrics: macroeconomics
    v. cm.
    Includes bibliographical references and index.
    Contents: edited by M. Hashem Pesaran and M. R. Wickens.
    ISBN 1–55786–208–7 (v. 1) — 0–631–21558–1 (pbk)
    1. Econometrics. I. Pesaran, M. Hashem, 1946– . II. Wickens, M. R.
HB 139.H35 1995   94–47425
330'.01'5195–dc20   CIP

Typeset in 10 on 12pt Times by Pure Tech Corporation, Pondicherry, India
Printed and bound in Great Britain by MPG Books Ltd, Bodmin, Cornwall

This book is printed on acid-free paper

Contents

Figures

Tables

Contributors

Michael Binder	University of Maryland
Tim Bollerslev	Northwestern University, Evanston, IL
Fabio Canova	Universitat Pompeu Fabra, Barcelona
Robert J. Hodrick	Northwestern University, Evanston, IL
K. Kim	Victoria University of Wellington, Wellington
Guy Laroque	INSEE, Paris
Ralph Lattimore	Department of Industry, Canberra
Agustín Maravall	European University Institute,
M. Hashem Pesaran	University of Cambridge
John Muellbauer	Nuffield College, Oxford
A. R. Pagan	Australian National University, Canberra
Bernard Salanié	ENSAE, Paris
Kenneth F. Wallis	University of Warwick, Coventry
Kenneth D. West	University of Wisconsin, Madison
Mike Wickens	University of York, York

Preface

This volume launches a series of handbooks which aims to survey the latest developments in the various areas of applied econometrics, both at micro and macro levels. In preparing this volume we have benefitted greatly from the help and advice of the members of the Advisory Committee of the series, Jerry Hausman, Edward Leamer, Adrian Pagan, Richard Quandt and Lawrence Summers.

In addition, we would like to thank Frank Diebold, Clive Granger, Jim Hamilton, Brian Henry, Kevin Lee, Helmut Lutkepohl, Hassan Molana, Peter Schmidt, Ron Smith and Ken West for helpful comments on draft chapters.

Finally, we would like to acknowledge the full support of Blackwell in this venture. We are also grateful for expert secretarial help from Gill Smith at all stages of the preparation of this volume.

BK Title → N/A

Introduction

M. Hashem Pesaran and M. R. Wickens

This is the first volume in what is planned to be a regular series of handbooks surveying the latest developments in applied econometrics. This volume covers topics related to macroeconomics and finance, and a companion volume will cover topics in the field of microeconometrics.[1] The emphasis of the series will be on rigorous applications of econometric and statistical methods to economic problems, and the methodological issues that arise from such applications, not on contributions of econometric and statistical theory. The impetus for this series comes from our perception that there is a body of knowledge about the problems of undertaking empirical work in the field of economics, and in general this knowledge is common to more than one application area. As a result, especially in this volume, the concern will not be with specific applications, although this distinction is bound to become blurred because each application area has a tendency to generate its own methodological problems.

There is, of course, no agreement over the appropriate methodology to use in applied work, and this is particularly applicable to empirical research in macroeconomics. There are currently five major approaches to macroeconometric modeling: the traditional Cowles Commission structural equations approach, unrestricted and Bayesian VARs, "structural" VARs, linear rational expectations models, and the calibration approach associated with real business cycle theories. In all these approaches, the main area of disagreement is over the relative roles of economics and statistics: should one aim to estimate a model derived from formal economic theory, or is it sufficient to find a model that accords well with the data? (On this, see also Pesaran and Smith, 1995) Compared with the natural sciences, where applied work has a profound influence in setting the theoretical agenda by uncovering empirical puzzles that require new theoretical tools to deal with them, in economics, notwithstanding data problems, applied research does not receive the attention that it deserves. The lack of a widely accepted methodological framework for applied economics is a major reason for this. In this handbook series we aim to provide a timely corrective by examining the many problems associated with bringing empirical evidence to bear in economics.

In this volume various methodological issues, more or less peculiar to applied macroeconometrics, are discussed, either explicitly or implicitly: the source of the stochastic structure of economic models, and especially the role of expectations; the stochastic properties of economic data and the implications for modeling, estimation, and testing; the role of economic theory in model building and the relation between statistical models and economic theory; equilibrium and disequilibrium models; the best way to bring evidence to bear; classical statistical methods or calibration, and the connection between the two; and forecasting with large models. It is planned that future volumes will add to this list of topics.

In applied econometrics there is a continual tension between the requirements of economic theory and the need to take account of the properties of the data. A theory that predicts a relation between variables with very different time series properties will often result in econometric models that have poor empirical properties: trying to explain a nonstationary series with a stationary series, or a seasonally adjusted series by a seasonally unadjusted series, are two examples. An understanding of the properties of the time series observations is therefore essential at the outset. In chapter 1 Agustín Maravall discusses the characteristics of economic time series from the perspective of unobserved component models. A study of unobserved component models can be justified in its own right as they have been used widely in macroeconomics. Two notable examples are the permanent income hypothesis and real business cycle theory. They are also used in short-term policy analysis, and trend and seasonal analysis. The chapter begins with a discussion of linear filters, and points out some of the dangers of the application of *ad hoc* filters to economic time series data. For example, using filters like the Hodrick-Prescott filter for trend removal or the X11 filters for seasonal adjustments may result in a process with very different characteristics from those that are wanted or even anticipated. To make matters worse, the filtered values may change as new observations are added to the data set. An alternative approach is to base seasonal adjustment or detrending of economic time series on parametric models such as the ARIMA model. This does not solve the problem entirely, however, as there is no agreement on the best way to model the components. The ensuing discussion on alternative ways of modeling the trend, seasonal, cyclical, and irregular components illustrates this. The chapter then turns to a discussion of the identification of one component from another, showing how additional restrictions can resolve the problem and using US GNP to provide an empirical example. This example helps to explain the common finding that within the class of linear models, a simple model is usually found to be adequate for US GNP.[2]

Having specified the components model, the next step is to estimate it. There follows a discussion of the determination of the optimal estimator and its implications for econometric analysis. These include the dangers of using detrended or deseasonalized data in econometric models, and using finite VAR models when the filter is invertible. The chapter concludes by warning against the use of seasonally adjusted series in econometric modeling and advances the view also emphasized by others, notably by Ken Wallis, that seasonality needs to be modeled explicitly in empirical analysis.

The VAR model was initially introduced into econometrics as a response to the difficulties surrounding the identification of the structural models favored by the Cowles Commission approach. The unrestricted VAR model and its various restricted derivative models are now among the most widely used time series models in macroeconometrics. As a result of introducing restrictions into the VAR, the distinction between structural models and time series models has become blurred. More recently, the cointegrated VAR (or VECM) has been used intensively in the analysis of nonstationary time series instead of structural systems. In chapter 2 Fabio Canova provides a comprehensive review of these developments. The chapter is therefore a complement to the univariate analysis presented in chapter 1. Canova starts by discussing various specification and estimation issues such as the ability of the VAR to represent a more general multivariate time series model and the related problem of how to choose the lag length. He also considers Bayesian specifications of the VAR (the BVAR) and its connection with the Kalman filter. Next he discusses how the VAR has been constrained to reflect the restrictions of economic theory. This method is widely used in the estimation and testing of real business cycle models (see chapter 7).

VAR analysis is commonly used as an atheoretical way of estimating the dynamic impact of economic shocks. Unfortunately, as with the structural systems approach it originally sought to replace, VARs suffer from a largely intractable identification problem that requires the use of, often arbitrary, restrictions. Canova examines various ways of achieving identification for stationary and nonstationary data. These include orthogonalization and alternative ways of bringing structural information to bear by exploiting short-run and long-run restrictions. He discusses the importance of this problem for testing exogeneity and causality, and for the variance decomposition of shocks. Another use of VAR analysis is for forecasting, both unconditional forecasting, which is the standard approach and is uncontroversial, and conditional forecasting, which is more problematical as it requires structural restrictions, and is subject to the Lucas critique. Of course, as Canova points out, once *a priori* information is used to identify a VAR, the distinction between the VAR modeling strategy and the standard simultaneous equation approach becomes a matter of degree, not of content. The issue then centers on the choice of *a priori* restrictions to be imposed on the VAR, and the extent to which they can be viewed as credible. Canova also discusses various recent methodological criticism of VAR analysis: the problems with using detrended, seasonally adjusted, or aggregated data; the fragility of VAR models for causality analysis; the effects of using a VAR of too low dimension; and the problems of using a VAR for policy analysis and the related implications of rational expectations and changes of policy regime. Finally, he provides an empirical application to illustrate many of his arguments, by estimating a trivariate VAR for the GNPs of the USA, Japan, and Germany.

There is a long history in econometrics of the modeling of expectations. In early work the expectations formation processes used in macroeconomic analysis tended to be *ad hoc*. Partly for estimation convenience, schemes such as static and adaptive expectations were widely adopted, even though they usually had the disadvantage of implying that economic agents made systematic mistakes. Although rational expectations is a very strong assumption, it has the merit of endogenizing expectations in a model-consistent manner, thereby putting expectations formation on the same footing as the rest of the model. For example, in a dynamic intertemporal optimizing framework, where the optimand contains lagged decision variables, the first-order conditions (or the Euler equations) will involve expectational variables that satisfy the requirement of the rational expectations hypothesis. These can be solved for, and the rational expectations variables solved out of the model, or the Euler equations can be estimated directly together with the constraints. Either way the rationally expected variables will be a function of the structural parameters – as well as the other variables in the model – and so efficient estimation of the structural parameters will require the use of this information. It will therefore be necessary to use nonlinear estimation methods. Whichever approach to estimation is chosen, the rational expectations solution will be needed either explicitly, or implicitly in the estimation process.

In chapter 3 Michael Binder and Hashem Pesaran survey existing rational expectations solution methods and suggest a new, more general yet straightforward procedure capable of handling both current and future expectations variables which is also applicable in a multivariate context. The proposed method decomposes the solution into a backward and a forward component and uses a martingale difference technique to solve the forward component. The proposed solution method provides a complete characterization of all the possible classes of solutions (namely the unique stable solution, multiple stable solutions, and the case where no stable solution exists), and allows the incorporation of many forms of nonstationarity and non-linearity of the model's forcing variables. It also produces a convenient VAR framework for the purposes of full information estimation and the analysis of the cointegration properties of multivariate linear rational expectations models. Two applications of the proposed method are given. One is for the small, standard real business cycle model of Christiano and Eichenbaum (1992) in which a comparison is made with other methods. Estimates of the model based on Christiano and Eichenbaum's data are presented. The other is an application to a broad class of dynamic optimization models of consumers' and/or firms' behavior in which complete characterization of the solution is analyzed. This model is not estimated. The chapter concludes with a brief review of three other important recent developments in the rational expectations literature not covered in this volume, namely learning, heterogeneous information and multivariate nonlinear rational expectations models.

Another important strand in the rational expectations literature is how to estimate Euler equations. In chapter 4 Kenneth West discusses this problem in the context of econometric models of inventory behavior, but the results have general applicability. He considers the linear quadratic model first used to analyze inventories by Holt et al. (1960). This model has also been widely applied to other problems (see also the multivariate adjustment cost example in chapter 3). Expected discounted net revenues are maximized subject to a quadratic cost function that depends on the level of output, its rate of change, the excess of inventories over sales and two stochastic terms which are proportional to the levels of output and inventories. This specification has the advantage of producing a first-order (Euler) condition with an intrinsic linear stochastic term. There is, therefore, no need to add a stochastic term to the Euler equation to produce an estimating equation as this is already included in the underlying optimization problem. As in most other studies of this type, the value of the discount rate is imposed *a priori* and not estimated.

Two approaches to the estimation are considered: a limited information approach, which avoids making any assumptions about the demand function; and a full information approach in which a demand function is specified and the estimating equation is the solution for the firm's equilibrium decision rule. The limited information estimation considers the choice of instruments, the estimation of the covariance matrix, and the implications of the presence of unit roots in the process of the forcing variables. The main complication here is that the disturbance term is a composite of current and expected future innovations, which presents problems both for finding (or constructing) instruments that are asymptotically uncorrelated with the disturbance term and suitably correlated with the regressors, and for the estimation of the covariance matrix. It is concluded that the usual tradeoff between full and limited information estimation methods is relevant here, namely, gains in efficiency versus computational complexity.

The chapter ends with a discussion of some existing empirical evidence, and, in particular, the common finding that inventories are procyclical and highly serially correlated. West observes that this is consistent with the cost function either being negatively related to the level of output, or having a large accelerator effect. He finds that existing evidence does not resolve the issue and that perhaps microeconomic evidence may be of help.

There are probably more econometric studies of the aggregate consumption function than of any other macroeconomic relation. This is because the consumption function is one of the main building blocks of the Keynesian model which is still the basis of most macroeconometric models. Despite this attention, there is still no settled view of how aggregate consumption should be modeled. The consumption function is an excellent example of the tendency, noted above, for applied econometrics to make more use of formal economic theory in constructing models. In the case of the consumption function, life-cycle theory has become the dominant theoretical framework. As with inventories, this has meant a concern for intertemporal optimization, the use of rational expectations, and a debate about whether it is better to estimate the associated Euler equation than the traditional (solved) consumption function. In chapter 5, John Muellbauer and Ralph Lattimore take a wide-ranging and critical look at the construction of consumption functions based on life-cycle theory.

They begin by deriving the standard two-period optimization model, and then extend this to many periods. Age and family effects, which are important for aggregation, are also considered. Using this framework, they then turn to a discussion of the stochastic structure of consumption and income and their interconnection – issues that have occupied much of the recent consumption function literature and draw heavily on the theory of nonstationary stochastic processes. Muellbauer and Lattimore provide a detailed analysis of the "excess sensitivity" and "excess smoothness" debate – i.e. why consumption appears to overrespond to anticipated changes in income, yet the variance of the growth in consumption is low relative to that of income – which further advances our understanding of the problems involved.

Muellbauer and Lattimore then turn to a discussion of the potential importance of income volatility and skewness for consumption and savings, how this might affect the appropriate rate of discount, and the implications for solving consumption from the Euler equation. Another finding not consistent with standard life-cycle theory is that changes in consumption are partly forecastable. Various explanations are suggested. One is that credit constraints induce an error-correction-type structure. Other explanations discussed are interactions between leisure and consumption, the presence of durable goods, the failure of the assumption of rationality, and aggregation. Finally, the practical implications of their previous arguments are drawn together and used to suggest how one might formulate econometric models of consumption. The authors take account of nonlinearities in functional form, a variable interest rate, credit constraints, and the effect of financial liberalization. They then comment on recent empirical work that embraces some of these features. This substantial chapter is completed with a discussion of data issues, including the measurement problems both in household surveys and in aggregate time series data.

Under the influence of the rational expectations hypothesis and the Lucas critique, large-scale macroeconometric modeling has undergone significant transformations, but still remains an important tool in economic forecasting and macroeconomic policy analysis. In chapter 6 Kenneth Wallis, drawing from his practical experiences at the Macroeconomic Modelling Bureau at the University of Warwick, provides a comprehensive account of the current state of the art of large-scale macroeconometric modeling. The chapter begins with a brief survey of some of the more important recent developments in the structures of macroeconomic models, especially those constructed for the US and UK economies. However, the main focus of the chapter is on various technical issues and the available methods of dealing with them. Three areas are considered: the evaluation of forecasts, the use of forecasts to evaluate models, and the use of stochastic simulation methods in the analysis of large-scale models incorporating rational expectations.

The discussion relating to forecasting considers the testing of forecast unbiasedness and efficiency, the combining of forecasts from different models or methods, the sources of forecast error, and the use of residual adjustments. The section on stochastic simulation provides a detailed description of the issues involved, including a discussion of the experimental design, the treatment of nonlinearities, and the usefulness of deriving variance measures. The examination of rational expectations in macroeconometric models focuses on model consistent solutions and comments on some of the implications for optimal control experiments. The implementation of rational expectations in large *nonlinear* macroeconometric models is still in its infancy. It raises a number of new issues for modelers, such as the time horizon, the information set assumed, and the treatment of nonlinearities. The chapter ends with a discussion of some of these questions.

Calibrated macroeconomic models have emerged in recent years as a major challenge to both the conventional system equation macroeconometric and VAR modeling approaches. Initially, under the influence of the pioneering work of Kydland and Prescott (1982), the primary emphasis of this approach was on "quantitative theory," where theory was the focus of the analysis, often at the expense of measurement. However, over the past decade important attempts have been made to place this approach in the context of traditional macroeconometric analysis, and chapter 7 by K. Kim and Adrian Pagan provides a systematic treatment which will go a long way towards defining the issues to be resolved and to answering many of the questions that have already arisen. Unlike previous commentators, Kim and Pagan highlight the similarities as well as the differences between the Cowles Commission system equation approach and the calibration method. They propose adopting the following five criteria that are familiar in traditional econometrics: specification, estimation, goodness of fit, quality, and usage of models. They argue that calibration is best thought of as an alternative research style which can be distinguished by its approach to four specification issues: whether the model possesses a steady state, the information available to agents, the dynamic specification, and the nature of the exogenous (forcing) variables. Calibrated models are often constructed from an intertemporal optimization and, as a result, have dynamics that are intrinsic, for example arising from the stock – flow relations implicit in the budget constraints. But they can also usually be represented as a VAR whose coefficients are a function of the deep structural parameters of the original optimization problem, and whose variables may be unobservable. Throughout their analysis Kim and Pagan heavily exploit this connection between the two approaches.

Next they discuss how models are calibrated, and compare estimation procedures based on matching unconditional moments with the more formal statistical procedures such as the generalized method of moments (GMM) and the maximum likelihood estimation methods that exploit conditional moment properties. A large part of the chapter is devoted to a discussion of assessing how well a calibrated model performs. Various criteria are considered such as replicating stylized facts of the time series properties of key variables (especially business cycle features), parameter restrictions, impulse response functions, and univariate representations of key variables. They note that errors in variables and the use of filtered data in the analysis of calibrated models can add considerably to the difficulties of their assessment. The chapter ends with a discussion of the sensitivity of calibrated models to parameter variation.

Modeling disequilibrium or the phenomenon of nonmarket clearing, with agents being constrained on one side of the market, provides a number of new conceptual problems for applied econometricians, as well as a different setting for many of the standard concerns. Guy Laroque and Bernard Salanié provide a review of the main issues in chapter 8. Their discussion is confined to market economies; the literature on planned economies is not covered.

They begin with a discussion of the most commonly studied case of static markets with fixed prices, without spillover effects, but with possible problems of aggregation across markets. These models have usually been estimated by maximum likelihood methods (either limited, full or pseudo maximum likelihood) but, as Laroque and Salanié note, simulation-based methods have recently been tried with some success. These are often less efficient but have the advantage of being more flexible, especially where closed-form solutions are either difficult or impossible to obtain. Apart from estimation, they touch on several specification issues, such as whether the regime (i.e. whether the market is demand or supply constrained) is known or unknown and requires estimation, the use of surveys to help resolve this, the functional form of the errors, and the relation between quantity and the demand and supply functions. They then review the empirical literature for these models.

Early work on disequilibrium models was often criticized for treating prices as given, and for ignoring the effect of price expectations and other dynamics. Laroque and Salanié next turn to a discussion of recent work on these problems. They comment favorably on the usefulness and good performance of simulation methods in the estimation of dynamic disequilibrium models. They close the chapter with a number of observations on areas where future work might successfully be directed. One of these is to take account of the econometric and specification problems that arise from the use of nonstationary data. At present there is virtually no work on this topic. They also remark on the need to model expectations, and taking better account of the role of inventories and buffer stocks.

Financial econometrics is another excellent example of how applied econometrics has led to new methodological developments in economics and econometrics. The different nature of much of financial data (they typically display different higher-order moments than conventional economic data and they are often nonstationary), the need for measures of new concepts (for example, volatility, present values, bubbles), for new estimators, and for new tests, and the puzzles thrown up by the empirical results, have all contributed to this. These considerations are very much in evidence in chapter 9 in which Tim Bollerslev and Robert Hodrick consider the problem of testing the efficiency of financial markets. They adopt a different approach to the other chapters. Instead of surveying the large number of published studies that exist, they have undertaken a systematic empirical analysis of the ability of different models to explain the distribution and, in particular, the temporal dependence of monthly data on the NYSE value-weighted price index. This is used as a vehicle to illustrate many of the alternative econometric tests and estimation procedures that are available for testing market efficiency. Their general conclusion is that a rational explanation of the behavior of stock returns requires an understanding of the link between conditional volatility of market fundamentals and the variability of expected returns.

The value of a test of market efficiency will depend on how good an explanation of the behavior of asset returns is provided by the underlying model. In common with most high-frequency financial data, the returns on the NYSE price index are characterized by periods of tranquility followed by periods of turbulence. Bollerslev and Hodrick provide a set of descriptive statistics for the stock index and then examine how well simulations of various models are capable of replicating these characteristics. These models are all based on alternative versions of the present value model of the relation between a stock price and expected future dividends, with real dividends being forecast either by an autoregressive or by a GARCH model. The basic model assumes a constant discount rate and no GARCH effects. Two variations on this are provided by adding a stochastic process to the fundamentals. One is the fads model in which the process added is stationary and serially correlated. The other is the (collapsing) bubbles model in which the process is nonstationary. Models with GARCH effects in the dividend process, and some specific formulations of time-varying discount rate, are also considered by Bollerslev and Hodrick. They find that over the period January 1928 through December 1987 actual monthly returns have strong dependence due to highly significant conditional heteroskedasticity, rather than serial correlation, which is mild. The returns also have significant positive skewness and pronounced leptokurtosis due to the heteroskedasticity in the dividend process. Using simulations of the various models, only the GARCH and time-varying discount rate models come close to replicating the behavior of actual returns, especially the volatility clustering.

The chapter then turns to long-run evidence on stock market predictability. The first question addressed is the predictability of future returns from current returns over alternative horizons ranging from 1 to 48 months for each of the various models. It is found that the results are sensitive to the forecast horizon, but not in any systematic way, suggesting that there may be small-sample problems with the distributions of the test statistics. After investigating different ways of estimating the models, and correcting the test statistics, the general conclusion to emerge is that past returns are not statistically significant in predicting future returns. This conclusion is reached using information on lagged prices and dividends, and may be contrasted with that of other studies, for example by Breen, Glosten, and Jagannathan (1990), Campbell, (1987), Fama and French (1989), Sentana and Wadhwani (1991), Granger (1992), and Pesaran and Timmermann (1994, 1995) which find much stronger statistical evidence of the predictability of excess returns (over short as well as long horizons) when other information such as lagged interest rates, output growth, or inflation are also included in the analysis.

Unlike studies based on annual data, a cointegration analysis of real stock prices and real dividends on these monthly data do not reject the cointegrating vector $(1, -1)$, but do reject the presence of a bubble. The study ends by performing a volatility test. The particular test chosen is a variant of that by Mankiw, Romer, and Shapiro (1991) which is based on a comparison of the actual and the *ex post* rational stock price, the latter being constructed by discounting actual dividends for a finite horizon. For all of the models, except the model with a time-varying discount rate, the *p*-values are small, indicating rejection of the standard asset pricing model. It is inferred from this – and this is supported by further tests – that the time-varying discount rate model contains information, such as the current level of dividends, time variation in the conditional variance of dividends, and a variable discount rate, that is relevant to portfolio decisions.

Clearly, no single volume could do justice to the wide variety of topics that are currently of interest in applied macroeconometrics. Important areas of research not covered in this volume include recent developments in growth theory, international trade and finance, and nonlinear dynamic modeling. Nevertheless, the included chapters provide a rich selection of the techniques that are currently in use in macroeconometrics.

Notes

1 Volume II of the handbook is edited by Pesaran and Schmidt and includes chapters on consumer demand (Lewbel), labor supply (Blundell), search and dynamic event history models (Neumann), inequality and welfare (Maasoumi), household firm models (Pitt), analysis of business surveys (Zimmermann), measurement of productivity (Berndt and Fuss), frontier production functions (Greene), and models of count data (Wooldridge).
2 This is not, however, necessarily the case once the linearity assumption is relaxed. See, for example, Potter (1995) and Pesaran and Potter (1994).

References

Breen, W., L. R. Glosten and R. Jagannathan (1990), Predictable Variations in Stock Index Returns, *Journal of Finance*, 44, pp. 117–89.

Campbell, J. Y. (1987), Stock Returns and the Term Structure, *Journal of Financial Economics*, 18, pp. 373–99.

Christiano, L. J. and M. S. Eichenbaum (1992), Current Real-Business-Cycle Theories and Aggregate Labor-Market Fluctuations, *American Economic Review*, 82, pp. 430–50.

Fama, E. F. and K. R. French (1989), Business Conditions and Expected Returns on Stocks and Performance, *Journal of Business and Economic Statistics*, 10, pp. 461–5.

Granger, C. W. J. (1992), Forecasting Stock Market Prices: Lessons for Forecasters, *International Journal of Forecasting*, 8, pp. 3–13.

Holt, Charles C., Franco Modigliani, John F. Muth and Herbert A. Simon (1960), *Planning Production, Inventories and Work Force*, Englewood Cliffs, NJ, Prentice-Hall.

Kydland, F. and E. C. Prescott (1982), Time to Build and Aggregate Fluctuations, *Econometrica*, 50, 1345–70.

Mankiw, N. G., D. Romer and M. D. Shapiro (1991), Stock Market Forecastability and Volatility: A Statistical Appraisal, *Review of Economic Studies*, 58, pp. 455–77.

Pesaran, M. H. and Simon M. Potter (1994), A Floor and Ceiling Model of UK Output, DAE Working Paper no. 9407, Department of Applied Economics, University of Cambridge.

Pesaran, M. H. and R. Smith (1995), The Role of Theory in Econometrics, *Journal of Econometrics*, 67, pp. 61–79.

Pesaran, M. H. and A. Timmermann (1994), Forecasting Stock Returns: An Examination of Stock Market Trading in the Presence of Transaction Costs, *Journal of Forecasting*, 13, pp. 335–67.

Pesaran, M. H. and A. Timmermann (1995), Predictability of Stock Returns: Robustness and Economic Significance, *Journal of Finance* (forthcoming).

Potter, Simon M. (1995), A Non-Linear Approach to US GNP, *Journal of Applied Econometrics*, 10, pp. 109–25.

Sentana, E. and S. B. Wadhwani (1991), Semi-Parametric Estimation and the Predictability of Stock Market Returns, Some Lessons from Japan, *Review of Economic Studies*, 58, pp. 547–64.

1

Unobserved Components in Economic Time Series

Agustín Maravall

C₂₂

1 Introduction

The chapter addresses the situation in which an economic variable, for which a time series of observations is available, can be seen as the combination of several components. Having only observations on the aggregate variable, the analyst wishes to learn about the unobserved components and, in particular, about the joint distribution of their estimators and forecasts.

Unobserved components in time series have been of interest to economists for some time, and a good review of the early developments and applications is contained in Nerlove, Grether, and Carvalho (1979). Although the treatment and modeling of unobserved components (be that in the context of business cycle analysis or of seasonal adjustment, to quote two important applications) lack an economic theory foundation (see Ghysels, 1990), they are nevertheless used extensively by economists and statisticians when dealing with economic time series. The interest has developed along two separate (although related) fronts. First, unobserved component models are used in economic research in a variety of problems when a variable, supposed to play some relevant economic role, is not directly observable. For example, unobserved components have been used in modeling agents' reaction to (permanent or transitory) changes in the price level (Lucas, 1976), in analyzing the stability of some of the macroeconomic "big ratios" (Pagan, 1975), in relation to the "natural" level of the labor supply (Bull and Frydman, 1983), in modeling technical progress (Slade, 1989; Harvey and Marshall, 1991), in modeling credibility of the monetary authority (Weber, 1992), in measuring the persistence (or long-term effects) of economic shocks (Cochrane, 1988), or in estimating the underground economy (Aigner, Schneider, and Ghosh, 1988).

Where, unquestionably, unobserved components have been most widely employed in economic research is in the area of macroeconomics. An important example is in the context of the permanent income hypothesis, where permanent and transitory components play a central role (some references are Muth, 1960; Fama and French, 1988; Stock and Watson, 1988; Christiano and Eichenbaum, 1989; Quah, 1990). More generally, unobserved components are heavily used in the business cycle literature, in the detection and analysis of the business cycle both at the methodological and applied levels (see, for example, Sargent and Sims, 1977; Beveridge and Nelson, 1981; Nelson and Plosser, 1982; Kydland and Prescott, 1982; Harvey, 1985; Prescott, 1986; Watson, 1986; Clark, 1987; Crafts, Leybourne, and Mills, 1989; Stock and Watson, 1988; 1991).

Most often, in the applications we have mentioned, a series is expressed as the sum of two components, such as a permanent and a transitory (or temporary) component, or as a trend and a cycle component. Typically, one of the components attempts to capture the trend-type nonstationarity of the series, while the other is a stationary component. Often, moreover, the series to be decomposed has been previously seasonally adjusted, and hence a third component containing the seasonal variation is also implicit in the decomposition.

But, besides their use in applied econometric research, unobserved components play an important role in short-term economic policy-making and monitoring of the economy. Typically, short-term policy and evaluation are based on the seasonally adjusted series. (Often, seasonal adjustment simply aims at providing a better picture of the underlying evolution of the series of interest. On occasion, it plays a direct role in the design of economic policy. An example is found in short-term monetary policy, where the money supply is set up so as to accommodate seasonal fluctuations in the demand for money, in order to avoid seasonal fluctuations in interest rates; see Pierce, 1983.) It is indeed the case that, for many important macroeconomic series, seasonal movements dominate the short-term evolution of the series. When the seasonally adjusted series displays undesirable erraticity, some further smoothing may be performed, attempting to capture the trend component. In fact, the standard decomposition of macroeconomic variables, as used in applied institutions or agencies, can be seen as decomposing the series into a nonstationary trend, a nonstationary seasonal, and a stationary irregular component (see, for example, Moore et al., 1981). This practical need for unobserved components estimation has also generated a large amount of research, most of it developed in the statistics field (see, for example, Zellner, 1978; 1983; and the references in Den Butter and Fase, 1991).

Unobserved components used in these two fields of applications (applied econometric research and statistical practical applications) often share the same basic structure. This chapter deals with unobserved component models displaying that type of structure. First, linear filters are introduced and *ad hoc* fixed filters are briefly discussed. Attention is focused on the Hodrick-Prescott filter to detrend a series, and on the X11 filter to seasonally adjust a series. Some dangers of *ad hoc* filtering are illustrated, in particular the risk of spurious results and the effects of over- and underestimation of a component. Some limitations are also pointed out, such as its incapacity to provide estimation standard errors and forecasts (with their associated standard errors). This is discussed in sections 2 and 3.

Section 4 presents the general set-up for a model-based approach common to the vast majority of unobserved component model applications. The basic feature is that the components follow linear stochastic processes. Section 5 reviews and compares some of the most frequent specifications for the most common components (such as the trend, cyclical, seasonal, transitory, or irregular components). For a given series, the lack of a unique decomposition reflects a general underidentification problem inherent in unobserved component models. This problem is addressed in section 6; the most relevant solutions are discussed and the implied decompositions compared. Section 7 illustrates the presentation with an example, the quarterly series of US GNP, which has been the center of attention in business cycle research. One "philosophical" point should perhaps be stressed: my discussion is not based on the prior belief that there is a unique (though unknown) data generating process for, say, the trend or the seasonal component, and that the analysis will attempt to reveal its true nature. An unobserved component is rather viewed as a (statistical) tool that we devise in order to provide sensible answers to questions of applied interest.

Estimation of the components is considered in section 8. The optimal estimator is the conditional expectation of the component given the observed series. Since it is well suited for analytical discussion, the Wiener-Kolmogorov representation of that conditional expectation is considered. First, we present the case of an infinite realization of the series and look at the component estimation filter; for most applied cases, it will be close to the one that yields the estimator of the component for the central years of the series (the historical estimator), independently of whether it has been obtained with the Wiener-Kolmogorov or with the Kalman filter.

Section 9 analyzes the properties of the estimator. It is seen to be generated by a linear stochastic process, structurally different from the process assumed to generate the component. This difference is analyzed in terms of the direction of the bias, the auto- and crosscorrelation structure, and the corresponding spectra. An application to diagnostic checking of the model, and some estimation extensions, are also considered. Two important implications for applied econometric research are discussed at the end of the section. One concerns the use of seasonally adjusted series (also of other components such as the trend or the detrended series) in econometric testing and model building, as well as in some commonly used unobserved component models. The second concerns the procedure of looking for business cycles in a detrended series which has been seasonally adjusted.

Estimation and forecasting of unobserved components for a finite sample, as well as preliminary estimators, are considered in section 10. Analytical expressions are derived and the structure of the preliminary estimator and associated revisions are discussed. Some illustrations are provided in the field of applied econometrics and in the field of statistical practical applications.

Section 11 deals with estimation errors. The models generating the errors in the historical and preliminary estimators are presented. Since the errors depend on the model specification, some relevant implications concerning identification of the unobserved component model are derived. Finally, the use of an unobserved component model in inference is illustrated with the monthly series of the UK money supply and the standard procedures used in monitoring monetary aggregate series.

2   Linear Filters

Consider an observed time series x_t which we wish to express as

$$x_t = \sum_{i=1}^{k} x_{it},$$ (1.1)

where $x_{1t}, \ldots, x_{kt}$ denote k unobserved components. Since often interest centers on one of the components, it will prove useful to rewrite (1.1) as the sum of two components:

$$x_t = m_t + n_t,$$ (1.2)

where m denotes the component of interest (the "signal") and n denotes the sum of the other components (the nonsignal or "noise").

For components such as a trend or a seasonal component, deterministic specifications, such as fixed polynomials in time or cosine functions, have been employed, and references can be found in Stephenson and Farr (1972), Fuller (1976), and Hylleberg (1986). The gradual realization that economic time series display moving or evolving trend and seasonal behavior led to the replacement of deterministic models by the so-called moving average methods, which can be seen as approximating the trend by local polynomials (see Kendall, 1976) and the seasonal by local cosine functions (see Box, Hillmer, and Tiao, 1978).

The most widely used moving average filters are linear (except for some possible tapering of outliers) and, for the observations not close to either end of the series, centered and symmetric. This last property is due to the requirement that the filter should not induce a phase-shift in the estimation of the component; since it is most desirable that the underlying seasonal or cyclical ups and downs of the series be properly timed, the requirement seems a sensible one (a good presentation of moving average filters can be found in Gouriéroux and Monfort, 1990). If B denotes the lag operator and $F = B^{-1}$

denotes the forward operator, such that $B^k x_t = x_{t-k}$ and $F^k x_t = x_{t+k}$, a linear symmetric moving average filter is of the form

$$\hat{x}_{it} = C_i(B)x_t, \qquad (1.3)$$

$$C_i(B) = c_0 + \sum_{j=1}^{r} c_j(B^j + F^j). \qquad (1.4)$$

A filter for a trend component will naturally be designed to capture the series variation associated with the long-term movements (i.e. the movements displaying very low frequencies), and the seasonal component filter will be constructed to capture variability associated with seasonal frequencies. Since the components are often associated with specific frequencies, the frequency domain view will be of help in analyzing the properties of the filters. Broadly, if a component is designed to capture the series variation for a specific frequency region, the moving average filter to estimate the component can be seen as a bandpass filter that should have a gain close to one in that region, and a zero gain for other frequencies. Filters have been constructed in an *ad hoc* manner to display that bandpass structure. These filters are fixed (perhaps

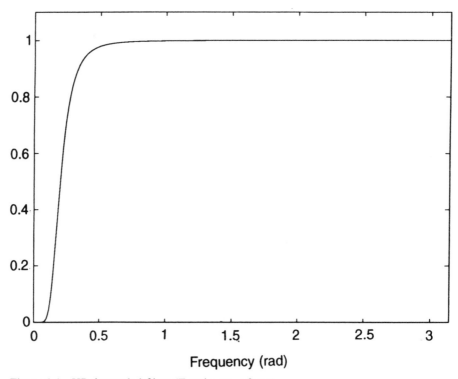

Figure 1.1 HP detrended filter (Fourier transform)

allowing for a few options), and independent of the time series under analysis. One important example in the area of applied economic research, where interest centers on detrending of series, is the Hodrick-Prescott (HP) filter; see Hodrick and Prescott (1980) and Prescott (1986). In the area of data treatment for policy and monitoring of the economy, where seasonal adjustment is the most frequent application, massive use is made of X11-type filters; see Shiskin, Young, and Musgrave (1967) and Dagum (1980). (A linear expression for the central X11 filter can be found in Ghysels and Perron, 1993.)

Let ω denote frequency, measured in radians; the frequency domain representation of the HP filter (for the recommended value of $\lambda = 1,600$) and of the symmetric X11 quarterly filter are displayed in figures 1.1 and 1.2, which evidence the bandpass character of the two filters. The HP filter is seen to remove variation near the 0 frequency and has a value of 1 for frequencies associated with periods of less than 4 or 5 years. The X11 filter removes the variance in the neighborhood of $\omega = \frac{\pi}{2}$ and $\omega = \pi$, the once- and twice-a-year seasonal frequencies.

An important property of two-sided symmetric filters of the type (1.4) is that the estimator of the component x_{it} cannot be obtained with (1.3) when t is

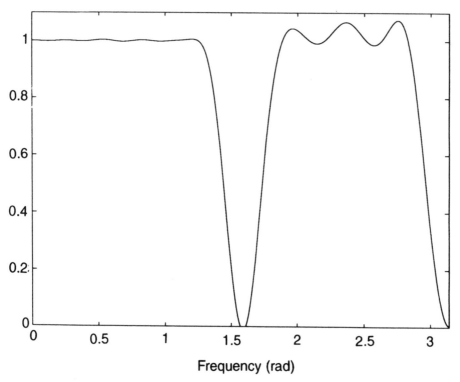

Figure 1.2 X11 seasonally adjusted filter (Fourier transform)

close enough to either end of the series. If $[x_t] = [x_1, x_2, \ldots, x_T]$ denotes the observed series, when $t < r$, unavailable starting values of x are required; when $t > T - r$, future observations are needed to complete the filter. *Ad hoc* filters (except for X11 ARIMA) truncate the filter for those end observations with *ad hoc* weights. Therefore, the centered and symmetric filter characterizes "historical" or final estimators. For recent enough periods, asymmetric filters have to be used, which yield preliminary estimators. As time passes and new observations become available, those preliminary estimators will be revised until the final estimator is eventually obtained. To this issue I shall come back later.

It would seem that a convenient feature of *ad hoc* filters could be that, by defining the component as the outcome of the filter (see Prescott, 1986), the issue of properly defining the component is simplified. The simplification, however, is misleading. To illustrate the difficulties involved in using that definition, consider an example: the trend component obtained with the HP filter applied to the series of US GNP. The series is discussed in detail in section 7; it consists of 35 years of quarterly observations. Assume we are in the middle of year 18 ($t = 70$), and use the HP filter to estimate the trend for that period. According to the definition of Prescott, this estimator is the trend for $t = 70$. But if one more quarter is

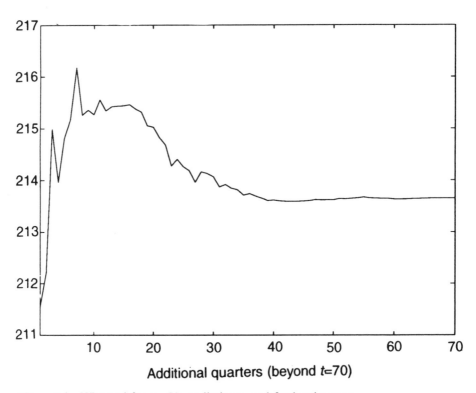

Figure 1.3   HP trend for $t = 70$: preliminary and final estimators

observed, the HP filter yields a different estimator for $t = 70$. Additional quarters will further change the estimator, and the HP filter is in fact a filter that implies a very long revision period. Figure 1.3 displays the trend estimated for $t = 70$ as the length of the series increases from 70 to 140 observations. The estimator is seen to fluctuate considerably, and takes nearly 10 years to converge. Which of these estimators is the trend? Obviously, a preliminary estimator is inadequate, since one would then conclude that new information deteriorates the estimator. If the trend is defined as the historical estimator, then it will take 10 years into the future to know today's trend.

More relevant virtues of *ad hoc* filters are that they are simple and easy to use. This is an important property when there is an actual need of estimating components for a large number of series. Thus one can understand that in a statistical agency, having to routinely seasonally adjust thousands of series, heavy use is made of an *ad hoc* filter such as X11. In applied economic research, where attention centers on methodological issues having to do with few series, the convenience of using *ad hoc* filters is far less clear.

3 *Ad Hoc* Filtering: Dangers and Limitations

The dangers and limitations of *ad hoc* filtering have been often pointed out. Here we illustrate with simple examples some of the most important ones.

3.1 Spurious Results

The danger of spurious adjustment is illustrated in figures 1.4 and 1.5. For a white-noise series with unit variance (expressed, for convenience, in units of 2π), the HP filter yields a trend component with spectrum that of figure 1.4. Yet, by construction, there is no trend in the white-noise series. For the same type of input, X11 extracts a seasonal component with spectrum that of figure 1.5. The spectrum is certainly that of a seasonal component, but it is spurious since the white-noise series contained no seasonality.

For a white-noise series, it is obvious that the filter that seasonally adjusts the series should simply be 1. On the other hand, if the series under analysis has a spectrum like that of figure 1.5, the filter to seasonally adjust the series should be 0, since all variation is seasonal. The filter should depend, thus, on the characteristics of the series. To illustrate this dependence, consider the model

$$\nabla\nabla_4 x_t = (1 - \theta_1 B)(1 - \theta_4 B^4)a_t, \qquad (1.5)$$

where a_t is a white-noise innovation (with variance V_a), $\nabla = 1 - B$, $\nabla_4 = 1 - B^4$, and the two moving average parameters lie between -1 and 1. It is a model similar to the so-called airline model of Box and Jenkins (1970, chapter 9) for quarterly series. On the one hand, it is often encountered in practice; on the other hand, it provides an excellent reference example. For

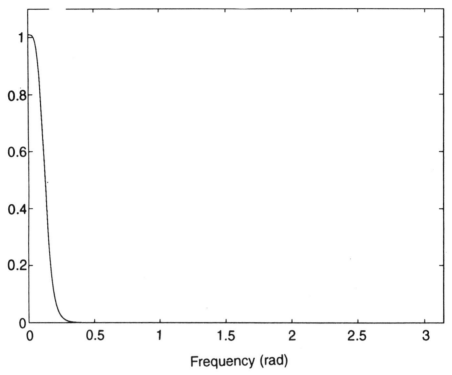

Figure 1.4   Trend extracted from white noise with HP filter

$\theta_4 > -0.15$, the model accepts a sensible decomposition into trend, seasonal, and irregular components (see Hillmer and Tiao, 1982). As θ_1 approaches 1, model (1.5) tends towards the model

$$\nabla_4 x_t = (1 - \theta_4 B^4)a_t + \mu_o,$$

with a more deterministic trend. (Notice that, since ∇_4 contains the root $(1 - B)$, μ_o is the – now deterministic – slope of the trend.) Similarly, when θ_4 becomes 1, the seasonality in (1.5) becomes deterministic. Thus, broadly, the parameters θ_1 and θ_4 can be interpreted as a measure of how close to deterministic the trend and the seasonal components, respectively, are. The behavior of a component is easily illustrated in the frequency domain. Model (1.5) does not have a proper spectrum, since it is nonstationary; it will be useful however to use its pseudo-spectrum (see Hatanaka and Suzuki, 1967; or Harvey, 1989). For a linear model $x_t = \Psi(B)a_t$, with $\Psi(B) = \theta(B)/\phi(B)$, where $\theta(B)$ and $\phi(B)$ are finite polynomials in B, the pseudo-spectrum is the Fourier transform of $\Psi(B)\Psi(F)V_a$; it will display infinite peaks for the frequencies associated with the unit roots of $\phi(B)$. In what follows, the term "spectrum" will be used also to denote a pseudo-spectrum.

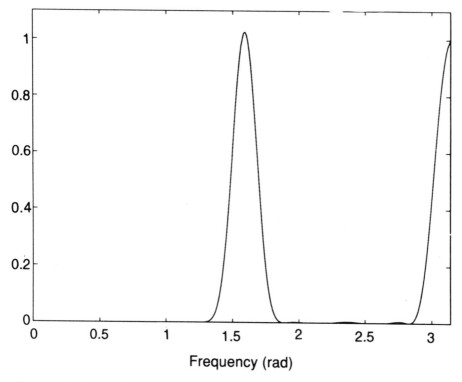

Figure 1.5 Seasonal component extracted from white noise with X11

The closeness to deterministic behavior of a component is revealed by the width of the spectral peak for the relevant frequency. Thus, for example, figure 1.6 displays the spectra of two series both following models of the type (1.5) with $V_a = 1$, one with $\theta_1 = -0.1$, $\theta_4 = 0.7$, and the other with $\theta_1 = 0.7$, $\theta_4 = -0.1$. Comparing the two spectra, the one with the continuous line contains a more stable (closer to deterministic) trend, and a more unstable seasonal. Since an *ad hoc* filter displays holes of a fixed width, the filter will underadjust when the width of the spectral peak in the series is larger than the width of the filter hole. Alternatively, it will overadjust when the spectral peak in the series is narrower than that for which the filter has been designed. Figure 1.7 illustrates the effect of using X11 on the series with unstable seasonality of figure 1.6. In part (a) it is seen how the width of the filter is narrower than the spectral peak in the series. Part (b) shows how the underestimation of the seasonal component has spillover effects, reflected by peaks in the seasonally adjusted series spectrum in the vicinity of the seasonal frequencies. For the case of the HP filter, figure 1.8 illustrates its application to the series with a relatively unstable trend of figure 1.6. (Since the HP trend filter becomes zero much before the first seasonal frequency, it will have no

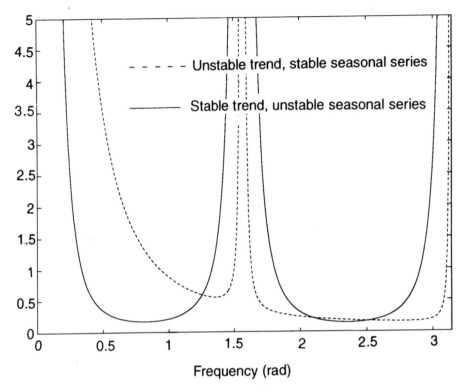

Figure 1.6   Two examples with stable and unstable components

effect on the spectrum for the seasonal frequencies.) As seen in part (a) of the figure, the filter underestimates the peak around the zero frequency contained in the series, and part (b) shows the effect of this underestimation: the detrended series will be overestimated, and will exhibit a strong cycle, induced entirely by the underestimation of the trend. The spurious cycle is associated with a period of approximately 6 years. (It is worth mentioning that the quarterly airline model used to illustrate the danger of underestimation with the HP filter is in fact very close to the model appropriate for the US GNP series, which has been the center of attention in business cycle research; see section 7.) The danger of spurious results induced by the HP filter has been often pointed out; examples are found in King and Rebelo (1993), Cogley (1990), Canova (1991), and Harvey and Jaeger (1991).

3.2 Statistical Problems

The lack of a proper statistical model limits in many important ways the usefulness of *ad hoc* filters. First, it makes it difficult to detect the cases in which the filter is not appropriate for the series at hand. Moreover, if such is

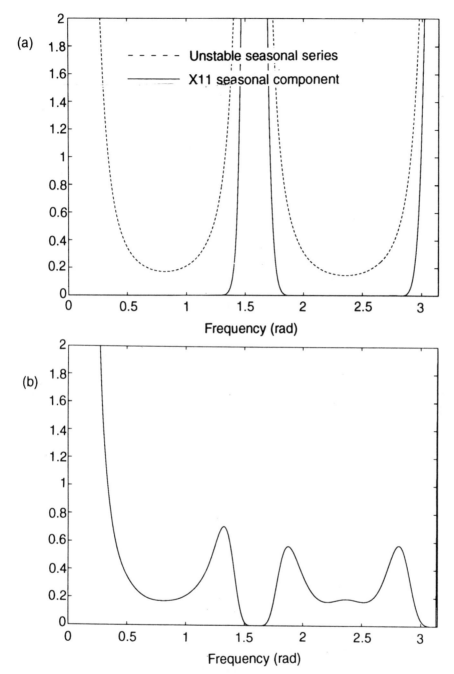

Figure 1.7 (a) Unstable seasonal series and X11 seasonal component (b) seasonally adjusted series

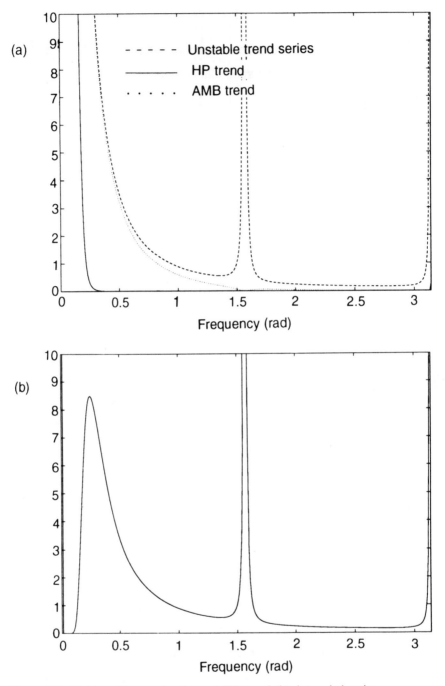

Figure 1.8 (a) Unstable trend series and HP trend (b) detrended series

the case, there is no systematic procedure to overcome the filter inadequacies. Second, even when appropriate, *ad hoc* filtering does not provide the basis for rigorous inference. Given that the filter yields an estimator of the unobserved component, it would be desirable to know the properties of the estimator, and in particular the underlying estimation errors; as shall be seen later, this knowledge may have relevant policy implications. Further, *ad hoc* filters do not provide the basis for obtaining forecasts of the components, which can also be of interest. Forecasts and estimation (and forecasting) errors of the components will be discussed in sections 10 and 11.

4 The Model-Based Approach

To overcome the black-box character of *ad hoc* filtering, and the limitations mentioned in the previous section, over the last 15 years new approaches to unobserved component estimation, based on parametric models, have been developed. These models are closely related to the autoregressive (AR) integrated (I) moving average (MA) models (ARIMA models) popularized by Box and Jenkins (1970). They have been the subject of considerable statistical research having to do with practical applications, such as seasonal adjustment. They have also been used intensively in applied econometric research and, in fact, most of the references given in section 1 contain model-based applications.

Except for some nonlinear extensions (examples are Carlin and Dempster, 1989; Hamilton, 1989; Harvey, Ruiz, and Sentana, 1992; Fiorentini and Maravall, 1994), the vast majority of model-based approaches use a linear assumption, which I shall state as follows:

Assumption 1 Each component in expression (1.1) can be seen as the outcome of a linear stochastic process of the type

$$\delta_i(B)x_{it} = \psi_i(B)a_{it}, \tag{1.6}$$

where a_{it} denotes a white-noise variable and the polynomial $\psi_i(B)$ can be expressed as $\psi_i(B) = \theta_i(B)/\varphi_i(B)$. The polynomials $\delta_i(B)$, $\theta_i(B)$, and $\varphi_i(B)$ are of finite order. The roots of $\delta_i(B)$ are on the unit circle; those of $\varphi_i(B)$ lie outside; and, finally, $\theta_i(B)$ has all roots on or outside the unit circle. For each i, the three polynomials are prime. ∎

Throughout the chapter, a white-noise variable will denote a zero-mean, normally, identically, and independently distributed variable. I shall refer to a_{it} as the p-innovation (pseudo-innovation) associated with component i. The variable $z_{it} = \delta_i(B)x_t$ represents the stationary transformation of x_t, and the parametric expression for the component will be

$$\varphi_i(B)\delta_i(B)x_{it} = \theta_i(B)a_{it}, \tag{1.7}$$

or, in compact form,

$$\phi_i(B)x_{it} = \theta_i(B)a_{it},\tag{1.8}$$

where $\phi_i(B)$ is the product of the stationary and the nonstationary AR polynomials. The orders of the polynomials $\phi_i(B)$ and $\theta_i(B)$ are p_i and q_i, respectively. Since different roots of the AR polynomial induce peaks in the spectrum of the series for different frequencies, and given that different components are associated with spectral peaks for different frequencies, the following assumption will be made.

Assumption 2   The polynomials $\phi_i(B)$ and $\phi_j(B)$, $i \neq j$, share no common root.   ∎

From (1.1) and (1.8),

$$x_t = \sum_{i=1}^{k} \frac{\theta_i(B)}{\phi_i(B)} a_{it},$$

which implies, under assumption 2, that x_t is also the outcome of a linear process, namely

$$\varphi(B)\delta(B)x_t = \theta(B)a_t,\tag{1.9}$$

where $\delta(B) = \Pi_{i=1}^{k} \delta_i(B)$, $\varphi(B) = \Pi_{i=1}^{k} \varphi_i(B)$, $\theta(B)$ is a polynomial of finite order in B (say, of order q), and a_t is a white-noise innovation. Expression (1.9) can be rewritten as

$$\phi(B)x_t = \theta(B)a_t,\tag{1.10}$$

and consistency between the overall model and the ones for the components implies the two constraints:

$$\phi(B) = \prod_{i=1}^{k} \phi_i(B),\tag{1.11}$$

$$\theta(B)a_t = \sum_{i=1}^{k} \theta_i(B)\phi_{ni}(B)a_{it},\tag{1.12}$$

where $\phi_{ni}(B)$ is the product of all AR polynomials excluding $\phi_i(B)$, that is

$$\phi_{ni}(B) = \prod_{j=1(j \neq i)}^{k} \phi_j(B).$$

Assumption 1 allows for noninvertible components. I shall require, however, the model for the observed series to be invertible. Since noninvertibility is associated with a spectral zero, there should be no frequency for which all component spectra become zero. The following assumption guarantees invertibility of the overall series.

Assumption 3   The polynomials $\theta_i(B)$, $i = 1, \ldots, k$, share no unit root in common.
∎

5 Characterization of the Components

In the same way that there is no universally accepted definition of a trend or of a seasonal component, there is no universally accepted model specification for a particular component. When building the overall model, one can proceed by directly specifying a model for each unobserved component that in some way captures the prior beliefs about the component. This is the so-called structural time series (STS) approach, and some basic references are Engle (1978), Gersch and Kitagawa (1983), Harvey and Todd (1983), and Harvey (1989); direct specification of the component model is also the most used approach in applied econometrics. Alternatively, since observations are only available on the overall series, one can proceed by first identifying a model for it, and then deriving appropriate models for the components that are compatible with the overall one. This is the so-called ARIMA model based (AMB) approach, and basic references are Box, Hillmer, and Tiao (1978), Burman (1980), Hillmer and Tiao (1982), Bell and Hillmer (1984), and Maravall and Pierce (1987). It is of interest to review some of the most common specifications used to characterize some of the most common components.

5.1 Trend Component

Consider the deterministic linear trend $m_t = a + \mu t$, for which

$$\nabla m_t = \mu, \tag{1.13}$$

$$\nabla^2 m_t = 0. \tag{1.14}$$

A moving or stochastic trend will not satisfy (1.13) and (1.14) exactly at every period; instead, one can assume that the above relationships are perturbated every period by a zero-mean random shock, with a small variance. When the shock is a white-noise variable, (1.13) becomes

$$\nabla m_t = \mu + a_{mt}, \tag{1.15}$$

where a_{mt} is the white-noise shock. Its variance V_m will reflect how important is the random element in the trend. Model (1.15) is the standard "random walk plus drift" specification, widely used in econometric applications (see, for example, Stock and Watson, 1988). Alternatively, (1.14) can generate the stochastic trend model

$$\nabla^2 m_t = a_{mt}, \tag{1.16}$$

similar to the one in Gersch and Kitagawa (1983). The STS approach of Harvey and Todd (1983) models the trend as a random walk plus drift process,

$$\nabla m_t = \mu_t + a_{mt}, \tag{1.17a}$$

where the drift is also generated by a random walk, as in

$$\nabla \mu_t = a_{\mu t}, \tag{1.17b}$$

with $a_{\mu t}$ white noise. (Similar types of "second-order" random walks are also found in the trend models of Harrison and Stevens, 1976; and of Ng and Young, 1990.) Writing (1.17) as $\nabla^2 m_t = a_{\mu t} + \nabla a_{mt}$, it is seen to be equivalent to an IMA(2, 1) model of the type

$$\nabla^2 m_t = (1 - \theta_m B) a_{mt}, \qquad (1.18)$$

with the constraint $\theta_m > 0$. Notice that as θ_m approaches 1, model (1.18) tends to the standard random walk plus drift model (1.15). Since μ is the slope of the linear trend, the choice between an I(1) and an I(2) trend reflects thus the choice between a constant and a time-varying slope. Finally, in the AMB approach, the model for the trend will depend on the model for the observed series and, in particular, its order of integration at $\omega = 0$ will be the same. As an example for the quarterly airline model (1.5), the trend follows an IMA(2, 2) model.

In general, stochastic trends are modeled as in

$$\nabla^d m_t = \psi_m(B) a_{mt}, \qquad (1.19)$$

with $d = 1$ or 2, and $\psi_m(B) a_{mt}$ a low-order ARMA process. The same type of stochastic linear trend specification is often used to model economic variables that are treated as unobserved components. Some examples are the model for the permanent component in permanent/transitory types of decomposition (Muth, 1960; Pagan, 1975; Clark, 1987; Stock and Watson, 1988; and Quah, 1990); the model for the unobserved planned policy targets (Weber, 1992); for technical progress (Slade, 1989); for productivity effects (Harvey et al., 1986); or for the general "state of the economy" in Stock and Watson (1989). (A more complete discussion of stochastic linear trends is contained in Maravall, 1993a.)

5.2   Seasonal Component and Seasonally Adjusted Series

In most economic applications of unobserved components, the seasonal component is not explicitly dealt with. If the series contains seasonality, as many macroeconomic series do, the seasonally adjusted data are typically employed. Although not explicitly modeled, the seasonal component may certainly affect the results of the analysis, and some limitations associated with the use of seasonally adjusted data have been pointed out (see, for example, Wallis, 1974; Ghysels and Perron, 1993; Miron, 1986; and Osborn, 1988). As shall be seen later, moreover, the seasonally adjusted series are likely to be particularly inadequate for business cycle analysis. Since, within the model-based framework, it can be done in a straightforward manner, it is preferable to incorporate the seasonal component as part of the model to be estimated, jointly with the rest of the components (a good example, in the context of an econometric model, is provided by Harvey and Scott, 1994). In the statistical applications having to do with economic policy or monitoring, explicitly modeling the seasonal component is certainly important, since seasonal adjustment is the most common application.

The structure of the model for the stochastic seasonal component can be motivated in a manner similar to that used for the trend. Let s denote the number of observations per year, and m_t a deterministic seasonal component (expressed as the sum of dummy variables or of cosine functions). Then the sum of s consecutive seasonal components will exactly cancel out, that is

$$S m_t = 0, \tag{1.20}$$

where $S = 1 + B + \ldots + B^{s-1}$. If the component is moving in time, (1.20) cannot be expected to be satisfied at each period, although the deviation should average out and be relatively small. If we assume that equation (1.20) is subject each period to a random shock, a stochastic model for the seasonal component is obtained. If the shock, for example, is the white-noise variable a_{mt}, the model becomes

$$S m_t = a_{mt}, \tag{1.21}$$

which is the model for the seasonal component in the STS approach of Harvey and Todd (1983), and also the seasonal model specification used in the approach of Gersch and Kitagawa (1983). There is no compelling reason for the deviations from zero in $S m_t$ to be uncorrelated and, for example, in the AMB approach, the seasonal component obtained in the decomposition of (1.5) is of the form

$$S m_t = \theta_m(B) a_{mt}, \tag{1.22}$$

where $\theta_m(B)$ is of order 3. Similar types of models can be found in, for example, Aoki (1990) and Kohn and Ansley (1987). More generally, expression (1.6), with $\delta_s(B) = S$ and $\psi_s(B)$ a relatively low-order ARMA process, is indeed a frequent specification for the seasonal component.

Some departures are found in Burridge and Wallis (1984), where $\theta_s(B)$ is of a relatively high order (although parsimonious), or in Hylleberg et al. (1990), where some seasonal harmonics are allowed not to be present, and hence some of the unit roots in S may be missing. In many of the earlier model-based approaches, the seasonal component was modeled as having ∇_S in its AR part. In the presence of a trend, this specification would be ruled out by assumption 2. In fact, ∇_S includes the root $(1-B)$, which should not be a part of the seasonal component, otherwise the filter that yields the seasonal estimator would contain part of the trend. (A more complete discussion of the seasonal component model specification is contained in Maravall, 1989.)

As for the seasonally adjusted series (also an unobserved component), its structure will depend on which components, other than the seasonal, are present in the series. For example, in the AMB decomposition of model (1.5), the seasonally adjusted series equals the sum of an IMA(2, 2) trend and a white-noise irregular. Thus the adjusted series will also follow an IMA(2, 2) model. In the STS decomposition of Harvey and Todd (1983), when no cycle is present, the adjusted series (the sum of an IMA(2, 1) trend and a white-noise irregular) also follows an IMA(2, 2) model.

5.3   Cyclical Component

There have been two different ways of characterizing the cyclical component. One has been as a periodic stochastic component, which can be rationalized as in the two previous cases. It is well known that, for $\phi_1^2 < 4\phi_2$, the difference equation

$$x_t + \phi_1 x_{t-1} + \phi_2 x_{t-2} = 0 \qquad (1.23)$$

displays deterministic periodic behavior of the type $x_t = A_0 r^t \cos(\omega t + A_1)$, where $r = \sqrt{\phi_2}$ is the modulus and $\omega = \arccos[-\phi_1/2\sqrt{\phi_2}]$ is the frequency (in radians). For some values of ϕ_1 and ϕ_2, ω will fall in the interval $0 < \omega < \omega_1$, where ω_1 is the fundamental seasonal frequency $\omega_1 = 2\pi/s$, with period equal to s. Values of ω inside that interval will generate deterministic cycles of period longer than a year. As before, if the cyclical component is of the moving type, (1.23) will not be satisfied exactly. If it is assumed that the deviations from zero are white noise, the linear stochastic model for the cycle becomes an AR(2) model; more generally, allowing for some autocorrelation in the deviations, the model for the cycle can be written as:

$$m_t + \phi_1 m_{t-1} + \phi_2 m_{t-2} = \theta_m(B) a_{mt}, \qquad (1.24)$$

where $\theta_m(B)$ is a low-order MA polynomial. Models of this type will be referred to as "periodic cycles," and they have been used in many applications (examples are Jenkins, 1979; Kitchell and Peña, 1984; Harvey, 1985; Crafts, Leybourne, and Mills, 1989).

In macroeconomics, however, the cycle is seldom seen as a periodic behavior in the previous sense. Typically, the cycle represents the deviations (that are not seasonal) from a long-term component or trend. The cycle is therefore measured as the residuals obtained after detrending a seasonally adjusted series. Of course, these residuals need not exhibit periodic cyclical behavior, and may follow, in general, a stationary ARMA process. What characterizes this concept of the cycle is that it represents in some sense the stationary variations of the series. I shall refer to this view of the cycle as the "business cycle" view.

Within the model-based approach, a different concept of the cycle has been recently proposed by Stock and Watson (1989; 1991; 1993). The cycle is given by sequences of growth of an unobserved component (the state of the economy) above or below some threshold. The unobserved component is then modeled as a stochastic trend.

5.4   Irregular and Transitory Component

In statistical decompositions of economic time series, the series is often expressed as the sum of a trend, a seasonal, and an irregular component. In practice, the irregular component is obtained as the residual after the trend and seasonality have been removed. In the model-based approach, the irregular component is a stationary low-order ARMA process, quite frequently simply white noise.

Transitory (or temporary) components are used in econometrics to capture short-term variability of the series and are equal to the series minus its permanent component. The permanent component, as already mentioned, is typically modeled as a stochastic trend, and hence the transitory component can also be seen as the detrended (often seasonally adjusted) series. Again, the transitory component will be a stationary ARMA process; in econometrics, it is frequently modeled as a finite AR process.

5.5   A Remark on Stationarity and Model Specification

Nonstationarity of the trend and of the seasonal component is somewhat implied by the very nature of the component. If the trend is stationary, in which way can it measure the long-term evolution of the series? As for the seasonal component, the basic requirement that its sum over a year span should, on average, be zero, implies the presence of the operator S in the AR expression for the component, as in (1.22), and hence the presence of nonstationary seasonality. For the case of the periodic cyclical component, if $\phi_2 = 1$ the component will be nonstationary. In practice, however, most cycles detected using models of the type (1.24) are found to be stationary.

The business cycle, the irregular, and the transitory components are modeled as stationary processes and, basically, can be seen as the residual obtained after the trend and seasonal components have been removed from the series. This common basic structure does not imply that, for the same series, the three components have to follow necessarily the same model. A simple example will illustrate the point.

Let x_t be a (nonseasonal) series, the output of the process $(1 - 0.7B)\nabla x_t = \theta(B)a_t$, where $\theta(B)$ is a low-order MA. If one is interested in short-term analysis (as is the case in statistical practical applications) and wishes to remove from x_t only white-noise variation, one may consider the model $x_t = m_t + n_t$, where

$$(1 - 0.7B)\nabla m_t = a_{mt}$$

$$n_t = a_{nt}.$$

On the contrary, if interest centers in long-run analysis (as in some econometric applications), one may prefer an alternative specification of the type

$$\nabla m_t = a_{mt}$$

$$(1 - 0.7B)n_t = a_{nt}.$$

Both specifications are perfectly reasonable; the second one will yield a smoother stationary component. In fact, it is a virtue of the model-based approach that the purpose of the analysis can be incorporated in the specification of the models.

6 Identification

6.1 The General Problem

Conditional on some starting conditions, and under assumptions 1–3, the overall ARIMA expression (1.10) determines entirely the joint distribution of the observations (or of the transformation $\delta(B)x_t$). Since the parameters of (1.10) can be estimated consistently, and given that our interest centers on estimation of the unobserved components, for most of the remaining discussion I shall make the following assumption.

Assumption 4 The polynomials $\phi(B)$ and $\theta(B)$, as well as the variance of a_t (V_a) in model (1.10), are known. ∎

Considering expression (1.11) and assumption 2, factorization of $\phi(B)$ directly yields the polynomials $\phi_i(B)$ of the unobserved components. The different roots may be allocated to the different components according to the behavior they induce in the series. Thus, the AR polynomials of the components are identified and can be obtained from the AR polynomial in the model for the observed series. The parameters that remain to be determined are those in the MA polynomials $\theta_i(B)$, $i = 1, \ldots, k$, and in the contemporaneous covariance matrix of the vector of p-innovations, namely those in $\Sigma = [\text{cov}(a_{it}, a_{jt})]$. These parameters have to be obtained from the identity (1.12). Under the normality assumption, if the system of equations that results from equating the auto-covariances of the left-hand side (LHS) to the autocovariances of the right-hand side (RHS) of the identity (1.12) has a locally isolated solution for the parameters in $\theta_i(B)$ and Σ the models for the components are identified. Obviously, without any additional assumption there will be an infinite number of possible specifications that will satisfy (1.12) (and the implied system of covariance equations). In order to isolate a particular solution (i.e. in order to reach identification), additional restrictions are needed.

6.2 Restrictions on the Covariance Matrix Σ

On occasion, the components are allowed to be correlated; see, for example, Watson (1986) and Ghysels (1987). The most widely used decomposition that allows for correlated components is the one proposed by Beveridge and Nelson (1981). If x_t denotes an I(1) variable such that ∇x_t has the Wold representation $\nabla x_t = \Psi(B)a_t$, then x_t can always be expressed as the sum of a permanent and a transitory component, where the permanent component is given by $\nabla m_t = \Psi(1)a_t$, and the transitory component is equal to $n_t = \Psi^*(B)a_t$, where $\Psi^*(B)$ satisfies $(1 - B)\Psi^*(B) = \Psi(B) - \Psi(1)$. The Beveridge-Nelson decomposition can be seen as an ingenious decomposition of an I(1) variable, but it does not properly fit into the unobserved components framework, since the components are, in fact, observable. This is easily seen by rewriting, for example, m_t as $m_t = \Psi(1)\Psi(B)^{-1}x_t$, and hence both components are defined as linear combinations of the observed series. The assumption, besides, that the permanent and transitory component share, at every period, the same innovation is a strong assumption, of limited appeal. Instead, I shall assume that what causes the underlying long-term evolution of an economic variable is different from what causes it to display seasonal variation, and from what causes the transitory deviations. Accordingly, the following constraint will be imposed.

Assumption 5 The p-innovations a_{it} and a_{jt} are uncorrelated for $i \neq j$. That is, $\Sigma = \text{diag}(V_i)$. ∎

Assumption 5 is a standard assumption in statistical practical applications. The choice between correlated and orthogonal p-innovations, as shall be seen in section 9, is less drastic than it may appear. Ultimately, the component estimators will be linear projections on the observed time series x_t, and hence linear filters of the innovations a_t. In fact, the Beveridge-Nelson decomposition can be seen as the estimators that are obtained for a particular permanent/transitory decomposition with uncorrelated components (Watson, 1986).

6.3   Additional Restrictions

Assumption 5 is not enough to identify the model, and more restrictions are needed. The discussion will be clearer if we look at a particular example, namely the quarterly airline model (1.5). Assume we wish to decompose x_t into a trend (x_{mt}), a seasonal (x_{st}), and an irregular component x_{ut}, as in (1.1). Since the AR part of (1.5) can be rewritten $\nabla\nabla_4 = \nabla^2 S$, the trend and seasonal components can be assumed to be the outcomes of the models $\nabla^2 x_{mt} = \theta_m(B)a_{mt}$, and $Sx_{st} = \theta_s(B)a_{st}$, respectively; the irregular component can be assumed to be white noise, $x_{ut} = a_{ut}$. Thus, letting $\theta(B) = (1 - \theta_1 B)(1 - \theta_4 B^4)$, consistency with the overall model (i.e. equation (1.12)) implies

$$\theta(B)a_t = S\theta_m(B)a_{mt} + \nabla^2\theta_s(B)a_{st} + \nabla\nabla_4 a_{ut}. \tag{1.25}$$

Since the LHS of (1.25) is an MA of order 5, we can set $\theta_m(B)$ and $\theta_s(B)$ to be of order 2 and 3, respectively, so that the three terms in the RHS of (1.25) are also of order 5. The component models will then be of the type:

$$\nabla^2 x_{mt} = (1 + \theta_{m,1}B + \theta_{m,2}B^2)a_{mt}, \tag{1.26a}$$

$$Sx_{st} = (1 + \theta_{s,1}B + \theta_{s,2}B^2 + \theta_{s,3}B^3)a_{st}, \tag{1.26b}$$

and $x_{ut} = a_{ut}$. Equating the covariances of the LHS and the RHS of (1.25), a system of six equations is obtained. These equations express the relationship between the parameters of the overall model and the unknown parameters in the component models. Since the number of the latter is eight ($\theta_{m,1}$, $\theta_{m,2}$, $\theta_{s,1}$, $\theta_{s,2}$, $\theta_{s,3}$, V_m, V_s, V_u), there is an infinite number of structures of the type (1.26) that are compatible with the same model (1.5). The identification problem is similar to the one that appears in standard econometric models (see, for example, Fisher, 1966). The model for the observed series is the reduced form, whereas the models for the components represent the associated structural form. For a particular reduced form, there is an infinite number of structures from which it can be generated. In order to select one, additional information has to be incorporated.

The traditional approach in econometrics has been to set *a priori* some parameters in the structural model equal to zero (see, for example, Theil, 1971). Identification by zero-coefficient restrictions in unobserved component models has been analyzed in Hotta (1989). The ith component model is identified if the order of its AR polynomial (p_i) exceeds that of its MA polynomial (q_i). In fact, setting, for example, $\theta_{m,2} = 0$ and $\theta_{s,3} = 0$, the system of six equations has now six unknowns, and the model becomes identified. This way of reaching identification is the approach most widely used in practice. For example, the STS decomposition would set *a priori* components with $p_m = 2 > q_m = 1$ and $p_s = 3 > q_s = 0$; Pauly (1989) sets $p_i = q_i + 1$ for all components (apart from the noise x_{ut}); and in econometrics, the practice of using random-walk trends (with $p = 1 > q = 0$) guarantees that the trend component is identified. But if traditional econometric models rationalize setting *a priori* some coefficients equal to zero on the grounds of economic theory (for example, some variables may not affect demand), no such rationalization holds for the unobserved component case.

However, despite the lack of *a priori* information on the components MA parameters, other types of considerations may be brought into the picture. In the decomposition of x_t into components, let u_t represent a noise component, and assume that for all components, except for u_t, $p_i \geqslant q_i$ in (1.8). Thus, when $p \geqslant q$ in the overall model, u_t will be white noise; when $q > p$, u_t will be an MA($q - p$), and hence colored noise. Then, consider all possible model specifications (under assumptions 1–5) that satisfy the identity (1.25), and have nonnegative component spectra. For a given model for the observed series, they form the set of "admissible" decompositions. Different admissible decompositions have different model specifications for the components, and therefore will display different properties. Since, as mentioned earlier, the component is a tool that we devise, we can choose, among the different admissible decompositions, the one that presents certain desirable features. As I proceed to show, this is the approach followed in the AMB method to achieve identification.

In the decomposition of model (1.5) into three orthogonal components as in (1.26), the sum of the components spectra should be equal to the spectrum for

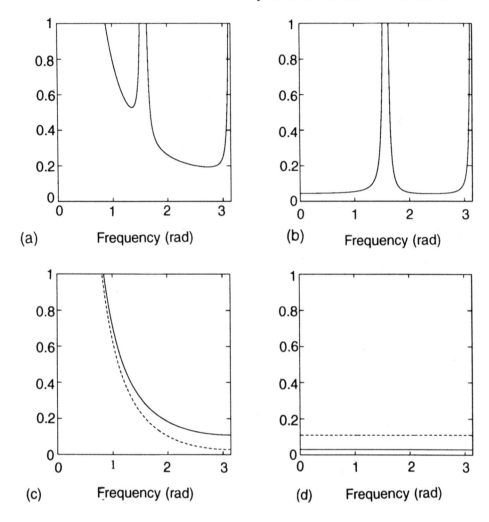

Figure 1.9 Two admissible decompositions: (a) series (b) seasonal component
(c) trend (d) irregular

the observed series. Figure 1.9 displays (with the continuous line) the spectra
of the components of an admissible decomposition for a particular case of
model (1.5), namely that given by (1.28). Let $g_m(\omega)$ denote the trend component spectrum. By noticing that its minimum is $g_m(\pi) = 0.1$, it follows that
x_{mt} can be further decomposed into a trend and an orthogonal white-noise
irregular, with the variance of the latter in the interval (0, 0.1). Removing
white noise with variance. 0.07 from x_{mt}, and assigning this noise to the
irregular component, another admissible decomposition is obtained, and it is
given by the dashed line in figure 1.9 (the seasonal component has not

changed). If x^1_{mt} and x^2_{mt} denote the trends in the first and the second decompositions, respectively, then x^1_{mt} can be expressed as $x^1_{mt} = x^2_{mt} + n_t$, where n_t is white noise, orthogonal to x^2_{mt}. Thus the trend x^1_{mt} can be seen as obtained from the trend x^2_{mt} by simply adding white noise. The latter trend would seem preferable since it contains less noise.

The previous consideration leads to the idea of choosing, within the set of admissible decompositions, the one that provides the smoothest trend. Since the spectrum of a trend component should be monotonically decreasing in ω, its minimum will be obtained for $\omega = \pi$. If this minimum is larger than zero, further white noise could still be removed from the trend. Therefore, the noise-free condition implies $g_m(\pi) = 0$, which is equivalent, in the time domain, to the presence of the root $B = -1$ in the polynomial $\theta_m(B)$. Components from which no additive noise can be extracted were first proposed by Box, Hillmer, and Tiao (1978), and Pierce (1978); they have been termed "canonical components." The canonical component has the important property that any other admissible component can be seen as the canonical one plus superimposed (orthogonal) noise. If an admissible decomposition exists, moreover, the canonical requirement identifies the component, since the canonical component is uniquely obtained by simply substracting from any admissible component spectrum its minimum. As Hillmer and Tiao (1982) show, the canonical condition also minimizes the variance of the component p-innovation a_{mt}; since a_{mt} is the source of the stochastic variability, the canonical component can be seen as the closest to a deterministic component that is compatible with the stochastic structure of the series. (Some additional interesting properties of canonical components will be seen in section 11.)

It is worth noticing that the random-walk trend, popular in econometrics, is not a canonical component. In particular, for the model $\nabla x_t = a_t$ with $V_a = 1$, x_t can be decomposed as in (1.2), with m_t and n_t orthogonal, the first given by

$$\nabla m_t = (1 + B)a_{mt} \qquad (V_m = 0.25), \qquad (1.27)$$

and n_t white noise, with variance $V_n = 0.25$. Model (1.27) is the canonical trend within a random-walk trend.

Back to the admissible decomposition of figure 1.9, and noticing that the spectrum of the seasonal component has a positive minimum, it follows that that component can, in turn, be expressed as the sum of a smoother seasonal component and an orthogonal white noise. Again, maximizing the smoothness of the component leads to a noninvertible component model. As with the trend, any admissible seasonal component can be seen as the canonical one with superimposed noise, and hence, if an admissible component is available, the canonical one can be trivially obtained. Finally, if, in the decomposition of (1.5), the canonical trend and seasonal components are specified, then the variance of the irregular (white-noise) component is maximized.

In the time domain analysis, the canonical requirement replaces the zero-coefficient restrictions with more general constraints among the coefficients. A canonical trend implies $\theta_m(-1) = 1 - \theta_{m.1} + \theta_{m.2} \doteq 0$, and if, for example, the spectral zero of the canonical seasonal component occurs at $\omega = 0$, then $\theta_s(1) = 1 + \theta_{s.1} + \theta_{s.2} + \theta_{s.3} = 0$. The two constraints, added to the system of six covariance equations associated with (1.25), provide now a system of eight equations which can be solved for the eight unknown parameters, and hence the model becomes identified.

Other solutions to the identification problem have been suggested, having to do for example with the different size of the component estimation error for different admissible decompositions (see, for example, Watson, 1987; and Findley, 1985). To this issue I shall return in section 11; what is worth stressing now is that the underidentification problem I have discussed affects equally the AMB and the STS approaches. To see how it applies to the latter, let the component models be of the type (1.8), and compute, for every i, $k_i = \min g_i(\omega)$, $\omega \in [0, \pi]$, and set $V_u = \sum_i k_i$. Then the set of admissible decompositions is given by the different ways of allocating a white-noise component with variance V_u among the different components (preserving the nonegativity of the spectrum). All admissible decompositions imply, of course, the same overall model, and the particular STS model identified can be seen as the choice of a particular distribution of the noise.

Although the examples will often use canonical components, the general discussion that follows makes no assumption on the particular identification criterion used. It applies to any unobserved component model under assumptions 1–5, independently of whether it is of the STS type or it has been derived within an AMB approach.

7   An Example

7.1   The Quarterly US GNP Series

I shall illustrate some of the previous discussion and, in particular, the AMB decomposition with the series that has attracted more attention in the business cycle (and permanent component) literature: the quarterly series (y_t) of (nominal) US GNP. I shall consider the original, not seasonally adjusted, series, and seasonality will explicitly be a part of the model. (The series contains 140 observations, from January, 1951 to December, 1985, and was kindly supplied to me by Fabio Canova.) Letting $x_t = \log y_t$, the model

$$\nabla\nabla_4 x_t = (1 - 0.702 B^4) a_t, \tag{1.28}$$

provides a very good fit. The residual standard deviation is $\sigma_a = 0.015$, and the only anomaly is a slightly high kurtosis value of 4.02 (SE $= 0.42$), due to two outlier observations, of opposite signs, for 1958/1 and 1984/1. Following the procedure of Chen and Liu (1993), the two are identified as temporary changes. Correcting for the outliers, the model varies very little with respect to (1.28). Since the two outliers are of moderate size and have little effect on the model, for illustration purposes we opt for the uncorrected series.

Model (1.28) is a particular case of (1.5), and hence the series x_t can be expressed as the sum of a trend, a seasonal, and an irregular (mutually uncorrelated) component, with models as in (1.26). We proceed to show a simple way to obtain, from (1.28), the unknown parameter values of (1.26) for the canonical specification of the components. Let $\zeta(B)$ denote a finite polynomial in B, and denote by $\gamma(\zeta, B)$ the product

$$\gamma(\zeta, B) = \zeta(B)\zeta(F) = \gamma_0 + \sum_j \gamma_j(B^j + F^j).$$

(γ is the autocovariance generating function (ACGF) of the process $\zeta(B)e_t$, with $V_e = 1$). Denote by $G(\zeta, \omega)$ the Fourier transform of γ, that is

$$G(\zeta, \omega) = g_0 + \sum_j g_j \cos(j\omega),$$

where $g_0 = \gamma_0$, and $g_j = 2\gamma_j (j \neq 0)$. (Note that G is the spectrum of the same process $\zeta(B)e_t$.) From (1.26) and (1.10) we have the identity:

$$\frac{G(\theta, \omega)}{G(\phi, \omega)} = \frac{G(\theta_m, \omega)}{G(\nabla^2, \omega)} + \frac{G(\theta_s, \omega)}{G(S, \omega)} + k, \tag{1.29}$$

where the only unknowns are the g-parameters in

$$G(\theta_m, \omega) = g_{m,0} + g_{m,1} \cos\omega + g_{m,2} \cos 2\omega$$

$$G(\theta_s, \omega) = g_{s,0} + g_{s,1} \cos\omega + g_{s,2} \cos 2\omega + g_{s,3} \cos 3\omega,$$

and the constant $k = V_u$. Removing denominators in (1.29), and using the relationship $\cos(r_1\omega)\cos(r_2\omega) = \{\cos(r_1 - r_2)\omega + \cos(r_1 + r_2)\omega\}/2$, $r_1 > r_2$, an identity is obtained between two harmonic functions of the type $\sum_{j=0}^5 g_j \cos(j\omega)$. The function in the LHS of the identity is known, and the one in the RHS contains the unknown parameters. Equating the coefficients of $\cos(j\omega)$, $j = 0, \ldots, 5$, in both sides of the identity yields a linear system of six equations in eight-unknown parameters. A simple way to obtain a first solution is by setting, for example, $\theta_{m,2} = \theta_{s,3} = 0$, which implies $g_{m,2} = g_{s,3} = 0$. Solving now the system of equations yields

$$G(\theta_m^0, \omega) = 1.424 - 1.418\cos\omega, \tag{1.30}$$

$$G(\theta_s^0, \omega) = 0.036 + 0.044\cos\omega + 0.014\cos 2\omega$$

and $k = V_u^0 \doteq 0$. Replacing these values in (1.29), a first decomposition is obtained; since none of the three spectra in the RHS of (1.29) is negative for $\omega \in [0, \pi]$, the decomposition is admissible. It is given by

$$g_m^0(\omega) = G(\theta_m^0, \omega)/G(\nabla^2, \omega), \tag{1.31}$$

$$g_s^0(\omega) = G(\theta_s^0, \omega)/G(S, \omega)$$

and $V_u^0 \doteq 0$. Let $k_m = \min g_m^0(\omega)$ and $k_s = \min g_s^0(\omega)$, for $\omega \in [0, \pi]$. Then the canonical trend and seasonal components are obtained through

$$g_m(\omega) = g_m^0(\omega) - k_m$$

$$g_s(\omega) = g_s^0(\omega) - k_s$$

and $V_u = V_u^0 + k_m + k_s$. To find the ARIMA expression for each component, one simply needs to factorize the corresponding spectrum (an easy and accurate procedure for spectral factorization is described in appendix A of Maravall and Mathis, 1994). It should be pointed out that knowledge of the component models, although of interest, is not needed in order to obtain the component estimation filter, which can be trivially computed from the spectra (see section 8).

For the US GNP series, the models obtained for the canonical components are:

$$\nabla^2 x_{mt} = (1 + 0.085 B - 0.915 B^2) a_{mt}, \qquad V_m = 0.194 V_a \qquad (1.32a)$$

$$S x_{st} = (1 + 0.996 B + 0.338 B^2 - 0.456 B^3) a_{st} \qquad V_s = 0.009 V_a \qquad (1.32b)$$

and $V_u = 0.182 V_a$. The trend MA polynomial can be factorized as $(1 - 0.915 B)(1 + B)$, and hence the trend spectrum has a minimum of zero for $\omega = \pi$. The zero in the seasonal component spectrum occurs for $\omega = 0.76\pi$. As the variances of the p-innovations indicate, the series is characterized by a relatively strong stochastic trend, and a fairly stable seasonal component. Since the variance of the white-noise irregular is 18% of the variance of the one-period-ahead forecast error of the series, the stochastic variability of the seasonal and (in particular) of the trend component contributes in an important way to the error in forecasting the series.

The model for the seasonally adjusted series, x_{dt}, is easily derived from $x_{dt} = x_{mt} + u_t$. It is an IMA(2, 2) model, given by

$$\nabla^2 x_{dt} = (1 - 0.921 B + 0.005 B^2) a_{dt}, \qquad V_d = 0.783 V_a. \qquad (1.32c)$$

7.2   Some Comments on the Specification of the Component Model

7.2.1   *First step of the decomposition*   From (1.30) and (1.31), the first admissible decomposition yielded the trend spectrum

$$g_m^0(\omega) = \frac{1.424 - 1.418 \cos \omega}{6 - 8 \cos \omega + 2 \cos 2\omega},$$

which, upon factorization, implies the IMA(2, 1) model:

$$\nabla^2 x_{mt}^0 = (1 - 0.912 B) a_{mt}^0, \qquad V_m^0 = 0.777 V_a.$$

The model is as (1.18), and can be expressed as an STS second-order random-walk model of the type (1.17), with $V_m = 0.709 V_a$ and $V_\mu = 0.006 V_a$. Since estimation may well indicate that V_μ can be accepted as zero, the trend model would again be given by the random-walk plus drift model, in accordance with the results in Harvey and Jaeger (1991). Notice, however, that restricting the order of the MA implies a considerable increase in the variance of the p-innovation when compared to that for the canonical trend (0.777 versus 0.194); the canonical trend is therefore considerably smoother.

7.2.2 Near cancellation of units roots

Compatibility with the observed series model implies that an overall ARIMA model with $\nabla \nabla_4$ in its AR part will always produce an I(2) trend. Yet if we consider (1.32a), factorize the MA part, and cancel the MA root 0.915 with one of the unit AR roots, the trend model becomes $\nabla x_{mt} = (1 + B) a_{mt} + \mu$, an I(1) model, similar to the "trend in a random-walk trend" of equation (1.27). Furthermore, looking at the model for the seasonally adjusted series given by (1.32c), it is immediately seen that it can be approximated by $\nabla x_{dt} = a_{dt} + \mu$, and hence is very close to the standard "random-walk plus drift" trend used in econometrics.

The near cancellation of a unit root in the trend of ARIMA models with a $\nabla \nabla_s$ stationarity-inducing transformation is often found in practice, and explains the apparent discrepancy between the I(1) models of econometricians and the I(2) trends of most statistical decompositions (see Maravall, 1993a). For the usual number of observations in quarterly or monthly series, it is most unlikely that sample information can reliably discriminate between the two models:

$$\nabla^2 m_t = (1 - 0.92B) a_{mt} \tag{1.33}$$

$$\nabla m_t = a_{mt} + \mu. \tag{1.34}$$

Model (1.33) can be expressed as model (1.34) by replacing the constant slope μ by a slowly changing μ_t. This flexibility is achieved at the cost of losing one observation, due to the additional differencing. Be that as it may, the short-term adaptability of the slope makes model (1.33) more suitable for short-term analysis; on the other hand, it is likely that this short-term flexibility is un-suitable for long-term inference. Since statistical practical applications are aimed at short-term monitoring, while the applications of unobserved compo-nent models by econometricians look at longer-term horizons, the use of specification (1.33) by the former and (1.34) by the latter seems justified. Still, the use of ARIMA models for long-term inference in economics has often been questioned; see, for example, Cochrane (1988), Quah (1990), Christiano and Eichenbaum (1989), Diebold and Rudebusch (1991), and Maravall (1993b).

7.2.3 MA parameters and p-innovation variances

Setting, without loss of generality, $V_a = 1$, it follows that, in the canonical decomposition of model (1.5), although the model for the trend depends on two parameters, the model for the seasonal component on three, and the model for the irregular on one, all those parameters are simply functions of θ_1 and θ_4. It can be seen that different values of θ_1 and θ_4 have little effect on the MA parameters of the trend and seasonal component models, and a strong effect on the variance of the component p-innovations. More stable trends (i.e. larger values of θ_1) yield smaller values of V_m, and more stable seasonal components (i.e. larger values of θ_4) yield smaller values of V_s.

7.2.4 A remark   The decomposition of the GNP series we have performed and discussed is simply meant to represent a reasonable decomposition; other specifications may be reasonable as well. What seems clear, however, is that the series does not contain evidence of periodic cycles; there is none in the model, none in the residuals.

8 Optimal Estimation of Unobserved Components

8.1 Minimum Mean-Squared Error Estimators

For the model consisting of equation (1.1) and the set of assumptions 1–5, the next assumption defines the estimator of interest.

Assumption 6   Denote by $X_T = [x_1, \ldots, x_T]$ the series of available observations. The optimal estimator of the unobserved component x_{it} is given by $x_{it|T} = E(x_{it}/X_T)$.   ∎

Assumption 6 is a standard assumption in model-based estimation of unobserved components; together with the other assumptions, it implies that $x_{it|T}$ is a linear projection and will be the MMSE estimator.

There are two well-known procedures to compute the above conditional expectation. One is based on the Kalman filter, the other on the Wiener-Kolmogorov (WK) filter. Both were first derived for stationary series (see, for example, Whittle, 1963; and Anderson and Moore, 1979) and subsequently extended to the nonstationary case (see Cleveland and Tiao, 1976; Bell, 1984; Ansley and Kohn, 1985; Maravall, 1988b; De Jong, 1988; among others).

The Kalman filter approach starts by setting the model in a state-space format, and runs a set of recursions after having established appropriate starting conditions. (For nonstationary models, those conditions have been the subject of considerable research; see Kohn and Ansley, 1986; De Jong, 1991; Bell and Hillmer, 1991; and Gómez and Maravall, 1993.) The Kalman filter provides an easy to program, computationally efficient algorithm, and is used in estimation of unobserved components in, for example, the approaches of Harrison and Stevens (1976), Engle (1978), Gersch and Kitagawa (1983), Harvey and Todd (1983), Burridge and Wallis (1985), Dagum and Quenneville (1993) and, in general, in the STS methodology. It is also the standard procedure in most econometric applications; a good general reference is Harvey (1989). Although less popular, the WK filter is also used on occasion. Examples are found in Nerlove, Grether, and Carvalho (1979), Sargent (1987) and, in particular, in the AMB methodology (see Burman, 1980). Ultimately, the two filters provide computationally efficient ways to obtain the same linear projection (that implied by the conditional expectation of assumption 6). The WK filter offers the advantage of providing more information on the structure of the filter and is better suited for analytical discussion; for this reason, it shall be used for the rest of the chapter. The discussion, however, will also apply to components estimated with the Kalman filter, although there may be some typically very small discrepancies due to the effect of different starting conditions.

8.2 The Wiener-Kolmogorov Filter

When considering estimation of a component, it will prove convenient to work with the two-component representations (1.2), where m_t denotes the component of interest, and n_t is the sum of the remaining components. The two components follow the models:

$$\phi_m(B)m_t = \theta_m(B)a_{mt}, \tag{1.35a}$$

$$\phi_n(B)n_t = \theta_n(B)a_{nt}, \tag{1.35b}$$

and (1.11) and (1.12) become $\phi(B) = \phi_m(B)\phi_n(B)$, and $\theta(B)a_t = \theta_m(B)\phi_n(B)a_{mt} + \theta_n(B)\phi_m(B)a_{nt}$. It will facilitate the presentation to begin by considering the case of a complete realization of the series x_t, extending from $t = -\infty$ to $t = \infty$. Denote this realization by X. Assume, first, the case of a stationary series (and hence stationary components), and write (1.10) and (1.35) as $x_t = \Psi(B)a_t$, $m_t = \Psi_m(B)a_{mt}$, $n_t = \Psi_n(B)a_{nt}$. Then, the WK filter is given by

$$\hat{m}_t = m_{t|\infty} = E(m_t|X) = k_m \frac{\Psi_m(B)\,\Psi_m(F)}{\Psi(B)\,\Psi(F)}\,x_t, \tag{1.36}$$

where $k_m = V_m/V_a$. Replacing the Ψ-polynomials by their rational expressions, after cancellation of roots, it is obtained that

$$\hat{m}_t = v(B, F)x_t, \tag{1.37a}$$

$$v(B, F) = k_m \frac{\theta_m(B)\theta_m(F)\phi_n(B)\phi_n(F)}{\theta(B)\theta(F)}, \tag{1.37b}$$

where $v(B, F)$ is the WK filter. It is seen that no AR roots appear in the denominator of the filter, which, under assumption 3, will always converge. In fact, expression (1.37) also yields the optimal estimator of m_t in the (unit roots) nonstationary case. Direct inspection of $v(B, F)$ shows that the filter is centered at t, symmetric, and convergent in B and F. In particular, the filter will be finite when the overall model (1.10) is a finite AR process. Expression (1.37b) shows that the filter is precisely the ACGF of the ARIMA model

$$\theta(B)z_t = \theta_m(B)\phi_n(B)b_t, \tag{1.38}$$

where var$(b_t) = k_m$. Assumption 3 guarantees stationarity; as for invertibility, the filter that yields m_t will be noninvertible when n_t is nonstationary.

Since $v(B, F)$ is a two-sided filter, it will be subject to the problem of preliminary estimation and revisions mentioned in section 2. This problem will be addressed in section 10; preliminary estimation typically affects a few years at the beginning and at the end of the series, and the historical estimator can be assumed to apply to the center years. For example, in the quarterly US GNP series of section 7, it can be seen that 95% of the variance of the revision in the trend concurrent estimator has been completed after 3 years of additional data. Thus, in the 35 years of available data, the historical estimator can be assumed to be approximately valid for the 116 central observations.

By construction, the WK filter adapts itself to the series under consideration, and this adaptability avoids the dangers of under- and overestimation mentioned in section 3, and associated with *ad hoc* filtering. As an illustration, if the AMB method is used in the two extreme cases of unstable seasonality and unstable trend of figure 1.6, then figure 1.7 becomes figure 1.10. For the series with a highly stochastic seasonal, the filter adapts to the width of the seasonal peak, and the seasonally adjusted series does not display any spurious spectral peaks, as was the case in figure 1.7b. For the unstable trend case, figure 1.8 also displays the AMB trend filter. From its closeness to the spectral peak around $\omega = 0$ in the series model, it is apparent that no spurious cycle will be induced in the detrended series.

It is worth mentioning that many *ad hoc* filters, including the HP and the X11 ones, have been given an (approximate) model-based interpretation under assumptions 1–6. Examples can be found in Cleveland and Tiao (1976), Tiao (1983), Burridge and Wallis (1984), King and Rebelo (1993), and Cogley (1990). In general, for a symmetric *ad hoc* filter, it will be possible to find an approximation derived from a model-based approach under assumptions 1–6.

9 The Structure of the Optimal Estimator

9.1 The Model for the Estimator

Consider the optimal estimator (1.37a), with $v(B, F)$ given by (1.37b). Using (1.10), the estimator of m_t can be expressed in terms of the innovations (a_t) in the observed series as

$$\phi_m(B)\hat{m}_t = \theta_m(B)\alpha_m(F)a_t, \tag{1.39a}$$

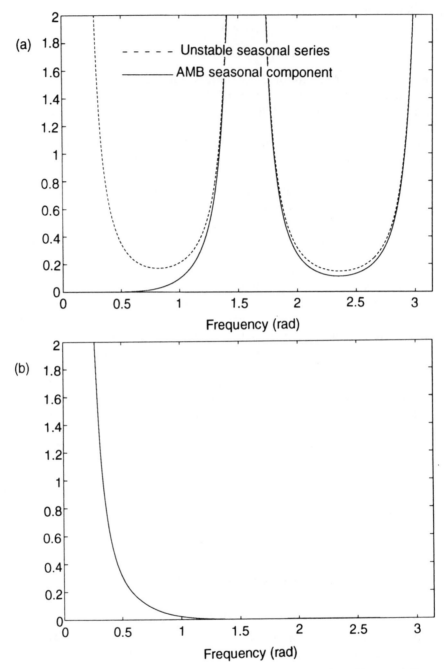

Figure 1.10 (a) Unstable seasonal and AMB seasonal component (b) seasonally adjusted series

where $\alpha_m(F)$ is the (invertible) forward filter

$$\alpha_m(F) = k_m \frac{\theta_m(F)\phi_n(F)}{\theta(F)}. \tag{1.39b}$$

Comparing (1.35a) with (1.39a), it is seen that the expressions for the unobserved component (m_t), and for its estimator $(\hat{m}_t)$, share the same AR polynomial. The stationarity-inducing transformation is the same for both, and component and estimator have the same order of integration. Moreover, the two models (1.35a) and (1.39a) share the same polynomials in the operator B. The basic difference between the two models is the presence of the polynomial $\alpha_m(F)$ in the model for the estimator. This forward filter expresses the two-sided character of the WK filter, that is, the dependence of the final estimator $\hat{m}_t$ on innovations posterior to period t (this dependence goes to zero as the time distance increases.)

In any event, the models for m_t and $\hat{m}_t$ are structurally different. They will display different variances and covariances (for the stationary transformation), and different spectra. These differences are illustrated in Figure 1.11, which compares the component and estimator spectra for the trend and seasonal components of the US GNP series. It is seen that the spectrum of a component is similar to that of its estimator, except for the dips displayed by the latter at the frequencies for which the other components present spectral peaks.

To understand the differences between the component spectrum and that of its estimator, from (1.36), the spectrum of $\hat{m}_t$ is equal to

$$g_{\hat{m}}(\omega) = R^2(\omega)g_x(\omega), \tag{1.40}$$

where

$$R(\omega) = \frac{g_m(\omega)}{g_x(\omega)} = \frac{1}{1 + 1/r(\omega)}, \tag{1.41}$$

and $r(\omega) = g_m(\omega)/g_n(\omega)$. Since m_t is the component of interest, we shall refer to it as the signal; accordingly, n_t will be denoted the noise. Therefore, $r(\omega)$ represents the signal-to-noise ratio, and MMSE estimation proceeds as follows. For each ω, it computes the signal-to-noise ratio. If the ratio is high, then the contribution of that frequency in the estimation of the signal will also be high. Thus, for the US GNP example, if the trend is the signal, then $R(0) = 1$, and the frequency $\omega = 0$ will only be used for trend estimation. Since the noise, in this case, contains seasonal nonstationarity, for the seasonal frequencies, $R(\omega) = 0$, so that these frequencies are ignored in computing the trend. The associated spectral zeros in $g_{\hat{m}}(\omega)$ explain the dips in the spectra of figure 1.11a; they also imply that model (1.39a) is noninvertible. This noninvertibility of the estimator is also evident from the unit seasonal roots of $\phi_n(B)$ in (1.39b), which appear in the MA part of model (1.39a).

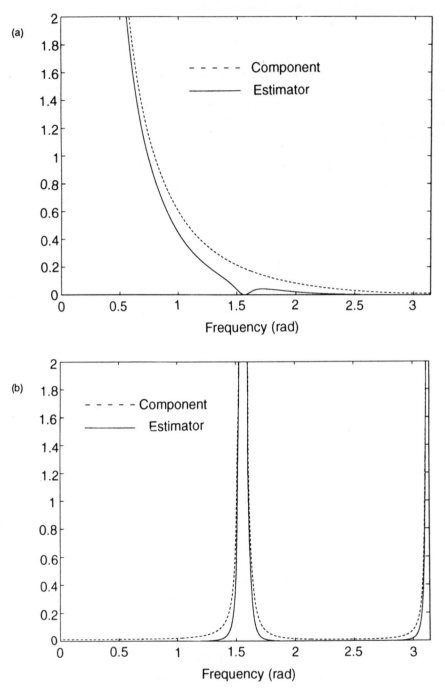

Figure 1.11 (a) Trend (b) seasonal

9.2 Structural Underestimation and Bias towards Stability

Since $r(\omega) \geq 0$, then $0 \leq R(\omega) \leq 1$, and considering that (1.40) and (1.41) imply $g_{\hat{m}}(\omega) = R(\omega)g_m(\omega)$, it follows that the estimator will always underestimate the component. The amount of that underestimation depends on the particular model under consideration. From (1.40) and (1.41), it can be seen that $g_{\hat{m}}(\omega)/g_m(\omega)$ is an increasing function of V_m/V_a. Therefore, the relative underestimation will be large (i.e. $g_{\hat{m}}(\omega)/g_m(\omega)$ will be small) when the variance of the component innovation V_m is relatively small. Table 1.1 illustrates, for the two examples of figure 1.6, the effects of underestimation of the seasonally adjusted series (m_t) and of the seasonal component (n_t), where underestimation is measured as the ratio of the variance of the stationary transformation of the estimator to that of the component.

Table 1.1 Underestimation of the component ($V_a = 1$)

	Stable m_t, unstable n_t		Unstable m_t, stable n_t	
	m_t	n_t	m_t	n_t
Variance of the component innovation	0.08	0.20	0.78	0.01
Estimator variance as fraction of component variance (stationary transformation)	0.09	0.77	0.85	0.08

It is seen that underestimation of the component will be particularly intense when the stochastic variability of the component is already small. Thus the estimator will always be biased towards producing a series more stable than the component. As a consequence, even though the component and its estimator have the same order of integration, the bias towards stability displayed by the latter should warn against using trends or seasonally adjusted series to test for difference versus time stationary series. It is also worth noticing that departures between estimator and component will be large when the component is of little importance, and vice versa.

In the model-based approach, the possibility of deriving the model that generates the component estimator can be a useful tool for diagnosis. In a particular application, the theoretical variance and autocorrelation function (ACF) of the stationary transformation of the estimator can be easily obtained from (1.39), and compared to those of the estimate actually obtained. As seen in Maravall (1987), large departures between the theoretical and empirical values would indicate misspecification of the overall model and, as a consequence, of the estimation filters employed.

As an illustration, table 1.2 compares, for the US GNP series example, the theoretical and empirical variances of the stationary transformation of the

Table 1.2   Variance of the stationary transformation of the estimator

		Correct filter	*Incorrect filter*
Trend estimator	Theoretical value	0.102	0.003
	Estimate (SE)	0.111 (0.012)	0.029 (0.0004)
Seasonal estimator	Theoretical value	0.001	0.143
	Estimate (SE)	0.001 (0.0001)	0.208 (0.017)
Irregular estimator	Theoretical value	0.052	0.001
	Estimate (SE)	0.040 (0.006)	0.002 (0.0001)
Seasonally adjusted	Theoretical value	0.825	0.009
series estimator	Estimate (SE)	0.645 (0.100)	0.039 (0.001)

estimated components for two filters: one is a "correct" filter, given by the AMB approach applied to model (1.28); the other is the AMB filter of the stable trend with unstable seasonal example of figure 1.5 (i.e. an "incorrect filter"). The variances have been standardized by dividing them by the variance of $\nabla \nabla_4 x_t$, and the reported standard errors (SEs) are asymptotic approximations (under the assumption that the underlying model is the one generating the filter). The table clearly indicates that, for the correct filter, the empirical variances are in close agreement with the theoretical ones; on the contrary, the two variances strongly disagree when the incorrect filter is employed.

9.3   Covariance between the Estimators

Since the sum of the components is equal to the sum of their estimators, the under estimation of the component implies that, while the crosscovariances between different components are always zero, this will not be the case for the estimators. For the two component decompositions (1.2), let $\Gamma(B, F)$ denote the crosscovariance generating function (CCGF) between $\hat{m}_t$ and $\hat{n}_t$; that is, $\Gamma(B, F) = \sum_{j=-\infty}^{\infty} \gamma_j B^j$, where $\gamma_j = E(\hat{m}_t \hat{n}_{t-j})$. Then, from (1.39) and the equivalent expression for $\hat{n}_t$,

$$\Gamma(B, F) = (k_m k_n) \frac{\theta_m(B) \alpha_m(B) \theta_n(F) \alpha_n(B)}{\phi_m(B) \phi_n(F)} V_a,$$

or, after simplification,

$$\Gamma(B, F) = \frac{\theta_m(B) \theta_n(B) \theta_m(F) \theta_n(F)}{\theta(B) \theta(F)} (V_m V_n / V_a). \qquad (1.42)$$

Therefore, the CCGF between the two estimators is symmetric and convergent; in particular, it is equal to the ACGF of the model

$$\theta(B) z_t = \theta_m(B) \theta_n(B) g_t, \qquad (1.43)$$

where g_t is white noise with variance $(V_m V_n)/V_a$. Even when the components are nonstationary, the crosscovariance between the estimators are finite.

The discrepancy between theoretically uncorrelated components and the existence of nonzero crosscovariances between their MMSE estimators in the model-based approach has been a cause of concern (see, for example, Nerlove, 1964; Granger, 1978; and García Ferrer and Del Hoyo, 1992). This concern, however, should be somewhat limited: for a complete realization of the series, the fact that the crossvariance is finite implies that, when at least one of the components is nonstationary (overwhelmingly the case of applied interest), the crosscorrelation between the estimators is also zero. Thus, model-based MMSE estimators of uncorrelated components are also un-correlated.

Table 1.3 Crosscorrelation between the stationary transformations of the estimators

		Correct filter	*Incorrect filter*
Between trend and	Theoretical value	−0.22	−0.30
seasonal estimators	Estimate	−0.21	−0.63
Between trend and	Theoretical value	−0.01	−0.36
irregular estimators	Estimate	−0.09	−0.71

It is nevertheless interesting to notice that, although the estimators (in levels) will be uncorrelated, their stationary transformations will be correlated. This peculiar feature can be exploited at the diagnostics stage in a manner similar to that used for the ACF of the estimators. Corresponding to the particular model at hand, the theoretical crosscorrelations between the stationary transformation of the estimators can be easily derived from (1.42) or (1.43), and then compared to the ones obtained empirically. As an illustration, table 1.3 displays the theoretical value and the estimate obtained for the lag-0 cross-correlation between the components for the US GNP series, using the correct and incorrect filters of table 1.2. Again, for the correct filter, the theoretical and empirical values are quite close. Since the incorrect filter is aimed at capturing a more stable trend than the one present in the GNP series, it underestimates the GNP trend, which contaminates then the seasonal and irregular estimates.

9.4   The Component Pseudo-Innovation

Estimation of the component p-innovation, a_{mt}, can be of some interest (an example is found in Harvey and Koopman, 1992), and the model-based approach can provide optimal estimators of the component p-innovations, a_{mt}. Taking conditional expectations in (1.35a), it is obtained that $\phi_m(B)\hat{m}_t = \theta_m(B)\hat{a}$, and considering (1.39), after simplification, the optimal estimator of the p-innovation can be expressed as

$$\hat{a}_{mt} = V_m \frac{\theta_m(F)\phi_n(F)}{\theta(F)} a_t,$$

a convergent forward filter of the innovations in the observed series. Therefore, the estimator of the p-innovation has a stochastic structure quite different from that of the white-noise p-innovation in the model. In fact, comparing the filter above with (1.38), it is seen that the ACGF of the standardized p-innovation estimator is precisely the WK filter.

9.5   Implications for Econometric Analysis

The properties of the optimal estimator have two relevant implications for applied econometric work. One has to do with the use of seasonally adjusted series (also of trends and of detrended series) in univariate or vector AR models, and in some commonly used unobserved component models. The second implication concerns the practice of identifying cycles by detrending seasonally adjusted series.

From expression (1.39), which expresses the estimator as a function of the innovations in the observed series, it is obtained that

$$\theta(F)\phi_m(B)\hat{m}_t = k_m\theta_m(B)\theta_m(F)\phi_n(F)a_t. \tag{1.44}$$

The MA part in (1.44) will be noninvertible when $\theta_m(B)$ and/or $\phi_n(B)$ contain one or more unit roots. As seen before, $\theta_m(B)$ will contain a unit root when m_t is a canonical component. More relevantly, $\phi_n(B)$ will contain unit roots whenever n_t is nonstationary. Thus, for example, if m_t denotes the seasonally adjusted series of the US GNP example of section 7, then, as implied by (1.32b), $\phi_n(B)$ is the polynomial S. The same is true when m_t denotes the trend component. Further, if m_t denotes the seasonal component, then $\phi_n(B) = \nabla^2$; finally, if m_t denotes the seasonally adjusted and detrended series (i.e. the irregular), then $\phi_n(B) = \nabla\nabla_4$. Therefore, the estimator of the seasonally adjusted series, of the trend, of the seasonal component, and of the irregular component will all be noninvertible. More generally, since, as was argued in section 5, for series exhibiting seasonality, typically S is included in the AR polynomial of the seasonal component, seasonally adjusted series and trend estimators will typically be noninvertible.

Noninvertibility of the estimator of a component (when some of the other components are nonstationary) is a property of model-based estimation satisfying assumptions 1–6, and hence is valid for the AMB as well as the STS approach. It will also characterize estimators obtained with *ad hoc* filters for which a model-based interpretation with nonstationary components can be given. For example, the filter $C_i(B)$ in (1.3) that provides the detrended series of the HP filter can be written as (see Cogley, 1990)

$$C_{HP}^2(B) = \alpha_{HP}(B, F)(1 - B)^2(1 - F)^2,$$

where $\alpha_{HP}(B, F)$ is symmetric and convergent in B and F, and hence for series that are $I(d)$ with $d < 4$, the detrended series will be noninvertible. For X11, the filter that provides the seasonally adjusted series can be expressed as (see Cleveland, 1972)

$$C_{X11}(B) = \alpha_{X11}(B, F)S(B)S(F),$$

where, again, $\alpha_{X11}(B, F)$ is symmetric and convergent in B and F, and hence the adjusted series will also be noninvertible.

An immediate implication of the noninvertibility property is that the seasonally adjusted series will not have a convergent AR representation, and hence to fit finite AR models to seasonally adjusted series will not be appropriate. Furthermore, a vector autoregression (VAR) model should not be used to model a vector of time series some of which have been seasonally adjusted. Given the reluctance, often encountered in applied econometrics, to deal explicitly with seasonality, the practice of using adjusted series when fitting AR or VAR models has become, since the influential work of Sims (1980), a close to universal practice (see, for example, Lütkepohl, 1991). Given that noninvertibility implies nonconvergence of the AR representation, no finite AR or VAR can be justified as an approximation when seasonally adjusted or detrended series are used. As a by-product, unit root tests based on AR representations (such as the augmented Dickey-Fuller test) or tests for cointegration based on VAR representations (such as Johansen tests) should not be applied to seasonally adjusted series. Here, too, since the work of Campbell and Mankiw (1987) and Stock and Watson (1986), among many others, testing for unit roots or cointegration on seasonally adjusted series is also standard econometric practice.

The error incurred when AR models are fit to noninvertible seasonally adjusted series can be both insidious and devastating, since it may easily pass undetected. These two important features are easily illustrated with the (X11 seasonally adjusted) US GNP series itself, a series which has often been the victim of this misspecification error. Following standard procedure, I consider the entire series, without truncation to remove preliminary estimators. Taking first differences of the log of the series, the ACF converges fast, and a low-order model seems appropriate. In fact, a simple "AR(1) + constant" model provides a reasonable fit, as evidenced by the relatively clean ACF of the residuals. This low-order AR specification is often found in applied econometrics work (see, for example, Campbell and Mankiw, 1987; or Evans, 1989). The choice of the parsimonious AR(1) specification seems to be confirmed by looking at what happens when the order of the AR polynomial is increased to 2, 3, or 4 lags. The additional AR coefficients are not significant, and the residual variance and Box-Ljung-Pierce Q-statistics for the residuals ACF remain roughly the same; this is shown in the first two columns

Table 1.4   AR fits to US GNP seasonally adjusted (rate of change)

	AR(1)		AR(4)		AR(9)		AR(13)	
$\mu(\times 10^2)$	1.28	(0.18)	1.38	(0.25)	0.83	(0.31)	0.79	(0.32)
ϕ_1	0.303	(0.081)	0.310	(0.085)	0.445	(0.083)	0.382	(0.087)
ϕ_2	–		0.039	(0.088)	−0.045	(0.086)	−0.097	(0.091)
ϕ_3	–		0.054	(0.087)	0.131	(0.084)	0.183	(0.089)
ϕ_4	–		−0.152	(0.084)	−0.302	(0.084)	−0.414	(0.090)
ϕ_5	–		–		0.143	(0.084)	0.222	(0.092)
ϕ_6	–		–		0.013	(0.081)	−0.047	(0.086)
ϕ_7	–		–		0.213	(0.081)	0.245	(0.083)
ϕ_8	–		–		−0.362	(0.085)	−0.445	(0.090)
ϕ_9	–		–		0.319	(0.083)	0.349	(0.092)
ϕ_{10}	–		–		–		0.030	(0.091)
ϕ_{11}	–		–		–		0.226	(0.090)
ϕ_{12}	–		–		–		−0.230	(0.090)
ϕ_{13}	–		–		–		0.203	(0.085)
$V_a(\times 10^4)$	1.49		1.44		1.12		0.97	
Q_{20}	28.6		28.2		19.4		9.8	

Significant AR coefficients are underlined.

of table 1.4. (The small negative value for lag 4 reflects the negative lag-4 autocorrelation often induced by seasonal adjustment.) Thus it is easy to conclude that the AR(1) approximation is reasonable. Yet it is not. If the order of the AR is further and further increased, additional significant coefficients keep showing up for large lags. Simultaneously, the residual variance and Q-statistics tend towards zero. This is evidenced in the last two columns of table 1.4; notice that in the AR(13) model, 10 of the 13 coefficients are significant. (This behavior could be expected since, for noninvertible series, the partial ACF does not converge.) The example illustrates thus the potentially devastating effects of noninvertibility (or close to noninvertibility) on estimation of AR models, and its perverse nature since, unless one is on the lookout, it may well pass undetected. (Good protection is provided by consideration of the sample partial and inverse ACF which, for noninvertible series, will converge slowly.)

The noninvertibility of the seasonally adjusted series also affects the specification of some unobserved component models commonly used in business cycle analysis. An example is model (2) in Stock and Watson (1988), where income is the sum (as in (1.2)) of a permanent and a transitory component (mutually orthogonal); the permanent component (m_t) follows a random walk plus drift model, as in (1.15), and the transitory component (n_t) is a stationary AR(2) model. The series has been seasonally adjusted with X11, and hence is noninvertible. On the contrary, the two components m_t and n_t in the RHS of (1.2) are invertible, so that their invertible sum cannot be equal to a noninvertible series. What the analysis also shows is that the use of the seasonally adjusted series on the belief that dimensionality will be reduced is unjustified. As (1.44) indicates, the filtered series, even when the underlying component has a very simple structure, will follow a rather complicated model, and may contain nonzero coefficients at relatively high-order lags.

I proceed now to discuss the second implication of interest for applied econometric research. As mentioned before, business cycle analysis often uses seasonally adjusted data, which are further detrended. The seasonally adjusted and detrended series is then analyzed, perhaps by fitting an ARMA model where the AR part may contain a cycle. This way of proceeding can be extremely misleading, as the following example illustrates.

Under assumptions 1–6, consider a quarterly series which is the sum of a trend, a seasonal, and an irregular component. The model for the trend is given by (1.16), that for the seasonal component by (1.21), and the irregular is white noise. The trend model is similar to that of the model-based version of the HP filter (King and Rebelo, 1993), and the seasonal component model is as in the STS model of Harvey and Todd (1983). This unobserved components model is, in fact, the type of model used in Gersch and Kitagawa (1983). The innovation variances are set equal to $V_m = V_u/1600$ (the standard value in the HP filter), $V_s = 2V_u$, and $V_u = 1$, and hence the series contains a very stable trend and a highly moving seasonal. By construction, it does not contain any periodic cycle, and the seasonally adjusted and detrended series is simply white noise. The model implies that the observed series x_t follows a model of the type

$$\nabla \nabla_4 x_t = \theta(B) a_t, \qquad (1.45)$$

where $\theta(B)$ is of order 5. If the series is seasonally adjusted and detrended by removing the MMSE estimators of the trend and of the seasonal component, then the residual obtained is the MMSE estimator of the white-noise irregular component x_{ut}. For a white-noise irregular component (x_{ut}) extracted from model (1.45), proceeding as in section 9.1 it is found that its MMSE estimator can be seen as generated by the model

$$\theta(F) \hat{x}_{ut} = k_u(1 - F)(1 - F^4) a_t. \qquad (1.46)$$

Thus $\hat{x}_{ut}$ will have the ACF of a stationary process; in particular, that of the inverse or dual model of (1.45). For the example considered, figure 1.12 exhibits the spectrum of $\hat{x}_{ut}$. It is certainly far from being that of white noise, and it is of interest to notice the large spectral peak for a frequency between 0 and the first seasonal frequency. This peak implies a relatively important cycle (with a period of approximately 5 years) that may easily show up in ARMA or even AR fits to $\hat{x}_{ut}$. The cyclical behavior detected in this way is entirely spurious, since it was not in the series. Notice that the spuriousness, in this case, is due to an incorrect interpretation of the filtered residuals, and not to the use of inappropriate filters to detrend and seasonally adjust the series.

The example illustrates a fairly general result. For models containing ∇_4 as part of the stationary transformation, the MMSE of a white-noise component will typically present a spectrum with two pronounced peaks towards the center of the frequency ranges $(0, \pi/2)$ and $(\pi/2, \pi)$. This is a result of the spectral zeros at $\omega = 0$, $\pi/2$, and π, induced by the presence of ∇_4 in the MA part of the model for $\hat{x}_{ut}$. The first peak, of course, will be associated with a cyclical frequency, and will produce a spurious cyclical-type behavior. As a consequence, the two-step procedure of fitting a model to a seasonally adjusted and detrended series is inappropriate for detecting periodic cycles. If a cycle is suspected, it should be estimated on the observed series, in a joint model with the rest of the components. When *ad hoc* filters (such as the HP and the X11 filters) are used to detrend and seasonally adjust white noise, a spectrum similar to that of figure 1.12 is obtained (with the peaks possibly more pronounced).

The effect of filters on the spectrum of the series has also implications for a methodology that has become popular in macroeconomics, in which, first, the

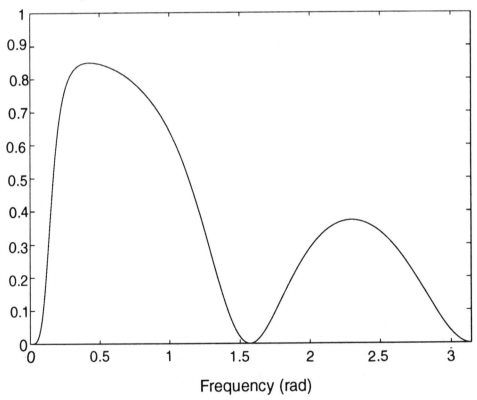

Figure 1.12 Seasonally adjusted and detrended white noise

so-called stylized facts of macroeconomic variables are identified and, second, an economic model is calibrated with the purpose of reproducing those facts (see, for example, Kydland and Prescott, 1982; and Danthine and Donaldson, 1993). The stylized facts typically consist of second-order moments of the seasonally adjusted and detrended series (most often, with X11 and the HP filter). As we have seen, the filters will have an effect on those second-order moments. This effect will affect the comparison since, to start with, the series produced by the calibrated model are not seasonally adjusted. Moreover, if the two filters are applied to two independent white-noise variables, the spectra of the two filtered series will display identical peaks and holes, and this fact will induce spurious crosscorrelation between the two (independent) series.

10   Preliminary Estimator and Forecast

10.1   General Expression

In the previous section, attention was centered on the historical estimator, i.e. on the estimator obtained applying the WK filter (1.37) to a complete realization on the series. As before, let X and X_T denote the complete and finite realization of the time series, respectively, and let m_t be the component or signal of interest. To project m_t on the finite realization X_T, since $X_T \subset X$, the optimal estimator can be expressed as

$$m_{t|T} = E(m_t|X_T) = E(E(m_t|X)|X_T)$$
$$= E(\hat{m}_t|X_T), \qquad (1.47)$$

which implies that $m_{t|T}$ can be expressed as

$$m_{t|T} = v(B, F)x_{t|T}, \qquad (1.48)$$

where $v(B, F)$ is the WK filter given by (1.37b), B and F operate on t, and $x_{t|T} = E(x_t|X_T)$. Since $x_{t|T}$ is the forecast of x_t done at time T (equal to x_t if $T \geq t$), the estimator (1.48) can be seen as the WK filter applied to the available series extended at both ends with forecasts and backcasts (i.e. applied to the "extended series"). For a large enough (positive) $T - t$ (1.48) provides in practice the final or historical estimator of m_t, equivalent to (1.37). As t approaches T, (1.48) provides preliminary estimators of recent signals; for $t > T$ (1.48) yields the $(t - T)$-periods-ahead forecast of the signal. Forecasts can thus be seen as particular cases of preliminary estimation (and can be computed in a simple recursive way; see Burman, 1980).

Consider the model for the observed series, given by (1.10), and let p and q be the orders of the AR and MA polynomials. Unless $q = 0$, the filter in (1.48) will contain an infinite number of weights. Since the filter is convergent, it could be safely truncated and approximated by a finite filter of the type (1.4). (The finite approximation can also be viewed as the WK filter for the AR approximation to the invertible model (1.10).) In practice, however, there is no need to truncate the filter: the exact filter (1.37b) can be applied in an efficient and easy manner using an algorithm due to Wilson and Burman (detailed in Burman, 1980). The algorithm requires only $[q + \max(q, p)]$ forecasts and backcasts of the observed series, the solution of two sets of $(p + q)$ linear equations, and some simple recursions. Besides its computational efficiency, the problem of the starting conditions is simplified since it reduces to the conditions associated with the assumptions $E_t a_{t+k} = 0$ and $E_t a^b_{t-k} = 0$ (for $k > 0$), where a_t and a^b_t are the forward and backward innovations in the series. Thus the assumptions required are the same ones as those underlying ARIMA forecasting (see Box and Jenkins, 1970; Bell, 1984; and Brockwell and Davis, 1987).

To simplify the discussion, I shall consider the finite approximation (1.4) applied to the series extended with forecasts and backcasts, and assume $T > 2r + 1$, so that the estimator of the component for the center periods of the series can be taken as the historical estimator. For $1 < t < r$, the estimator will make use of the backcasts and will yield "preliminary" estimators for the starting periods. When $T - r < t < T$, the estimator will use forecasts of the series and will thus yield preliminary estimators for recent periods. The two types of preliminary estimators are mirror images of each other; I shall focus attention on the preliminary estimator of recent periods, the one of applied interest.

It is easily seen (Box and Jenkins, 1970) that the forecast of the series $(x_{t|T}, t > T)$ can be expressed as

$$x_{t|T} = \prod_{(t-T)}(B)x_T, \tag{1.49}$$

where the subindex $(t - T)$ indicates the dependence of the filter on the forecast horizon. Combining (1.48) and (1.49), the preliminary estimator of the component can also be expressed as

$$m_{t|T} = \lambda_{(t-T)}(B)x_T, \tag{1.50}$$

which has a relevant implication for applied work. Let the component of interest be the seasonally adjusted series. If the observed series is $X_T = [x_1, \ldots, x_T]$, and the adjusted series used is $[m_{1|T}, \ldots, m_{T|T}]$, as is standard procedure, then the adjusted series is nonstationary in the sense that, as (1.50) shows, the underlying linear process generating the latter has time-varying coefficients.

If (1.48) is rewritten as

$$m_{t|T} = \nu^{(0)}(B)x_T + \sum_{j>0} \nu_{T-t+j} x_{T+j|T},$$

when a new observation, x_{T+1}, becomes available, the forecast $x_{T+1|T}$ is replaced by the observation, and the forecasts, $x_{T+j|T}$, $j > 1$, are updated to

$x_{T+j|T+1}$. The new estimator obtained will be $m_{t|T+1}$, and the one-period revision in the estimator is

$$d_{t|T}(1) = m_{t|T+1} - m_{t|T} = \sum_{j>0} v_{T-t+j}(x_{T+j|T+1} - x_{T+j|T}) = \left(\sum_{j>0} v_{T-t+j}\Psi_{j-1}\right)a_{T+1},$$

(1.51)

and hence the one-period revision is a constant fraction of the series innovations. More generally, as seen in Pierce (1980), the revision between two periods T and $T + k$ is an MA($k - 1$) process, which can be expressed in terms of the innovations $a_{T+1}, \ldots, a_{T+k}$.

When $T \to \infty$, the estimator $m_{t|T}$ becomes the historical estimator $\hat{m}_t$. It will prove useful to rewrite expression (1.39) as

$$\hat{m}_t = \eta^{(0)}(B)a_T + \eta^{(1)}(F)a_{T+1},$$

(1.52)

where the first term in the RHS includes the effect of the starting conditions and of the innovations up to and including a_T, and the second term contains the innovations posterior to T. From (1.39b), the filter $\eta^{(1)}(F)$ is convergent; its weights are easily obtained as the coefficients $\eta_{T-t+j}(j = 1, 2, 3, \ldots)$ of the polynomial $\eta(B, F)$ obtained through the identity

$$\theta_m(B)\theta(F)\eta(B, F) = V_m\theta_m(B)\theta_m(F)\phi_n(F)$$

(see Maravall, 1994). From (1.52) and (1.47), the preliminary estimator is then equal to

$$m_{t|T} = \eta^{(0)}(B)a_T,$$

(1.53)

and subtracting this expression from (1.52), the full revision that the estimator will undergo is found to be:

$$d_{t|T} = \eta^{(1)}(F)a_{T+1},$$

(1.54)

and hence, due to the invertibility of $\theta(B)$, the full revision is a stationary process.

10.2   Some Applications of Interest

Among the many preliminary estimators, of particular relevance in economic policy making and monitoring is the so-called concurrent estimator, obtained when $t = T$. The concurrent estimator yields the estimator of the component for the most recent period, and is obtained with the one-sided filter $m_{t|t} = \eta^{(0)}(B)a_t$. In practice, revision in the concurrent estimator of the seasonally adjusted series is an issue of concern for policy makers. An example is provided by Maravall and Pierce (1983), in the context of the conduct of monetary policy by the Federal Reserve during the period of the seventies. We compared the concurrent estimator of the seasonally adjusted M1 monthly growth with its final estimator, and with the tolerance bands set every month by the Federal Open Market Committee, and obtained that the concurrent estimator gave a false signal (in the sense of indicating unacceptable growth when the final estimator eventually showed that growth was within the tolerance range, or vice versa) 40% of the time. We further argued that this proportion could be reduced with improved seasonal adjustment methods; still, the percentage could not go below 20%. Thus an important percentage of false signals given by the concurrent estimator could be attributed to the single effect of the revision error it contains.

Although damaging, revisions are unavoidable when two-sided filters are employed. (Figure 1.3 illustrated, for example, the revisions in the concurrent trend estimator for the HP filter.) Their properties – in particular, their size – will depend on the characteristics of the series and of the filter used to estimate the component. In the model-based approach, this filter depends, in turn, on the series, and hence revisions are a property of the series. For some, they will be small; for others, large.

Besides interest in estimating components for recent periods, on occasion it is the component forecast that is of interest. An example in the area of economic policy is the role played by the forecasts of the monetary aggregate seasonal component, used in short-term control of the money supply, which shall be illustrated in the next section. In the area of applied econometrics, an example of an application of unobserved component forecasting is the work of Stock and Watson (1989; 1991; 1993) on forecasting the business cycle using a model-based unobserved component model. Although an ingenious and attractive approach, care should be taken when interpreting the results precisely because of the unobserved component structure of the model. This is illustrated with the following example, consisting of the simplest nontrivial case of Stock and Watson's model, namely the model

$$\nabla y_t = \nabla c_t + n_t \qquad\qquad (1.55a)$$

$$(1 - \phi B)\nabla c_t = b_t, \qquad\qquad (1.55b)$$

where n_t and b_t are independent white-noise variables. (Notice that, since the RHS of (1.55a) is the sum of two invertible processes, and hence invertible, once again the model cannot be applied to seasonally adjusted series.) The unobserved component c_t represents "the state of the economy" and it is modeled as an I(1) trend. A recession (expansion) is then defined as a sequence of ∇c_t that are below (above) a certain threshold. The definition is made, thus, in terms of the "true" unobserved component. (Associating the business cycle with the behavior of a trend is an important departure from the traditional procedure of identifying the business cycle on the detrended series, as in Watson, 1986, or Clark, 1987; and from the periodic stochastic cycle component of Harvey, 1985.)

Stock and Watson attempt to capture in their model the official dating of recessions by the NBER Business Cycle Dating Committee (BCDC). Thus, assuming that (1.55) actually duplicates BCDC behavior, since the component is never observed, the BCDC is forced to operate with the best possible estimator, that is with the historical estimator (BCDC behavior reveals, in fact, a two-sided, relatively long, filter, typical of a historical estimator). Finally, in order to obtain recession forecasts, Stock and Watson consider the joint distribution of future sequences of ∇c_t conditional on the available information. By letting $x_t = \nabla y_t$ and $m_t = \nabla c_t$, the model is seen to be a particular case of the model-based procedure under assumptions 1–6: the simple "AR(1) + noise" decomposition. From previous results, the differences in the distributions of the component, the preliminary and the final estimator will imply that the probability of positive sequences of the component will be structurally different from that of the historical estimator (see Maravall, 1994). Thus, a systematic bias will show up when matching the forecasted probabilities with the series of historical estimators (in accordance with what Stock and Watson find).

11 Estimation Errors and Inference

11.1 Historical Estimation Error and Revision Error

Point estimators or forecasts of the components are of limited interest unless some information is provided about their precision. This information is unavailable when *ad hoc* filters are applied. The model-based approach provides the framework for obtaining the standard error of the components estimators. Within an STS approach, Burridge and Wallis (1985) show how the Kalman filter can be used to compute those errors; alternatively, they can be computed, within the AMB approach, using the procedure in Hillmer (1985). More generally, the model-based method allows us to derive, under our assumptions, the full distribution of the different estimation errors (associated with the final or with some preliminary estimator).

Consider the two-component decomposition (1.2), and let m_t be the component of interest, whose estimator is given by (1.48). The estimation error is

$$e_{t|T} = m_t - m_{t|T}, \tag{1.56}$$

which can be rewritten as

$$e_{t|T} = d_t + d_{t|T}, \tag{1.57}$$

where $d_t = m_t - \hat{m}_t$, and $d_{t|T} = \hat{m}_t - m_{t|T}$. Thus, d_t is the error in the historical estimator, and $d_{t|T}$ is the revision error contained in the estimator $m_{t|T}$. As shown in Pierce (1979), the two errors d_t and $d_{t|T}$ are independent (under assumptions 1–6), and the historical estimation error can be seen as generated by the stationary ARIMA model

$$\theta(B)d_t = \theta_m(B)\theta_n(B)g_t, \tag{1.58}$$

with $V_g = V_m V_n / V_a$. The variance of d_t is therefore finite; both variance and ACF can be easily computed from (1.58). (The ACF of the error is of interest when computing approximate standard errors for the rates of growth of the component.) As noticed in Maravall and Planas (1994), model (1.58) is identical to model (1.43), and hence the CCGF between the estimators $\hat{m}_t$ and $\hat{n}_t$ is the same as the ACGF of the historical estimation error of m_t (and of n_t). This result has an implication of interest: when searching for a criterion to select a unique decomposition among the set of admissible ones, one could think of selecting the specification for which the (lag-0) crosscovariance between the two estimators is minimized, given that the components are assumed orthogonal. On the other hand, one may select the decomposition for which the historical estimation error is minimum. What the previous result tells us is that both criteria lead to the selection of the same decomposition. Moreover, Maravall and Planas show that, in the selected decomposition, one of the two components is always a canonical one.

As for the revision error, $d_{t|T}$, from expression (1.54) its properties (in particular variance and ACF) can be easily derived, for any pair (t, T). From the orthogonality of d_t and $d_{t|T}$, the variance and ACF of the total estimation error $e_{t|T}$ are, then, straightforward to obtain. Notice that the fact that d_t and $d_{t|T}$ have finite variance implies that the theoretical component, m_t its historical estimator, $\hat{m}_t$ and its preliminary estimator or forecast, $m_{t|T}$ are all pairwise cointegrated.

11.2   An Example: the UK Money Supply Series

To illustrate the use of the model-based approach in inference, I consider an example within the area of monetary policy, where the need for a measure of the estimator's uncertainty has been repeatedly pointed out (see, for example, Bach et al., 1976; Moore et al., 1981; and Hibbert Committee, 1988). The example is the monthly series of the monetary aggregate M_1 in the UK from January, 1983 to December, 1991; seasonal adjustment of the UK monetary aggregate has been, in fact, an issue of recent concern (see Bank of England, 1992).

Letting x_t denote the log of the series, the model

$$\nabla \nabla_{12} x_t = (1 - 0.738 B^{12}) a_t, \tag{1.59}$$

with $\sigma_a = 0.00674$, fits the series very well; its structure is the monthly equivalent of that of model (1.28), obtained for the quarterly GNP series. As was the case then, the model reveals a relatively stochastic trend and a fairly stable seasonal component. Using the AMB approach, and standardizing units by setting $V_a = 1$, the models for the trend and seasonally adjusted series are, respectively, given by the IMA(2, 2) models:

$$\nabla^2 x_{mt} = (1 - 0.975B)(1 + B) a_{mt} \qquad (V_m = 0.191)$$

$$\nabla^2 x_{dt} = (1 - 0.975B)(1 - 0.004B) a_{dt} \qquad (V_d = 0.768).$$

Table 1.5 Variance of estimation errors: concurrent estimator (in units of V_a)

Type of error	Trend	Seasonally adjusted series
Final estimation error	0.169	0.110
Revision error	0.163	0.114
Total estimation error	0.332	0.224

Both are indistinguishable from an "I(1) + drift" model and, in particular, the seasonally adjusted series can be seen as a random walk with a slowly changing drift. The seasonal component model is of the type $Sx_{st} = \theta_s(B)a_{st}$, where $S = 1 + B + \ldots + B^{11}$, $\theta_s(B)$ is of order 11, and $V_s = 0.024$. The irregular component x_{ut} is simply white noise with $V_u = 0.189$.

For this decomposition, the variance of the different estimation errors for the concurrent and historical estimators of the trend and of the seasonally adjusted series are displayed in table 1.5. For both components, the variance of the historical estimation error is close to that of the revision error; both types of error are smaller for the seasonally adjusted series than for the trend. The variance of the concurrent estimator of the trend is roughly one-third of the variance of the one-period-ahead forecast error of the series x_t; this fraction becomes one-quarter for the seasonally adjusted series estimator.

Besides the magnitude of the revision error in the concurrent estimator, it is also of interest to know the duration of the revision period, that is, how many periods it takes for a new observation to no longer significantly affect the estimate. From (1.54) it is easily found that, for the example considered, after one more year of additional data, the variance of the trend revision error has decreased by 70%; for the seasonally adjusted series this percentage is 50%. After three years of additional data, 85% of the trend revision error variance has been removed; 77% for the seasonally adjusted series. After 5 years, the percentages become 92% for the trend and 88% for the adjusted series. In 5 years, thus, both estimators have practically converged. Notice that, despite its larger revision error in the concurrent estimator, the trend estimator converges faster than that of the seasonally adjusted series. Recalling that the trend component was highly stochastic, while the seasonal component was fairly stable, the example illustrates a general result: highly stochastic components are characterized by large revision errors which converge relatively fast, while the removal of stable components implies smaller revision errors, which tend to converge slowly. Thus the revision lasts long when the removed component is of little importance in explaining the series variability. This "compensation" effect (i.e. large revisions converge fast) is easily understood from the following consideration. As mentioned in section 4, the stability of a

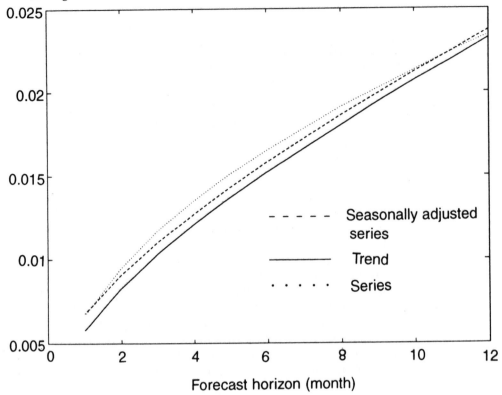

Figure 1.13 Standard error of forecast

component is associated with roots in $\theta(B)$, the MA part of the model for x_t, that are close to the unit AR roots. Due to these large roots, $\theta(B)^{-1}$ will converge slowly and hence, according to (1.37b), the estimation filter of stable components will be long. Moreover, since $\theta(F)$ is also present in the denominator of $\eta(B, F)$, expression (1.54) implies that the revision in the estimator will also last long.

We have seen convergence of the concurrent estimator to the historical one; it is also of interest to look at how fast the estimation error increases when we consider the forecasts. For the log of the M1 series, figure 1.13 presents the standard errors for the 1-to-12-periods-ahead forecasts, for the trend, seasonally adjusted and original series. The (small but consistent) gain in precision from using the trend in short-term forecasting is apparent. All considered, comparing the seasonally adjusted series and the trend component, although the concurrent estimator of the latter has a larger error variance, it converges faster to the final estimator, and it provides more precise forecasts. These are important features to consider when deciding which of the two components provides a more adequate signal to measure the underlying evolution of the series.

Assume now that at the beginning of a new year (with the last observation that of December), an annual money growth target is set. As time passes, new observations become available and it is of interest to see what growth these new data imply, once they have been cleaned of seasonality. The most frequent operating procedure is to compute, at the beginning of the year, seasonal factors for the next months (in X11, with an *ad hoc* formula), and adjust incoming monthly data with these factors. (At some institutions, such as the Federal Reserve Board and the Bank of England, seasonal adjustment is done with a higher than once-a-year frequency.) There is an obvious loss of precision in using a forecasted factor instead of the one obtained every month with concurrent estimation. Since concurrent adjustment is a costly procedure for data-producing agencies (the series have to be constantly modified), as stressed by the Bank of England (1992), it is important to quantify the loss in precision associated with intermittent adjustment. This quantification is easily done in the model-based approach by comparing the error in the seasonal component concurrent estimator with the average of the errors for the forecasted seasonal component. For the example considered and the once-a-year versus concurrent adjustment comparison, it is found that concurrent adjustment produces an average reduction of 11.2% in the root MSE of the seasonal component estimator. This relatively small gain is explained by the fact that the seasonal component is fairly stable and displays relatively small forecasting errors.

As new monthly observations become available, the forecast of the annual rate of growth will be updated. The standard errors associated with these updated forecasts for a fixed horizon (that of the end of the year) are easily obtained from the standard errors in figure 1.13. At the beginning of the year, the forecasted rate of growth for the year has approximately the same error whether the forecast is computed with the series, with the trend, or with the seasonally adjusted series; this standard error equals 2.35% of growth. For intrayear updating, after 4 months, for example, the standard error of the rate of growth is down to 1.83% if the trend is used, and to 1.91% for the forecast computed with the observed series. After 8 months, these standard errors become 1.24% and 1.35%.

Although, as pointed out in Box, Pierce, and Newbold (1987), the updated forecast of the trend rate of growth provides possibly the most natural tool for monitoring the underlying evolution of the series throughout the year, standard operating procedures rely heavily on a battery of different rate-of-growth measurements. Using linear approximations, the model-based approach can be used to derive the variances of the associated estimation errors. Consider, for example, the concurrent estimator of the most commonly used rate: the monthly rate of growth of the monthly estimator (typically, of the seasonally adjusted series), and denote this rate by R. (The wording of the Federal Open Market Committee Record of Policy Action, for example, states that modifications to the Federal funds rate had to be based on the evolution of this month-to-month rate of growth of the seasonally adjusted series.) If capital letters denote levels and small letters denote logs, the rate can be expressed as

$$R_t = (M_t - M_{t-1})/M_{t-1} \doteq m_t - m_{t-1},$$

where m_t is the signal of interest in the decomposition of (1.59). The concurrent estimator of R_t is

$$R_{t|t} = m_{t|t} - m_{t-1|t}.$$

Consider the auxiliary rate $R_A = m_{t|t} - m_{t-1|t-1}$ and its estimation error, e_t^A which can be expressed as:

$$e_t^A = R_t - R_A = (R_t - R_{t|t}) + (R_{t|t} - R_A). \tag{1.60}$$

The second parenthesis in the RHS of (1.60) is equal to $R_{t|t} - R_A = -(m_{t-1|t} - m_{t-1|t-1})$, and represents, thus, the one-period update in the concurrent estimator of m_{t-1}. From (1.51), $R_{t|t} - R_A = d_{t-1|t}(1) = -\eta_1 a_t$ where η_1 is the coefficient of F in the polynomial $\eta^{(1)}(F)$ of (1.54). For the M1 example, $\eta_1 = 0.300$ when m_t is the trend, and $\eta_1 = 0.112$ when m_t is the seasonally adjusted series. The first parenthesis in the RHS of (1.60) is the estimation error in $R_{t|t}$; denote this error by e_t^R. Since this error is the sum of the historical estimation error and a revision error which is a linear filter of innovations a_{t+k}, $k > 0$, it follows that the two expressions in parentheses in (1.60) are independent, and hence the variances will satisfy

$$V(e_t^R) = V(e_t^A) - \eta_1^2 V_a. \tag{1.61}$$

To obtain $V(e_t^A)$, notice that e_t^A can be expressed as $e_t^A = (m_t - m_{t|t}) - (m_{t-1} - m_{t-1|t-1})$, and hence is equal to the difference between two consecutive concurrent estimation errors $e_{t|t}$ and $e_{t-1|t-1}$ of (1.56). To simplify notation, let $[e_t]$ denote the series of concurrent estimation errors $[e_{t|t}]$. Then,

$$V(e_t^A) = V(e_t - e_{t-1}) = 2(1 - \rho_1^e) V_e, \tag{1.62}$$

where V_e is the variance of $e_{t|t}$, and ρ_1^e its lag-1 autocorrelation. As described earlier, both parameters can be easily obtained, and for the M1 example it is found that $V_e = 0.333 V_a$, $\rho_1^e = 0.574$, when m_t is the trend component, and $V_e = 0.224 V_a$, $\rho_1^e = 0.584$, when m_t is the seasonally adjusted series. Inserting (1.62) in (1.61), the variance of the error in the concurrent estimator of R_t is $V(e_t^R) = 2(1 - \rho_1^e) V_e - \eta_1^2 V_a$.

In order to compare R_t with the annual target, the rate is multiplied by 12 and expressed in per cent. The standard errors of the rate computed in this way, for the trend and for the seasonally adjusted series, are given in the first row of table 1.6. For both components, the standard error is close to 3.5%, and hence, at the 95% confidence level, a measurement of (say) 10% growth would be compatible with a target between, roughly, a 3% and a 17% annual growth. The implied range is certainly wider than the tolerance ranges used in

Table 1.6 Standard error of the rate of growth: concurrent estimator (in %
of annualized growth)

	Trend component	*Seasonally adjusted series*
Monthly growth of the monthly series	3.56	3.38
Monthly growth of a centered 3-month moving average	2.60	2.83
Monthly growth of the last 3 months	1.99	1.79
Centered estimator of 12-month growth	1.61	1.64

practice. The rate R_t is therefore too volatile and does not provide a precise
tool for short-term monitoring.

Rates computed over longer periods will of course be more stable. Within
the model-based approach, linearizing the rate, the standard error of the
estimators can be computed in a similar manner to that of the rate R_t. Table
1.6 presents some examples. First, the second row contains the standard error
of the estimator of the monthly rate of growth of a 3-month moving average.
In order to minimize the phase effect, the moving average is centered, and
hence the one-period-ahead forecast of the component is included in its
computation. The third row of table 1.6 presents the standard error of the
estimator of the rate of growth of a one-sided 3-month moving average,
formed by the last three periods. Finally, the last row contains the standard
errors of a rate that measures the annual growth by comparing the 6-month-
ahead forecast of the component with its value 1 year before this horizon. This
rate, which smoothes the data over a 12-month period, is clearly the most
stable one, and provides more sensible tolerance ranges ($\pm 3\%$, approximately).
The rate, however, can also be computed directly on the original series,
without having to estimate the components; the standard error of the estimator when the series is used equals 1.65%, slightly larger than the one obtained
when the trend is used.

These are some examples that illustrate inference in model-based unobserved component estimation procedures; additional examples can be found in
Cleveland and Pierce (1981), Bell and Hillmer (1984), Hillmer (1985), Burridge
and Wallis (1985), and Maravall (1988a).

11.3   A Final Remark

In the previous paragraphs we have seen how the model-based approach
provides the tools to apply, in a simple way, proper statistical inference to
answer relevant questions concerning the series components. Be that as it may,
we had seen previously that the use of unobserved components in econometric
models has strong implications concerning the specification of the model
and interpretation of the results. We saw, for example, that the seasonally

adjusted, trend, or detrended series will typically be noninvertible and will not accept, as a consequence, a finite AR representation or approximation. Thus, AR and VAR models should not be applied to such filtered series. We saw that the same was true for some other type of models popular in business cycle analysis, and that some popular unit root tests cannot be applied to the trend or to the seasonally adjusted series. We also showed how the stylized facts of the series can be seriously distorted when some components are removed, and how the component estimator filters induce a spurious spectral peak for the cyclical frequency in the detrended and seasonally adjusted series. Besides, spurious crosscorrelations among the filtered series are also created. To make matters worse, the use of the seasonally adjusted series is not likely to reduce the dimensionality of the model, and, if the model for the series is linear and the full set of adjusted values is used, the underlying model for the seasonally adjusted series will have time-varying parameters.

Added to already documented limitations (referred to in section 5.2), the previous results strongly suggest that seasonally adjusted series, rather than helping economists in their analysis and research, make life considerably harder. From the set of available tools, they severely limit those that can be applied, and, besides, they may seriously contaminate the measurements. The practice followed by many data-producing agencies of only publishing seasonally adjusted series for economic variables is, as a consequence, damaging and deeply regrettable.

Notes

All the computations reported in the chapter are the output of a program Signal Extraction in ARIMA Time Series (SEATS), described in Maravall and Gómez (1994), and available upon request. The program originated from one developed by J.P. Burman for seasonal adjustment at the Bank of England; to him I wish to express my gratitude. Thanks are also due to V. Gómez, G. Fiorentini, G. Caporello, F. Canova, A.C. Harvey, and three anonymous referees.

References

Aigner, D.J., Schneider, F. and Ghosh, D. (1988), "Me and My Shadow: Estimating the Size of the U.S. Hidden Economy From Time Series Data," in Barnett, W., Berndt, E. and White, H. (eds), *Dynamic Econometric Modeling*, Cambridge: Cambridge University Press, 297–334.
Anderson, B. and Moore, J. (1979), *Optimal Filtering*, New Jersey: Prentice-Hall.
Ansley, C.F. and Kohn, R. (1985), "Estimation, Filtering and Smoothing in State Space Models with Incompletely Specified Initial Conditions," *Annals of Statistics* 13, 1286–1316.
Aoki, M. (1990), *State Space Modeling of Time Series* (2nd edn), Berlin/Heidelberg/New York: Springer-Verlag.

Bach, G.L., Cagan, P.D., Friedman, M., Hildreth, C.G., Modigliani, F. and Okun, A. (1976), *Improving the Monetary Aggregates: Report of the Advisory Committee on Monetary Statistics*, Washington, DC: Board of Governors of the Federal Reserve System.

Bank of England (1992), "Report of the Seasonal Adjustment Working Party," Occasional Paper no. 2, October 1992.

Bell, W.R. (1984), "Signal Extraction for Nonstationary Time Series," *Annals of Statistics* 12, 646–64.

Bell, W.R. and Hillmer, S.C. (1984), "Issues Involved with the Seasonal Adjustment of Economic Time Series," *Journal of Business and Economic Statistics* 2, 291–320.

Bell, W.R. and Hillmer, S.C. (1991), "Initializing the Kalman Filter for Nonstationary Time Series Models," *Journal of Time Series Analysis* 4, 283–300.

Beveridge, S. and Nelson, C.R. (1981), "A New Approach to Decomposition of Economic Time Series into Permanent and Transitory Components with Particular Attention to Measurement of the 'Business Cycle'," *Journal of Monetary Economics* 7, 151–74.

Box, G.E.P., Hillmer, S.C. and Tiao, G.C. (1978), "Analysis and Modelling of Seasonal Time Series," in Zellner, A. (ed.), *Seasonal Analysis of Economic Time Series*, Washington, DC: US Dept. of Commerce, Bureau of the Census, 309–34.

Box, G.E.P. and Jenkins, G.M. (1970), *Time Series Analysis: Forecasting and Control*, San Francisco: Holden-Day.

Box, G.E.P., Pierce, D.A. and Newbold, P. (1987), "Estimating Trend and Growth Rates in Seasonal Time Series," *Journal of the American Statistical Association* 82, 276–82.

Brockwell, P. and Davis, R. (1987), *Time Series: Theory and Methods*, Berlin: Springer-Verlag.

Bull, C. and Frydman, R. (1983), "The Derivation and Interpretation of the Lucas Supply Function," *Journal of Money, Credit, and Banking* 15, 82–95.

Burman, J.P. (1980), "Seasonal Adjustment by Signal Extraction," *Journal of the Royal Statistical Society* A, 143, 321–37.

Burridge, P. and Wallis, K.F. (1984), "Unobserved Components Models for Seasonal Adjustment Filters," *Journal of Business and Economic Statistics* 2, 350–9.

Burridge, P. and Wallis, K.F. (1985), "Calculating the Variance of Seasonally Adjusted Series," *Journal of the American Statistical Association* 80, 541–52.

Campbell, J.Y. and Mankiw, N.G. (1987), "Permanent and Transitory Components in Macro-Economic Fluctuations," *American Economic Review Proceedings 1987*, 111–17.

Canova, F. (1991), "Detrending and Business Cycle Facts," EUI Working Paper ECO no. 91/58.

Carlin, J.B. and Dempster, A.P. (1989), "Sensitivity Analysis of Seasonal Adjustments: Empirical Case Studies," *Journal of the American Statistical Association* 84, 6–20.

Chen, C. and Liu, L.M. (1993), "Joint Estimation of Model Parameters and Outlier Effects in Time Series," *Journal of the American Statistical Association* 88, 284–97.

Christiano, L.J. and Eichenbaum, M. (1989), "Unit Roots in Real GNP: Do We Know, and Do We Care?," mimeo, Federal Reserve Bank of Minneapolis, Research Department.

Clark, P.K. (1987), "The Cyclical Component of U.S. Economic Activity," *The Quarterly Journal of Economics* 102, 797–814.

Cleveland, W.P. (1972), "Analysis and Forecasting of Seasonal Time Series," PhD Dissertation, Department of Statistics, The University of Wisconsin–Madison.

Cleveland, W.P. and Pierce, D.A. (1981), "Seasonal Adjustment Methods for the Monetary Aggregates," *Federal Reserve Bulletin*, Board of Governors of the Federal Reserve System, December 1981, 875–87.

Cleveland, W.P. and Tiao, G.C. (1976), "Decomposition of Seasonal Time Series: A Model for the X-11 Program," *Journal of the American Statistical Association* 71, 581–7.

Cochrane, J.H. (1988), "How Big is the Random Walk in GNP?," *Journal of Political Economy* 96, 893–920.

Cogley, T. (1990), "Spurious Business Cycle Phenomena in HP Filtered Time Series," mimeo, University of Washington.

Crafts, N.F.R., Leybourne, S.J. and Mills, T.C. (1989), "Trends and Cycles in British Industrial Production, 1700–1913," *Journal of the Royal Statistical Society* A, 152, 43–60.

Dagum, E.B. (1980), "The X11 ARIMA Seasonal Adjustment Method," Statistics Canada, Catalogue 12–564E.

Dagum, E.B. and Quenneville, B. (1993), "Dynamic Linear Models for Time Series Components," *Journal of Econometrics* 55, 333–53.

Danthine, J.P. and Donaldson, J.B. (1993), "Methodological and Empirical Issues in Real Business Cycle Theory," *European Economic Review* 37, 1–35.

De Jong, Piet (1988), "The Likelihood for the State Space Model," *Biometrika* 75, 165–9.

De Jong, Piet (1991), "The Diffuse Kalman Filter," *Annals of Statistics* 19, 1073–83.

Den Butter, F.A.G. and Fase, M.M.G. (1991), *Seasonal Adjustment as a Practical Problem*, Amsterdam: North-Holland.

Diebold, F.X. and Rudebusch, G.D. (1991), "Is Consumption Too Smooth? Long Memory and the Deaton Paradox," *The Review of Economics and Statistics* LXXIII, 1–9.

Engle, R.F. (1978), "Estimating Structural Models of Seasonality," in Zellner, A. (ed.), *Seasonal Analysis of Economic Time Series*, Washington, DC: US Dept. of Commerce, Bureau of the Census, 281–97.

Evans, G.W. (1989), "Output and Unemployment Dynamics in the United States: 1950–1985," *Journal of Applied Econometrics* 4, 213–37.

Fama, E.F. and French, K.R. (1988), "Permanent and Temporary Components of Stock Prices," *Journal of Political Economy* 96, 246–73.

Findley, D.F. (1985), "An Analysis and Generalization of M. Watson's Minimax Procedure for Determining the Component Estimates of a Seasonal Time Series," Washington, DC: Statistical Research Division, Bureau of the Census.

Fiorentini, G. and Maravall, A. (1994), "Unobserved Components in ARCH Models: An Application to Seasonal Adjustment," EUI Working Paper ECO no. 94/7 (forthcoming in the *Journal of Forecasting*).

Fisher, F.M. (1966), *The Identification Problem in Econometrics*, New York: McGraw-Hill. Book Co.

Fuller, W.A. (1976), *Introduction to Statistical Time Series*, New York: John Wiley and Sons.

García Ferrer, A. and Del Hoyo, J. (1992), "On Trend Extraction Models: Interpretation, Empirical Evidence and Forecasting Performance," *Journal of Forecasting* 11, 645–65.

Gersch, W. and Kitagawa, G. (1983), "The Prediction of Time Series with Trends and Seasonalities," *Journal of Business and Economic Statistics* 1, 253–64.

Ghysels, E. (1987), "Seasonal Extraction in the Presence of Feedback," *Journal of Business and Economic Statistics* 5, 191–4.

Ghysels, E. (1990), "On the Economics and Econometrics of Seasonality," Invited Lecture at the Sixth World Congress of the Econometrics Society, Barcelona, August 1990.

Ghysels, E. and Perron, P. (1993), "The Effect of Seasonal Adjustment Filters on Tests for a Unit Root," *Journal of Econometrics* 55, 57–98.

Gómez, V., and Maravall, A. (1993), "Initializing the Kalman Filter with Incompletely Specified Initial Conditions," in Chen, G.R. (ed.), *Approximate Kalman Filtering (Series on Approximation and Decomposition)*, London: World Scientific Publ. Co.

Gouriéroux, C. and Monfort, A. (1990), *Séries Temporelles et Modèles Dynamiques*, Paris: Economica.

Granger, C.W.J. (1978), "Seasonality: Causation, Interpretation and Implications," in Zellner, A. (ed.), *Seasonal Analysis of Economic Time Series*, Washington, DC: US Dept. of Commerce, Bureau of the Census, 33–46.

Hamilton, J.D. (1989), "A New Approach to the Economic Analysis of Nonstationary Time Series and the Business Cycle," *Econometrica* 57, 357–84.

Harrison, P.J. and Stevens, C.F. (1976), "Bayesian Forecasting," *Journal of the Royal Statistical Society* B, 38, 205–47.

Harvey, A.C. (1985), "Trends and Cycles in Macroeconomic Time Series," *Journal of Business and Economic Statistics* 3, 216–27.

Harvey, A.C. (1989), *Forecasting, Structural Time Series Models and the Kalman Filter*, Cambridge: Cambridge University Press.

Harvey, A.C., Henry, B., Peters, S. and Wren-Lewis, S. (1986), "Stochastic Trends in Dynamic Regression Models: An Application to the Output–Employment Equation," *Economic Journal* 96, 975–85.

Harvey, A.C. and Jaeger, A. (1991), "Detrending, Stylized Facts and the Business Cycle," STICERD, London School of Economics Discussion Paper EM/91/230.

Harvey, A.C. and Koopman, S.J. (1992), "Diagnostic Checking of Unobserved Components Time Series Models," *Journal of Business and Economic Statistics* 10, 377–90.

Harvey, A.C. and Marshall, P. (1991), "Inter-Fuel Substitution, Technical Change and the Demand for Energy in the UK Economy," *Applied Economics* 23, 1077–86.

Harvey, A.C., Ruiz, E. and Sentana, E. (1992), "Unobserved Component Time Series Models with ARCH Disturbances," *Journal of Econometrics* 52, 129–57.

Harvey, A.C. and Scott, A. (1994), "Seasonality in Dynamic Regression Models," *The Economic Journal* 104, 1324–45.

Harvey, A.C. and Todd, P.H.J. (1983), "Forecasting Economic Time Series with Structural and Box-Jenkins Models: A Case Study," *Journal of Business and Economic Statistics* 1, 299–306.

Hatanaka, M. and Suzuki, M. (1967), "A Theory of the Pseudospectrum and its Application to Nonstationary Dynamic Econometric Models," in Shubik, M. (ed.), *Essays in Mathematical Economics in Honor of Oskar Morgenstern*, Princeton: Princeton University Press.

Hibbert Committee (1988), "Report of the Working Party on Seasonal Adjustment of the Monetary Aggregates," CSO 8.

Hillmer, S.C. (1985), "Measures of Variability for Model-Based Seasonal Adjustment Procedures," *Journal of Business and Economic Statistics* 3, 60–8.

Hillmer, S.C. and Tiao, G.C. (1982), "An ARIMA-Model Based Approach to Seasonal Adjustment," *Journal of the American Statistical Association* 77, 63–70.

Hodrick, R. and Prescott, E. (1980), "Post-War U.S. Business Cycles: An Empirical Investigation," Carnegie Mellon University manuscript.

Hotta, L.K. (1989), "Identification of Unobserved Components Models," *Journal of Time Series Analysis* 10, 259–70.

Hylleberg, S., (1986), *Seasonality in Regression*, New York: Academic Press.

Hylleberg, S., Engle, R.F., Granger, C.W.J. and Yoo, B.S. (1990), "Seasonal Integration and Cointegration," *Journal of Econometrics* 44, 215–38.

Jenkins, G.M. (1979), "Practical Experiences with Modelling and Forecasting Time Series," GJP Publ.; also in Anderson, O.D. (ed.), *Forecasting*, Amsterdam: North-Holland.

Kendall, M. (1976), *Time Series*, London: Griffin and Co.

King, R.G. and Rebelo, S.T. (1993), "Low Frequency Filtering and Real Business Cycles," *Journal of Economic Dynamics and Control* 17, 207–33.

Kitchell, J. and Peña, D. (1984), "Periodicity of Extinction on the Remote Past: Deterministic versus Stochastic Explanation," *Science* 226, 689–92.

Kohn, R. and Ansley, C.F. (1986), "Estimation, Prediction and Interpolation for ARIMA Models with Missing Data," *Journal of the American Statistical Association* 81, 751–61.

Kohn, R. and Ansley, C.F. (1987), "Signal Extraction for Finite Nonstationary Time Series," *Biometrika* 74, 411–21.

Kydland, F.E. and Prescott, E.C. (1982), "Time to Build and Aggregate Fluctuations," *Econometrica* 50, 1345–70.

Lucas, R.E. (1976), "Understanding Business Cycles," in Brunner, K. and Meltzer, A. (eds), *Stabilization of the Domestic and International Economy*, Amsterdam: North-Holland.

Lütkepohl, H. (1991), *Introduction to Multiple Time Series Analysis*, Berlin: Springer-Verlag.

Maravall, A. (1987), "On Minimum Mean Squared Error Estimation of the Noise in Unobserved Component Models," *Journal of Business and Economic Statistics* 5, 115–20.

Maravall, A. (1988a), "The Use of ARIMA Models in Unobserved Components Estimation," in Barnett, W., Berndt, E. and White, H. (eds), *Dynamic Econometric Modeling*, Cambridge: Cambridge University Press.

Maravall, A. (1988b), "A Note on Minimum Mean Squared Error Estimation of Signals with Unit Roots," *Journal of Economic Dynamics and Control* 12, 589–93.

Maravall, A. (1989), "On the Dynamic Structure of a Seasonal Component," *Journal of Economic Dynamics and Control* 13, 81–91.

Maravall, A. (1993a), "Stochastic Linear Trends: Models and Estimators," *Journal of Econometrics* 54, 1–33.

Maravall, A. (1993b), "Short-Term Analysis of Macroeconomic Time Series," EUI Working Paper ECO no. 93/15 (forthcoming in *Economics: The Next Ten Years*, Proceedings of a September 1992 Conference at the GREQE, Marseille. Oxford: Oxford University Press).

Maravall, A. (1994), "Use and Misuse of Unobserved Components in Economic Forecasting," *Journal of Forecasting* 13, 157–78.

Maravall, A. and Gómez, V. (1994), "Signal Extraction in ARIMA Time Series: Program SEATS," EUI Working Paper ECO no. 94/28, Department of Economics, European University Institute.

Maravall, A. and Mathis, A. (1994), "Encompassing Univariate Models in Multivariate Time Series: A Case Study," *Journal of Econometrics* 61, 197–233.

Maravall, A. and Pierce, D.A. (1983), "Preliminary-Data Error and Monetary Aggregate Targeting," *Journal of Business and Economic Statistics* 1, 179–86.

Maravall, A. and Pierce, D.A. (1987), "A Prototypical Seasonal Adjustment Model," *Journal of Time Series Analysis* 8, 177–93.

Maravall, A. and Planas, C. (1994), "Estimation Error and the Specification of Unobserved Component models," EMI working paper ECO no. 94/34, Department of Economics, European University Institute.

Miron, J.A. (1986), "Seasonal Fluctuations and the Life Cycle–Permanent Income Model of Consumption," *Journal of Political Economy* 94, 1258–79.

Moore, G.H., Box, G.E.P., Kaitz, H.B., Stephenson, J.A. and Zellner, A. (1981), *Seasonal Adjustment of the Monetary Aggregates: Report of the Committee of Experts on Seasonal Adjustment Techniques*, Washington, DC: Board of Governors of the Federal Reserve System.

Muth, J.F. (1960), "Optimal Properties of Exponentially Weighted Forecasts," *Journal of the American Statistical Association* 55, 299–306.

Nelson, C.R. and Plosser, G.J. (1982), "Trends and Random Walks in Macroeconomic Time Series," *Journal of Monetary Economics* 10, 139–62.

Nerlove, M. (1964), "Spectral Analysis of Seasonal Adjustment Procedures," *Econometrica* 32, 241–86.

Nerlove, M., Grether, D.M. and Carvalho, J.L. (1979), *Analysis of Economic Time Series: A Synthesis*, New York: Academic Press.

Ng, C.N. and Young, P.C. (1990), "Recursive Estimation and Forecasting of Nonstationary Time Series," *Journal of Forecasting* 9, 173–204.

Osborn, D.R. (1988), "Seasonality and Habit Persistence in a Life Cycle Model of Consumption," *Journal of Applied Econometrics* 3, 255–66.

Pagan, A. (1975), "A Note on the Extraction of Components from Time Series," *Econometrica* 43, 1, 163–8.

Pauly, R. (1989), "A General Structural Model for Decomposing Time Series and its Analysis as a Generalized Regression Model," *Statistical Papers* 30, 245–61.

Pierce, D.A. (1978), "Seasonal Adjustment when Both Deterministic and Stochastic Seasonality are Present," in Zellner, A. (ed.), *Seasonal Analysis of Economic Time Series*, Washington, DC: US Dept. of Commerce, Bureau of the Census, 242–69.

Pierce, D.A. (1979), "Signal Extraction Error in Nonstationary Time Series," *Annals of Statistics* 7, 1303–20.

Pierce, D.A. (1980), "Data Revisions in Moving Average Seasonal Adjustment Procedures," *Journal of Econometrics* 14, 1, 95–114.

Pierce, D.A. (1983), "Seasonal Adjustment of the Monetary Aggregates: Summary of the Federal Reserve's Committee Report," *Journal of Business and Economic Statistics* 1, 37–42.

Prescott, E.C. (1986), "Theory Ahead of Business-Cycle Measurement," *Carnegie-Rochester Conference Series on Public Policy* 25, 11–44.

Quah, D. (1990), "Permanent and Transitory Movements in Labor Income: An Explanation for 'Excess Smoothness' in Consumption," *Journal of Political Economy* 98, 449–75.

Sargent, T. (1987), *Macroeconomic Theory* (2nd edn), New York: Academic Press.

Sargent, T. and Sims, C. (1977), "Business Cycle Modeling without Pretending to Have Too Much *A Priori* Economic Theory," in Sims, C. (ed.), *New Methods in Business Cycle Research*, Minneapolis: Federal Reserve Bank of Minneapolis.

Shiskin, J., Young, A.H. and Musgrave, J.C. (1967), "The X11 Variant of the Census Method II Seasonal Adjustment Program," Technical Paper 15, Washington, DC: Bureau of the Census.

Sims, C.A. (1980), "Macroeconomics and Reality," *Econometrica* 48, 1–48.

Slade, M.E. (1989), "Modelling Stochastic and Cyclical Components of Structural Change: An Application of the Kalman Filter," *Journal of Econometrics* 41, 363–83.

Stephenson, J.A. and Farr, H.T. (1972), "Seasonal Adjustment of Economic Data by Application of the General Linear Statistical Model," *Journal of the American Statistical Association* 67, 37–45.

Stock, J.H. and Watson, M.W. (1986), "Does GNP Have a Unit Root? A Re-Evaluation," *Economics Letters* 22, 147–51.

Stock, J.H. and Watson, M.W. (1988), "Variable Trends in Economic Time Series," *Journal of Economic Perspectives* 2, 147–74.

Stock, J.H. and Watson, M.W. (1989), "New Indexes of Leading and Coincident Economic Indicators," *NBER Macroeconomics Annual*, 351–94.

Stock, J.H. and Watson, M.W. (1991), "A Probability Model of the Coincident Economic Indicators," in Lahiri, K. and Moore, G.H. (eds), *Leading Economic Indicators: New Approaches and Forecasting Records*, Cambridge: Cambridge University Press.

Stock, J.H. and Watson, M.W. (1993), "A Procedure for Predicting Recessions with Leading Indicators: Econometric Issues and Recent Performance," in Stock, J.H. and Watson, M.W. (eds), *New Business Cycle Indicators and Forecasting*, Chicago: Chicago University Press.

Theil, H. (1971), *Principles of Econometrics*, New York: John Wiley and Sons.

Tiao, G.C. (1983), "Study Notes on Akaike's Seasonal Adjustment Procedures," in Zellner, A. (ed.), *Applied Time Series Analysis of Economic Data*, Washington, DC: US Department of Commerce, Bureau of the Census, 44–5.

Wallis, K.F. (1974), "Seasonal Adjustment and Relations between Variables," *Journal of the American Statistical Association* 69, 18–31.

Watson, M.W. (1986), "Univariate Detrending Methods with Stochastic Trends," *Journal of Monetary Economics* 18, 49–75.

Watson, M.W. (1987), "Uncertainty in Model-Based Seasonal Adjustment Procedures and Construction of Minimax Filters," *Journal of the American Statistical Association* 82, 395–408.

Weber, A.A. (1992), "The Role of Policymakers' Reputation in the EMS Disinflations. An Empirical Evaluation," *European Economic Review* 36, 1473–92.

Whittle, P. (1963), *Prediction and Regulation by Linear Least-Squares Methods*, London: English Universities Press.

Zellner, A. (ed.) (1978), *Seasonal Analysis of Economic Time Series*, Washington, DC: US Dept. of Commerce, Bureau of the Census.

Zellner, A. (ed.) (1983), *Applied Time Series Analysis of Economic Data*, Washington, DC: US Department of Commerce, Bureau of the Census.

2

(selected
covariances)

C32
C50
EJA

Vector Autoregressive Models: Specification, Estimation, Inference, and Forecasting

Fabio Canova

I have understood that the world is a vast emptiness built upon emptiness . . .
And so they call me the master of wisdom. Alas! Does anyone know what
wisdom is?

Song of the Owl: The Thousand and One Nights

1 Introduction

The seminal work of Sims (1972; 1980a; 1980b; 1982) introduced the vector
autoregressive (VAR) methodology into the mainstream of applied macroeconomic research as an alternative to large scale macroeconometric models.
The influence of Sims' ideas in the profession has been pervasive and the
approach has found a permanent position in the tool kit of applied time series
and macroeconomic analysts. The methodology, criticized in terms of its
validity both for characterizing historical data and for conducting useful
policy analyses, has spurred endless debates and has evolved to account for
some of the shortcomings pointed out by critics.

The task of this chapter is to provide a self-contained presentation of the
early developments of the VAR methodology and a summary of its current
state. The chapter is divided in eight sections: section 2 briefly reports some
results from time series analysis which are useful to understand why VAR
models are used so extensively, and discusses issues connected with the
multiplicity of moving average representations. Section 3 deals with the
specification and estimation of VARs. There, I discuss four approaches to
model selection which have appeared in the literature and the estimation and
testing procedures connected with each of them. The first part of section 4
deals with data analysis. Here I discuss the use of impulse responses and
variance decompositions to characterize the interrelationships among variables and the computation of standard errors of these two statistics. The
second part of this section examines issues connected with identification.
Semistructural, economic and informational procedures are compared and

contrasted. While VAR models are generally regarded as useful tools for unconditional forecasting and, in certain situations, produce forecasts which are more accurate than those of large scale macro models or univariate time series models, several criticisms have been raised to using their conditional forecasts for policy analysis. Section 5 therefore discusses how to implement both unconditional forecasts and conditional policy projections with VAR models. Section 6 reviews the major criticisms and objections raised to the VAR methodology. Section 7 lists a number of applications which have appeared in the literature and discusses extensions of the technique to panel data, to random fields, to the use of VARs as "windows" for simulation exercises conducted with dynamic general equilibrium models, and to the use of VARs for computing probabilities of future events. To illustrate some aspects of the methodology, section 8 presents an example studying the properties of the transmission mechanism of business cycles in the world economy. Other papers have critically surveyed some of the material covered in this chapter, although their focus is different. The interested reader is invited to consult Watson (1994), who deals primarily with model specification in the presence of cointegration, and Canova (1995), who extensively discusses economic issues connected with VAR analyses.

2   Some Time Series Results

This section briefly describes the mathematical apparatus underlying the VAR technique. Because of space limitations only major results are emphasized. Extensive details and mathematical proofs are contained in e.g. Rozanov (1967), Brockwell and Davis (1989), or Quah (1993). A simple and thorough presentation of the theory contained in this section also appears in Sargent (1986, chapter 11).

The major building block of the analysis is the Wold theorem. Using properties of Hilbert spaces (see e.g. Kreyszig, 1989), one can decompose any vector stochastic process x_t of dimension m into the sum of two orthogonal components: one which is linearly predictable based on the information available at time $t - 1$ and one which is linearly unpredictable. For this purpose let $\mathcal{F}_t$ to be the information set available at time t and note that $\mathcal{F}_t = \mathcal{F}_{t-1} \oplus \mathcal{E}_t$, where $\mathcal{F}_{t-1}$ is the information set available at time $t - 1$, $\mathcal{E}_t$ is the space spanned by new information, and $\oplus$ indicates direct sum. Because $\mathcal{F}_{t-1}$ is orthogonal to $\mathcal{E}_t$, we can write:

$$x_t \equiv P_t[x_t|\mathcal{F}_t] = P_t[x_t|\mathcal{F}_{t-1}] + P_t[x_t|\mathcal{E}_t], \qquad (2.1)$$

where $P_t[.]$ is the linear projection operator and the equivalence between the first two expressions comes from the fact that x_t is adapted to $\mathcal{F}_t$. Since, at each t, $\mathcal{F}_t$ can be decomposed into the sum of two orthogonal components, one containing information available one period in advance and one containing new information, (2.1) can be solved backward to obtain:

$$x_t = P_t[x_t|\mathcal{F}_{-\infty}] + \sum_{j=0}^{\infty} P_t[x_t|\mathscr{E}_{t-j}], \tag{2.2}$$

where the first term on the right hand side of (2.2) is the "linearly deterministic" part of x_t, i.e. the part that is predictable given the infinite past, where $\mathcal{F}_{-\infty} = \cap_{j=0}^{\infty}\mathcal{F}_{t-j}$, and the second term is the "linearly regular" part. Since P is a linear operator, we write $P_t[x_t|\mathscr{E}_{t-j}] = B_{jt}\varepsilon_{t-j}\forall j$, where ε_{t-j} is an element of $\mathscr{E}_{t-j}$ and it is defined by $\varepsilon_{t-j} = x_{t-j} - P_{t-j}[x_{t-j}|\mathcal{F}_{t-j-1}]$. The innovation sequence $\{\varepsilon_t\}_{t=0}^{\infty}$ is a white noise process (i.e. $E(\varepsilon_t) = 0$ and $E(\varepsilon_t\varepsilon'_{t-s}) = \Sigma_t$ if $s = 0$ and zero otherwise) and the coefficients of the projection satisfy $\Sigma_{j=0}^{\infty}B_{jt}^2 < \infty$ and $B_{j0} = I$.

It is typical to assume that x_t is a mean zero process (possibly after appropriate transformations such as deseasonalization with deterministic periodic functions, removal of constants, etc.) and to omit the linearly deterministic component from (2.2). It is also typical to assume that x_t is covariance stationary (i.e. $E(x_t x'_{t-s})$ depends on s but not on t so that the projections in (2.2) are independent of t. However, it should be clear that (2.2) holds independently of the covariance stationary assumption. In general, economic time series do not satisfy the covariance stationarity assumption and transformations are required. For example, if the data contain a unit root, the theory described in the rest of this section applies to the first differences of the original process, i.e. $x_t = y_t - y_{t-1}$.

For a covariance stationary vector process x_t it is convenient to rewrite (2.2) in a moving average (MA) form as:

$$x_t = Dw_t + B(\ell)\varepsilon_t, \tag{2.3}$$

where w_t is a vector (possibly equal to zero) including all deterministic components of the process, D is a vector of coefficients, $w_t \in \mathcal{F}_{-\infty}$, $B(\ell) = I + B_1\ell + B_2\ell^2 \dots$, with $\ell\varepsilon_t = \varepsilon_{t-1}$, and each B_j matrix $j = 1, 2, \dots$ is of dimension $m \times m$ and rank m. For any nonsingular matrix $H(\ell)$ such that $H(z)$ has no poles (singularities) for $|z| \leq 1$ and satisfying $H(\ell)H^*(\ell^{-1}) = I$, where $H^*(\ell^{-1})$ is the transpose (and possibly complex conjugate) of $H(\ell)$, there exists an MA representation for x_t of the form:

$$x_t = Dw_t + \tilde{B}(\ell)\tilde{\varepsilon}_t, \tag{2.4}$$

where $\tilde{B}(\ell) = B(\ell)H(\ell)$ and $\tilde{\varepsilon}_t = H^*(\ell^{-1})\varepsilon_t$. Note that $E(\tilde{\varepsilon}_t\tilde{\varepsilon}'_t) = E(\varepsilon_t\varepsilon'_t)$ so that the two representations are equivalent from the point of view of the autocovariance function of x_t. Matrices like $H(\ell)$ are called Blaschke factors and are of the form:

$$H(\ell) = \prod_{r=1}^{R} k_r Q(\lambda_r, \ell), \tag{2.5}$$

where λ_r are the roots of $B(\ell)$, $|\lambda_r| < 1$, $k_r k_r' = I$, and, for each r, $Q(\lambda_r, \ell)$ is given by:

$$Q(\lambda_r, \ell) = \begin{bmatrix} 1 & 0 & \cdots & 0 \\ \cdots & & \cdots & \cdots \\ 0 & \dfrac{\ell - \lambda_r}{1 - \lambda_r^{-1}\ell} & \cdots & 0 \\ 0 & 0 & \cdots & 1 \end{bmatrix}.$$

Among the class of equivalent MA representations for x_t it is typical to consider the one which is "fundamental," i.e. one for which $\det(B_0 E_t \varepsilon_t \varepsilon_t' B_0)$ is maximal. Fundamental representations, also termed Wold representations, are identified by the requirement that the completion of the space spanned by linear combinations of the x_ts has the same amount of information as the completion of the space spanned by linear combinations of ε_ts. Let (2.3) be such a representation.

Since the covariance matrix of the εs is, in general, nondiagonal, it is useful in certain situations to transform (2.3) to have innovations which are contemporaneously uncorrelated. This representation is obtained by appropriately renormalizing the system and is also observationally equivalent to (2.3) from the point of view of the autocovariance function of x_t. To obtain such a representation let Σ be the covariance matrix of ε_t in (2.3) and let $\Sigma = LVL'$, where V is a diagonal matrix. Then the system:

$$x_t = Dw_t + \hat{B}(\ell)\hat{\varepsilon}_t \tag{2.6}$$

is equivalent to (2.3) for $\hat{B}(\ell) = B(\ell)L$ and $\hat{\varepsilon}_t = L^{-1}\varepsilon$ and $V = E(\hat{\varepsilon}_t \hat{\varepsilon}_t')$.

When the polynomial $B(z)$ has all its roots greater than one in modulus,[1] it is invertible and there exists an autoregressive (AR) representation which expresses ε_t as a linear combination of current and past x_ts of the form

$$A(\ell)^* x_t = C(\ell)w_t + \varepsilon_t, \tag{2.7}$$

where $A(\ell)^* = (B(\ell))^{-1}$, and $C = (B(\ell))^{-1}D$ and $A(0)^* = I$. Moving lagged x's on the right hand side and grouping, we obtain a vector autoregressive (VAR) representation

$$x_t = C(\ell)w_t + A(\ell)x_{t-1} + \varepsilon_t, \tag{2.8}$$

where $A(\ell) = [\ell^{-1}A^*(\ell)]_+$ and the notation $[.]_+$ indicates the annihilator operator (see Sargent, 1986). In general, the polynomials $C(\ell)$ and $A(\ell)$ will have infinite length for any reasonable specification of the polynomial $B(\ell)$.

An example illustrating the issues of fundamentalness and renormalization can be informative here. Suppose $m = 2$, $w_t = 0$, $\forall t$ and that (2.3) has the form:

$$\begin{pmatrix} x_{1t} \\ x_{2t} \end{pmatrix} = \begin{pmatrix} (1 + 4\ell) & 0 \\ 0 & (1 + 5\ell) \end{pmatrix} \begin{pmatrix} \varepsilon_{1t} \\ \varepsilon_{2t} \end{pmatrix} \tag{2.9}$$

with $E(\varepsilon_{1t}\varepsilon_{2t}) = \Sigma$. The roots of $B(z) = 0$ are -0.25 and -0.2, which are both less than 1 in modulus. In this case it is not possible to express e_ts as a convergent linear combination of current and past x_ts because the space spanned by the completion of linear combinations of ε_ts is larger than the space spanned by linear combinations of the x_ts. Therefore (2.9) is not a fundamental MA representation for x_t. It is easy to check that the vector x_t defined by (2.9) and

$$\begin{pmatrix} x_{1t} \\ x_{2t} \end{pmatrix} = \begin{pmatrix} (1 + 0.25\ell) & 0 \\ 0 & (1 + 0.2\ell) \end{pmatrix} \begin{pmatrix} u_t \\ \varepsilon_{2t} \end{pmatrix} \tag{2.10}$$

have the same autocovariance function, where $u_t = \varepsilon_{1t} - \gamma\varepsilon_{2t}$ and $\gamma = \mathrm{cov}(\varepsilon_{1t}\varepsilon_{2t})/\mathrm{var}(\varepsilon_t)$. Note however that the roots of $B(\ell)$ are all greater than one in modulus, so that there exists an AR representation for (2.10) where current innovations can be expressed in terms of current and past x_ts with coefficients which are square summable. In addition (2.10) is fundamental for x_t since $\det(B_0 E_t \varepsilon_t \varepsilon_t' B_0)$ is maximal. Finally, the innovations are contemporaneously uncorrelated because $E(u_t\varepsilon_{2t})$ is zero by construction.

Two concepts which will be used later on in the chapter and are stated without proofs are those of Granger (1988) noncausality and Sims (econometric) exogeneity (see Sims, 1972 for proofs; and Hamilton, 1994 for the statistical apparatus needed to test them). Let (x_{1t}, x_{2t}) be a partition of a covariance stationary linear vector process x_t with fundamental innovations ε_{1t} and ε_{2t}. Let Σ_ε be diagonal and partition $B(\ell)$ as

$$B(\ell) = \begin{pmatrix} B_{11}(\ell) & B_{12}(\ell) \\ B_{21}(\ell) & B_{22}(\ell) \end{pmatrix}.$$

Granger noncausality x_{2t} fails to Granger-cause x_{1t} if and only if $B_{12}(\ell) = 0$.

Sims exogeneity x_{2t} can be expressed as a distributed lag regression involving only current and past x_{1t} with $E_t[u_{2t}x_{1t-s}] = 0 \;\forall s$ if and only if x_{2t} fails to Granger-cause x_{1t} and $B_{21}(\ell) \neq 0$.

3 Specification and Estimation of VAR Models

Macroeconomic analysis with VAR models was first introduced in the mainstream of applied macroeconometrics because of the dissatisfaction with existing econometric practice. Sims (1980a) raised three basic criticisms against traditional macroeconometric models. First, the identifying restrictions employed by model builders were deemed "incredible" in the sense that economic theory is weak in deciding what variables should enter a reduced form model and exclusion restrictions were routinely imposed with little attention to the underlying economic structure. Sims considered these restrictions inessential to construct a model which is useful for policy analysis and forecasting (see also Liu, 1960). Second, many variables were taken to be exogenous with respect to the system by default rather than as a result of solid economic or statistical arguments. Finally, because the outcomes of traditional macroeconometric models are typically amended by their users with judgmental *ex post* decisions, the results of policy exercises are both nonreproducible and hard to compare with those of other researchers even when they employ the same type of models.

As an alternative to the traditional style of identification and estimation, Sims suggested formulating unrestricted VAR models, treating all variables as endogenous at a first stage in order to avoid infecting the model with spurious or false identifying restrictions. Contrary to standard macroeconometric practice, the analyst's prior knowledge is used only to decide what variables should enter the reduced form and, in some cases, the time series transformations to be used (log or ratios of variables). Statistical procedures can then be used to determine the lag length and an appropriate treatment of trending variables. Estimation of unrestricted VAR models is simple since single equation methods like OLS are consistent and, under normality of the errors, efficient. When a statistical model free of restrictions based on alleged *a priori* knowledge has been devised to summarize the data, economic hypotheses can be formulated and tested and the historical dynamics of the data can be examined. Policy advice can also be offered at this second stage of the analysis.

Typical applications of the early VAR literature comprised ways to assess the in-sample additional predictive content of one variable for another (see e.g. Sims, 1972; Sargent, 1978; Hamilton, 1983). More recently, the computation of impulse responses and variance decompositions to assess the in-sample effect of a typical shock on the rest of the system has become a widespread practice (e.g. Sims, 1980b; Litterman and Weiss, 1985). In several papers interested in policy questions, out-of-sample unconditional and conditional forecasts were carried out to provide numerical assessments of the effect of policy changes (see e.g. Gordon and King, 1982; Litterman, 1984; Sims, 1982; 1988a). In addition, various hypotheses concerning structural dynamics have been examined within the context of reduced form VARs using the encompassing principle (see e.g. Clements and Mizon, 1991). Finally, researchers have used VARs as "windows" to compare the properties of actual data and data simulated from dynamic general equilibrium models (see e.g. Smith, 1993; Canova, Finn, and Pagan, 1994).

Criticisms of the VAR methodology appeared at all stages of the analysis. Some authors (see e.g. Runkle, 1987; Ohanian, 1988; Spencer, 1989; Maravall, 1993) raised doubts about the usefulness of the methodology to robustly characterize the dynamics of the data. The major bulk of the critiques, however, has focused on the meaning and on the limitations of hypothesis testing and policy analyses with VARs. Attacks were mounted on its "atheoretical" underpinning (see e.g. Cooley and LeRoy, 1985; Leamer, 1985), on the implicit and hardly justifiable contemporaneously recursive structural model which underlay early exercises with VARs (see e.g. Bernanke, 1986; Blanchard and

Watson, 1986), on the type of policy interventions which were reasonable in light of the Lucas critique and on the way they were engineered (see e.g. Sachs, 1982; Engle, Hendry, and Richard, 1983; Cooley and LeRoy, 1985) and, in general, on the usefulness of providing policy advice with VARs (see e.g. Sargent, 1984).

In response to these criticisms the methodology has evolved to include at least four different ways of formulating and estimating VAR models (and, as a consequence, of undertaking historical and policy analyses). The rest of this section will characterize and compare these different approaches.

Throughout the rest of the chapter and for the sake of exposition, I will refer to a finite order bivariate VAR model of order p of the form:

$$\begin{pmatrix} x_{1t} \\ x_{2t} \end{pmatrix} = \begin{pmatrix} C_{11}(\ell) & C_{12}(\ell) \\ C_{21}(\ell) & C_{22}(\ell) \end{pmatrix} \begin{pmatrix} w_{1t} \\ w_{2t} \end{pmatrix} + \begin{pmatrix} A_{11}(\ell) & A_{12}(\ell) \\ A_{21}(\ell) & A_{22}(\ell) \end{pmatrix} \begin{pmatrix} x_{1t-1} \\ x_{2t-1} \end{pmatrix} + \begin{pmatrix} \varepsilon_{1t} \\ \varepsilon_{2t} \end{pmatrix}, \quad (2.11)$$

where x_{1t} and x_{2t} are vectors of dimensions $m_1 \times 1$ and $m_2 \times 1$, respectively, with $m_1 + m_2 = m$. The matrix $C(\ell)$ contains the coefficients on $w_t' = [w_{1t}, w_{2t}]'$, which include all deterministic components in the two blocks of equations; $\varepsilon_t' = [\varepsilon_{1t}, \varepsilon_{2t}]'$ and, conditional on $\mathcal{F}_t$, is a white noise vector (the innovations in predicting x_t) with covariance matrix Σ; $\mathcal{F}_t$ represents the information set available at time t to the econometrician; and $A_{ij}(\ell) = A_{ij1} + A_{ij2}\ell + \ldots + A_{ijp}\ell^{p-1}$, $\forall i, j$ where ℓ is the lag operator. I will write the MA representation of the system (2.11) as:

$$\begin{pmatrix} x_{1t} \\ x_{2t} \end{pmatrix} = \begin{pmatrix} D_{11}(\ell) & D_{12}(\ell) \\ D_{21}(\ell) & D_{22}(\ell) \end{pmatrix} \begin{pmatrix} w_{1t} \\ w_{2t} \end{pmatrix} + \begin{pmatrix} B_{11}(\ell) & B_{12}(\ell) \\ B_{21}(\ell) & B_{22}(\ell) \end{pmatrix} \begin{pmatrix} \varepsilon_{1t} \\ \varepsilon_{2t} \end{pmatrix}, \quad (2.12)$$

where $B(\ell) = (I - A(\ell)\ell)^{-1}$ and $D(\ell) = B(\ell)C(\ell)$.

The finite order VAR model (2.11) can be taken to be the true data generating process (DGP) for x_t, a finite order approximation to an underlying infinite order linear model, or a first-order Taylor approximation of a (in)finite order nonlinear model. The issue of nonlinearities in the conditional mean is of only marginal interest here, since monthly and quarterly macroeconomic time series are usually well approximated by linear processes (see e.g. Brock and Sayers, 1988). In addition, in many instances it will not matter which of the first two points of view is taken. One case where the distinction is relevant is in computing asymptotic standard errors and in determining the finite sample properties of estimators of functions of the parameters (see e.g. Lutkepohl, 1991). In the rest of this chapter (2.11) is assumed to be the true DGP. However, I will discuss the differences with the infinite-true VAR methodology when they arise. The four approaches to specification and estimation discussed here will differ in the type of restrictions placed on the $A(\ell)$ matrix.

3.1 Specification Using Classical Statistical Theory

Given the VAR (2.11), one may appeal to economic theory, empirical observations or experience to choose the variables to include in x_t. In principle, one would like to include all series which are likely to have important interdepend-encies. In practice, the limited size of existing data sets requires the use of small scale models. Implicit in the choice of variables is therefore a process of marginalization: i.e. the joint probability density of the VAR must be inter-preted as having been marginalized with respect to some potentially "relevant" variables (see e.g. Clements and Mizon, 1991). This assumption has raised some controversy. Some (see e.g. McNees, 1986b; Fair, 1988; Kirchgassner, 1991; Sims, 1991a) consider it dubious, just as "incredible" as the exclusion restrictions employed in standard simultaneous equation models and a potential source of incorrect inference in small scale VAR models. Others (see e.g. Mizon, 1990) consider it innocuous as long as the selected VAR is statistically well specified.

In addition to choosing the components of x_t, a researcher must specify:

1   the lag length p of the autoregression
2   the type of deterministic components to be included in w_t
3   what to do if nonstationary or explosive roots appear in the $A(\ell)$ matrix.

In choosing the lag length p one must weigh two opposing considerations: the "curse of dimensionality" and the correct specification of the model. Since the number of parameters to be estimated quickly increases with the number of lags of the system, and because the relevant number of degrees of freedom in a VAR depends on the total number of free parameters appearing in the system, moderately sized systems become highly overparameterized relative to the number of observations, leading to insignificant or inefficient estimates of short run parameters. A lag length which is too short, on the other hand, produces a statistical model where only a subset of the relevant information is used to characterize the data and leaves serial correlation in ε_ts, which may induce spurious significance and inefficient estimates. This trade-off between overparameterization and oversimplification is at the heart of the selection criteria designed to choose p.

In specifying the lag length of the VAR, Sims (1977; 1980a) suggests keeping in mind that a VAR effectively belongs to an infinite-dimensional parameter space and that finite parameter methods are justified as part of a procedure in which the number of parameters is a function of the sample size. He argues in favour of arbitrary smoothing rules to control the decay of information. Lutkepohl (1991, p. 308) proceeds along the same lines but suggests linking the number of parameters in each equation to both the sample size (T) and the dimension of the time series (m) according to the rule $mp = T^{1/3}$.

Formal selection criteria to determine the maximum order of p in a multiple autoregression are well established (see the criteria of e.g. Akaike (AIC), 1974; Parzen, 1976; McClave, 1978; Hannan and Quinn, 1978; or the modified likelihood ratio (MLR) procedure of Sims, 1980a) and some of them have Bayesian justifications (see the SIC criterion of Schwarz, 1978).[2] While the asymptotic properties of these criteria are well established, their small sample properties are still under investigation. In general, they appear to differ significantly depending on the true lag structure of the generating process and the exact size of the sample (see e.g. Nickelsburg, 1985; Lutkepohl, 1986).

The essence of these procedures is straightforward: given a sample size T, the value $\bar{p}$ is chosen if the reduction of the loss function of the system (in all cases the mean square error) due to the addition of the $\bar{p} + 1$ lag is smaller than the increase in the loss function caused by the additional uncertainty introduced (more parameters need to be estimated). All these methods choose the $\bar{p}$ which jointly best explains all the variables of the system. The various criteria differ primarily in the way the two effects are weighted.

Choosing the lag length according to one of these asymptotically consistent criteria has an advantage. Because only predetermined variables and deterministic functions of time appear as right hand side variables, and $E(\varepsilon_t \varepsilon'_{t-s}) = E(\varepsilon_t x'_{t-s})) = 0 \forall s$, OLS estimates of the coefficient matrix $A(\ell)$ are consistent. In addition, because no restrictions are imposed on $A(\ell)$, single equation methods are (asymptotically) efficient. To see this it is sufficient to rewrite (2.11) as a dynamic seemingly unrelated system (DSUS) (see e.g. Harvey, 1989; Judge et al., 1980)

$$x_t = (I \otimes y_t)\beta + \varepsilon_t, \qquad (2.13)$$

where $y'_t = [\tilde{x}_{1t}, \tilde{x}_{2t}]$, $\tilde{x}_{it} = [x_{it-1}, x_{it-2}, \ldots, x_{it-p}]$, $\beta = [\beta_{11}, \beta_{12}, \beta_{21}, \beta_{22}]$, $\beta_{ij} = [a_{ij1}, a_{ij2}, \ldots, a_{ijp}]$, I is the identity matrix of dimension m and $\otimes$ is the Kroneker product. The DSUS (2.13) has the property that the same right hand side variables appear in each equation. Under this condition Zellner (1962) showed that single equation methods are as efficient as system wide methods, no matter what the contemporaneous correlations among the εs are. If, in addition, the εs are normal, then OLS is efficient.

The major drawback of these procedures is that all the variables entering the system have identical lag lengths, which need not be a valid economic or statistical restriction, may reduce the efficiency of the estimates and, in some cases, may even bias the choice of p (see Akaike, 1970). To overcome this problem Hsiao (1981; 1982) suggested combining Akaike's (1969) final prediction error (FPE) approach for univariate autoregression[3] with Granger causality testing to decide what variables should enter each autoregression and with what number of lags.

The major advantage of Hsiao's sequential procedure is that by imposing statistical exclusion restrictions, it substantially reduces the number of parameters to be estimated. Three drawbacks should also be mentioned. First, the approach breaks separation between the specification of the model and tests of economic hypotheses (such as Granger causality). Second, since the results of testing statistical hypotheses are treated as exact, second stage hypothesis testing may be sensitive to type I errors committed at the first stage. Third, since the same variables do not appear in all equations, system wide methods (such as full information maximum likelihood (FIML)) are needed for efficient estimation of the parameters.

An alternative procedure to select p, which goes in the opposite direction of Hsiao's "specific-to-general" approach, has been popularized in the works of Hendry (1990), Hendry and Mizon (1990), and Clements and Mizon (1991). The key to this approach is to select a VAR which is statistically well specified. Given available information, econometricians attempt to select an unrestricted "congruent" VAR. A model is termed "congruent" if it captures the dynamic relationships existing in the data, if it is free from specification errors, and if it has constant parameters. Once such a model is found, the dimensionality of the VAR is reduced with a number of t-tests and F-tests designed to examine the significance of the lag of one variable in one or all the equations. Insignificant lags are purged from the original specification to produce a parsimonious VAR (PVAR) representation with specification tests used as an essential part of the simplification procedure.

One difference between the Hsiao or SIC approaches and the Hendry and Mizon procedure in selecting lag length lies in the way hypothesis testing is conducted. In the former tests are based on recursive, in-sample estimates of the parameters. In the latter F-tests (or t-tests) on the coefficients are computed using full sample estimates of the coefficients. In other words, while the former criteria use the size of recursive residuals to decide $\bar{p}$, the latter uses *ex post* residuals to judge the relevance of lags or variables.[4]

Under the fairly general conditions summarized in section 2 (see e.g. Rozanov, 1967 for more details), a vector of stationary time series admits an autoregressive representation. The idea that macroeconomic time series are stationary around say, a deterministic polynomial function of time, has come under debate in the last decade (see e.g. the original study by Nelson and Plosser, 1982). However, recent work by Perron (1989), DeJong and Whiteman (1991), and Christiano (1992) suggests that the evidence on unit roots is not so overwhelming. In specifying a stationary VAR model it is therefore necessary to take a stance on the sources of nonstationarity (deterministic or stochastic), on whether structural breaks in time trends are present, and, in general, on the methodology needed to deal with those shifts which occur from time to time in economic variables.

The choice has implications for estimation and testing. Phillips (1988) shows that knowledge of the order of integration of the variables in a regression and of the nature of the deterministic components can be important in designing optimal inference. Because testing hypotheses on coefficients of integrated variables requires nonstandard asymptotic theory (see e.g. Phillips and Durlauf, 1988), determining the order of integration is crucial for correct inference (see Phillips, 1991 and Sims, 1991b for a recent update of this discussion). These considerations suggest that the appropriate modeling strategy to determine the long run properties of each variable of the VAR model should be based on univariate unit roots tests (such as those of Dickey and Fuller, 1979; Phillips and Perron, 1986; or Stock and Watson, 1989). Based on the results of univariate unit root tests, one generally ends up choosing a VAR in first difference. Tiao and Box (1981), however, recommend against differencing individual series to achieve stationarity in multivariate models. In addition, Engle and Granger (1987) indicate that univariate unit root procedures may generate "too many" unit roots in a VAR and suggest checking for the presence of cointegrating restrictions to avoid this and the consequent loss of information, particularly about long run parameters. According to Engle and Granger, one should first test for the presence of stochastic trends in each of the variables and for the possibility of common long run patterns and then, taking the OLS estimates of the coefficients of the long run relationships as if they were the true ones, transform the VAR into a stationary vector error correction model (VECM) and proceed with standard estimation and inference.

An alternative approach to Engle and Granger's two step procedure has been championed by Johansen (1988) and Johansen and Juselius (1990) (for applications see e.g. Hendry and Mizon, 1990; Clements and Mizon, 1991; Johansen and Juselius, 1992). In this approach one determines the order of integration and cointegration of the system using standard unit root and cointegration tests and models the VAR in the space of integrated processes of order zero (I(0)). One way of doing so is to choose a VECM form. After this one distinguishes three cases: one where the rank of the matrix containing the factor loadings for the cointegrating vectors (say Π) is equal to m, in which case all variables of the system are I(0); one where the rank of the matrix is 0, so that all variables are stationary in first difference (I(1)); and an intermediate case where the rank of the matrix is between 0 and m, in which case there are some linear combinations of the variables which act as a common statistical trend. In this third case, Π can be factored into $\Pi = \alpha\beta'$ and one jointly estimates the cointegrating vector and the coefficients of the VAR model under the rank restrictions on Π with a maximum likelihood technique (see e.g. Johansen, 1988; Stock and Watson, 1993). Because restrictions are imposed on the coefficients in the $A(\ell)$ matrix, system wide methods (such as FIML) are needed for efficient estimation. King et al. (1991) and Giannini (1992) provide useful insights on the economic interpretability of the β' vector in the factorization.

Sims, Stock, and Watson (1990), developing results presented in Fuller (1976), provide a comprehensive solution to the testing problem in the context of VARs with polynomial functions of time and one or more unit roots. They argue that Engle and Granger's two step procedure is not necessary by showing (i) coefficients are consistently estimated, independently of the order of integration of the variables; (ii) any hypothesis which can be written as a restriction on a mean zero stationary canonical regressor in a transformed VAR model can be tested using standard asymptotic theory; and (iii) hypotheses which involve one or more coefficients on canonical variates which are dominated by a stochastic trend must be tested using a nonstandard distribution. In this procedure the order of integration of the variables and the number of cointegrating restrictions is important to determine which distribution applies (see e.g. Stock and Watson, 1989 for an application sorting out the existing evidence on money–income causality; and Sims, 1988b and Sims and Ulhig, 1991 for a critical view on the usefulness of this characterization), but the presence of nonstationarities does not require the transformation of the VAR into a VECM form for meaningful economic inference to be carried out.

To summarize, the classical approach to specification and estimation of VAR models involves two steps. First, one chooses a model which is dynamically well specified (in terms of functional forms, variables included, lag length, noncorrelation and, possibly, normality of the residuals), extracts as much information as possible from the data, and tests for the presence of unit roots and cointegrating restrictions, taking into account the possibility of regime shifts, segmented trends, etc. Second, one can either transform the system and estimate the VAR coefficients using the two step procedure of Engle and Granger, or estimate the original VAR model under rank restrictions using the maximum likelihood approach of Johansen. Testing of hypotheses on the coefficients of the transformed system can be undertaken using standard asymptotic theory. The coefficients of the untransformed, unrestricted model can be estimated with OLS, equation by equation, and the results of Sims, Stock, and Watson (1990) applied to test hypotheses of interest. As an intermediate step, it is possible to reduce the dimensionality of the system by eliminating either variables or lags which appear to be unimportant in explaining variations of the endogenous variables in one or more equations while maintaining a dynamically well specified system. If this intermediate step is taken, it should be kept in mind that single equation methods of estimation of the second step regression in Engle and Granger's procedure or of the untransformed system are no longer efficient.

One major shortcoming of the procedures described in this subsection, which is applicable to any sequential testing approach undertaken with classical methods, is that tests of economic hypotheses are conditional on the results of testing for the model specification (e.g. for integration and cointegration, for lag length, etc.). In other words, if the procedures used to select a model have size and/or power problems in small samples (as is the case e.g. with unit root tests), the consistency of the first round testing is in jeopardy and inference based on the results of the second round of tests may be flawed. For a more detailed analysis of the implications of cointegration for the specification of a VAR model, the reader is invited to consult Watson (1994).

3.2   Specification Using Bayesian Methods

An alternative strain of literature, originating from Litterman (1980; 1986a; 1986b) and described in Todd (1984), takes a Bayesian perspective to the specification of VAR systems. The starting point of the approach is that in specifying econometric models one attempts to filter as much information as possible from the data. However, instead of relying on classical hypothesis testing or economic theory to decide whether a particular variable or lag should enter the autoregression, these authors use a symmetric "atheoretical" prior on all variables to trade off overparameterization with oversimplification. The reason for taking an alternative route to the specification problem is that there is a very low signal-to-noise ratio in economic data and economic theory leaves a great deal of uncertainty concerning which economic structures are useful for inference and forecasting. Because highly parameterized unrestricted VAR models include many variables in each equation, the extraction filter is too wide and noise obscures the relatively weak signal present in the data: the prior acts as an orientable antenna which, when appropriately directed, may clarify the signal. The prior is characterized by a small number of parameters. A specification search *à la* Leamer (1978) over these parameters tunes up the filter for an "optimal" extraction of information from a given data set.

The prior is nonstandard from the point of view of Bayesian analysis; it is "objective" in the sense that it is based on experience and reflects accepted rules in the forecasting community and it is, in most cases, "atheoretical" because the restrictions built in the prior have no economic interpretation. To clarify the discussion, a Bayesian VAR (BVAR) is typically composed of two sets of equations:

$$x_t = C_t(\ell)w_t + A_t(\ell)x_{t-1} + \varepsilon_t \tag{2.14}$$

$$\beta_t = G\beta_{t-1} + F\bar{\beta} + u_t, \tag{2.15}$$

where β_t is the stacked version of $A_t(\ell)$ and $C_t(\ell)$, $\bar{\beta}$ is the unconditional mean of β, G and F are $mp \times mp$ matrices, and u_t is a white noise process with covariance matrix Ω_t.

In (2.14) the coefficients of the autoregressive process are, in principle, allowed to be time varying. Equation (2.15) represents the prior law of motion of the coefficients and is very generally formulated. Several special cases are included. For $G = 0$ and $F = I$ the coefficients are random around the unconditional mean. For $F = 0$ and $G = I$, the coefficients are random walks. For $\Omega_t = 0$ the coefficients are deterministically evolving over time. For $G = 0$, $F = I$ and $\Omega_t = \Omega$, the unconditional distribution of the β_ts is constant. Finally, for $G = 0$, $F = 0$, and $\Omega_t = 0$, the coefficients are constant over time.

For (2.14) and (2.15) to be operational we need to specify the $3m^2(p + 1)(m^2(p + 1) + 1)$ parameters contained in the matrices G, F, Ω_0, $\bar{\beta}$ plus the law of motion linking Ω_t to Ω_0. The idea of the approach is to make the parameters of these matrices depend on a low dimensional vector of hyperparameters θ which indexes various extraction filters. One specification found to be useful in forecasting is the following:

$$G = \theta_0 I \tag{2.16}$$

$$F = I - G \tag{2.17}$$

$$\bar{\beta}_{ij\ell} = 1 \qquad \text{if } i = j, \, \ell = 1 \tag{2.18}$$

$$\bar{\beta}_{ij\ell} = 0 \qquad \text{otherwise} \tag{2.19}$$

$$\Omega_{0ij\ell} = \theta_1 f(i, j) h(\ell) \frac{\sigma_i}{\sigma_j} \tag{2.20}$$

$$\Omega_t = \theta_2 \Omega_0. \tag{2.21}$$

Some explanations may be useful at this point. With (2.16) and (2.17) it is assumed that the coefficients are AR(1) processes with some decay toward the mean. Equations (2.18) and (2.19) assume that the time zero mean is one on the first lag own coefficient and zero otherwise. Equation (2.20) assumes that the time zero variance of the coefficients shrinks with lags (the function $h(\ell)$ is typically chosen to have a geometric decay of the form $h(\ell) = 1/\ell$), is smaller for coefficients of other variables in each equation ($f(i, j) < f(i, i) \forall i \neq j$), is scaled by the ratio of standard deviations of x_i and x_j, and is regulated by a tightness parameter θ_1. Equation (2.21) assumes that the covariance matrix of the coefficients at each t is a fixed function of the covariance matrix at time zero.

In this formulation the VAR coefficients are assumed to be time varying. The $\theta = [\theta_0, \theta_1, \theta_2]$ vector describes the time invariant features of the system. Since θ is unrestricted, the specification allows for very general structures for the evolution of the coefficients and "lets the data speak" if there is enough information in the data to pull the model away from the prior specification.

This approach to specification is advantageous in two respects: it avoids strong restrictions on which lags should enter the autoregression and refrains from specification testing procedures which may bias the tests of economic hypotheses. In addition, the approach is flexible enough to allow different lag lengths in different equations.

The specification search over the θ vector can be carried out numerically, passing through the sample recursively with the Kalman filter algorithm. Since the Kalman filter automatically yields the two components of the prediction error decomposition of the likelihood under normality of the residuals (see e.g. Harvey, 1989), one can use a likelihood based statistic to select an "optimal" specification for the θ (see e.g. Doan, Litterman, and Sims, 1984). Sims (1986b) provides a computer program which mechanizes the search algorithm for the θ vector using a likelihood based statistics.

One special case, originally considered by Litterman (1986b), needs to be considered in particular. When $\Omega_t = \Omega_0$ and $G = 0$ the system of equations (2.14)–(2.15) forms a VAR model with a set of uncertain linear restrictions on the coefficients. If (2.15) is regarded as a dummy observation appended to the system, estimation of the model parameters can be carried out with mixed-type estimation (see e.g. Theil, 1971). The result is a restricted estimator which shrinks the data toward the information contained in the prior restriction. This interpretation of (2.14)–(2.15) suggests an alternative way of looking at a BVAR model which is similar to single equation ridge regressions: when the noise in the data is substantial, the set of uncertain linear restrictions acts as a constraint on the filter extracting information from the data.

Contrary to the approach of section 3.1, the presence of trending variables in the system does not cause particular problems to this or any generic Bayesian approach (see e.g. Sims, 1988b; Sims and Ulhig, 1991). Inference in BVAR models is based on the likelihood principle. The approach requires normal residuals (which may not always be a reasonable assumption) and good priors (which are not always easy to obtain) but is entirely invariant to the size of the dominant root of the system. The aim of the analysis here is to provide conditional probability statements given observations. Therefore, contrary to classical statistical analysis, probabilities of events which have not yet occurred are treated as irrelevant to assessing uncertainty about parameters given what has occurred (see e.g. Sims, 1991b). As a consequence, no pretesting is needed to determine which asymptotic distribution applies and inferential procedures are considerably simplified.

The prior builds into the model the fact that univariate near random walk models well represent the features of many series. Although this may be a good starting point for forecasting – and, as Nickelsburg and Ohanian (1987) have indicated, they work well in many applied situations since they approximate several DGPs – there has been recent debate on the presence of unit roots in macroeconomic time series (see e.g. Perron, 1989) and on their statistical properties when structural breaks are present. Put in another way, although BVAR models avoid biases due to incorrect size and/or power of specification testing, they potentially introduce an alternative source of bias when they shrink the model to an incorrect parameter vector. An alternative approach, which does not rely on a prior specification of this type, emerges from the work of Geweke (1989) and DeJong and Whiteman (1991). The idea here is to specify a prior distribution over different trend specifications, make distributional assumptions on the innovations of the VAR model, and compute pairwise posterior odd ratios using numerical integration. This approach, which allows for a second layer of hyperparameters to control the specification of the trend in the variables, may be useful for the testing stage of the analysis. Since the choice of trend specification has economic content (e.g. unit root processes have no tendency to return to any particular level), it can be included, together with other restrictions, as a part of the second stage testing and used to examine the implication of economic theories. The major disadvantage of the approach lies in the computational burden of the numerical integration exercise. Recent development in computer technology and new algorithms constructed in the space of densities (see Gelfand and Smith, 1990), however, make numerical integration feasible for small scale systems on current desktop computers.

It is useful to highlight some relationships with existing literature in order to bring out some important aspects of the BVAR methodology. Although (2.15) is treated as a prior, it may also be considered as part of the model, i.e.

functional choices for the law of motion of the coefficients. This is exactly what the literature on time varying coefficient (TVC) models does (see Sarris, 1973; Andel, 1976; Feigin and Tweedie, 1980; Quinn and Nicholls, 1981; 1982; Nicholls and Quinn, 1982; Nicholls, 1986). Since it is a philosophical matter to determine where the model stops and where the prior begins, and since inferential procedures are identical in both frameworks, all of the tools developed in the TVC literature can also be applied to this framework.

As emphasized by Nickelsburg and Ohanian (1987) and Canova (1993a), a BVAR model is flexible enough to include as special cases several time series models which have been used to characterize the properties of macro and financial time series. In particular, ARCH (Engle, 1982) and ARCH-M (Engle, Lilien, and Robbins, 1987) models, bilinear models (Granger and Anderson, 1978), discrete regime shift models (Hamilton, 1989), and subordinated models (see Clark, 1973; or Gallant, Hsieh, and Tauchen, 1991) can be nested and tested using (2.14)–(2.21).[5]

Several modifications of the basic scheme contained in equations (2.16)–(2.21) exist in the literature, including modifications to deal with series which are seasonal (see e.g. Burbidge, Magee, and Neall, 1985; Canova, 1992; Raynauld and Simonato, 1993), to allow for structural breaks in the unconditional distribution of the coefficients (see Sims, 1989b), to account for the presence of discrete time approximations to continuous time processes (see Sims, 1989b), to allow for geometrical evolution of the variance of the coefficients, which seems useful to forecast financial variables (see Canova and Ito, 1991), and to account for the fact that variables may display common patterns at particular frequencies (see Canova, 1993b). Finally, Ingram and Whiteman (1994) have modified (2.16)–(2.21) to include restrictions derived from economic theory.

3.3   Specification Based on Dynamic Economic Theory

An alternative approach to the specification of VAR models, which is firmly rooted in dynamic economic theory, has been suggested e.g. by Sargent (1978), Hansen and Sargent (1980; 1982), Kydland and Prescott (1982), and Long and Plosser (1983). The approach starts from a fully specified dynamic model of the economy, where tractable functional forms for the primitives of the model (preferences, technology, and the stochastic processes for the exogenous variables) have been selected. Optimization and market clearing imply decision rules (reduced forms) for the endogenous variables of the model which can be written in terms of the states of the problem and the driving shocks of the economy. In early applications (e.g. Sargent, 1978) the linear quadratic structure of preferences and constraints delivered closed form decision rules which come nicely packaged as VAR models. In more recent versions VAR models emerge from specific assumptions about preferences and the rate of depreciation of the capital stock (see e.g. Long and Plosser, 1983) or from taking linear approximations of nonlinear decision rules around the steady states (e.g. Kydland and Prescott, 1982; King, Plosser, and Rebelo, 1988). In both cases the final form representation of the decision rule (one in which lagged endogenous variables are solved out) is an MA model similar to (2.12), with restrictions on the locations of the roots of the $B(\ell)$ matrix polynomial and extensive cross-equation restrictions on its elements.

To be specific, many of these models (see e.g. Hansen and Sargent, 1991) come in the form:

$$H(\ell)x_{1t} = M(K(\ell))\varepsilon_{2t} \tag{2.22}$$

$$x_{2t} = K(\ell)\varepsilon_{2t}, \tag{2.23}$$

where $H(\ell)$, $M(\ell)$ and $K(\ell)$ are one-sided polynomial matrices in the lag operator. The elements of these matrices are reduced form parameters which are, in general, complicated nonlinear functions of the parameters of interest (preferences and technologies). Because there are only $m_2 < m$ shocks, the model is singular. To undertake estimation it is typical to assume either that the econometrician observes only a subset of the variables appearing in x_{2t}, so that an additional vector of errors is added to the second equation, or that the x_{1t} variables are measured with error, so that we have an additional m_1 sources of disturbances.

When the model has been completed probabilistically so that there at least as many sources of shocks as variables in the system, estimation can be conducted by constrained maximum likelihood and using the nonlinear constraints to identify the parameters of the economic model. The VAR coefficients in this approach are of no interest except for unconditional forecasting exercises (see discussion in section 6). The task of the econometrician is to estimate the parameters of the preferences and technologies which are hidden through complicated nonlinear restrictions in the VAR coefficients.

In this line of research the judgmental role of the econometrician is limited to the specification of the lag length of the $H(\ell)$, $M(\ell)$ and $K(\ell)$ matrix polynomials. In addition, since the economic model typically specifies that the roots of the $H(\ell)$, $M(\ell)$, and $K(\ell)$ polynomials all have modulus greater than one, the econometrician must undertake suitable transformations of variables to insure that this is the case (for a study where (2.22) and (2.23) may contain unit roots see Gregory, Pagan, and Smith, 1990).

Although this approach yields VAR models which are similar to those used in the previous sections, a substantial philosophical difference sets the approaches apart. The methodologies of sections 3.1 and 3.2 choose model specifications with little reference to economic theory, which is used only to select the variables which may be relevant in characterizing the interdependencies in the data. In that case, the VAR is a (unconstrained) description of the probabilistic distribution of the data.

Here, the econometrician is provided with a list of strictly exogenous variables (the x_{2t}s) and with a set of cross-equation constraints from a dynamic economic model. The resulting VAR is therefore a (constrained) representation of the dynamic theory underlying the model. Examining the usefulness of these constraints becomes a way to test the theory (see e.g. Miller, 1983).

3.4   VAR as Index Models

An alternative modelling approach for VARs is constituted by the observable "index" model literature (see Sargent and Sims, 1977; Geweke, 1977; Reinsel, 1983; Quah and Sargent, 1993). The idea is to start from an unrestricted VAR model and examine whether an m-dimensional process x_t can be explained or predicted by past values of an index series η_t of dimension $r < m$. The economic rationale behind this scheme is that there is a low dimensional vector of economic variables (the states of the economy) which is responsible for most of the dynamic interdependencies of the economy. In practice, an index model can be obtained by factoring the $A(\ell)$ polynomial in (2.11) as $A(\ell) = \Phi(\ell) \Psi(\ell)$, where $\Phi(\ell)$ is of dimension $m \times r$ and $\Psi(\ell)$ is of dimension $r \times m$. By taking $\eta_t = \Psi(\ell) x_{t-1}$ we have the representation:

$$x_t = C(\ell) w_t + \phi(\ell) \eta_t + \varepsilon_t. \tag{2.24}$$

As it stands (2.24) is simply a reparameterization of (2.11). We can give content to the index model by normalizing, by imposing dimensionality restrictions on r (e.g. $r \leq 2$) and by model selection procedures (i.e. by choosing the lag length of $\Phi(\ell)$ and $\Psi(\ell)$). As pointed out in Quah and Sargent (1993), if we require that η_t is an r-dimensional vector of random walks and $\Phi(\ell) = \Phi$, (2.24) is a common trend representation for x_t (see e.g. Stock and Watson, 1988). The major difference between the two setups is that in the index model η_t are orthogonal to ε_t while in the common trend representation η_t and ε_t are perfectly correlated. Reinsel (1983) describes selection procedures for these types of index models together with the theory for identification of the parameters and their maximum likelihood estimation and for testing for the cross-equation restrictions implied by the index structure. Litterman (1982) describes a Bayesian version of the index models and Brillinger (1981, chapter 10) the estimation of parameters by frequency domain methods.

From the point of view of this chapter, observable index models are specifications which statistically restrict the entries of the $A(\ell)$ matrix to lie in a lower dimensional space. Therefore index models can be interpreted as providing an alternative focus to the overparameterization/oversimplification trade-off. It is also worth emphasizing that while structural interpretations of these models are often attempted (the indices are sometimes termed demand or supply, real or monetary factors), there is nothing in the approach that grants such interpretations.

4 Data Analysis and Tests of Economic Hypotheses

Unconstrained VAR models are a convenient way to summarize the statistical properties of the data, the relationships across variables, and the second moments of the innovations. Spanos (1989), for example, treats VAR models of this type as representing the Haavelmo distribution, i.e. a model which is a valid basis for inference. A standard first round of data analysis typically involves the estimation of the covariance matrix of innovations and exclusion tests (*F*-tests) for the significance of certain variables in one equation. The former statistic summarizes how innovations are correlated across variables, whether there are common contemporaneous patterns or a natural contemporaneous ordering of the variables of the system, etc. The latter tells us whether, in addition to their own lags, lags of other variables are statistically useful in predicting the left hand side variables. Although the power of these *F*-tests may be low in small samples (see e.g. Geweke, 1984), and their Wald test counterpart has asymptotic distribution which depends on the number of unit roots in the system and on nuisance parameters (see Toda and Phillips, 1992; 1993), they constitute a simple limited information test to confront the data with some well established economic propositions (see e.g. Sargent, 1978; 1979; Hamilton, 1983; King and Watson, 1992). For example, *F*-tests in a bivariate VAR or between two blocks of a VAR are identical to standard Granger noncausality tests (see e.g. Sims, 1972). This is not the case in multivariate settings since indirect effects may come through other variables. There *F*-tests examine whether the one-step-ahead predictor of x_{11t} based on lagged x_{11t} and x_{1kt}, $k \geq 3$ is as good as the one-step-ahead predictor based on lagged x_{11t} and, say, lagged x_{12t} and x_{1kt}, $k \geq 3$ (see e.g. Lutkepohl, 1990b). Considerable debate in the earlier VAR literature has been given to the relationships between Granger noncausality and the concepts of strict exogeneity, predeterminateness, weak exogeneity, strong exogeneity and super exogeneity (Sims, 1972; Zellner, 1979; Granger, 1988; Engle, Hendry, and Richard, 1983; Florens and Mounchart, 1983). Engle, Hendry, and Richard point out that the relevant concept of exogeneity depends on what use we make of an econometric model. For inference, weak exogeneity is required. That is, we need to be able to factorize the joint likelihood function of x_{1t} and x_{2t} in such a way that the partitions are completely independent of each other. For conditional forecasting involving no changes in the conditional distribution of the data, strong exogeneity is relevant, i.e. we need weak exogeneity plus the condition that the two sets of variables we care about do not Granger cause the set of variables which are manipulated. Finally, to design policy interventions which involve changes in the conditional distribution of the variables, super exogeneity is needed. In other words, together with weak exogeneity we also need that all the parameters of the model are invariant with respect to a specific class of interventions.

Coefficient estimates and their standard errors are in general not reported by users of unrestricted VAR models for two reasons. First, with a highly parameterized model and a limited data set the number of degrees of freedom is small and coefficient estimates are uninformative. Second, because of the highly parameterized nature of the model, near-collinearity of the regressors may lead to very imprecise estimates of the short run relationships.

For a more sophisticated data analysis a researcher may compute encompassing tests or examine the variance decomposition and the impulse response function of the system. The encompassing approach (see e.g. Hendry and Mizon, 1990) involves formulating a structural model within the framework of a well specified reduced form PVAR (see section 3.1) and using encompassing tests to select the specification which is, on one hand, most consistent with the data and, at the same time, coherent with economic theory. Structural equations are identified using a standard simultaneous equation approach, i.e. placing zero restrictions on either lagged relationships or the covariance matrix of innovations. The essence of the test is to select the structural model whose residuals contain the least amount of unexplained information.

A researcher analyzing the variance decomposition and the impulse response, on the other hand, attempts to describe the dynamic properties of the model following certain shocks: the variance decomposition tells us how much of the average squared forecast error variance of one variable at the kth step ahead is associated with surprise movements in each variable of the model. The impulse response function essentially traces out the moving average representation of the system and describes how one variable responds over time to a single surprise increase in itself or in any other variable. As noted by Sims (1980a), examining the impulse response function may be the most effective way of checking for Granger noncausality in multivariate frameworks.

For both exercises to be meaningful, it is essential to transform the innovations of the system into a contemporaneously uncorrelated form. Because all the variables of the system are endogenous, the sequence of forecast errors in predicting them is an amalgam of many economically meaningful disturbances (e.g. supply and demand shocks, money demand and money supply shocks, etc.). For the variance decomposition and the impulse responses to be interpretable, it is necessary to be able to distinguish the response of, say, output to a money demand shock from its response to a money supply shock. But, if disturbances are correlated, the response of output to an innovation in one of the VAR equations describes its dynamic response to a combination of several economically interpretable disturbances.

To transform VAR innovations into an orthogonal form with economically interpretable shocks it is necessary to "identify" the model: that is, it is necessary to link the observed innovations which have ambiguous economic interpretation with unobservable variables which have a clearer economic meaning. This identification process is analogous to the procedure employed in standard simultaneous equation systems (SESs) to recover an economic model from a set of reduced form equations. As in that framework, it is impossible to distinguish, for example, the effect of movements in the demand or supply equations without imposing economic restrictions. The major difference between the two setups is that in SESs restrictions are places on lagged relationships while here restrictions are typically placed either on the contemporaneous or on the long run relationships across variables. The focus on contemporaneous or long run restrictions comes from the fact that dynamic economic theory offers very little guidance about lagged behavioral relationships but, in general, places interesting contemporaneous or long run restrictions on the variables of the system (see Orden and Fackler, 1989). Another important difference between the two approaches is that while in unrestricted VARs there is a clear separation between the uncertainty due to the imperfect knowledge of the probability distribution of the data and the uncertainty due to the economic restrictions used to identify the model, in simultaneous equation models the distinction is blurred.

Structural innovations can be recovered using a semi-automatic normalization scheme which imposes a recursive structure on the contemporaneous innovations (a Wold causal chain), "economic" restrictions such as the homogeneity restriction on real variables in the long run, or other long run (e.g. cointegration) and/or short run restrictions based on informational delays.

The next section discusses identification by means of a Wold causal chain. The following one examines alternative identification schemes and compares them.

4.1   Identification Achieved Using a Semi-Automatic Scheme

Suppose x_t is a covariance stationary stochastic process (possibly after some transformation) with a MA representation (2.12). For such an x_t, Σ is, in general, nondiagonal. To transform the system in such a way that shocks to each equation are uncorrelated one can use a Choleski decomposition of Σ. Let L be a nonsingular lower triangular orthogonal matrix with ones on the main diagonal and let V be a diagonal matrix. If we choose $L^{-1}VL^{-1'} = \Sigma$, (2.12) can be renormalized as:

$$\begin{pmatrix} x_{1t} \\ x_{2t} \end{pmatrix} = \begin{pmatrix} D_{11}(\ell) & D_{12}(\ell) \\ D_{21}(\ell) & D_{22}(\ell) \end{pmatrix} \begin{pmatrix} w_{1t} \\ w_{2t} \end{pmatrix} + \begin{pmatrix} G_{11}(\ell) & G_{12}(\ell) \\ G_{21}(\ell) & G_{22}(\ell) \end{pmatrix} \begin{pmatrix} v_{1t} \\ v_{2t} \end{pmatrix}, \qquad (2.25)$$

where $G(\ell) = B(\ell)L$ and $v_t = L^{-1}\varepsilon_t$. Because L is lower triangular, $G(0) = G(\ell = 0)$ is lower triangular and innovations in variable i do not contemporaneously affect variable k if variable k precedes variable i in the list of elements of x_t. The VAR system (2.25) has a so-called Wold causal chain form. If i and k are the only two variables in the system, then variable i fails to instantaneously Granger cause variable k (see e.g. Geweke, 1982).

Recovering an interpretable MA representation for the vector x_t with the Choleski decomposition has the advantage of reducing the investigator's discretion and the scope for data mining. However, it has the disadvantage of implicitly assuming that there exists an underlying interpretable model which has a contemporaneously recursive form: i.e. the variables on the top of the triangle contemporaneously feed into all the other variables and the variables on the bottom of the triangle contemporaneously affect only themselves. Two types of objections are typically raised to this identification scheme. First, economic theory rarely delivers models in which the contemporaneous relationships among variables are of this recursive type (a point stressed by Leamer, 1985; Bernanke, 1986). This objection is important because the point of identification is to recover a class of models which is economically interpretable. A solution to this type of problem is provided in the next section. Second, the Choleski decomposition is unique only up to a premultiplication by an orthonormal matrix. This implies that the space of semi-automatic transformations is of dimension $m!$ (the number of possible permutations of the variables of the system) and selecting one of the many transformations imposes a particular causal ordering on the variables of the system. Since there is no *a priori* reason to believe that economic variables can be ranked according to a particular causal ordering, any identification scheme is arbitrary and needs validation.

Validation can be carried out by trying alternative orderings of the variables of the system (see e.g. the RATS manual by Doan, 1993). If the covariance matrix of the innovations is approximately diagonal, the ordering of the variables will be unimportant. A Wold causal chain is a reasonable approximation on such an occasion and the results will be independent of the ordering chosen. However, if Σ has large off-diagonal elements, different orderings of the variables will give different approximations and results must be interpreted with caution.

Once meaningful innovations are recovered from reduced form VAR innovations, the variance decomposition and the impulse response of the system can be computed. For example, the matrix $G(\ell)$ in (2.25) represents the impulse response functions and is useful in examining the effects of typical shocks to the variables of the system in the short and long run. Each G_j describes the response of the vector x_t to innovations j periods ago. The kth row of each G_j measures the responses of x_{kt} to innovations in the system which occurred j periods ago, $j = 0, 1, \ldots$ Finally, the hth element of the kth row of $G(1)$ measures the cumulative effect on x_{kt} of an innovation in x_{ht} that occurred j periods ago, where $j \to \infty$.

The variance decomposition provides similar information. To compute the variance decomposition of x_t note that from (2.25)

$$\text{var}(x_t) = G(1)Ev_t v_t' G(1)'. \tag{2.26}$$

To see exactly what the above expression entails, consider the case where $m_1 = m_2 = 1$. Then, the variance of x_{1t} has two components: one due to the impact of its own innovations from time t to time $t - j, j = 1, 2, \ldots$; and one due to innovations in x_{2t} from time t to time $t - j$. If x_{2t} is shocked at time

$t - j$ and left unperturbed afterward, we can examine how much of the variability of x_1 at time t is due to that innovation, for all j. As (2.26) makes clear, the variance decomposition does not add new information to the impulse response analysis but, instead, presents it in an alternative form.

The variance decomposition and the impulse response function are in-sample forecasting exercises. They describe the effect on the system of a "typical" shock to a variable or to an economically interpretable entity, where by "typical" one usually means a one standard error shock, or a sequence of shocks which, on average, have occurred during the sample period. It is important to emphasize the distinction between these types of exercise and the more complicated conditional forecasting exercises considered in section 5 in order to understand the relevance of Lucas' critique to policy analyses undertaken with VARs.

Runkle (1987) pointed out that point estimates of the impulse responses and of the variance decomposition are not very useful. As in the simple regression framework, the presentation of point estimates of the coefficients is unrevealing unless standard errors are also provided. This is particularly important when the economic analysis is based on large j (i.e. when we test long run restrictions such as neutrality of money as in King and Watson, 1992 or Weber, 1993). Runkle shows that the G_j matrices for moderately large j tend to be very imprecisely estimated, with the measure of dispersion around the point estimate increasing with the lag length p of the autoregression and the size m of the system.

Because of the complicated structure of the G_j matrices, the asymptotic distribution of estimators of G_j has been worked out only relatively recently. Baillie (1987a; 1987b) derives a general form for the asymptotic distribution of estimators of the impulse response function. The major drawback of his approach is that no closed form solution for the covariance matrix of the estimators of the G_j is provided. In a series of works Lutkepohl (1988; 1989; 1990a; 1990b; 1991) and Lutkepohl and Proskitt (1991) derive a simpler expression for the asymptotic covariance matrix of estimators of the impulse response function under two alternative assumptions: that the data are truly generated by a finite order VAR(p) model and that a VAR(p) is a small sample approximation to an infinite order model. Both Baillie and Lutkepohl require that the parameters of the $C(\ell)$ and $A(\ell)$ matrices be estimated by maximum likelihood.[6] For unrestricted systems maximum likelihood is equivalent to OLS on each equation separately. For models constrained by statistical or economic restrictions, system wide estimation procedures are needed (see also Mittnik and Zadrozny, 1993 for an alternative set of formulas).

To determine the small sample properties of estimators of the impulse response function, Runkle uses a bootstrap technique and an approximate Monte Carlo approach. Sims (1987) argues that neither procedure is appropriate even as an approximation and suggests basing inference on posterior standard errors computed using Monte Carlo methods. His procedure simplifies the approach that Kloek and Van Djik (1978) employ to compute the posterior distribution for interim multipliers in simultaneous equation systems. It requires the assumption of normality for the innovations (which may not be warranted in certain applications) and draws Monte Carlo replications directly from the joint posterior of VAR coefficients and innovations. A comparative study of the small sample properties of different procedures appears in Griffiths and Lutkepohl (1990). They find that the asymptotic theory works well in small samples when near unit roots are present and even when the normality assumption is violated. They also find that among bootstrap, normal simulation, and asymptotic procedures there is no procedure which is superior for all lags and all parameter configurations.

Blanchard (1987) and Watson (1987) consider possible ways to reduce the uncertainty around the point estimates of these statistics. They both find that meaningful economic restrictions (such as homogeneity of real variables with respect to nominal shocks or common trends in the variables) do not seem to help in reducing the size of the standard errors of the estimated impulse responses and variance decompositions. Watson, however, conjectures that constraints on the lag polynomials may be useful and presents a simple example where this is the case. These constraints may come from Granger causal orderings of the variables, uncertain restrictions like those imposed by BVAR models, or fully Bayesian priors. The results contained in Canova (1991) confirm Watson's conjecture. Although the standard errors around the point estimates of the variance decomposition are large, the presence of uncertain linear constraints (of BVAR type) reduces the intrinsic uncertainty in the model and makes the results more easily interpretable.

4.2   Identification Using Economic and/or Informational Restrictions

From the point of view of economic theory the identification of meaningful disturbances by means of a Choleski normalization is arbitrary and has drawn substantial criticism (see section 6). An alternative method of identification was pioneered by Blanchard and Watson (1986) and Bernanke (1986) (see Orden and Fackler, 1989 for a simple description of the approach). The basic idea of the approach is that a large class of dynamic models have a VAR representation of the form:

$$R_0 x_t = Q(\ell)w_t + R(\ell)x_{t-1} + Su_t, \tag{2.27}$$

where the us are primitive exogenous forces not directly observed by the econometrician which buffet the system and cause oscillation. Because the us are among the primitives of the model they are assumed to be contemporaneously and serially uncorrelated and can be given fairly specific economic interpretation. VAR users are generally interested in the us from (2.27) since they are the primitives they want to manipulate (e.g. to compute impulse response functions, conditional forecasts, etc.) and not in the εs in (2.11) which are reduced form shocks. Note that (2.11) and (2.27) imply, among other things, that:

$$R_0 \varepsilon_t = S u_t. \tag{2.28}$$

Given estimates of ε_t and Σ from (2.11) an investigator must commit himself to a particular class of structures (i.e. particular R_0 and S matrices) to obtain an estimate of u_t from (2.28).[7]

Dynamic structural economic models may place restrictions on the correlation among observables (the R_0 matrix), on the correlation among unobservables (the S matrix), or both. A recursive structural model (i.e. a model where $S = I$ and R_0 is lower triangular) is one possible choice but there are many alternative structures which will do as well. In choosing one of these structures one must select a particular model for the correlation among variables. In the absence of meaningful economic motivation such a choice is arbitrary (see Blanchard, 1989 for this issue).

Typically, the relationship between a particular structure and the reduced form VAR model holds for all lags. When the variables of the VAR system and of the structural model are nonstationary, one is free to choose restrictions for contemporaneous correlations, for long run correlations, or for both. For example, Blanchard and Watson (1986), Bernanke (1986), Evans (1989), Orden and Fackler (1989), and Gali and Hammour (1991) used economic theory to pin down a model for contemporaneous correlations across variables. Blanchard and Quah (1989), Shapiro and Watson (1989), Amhed (1990), King et al. (1991), Amhed et al. (1993), and others employed long run economic restrictions to identify structural disturbances. Finally, Gali (1992) and Checchetti and Karras (1994) used a mixture of contemporaneous and long run restrictions. To see exactly what the set of restrictions is which hold when variables are nonstationary, rewrite (2.11) and (2.27) as:

$$y_t = D(\ell)w_t + B(\ell)\varepsilon_t$$

$$= D(\ell)w_t + B(1)\varepsilon_t + B^*(\ell)\Delta\varepsilon_t \tag{2.29}$$

$$y_t = M(\ell)w_t + N(\ell)R_0^{-1}S u_t$$

$$= M(\ell)w_t + N(1)R_0^{-1}S u_t + N^*(\ell)R_0^{-1}S \Delta u_t \tag{2.30}$$

where y_t is a stationary inducing transformation of x_t, e.g. $y_t = (I - \ell)x_t$, $\Delta u_t = u_t - u_{t-1}$, $\Delta \varepsilon_t = \varepsilon_t - \varepsilon_{t-1}$, $M(\ell) = Q(\ell)\hat{R}(\ell)^{-1}$, $N(\ell) = \hat{R}(\ell)^{-1}$, and where $N^*(\ell) \equiv (N(\ell) - N(1))/(1 - \ell)$, $B^*(\ell) \equiv (B(\ell) - B(1))/(1 - \ell)$ and $\hat{R}(\ell) = (1 - \ell)\tilde{R}(\ell) = (R_0 - R(\ell)\ell)$.

Matching the coefficients of the moving average representations (2.30) and (2.29) we have:

$$M(\ell) = D(\ell) \tag{2.31}$$

$$N(\ell)R_0^{-1}S u_t = B(\ell)\varepsilon_t. \tag{2.32}$$

Note that (2.28) can be obtained from (2.32) by setting $N(\ell) = B(\ell)$. An alternative formulation of the second restriction, which can be derived from the second equality appearing in (2.30) and (2.29), is in terms of the long run multipliers $N(1)$ and $B(1)$ and/or of innovations to the theoretical and VAR model:

$$N(1) R_0^{-1} S = B(1) \tag{2.33}$$

$$R_0^{-1} S u_t = \varepsilon_t. \tag{2.34}$$

Clearly, when x_t is stationary, $N(1)$ and $B(1)$ are equal to zero and (2.33) and (2.34) are vacuous.

The use of long run restrictions to identify a VAR has been motivated as a way of generating an unrestricted "permanent-transitory" decomposition for time series with unit roots which overcomes the lack of interpretability of traditional decompositions such as those of Beveridge and Nelson (1981) or Watson (1986). A VAR identified with long run restrictions, in fact, imposes a specific but arbitrary structure on the permanent components and provides a meaningful measure of the relative importance of permanent components in explaining cyclical fluctuations in the system (see e.g. King et al., 1991; Quah, 1992).[8] However, while the use of long run restrictions to identify the system has appealing features from the point of view of economic theory, it is often hard to determine the long run properties of a time series, so the results may be very sensitive to the treatment of trends. In addition, for systems of medium or large size one hopes to have, at best, enough constraints to be able to just identify the model since the number of meaningful long run restrictions is limited.

From a statistical point of view a structural system can be recovered from the VAR if the order and/or rank conditions derived from a set of nonhomogeneous linear constraints are satisfied (see e.g. Giannini, 1992). Loosely speaking, because there are $m(m + 1)/2$ independent elements in Σ, a necessary (order) condition requires that $m(m - 1)/2$ restrictions are needed in a VAR system of m equations. A necessary and sufficient (rank) condition requires that such restrictions are "correctly" placed. If the statistical conditions for identification are satisfied, one can employ either an indirect least squares (ILS) procedure as in Sims (1986a) or a two stage least square procedure (2SLS) as in Blanchard (1989) to estimate the free parameters of (2.26). When a system is just identified the two procedures yield the same estimators (see Shapiro and Watson, 1989). If the restrictions are placed on both the R_0 and the S matrices, the ILS and 2SLS procedures may be inapplicable, in which case one could employ the method of moments to estimate the free parameters (as in Bernanke, 1986). Finally, for systems which do not have a special recursive structure or zeros appropriately placed and for overidentified systems, Giannini (1992) develops a full information maximum likelihood (FIML) estimator of the structural parameters and a formal test for overidentifying restrictions.

It has become increasingly popular in the last few years to attempt to identify VAR models using cointegration restrictions (see e.g. King et al., 1991; Giannini, 1992; Wickens, 1992). The basic idea of the approach is simple. If there are cointegrating restrictions among the variables of the system, the number of shocks driving the structural system is smaller than the dimension of the time series. Hence, to identify structural disturbances and their covariance matrix, we need a smaller number of restrictions. In this case, the order condition requires that $(m - r)(m - r - 1)/2$ restrictions are imposed on the system, where r is the number of common trends since the rank of $N(1)$ is $m - r$. The advantage of this approach is obvious since the burden of finding meaningful economic restrictions is lightened and identification of the structural disturbances becomes possible also in systems of medium size. On the other hand, although the imposition of cointegrating restrictions helps identification by decreasing the number of restrictions needed to undertake structural analyses, it helps in an uninteresting way by shifting the emphasis of identification from finding interesting economic restrictions to characterizing the statistical properties of economic time series.

Sims (1986a) takes an alternative approach to the question of identifying a structural form. Instead of using explicit economic restrictions which may be both debatable and scarce, one can use knowledge about the flows of information in the economy to recover generic structural forms. For example, it is known that data on GNP become available only once every three months. Therefore, it is reasonable to suppose that within a month, GNP is not a variable in the reaction function of the monetary authorities. This, however, does not imply that over longer horizons (even a quarter) the monetary authorities do not use information about GNP in setting targets for e.g. the growth rate of the money supply (see also Gordon and Leeper, 1995). Because informational delays are very common, there are often more than enough restrictions to identify either particular shocks or, in some cases, the entire system. In situations where the system is just identified, ILS or 2SLS procedures may be used to estimate the free parameters. However, when there are overidentifying restrictions, a maximum likelihood procedure should be used to efficiently estimate the free parameters of R_0 and S. Canova (1991) describes a latent variable procedure which accomplishes this.

This approach is less theoretically bound than previous ones, is the natural extension of Sims' original work, and can be more useful in investigating controversial relationships which may otherwise require stringent assumptions on the nature of the shocks impinging on the system.

One important issue, often neglected in all the literature on structural VAR analysis, is the correct number of relevant shocks buffeting the system. In many cases bivariate systems are analyzed and identification is limited to one source of supply and of demand disturbances. It should be clear, however, that a misspecification of the number of shocks driving the structural system is likely to confuse different sources of structural disturbances and is bound to produce uninterpretable impulse responses (see e.g. Blanchard and Quah, 1989).

Finally, one should note that once informational or economic restrictions are used to identify a VAR, the distinction between a structural VAR, a PVAR which is congruent with economic theory, and a standard simultaneous equation model becomes a matter of degree, not of content. The two basic questions are: (i) whether prior information should be imposed at the stage of construction/estimation of the model or if one should wait to extract as much information as possible from the data and use the *a priori* information at a later stage of the analysis; and (ii) whether economic restrictions are more sensibly placed on lagged relationships, on contemporaneous correlations, or on long run correlations.

5   Forecasting

Because of their simplicity, unrestricted VAR models are particularly well suited for forecasting. In this task Litterman (1986b) lists two main advantages of VARs over standard simultaneous equation systems. VARs give on objective summary of the uncertainty of the forecasts in the sense that they are very weakly contaminated by the modeler's judgmental decisions and, because of this, they provide realistic multivariate probability distributions for future paths of the economy. For the purposes of this section I distinguish between unconditional forecasts, which are uncontroversially conducted in the context of VAR models, and conditional forecasts. Under the heading of conditional forecasts I will distinguish between simple innovation accounting exercises and policy analysis exercises.

5.1   Unconditional Forecasts

Once it is consistently and efficiently estimated, the system (2.11) is in a format which allows the application of the Wiener-Kolmogorov prediction formulas (see Sargent, 1986) to obtain forecasts of future variables. I call this activity unconditional forecasting. This terminology may be confusing because forecasts are indeed conditional on information up to time t. Perhaps a better way of characterizing this activity would be to call it "baseline" forecasting, in the sense that the stochastic process underlying the model is assumed to perpetuate into the future. However, because this is the terminology commonly used in the debate concerning the appropriateness of policy analysis with VARs, I will maintain it. For future comparison, it may be useful to restate the concept in a somewhat different way: I will call unconditional forecasts those exercises computed without interventions on the realization or on the parameters of the estimated stochastic processes.

Unrestricted VAR models selected so as to satisfy the white noise assumption for the disturbances typically forecast very poorly. To insure that the disturbances are white noise innovation one should include, in principle, a large number of lags. Because the number of parameters to be estimated may be large for a fixed sample size, the precision of the estimates is very dubious (see e.g. Litterman, 1980 or Todd, 1984 for this type of argument). In other words, although the in-sample fit of the model as measured, for example, by the R^2 coefficient may be extremely good (VARs have R^2 of the order of 0.999), the out-of-sample performance can be very poor because of very poor parameter estimates. In comparison with parsimoniously parameterized uni-variate ARIMA models, standard out-of-sample measures (like the Theil U or the root mean square error) generally discard unrestricted VAR models. The approach of Hsiao may reduce the dimensionality of the model but will not help in forecasting because model specification choices are based on the in-sample fit of various specifications.

One solution to this problem is to select the lag length of the model bearing in mind that the specification will be used for forecasting. Information criteria such as the MLR test of Sims, the AIC, or the SIC are helpful here. These last two methods in particular are useful because they measure adequacy by trading off in a nonlinear way the divergent considerations of accuracy in the forecasts and the "best" approximation to reality. They do so by sacrificing unbiasedness of parameter estimates in exchange for a reduction in the variance of the estimates, along the line of James-Stein-type estimators (see e.g. Stein, 1974; Judge et al., 1980). The result is that although the selected model is inaccurate to describe reality, it may turn out to be useful in forecasting. An alternative solution is to use the BVAR approach of Litterman (1986a; 1986b) discussed in section 3.2.

5.1.1 Forecasting performance of VAR models The literature documenting the unconditional forecasting performance of VAR models is constantly growing. From the seminal works of Fair (1979), Webb (1984), Kling and Bessler (1985), Litterman (1986b), McNees (1986a; 1986b), and Sims (1989b) to the recent articles by Hafer and Sheehan (1989), McNees (1990), Fair and Shiller (1989; 1990), and Artis and Zhang (1990), numerous researchers have documented three basic regularities concerning the forecasting performance of VAR models. First, relative to large scale structural models, unrestricted VARs are superior in long run forecasting (see e.g. Luppoletti and Webb, 1986). Relative to other time series models the evidence for long run forecasting is more mixed. Second, BVARs are, at least, competitive with large scale structural models and outperform univariate ARIMA models in forecasting real variables. For the most recent experience, however, NcNees (1990) notes a deterioration of the forecasting ability of BVAR models which is especially evident for monetary variables. Third, both unrestricted VARs and BVARs usually contain information which is not present in the forecasts of structural models. This indicates that neither specification is totally adequate and that a pooling of the forecasts may improve the quality of the predictions.

Within the VAR methodology, Todd (1984), Litterman (1986a; 1986b), Kunst and Neusser (1986), Trevor and Thorp (1988), and Funke (1990) favour BVAR models over unrestricted VARs. Luppoletti and Webb (1986), on the other hand, suggest that shrewdly chosen unrestricted models are as good as more elaborate BVAR models in forecasting key macro variables.

The forecasting performance of BVAR models with asymmetric priors has been examined in Litterman (1984) and Funke (1990). However, these studies employ single equation methods to estimate the parameters despite the fact that they are inefficient. Therefore, a clear assessment of their forecasting performance is still missing. Recently, Kadiyala and Karlsson (1989) show that one may obtain substantial improvements over the forecasts of a symmetric BVAR model and estimate its parameters with multivariate methods restricting VAR models with a tractable family of asymmetric priors.

The asymptotic properties of the forecasts of a VAR system which display cointegrating relationships have been analyzed by Engle and Yoo (1987) and Hendry and Clements (1991). Monte Carlo studies of the small sample properties of the forecasts in the short and long run appear in Brandner and Kunst (1990) and Clements and Hendry (1991).

5.2   Conditional Forecasting

Following Litterman (1984) I distinguish between two types of conditional forecasts: those which involve no explicit policy assumption and those requiring it.

Suppose one equation of the system has output as the left hand side variable. The first type of question may involve an experiment such as: what is the effect on the system of a once-and-for-all shock to output? Suppose one equation represents the behavior of the fiscal authorities. The second type of question may be formulated as: what is the effect of a 10% cut in taxes in the economy?

The first type of question can be answered by analyzing the impulse response function of the system. Alternatively, one could input a vector of shocks and examine the change in the baseline forecasts that would occur as a result of the vector of shocks.

In answering the second question it is necessary to identify one equation as describing the behavior of the fiscal authorities and, more importantly, define what is meant by the supposed policy change. To identify the reaction function of the fiscal authority one could use one of the identification schemes discussed in section 4. A policy change is then defined as a sequence of shocks to a policy equation (i.e. the alteration of the path of innovations in one equation: see Sims, 1982). For the answer to be meaningful two conditions must be satisfied: (i) that the actions contemplated do not involve changes in the conditional distribution of the policy instrument; and (ii) that the size of the prospective policy change is within the historical experience of changes that actually occurred.

If the first condition is not satisfied, the well known Lucas critique would invalidate the conditional forecasting exercise (see Miller and Roberds, 1991 for a recent evaluation of the quantitative significance of the Lucas critique for VAR models). If the second condition is not satisfied, great care must be taken in extrapolating results which are very far away from what the economy has experienced in the past.

6 Some Critiques

A number of critiques have been raised to the VAR methodology. The objections come at all stages of the analysis and involve the robustness of data characterizations with VARs, their usefulness in analyzing historical episodes and their significance for policy analyses.

Maravall (1993) has suggested that, when the underlying structural model contains unobservable components with unit roots, seasonal adjustment procedures will induce noninvertible MA components in the seasonally adjusted data. This implies that seasonally adjusted data cannot be approximated with VAR systems, that VARs fitted to seasonally adjusted series are misspecified, and that most of the statistical specification tests for dimensionality, encompassing, etc. are inappropriate. Although this theoretical result casts doubts on the ability of VARs to effectively capture the interdependencies present in seasonally adjusted data, its relevance for empirical analysis still needs to be demonstrated.

Another objection to the characterization of the data comes from the work of Eichenbaum and Singleton (1986), Runkle (1987), Ohanian (1988), and Spencer (1989). They examine the robustness of variance decomposition and impulse response results obtained in VARs identified with a semi-automatic scheme to alternative and apparently innocuous (from the point of view of economic theory) changes in the statistical specification of the model. They find that the ordering of the variables, the method of trend removal, the level of aggregation, the lag length employed, and the choice among variables that measure the same concept over the same period of time (e.g. GNP deflator or the personal consumption expenditure price index) all have substantial effects in determining the actual features of business cycles in the US since World War II.

Runkle and Spencer speculate that the nonrobustness of VAR evidence could be a widespread phenomenon and question the usefulness of the technique as a way to characterize data. Todd (1990) demonstrates that although these criticisms are well taken, the strong conclusions Runkle and Spencer draw may be unfounded. He shows that although numerical measures of the importance of certain shocks are subject to robustness problems, the major qualitative conclusions regarding money/income/interest-rate causality are independent of model specification. In addition, he argues that some of the specifications examined in the literature induce impulse responses which do not conform to the notion of monetarism examined by Sims (1980a) or formulated in Friedman and Schwartz (1963) (e.g. when an innovation in monetary aggregates induces a *negative* response in output). Sims (1987) objects to some of these robustness exercises because they are not as innocuous as they seem, in the sense that they alter the uncertainty in the long run responses of output to interest rates. He also objects to the conclusion that VARs are unreliable because of the inherent imprecision of point estimates of statistics of interest, claiming that this imprecision is characteristic of any methodology which gives an honest account of the effects of specification uncertainty on the uncertainty of the results. In other words, if the data appear to speak more softly than in standard models, it is because no artificial "megaphone" is imposed on them (an opinion shared by Blanchard, 1987).

Another objection to the usefulness of VARs comes from their fragility in conducting analyses of Granger noncausality issues. Christiano and Ljungvist (1987) find that inference based on these tests may depend on the model specification (log level verses first differences). Using a bootstrap methodology they show that the resulting differences are due to the lack of power of standard Granger causality tests to detect unidirectional causation when the data are measured in first differences. Toda and Phillips (1992; 1993) object to the use of VAR models in levels to examine Granger noncausality. They show that the limiting distribution of the tests is nonstandard, depends on a nuisance parameter, and conclude that there is no sound statistical basis for noncausality testing. They recommend testing noncausality in VECM models. Finally Lutkepohl and Proskitt (1992) show that if the data generating process is an infinite order VAR, the size of standard noncausality tests computed estimating finite order VAR models may be far from the nominal size and tends to overreject the null of no causality.

Finally, Gordon and King (1982), Fair (1988), and Kirchgassner (1991) stress that although VAR users do not employ exclusion restrictions to specify and estimate the model, they implicitly assume that there exist a small number of variables which span the information available to the econometrician. Fair, for example, shows that if some of the omitted variables are correlated with the included ones, the estimated coefficients will be wrong. In this case the VAR model will be a poor approximation to the underlying structural model, in the sense that noncausality tests, variance decomposition, impulse responses, and various multipliers will be misspecified.

The usefulness of policy analyses with VARs has been considered, at a minimum, debatable. The major objections stem from two different points of view: (i) the rational expectation econometric program (REE) (see e.g. Sargent and Lucas, 1980; Sargent, 1984; Keating, 1990; see Kocherlakota, 1988 for a counterargument) which uses the Lucas' critique as a building block for designing the effect of regime changes; and (ii) a line of thought which interprets the concepts of causality and of structural model in a more orthodox way than Sims (1972; 1980a) (see e.g. Jacobs, Leamer, and Ward, 1979; Sachs, 1982; Cooley and LeRoy, 1985; Leamer, 1985).

The REE criticism comes from the observation that some difference between the estimated sample and the future must be posited by anyone recommending a change in policy (an argument disputed e.g. by Sims, 1988a). According to this view, thoroughly expressed in Sargent (1984), proponents of VAR models cannot give advice to governments (in the sense of proposing an optimal strategy for government behavior), not because VARs are atheoretical, but because VAR econometricians regard current strategies as nearly optimal.

In rational expectations models the public and the government play a dynamic game. Constrained VARs emerge as reduced form models of these dynamic optimizing exercises. A rational expectations (RE) econometrician recommends for policy the optimal solution to the dynamic game that describes government decisions (see e.g. Lucas and Stokey, 1983; Epple, Hansen, and Roberds, 1985). His choice is therefore among deterministic strategies which describe the distribution of government variables. The major difference in the philosophy underlying a constrained RE-VAR and an unconstrained VAR model is in the way the dynamic game is assumed to be played before and after the estimation period. RE econometricians assume that, over the past history, government variables follow arbitrary (suboptimal) stochastic processes. Proponents of "unrestricted" VAR models assume that government behavior has been, historically, nearly optimal.

Because of this near optimality of government behavior, unrestricted VAR econometricians claim that everyday policy interventions do not occur in the form of changes in government strategies (i.e. changes in the entire probability distribution of government variables). Changes of this type are rare and, in general, impossible to analyze with statistical models because they require extrapolation for conditions far outside the range experienced in the sample. Instead, after accounting for political rhetoric, agents' discounting of false signals, the fact that many policy announcements are rarely carried out, and the fact that true policies are unknown, VAR econometricians believe that policy interventions are better portrayed as alternative implementations of the existing rule rather than a change in the choice of permanent rules of behavior for policy authorities. In other words, policy interventions may be thought of as modifications of the realizations of the stochastic processes for government variables, not as modifications of their probability distribution (see e.g. Sims, 1982; Doan, Litterman, and Sims, 1984).

An example could illustrate the difference more clearly. Suppose that in (2.11) $m_1 = m_2 = 1$, x_{1t} is the growth rate of output, and x_{2t} is the growth rate of the money supply, and that $A_{12}(\ell) \neq 0$ and $A_{21}(\ell) = 0$, so that money supply growth Granger-causes output growth. Suppose also for simplicity that Σ_{12} is equal to zero (if it is not, transform the system (2.11) so that this is true). A valid policy exercise in the context of the VAR framework is the following: "What would happen to future output growth if the current and future growth

rate of the money supply would be 5% higher than they have been in the past?"
This exercise would be implementable if historically the money supply growth
has been 5% higher than what it is currently and can be carried out by
selecting a path for ε_{2t} which would give this growth rate for x_{2t} and examining
the effect of this altered path for x_{2t} on x_{1t}. On the other hand, a typical
exercise that an REE is concerned with might be: "What would happen to the
growth rate of output if we switch from an autoregressive rule for the money
supply growth to, say, a constant growth rate rule?" This type of intervention
cannot be modelled by simply altering the ε_{2t} path with the same $A_{22}(\ell)$
previously estimated. Its effect cannot be evaluated within the VAR framework since this change in the money supply rule will alter agents' decisions
which underlay the $A_{12}(\ell)$ coefficients. In the terminology of Cooley and
LeRoy (1985), and for this type of intervention, $A_{12}(\ell)$ are "shallow" parameters and the effect of policy is ambiguous since both x_{2t} *and* $A_{12}(\ell)$ will change.

Kocherlakota (1988) presents an example where policy analyses involving
interventions on the distribution of the stochastic processes conducted within
VARs are as good as those conducted along the dictate of the Lucas' critique.
His argument is that there are situations when an RE econometrician can
select an economic model up to a range of observationally equivalent structures. In choosing one of these structures he makes assumptions which are as
strong (and in some cases stronger) than the assumption of invariant structure
under intervention used by a VAR econometrician. These assumptions may
lead to errors which are larger in the MSE sense than those made by a VAR
econometrician. Although with limited data sets from a small number of
regimes a VAR econometrician may provide better predictions of regime
changes, adding observations from more policy regimes helps an RE econometrician to reduce the set of observationally equivalent structures and to
decrease the size of the prediction errors. A VAR econometrician, on the other
hand, cannot improve his prediction by obtaining data from different regimes
because his errors are independent of the number of regimes observed (see also
Cooley, LeRoy, and Raymon, 1984).

Although very controversial at the time of their appearance, Sims' ideas
regarding exogeneity and causality are tightly linked to those of the Cowles
Commission. In my opinion the major contribution of Sims is to use data to
examine these issues instead of loosely arguing in favor of the exogeneity of
one variable or another. In some extreme interpretations Sims' approach is
implied to mean that the effect of changing exogenous variables on the system
can be analyzed without explicit reference to economic theory. Cooley and
LeRoy (1985) criticize this point of view. They claim that neither strict
exogeneity nor Granger causality is relevant to conducting policy experiments
which are unambiguous. A change in a policy variable has a well defined effect
on an endogenous variable if the variable is predetermined (i.e. can be
conditioned upon because it is determined outside the system). In the VAR
system (2.11), for x_{2t} to be a reasonable policy variable it is necessary that

$A_{210} = 0$ and that the structural innovations in the system be contemporaneously uncorrelated.[9] These requirements cannot be examined in the context of nonstructural VAR models because they are nontestable without *a priori* economic restrictions.

An implication of Cooley and LeRoy's argument is that conclusions drawn by analyzing causal orderings and policy analyses undertaken in VARs, where identification is achieved using a semi-automatic triangular decomposition, are misleading and meaningless. Structural analyses in VAR models are justified when the restrictions on the covariance matrix of the residuals are *a priori* imposed from economic theory (see also Sachs, 1982 and Leamer, 1985 for this point). Such restrictions cannot be simple renormalizations of the distribution of the innovations.

Monfort and Rabemananjara (1990) demonstrate that the above argument holds only partially. Given the VAR coefficients and the covariance matrix of innovations, a nonstructural VAR econometrician can recover an economic structure, test predeterminateness (along with weak structurality of the model) and undertake policy analyses by choosing a structure from a class of overidentified models. Instead of *a priori* selecting a structural form, the econometrician can extract that overidentified model which is most consistent with the historical data through a set of nested hypothesis tests. For just identified models the arguments of Cooley and LeRoy still apply.

Cooley and LeRoy's and Leamer's criticisms have been pervasive and most of the current VAR literature now uses structural or informational approaches to identification: e.g. Blanchard and Watson (1986), Sims (1986a), Blanchard and Quah (1989), Evans (1989), Blanchard (1989), Shapiro and Watson (1989), King et al. (1991), Gali (1992), West (1990; 1991), and Canova (1991), among others.

The most effective and articulate answers to these correct and logically consistent critiques are contained in Litterman (1984) and Sims (1982; 1986a; 1988a). In essence they argue that such critiques are "cautionary footnotes" which should not deter sophisticated users of VARs from continuing to use them for data analyses and policy purposes. They demonstrate how one can ingeniously use informational delays, which are consistent with rational expectations, while refraining from using dubious theoretical restrictions to identify an economic structure; how policy analyses can be effectively and meaningfully carried out in such "weakly" identified VAR models; how and when the assumption of stable structure under intervention is appropriate and reasonable; and how one can resolve within VAR models the question of policy endogeneity, an issue neglected in all traditional and most RE models.

It is worth emphasizing the issue of policy endogeneity. In almost all models policy variables are treated as predetermined (one exception is Gordon and King, 1982). This means that if one wishes to use x_{2t} in (2.11) as a policy variable, one must insure that A_0 is upper block triangular and that the innovations in the two blocks are uncorrelated. Predeterminateness of x_{2t} is, however, an unreasonable assumption when there are feedbacks on government behavior. Taking into account the endogeneity of many policy instruments is one of the major advantages of policy analyses conducted with VAR. When policy variables are endogenous Sims (1988a) shows that predetermineteness (in the sense of Cooley and LeRoy) is not a necessary condition for policy analysis to be meaningful. Alternative interventions can be carried out using a structural model which is identified using e.g. informational delays.

Finally, criticisms have been raised to the way identification is carried out in VAR models. Keating (1990) has criticized the practice of placing zero restrictions on the covariance matrix of innovations to achieve identification because it is inconsistent with certain models where agents have rational expectations. This criticism applies to VAR models identified with a semi-automatic scheme as well as to those "structural" VAR models identified using contemporaneous zero restrictions derived from economic theories (e.g. by Evans, 1989; Gali and Hammour, 1991). In the context of (2.11), Keating's result can be obtained if x_{1t} and x_{2t} are contemporaneously observable and agents use say x_{2t} in constructing the optimal decision rule for x_{1t}. Instead of placing zero restrictions on the R_0 or S matrices, Keating suggests using implicit cross-equation restrictions that the model imposes to identify structural disturbances and coefficients.

An important point related to the recoverability of structural forms emerges from the work of Leeper (1989), Quah (1990), Hansen and Sargent (1991), Hansen, Roberds, and Sargent (1991), and Lippi and Reichlin (1993). The basic message of their argument is the following: in recovering an interpretable MA representation from an unrestricted VAR model, a researcher implicitly assumes that there exists an economic structure with a Wold MA representation. These authors point out that there are many interesting structural models which need not have a Wold MA representation, in the sense that the linear space spanned by the innovations is strictly larger than the space spanned by current and lagged variables (i.e. the sequence of B_j matrices in (2.12) is not square summable). Structural inference conducted within the framework of a fundamental MA model is therefore unable to capture the dependencies of the true behavioral model. In particular, innovations and impulse responses recovered through standard innovation accounting exercises have little to do with the innovations and responses of the underlying behavioral structure.

Hansen and Sargent show that when a theoretical model has a non-Wold representation the structural innovations recovered by a VAR econometrician will be a complicated function of past, current, and future innovations to the system. Hansen, Roberds, and Sargent argue that present value relationships are untestable under some commonly used assumptions since they apply to nonfundamental MA representations. Lippi and Reichlin (1993) show that when one takes into account the possibility that technological progress comes in the form of diffusion (in which case the structural model has at least one root outside the unit circle), then Blanchard and Quah's (1989) results concerning the relative importance of demand and supply shocks are not robust (see also comment by Blanchard and Quah, 1993). Leeper (1989) demonstrates that fiscal effects can mistakenly be attributed to monetary surprises if one does not take into account the fact that because of institutional arrangements, actual shocks to fiscal variables are known before they actually occur. Quah (1990), finally, explains Deaton's (1987) paradox using a decomposition of labor income in transitory and permanent components which imply a theoretical nonfundamental representation for the joint consumption–income process.

Another difficulty that a VAR econometrician encounters in attempting to recover behavioral disturbances from the reduced form VAR evidence has been pointed out by Hansen and Sargent (1991) and concerns the effects of time aggregation. Hansen and Sargent show that if an economic model is truly in continuous time a VAR econometrician has little hope of recovering innovations to the agents' information set and of making sense of the discrete time version of the MA coefficients recovered with standard innovation accounting exercises. This is because discrete time innovations at t need not reflect the behavior of continuous time innovations near t, because the components of the discrete time innovation vector are mixtures of the vector of continuous time innovations – a result which implies that Granger causality in discrete time may emerge even though in continuous time the components of vector processes are contemporaneously and serially uncorrelated among each other – and because the discrete time MA coefficients will look like the sampled version of the continuous time coefficients if and only if the equilibrium process for the endogenous variables in continuous time is a VAR where only the coefficient on the first lag is different from zero.

These results have several implications for standard practice. First, discrete time innovations tend to be distributed lags of the innovations in continuous time with memory which can go arbitrarily far into the past. This feature therefore implies that "news" in discrete time is a weighted average of the news hitting agents' information set over a possible large interval of time and, as such, need not have much relationship with the true innovations at each t. Second, evidence of Granger causality in discrete time data need not bear a relationship with the Granger causality existing in continuous time, unless the VAR econometrician finds no evidence of causality. Third, and as a consequence of the above, the impulse response analysis conducted in discrete time may have little relationship with the true continuous time impulse responses.

7 Applications and Extensions

The VAR methodology has been used in recent years to examine a number of issues. Among them researches have been concerned with the occurrence and the impact of specific shocks to interpret economic history (e.g. Burbidge and Harrison, 1984 study the effects of the first oil shock; and Canova, 1991 studies the creation of the Federal Reserve System), the examination of the empirical distribution of shocks to check some general hypothesis about the sources of cycles (see e.g. Genberg, Salemi, and Swoboda, 1986; Blanchard and Watson, 1986; Shapiro, 1987; Shapiro and Watson, 1989; Blanchard and Quah, 1989; Blanchard, 1989; Evans, 1989; King et al., 1991; Englund, Vredin, and Warne, 1991; Quah, 1991; Evans, 1992; Gali, 1992; Gali and Hammour 1991; Checchetti and Karras, 1994; West, 1990; 1991; Amhed et al., 1993, their properties (Simkins, 1991), and persistence of shocks (see Campbell and Mankiw, 1989; Evans, 1989). Other studies examine more specialized hypotheses concerning stylized correlations. For example Sims (1980b), McCullum (1983), Stock and Watson (1989), and Friedman and Kuttner (1992; 1993) examine money/income/interest-rate relationships; Ashenfelter and Card (1982) study employment over the business cycle; Friedman (1983), Porter and Offenbacher (1983), and Litterman and Weiss (1985) discuss passive money supply rules; Dorbny and Gausden (1988) study the relationship between factor prices and employment; Bernanke (1986) and Amhed (1990) study theories of inside–outside money on GNP; King and Watson (1992) and Weber (1993) consider neutrality propositions; Bernanke and Blinder (1992) study the predictive power of interest rates for economic activity; and Roberds and Whiteman (1992) look at the effect of targeting monetary aggregates on real variables. Backus (1986) (correlation of US$/Can$ exchange rate), Bayoumi and Eichengreen (1992), and Robertson and Wickens (1992) consider monetary effects under alternative exchange rate regimes, and Litterman and Supel (1983) study the problem of forecasting state revenues. Wolff (1987) examines the correlations among exchange rates; Canova and Ito (1991), Bekaert and Hodrick (1992) predictability issues in foreign exchange and equity markets; Lee (1992) and Campbell and Ammer (1993), the relationship between stock and bond returns and inflation; Campbell and Shiller (1988a; 1988b), volatility issues in financial markets; Calomiris and Hubbard (1989), credit and fluctuations over the 1894–1909 period; Lawrence and Siow (1985), the relationship between investment and interest rates; Macunovich and Easterlin (1988) and Mocai (1990), the procyclicity of fertility; and Eckstein, Schultz, and Wolpin (1985), the relationship between fertility and mortality. Other studies have concentrated on the effects of structural changes in policy variables on reduced form coefficients (see e.g. Miller, 1983; Miller and Roberds, 1991). Finally, welfare and general policy questions have received substantial coverage (see e.g. Fisher, 1981; Gordon and King, 1982; Sims, 1982; Litterman, 1984; Leeper, 1989; Gordon and Leeper, 1992).

Although the VAR methodology is based on time series principles and has been extensively applied to a variety of macroeconomic problems, it has been extended to analyze panel macro data (see e.g. Canova and Dellas, 1993), panel micro data (see e.g. Holtz-Eakin, Newey, and Rosen, 1988; 1989;

Holtz-Eakin, 1989) and data that come in the form of "random fields" where the length of the vector of time series is approximately of the same size as the dimension of the panel (see Quah and Rauch, 1990; Quah and Sargent, 1993).

As we have seen, VARs provide a summary of the correlation structure of the observed data. VARs can also be used to summarize the properties of data simulated from a dynamic general equilibrium model and to statistically evaluate its properties. Given a set of "deep parameters," a fully specified general equilibrium model is taken to represent the correct data generating process for the actual data if observed and simulated time series look alike when viewed through the VAR "window" (Sims, 1989a). From this point of view, a VAR is an analytically tractable but possibly misspecified approximation of the true underlying model. The parameters of the VAR define the measure of fit for the problem: the observed and the simulated time series are deemed alike if the VAR parameters of the observed and observed and simulated data are similar. The precise definition of what "similar" means depends on the particular application. In the current literature, a quasi log likelihood distance and a least squares distance have been used (see e.g. Smith, 1993; King and Watson, 1993; Gouriéroux and Monfort, 1991). One could also use a metric based on the simulated distribution of the VAR parameters (as in Kwan, 1990; Canova, 1994; Gregory and Smith, 1992). Note that one can also compare actual and simulated data imposing theoretical restrictions on the VAR system (as in Canova, Finn, and Pagan, 1994).

An additional useful application of VAR models is to compute probabilities of events (see Howrey, 1991). For example, Litterman (1984) has used BVARs to generate the probability of turning points in US economic activity, while Miller (1983) computes the probability that the residuals from two VAR regressions come from the same distribution. The idea is that, by defining an event in a particular way (e.g. calling two consecutive declines in the growth rate of output a recession) and randomizing both on the innovations and the estimated parameters of the VAR, it is possible to construct probability distributions for the event by Monte Carlo. In this function, a VAR is a vehicle to describe the uncertainty existing at some point in time in characterizing a future event.

8 An Example

To provide an illustrative example of some of the arguments I have discussed in this chapter, I will consider a trivariate VAR of GNPs of the USA, Japan, and Germany. This VAR can be used to examine questions concerning the transmission and generation of international business cycles. In particular, I would like to know whether international business cycles are due to the transmission of independently generated shocks or if they are due to common shocks contemporaneously impinging on the economy.

I specify and estimate two different VAR models: one selected using the classical procedure outlined in section 3.1, and a BVAR model. From the point of view of the specification procedure of section 3.3, a VAR on the GNPs of these three countries can be obtained with an international version of the Long and Plosser (1983) economy as is done e.g. in Canova and Dellas (1993). The data we use in this exercise are quarterly figures on gross national products for the three countries for the period 1955/1 to 1986/4 which are obtained from the Citibase Tape and converted into 1980 real indices.

8.1 Results Obtained Using Classical Specification Methods

Table 2.1 presents univariate unit root and cointegration tests on the log of the three series. All three GNPs appear to have one unit root after a deterministic trend is accounted for. However, no cointegrating vector seems to exist. Therefore, I specify a VAR in first differences and proceed using the Hendry and Mizon methodology to examine the congruence of a six lag version of the model. From table 2.2 no evidence of incongruence appears: residuals are serially uncorrelated and homoskedastic, and recursive residuals display no evidence of structural breaks or nonnormalities except, perhaps, for Japan. Next, I proceed to decrease the dimensionality of the model by testing the joint significance of one lag of each variable in all the equations using F-tests. I find that lags 5 and 6 of all variables are insignificantly different from

Table 2.1 Unit roots and cointegration tests of the log of the variables: sample 1955/1 to 1986/4

Series	ADF1(4)	ADF2(4)	SW1	SW2
USAGNP80	−2.77	−1.69	−9.94	−1.20
DUSAGNP80	−4.52	−4.29	−74.22	−72.41
GERGNP80	−1.89	−2.04	−6.60	−1.41
DGERGNP80	−4.63	−4.12	−109.08	−104.63
JAPGNP80	−1.37	−3.21	−2.70	−1.57
DJAPGNP80	−3.95	−2.74	−104.92	−87.17
USA-GER	−2.54	−2.53	−12.50	−12.12
USA-JAP	−1.75	−1.58	−7.62	−6.36
GER-JAP	−2.04	−1.84	−12.59	−11.65

ADF1(4) refers to the augmented Dickey-Fuller test with a constant and augmentation of four lags; ADF2(4) to the augmented Dickey-Fuller test with a time trend and augmentation of four lags; SW1 to the Stock and Watson test with a constant; and SW2 to the Stock and Watson test with a time trend. DUSAGNP80, DGERGNP80, and DJAPGNP80 refer to the tests on the growth rates of the variables. USA-GER, USA-JAP, and GER-JAP refer to the tests performed on the residuals of an OLS cointegrating regression of these variables.

Table 2.2 Diagnostic tests on the VAR residuals: sample 1955/1 to 1986/4

Variable	Q(30)	BP(8)	ARCH(6)	Skewness	Kurtosis
Six lags					
DUSGNP80	33.23	1.95	5.70	−0.33	0.83
	(0.31)	(0.97)	(0.45)	(0.18)	(0.10)
DGERGNP80	23.66	1.34	3.42	−0.28	−0.05
	(0.78)	(0.99)	(0.75)	(0.26)	(0.90)
DJAPGNP80	17.21	1.98	0.21	2.58	17.48
	(0.96)	(0.97)	(0.99)	(0.00)	(0.00)
Four lags					
DUSGNP80	31.95	1.92	5.17	−0.22	0.80
	(0.36)	(0.97)	(0.52)	(0.38)	(0.12)
DGERGNP80	27.62	1.38	3.72	−0.13	−0.39
	(0.59)	(0.99)	(0.71)	(0.59)	(0.44)
DJAPGNP80	17.50	1.66	0.22	2.85	19.71
	(0.96)	(0.98)	(0.99)	(0.00)	(0.00)

Q is the Box-Ljung test for serial correlation; BP is the Breush-Pagan test for heteroskedasticity; ARCH is the ARCH test for conditional heteroskedasticity; Skewness and Kurtosis are the skewness and kurtosis coefficients. In parentheses are the degrees of freedom of the chi-square test. *P*-values are reported under each statistic.

zero. The next round of specification tests is then concerned with the congruence of a four lag VAR model in first difference. The results of the second set of tests also appear in table 2.2. Again there is no evidence of serial correlation or heteroskedasticity in the residuals. Figure 2.1 indicates that recursive residuals are stable over time (except again for Japan's GNP in 1974/1). Finally, evidence of deviations from normality appears only for Japanese GNP and seem to be entirely due to the 1974/1 episode. Therefore, I will use a four lag VAR model with a constant on the first difference of the log of the variables and a dummy for 1974/1 as the preferred specification to examine the hypotheses of economic interest

The question of what causes international business cycles can be analyzed by examining the matrix of contemporaneous correlations of innovations, Granger noncausality tests for blocks of equations, and the impulse response function of the system. If international business cycles are mainly due to common sources, the contemporaneous correlation among innovations should be high and there should be little evidence of Granger causality from any two variable block to the remaining variable or of transmission over time. Table 2.3 presents the matrix of contemporaneous correlations and the results of Granger noncausality testing. Figure 2.2 presents the asymptotic 95% normal confidence band for the impulse responses where standard errors are computed using Lutkepohl's procedure together with the point estimate of the function.

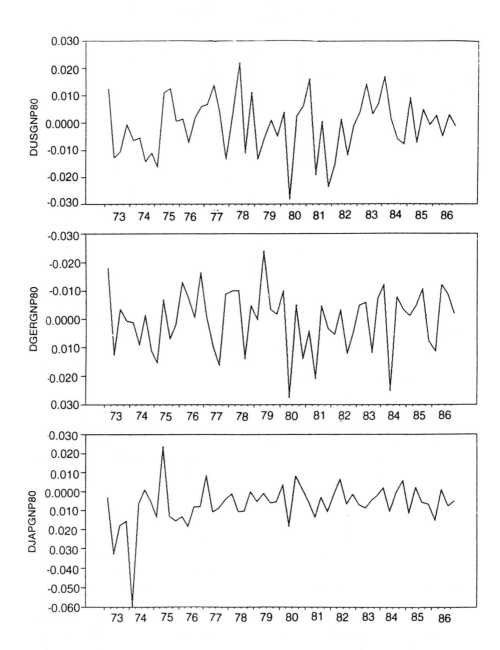

Figure 2.1 VAR recursive residuals

Table 2.3 VAR covariance and Granger results

Covariance matrix of innovations

	DUSAGNP80 residuals	*DGERGNP80* residuals	*DJAPGNP80* residuals
DUSGNP80 residuals		0.3023	0.1907
DGERGNP80 residuals			0.2416

Granger causality tests

	F-statistics	*Significance*
DUSGNP80	3.802	0.126
DGERGNP80	3.794	0.126
DJAPGNP80	2.411	0.337

The *F*-test is for the joint significance of the lags of the other two variables in the equation.

The data confirm the presence of an international business cycle, in the sense that growth rates of outputs in different countries move together over time, but the size of the comovements is not overwhelming. Contemporaneous correlations are rather small and only the one between US and German GNP innovations appears to be significantly different from zero. Granger causality tests indicate that, except for German GNP, there appears to be little evidence of transmission and that the time series properties of outputs are well represented by univariate random walks. This impression is confirmed by the impulse response plots where, except for the response of Japan GNP growth to an innovation in German GNP growth in the first few lags, all bands include zero. The 95% bands for the cumulative effect of a 1% shock to US GNP growth on the growth rates of US, Germany, and Japan are [−0.23, 3.41], [−1.74, 3.65,], [−2.53, 4.73], respectively.

With the selected model and the information available at 1983/4, I conducted two forecasting exercises. First, I computed the probability of a recession over the next three years. Here a recession is assumed to start on the first of two consecutive declines in the detrended growth rate of output. Probabilities are computed by randomizing on the asymptotic distribution of parameters and innovations. Second, I compute conditional and unconditional forecasts. Conditional forecasts were obtained assuming that innovations in US GNP growth were uniformly higher by 1% over the next 12 quarters. This exercise can be interpreted as trying to assess the effect of a 1% permanent technological shift in the growth rate of aggregate US production function. The results of these two exercises are presented in figures 2.3 and 2.4. With the information available at 1983/4 there was not very much evidence of an emerging recession over the next three years in any of the three countries. The maximum probability of recession occurred around the first two quarters of

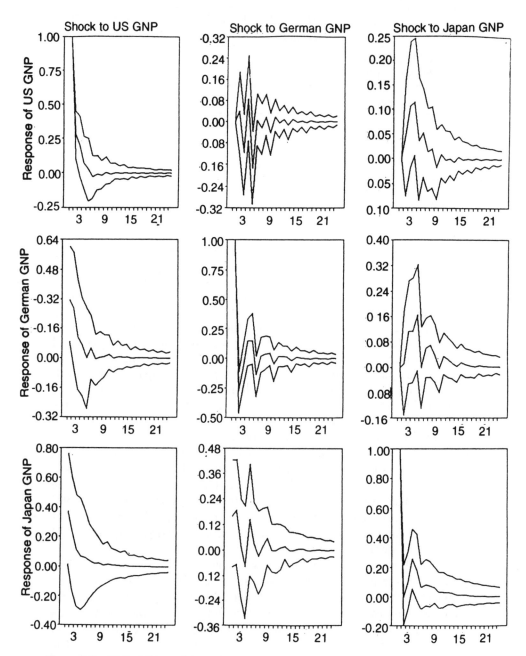

Figure 2.2 VAR 95% confidence bands

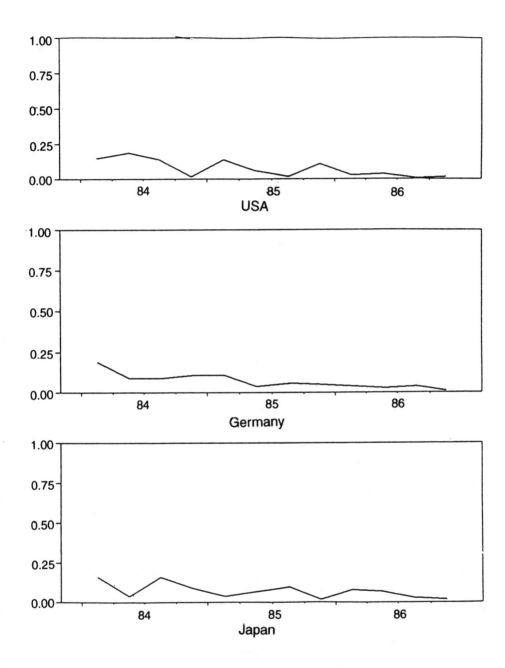

Figure 2.3 VAR probability of a recession

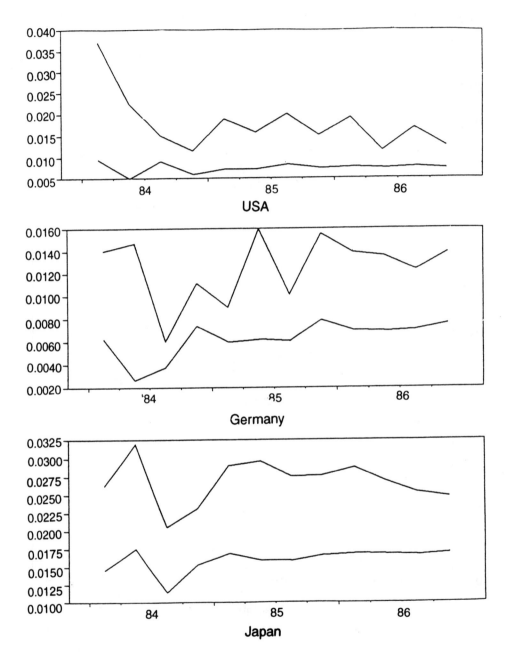

Figure 2.4 VAR conditional and unconditional forecasts for GNP growth

1984 and was of 22%, 21%, and 17% for the three countries, respectively. Unconditional forecasts suggest that with the information available in 1983/4 one should have expected an average growth rate of 3% in the next three years in the US, 2.5% in Germany, and 6% in Japan. With a permanent increase in the innovations of US GNP growth over the next three years, all three average growth rates over the next three years shift up to about 6% in the US, 4.2% in Germany, and 10% in Japan. Note, however, that the shift is nonmonotone over time and that the average increase is larger in Japan and Germany, possibly indicating the presence of transmission of permanent shocks.

8.2 Results Using a BVAR Model

I specify a BVAR model on the logs of the variables with five hyperparameters only. I set $\theta_0 = 1$, and $\theta_1 = 0.2$, $\theta_2 = 0.000001$, $f(i, j) = 0.5$, $\forall i \neq j$, $f(i, i) = 1.0$ and $h(\ell) = \ell^{-0.5}$ after a rough specification search. The model is estimated with nine lags to capture possible seasonal patterns and includes a time trend, following Sims, Stock, and Watson (1990).[10] In table 2.4 I check for the appropriateness

Table 2.4 Diagnostic tests on the BVAR residuals: sample 1955/1 to 1986/4

Variable	$Q(27)$	$BP(8)$	$ARCH(6)$	Skewness	Kurtosis
Nine lags					
USGNP80	20.09	1.93	1.45	−0.28	0.47
	(0.82)	(0.99)	(0.96)	(0.77)	(0.63)
GERGNP80	20.17	0.74	8.41	−0.36	0.32
	(0.83)	(0.69)	(0.20)	(0.71)	(0.74)
JAPGNP80	15.27	1.15	0.55	2.77	2.55
	(0.96)	(0.98)	(0.99)	(0.005)	(0.006)

Q is the Box-Ljung test for serial correlation; BP is the Breush-Pagan test for heteroskedasticity; ARCH is the ARCH test for conditional heteroskedasticity; Skewness and Kurtosis are the skewness and kurtosis coefficients. In parentheses are the degrees of freedom of the chi-square test. *P*-values are reported under each statistic.

of the specification using several diagnostics on the residuals of the estimated BVAR. There is no evidence of serial correlation or heteroskedasticity and, except for the residuals of the Japan GNP equation, little evidence of nonnormality. From the plot of the recursive residuals (figure 2.5), it is evident that the strongly negative residuals of 1974/1 are responsible for the nonnormality of Japanese GNP residuals.

Next I turn to examine some economic hypotheses. Table 2.5 presents the covariance matrix of contemporaneous innovations and the Granger noncausality tests for the model, while figure 2.6 plots the 95% confidence band for the impulse response function, together with a point estimate of the response

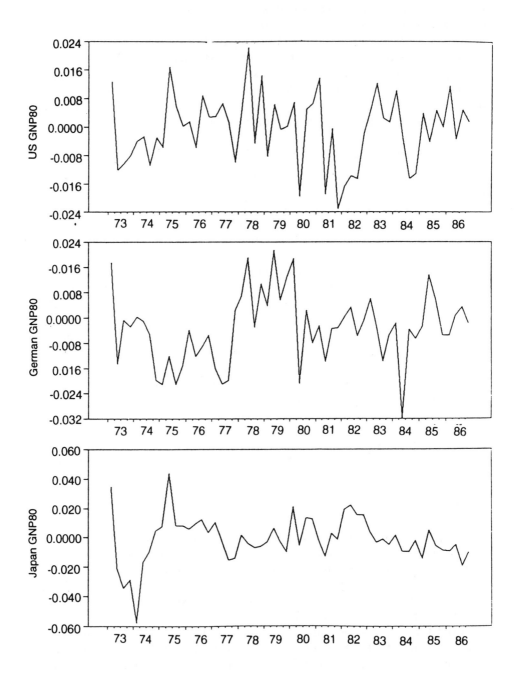

Figure 2.5 BVAR recursive residuals

Table 2.5 BVAR covariance and Granger results

Covariance matrix of innovations

	USGNP80 residuals	*GERGNP80 residuals*	*JAPGNP80 residuals*
USGNP80 residuals		0.2023	0.1929
GERGNP80 residuals			0.1565

Granger causality tests

	F-statistics	*Signiẁcance*
USAGNP80	0.480	0.986
GERGNP80	1.523	0.967
JAPGNP80	1.211	0.987

The *F*-test is for the joint significance of the lags of the other two variables in the equation.

where the bands are computed with an approximate Monte Carlo exercise. With this specification I find more support for the presence of international business cycles in the sense that the logs of outputs tend to move together. Also, I find very little evidence of common generation and some support for the presence of transmission. For example a shock in US GNP is likely to have a positive impact on German and Japanese GNP for at least two years. The 95% band for the cumulative effect of this shock on the three GNPs are [-3.99, 20.97], [-3.86, 19.10], [-8.17, 38.36]. The evidence for the transmission of shocks in German and Japanese GNPs is much weaker.

Also in this case, and given information at 1983/4, I conducted two forecasting exercises, computing the probability of a recession (figure 2.7), and unconditional forecasts and forecasts conditional on a 1% permanent increase in USA GNP shocks for the next 12 months (figure 2.8). I find that the probability of a recession for the period 1984–6 was in general small. The maximum probabilities occurred for USA GNP at 1984/2 with 18%, for German GNP at 1984/3 with 15%, and for Japan at 1985/2 with 19%.

Unconditional forecasts indicate a smooth decline in the growth rate of output of all countries. Conditional on the supposed path for innovations in USA GNP, GNP growth rates are more seasonal, and in general higher. The average unconditional forecasts for GNP growth over the next three years were 2.3%, 2.4%, and 4.1% respectively. Conditional on the path for innovations in the US GNP equation, the average growth rates are 2.5%, 2.3%, and 4.4% respectively.

Finally, it is worth noting that, although a VAR selected using classical methods and a BVAR deliver substantially similar probabilities of recessions as far as timing and magnitude are concerned, the two models give a very

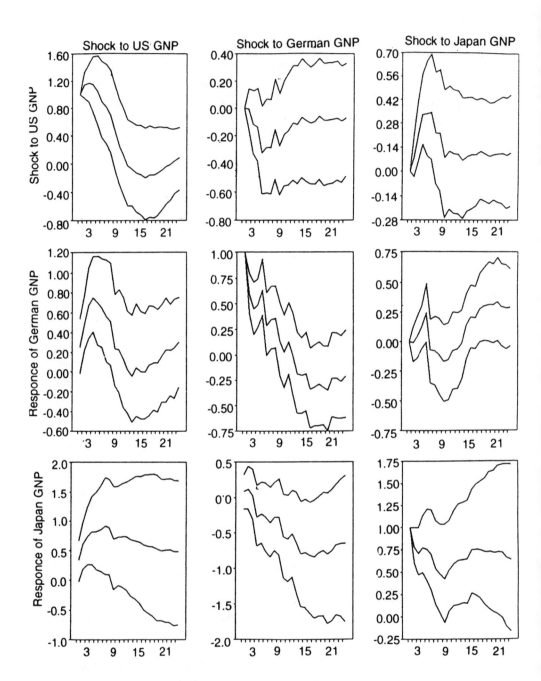

Figure 2.6 BVAR 95% confidence bands

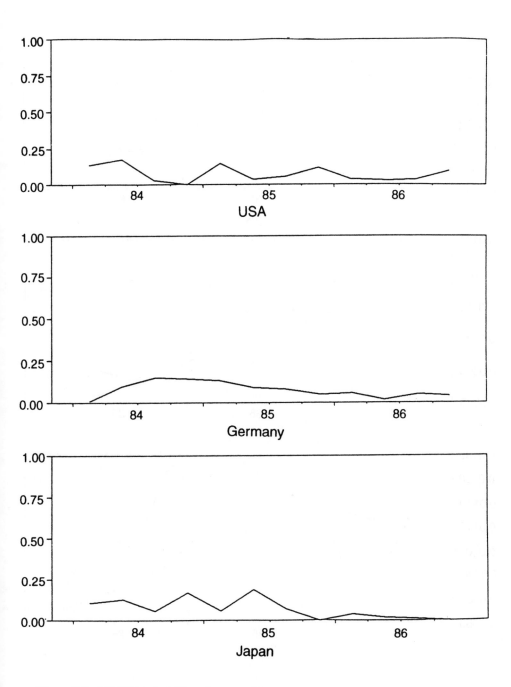

Figure 2.7 BVAR probability of a recession

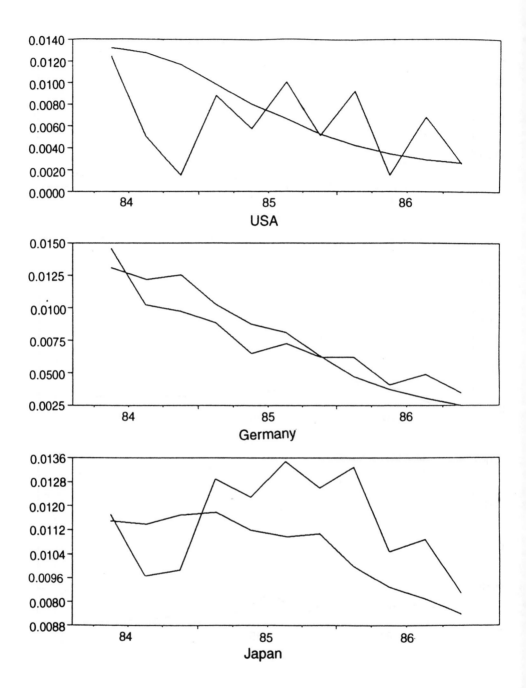

Figure 2.8 BVAR conditional and unconditional forecasts for GNP growth

different picture of the conditions expected to occur in the last three years of the sample. In particular, the BVAR is more pessimistic on the expected growth patterns of GNPs in the US and Japan.

Notes

Part of the work for this chapter was undertaken while the author was associated with the European University Institute in Florence, Italy. I have benefited from extensive discussions and comments from a number of people including R. Fair, J. Gali, C. Giannini, E. Leeper, H. Lutkepohl, S. McNees, J. Marrinan, G. Mizon, L. Ohanian, A. Pagan, D. Quah, R. Todd, M. Wickens, and an anonymous referee. A special thanks to C. Sims and T. Sargent for getting me interested in the topic and for providing invaluable intellectual stimulus over a number of years.

1   This condition is ensured by the restriction that $\{B_j\}_{j=0}^{\infty}$ is a Cauchy sequence, i.e. $\Sigma_{j=0}^{\infty} B_j^2 < \infty$. Rozanov (1967) provides weaker restrictions.
2   When AIC is used, p is chosen to minimize log det $\Sigma_i + 2K/T$; when SIC is used p is chosen to minimize log det $\Sigma_i + K \log(T)/T$; and when MLR is used, p minimizes $(T - \gamma)|\log \det \Sigma_i|$; where K is the number of estimated parameters, T the sample size, γ a correction factor, and Σ_i the estimated covariance matrix of the residuals for specification i.
3   FPE minimizes

$$\frac{SSR_k}{t} \frac{T + K - 1}{T - K - 1}, \quad k = 1, 2, \ldots, p^*,$$

where p^* is the maximum number of lags, $k = p - j$, and j is the number of lags constrained to be zero.
4   A much less formal version of this procedure has been employed by Gordon and King (1982), who set up an unrestricted VAR model and, as a second step, "edit" insignificant variables and lags to obtain a model of tractable size.
5   To be precise the Hamilton model will not be efficiently estimated within the BVAR framework since nonlinearities in the parameters will not be taken into account in estimation.
6   Lutkepohl assumes also that x_t is a Gaussian vector process even though this is not necessary to derive the asymptotic distribution of impulse responses.
7   The terms "structure" and "structural" have many meanings in the literature. Some economists lable structural a model where all parameters have economic interpretations in terms of preferences and technologies (e.g. Hansen and Sargent, 1980). Others claim that a model is structural if the consequence of a specific class of actions can be predicted by modifying part of the model (see e.g. Koopmans, 1963; Hurwicz, 1962), if it is invariant to a specific class of actions (see e.g. Sargent and Lucas, 1980) or if it refers to the use of economic *a priori* hypothesis (Hendry and Mizon, 1990). Finally, some claim that a model is structural if it is in a particular mathematical form (see e.g. Harvey, 1985). In this section, a model is labelled structural if it is possible to give distinct behavioral interpretations to its stochastic disturbances. For the discussion contained in section 6 I make clear which of the meanings I will refer to.

8　I would like to thank Jordi Gali and Adrian Pagan for pointing out this argument to me.
9　It is worth noting that the concept of predeterminateness in Cooley and LeRoy corresponds to the concept of super exogeneity in Engle, Hendry, and Richard (1983) for the case of linear models.
10　I experimented also with a model with no time trend and found explosive behavior in the impulse response function.

References

Akaike, H. (1969), "Fitting Autoregressions for Prediction," *Annals of the Institute of Statistical Mathematics*, 21, 243–7.
Akaike, H. (1970), "Autoregressive Model Fitting for Control," *Annals of the Institute of Statistical Mathematics*, 22, 163–80.
Akaike, H. (1974), "A New Look at the Statistics Model Identification," *IEEE Transactions on Automatic Control*, AC-19, 716–23.
Amhed, S. (1990), "Sources of Money–Output Correlation," The Pennsylvania State University, working paper 90–5.
Amhed, S., Ickes, B., Wang, P. and Yoo, S. (1993), "International Business Cycles," *American Economic Review*, 83, 335–60.
Andel, J. (1976), "Autoregressive Series with Random Parameters," *Mathematische Operationforschung und Statistik*, 7, 736–41.
Artis, M. and Zhang, W. (1990), "BVAR forecasts for the G-7," *International Journal of Forecasting*, 6, 349–62.
Ashenfelter, O. and Card, D. (1982), "Time Series Representations of Economic Variables and Alternative Models of the Labor Market," *Review of Economic Studies*, 49, 761–82.
Backus, D. (1986), "The Canadian–US Exchange Rate: Evidence from a Vector Autoregression," *The Review of Economics and Statistics*, 68, 628–37.
Baillie, R.T. (1987a), "Inference in Dynamic Models Containing Surprise Variables," *Journal of Econometrics*, 35, 101–17.
Baillie, R.T. (1987b), "Asymptotic Prediction Mean Square Errors for Vector Autoregressive Models," *Biometrika*, 66, 675–8.
Bayoumi, T. and Eichengreen, B. (1992), "Macroeconomic Adjustment under Bretton Woods and the Past Bretton Woods Float: An Impulse Response Analysis," NBER working paper 4169.
Bekaert, G. and Hodrick, R. (1992), "Characterizing Predictable Components in Excess Returns on Equities and Foreign Exchange Markets," *Journal of Finance*, 47, 467–510.
Bernanke, B. (1986), "Alternative Explorations of the Money–Income Correlation," *Carnegie Rochester Conference in Public Policy*, 25, 49–100.
Bernanke, B. and Blinder, A. (1992), "The Federal Funds Rate and the Channels of Monetary Transmission," *American Economic Review*, 82, 901–21.
Beveridge, S. and Nelson, C. (1981), "A New Approach to Decomposition of Economic Time Series into Permanent and Transitory Components with Particular Attention to Measurement of Business Cycle," *Journal of Monetary Economics*, 7, 151–74.

Blanchard, O. (1987), Comment to Runkle's "Vector Autoregression and Reality," *Journal of Business and Economic Statistics*, 5, 449–51.

Blanchard, O. (1989), "A Traditional Interpretation of Macroeconomic Fluctuations," *American Economic Review*, 79, 1146–64.

Blanchard, O. and Quah, D. (1989), "The Dynamic Effects of Aggregate Demand and Supply Disturbances," *American Economic Review*, 79, 655–73.

Blanchard, O. and Quah, D. (1993), "Fundamentalness and the Interpretation of Time Series Evidence: A Reply to Lippi and Reichlin," *American Economic Review*, 83, 653–8.

Blanchard, O. and Watson, M. (1986), "Are Business Cycles all Alike?," in R. Gordon, ed., *The American Business Cycle*, Chicago, Il.: University of Chicago Press.

Brandner, P. and Kunst, R. (1990), "Forecasting Vector Autoregressions – The Influence of Cointegration: A Monte Carlo Study," Research Memorandum 265, Institute of Advanced Studies, Vienna.

Brillinger, D. (1981), *Time Series: Data Analysis and Theory*, San Francisco, Ca.: Holden-Day.

Brock, W. and Sayers, C. (1988), "Is the Business Cycle Characterized by Deterministic Chaos?," *Journal of Monetary Economics*, 22, 71–90.

Brockwell, P. and Davis, R. (1989), *Time Series: Theory and Methods*, Springer Verlag.

Burbidge, J. and Harrison A. (1984), "Testing for the Effect of Oil Price Rises Using Vector Autoregression," *International Economic Review*, 25, 459–84.

Burbidge, J., Magee, L. and Neall, M. (1985), "On the Seasonality in VAR models," *Economic Letters*, 18, 137–41.

Calomiris, C. and Hubbard, G. (1989), "Price Flexibility, Credit Availability and Economic Fluctuations: Evidence from the United States: 1894–1909," *Quarterly Journal of Economics*, 96, 429–52.

Campbell, J. and Ammer, J. (1993), "What Moves the Stock and Bond Markets: A Variance Decomposition of Long Term Asset Returns," *Journal of Finance*, 48, 3–38.

Campbell, J. and Mankiw, G. (1989), "Permanent and Transitory Components in Macroeconomic Fluctuations," *American Economic Review, Papers and Proceedings*, 77, 111–17.

Campbell, J. and Shiller, R. (1988a), "Cointegration and Tests of the Present Value Model," *Journal of Political Economy*, 95, 1062–88.

Campbell, J. and Shiller, R. (1988b), "Interpreting Cointegrated Models," *Journal of Economic Dynamics and Control*, 12, 505–22.

Canova, F. (1991), "The Sources of Financial Crises: Pre and Post Fed Evidence," *International Economic Review*, 32, 689–713.

Canova, F. (1992), "An Alternative Approach to Modelling and Forecasting Seasonal Time Series," *Journal of Business and Economic Statistics*, 10, 1–12.

Canova, F. (1993a), "Modelling and Forecasting Exchange Rates with Bayesian Time Varying Coefficient Model," *Journal of Economics Dynamic and Control*, 17, 233–61.

Canova, F. (1993b), "Forecasting a Multitude of Time Series with Common Seasonal Patterns," *Journal of Econometrics*, 55, 173–200.

Canova, F. (1994), "Statistical Inference in Calibrated Models," *Journal of Applied Econometrics*, 9, S123–S42.

Canova, F. (1995), "On the Economics of VAR Models," in K. Hoover, ed., *Macroeconometrics: Developments, Tensions and Prospects*, Kluwer Press.

Canova, F. and Dellas, H. (1993), "Trade Interdependence and International Business Cycles," *Journal of International Economics*, 34, 23–47.

Canova, F., Finn, M. and Pagan, A. (1994), "Evaluating a Real Business Cycle Model," in C. Hargreaves, ed., *Nonstationary Time Series Analysis and Cointegration*, Oxford University Press.

Canova, F. and Ito, T. (1991), "Time Varying Risk Premium in the Yen/Dollar Exchange Market," *Journal of Applied Econometrics*, 6, 125–42.

Checchetti, S. and Karras, G. (1994), "Sources of Output Fluctuations during the Interwar Period: Further Evidence on the Causes of the Great Depression," *Review of Economics and Statistics*.

Christiano, L. (1992), "In Search for Break in GNP," *Journal of Business and Economics Statistics*, 10, 237–50.

Christiano, L. and Ljungvist, L. (1987), "Money does Granger Cause Output in the Bivariate Output–Money Relation," *Journal of Monetary Economics*, 22, 217–35.

Clark, P. (1973), "A Subordinated Stochastic Process Model with Finite Variance with Speculative Prices," *Econometrica*, 41, 136–56.

Clements, M.P. and Hendry, D.F. (1991), "Forecasting in Cointegrated Systems," Oxford Institute of Economics and Statistics, manuscript.

Clements, M.P. and Mizon G.E. (1991), "Empirical Analysis of MacroEconomic Time Series: VAR and Structural Models," *European Economic Review*, 35, 887–917.

Cooley, T. and LeRoy, S. (1985), "Atheoretical Macroeconometrics: A Critique," *Journal of Monetary Economics*, 16, 283–308.

Cooley, T., LeRoy, S. and Raymon, N. (1984), "Econometric Policy Evaluation: A Note," *American Economic Review*, 74, 467–70.

Deaton, A. (1987), "Life Cycle Models of Consumption: Is the Evidence Consistent with Theory," in T. Bewley, ed., *Advances in Econometrics: Fifth World Congress*, vol. 2, New York, NY: Cambridge University Press.

Dickey, D. and Fuller, W. (1979), "Distribution of the Estimators for a Autoregressive Time Series with a Unit Root," *Journal of the American Statistical Association*, 74, 427–31.

DeJong, D. and Whiteman, C. (1991), "Reconsidering Trends and Random Walks in Macroeconomic Time Series," *Journal of Monetary Economics*, 28, 221–54.

Doan, T. (1993), *RATS Manual, Version 4.02*, Evanston, Il.

Doan, T., Litterman, R. and Sims, C. (1984), "Forecasting and Conditional Projections Using Realist Priori Distributions," *Econometric Reviews*, 3(1), 1–100.

Dorbny, A. and Gausden, R. (1988), "Granger-Causality, Real Factor Prices and Employment: A Reappraisal with UK Data," *European Economic Review*, 32, 1261–83.

Eckstein, Z., Schultz, T. and Wolpin, K. (1985), "Short Run Fluctuations in Fertility and Mortality in Pre-Industrial Sweden," *European Economic Review*, 26, 295–317.

Eichenbaum, M. and Singleton, K. (1986), "Do Equilibrium Real Business Cycle Theories Explain Postwar US Business Cycles?," in S. Fisher, ed., *NBER Macroeconomic Annual*, Cambridge, Mass.: MIT Press, 1, 91–135.

Engle, R. (1982), "Autoregressive Conditional Heteroskedasticity with Estimates of the Variance of the UK Inflation," *Econometrica*, 50, 987–1006.

Engle, R. and Granger, C. (1987), "Co-Integration and Error Correction: Representation, Estimation and Testing," *Econometrica*, 55, 251–76.

Engle, R., Hendry, D. and Richard, J.F. (1983), "Exogeneity," *Econometrica*, 51, 277–304.

Engle, R., Lilien, D. and Robbins R. (1987), "Estimating Time Varying Risk Premia in the Term Structure: The ARCH-M model," *Econometrica*, 55, 191–408.

Engle, R. and Yoo, S. (1987), "Forecasting and Testing in Cointegrated Systems," *Journal of Econometrics*, 35, 143–59.

Englund, P., Vredin, A. and Warne, A. (1991), "Macroeconomic Shocks in Sweden 1925–1986," University of Stockholm, manuscript.

Epple, R., Hansen, L. and Roberds, W. (1985), "Linear Quadratic Games of Resource Depletion," in T. Sargent, ed., *Energy, Foresight and Strategy: Resources for the Future*, Washington, DC: Resources for the Future.

Evans, G. (1989), "Output and Unemployment Dynamics in the United States: 1950–1985," *Journal of Applied Econometrics*, 4, 213–237.

Evans, G. (1992), "Productivity Shocks and Real Business Cycles," *Journal of Monetary Economics*, 29, 191–208.

Fair, R. (1979), "An Analysis of the Accuracy of Four Macro Models," *Journal of Political Economy*, 87, 375–89.

Fair, R. (1988), "VAR Models and Structural Approximations," Cowles Foundation, Discussion Paper 856.

Fair, R. and Shiller, R. (1989), "The Informational Content of Ex-Ante Forecasts," *Review of Economic and Statistics*, LXXI, 325–31.

Fair, R. and Shiller, R. (1990), "Comparing the Information Forecasts from Econometric Models," *American Economic Review*, 80, 375–89.

Feigin, P.D. and Tweedie, R.L. (1980), "Random Coefficient Autoregressive Processes: A Markov Chain Analysis of Stationarity and Finiteness of Moments," *Journal of Time Series Analysis*, 6, 1–14.

Fisher, S. (1981), "Relative Shocks, Relative Price Variability and Inflation", *Brooking Papers of Economic Activity*, 2, 341–431.

Florens, J.P. and Mounchart, A. (1983), "A Note on Noncausality," *Econometrica*, 50, 583–91.

Friedman, B. (1983), "The Roles of Money and Credit in Macroeconomic Analysis," in J. Tobin, ed., *Macroeconomics, Prices and Quantities*, Washington, DC: Brookings Institution.

Friedman, B. and Kuttner, K. (1992), "Money, Income, Prices and Interest Rates," *American Economic Review*, 82, 472–92.

Friedman, B. and Kuttner, K. (1993), "Another Look at the Evidence on Money–Income Causality," *Journal of Econometrics*, 57, 189–204.

Friedman, M. and Schwartz, A. (1963), *A Monetary History of the United States, 1867–1960*, Princeton, NJ: Princeton University Press.

Fuller, W. (1976), *Statistical Analysis of Time Series*, New York, NY: Wiley and Sons.

Funke, M. (1990), "Assessing the Forecasting Accuracy of Monthly Vector Autoregressive Models: The Case of Five OECD Countries," *International Journal of Forecasting*, 6, 363–78.

Gali, J. (1992), "How Well Does the ISLM Model Fit Postwar U.S. Data?," *Quarterly Journal of Economics*, CVII, 709–35.

Gali, J. and Hammour, M. (1991), "Long Run Effects of Business Cycles," Columbia University, manuscript.

Gallant, R. Hsieh, D. and Tauchen, G. (1991), "On Fitting Recalcitrant Series: The Pound/Dollar Exchange Rate, 1974–1983," in W. Barnett, J. Powell and G. Tauchen, eds, *Nonparametric and Semiparametric Methods in Econometrics and Statistics*,

Proceedings of the 5th International Symposium in Economic Theory and Econometrics, Cambridge, Mass.: Cambridge University Press.

Gelfand, A. and Smith, A. (1990), "Sampling Based Approaches to Calculating Marginal Densities," *Journal of the American Statistical Association*, 85, 398–409.

Genberg, H., Salemi, M. and Swodoba, A. (1986), "The Relative Importance of Foreign and Domestic Disturbances for Aggregate Fluctuations in Open Economies: Switzerland 1964–1981," *Journal of Monetary Economics*, 19, 45–67.

Geweke, J. (1977), "Labor Turnover and Employment Dynamics in US Manufacturing Industry," in C. Sims, ed., *New Methods in Business Cycle Research*, Mn.: Federal Reserve Bank.

Geweke, J. (1982), "The Measurement of Linear Dependence and Feedback between Multiple Time Series," *Journal of the American Statistical Association*, 77, 304–13.

Geweke, J. (1984), "Inference and Causality in Economic Time Series Model," in Z. Grilliches and M. Intrilligator, eds, *Handbook of Econometrics*, vol. II, Amsterdam: North-Holland.

Geweke, J. (1989), "Bayesian Inference in Econometric Models using Monte Carlo Integration," *Econometrica*, 57, 1317–40.

Giannini, C. (1992), *Topics in Structural VAR Econometrics*, Berlin: Springer Verlag.

Gordon, D. and King, S. (1982), "The Output Costs of Inflation in Traditional and Vector Autoregressive Models," *Brookings Papers on Economic Activity*, 1, 205–44.

Gordon, D. and Leeper, E. (1992), "In Search of the Liquidity Effects," *Journal of Monetary Economics*, 29, 341–71.

Gordon, D. and Leeper, E. (1995), "The Dynamic Impact of Monetary Policy: An Exercise in Tentative Identification," *Journal of Political Economy* (forthcoming).

Gouriéroux, C. and Monfort, A. (1991), "Simulation Based Econometrics in Models with Heterogeneity," *Annales d'Economic at de Statistique*, 20–21.

Granger, C. (1988), "Some Recent Developments in a Concept of Causality," *Journal of Econometrics*, 39, 199–211.

Granger, C. and Anderson, B. (1978), *Introduction to Bilinear Time Series*, Gottingen, Germany: Vandenhoeck and Ruprecht.

Gregory, A., Pagan, A. and Smith, G. (1990), "Linear Rational Expectations Models with Integrated Regressors," in P.C.B. Phillips and V.B. Hall, eds, *Models, Methods and Applications of Econometrics, Essays in the Honor of Rex Bergstrom*, Oxford: Oxford University Press.

Gregory, A. and Smith, G. (1992), "Calibration in Macroeconomics," in G.S. Maddala, ed., *Handbook of Statistics*, vol. 10, Amsterdam: North-Holland.

Griffiths, W. and Lutkepohl, H. (1990), "Confidence Interval for Impulse Responses from VAR Models: A Comparison of Asymptotic Theory and Simulation Approaches," University of New England, manuscript.

Hafer, R.W. and Sheehan, R. (1989), "The Sensitivity of VAR Forecasts to Alternative Lag Structures," *International Journal of Forecasting*, 5, 399–408.

Hamilton, J. (1983), "Oil and the Macroeconomy since WWII," *Journal of Political Economy*, 91, 228–48.

Hamilton, J. (1989), "A New Approach to Economic Analysis of Nonstationary Time Series and the Business Cycles," *Econometrica*, 57, 357–84.

Hamilton, J. (1994), *Time Series Analysis*, Princeton, NJ: Princeton University Press.

Hannan, J. and Quinn, B.G. (1978), "The Determinants of the Order of an Autoregression," *Journal of the Royal Statistical Society*, Series B, 41, 190–5.

Hansen, L., Roberds, W. and Sargent, T. (1991), "Time Series Implications of Present Value and Balanced Budget and Martingale Models of Consumption and Taxes," in L. Hansen and T. Sargent, eds, *Rational Expectations Econometrics*, Boulder & London: Westview Press.

Hansen, L. and Sargent, T. (1980), "Formulating and Estimating Linear Rational Expectations Models," *Journal of Economic Dynamics and Control*, 2, 1–46.

Hansen, L. and Sargent, T. (1982), "Instrumental Variable Procedures for Estimating Linear Rational Expectations Models," *Journal of Monetary Economics*, 9, 263–96.

Hansen, L. and Sargent, T. (1991), "Two Difficulties in Interpreting Vector Autoregressions," in L. Hansen and T. Sargent, eds, *Rational Expectations Econometrics*, Boulder & London: Westview Press.

Harvey, A.C. (1985), "Trends and Cycles in Macroeconomics," *Journal of Business and Economic Statistics*, 3, 216–27.

Harvey, A.C. (1989), *The Econometric Analysis of Time Series* (2nd edn) (Halsted Press).

Hendry, D. (1990), *Lectures on Econometric Methodology*, Oxford: Oxford University Press.

Hendry, D. and Clements, M.P. (1991), "On the Theory of Economic Forecasting," Oxford Institute of Economics and Statistics, manuscript.

Hendry, D. and Mizon, G. (1990), "Evaluating Dynamic Econometric Models by Encompassing the VAR," in P.C.B. Phillips and V.B. Hall, eds, *Models, Methods and Applications of Econometrics, Essays in the Honor of Rex Bergstrom*, Oxford: Oxford University Press.

Holtz-Eakin, D. (1989), "Testing for Individual Effects in Autoregressive Models," *Journal of Econometrics*, 39, 297–307.

Holtz-Eakin, d., Newey, W. and Rosen, H. (1988), "Estimating Vector Autoregressions with Panel Data," *Econometrica*, 56, 1371–95.

Holtz-Eakin, D., Newey, W. and Rosen, H. (1989), "The Revenue Expenditure Nexus: Evidence from Local Government Data," *International Economic Review*, 30, 415–29.

Howrey, P. (1991), "A Note on Estimating Event Probabilities from a VAR Model," University of Michigan, manuscript.

Hsiao, C. (1981), "Autoregressive Modelling and Money–Income Causality Detection," *Journal of Monetary Economics*, 7, 85–106.

Hsiao, C. (1982), "Autoregressive Modelling and Causal Ordering of Economic Variables," *Journal of Economic Dynamics and Control*, 4, 243–59.

Hurwicz, L. (1962), "On the Structural Form of Interdependent Systems," in *Logic and Methodology in Social Sciences*, Stanford, Ca.: Stanford University Press, 232–9.

Ingram, B. and Whiteman, C. (1994), "Supplanting the Minnesota Prior: Forecasting Macroeconomic Time Series Using Real Business Cycle Priors," *Journal of Monetary Economics*, 34, 497–510.

Jacobs, R., Leamer, E. and Ward, M. (1979), "Difficulties with Testing for Causation," *Economic Inquiry*, 17, 401–13.

Johansen, S. (1988), "Statistical Analysis of Cointegrating Vectors," *Journal of Economic Dynamics and Control*, 12, 231–54.

Johansen, S. and Juselius, K. (1990), "Maximum Likelihood Estimation and Inference on Cointegration – with Application to the Demand for Money," *Oxford Bulletin of Economics and Statistics*, 52, 169–210.

Johansen, S. and Juselius, K. (1992), "Testing Structural Hypotheses in a Multivariate Cointegration Analysis of the PPP and UIP of UK," *Journal of Econometrics*, 53, 211–44.

Judge, G., Griffiths, W., Hill, R., Lutkepohl, H. and Lee, T. (1980), *The Theory and Practice of Econometrics* (2nd edn), New York, NY: Wiley and Sons.

Kadiyala, K. and Karlsson, L. (1989), "Forecasting with Bayesian VAR's," Purdue University, Krannert Graduate School of Management, working paper 962.

Keating, J. (1990), "Identifying VAR Models under Rational Expectations," *Journal of Monetary Economics*, 25, 453–76.

King, R., Plosser, C. and Rebelo, S. (1988), "Production, Growth and Business Cycles, I," *Journal of Monetary Economics*, 21, 309–42.

King, R., Plosser, C., Stock, J. and Watson, M. (1991), "Stochastic Trends and Economic Fluctuations," *American Economic Review*, 81, 819–40.

King, R. and Watson, M. (1992), "Testing Long Run Neutrality," NBER working paper 4156.

King, R. and Watson, M. (1993), "The Econometrics of Comparative Dynamics," University of Rochester, manuscript.

Kirchgassner, G. (1991), Comments to Clements, M.P. and Mizon, G.E. "Empirical Analysis of MacroEconomic Time Series: VAR and Structural Models," *European Economic Review*, 35, 918–22.

Kling, J. and Bessler, D. (1985), "A Comparison of Multivariate Forecasting Procedures for Economic Time Series," *International Journal of Forecasting*, 1, 5–24.

Kloek, T. and Van Djik, H. (1978), "Bayesian Estimates of Equations System Parameters: An Application of Integration by Monte Carlo," *Econometrica*, 46, 1–20.

Kocherlakota, N. (1988), "Evaluating Policy Innovations using Vector Autoregressions and Structural Methods," Northwestern University, manuscript.

Koopmans, T. (1963), "Identification Problems in Economic Model Construction," in W. Hood and T.J. Koopmans, eds, *Studies in Econometric Methods*, New Haven, Ct.: Yale University Press.

Kreyszig, E. (1989), *Introductory Functional Analysis with Applications*, New York, NY: Wiley and Sons.

Kunst, R. and Neusser, K. (1986), "A Forecasting Comparison of VAR Techniques," *International Journal of Forecasting*, 2, 447–56.

Kwan, Y.K. (1990), "Bayesian Calibration with an Application to a Nonlinear Rational Expectations Two Country Model," University of Chicago, working paper.

Kydland, F. and Prescott, E. (1982), "Time to Build and Aggregate Fluctuations," *Econometrica*, 50, 1345–70.

Lawrence, C. and Siow, A. (1985), "Interest Rates and Investment Spending: Some Empirical Evidence for Postwar US Producer Equipment," *Journal of Business*, 58, 359–75.

Leamer, E. (1978), *Specification Searches and Ad-Hoc Inference with Nonexperimental Data*, New York: Wiley and Sons.

Leamer, E. (1985), "Vector Autoregression for Causal Inference?," *Carnegie Rochester Conference Series on Public Policy*, 22, 255–304.

Lee, B.S. (1992), "Causal relationship among Stock Returns, Interest Rates, Real Activity and Inflation," *Journal of Finance*, 47, 1591–604.

Leeper, E. (1989), "Policy Rules, Information and Fiscal Effects in a 'Ricardian' Model," Board of Governors of the Federal Reserve System, International Finance Discussion Paper 360.

Lippi, M. and Reichlin, L. (1993), "A Note on Measuring the Dynamic Effects of Aggregate Demand and Supply Disturbances," *American Economic Review*, 83, 644–52.

Litterman, R. (1980), "Techniques for Forecasting with Vector Autoregressions," Unpublished PhD Thesis, University of Minnesota.

Litterman, R. (1982), "A Use of Index Models in Macroeconomic Forecasting," Federal Reserve of Minneapolis, Research Department, Staff Report 78.

Litterman, R. (1984), "Forecasting and Policy Analysis with Bayesian Vector Autoregression Models," *Quarterly Review*, Federal Reserve Bank of Minneapolis, 8, Fall, 30–41.

Litterman, R. (1986a), "Forecasting with Bayesian Vector Autoregressions – Five Years of Experience," *Journal of Business and Economic Statistics*, 4, 25–38.

Litterman, R. (1986b), "Specifying Vector Autoregressions for Macroeconomic Forecasting," in P. Goel and A. Zellner, eds, *Bayesian Inference and Decision Techniques*, Amsterdam: North-Holland.

Litterman, R. and Supel, T. (1983), "Using Vector Autoregressions to Measure the Uncertainty in Minnesota's Revenue Forecasts," *Quarterly Review*, Federal Reserve Bank of Minneapolis, 7, Spring, 10–22.

Litterman, R. and Weiss, L. (1985), "Money, Real Interest Rates and Output: A Reinterpretation of Postwar US Data," *Econometrica*, 52, 129–56.

Liu, T. (1960), "Underidentification, Structural Estimation and Forecasting," *Econometrica*, 28, 855–65.

Long, J. and Plosser, C. (1983), "Real Business Cycles," *Journal of Political Economy*, 91, 1345–70.

Lucas, R. and Stokey, N. (1983), "Optimal Fiscal and Monetary Policy in an Economy without Capital," *Journal of Monetary Economics*, 12, 55–93.

Luppoletti, W. and Webb, R. (1986), "Defining and Improving the Accuracy of Macroeconomic Forecasts: Contributions from a VAR Model," *Journal of Business*, 59, 263–85.

Lutkepohl, H. (1986), "Comparison of Criteria for Estimating the Order of a Vector Autoregressive Process," *Journal of Time Series Analysis*, 6, 35–52 and "Correction", 8, 373.

Lutkepohl, H. (1988), "Asymptotic Distribution of the Moving Average Coefficients of an Estimated Vector Autoregressive Process," *Econometrics Theory*, 4, 77–85.

Lutkepohl, H. (1989), "A Note on the Asymptotic Distribution of Impulse Response Functions of Estimated VAR Models with Orthogonal Residuals," *Journal of Econometrics*, 42, 371–6.

Lutkepohl, H. (1990a), "Asymptotic Distributions of Impulse Response Functions and Forecast Error Variance Decompositions of Vector Autoregressive Models," *Review of Economics and Statistics*, LXXII, 116–25.

Lutkepohl, H. (1990b), "Testing for Causation between Two Variables in Higher Dimensional VAR Models," University of Kiel, manuscript.

Lutkepohl, H. (1991), *Introduction to Multiple Time Series Analysis*, New York, NY: Springer Verlag.

Lutkepohl, H. and Proskitt, D. (1991), "Estimating Orthogonal Impulse Responses via Vector Autoregressive Models," *Econometric Theory*, 7, 487–96.

Lutkepohl, H. and Proskitt, D. (1992), "Testing for Causation using Infinite Order Vector Autoregressive Processes," manuscript, Christian University, Kiel, Germany.

McCallum, B. (1983), "A Reconsideration of Sims' Evidence Concerning Monetarism," *Economic Letters*, 13, 167–71.

McClave, J. (1978), "Estimating the Order of Autoregressive Models: The Max χ^2 Method," *Journal of the American Statistical Association*, 73, 122–8.

McNees, S. (1986a), "Forecasting Accuracy of Alternative Techniques: A Comparison of US Macroeconomic Forecasts" (with comments), *Journal of Business and Economic Statistics*, 4, 23–8.

McNees, S. (1986b), "The Accuracy of Two Forecasting Techniques: Some Evidence and Interpretation," *New England Economic Review*, March–April, 20–31.

McNees, S. (1990), "The Role of Judgement in Macroeconomic Forecasting Accuracy," *International Journal of Forecasting*, 6, 287–99.

Macunovich, D. and Easterlin, R. (1988), "Application of the Granger-Sims Causality tests to Monthly Fertility data, 1958–1984," *Journal of Population Economics*, 1, 71–88.

Maravall, A. (1993), "Stochastic Linear Trends: Models and Estimators," *Journal of Econometrics*, 56, 5–37.

Miller, P. (1983), "Higher Deficit Policies Lead to Higher Inflations," *Quarterly Review*, Federal Reserve Bank of Minneapolis, 7, Winter, 8–19.

Miller, P. and Roberds, W. (1991), "The Quantitative Significance of the Lucas Critique," *Journal of Business and Economic Statistics*, 9, 361–82.

Mittnik, S. and Zadrozny, P. (1993), "Asymptotic Distributions of Impulse Responses, Step Responses and Variance Decompositions of Estimated Linear Dynamic Models," *Econometrica*, 61, 857–70.

Mizon, G. (1990), "The Role of Measurement and Testing in Economics," in D. Greenway, M. Bleaney and I. Stewart, eds, *Economics in Perspective*, London: Routledge.

Mocai, N. (1990), "Business Cycle and Fertility Dynamics in the US: A VAR Model," NBER working paper 3177.

Monfort, A. and Rabemananjara, R. (1990), "From a VAR Model to a Structural Model, with an Application to Wage Price Spiral," *Journal of Applied Econometrics*, 5, 203–27.

Nelson, C. and Plosser, G. (1982), "Trends and Random Walks in Macroeconomic Time Series," *Journal of Monetary Economics*, 10, 139–62.

Nicholls, D.F. (1986), "The Box-Jenkins Approach to Random Coefficient Autoregressive Modelling," *Journal of Applied Probability*, 23A, 231–40.

Nicholls, D.F. and Quinn, B.G. (1982), *Random Coeỿcient Autoregressive Models: An Introduction*, New York, NY: Springer Verlag.

Nickelsburg, G. (1985), "Small Sample Properties of Dimensionality Statistics for Fitting VAR Models to Aggregate Economic Data," *Journal of Econometrics*, 28, 183–92.

Nickelsburg, G. and Ohanian, L. (1987), "VAR Priors and Economic Theory," *Papers and Proceedings: Business and Economic Section of the American Statistical Association*, 423–6.

Ohanian, L. (1988), "The Spurious Effects of Unit Roots on Vector Autoregressions: A Monte Carlo Study," *Journal of Econometrics*, 39, 251–66.

Orden, D. and Fackler, P. (1989), "Identifying Monetary Impacts on Agricultural Prices in VAR Models," *American Journal of Agricultural Economics*, 71, 495–502.

Parzen, E. (1976), "Multiple Time Series: Determining the Order of Approximating Autoregressive Schemes," in P.K. Krishnaiah, ed., *Multivariate Analysis IV*, New York, NY: Academic Press.

Perron, P. (1989), "The Great Crash, the Oil Price Shock and the Unit Root Hypothesis," *Econometrica*, 57, 1361–401.

Phillips, P.C. (1988), "Optimal Inference in Cointegrated Systems," *Econometrica*, 55, 277–301.

Phillips, P.C. (1991), "To Criticize the Critics: An Objective Bayesian Analysis of Stochastic Trends," (with discussion), *Journal of Applied Econometrics*, 6, 333–54.

Phillips, P.C. and Durlauf, S. (1988), "Trends vs. Random Walks in Time Series Analysis," *Econometrica*, 56, 1333–54.

Phillips, P.C. and Perron, P. (1986), "Testing for Unit Roots in Time Series Regressions," *Biometrika*, 70, 335–46.

Porter, R. and Offenbacher, E. (1983), "Empirical Comparison of Credit and Monetary Aggregates with Vector Autoregressive Methods," *Economic Review*, 69, 16–29.

Quah, D. (1990), "Permanent and Transitory Movements in Labor Income: An Explanation Based on Excess Smoothness in Consumption," *Journal of Political Economy*, 98(3), 449–75.

Quah, D. (1991), "Identifying VAR: A Discussion of P. Englund, A. Vredin and A. Warne: Macroeconomic Shocks in Sweden, 1925–1986," LSE manuscript.

Quah, D. (1992), "The Relative Importance of Permanent and Transitory Components: Identification and Some Theoretical Bounds," *Econometrica*, 60, 107–18.

Quah, D. (1993), "Lecture Notes in Macroeconomics," LSE manuscript.

Quah, D. and Rauch, P. (1990), "Openness and the Rate of Economic Growth," MIT, manuscript.

Quah, D. and Sargent, T. (1993), "A Dynamic Index Model for a Large Cross Section," in J. Stock and M. Watson, eds, *New Research in Business Cycles, Indicators and Forecasting*, Chicago, Il.: Chicago University Press.

Quinn, B.G. and Nicholls, D.F. (1981), "The Estimation of Random Coefficient Autoregressive Models, II," *Journal of Time Series Analysis*, 7, 185–203.

Quinn, B.G. and Nicholls, D.F. (1982), "Testing for the Randomness of Autoregressive Coefficients," *Journal of Time Series Analysis*, 8, 123–35.

Raynauld, J. and Simonato, A. (1993), "Seasonal BVAR Models: A Search along some Time Domain Priors," *Journal of Econometrics*, 55, 202–20.

Reinsel, G. (1983), "Some Results on Multivariate Autoregressive Index Models," *Biometrika*, 70, 145–56.

Roberds, W. and Whiteman, C. (1992), "Monetary Aggregates as Monetary Targets," *Journal of Money, Banking and Credit*, 24, 141–61.

Robertson, D. and Wickens, M. (1992), "Measuring Real and Nominal Macroeconomic Shocks and their International Transmission under Different Monetary Systems," London Business School, manuscript.

Rozanov, Y. (1967), *Stationary Random Processes*, San Francisco, Ca.: Holden-Day.

Runkle, D. (1987), "Vector Autoregression and Reality" (with discussion), *Journal of Business and Economic Statistics*, 5, 437–54.

Sachs, J. (1982), Comments to Sims "Policy Analysis with Econometric Models," *Brooking Papers of Economic Activity*, 2, 157–62.

Sargent, T. (1978), "Estimating Dynamic Labour Demand Schedules Under Rational Expectations," *Journal of Political Economy*, 86, 1009–44.

Sargent, T. (1979), "Estimating Vector Autoregressions using Methods not Based on Explicit Economic Theory," *Quarterly Review*, Federal Reserve Bank of Minneapolis, 3, Summer, 8–15.

Sargent, T. (1984), "Autoregression, Expectations and Advice," *American Economic Review, Papers and Proceedings*, 74, 408–15.

Sargent, T. (1986), *Macroeconomic Theory*, (2nd edn), New York, NY: Academic Press.

Sargent, T. and Lucas, R. (1980), *Rational Expectations and Econometric Practice*, Minneapolis, M.N.: University of Minnesota Press.

Sargent, T. and Sims, C. (1977), "Business Cycle Modelling without Pretending to Have Too Much *A-Priori* Economic Theory," in C. Sims, ed., *New Methods in Business Cycle Research*, Minneapolis, Mn.: Federal Reserve Bank.

Sarris, A. (1973), "Kalman Filter Models: A Bayesian Approach to Estimation of Time Varying Regression Coefficients," *Annals of Economic and Social Measurement*, 2/4, 501–23.

Schwarz, G. (1978), "Estimating the Dimension of a Model," *Annals of Statistics*, 6, 461–4.

Shapiro, M. (1987), "Are Cyclical Fluctuations in Productivity Due More to Supply Shocks or Demand Shocks," *American Economic Review, Papers and Proceedings*, 77, 118–24.

Shapiro, M. and Watson, M. (1989), "Sources of Business Cycle Fluctuations," *NBER Macroeconomic Annual*, Cambridge, Mass.: MIT Press, 3, 111–48.

Simkins, S. (1991), "What do VAR Models Tell Us about Business Cycle Behavior? Estimation of VAR Models subject to Business Cycle Restrictions," University of North Carolina at Greensboro, manuscript.

Sims, C. (1972), "Money, Income and Causality," *American Economic Review*, 62, 540–53.

Sims, C. (1977), "Exogeneity and Causal Ordering in Macroeconomic Models," in C. Sims, ed., *New Methods in Business Cycle Research*, Minneapolis, Mn.: Federal Reserve of Minneapolis.

Sims, C. (1980a), "Macroeconomics and Reality," *Econometrica*, 48, 1–48.

Sims, C. (1980b), "A Comparison of Interwar and Postwar Business Cycles: Monetarism Reconsidered," *American Economic Review Papers and Proceedings*, 70, 250–7.

Sims, C. (1982), "Policy Analysis with Econometric Models," *Brookings Papers of Economic Activity*, 2, 107–52.

Sims, C. (1986a), "Are Forecasting Models Usable for Policy Analysis," *Quarterly Review*, Federal Reserve Bank of Minneapolis, 10, Winter, 2–16.

Sims, C. (1986b), "Bayesmth: A Program for Bayesian Interpolation," University of Minnesota, working paper.

Sims, C. (1987), Comment to Runkle's "Vector Autoregression and Reality," *Journal of Business and Economic Statistics*, 5, 443–9.

Sims, C. (1988a), "Identifying Policy Effects," in R. Bryant, D. Henderson, G. Holtman, P. Hooper and A. Symansky, eds, *Empirical Macroeconomics for Interdependent Economies*, Washington, DC: Brookings Institution, 305–21.

Sims, C. (1988b), "Bayesian Perspective on Unit Roots Econometrics," *Journal of Economic Dynamics and Control*, 12, 436–74.

Sims, C. (1989a), "Models and their Users," *Journal of the American Agricultural Association*, 71, 490–4.

Sims, C. (1989b), "A Nine Variable Probabilistic Model of the US Economy," Institute for Empirical Macroeconomics, Federal Reserve of Minneapolis, discussion paper 14.

Sims, C. (1991a), Comment to Clements, M.P. and Mizon, G.E. "Empirical Analysis of Macroeconomic Time Series: VAR and Structural Models," *European Economic Review*, 35, 922–32.

Sims, C. (1991b), Comment to Phillips, P.C. "To Criticize the Critics," *Journal of Applied Econometrics*, 6, 423–34.

Sims, C., Stock, J. and Watson, M. (1990), "Inference in Linear Time Series Models with some Unit Roots," *Econometrica*, 58, 113–44.

Sims, C. and Ulhig, H. (1991), "Unit Rooters: A Helicopter Tour," *Econometrica*, 59, 1591–1600.

Smith, T. (1993), "Estimating Dynamic Economic Models by Simulations: A Comparison of two Approaches," *Journal of Applied Econometrics*, 8, s63–s85.

Spencer, D. (1989), "Does Money Matter? The Robustness of the Evidence from Vector Autoregressions," *Journal of Money, Banking and Credit*, 21, 442–54.

Spanos, A. (1989), "On Re-reading Haavelmo: A Retrospective View of Econometric Modelling," *Econometric Theory*, 5, 405–29.

Stein, C. (1974), "Multiple Regressions," chapter 37 in I. Olkin, ed., *Contribution to Probability and Statistics: Essays in Honor of Harald Hotelling*, Stanford: Stanford University Press.

Stock, J. and Watson, M. (1988), "Testing for Common Trends," *Journal of the American Statistical Association*, 83, 1097–107.

Stock, J. and Watson, M. (1989), "Interpreting the Evidence on Money–Income Causality," *Journal of Econometrics*, 40, 161–81.

Stock, J. and Watson, M. (1993), "A Simple Maximum Likelihood Estimator of Cointegrating Vectors," *Econometrica*, 61.

Theil, H. (1971), *Principles of Econometrics*, New York, NY: Wiley and Sons.

Tiao, G. and Box, G. (1981), "Modelling Multiple Time Series with Applications," *Journal of the American Statistical Association*, 75, 802–16.

Toda, H. and Phillips, P. (1992), "Vector Autoregression and Causality: A Theoretical Overview and a Simulation Study," *Econometric Reviews*, 10.

Toda, H. and Phillips, P. (1993), "Vector Autoregression and Causality," *Econometrica*, 61, 1367–93.

Todd, R. (1984), "Improving Economic Forecasting with Bayesian Vector Autoregression," *Quarterly Review*, Federal Reserve Bank of Minneapolis, 8, Fall, 18–29.

Todd, R. (1990), "Vector Autoregression Evidence on Monetarism: Another Look at the Robustness Debate," *Quarterly Review*, Federal Reserve Bank of Minneapolis, 14, Spring, 17–37.

Trevor, G.R. and S.J. Thorp (1988), "VAR Forecasting Models of the Australian Economy: A Preliminary Analysis," *Australian Economic Papers*, 27, 108–20.

Watson, M. (1986), "Univariate Detrending Methods with Stochastic Trends," *Journal of Monetary Economics*, 18, 49–75.

Watson, M. (1987), Comment to Runkle's "Vector Autoregression and Reality," *Journal of Business and Economic Statistics*, 5, 451–3.

Watson, M. (1994), "VARs and Cointegration," in R. Engle and D. McFadden, eds, *Handbook of Econometrics*, vol. 4, Amsterdam: North-Holland.

Webb, R. (1984), "Vector Autoregression as a Tool for Forecast Evaluation," *Economic Review*, Federal Reserve Bank of Richmond, 70, Jan–Feb, 3–11.

Weber, A. (1993), "Testing Long Run Neutrality: Empirical Evidence for G-7 Countries with Special Emphasis on Germany," forthcoming, *Carnegie Rochester Conference Series On Public Policy*.

West, K. (1990), "Fluctuations in Aggregate GNP and Inventories," *Quarterly Journal of Economics*, 105, 939–71.

West, K. (1991), "Sources of Cycles in Japan 1975–1987," University of Wisconsin, manuscript.

Wickens, M. (1992), "VAR Analysis in the Presence of Cointegration," London Business School, manuscript.

Wolff, C. (1987), "Time Varying Parameters and the Out-of-Sample Forecasting Performance of Structural Exchange Rate Models," *Journal of Business and Economic Statistics*, 5, 87–97.

Zellner, A. (1962), "An Efficient Method for Estimating Seemingly Unrelated Regressions and Tests for Aggregation Bias," *Journal of the American Statistical Association*, 57, 348–68.

Zellner, A. (1979), "Causality and Econometrics. Three Aspects of Policy and Policy-making: Knowledge, Data and Institutions," in K. Brunner and I. Meltzer, eds, *Carnegie Rochester Conference Series on Public Policy*, 10.

3

Multivariate Rational Expectations Models and Macroeconometric Modeling: A Review and Some New Results

Michael Binder and M. Hashem Pesaran

1 Introduction

This chapter provides a review of solution and estimation methods available in the literature for the analysis of multivariate linear rational expectations models, and proposes new techniques which are straightforward to implement and allow the incorporation of many forms of nonstationarity and nonlinearity (the latter being restricted to the models' forcing variables) into the analysis of multivariate rational expectations models.

The proposed method decomposes the solution into a backward and a forward component, and employs familiar martingale or martingale difference techniques to obtain all the solutions for the forward component. The method is relatively straightforward to apply and requires solution of a quadratic determinantal equation, the roots of which provide a complete characterization of all the possible classes of solutions, namely the unique stable solution, the multiple stable solutions, and the case where no stable solution exists. Since we only need to impose very weak assumptions on the forcing variables of the model, this solution method is applicable to cases where the forcing variables are first-order integrated, or display conditional variance dynamics, or other forms of nonstationarities or nonlinearities in the forcing variables. The quadratic determinantal equation solution method also renders a convenient (restricted) VAR framework for purposes of full information estimation and within which to analyze cointegration properties of the rational expectations models and the dynamics of the adjustment towards long-run equilibria. The proposed solution method is, however, subject to a limitation in that it does not allow for possible feedbacks from the decision to the forcing variables. This restriction can be relaxed though in an alternative solution method based on a factorization procedure.[1] The main contribution of this chapter is therefore to provide a comprehensive and straightforward to implement method for the solution and estimation of multivariate rational expectations models which are linear in the decision variables (or may be rewritten as such) but allow an investigation of all specifications of forcing variables which may be of interest to the applied researcher.

The solution methods and their use for model evaluation are illustrated with two applications which are at the core of much recent work in macroeconomic modeling under rational expectations. We analyze a standard real business cycle model and contrast the solution using the quadratic determinantal equation method with standard simulation methods employed in that literature. The second application considered is a broad class of dynamic adjustment cost problems as they may arise in a wide variety of intertemporal optimization models of consumers' and/or firms' behavior. The coefficient matrices in the Euler equations associated with this latter application exhibit a particular structure which may be exploited for a complete characterization of the solution of such models analytically.

The chapter concludes with a brief overview of the other important recent developments in the rational expectations literature, namely the analysis of the learning problem, rational expectations models with heterogeneously informed agents, and rational expectations models nonlinear in the decision variables.

2   Solution Methods for Multivariate Linear Rational Expectations Models

2.1   A General Characterization

Consider the following multivariate (structural) rational expectations model:

$$\sum_{i=0}^{n_1} \sum_{j=0}^{n_2} \mathbf{M}_{ij} E(\mathbf{x}_{t+j-i} | \Omega_{t-i}) = \mathbf{u}_t, \tag{3.1}$$

where $\mathbf{x}_t$ is a $p \times 1$ dimensional vector of decision variables, $\mathbf{u}_t$ represents a vector of "forcing variables" of the same dimension,[2] $\mathbf{M}_{ij}(i = 0, 1, \ldots, n_1; j = 0, 1, \ldots, n_2)$ are $p \times p$ dimensional matrices of fixed coefficients (with $\mathbf{M}_{00}$ being nonsingular), and Ω_t represents a nondecreasing information set at time t, containing at least current and lagged values of $\mathbf{x}_t$ and $\mathbf{u}_t$: $\Omega_t = \{\mathbf{x}_t, \mathbf{x}_{t-1}, \ldots; \mathbf{u}_t, \mathbf{u}_{t-1}, \ldots; \ldots\}$. The forcing variables $\{\mathbf{u}_t\}$ are assumed to be adapted to the information set Ω_t, and it is assumed that the conditional expectations $E(\mathbf{u}_{t+i} | \Omega_t)$ exist.[3] These are relatively weak assumptions and do not, for example, require the $\{\mathbf{u}_t\}$ process to be linear or covariance stationary.

The expectational difference equation system described by (3.1) encompasses a large variety of linear (homogeneous information) rational expectations models employed in the macro- and microeconometric literature. Examples include intertemporal models of firms' and households' behavior, neoclassical growth and business cycle models, neo-Keynesian models of price and wage setting, and simultaneous equation macroeconometric models *à la* Cowles Commission.[4] Notice that the above specification readily allows for inclusion of lagged dependent variables and future expectations of $\mathbf{x}_{t+i}$ based on information at different points in the past, as well as perception variables such as, say, $E(\mathbf{x}_{t-1}|\Omega_{t-2})$ or $E(\mathbf{x}_{t-2}|\Omega_{t-4})$. Therefore, it is easy to show that any of the above examples can be readily cast as a special case of the equation system (3.1). A detailed discussion of how this is done in the context of specific applications is provided in section 4.

In order to keep the notation tractable, in what follows it will be convenient to work with a first-order system involving only one-period-lagged dependent variables and one-period-ahead expectations of the dependent variables. As is well known, this involves no loss of generality, as the equation system described by (3.1) can always be reduced to such a form. For expositional clarity, it may be easiest to accomplish this transformation in two steps.[5] In the first step, (3.1) may be reduced to a system of expectational difference equations including lagged terms for the past n_1 periods and only one-period-ahead expectations. To this purpose, define the following auxiliary matrices and vectors:

$$
\mathbf{z}_t = \begin{pmatrix} \mathbf{x}_t \\ E(\mathbf{x}_{t+1}|\Omega_t) \\ \vdots \\ E(\mathbf{x}_{t+n_2}|\Omega_t) \end{pmatrix}, \quad
\Gamma_0 = \begin{pmatrix} \mathbf{M}_{00} & \mathbf{M}_{01} & \cdots & \mathbf{M}_{0n_2} \\ 0_p & I_p & \cdots & 0_p \\ & & \ddots & \\ 0_p & 0_p & \cdots & I_p \end{pmatrix},
$$

$$
\Gamma_i = \begin{pmatrix} \mathbf{M}_{i0} & \mathbf{M}_{i1} & \cdots & \mathbf{M}_{in_2} \\ 0_p & 0_p & \cdots & 0_p \\ & & \ddots & \\ 0_p & 0_p & \cdots & 0_p \end{pmatrix}, \quad
\Gamma_{-1} = \begin{pmatrix} 0_p & 0_p & \cdots & 0_p & 0_p \\ -I_p & 0_p & \cdots & 0_p & 0_p \\ & & \ddots & \\ 0_p & 0_p & \cdots & -I_p & 0_p \end{pmatrix}, \quad
\boldsymbol{\vartheta}_t = \begin{pmatrix} \mathbf{u}_t \\ 0_{p\times 1} \\ \vdots \\ 0_{p\times 1} \end{pmatrix},
$$

where 0_p and I_p respectively stand for zero and identity matrices of order p, Γ_0 is an $(n_2 + 1)p \times (n_2 + 1)p$ dimensional nonsingular matrix, the Γ_is and Γ_{-1} are also of dimension $(n_2 + 1)p \times (n_2 + 1)p$, and $\boldsymbol{\vartheta}_t$ is an $(n_2 + 1)p \times 1$ dimensional vector. Then (3.1) can be rewritten more compactly as

$$
\sum_{i=0}^{n_1} \Gamma_i \mathbf{z}_{t-i} + \Gamma_{-1} E(\mathbf{z}_{t+1}|\Omega_t) = \boldsymbol{\vartheta}_t. \tag{3.2}
$$

Using this result the desired reduction to a first-order system can be achieved by further defining

$$\mathbf{y}_t = \begin{pmatrix} \mathbf{z}_t \\ \mathbf{z}_{t-1} \\ \vdots \\ \mathbf{z}_{t-n_1+1} \end{pmatrix}, \qquad \Lambda_0 = \begin{pmatrix} \Gamma_0 & \Gamma_1 & \cdots & \Gamma_{n_1-1} \\ 0_{(n_2+1)p} & I_{(n_2+1)p} & \cdots & 0_{(n_2+1)p} \\ & & \ddots & \\ 0_{(n_2+1)p} & 0_{(n_2+1)p} & \cdots & I_{(n_2+1)p} \end{pmatrix},$$

$$\Lambda_1 = \begin{pmatrix} 0_{(n_2+1)p} & 0_{(n_2+1)p} & \cdots & 0_{(n_2+1)p} & \Gamma_{n_1} \\ -I_{(n_2+1)p} & 0_{(n_2+1)p} & \cdots & 0_{(n_2+1)p} & 0_{(n_2+1)p} \\ & & \ddots & & \\ 0_{(n_2+1)p} & 0_{(n_2+1)p} & \cdots & -I_{(n_2+1)p} & 0_{(n_2+1)p} \end{pmatrix},$$

$$\Lambda_{-1} = \begin{pmatrix} \Gamma_{-1} & 0_{(n_2+1)p} & \cdots & 0_{(n_2+1)p} \\ 0_{(n_2+1)p} & 0_{(n_2+1)p} & \cdots & 0_{(n_2+1)p} \\ & & & \vdots \\ 0_{(n_2+1)p} & 0_{(n_2+1)p} & \cdots & 0_{(n_2+1)p} \end{pmatrix}, \qquad \tilde{\boldsymbol{\vartheta}}_t = \begin{pmatrix} \boldsymbol{\vartheta}_t \\ 0 \\ \vdots \\ 0 \end{pmatrix},$$

where $\mathbf{y}_t$ is now an $n_1(n_2+1)p \times 1$ dimensional vector, and Λ_0, Λ_1, and Λ_{-1} are square matrices with dimensions conformable to $\mathbf{y}_t$. It then immediately follows that an equivalent expression for (3.2) is

$$\mathbf{y}_t = -\Lambda_0^{-1}\Lambda_1\mathbf{y}_{t-1} - \Lambda_0^{-1}\Lambda_{-1}E(\mathbf{y}_{t+1}|\Omega_t) + \Lambda_0^{-1}\tilde{\boldsymbol{\vartheta}}_t, \qquad (3.3)$$

or, with an obvious notation,

$$\mathbf{y}_t = A\mathbf{y}_{t-1} + BE(\mathbf{y}_{t+1}|\Omega_t) + \mathbf{w}_t, \qquad (3.4)$$

where the dimensionalities are now as follows: $\mathbf{y}_t$ and $\mathbf{w}_t$ are $m \times 1$ vectors, and A and B are $m \times m$ matrices, with $m = n_1(n_2+1)p$. For the remainder of the chapter, we focus our analysis on the compact version of (3.1) given by (3.4).

2.2   A Brief Review of Previously Suggested Solution Methods

In this section, we briefly discuss methods that are currently available in the literature for the solution of multivariate linear rational expectations models.[6] These solution methods differ in their degree of generality, and can be grouped under two headings. Methods in the first group are valid when the coefficient matrices A and B in (3.4) and the processes generating the forcing variables are subject to certain restrictions. The solution methods discussed in the seminal paper by Hansen and Sargent (1981a) fall in this category. These solution methods are therefore not generally applicable to (3.4).[7] A second group of solution methods suggested by Whiteman (1983), Salemi (1986), and Broze, Gouriéroux, and Szafarz (1985; 1990) are more generally applicable and do not require specific relationships to hold between the coefficient matrices A and B. In what follows we provide a review of the solution methods that fall in this latter group. While no claim is made that this is an exhaustive list of available solution methods, it is probably fair to say that these are currently the most widespread procedures that are used in the applied literature.[8]

2.2.1 Undetermined coefficients methods
The solution methods proposed by Whiteman (1983) and Salemi (1986) both employ the undetermined coefficients approach and exploit two basic premises which may be traced back to the seminal contribution of Muth (1961). First, these methods restrict themselves to stochastic processes for the forcing variables which are linearly regular covariance stationary, and thus have a Wold representation. Second, solutions are constrained *a priori* to fall into the class of (time-independent) absolute-summable linear combinations of the stochastic processes fundamental for the forcing variables. That is, the class of solutions considered is of the form $\mathbf{y}_t = \Sigma_{j=0}^{\infty} C_j \boldsymbol{\varepsilon}_{t-j}$, where the coefficient matrices C_j depend only on the displacement j but not the absolute position in time t, and are assumed to be absolute summable, thus satisfying the condition $\Sigma_{j=0}^{\infty} \operatorname{tr} C_j C_j' < \infty$. The processes $\boldsymbol{\varepsilon}_t$ are also taken to be fundamental for the forcing variables $\mathbf{w}_t$ (see equations (3.5) and (3.6)). To discuss the different undetermined coefficients solution procedures in more detail, let us consider without loss of generality our first-order set-up given by equation (3.4). In line with the two crucial assumptions made above, $\mathbf{w}_t$ is taken to be a covariance stationary process having the Wold moving average representation

$$\mathbf{w}_t = \sum_{j=0}^{\infty} A_j \boldsymbol{\varepsilon}_{t-j} \equiv A(L)\boldsymbol{\varepsilon}_t, \qquad (3.5)$$

where the A_js are of dimension $m \times m$, $A(L) = \Sigma_{j=0}^{\infty} A_j L^j$ is an infinite-order polynomial matrix lag operator, and $\boldsymbol{\varepsilon}_t$ is of dimension $m \times 1$. Solutions to (3.4) are then obtained by searching within the class

$$\mathbf{y}_t = \sum_{j=0}^{\infty} C_j \boldsymbol{\varepsilon}_{t-j} \equiv C(L)\boldsymbol{\varepsilon}_t, \qquad (3.6)$$

where $\{\mathbf{y}_t\}$ is also taken to be covariance stationary. Using the lag operator notation, (3.4) may now be written as:

$$E((I_m - BL^{-1} - AL)\mathbf{y}_t | \Omega_t) = \mathbf{w}_t. \qquad (3.7)$$

From (3.6), the optimal predictor of $\mathbf{y}_{t+1}$ given Ω_t in the mean squared error sense is given by

$$E(\mathbf{y}_{t+1} | \Omega_t) = C_1 \boldsymbol{\varepsilon}_t + C_2 \boldsymbol{\varepsilon}_{t-1} + \dots \qquad (3.8)$$

$$= L^{-1}(C(L) - C_0)\boldsymbol{\varepsilon}_t.$$

Substituting from (3.5), (3.6), and (3.8) in (3.7) now yields

$$(I_m - BL^{-1} - AL)C(L)\boldsymbol{\varepsilon}_t = (-BC_0 L^{-1} + A(L))\boldsymbol{\varepsilon}_t, \qquad (3.9)$$

which needs to be solved for the matrix lag operator polynomial $C(L)$ for all realizations of ε_t. Whiteman's (1983) and Salemi's (1986) methods differ in how this is achieved: Whiteman employs the "z-transform" technique, whereas Salemi uses direct matrix inversion techniques.

Consider first the z-transform method of Whiteman.[9] Since the lag polynomials on the left- and right-hand sides of (3.9) must be equal for all realizations of ε_t, it follows that the corresponding z-transforms must also be equal as analytic functions on the open unit disk:

$$(I_m - Bz^{-1} - Az)C(z) = -BC_0z^{-1} + A(z). \tag{3.10}$$

The next step is to factor the characteristic polynomial associated with the left-hand side of (3.10). This, under certain conditions, can be accomplished by making use of the Smith normal form:[10] as long as B is of full rank and the determinant of $I_m z - B - Az^2$ is nonzero on the unit circle and has distinct roots, it is always possible to factor $I_m z - B - Az^2$ into $S(z)T(z)$, where $S(z) = S_0 + S_1 z$, $T(z) = T_0 + T_1 z$ and S_0, S_1, T_0 and T_1 are $m \times m$ dimensional matrices. In this factorization all roots of $\det(S(z)) = 0$ and of $\det(T(z)) = 0$ will be distinct and will fall respectively inside and outside the unit circle.[11] Among the assumptions made to render the factorization feasible, particularly the requirement that B be nonsingular may be rather restrictive in practice. Whiteman indicates that one could relax this assumption by partitioning (3.10) conformably with the nonsingular portion of B; it should be clear that the necessary computations would become quite a bit more involved, though. Equating $S(z)T(z)$ with the first entry on the left-hand side of (3.10), all that remains, then, is to solve for $C(z)$ in

$$T(z)C(z) = S(z)^{-1}(-BC_0z^{-1} + A(z))z. \tag{3.11}$$

Whiteman suggests to compute the inverse of $S(z)$ using an algorithm due to Emre and Hüsseyin (1975) as adapted in Hansen and Sargent (1981a). This algorithm uses the identity $S(z)^{-1} = \mathrm{adj}(S(z))/\det(S(z))$,[12] and allows one to write

$$S(z)^{-1} = \sum_{j=1}^{m_1} \frac{N_j}{z - z_j}, \tag{3.12}$$

where $z_1, z_2, \ldots, z_{m_1}$ are the roots of $\det(S(z)) = 0$, the $m \times m$ dimensional matrices $N_1, N_2, \ldots, N_{m_1}$ are functions of $\mathrm{adj}(S(z_j))$, and m_1 is the number of roots of $\det((I_m z - B - Az^2)) = 0$ that fall inside the unit circle.

Using this expansion of $S(z)^{-1}$, (3.11) can be rewritten as

$$T(z)C(z) = \sum_{j=1}^{m_1} \frac{N_j}{z - z_j}(-BC_0 + A(z)z), \tag{3.13}$$

which holds for all z on the open unit disk except at $z = z_j$, $j = 1, 2, \ldots, m_1$. However, since $C(z)$ must exist for all $|z| < 1$, (3.13) implicitly places restrictions on C_0. In particular, it must be true that

$$(z - z_j)T(z)C(z)|_{z=z_j} = N_j(-BC_0 + A(z_j)z_j) = 0_{m \times 1}, \quad j = 1, 2, \ldots, m_1. \quad (3.14)$$

Equivalently, we obtain the $m_1 m$ dimensional equation system

$$\begin{pmatrix} N_1 A(z_1)z_1 \\ \vdots \\ N_{m_1} A(z_{m_1})z_{m_1} \end{pmatrix} = \begin{pmatrix} N_1 \\ \vdots \\ N_{m_1} \end{pmatrix} BC_0, \quad (3.15)$$

which can be solved for C_0. The solution for C_0, and consequently the solution to (3.4), is unique if $m_1 = m$ (what Sargan, 1983, 1984 has called the "regular case").

This may be seen by noting that the rank of

$$\begin{pmatrix} N_1 \\ \vdots \\ N_{m_1} \end{pmatrix} B$$

is less than or equal to the minimum of (m_1, m); standard arguments from linear algebra then imply the above result. Furthermore, there are infinitely many covariance stationary solutions to (3.4) if $m_1 < m$ (the "irregular case"), and no covariance stationary solution would exist if $m_1 > m$. Combining (3.13) and the restrictions (3.15), after some tedious algebra one obtains the solution in an econometrically implementable form. We confine ourselves here to reporting the main results, and refer to Whiteman (1983) for the computational details. If the solution is unique, it is given by

$$\mathbf{y}_t = T(L)^{-1} \sum_{j=1}^{m} N_j \left(\frac{LA(L) - z_j A(z_j)}{L - z_j} \right) \boldsymbol{\varepsilon}_t \quad (3.16)$$

where using (3.5) $\boldsymbol{\varepsilon}_t$ can be obtained in terms of the observable variables, $\mathbf{w}_t$, by inverting $A(L)$, namely $\boldsymbol{\varepsilon}_t = A(L)^{-1}\mathbf{w}_t$. In the case of multiple solutions, $m - m_1$ roots have to be "flipped" to find the appropriate factorization of $I_m z - B - Az^2$ into $S(z)T(z)$. Otherwise, the computations are exactly the same as in the case of a unique solution, and we again refer to Whiteman (1983) for the details.

Several remarks concerning this solution procedure seem in order. First, the restriction that solutions lie in the (Hilbert) space spanned by (time-independent) absolute-summable combinations of the stochastic processes fundamental for the forcing variables rules out the multiplicity of solutions due to a martingale component in the general solution.[13] In Whiteman's view, such a "strategy produces multiple, econometrically tractable solutions whenever the environment, embodied in the parameters of the model, so dictates."[14] Second, Whiteman's procedure requires the factorization of the characteristic polynomial associated with the first entry on the left-hand side of (3.10). There are several numerical algorithms available to accomplish this task. Whiteman himself suggests the algorithm developed by Pace and Barnett (1974). Third, it should be noted that the assumption of covariance stationarity of the stochastic processes generating the forcing variables could be relaxed by working with the appropriately differenced processes. For a detailed discussion of this in the univariate context, see Wickens (1993). Finally, we may also stress again that the complexity of the computations involved in arriving at (3.16) (or its equivalent in the case of multiple solutions) is directly dependent on whether the coefficient matrix B is invertible or not. Since, as we will see in section 4, B is in many applications generically singular, this is certainly a drawback of Whiteman's solution procedure.

We turn next to Salemi's (1986) implementation of the method of undetermined coefficients. Starting from (3.9), a solution, if it exists, is given by

$$\mathbf{y}_t = (- B + I_m L - AL^2)^{-1}(- BC_0 + A(L)L)\boldsymbol{\varepsilon}_t. \tag{3.17}$$

The implementation of (3.17) firstly involves computing the inverse of $(- B + I_m L - AL^2)$ and, in analogy to Whiteman's (1983) procedure, secondly requires obtaining possible restrictions on C_0. The first task may be accomplished quite easily using standard recursive methods. Denoting the inverse of $(- B + I_m L - AL^2)$ by the (infinite-order) lag polynomial $(H_0 + H_1 L + H_2 L^2 + \ldots)$, where H_0, H_1 etc. are $m \times m$ matrices, it readily follows that

$$(- B + I_m L - AL^2)(H_0 + H_1 L + H_2 L^2 + \ldots) = I_m. \tag{3.18}$$

The matrices H_0, H_1, H_2, ... are then recursively given by (assuming again that B is nonsingular)

$$H_i = - B^{-1}(H_{i-1} - AH_{i-2}), \quad i = 0, 1, 2, \ldots, \tag{3.19}$$

where $H_0 = - B^{-1}$ and $H_i = 0_m$ for $i < 0$.

To derive restrictions on C_0, Salemi proceeds by making the following two assumptions: the determinant of $I_m L - B - AL^2$ is nonzero on the unit circle, and B is of full rank. As with Whiteman's method, the requirement that B be nonsingular may be circumvented by partitioning (3.4) conformably with the nonsingular portion of B.[15] If B is nonsingular, we can premultiply the lag polynomials in (3.9) by B^{-1} to obtain

$$(B^{-1}L - I_m - B^{-1}AL^2)C(L) = - C_0 + B^{-1}A(L)L, \tag{3.20}$$

which can be equivalently represented as

$$\left(\begin{pmatrix} -I_m & 0_m \\ 0_m & -I_m \end{pmatrix} + \begin{pmatrix} B^{-1} & -B^{-1}A \\ I_m & 0_m \end{pmatrix}L\right)\begin{pmatrix} C(L) \\ C(L)L \end{pmatrix} = \left(\begin{pmatrix} -C_0 & 0_m \\ 0_m & I_m \end{pmatrix} + \begin{pmatrix} B^{-1}A(L) & 0_m \\ 0_m & I_m \end{pmatrix}L\right)\begin{pmatrix} I_m \\ 0_m \end{pmatrix},$$

$$\tag{3.21}$$

or, more compactly,

$$(I_{2m} - GL)\Theta(L) = (K_0 + K_1(L)L)P, \qquad (3.22)$$

where G, K_0, and K_1 are of dimension $2m \times 2m$, and the matrix lag polynomial $\Theta(L)$ and P have dimension $2m \times m$. This transformation is particularly useful in distinguishing between the three cases of no covariance stationary solution, a unique covariance stationary solution, and multiple covariance stationary solutions. One may readily see this by noting that (3.4) can be equivalently written as

$$\begin{pmatrix} E(\mathbf{y}_{t+1}|\Omega_t) \\ \mathbf{y}_t \end{pmatrix} = G\begin{pmatrix} \mathbf{y}_t \\ \mathbf{y}_{t-1} \end{pmatrix} - PA(L)\boldsymbol{\varepsilon}_t. \qquad (3.23)$$

It is immediate that no covariance stationary solution exists for the system given by (3.23) if more than m eigenvalues of

$$G = \begin{pmatrix} G_1 \\ G_2 \end{pmatrix}$$

(both G_1 and G_2 being $m \times 2m$ dimensional) lie outside the unit circle, since in that case the backward component $\mathbf{y}_t - G_2\mathbf{y}_{t-1}$ would explode. With analogous reasoning, if m eigenvalues of G lie outside the unit circle, and the remaining m inside the unit circle, a unique solution exists (the "regular case"). For the "irregular case" of more than m eigenvalues of G falling inside the unit circle, a multiplicity of solutions exists. For both the regular and irregular cases, the solution polynomials are given by

$$\Theta(L) = (I_{2m} - GL)^{-1}(K_0 + K_1(L)L)P. \qquad (3.24)$$

From (3.24), we can obtain the restrictions that are imposed on the elements of C_0 under the regular and irregular cases. To keep the argument simple, let us follow Salemi and assume that G has linearly independent elementary divisors. Then we can diagonalize G as $H^{-1}JH$ (where the eigenvalues of G are placed on the main diagonal of J in descending order based on their moduli), and rewrite (3.24) as

$$\Theta(L) = K_0P + H^{-1}(I_{2m} + JL + J^2L^2 + \ldots)(JHK_0 + HK_1)PL. \qquad (3.25)$$

Clearly, if at least one eigenvalue of G falls outside the unit circle (but at most m), for $\Theta(L)$ to have absolute-summable coefficients it will be necessary that a corresponding number of rows of $(JHK_0 + HK_1)P$ are identically equal to zero. Thus, to derive the exact algebraic form of the restrictions on C_0, all that remains is to partition the matrices J and H conformably with the number of entries on the main diagonal of J falling outside the unit circle. We refer to Salemi (1986) and Salemi and Song (1992) for the computational details.

2.2.2 *Martingale difference methods*

Broze, Gouriéroux, and Szafarz (1990) have recently introduced what they call the "adjoint operator method." It is an extension to the multivariate context of the martingale difference method introduced by the same authors in 1985. The basic idea is to replace rational expectations by their realizations plus the realization of a martingale difference process.[16] The adjoint operator method subsequently exploits properties of the characteristic polynomial of the resulting equation system. Again our discussion will be based on the equation system (3.4). Substituting $E(\mathbf{y}_{t+1}|\Omega_t) = \mathbf{y}_{t+1} - \boldsymbol{\xi}_{t+1}$, where each component of $\boldsymbol{\xi}_{t+1}$ is a martingale difference process with respect to the information set Ω_t, into (3.4), we obtain

$$\mathbf{y}_t - A\mathbf{y}_{t-1} - B\mathbf{y}_{t+1} = \mathbf{w}_t - B\boldsymbol{\xi}_{t+1}, \qquad (3.26)$$

The characteristic polynomial of (3.26) (in terms of nonnegative powers on the lag operators) is easily seen to be

$$\Xi(L) = -B + I_m L - AL^2. \qquad (3.27)$$

Broze, Gouriéroux, and Szafarz proceed by premultiplying both sides of (3.26) lagged one period by the adjoint matrix of $\Xi(L)$, $Y(L)$ to obtain

$$L^{m_1}\Phi(L)\mathbf{y}_t = -Y(L)B\boldsymbol{\xi}_t + Y(L)\mathbf{w}_{t-1}, \qquad (3.28)$$

where $L^{m_1}\Phi(L) = \det(\Xi(L))$, and m_1 equals the number of zero roots of $\det(\Xi(L))$ (we are thus assured that $\Phi(0) \neq 0$). Substituting for B on the right-hand side of (3.28) from (3.27) and multiplying through by L^{-m_1}, (3.28) can be rewritten as

$$\Phi(L)\mathbf{y}_t - L^{-m_1}Y(L)\Xi(L)\boldsymbol{\xi}_t = -Y(L)(I_m L - AL^2)\boldsymbol{\xi}_{t+m_1} + Y(L)\mathbf{w}_{t+m_1-1}, \qquad (3.29)$$

or, more compactly,

$$\Phi(L)(\mathbf{y}_t - \boldsymbol{\xi}_t) = -Y(L)(I_m L - AL^2)\boldsymbol{\xi}_{t+m_1} + Y(L)\mathbf{w}_{t+m_1-1}. \qquad (3.30)$$

Now note that the left-hand side of (3.30) only depends on information known at time $t - 1$ (recalling in particular that $\mathbf{y}_t - \boldsymbol{\xi}_t = E(\mathbf{y}_t|\Omega_{t-1})$); as Broze, Gouriéroux, and Szafarz argue, the same must then be true for the right-hand side, and we must therefore have

$$E((-Y(L)(I_m L - AL^2)\boldsymbol{\xi}_{t+m_1} + Y(L)\mathbf{w}_{t+m_1-1})|\Omega_{t-1})$$

$$= -Y(L)(I_m L - AL^2)\boldsymbol{\xi}_{t+m_1} + Y(L)\mathbf{w}_{t+m_1-1}. \qquad (3.31)$$

All solutions to the rational expectations model (3.4) are thus computed by finding the martingale difference processes $\boldsymbol{\xi}_t$ that satisfy (3.31), and subsequently solving the corresponding difference equation systems (3.26) for $\mathbf{y}_t$ in terms of $\mathbf{w}_t$ and $\boldsymbol{\xi}_t$. Generally, there will be infinitely many bounded solutions and the number of martingale difference processes $\boldsymbol{\xi}_t$ that can be chosen arbitrarily may be derived using the restrictions implied by (3.31). See Broze, Gouriéroux, and Szafarz (1990) for the computational details. They also show how the derivations involved can in principle be somewhat simplified if, as in Whiteman (1983) and Salemi (1986), one restricts attention to the class of solutions consisting of (time-independent) absolute-summable linear combinations of the stochastic processes driving the forcing variables. The Broze, Gouriéroux, and Szafarz solution method is applicable to covariance stationary as well as I(1) forcing variables and is easily adapted to the analysis of cointegrating properties of y_t and w_t, when the latter are I(1).[17] A drawback of their approach, however, is that it is not readily transparent from (3.26) and (3.31) when a unique solution will exist, and that the method does not provide a readily implementable algorithm for the computation of the solutions.

2.3 A Quadratic Determinantal Equation Method

Having reviewed available solution methods for multivariate linear rational expectations models, in this section we propose a new solution method which is capable of characterizing all possible solutions and is straightforward to implement computationally. Another attractive feature of this new solution procedure lies in the fact that it imposes considerably weaker assumptions on the forcing variables than the methods discussed in the previous section. The main difficulty with obtaining a solution for (3.4) is the simultaneous dependence of y_t on its past and future (expected) values. Our proposed method starts by transforming the equations in (3.4) so that the resultant system in terms of the transformed variables only depends on expected future values and can be solved using the martingale method developed in Pesaran (1981; 1987) and/or a variant of the martingale difference method of Broze, Gouriéroux, and Szafarz (1985) reviewed in the previous section. The remainder of this section is structured as follows. We first introduce the transformation of (3.4) to a system involving only current and expected future values. A discussion of the general solution of the resultant transformed system follows. The third subsection outlines the computational implementation of our method. Subsequently, we present several propositions linking the solution to characteristics of the matrices A and B, before concluding the section by establishing cointegrating properties for a stacked system in y_t and w_t either if w_t contains I(1) variables and/or if some eigenvalues of C are unity in absolute value.

2.3.1 A backward and forward decomposition Consider the (vector) quasi-difference transformation

$$\mathbf{Y}_t = \mathbf{y}_t - C\mathbf{y}_{t-1}, \tag{3.32}$$

where C is an $m \times m$ matrix to be defined momentarily. This transformation in effect decomposes the solution of (3.4) into a "backward" ($\mathbf{y}_{tb}$) and a "forward" component ($\mathbf{y}_{tf}$): $\mathbf{y}_t = \mathbf{y}_{tb} + \mathbf{y}_{tf}$, where $\mathbf{y}_{tb} = C\mathbf{y}_{t-1}$, and $\mathbf{y}_{tf} = \mathbf{Y}_t$. Our task in what follows therefore is to determine C, which in turn will yield the "backward" part, and to solve for $\mathbf{Y}_t$, which gives the "forward" part. Using the fact that $E(\mathbf{Y}_{t+1}|\Omega_t) = E(\mathbf{y}_{t+1}|\Omega_t) - C\mathbf{y}_t$, substituting (3.32) back into (3.4) and collecting terms, we readily obtain

$$(I_m - BC)\mathbf{Y}_t = BE(\mathbf{Y}_{t+1}|\Omega_t) + (BC^2 - C + A)\mathbf{y}_{t-1} + \mathbf{w}_t, \tag{3.33}$$

which implicitly characterizes the matrix C introduced in (3.32) as the solution to the second-order matrix polynomial equation

$$BC^2 - C + A = 0_m. \tag{3.34}$$

Assuming $(I_m - BC)$ is nonsingular,[18] then premultiplying both sides of (3.33) by its inverse yields

$$\mathbf{Y}_t = FE(\mathbf{Y}_{t+1}|\Omega_t) + \mathbf{W}_t, \tag{3.35}$$

where

$$F = (I_m - BC)^{-1}B \tag{3.36}$$

$$\mathbf{W}_t = (I_m - BC)^{-1}\mathbf{w}_t. \tag{3.37}$$

The equation system (3.35), which now depends only on future expectations, can be solved using the martingale or martingale difference methods.

2.3.2 *General solution*

The general solution of (3.35) crucially depends on whether B is invertible or not. We therefore distinguish between these two cases.

Case 1: B is invertible When B is nonsingular, so will be F, and the general martingale solution of (3.35) is given by[19]

$$\mathbf{Y}_t = -\sum_{j=1}^{t-1} F^{-j}\mathbf{W}_{t-j} + F^{-t}\mathcal{M}_t, \tag{3.38}$$

or, upon substituting for $\mathbf{Y}_t$ from (3.32),

$$\mathbf{y}_t = C\mathbf{y}_{t-1} - \sum_{j=1}^{t-1} F^{-j}\mathbf{W}_{t-j} + F^{-t}\mathcal{M}_t, \tag{3.39}$$

where $\mathcal{M}_t$ represents a vector martingale process comprising m distinct martingale processes with respect to the information set Ω_t.[20] Thus, independently of the eigenvalues of F, there is a multiplicity of solutions characterized by the m arbitrary martingale processes in $\mathcal{M}_t$.[21] We provide an alternative characterization of this multiplicity in the following proposition:

Proposition 1 If $\mathbf{y}_t^0$ is a solution of (3.4), so is $\mathbf{y}_t^1 = \mathbf{y}_t^0 + C(\mathbf{y}_{t-1}^1 - \mathbf{y}_{t-1}^0) + F^{-t}\mathcal{M}_t$, where $\mathcal{M}_t$ is an $m \times 1$ vector of martingale processes. ∎

Proof of proposition 1 Starting with the first expression on the right-hand side of (3.35) we have, noting that $\mathbf{Y}_t^1 = \mathbf{Y}_t^0 + F^{-t}\mathcal{M}_t$,

$$FE(\mathbf{Y}_t^1|\Omega_t) = FE(\mathbf{Y}_{t+1}^0 + F^{-t-1}\mathcal{M}_{t+1}|\Omega_t)$$

$$= FE(\mathbf{Y}_{t+1}^0|\Omega_t) + F^{-t}\mathcal{M}_t.$$

But since Y_t^0 is a solution of (3.35), it readily follows that

$$Y_t^1 = FE(Y_{t+1}^1 | \Omega_t) + W_t,$$

and thus Y_t^1 is also a solution of (3.35). Substituting $Y_t^1 = y_t^1 - Cy_{t-1}^1$ and $Y_t^0 = y_t^0 - Cy_{t-1}^0$ in $Y_t^0 = Y_t^1 + F^{-t}\mathcal{M}_t$ delivers the result of the proposition.   QED

Depending on the location of the eigenvalues of F, the general solution (3.39) can be written in different forms. Suppose first that all eigenvalues of F fall inside the unit circle. Assuming that $\{W_t\}$ is a sequence of (m-dimensional) random variables satisfying

$$E(W_t'\, W_t) \leq k, \quad t = 0, 1, 2, \ldots \tag{3.40}$$

for some finite constant k, then, since $\{F^i\}$ is an absolutely summable sequence, the infinite sum $\Sigma_{i=1}^{\infty} F^i W_i$ exists. Furthermore $\{\mathcal{M}_t^f\}$, defined as

$$\mathcal{M}_t^f = \mathcal{M}_t - E\left(\sum_{i=1}^{\infty} F^i W_i | \Omega_t\right), \tag{3.41}$$

will, as may easily be verified, also be a vector martingale process. Solving (3.41) for $\mathcal{M}_t$ and substituting into (3.39) yields

$$y_t = Cy_{t-1} + \sum_{i=0}^{\infty} F^i E(W_{t+i} | \Omega_t) + F^{-t}\mathcal{M}_t^f, \tag{3.42}$$

which is known as the forward solution. If, following Gouriéroux, Laffont, and Monfort (1982), one imposes the additional condition requiring the solution to be bounded in mean, namely $\sup E|y_t| < \infty$,[22] the component $F^{-t}\mathcal{M}_t^f$ on the right-hand side of (3.42) has to vanish since otherwise the solutions would explode as $t \to \infty$. To see this, note that if both Y_t^0 and Y_t^1 (as defined in the proof of proposition 1) were solutions to (3.4), then $Y_t^* = Y_t^0 - Y_t^1 = F^{-t}\mathcal{M}_t$, and $E|Y_t^*| = |F^{-t}|E|\mathcal{M}_t|$. For every component $\mathcal{M}_t^j$ of $\mathcal{M}_t$ being a martingale process ($j = 1, 2, \ldots, m$), we have that $E|\mathcal{M}_t^j| \leq E|\mathcal{M}_{t+1}^j| \leq E|\mathcal{M}_{t+2}^j| \leq \ldots$. Thus, with all eigenvalues of F falling inside the unit circle, the only choice of $\mathcal{M}_t^j$ for which $E|Y_t^*|$ is bounded is $\mathcal{M}_t^j = 0$ almost surely for all t ($j = 1, 2, \ldots, m$). Since this implies that $Y_t^0 = Y_t^1$ almost surely, then $(I_m - CL)(y_t^0 - y_t^1) = 0_{m \times 1}$ also has to hold almost surely, and as long as all roots of C fall inside the unit circle,[23] the unique stable solution is therefore given by

$$y_t = Cy_{t-1} + \sum_{i=0}^{\infty} F^i E(W_{t+i} | \Omega_t). \tag{3.43}$$

Secondly, we can write down a backward solution when all eigenvalues of F fall outside the unit circle. Assuming $\{W_t\}$ satisfies condition (3.40), then the infinite sum $\Sigma_{i=0}^{\infty} F^{-i} W_{-i}$ exists. Define

$$\mathcal{M}_t^b = \mathcal{M}_t + \sum_{i=0}^{\infty} F^{-i} \mathbf{W}_{-i}. \tag{3.44}$$

Again, it is easily seen that $\mathcal{M}_t^b$ is also a vector martingale process. Substituting $\mathcal{M}_t$ from (3.44) into (3.39) yields the "backward" solution

$$\mathbf{y}_t = C\mathbf{y}_{t-1} - \sum_{i=0}^{\infty} F^{-i} \mathbf{W}_{t-i} + F^{-t} \mathcal{M}_t^b. \tag{3.45}$$

It should be noted that since all eigenvalues of F are assumed to fall outside the unit circle, the martingale components $F^{-t}\mathcal{M}_t^b$ in (3.45) cannot be eliminated by an appeal to a stability criterion. The stable solutions are therefore characterized by an m-dimensional multiplicity through arbitrary choices for the m components of $\mathcal{M}_t^b$.

Finally suppose that F has $m_1(\neq 0)$ eigenvalues inside and $m_2(\neq 0)$ ($m_1 + m_2 = m$) eigenvalues outside the unit circle. Intuitively, to obtain a characterization of the general solution (3.39) which corresponds to the representations (3.43) and (3.45), one has to solve that part of (3.35) which is associated with the eigenvalues of F that fall inside the unit circle forward, and that part of (3.35) associated with the eigenvalues of F which fall outside the unit circle backward. This uncoupling may be accomplished by using the Jordan normal form of F, namely $F = T\Lambda T^{-1}$, where

$$\Lambda = \begin{pmatrix} \Lambda_{f_1} & 0_{m_1 \times m_2} \\ 0_{m_2 \times m_1} & \Lambda_{f_2} \end{pmatrix}, \tag{3.46}$$

T is an $m \times m$ nonsingular matrix, Λ_{f_1} (which is of order $m_1 \times m_1$) is the block associated with the eigenvalues of F which lie inside the unit circle, and Λ_{f_2} (which is of order $m_2 \times m_2$) represents the block associated with the eigenvalues of F which fall outside the unit circle.[24] Using (3.46), we may rewrite (3.35) in the form of two separate blocks of equations:

$$\bar{\mathbf{Y}}_{t1} = \Lambda_{f_1} E(\bar{\mathbf{Y}}_{t+1,1} | \Omega_t) + \bar{\mathbf{W}}_{t1}, \tag{3.47}$$

$$\bar{\mathbf{Y}}_{t2} = \Lambda_{f_2} E(\bar{\mathbf{Y}}_{t+1,2} | \Omega_t) + \bar{\mathbf{W}}_{t2}, \tag{3.48}$$

where

$$\bar{\mathbf{Y}}_t = T^{-1}\mathbf{Y}_t, \quad \bar{\mathbf{W}}_t = T^{-1}\mathbf{W}_t, \quad \bar{\mathbf{Y}}_t = \begin{pmatrix} \bar{\mathbf{Y}}_{t1} \\ \bar{\mathbf{Y}}_{t2} \end{pmatrix}, \quad \bar{\mathbf{W}}_t = \begin{pmatrix} \bar{\mathbf{W}}_{t1} \\ \bar{\mathbf{W}}_{t2} \end{pmatrix}.$$

Clearly, we could now proceed to derive a forward solution for (3.47) and a backward solution for (3.48). An alternative way to proceed is to derive a solution for (3.48) using the martingale difference technique. The general solution to (3.48), in analogy to (3.38), is given by

$$\bar{\mathbf{Y}}_{t2} = -\sum_{j=1}^{t-1} \Lambda_{f_2}^{-j} \bar{\mathbf{W}}_{t-j,2} + \Lambda_{f_2}^{-t} \mathcal{M}_{t2}, \tag{3.49}$$

where $\{\mathcal{M}_{t2}\}$ is a martingale vector process of order m_2. A different characterization of (3.49) may then be obtained by rewriting this equation system in
martingale difference form. This may be accomplished by solving (3.49) for
$\mathcal{M}_{t2}$ and subtracting the resultant expression from the same relation evaluated
at $t - 1$. Doing so, one obtains

$$\bar{\mathbf{Y}}_{t2} = \Lambda_{f_2}^{-1}\bar{\mathbf{Y}}_{t-1,2} - \Lambda_{f_2}^{-1}\bar{\mathbf{W}}_{t-1,2} + \boldsymbol{\xi}_t, \qquad (3.50)$$

where $\boldsymbol{\xi}_t = \Lambda_{f_2}^{-1}(\mathcal{M}_{t2} - \mathcal{M}_{t-1,2})$ is a martingale difference process of order m_2.
Combining (3.50) with the forward solution to (3.47) (assuming (3.40) holds),
an alternative characterization of the general solution in the case of F having
m_1 roots inside and m_2 roots outside the unit circle is given by (after stacking
the blocks of $\mathbf{Y}_t$ and substituting for $\mathbf{Y}_t$ from (3.32))

$$\mathbf{y}_t = (C + Q)\mathbf{y}_{t-1} - QC\mathbf{y}_{t-2} - Q\mathbf{W}_{t-1} + \sum_{i=0}^{\infty} G_i E(\mathbf{W}_{t+i}|\Omega_t) + \mathfrak{D}_t, \qquad (3.51)$$

where

$$Q = T\begin{pmatrix} 0_{m_1 \times m_1} & 0_{m_1 \times m_2} \\ 0_{m_2 \times m_1} & \Lambda_{f_2}^{-1} \end{pmatrix} T^{-1}, \quad G_i = T\begin{pmatrix} \Lambda_{f_1}^{i} & 0_{m_1 \times m_2} \\ 0_{m_2 \times m_1} & 0_{m_2 \times m_2} \end{pmatrix} T^{-1}, \quad \mathfrak{D}_t = T\begin{pmatrix} \Lambda_{f_1}^{-t}\mathcal{M}_{t1}^{f} \\ \boldsymbol{\xi}_t \end{pmatrix}.$$

If the stability criterion is imposed on the solution, the m_1 entries in $\mathcal{M}_{t1}^{f}$ have
to be equal to zero almost surely. The general stable solution will involve
multiplicity of dimension m_2, the order of the vector martingale difference
process $\boldsymbol{\xi}_t$.

Case 2: B is not invertible When B is singular, it is necessary to directly work
with the Jordan normal form of F, distinguishing between blocks corresponding
to the zero and nonzero eigenvalues of F. Let us set up the resultant transformation of (3.35) for the general case of respectively m_1 eigenvalues of F falling
inside the unit circle (but being nonzero), m_2 eigenvalues falling outside the
unit circle, and m_3 eigenvalues of F being zero ($m_1 + m_2 + m_3 = m$). The Jordan
normal form of F in this case is given by $F = T\Lambda T^{-1}$, where

$$\Lambda = \begin{pmatrix} \Lambda_{f_1} & 0_{m_1 \times m_2} & 0_{m_1 \times m_3} \\ 0_{m_2 \times m_1} & \Lambda_{f_2} & 0_{m_2 \times m_3} \\ 0_{m_3 \times m_1} & 0_{m_3 \times m_2} & \Lambda_{f_3} \end{pmatrix}, \qquad (3.52)$$

T is an $m \times m$ matrix, Λ_{f_1} (which is of order $m_1 \times m_1$) is the block associated
with the eigenvalues of F which lie inside the unit circle, Λ_{f_2} (which is of order
$m_2 \times m_2$) represents the block associated with the eigenvalues of F which fall
outside the unit circle, and Λ_{f_3} (which is of order $m_3 \times m_3$) is the block
associated with the eigenvalues of F which are zero. Using (3.52), we may
rewrite (3.35) in the form of three uncoupled blocks of equations:

$$\bar{\mathbf{Y}}_{t1} = \Lambda_{f_1} E(\bar{\mathbf{Y}}_{t+1,1}|\Omega_t) + \bar{\mathbf{W}}_{t1}, \qquad (3.53)$$

$$\bar{\mathbf{Y}}_{t2} = A_{f_2} E(\bar{\mathbf{Y}}_{t+1,2} | \Omega_t) + \bar{\mathbf{W}}_{t2}, \tag{3.54}$$

$$\bar{\mathbf{Y}}_{t3} = A_{f_3} E(\bar{\mathbf{Y}}_{t+1,3} | \Omega_t) + \bar{\mathbf{W}}_{t3}, \tag{3.55}$$

where

$$\bar{\mathbf{Y}}_t = T^{-1} \mathbf{Y}_t, \quad \bar{\mathbf{W}}_t = T^{-1} \mathbf{W}_t, \quad \bar{\mathbf{Y}}_t = \begin{pmatrix} \bar{\mathbf{Y}}_{t1} \\ \bar{\mathbf{Y}}_{t2} \\ \bar{\mathbf{Y}}_{t3} \end{pmatrix}, \quad \bar{\mathbf{W}}_t = \begin{pmatrix} \bar{\mathbf{W}}_{t1} \\ \bar{\mathbf{W}}_{t2} \\ \bar{\mathbf{W}}_{t3} \end{pmatrix}.$$

Equation systems (3.53) and (3.54) have the same general solutions as (3.47) and (3.48). The general solution to (3.55) is given by

$$\bar{\mathbf{Y}}_{t3} = A_{f_3}^j E(\bar{\mathbf{Y}}_{t+j,3} | \Omega_t) + \sum_{i=0}^{j-1} A_{f_3}^i E(\bar{\mathbf{W}}_{t+i,3} | \Omega_t)$$

for $j > 0$, which, by observing that A_{f_3} is a nil-potent matrix of order m_3,[25] can be rewritten as

$$\bar{\mathbf{Y}}_{t3} = \sum_{i=0}^{m_3-1} A_{f_3}^i E(\bar{\mathbf{W}}_{t+i,3} | \Omega_t). \tag{3.57}$$

Combining the general solutions for the three blocks (3.53) to (3.55), we obtain after substituting for Y_t from (3.32) (assuming (3.40) holds)

$$\mathbf{y}_t = (C + Q)\mathbf{y}_{t-1} - QC\mathbf{y}_{t-2} - Q\mathbf{W}_{t-1} + \sum_{i=0}^{\infty} G_i E(\mathbf{W}_{t+i} | \Omega_t) \tag{3.58}$$

$$+ \sum_{i=0}^{m_3-1} H_i E(\mathbf{W}_{t+i} | \Omega_t) + \mathfrak{D}_t,$$

where

$$Q = T \begin{pmatrix} 0_{m_1 \times m_1} & 0_{m_1 \times m_2} & 0_{m_1 \times m_3} \\ 0_{m_2 \times m_1} & A_{f_2}^{-1} & 0_{m_2 \times m_3} \\ 0_{m_3 \times m_1} & 0_{m_3 \times m_2} & 0_{m_3 \times m_3} \end{pmatrix} T^{-1}, \quad G_i = T \begin{pmatrix} A_{f_1}^i & 0_{m_1 \times m_2} & 0_{m_1 \times m_3} \\ 0_{m_2 \times m_1} & 0_{m_2 \times m_2} & 0_{m_2 \times m_3} \\ 0_{m_3 \times m_1} & 0_{m_3 \times m_2} & 0_{m_3 \times m_3} \end{pmatrix} T^{-1},$$

$$H_i = T \begin{pmatrix} 0_{m_1 \times m_1} & 0_{m_1 \times m_2} & 0_{m_1 \times m_3} \\ 0_{m_2 \times m_1} & 0_{m_2 \times m_2} & 0_{m_2 \times m_3} \\ 0_{m_3 \times m_1} & 0_{m_3 \times m_2} & A_{f_3}^i \end{pmatrix} T^{-1}, \quad \mathfrak{D}_t = T \begin{pmatrix} A_{f_1}^{-t} M_{t1}^f \\ \xi_t \\ 0_{m_3 \times 1} \end{pmatrix}.$$

If again the stability criterion is imposed on the solution (3.58), the entries in $\mathfrak{D}_t$ associated with the vector martingale process M_{t1}^f have to be equal to zero almost surely. Consequently, the general stable solution has a multiplicity of order m_2.

Obviously, the solution given by (3.58) may be further specialized if m_1 or m_2 equals zero.

2.3.3 Computational considerations In implementing the quadratic determinantal equation approach set out above, we need to address explicitly two practical problems. Firstly, the matrix C (and hence the matrix F) defined by the quadratic matrix equation (3.34) has to be computed. Secondly, the forward part of the solution, given by expressions such as $\sum_{i=0}^{\infty} F^i E(\mathbf{W}_{t+i}|\Omega_t)$ in (3.43), $\sum_{i=0}^{\infty} G_i E(\mathbf{W}_{t+i}|\Omega_t)$ in (3.51), and $\sum_{i=0}^{\infty} G_i E(\mathbf{W}_{t+i}|\Omega_i) + \sum_{i=0}^{m_3-1} H_i E(\mathbf{W}_{t+i}|\Omega_t)$ in (3.58), needs to be computed in a tractable manner.

Consider first possible ways of computing C. A brute force procedure would, of course, be to obtain a solution by applying numerical methods directly to (3.34). While this is very easy to implement in that one just has to iterate on an initial choice for C, such a procedure may be sensitive to the initial conditions employed.[26] An alternative algorithm is obtained if one observes[27] that every eigenvalue λ_c of a solution C to (3.34) satisfies the quadratic determinantal equation:

$$\det(B\lambda_c^2 - I_m\lambda_c + A) = 0. \tag{3.59}$$

Note that there are m pairs of such eigenvalues. Having solved for the eigenvalues, one can also compute the corresponding eigenvectors of C (using $(B\lambda_c^2 - I_m\lambda_c + A)e_j = 0$, $j = 1, 2, \ldots, m$), and, through "inverting" the appropriate canonical form, arrive at solutions for C.[28] The canonical form will be either a diagonal matrix with the eigenvalues along the main diagonal (if the eigenvectors are linearly independent) or a Jordan normal form (if at least two of the eigenvectors are linearly dependent). In both cases, the computations involved are rather straightforward, as one may without loss of generality assume that at most the eigenvalue zero is of geometric multiplicity greater than one. We will provide a justification for this assertion below.

An even simpler method of computing C is available in the special case where the matrices A and B commute and all their eigenvectors are linearly independent. In that case, there exists an $m \times m$ matrix T such that $T^{-1}AT = \Lambda_a$ and $T^{-1}BT = \Lambda_b$, where Λ_a and Λ_b are diagonal matrices with the diagonal elements being equal to the eigenvalues of A and B. Equation (3.34) therefore becomes

$$\Lambda_b T^{-1} C^2 T - T^{-1} CT + \Lambda_a = 0_m. \tag{3.60}$$

Solutions C to (3.60) can be chosen to be of a form such that $T^{-1}C^2T$ and $T^{-1}CT$ are diagonal. We then have

$$\Lambda_b \Lambda_c^2 - \Lambda_c + \Lambda_a = 0_m, \tag{3.61}$$

which is a simple alternative to (3.59) for computing the eigenvalues of C. One may then again convert the diagonal form of C, Λ_c, to arrive at a solution for C.

To actually compute solution paths of y_t, it is necessary to characterize the forward part of the solution (i.e. terms such as $\sum_{i=0}^{\infty} F^i E(\mathbf{W}_{t+i}|\Omega_t)$ in (3.43)) (if it arises) in a tractable finite order form. Here we suggest a recursive method to implement this task, which may be viewed as an alternative to the

Wiener-Kolmogorov optimal prediction formulae discussed in Whittle (1963) and subsequently adapted in Hansen and Sargent (1980; 1981b). We note, however, that the Whittle approach requires the $\{\mathbf{W}_t\}$ process to be linear or normally distributed, but our procedure does not. This method is also attractive in that it allows the user to determine a horizon within which expectations of future realizations of the forcing variables do matter for current decisions.[29] For expositional simplicity let us base our discussion on (3.43), imposing also the stability condition. Decompose (3.43) into its backward and forward part:

$$\mathbf{y}_t = \mathbf{y}_{tb} + \mathbf{y}_{tf}, \quad \text{where } \mathbf{y}_{tb} = C\mathbf{y}_{t-1}, \quad \mathbf{y}_{tf} = \sum_{i=0}^{\infty} F^i E(\mathbf{W}_{t+i}|\Omega_t). \qquad (3.62)$$

For an arbitrary choice of the terminal value $\mathbf{y}_{t+N+1,f} = \bar{\mathbf{y}}_f$, N is then chosen such that $\|F^{N+1}\bar{\mathbf{y}}_f\| < \varepsilon$, where ε is an arbitrary vector of small positive numbers chosen by the economic agent or the econometrician (its significance will become clear momentarily). Then from (3.62) it follows that

$$\mathbf{y}_{t+N,f} = F\mathbf{y}_{t+N+1,f} + E(\mathbf{W}_{t+N}|\Omega_t), \qquad (3.63)$$
$$\vdots$$
$$\mathbf{y}_{t,f} = F\mathbf{y}_{t+1,f} + E(\mathbf{W}_t|\Omega_t).$$

Working recursively backwards from time $t + N - 1$, one obtains

$$\mathbf{y}_{t+N-1,f} = F(F\bar{\mathbf{y}}_f + E(\mathbf{W}_{t+N}|\Omega_t)) + E(\mathbf{W}_{t+N-1}|\Omega_t) \qquad (3.64)$$
$$= F^2\bar{\mathbf{y}}_f + FE(\mathbf{W}_{t+N}|\Omega_t) + E(\mathbf{W}_{t+N-1}|\Omega_t),$$
$$\vdots$$
$$\mathbf{y}_{t,f} = F^{N+1}\bar{\mathbf{y}}_f + F^N E(\mathbf{W}_{t+N}|\Omega_t) + F^{N-1}E(\mathbf{W}_{t+N-1}|\Omega_t)$$
$$+ \ldots + FE(\mathbf{W}_t|\Omega_t) + E(\mathbf{W}_t|\Omega_t).$$

Rewriting the last equation yields

$$\mathbf{y}_{tf} = F^{N+1}\bar{\mathbf{y}}_f + \sum_{i=0}^{N} F^i E(\mathbf{W}_{t+i}|\Omega_t). \qquad (3.65)$$

Since the first term on the right-hand side of (3.65) was chosen so as to be negligible, the forward part of the solution does not depend on $\bar{\mathbf{y}}_f$, and all that remains is to evaluate the second term on the right-hand side of (3.65) for the specific representation chosen for the stochastic process generating the forcing variables (i.e. to solve forward for $E(\mathbf{W}_{t+i}|\Omega_t)$) (for $i = 0, 1, 2, \ldots, N$). However, the terminal condition chosen initially may not be a good one. One should therefore compute the forward solution $\mathbf{y}_{tf}$ (using the above backward recursive procedure) for different values of N and ensure that the forward solution $\mathbf{y}_{tf}$ is not sensitive to the choice of the terminal values, $\bar{\mathbf{y}}_f$.

2.3.4 Characterizing the nature of the solutions In this section we consider the conditions under which the canonical multivariate rational expectations model (3.4) has a unique stable solution. We have already seen that the general solution can be decomposed into a backward and a forward component, given respectively by $\mathbf{y}_{tb} = C\mathbf{y}_{t-1}$ and the solution to the multivariate rational expectations model $\mathbf{y}_{tf} = FE(\mathbf{y}_{t+1,f}|\Omega_t) + \mathbf{W}_t$. The matrices C and F are defined by (3.34) and (3.36). The stability of the solution $\mathbf{y}_t = \mathbf{y}_{tb} + \mathbf{y}_{tf}$ therefore depends crucially on whether these two components are stable. For a given stable forward solution (which, as one may recall from our discussion in the previous section, requires all eigenvalues of F to fall inside the unit circle and the condition (3.40)), the solution is stable if all eigenvalues of C fall inside the unit circle. In this case, referred to by Sargan (1983; 1984) as the "regular case", the unique stable solution is given by (3.43):

$$\mathbf{y}_t = C\mathbf{y}_{t-1} + \sum_{i=0}^{\infty} F^i E(\mathbf{W}_{t+i}|\Omega_t).$$

Since matrix C satisfies the second-order matrix polynomial equation $BC^2 - C + A = 0_m$ (see (3.34)), then every eigenvalue λ_c of a solution C to this matrix polynomial equation also satisfies the quadratic determinantal equation (3.59):

$$\det(B\lambda_c^2 - I_m\lambda_c + A) = 0,$$

and the existence of a unique solution will depend on whether (3.59) has pairs of eigenvalues which satisfy the regularity conditions. In what follows we first consider the case where A and B commute, distinguishing between cases where A and B are nonsingular and when they have zero eigenvalues. An immediate corollary can then be provided for the case when the even stronger relationship $B = \beta A$ $(0 < \beta < 1)$ holds and B is nonsingular. Finally, we discuss the general case where no specific relationships between A and B are assumed.

Consider first the case where A and B commute.

Proposition 2 Suppose that
  (i) the coefficient matrices A and B in (3.4) commute,
  (ii) all eigenvalues of A and B, denoted by λ_a and λ_b, are nonzero and satisfy

$$\left(\frac{1}{\lambda_b^2} + 2\left(\left|\frac{\lambda_a}{\lambda_b}\right| - \frac{\lambda_a}{\lambda_b}\right)\right)^{0.5} > \left|\frac{\lambda_a}{\lambda_b}\right| + 1, \tag{3.66}$$

    and
  (iii) all their eigenvectors are linearly independent.

Then the unique stable solution of (3.4) (assuming it exists) is given by (3.43):

$$\mathbf{y}_t = C\mathbf{y}_{t-1} + \sum_{i=0}^{\infty} F^i E(\mathbf{W}_{t+i}|\Omega_t).$$

        ■

Remark   The relevant pairs of eigenvalues of A and B referred to in condition (ii) are determined through the ordering of the eigenvalues along the main diagonal of the matrices $\Lambda_a = T^{-1}AT$ and $\Lambda_b = T^{-1}BT$, where T is a nonsingular $m \times m$ matrix that simultaneously diagonalizes A and B.

Proof of proposition 2   Recall that if A and B commute, the equation defining C, (3.34), can be simplified to (3.61):

$$\Lambda_b \Lambda_c^2 - \Lambda_c + \Lambda_a = 0_m.$$

Now we first show that, under condition (3.66), all m pairs of roots to

$$\Lambda_b \Lambda_c^2 - \Lambda_c + \Lambda_a = 0_m$$

will be such that one root falls inside the unit circle, and the other root falls outside the unit circle. Pick anyone of the roots of (3.61) falling inside the unit circle and denote it by $\tilde{\lambda}_c$, and denote its corresponding root falling outside the unit circle by $\tilde{\lambda}_c'$. Starting from (3.66), and noting from (3.61) that $\tilde{\lambda}_c \tilde{\lambda}_c' = \lambda_a/\lambda_b$ and $\tilde{\lambda}_c + \tilde{\lambda}_c' = 1/\lambda_b$, one easily arrives at $(1 - |\tilde{\lambda}_c|)(|\tilde{\lambda}_c'| - 1) > 0$, which verifies that the roots of (3.61) satisfy the regularity conditions, namely for each pair one root will fall inside the unit circle and the other outside it. To compute the eigenvalues of F, recall that F is defined as $F = (I_m - BC)^{-1}B$. It can then be easily seen that F will commute with A, B, and C as well. Consequently, T diagonalizes F as well. Denote the eigenvalues of F by λ_f. Then $\lambda_f = (1 - \lambda_b \lambda_c)^{-1}\lambda_b$. Evaluating this expression for $\tilde{\lambda}_c$, we have

$$\lambda_f = (1 - \lambda_c \tilde{\lambda}_c)^{-1}\lambda_b. \tag{3.67}$$

Using (3.67) and observing from (3.61) that $(1 - \lambda_b \tilde{\lambda}_c)^{-1} = \tilde{\lambda}_c/\lambda_a$, it follows that $\lambda_f = \tilde{\lambda}_c \lambda_b/\lambda_a$. Recalling that $\tilde{\lambda}_c \tilde{\lambda}_c' = \lambda_a/\lambda_b$, we obtain $\lambda_f = 1/\tilde{\lambda}_c'$, which establishes that λ_f is equal to the inverse of the root of (3.61) that falls outside the unit circle. Since $\tilde{\lambda}_c$ was an arbitrarily selected root falling inside the unit circle, we have thus proved that all eigenvalues of F will fall inside the unit circle, as required for the forward part of (3.43) to be well defined. Furthermore, $(I_m - BC)$ will be invertible since invertibility only requires $\tilde{\lambda}_c \lambda_b \neq 1$, which from (3.61) is equivalent to $\lambda_a \neq 0$.   QED

An immediate corollary arises when $B = \beta A$ $(0 < \beta < 1)$, the case analyzed by Hansen and Sargent (1981a).

Corollary 1   Suppose that
(i)   the coefficient matrices A and B in (3.4) are related through $B = \beta A$, and
(ii) B is nonsingular.

Then the unique solution (if it exists) to (3.4) is given by (3.43):

$$\mathbf{y}_t = C\mathbf{y}_{t-1} + \sum_{i=0}^{\infty} F^i E(\mathbf{W}_{t+i}|\Omega_t). \qquad \blacksquare$$

Proof of corollary 1 When $B = \beta A$, the matrices A and B trivially commute, and thus (3.61) holds. One may easily verify that the roots of (3.61) satisfy the regularity conditions. The remainder of the proof can follow exactly the same reasoning as that of proposition 2.[30]   QED

It may be useful to note that for the dynamic adjustment cost models considered in section 4.2, for which $B = \beta A$ is often satisfied, B will usually be nonsingular and therefore condition (ii) is also satisfied.

What happens if we allow for one or more eigenvalues of A and/or B to be zero? The arguments in proposition 2 then have to be modified as follows. First, if all eigenvalues of B are zero, then $B = 0_m$, and the model reduces to $y_t = Ay_{t-1} + w_t$, and no further computations are required. Consider the more interesting case where some (but not all) eigenvalues of B equal zero (see also proposition 3 below). Then the corresponding eigenvalues of C will be equal to that of A, as can be seen from (3.59). For stability, therefore, these eigenvalues need to fall inside the unit circle. Furthermore, from (3.59) we obtain, as expected, $\lambda_f = 0$. The requirement that $(I_m - BC)$ be invertible continues to be clearly satisfied if some eigenvalue of B equals zero, since $\tilde{\lambda}_c \lambda_b = 0$. Second, if all eigenvalues of A are equal to zero, then $A = 0_m$, and $y_t = BE(y_{t+1}|\Omega_t) + w_t$, which has a unique stable solution given by $y_t = \sum_{i=0}^{\infty} B^i E(w_{t+i}|\Omega_t)$ if all eigenvalues of B fall inside the unit circle and a condition analogous to (3.40) holds. If some (but not all) eigenvalues of A are equal to zero (see again proposition 3 below), observing (3.59) and imposing the requirement that $(I_m - BC)$ be invertible readily yields that the corresponding eigenvalues of C must be zero for (3.43) to be well defined.

The above reasoning does not exploit the assumption that all eigenvectors of A and B are linearly independent. We now relax this assumption more formally. While it is maintained that the eigenvectors corresponding to the nonzero eigenvalues of A and B are linearly independent, we allow for there being multiple zero eigenvalues which do not have linear elementary divisors. It may be added that assuming that the nonzero eigenvalues of A and B possess linear elementary divisors seems to be a rather innocuous assumption. This is because given any matrix M, we can always find a matrix M' with distinct eigenvalues such that $\|M - M'\| \leq \varepsilon$, where ε is any preassigned (arbitrarily small) positive quantity (see for example Bellman, 1960).

Proposition 3 Suppose that
(i) the coefficient matrices A and B in (3.4) commute,
(ii) the eigenvectors corresponding to the nonzero eigenvalues of A and B are linearly independent where the nonzero eigenvalues of A and B, denoted as λ_a and λ_b, satisfy (3.66):[31]

$$\left(\frac{1}{\lambda_b^2} + 2 \left(\left| \frac{\lambda_a}{\lambda_b} \right| - \frac{\lambda_a}{\lambda_b} \right) \right)^{0.5} > \left| \frac{\lambda_a}{\lambda_b} \right| + 1,$$

(iii) the eigenvalues of A corresponding to the zero eigenvalues of B fall inside the unit circle, and

(iv) the eigenvalues of C corresponding to the zero eigenvalues of A equal zero.

Then the unique solution to (3.4) (if it exists) is given by (3.43):

$$\mathbf{y}_t = C\mathbf{y}_{t-1} + \sum_{i=0}^{\infty} F^i (I_m - BC)^{-1} E(\mathbf{W}_{t+i}|\Omega_t). \qquad \blacksquare$$

The basic problem arising if not all eigenvectors of A and/or B are linearly independent is that these matrices are not diagonalizable, and equation (3.61) will not hold any longer. However, since A and B commute, we can again pick a solution C to (3.34) which will be commuting with A and B. Then it is still true that the eigenvalues of A, B, and C are related through[32]

$$\lambda_b \lambda_c^2 - \lambda_c + \lambda_a = 0. \qquad (3.68)$$

Proof of proposition 3   The reasoning advanced in the proof of proposition 2 which showed (assuming A and B were diagonalizable) that if the eigenvalues of C fall inside the unit circle, so must the eigenvalues of F, goes through unmodified, since (3.68) holds: B and C commute, and they thus possess property P, making possible the application of Frobenius' theorem as restated in Motzkin and Taussky (1952) (see the discussion in note 32). In summary, therefore, if A and/or B are not diagonalizable but still commute, nothing changes except that the computation of C becomes slightly more involved.   QED

Next consider the case where A and B do not commute. Then, conditions on the A and B matrices in a form as simple as (3.66) can no longer be established, as there are in general no procedures available to compute the eigenvalues of products and/or sums of matrices making use only of the eigenvalues and eigenvectors of the component matrices if the matrices involved do not possess property P (see note 32). The condition that the eigenvalues of C be inside the unit circle is therefore (implicitly) given by (3.59). Also, it is in general not possible to show that if the eigenvalues of C fall inside the unit circle, so do the eigenvalues of F (and therefore establish that the unique stable solution given by (3.43) has to hold). However, we can readily give an (implicit) condition when this will still be true. Recalling the definition of F, it is clear that its eigenvalues are given through

$$\det((I_m - BC)\lambda_f^2 - B\lambda_f) = 0. \qquad (3.69)$$

It therefore has to be determined on a case by case basis whether the unique stable solution (3.43) exists even if all eigenvalues of C fall inside the unit circle. See section 4.1 for a discussion of this case in the context of a real business cycle model. Should some of the eigenvalues of F fall outside the unit circle, a multiplicity of solutions will arise. These solutions can be readily computed using a martingale difference method to be discussed below.

We next turn our attention to the case where the roots of (3.59) do not satisfy the "regularity conditions."

Proposition 4 Suppose that more than m roots of (3.59)

$$\det(B\lambda_c^2 - I_m\lambda_c + A) = 0$$

fall outside the unit circle. Then no bounded solution exists. ∎

Proof of proposition 4 If more than m roots of (3.59) fall outside the unit circle, the matrix C will have some eigenvalues which fall outside the unit circle and the backward part of the general solution (3.38) is not bounded anymore.   QED

In what we have called the "irregular case" (more than m of the roots of (3.59) falling inside the unit circle), an infinite number of stable solutions is possible (the degree of multiplicity is given by the number of roots of (3.59) falling outside the unit circle). These solutions are derived in (3.51) and (3.58).

To summarize, in the "regular case" the unique stable solution (if it holds) is given by (3.43). The existence of this solution was proven for the case when A and B commute (and are not zero matrices). If this restriction on A and B does not hold, it has to be determined on a case by case basis whether (3.43) is well defined, using condition (3.69). Should some of the eigenvalues of F fall outside the unit circle, the Jordan normal form of F has to be split into blocks, one associated with the eigenvalues of F which fall inside the unit circle and the other with the eigenvalues of F which fall outside the unit circle. For the case of "irregular" roots, all possible multiple solutions are characterized by (3.51) (if B is invertible) and by (3.58) (if B is singular). The question of how many eigenvalues of F fall outside the unit circle (which we can answer analytically only in the case where A and B commute) only matters to the extent that it determines the dimensions of the blocks (associated with the eigenvalues falling inside or outside the unit circle) of Λ in (3.46) or (3.52). The multiplicity of the stable solutions is characterized by vector martingale (difference) processes such as $\mathcal{M}_t$ in (3.39) or $\mathcal{D}_t$ in (3.51) or (3.58): any martingale (difference) process involving innovations in the forcing variables can be a component of $\mathcal{M}_t$ or $\mathcal{D}_t$ (model-intrinsic multiplicity), as can any martingale (difference) process in variables other than w_t ("sunspots").

2.3.5 Cointegration properties of the rational expectations solution

One of the advantages of the quadratic determinantal equation solution method is not only that it allows for integrated stochastic processes driving the forcing variables, but that cointegrating restrictions on the solution processes for the decision variables can also be readily derived. Let us first turn to the case where (3.4) has the unique stable solution given by (3.43). Since in this section we need to be more precise about the number of forcing variables driving the system, we introduce the following additional notation: let

$\mathbf{w}_t = D\tilde{\mathbf{w}}_t$, where D is an $m \times s$ matrix of fixed coefficients, and s, the dimension of the column vector $\tilde{\mathbf{w}}_t$, represents the number of forcing variables. It is assumed that $\tilde{\mathbf{w}}_t$ follows a first-order VAR process:

$$\tilde{\mathbf{w}}_t = R\tilde{\mathbf{w}}_{t-1} + \mathbf{v}_t, \quad \mathbf{v}_t \sim \text{iid}(0_{s \times 1}, \Sigma_v). \tag{3.70}$$

Using (3.43), we now obtain the following VAR(1) model:

$$\begin{pmatrix} I_m & -\Sigma_{i=0}^{\infty} F^i (I_m - BC)^{-1} DR^i \\ 0_{s \times m} & I_s \end{pmatrix} \begin{pmatrix} \mathbf{y}_t \\ \tilde{\mathbf{w}}_t \end{pmatrix} = \begin{pmatrix} C & 0_{m \times s} \\ 0_{s \times m} & R \end{pmatrix} \begin{pmatrix} \mathbf{y}_{t-1} \\ \tilde{\mathbf{w}}_{t-1} \end{pmatrix} + \begin{pmatrix} 0_{m \times 1} \\ \mathbf{v}_t \end{pmatrix}. \tag{3.71}$$

It should be noted that unless an error term is tacked on to (3.43), the variance-covariance matrix of the innovations in (3.71) is singular. Suppose now that s_2 of the forcing variables are first-order integrated, while the remaining $s_1 (= s - s_2)$ are generated by covariance stationary processes. Thus

$$\tilde{\mathbf{w}}_t = \begin{pmatrix} \tilde{\mathbf{w}}_{1t} \\ \tilde{\mathbf{w}}_{2t} \end{pmatrix} = \begin{pmatrix} R_1 & 0_{s_1 \times s_2} \\ 0_{s_2 \times s_1} & I_{s_2} \end{pmatrix} \begin{pmatrix} \tilde{\mathbf{w}}_{1t-1} \\ \tilde{\mathbf{w}}_{2t-1} \end{pmatrix} + \begin{pmatrix} \mathbf{v}_{1t} \\ \mathbf{v}_{2t} \end{pmatrix}, \tag{3.72}$$

where all the roots of $\det(I_{s_1} - R_1\lambda)$ are greater than one in modulus. Substituting (3.72) back into (3.71) we obtain, after partitioning D as (D_1, D_2), with D_1 being $m \times s_1$ dimensional and D_2 being $m \times s_2$ dimensional,

$$\begin{pmatrix} I_m & -\Sigma_{i=0}^{\infty} F^i (I_m - BC)^{-1} D_1 R_1^i & -\Sigma_{i=0}^{\infty} F^i (I_m - BC)^{-1} D_2 \\ 0_{s_1 \times m} & I_{s_1} & 0_{s_1 \times s_2} \\ 0_{s_2 \times m} & 0_{s_2 \times s_1} & I_{s_2} \end{pmatrix} \begin{pmatrix} \mathbf{y}_t \\ \tilde{\mathbf{w}}_{1t} \\ \tilde{\mathbf{w}}_{2t} \end{pmatrix}$$

$$= \begin{pmatrix} C & 0_{m \times s_1} & 0_{m \times s_2} \\ 0_{s_1 \times m} & R_1 & 0_{s_1 \times s_2} \\ 0_{s_2 \times m} & 0_{s_2 \times s_1} & I_{s_2} \end{pmatrix} \begin{pmatrix} \mathbf{y}_{t-1} \\ \tilde{\mathbf{w}}_{1t-1} \\ \tilde{\mathbf{w}}_{2t-1} \end{pmatrix} + \begin{pmatrix} 0_{m \times 1} \\ \mathbf{v}_{1t} \\ \mathbf{v}_{2t} \end{pmatrix}, \tag{3.73}$$

or, in an obvious notation,

$$A_0 \mathbf{X}_t = A_1 \mathbf{X}_{t-1} + \mathbf{U}_t. \tag{3.74}$$

As is well known, the number of cointegrating relations in (3.73) is determined by the rank deficiency of the matrix $A_0 - A_1$. Noting that

$$A_0 - A_1 = \begin{pmatrix} I_m - C & -G_1 & -G_2 \\ 0_{s_1 \times m} & I_{s_1} - R_1 & 0_{s_1 \times s_2} \\ 0_{s_2 \times m} & 0_{s_2 \times s_1} & 0_{s_2} \end{pmatrix}, \tag{3.75}$$

where

$$G_1 = \sum_{i=0}^{\infty} F^i (I_m - BC)^{-1} D_1 R_1^i,$$

$$G_2 = (I_m - F)^{-1} (I_m - BC)^{-1} D_2,$$

it follows that the rank of $A_0 - A_1$ will be at most equal to $m + s_1$, thus suggesting that there are at most $m + s_1$ stationary relationships among the variables in the model.[33] However, s_1 of these "relations" refer to the $\tilde{w}_{1t}$ forcing variables that are I(0) by assumption. We are, therefore, left with m different cointegrating relations linking the endogenous variables, y_t, to the I(1) forcing variables, $\tilde{w}_{2t}$. The associated cointegrating vectors are given by

$$\beta' = (I_m - C, -G_2),$$

and may also be written equivalently as[34]

$$(I_m - A - B)y_t - D_2\tilde{w}_{2t} \sim I(0). \tag{3.76}$$

As is to be expected, only I(1) forcing variables enter the cointegrating relations. The number of I(1) forcing variables determine the number of common stochastic trends in the system.[35] The above result also suggests a simple method for obtaining the cointegrating relations for the structural model form (3.1). It simply involves abstracting from I(0) variables and ignoring the short-run dynamics implicit in the lagged and future expected values of y_t.

Let us next consider the case of multiple stable solutions as given by (3.58). Again stacking decision and forcing variables, and using (3.72), we obtain

$$
\begin{pmatrix}
I_m & -\sum_{i=0}^{\infty}(G_i + H_i)(I_m - BC)^{-1}D_1R_1^i & -\sum_{i=0}^{\infty}(G_i + H_i)(I_m - BC)^{-1}D_2I_{s_2} \\
0_{s_1 \times m} & I_{s_1} & 0_{s_1 \times s_2} \\
0_{s_2 \times m} & 0_{s_2 \times s_1} & I_{s_2}
\end{pmatrix}
\begin{pmatrix}
y_t \\
\tilde{w}_{1t} \\
\tilde{w}_{2t}
\end{pmatrix}
$$

$$
=
\begin{pmatrix}
C + Q & -Q(I - BC)^{-1}D_1 & -Q(I - BC)^{-1}D_2 \\
0_{s_1 \times m} & R_1 & 0_{s_1 \times s_2} \\
0_{s_2 \times m} & 0_{s_2 \times s_1} & I_{s_2}
\end{pmatrix}
\begin{pmatrix}
y_{t-1} \\
\tilde{w}_{1t-1} \\
\tilde{w}_{2t-1}
\end{pmatrix}
$$

$$
+
\begin{pmatrix}
-QC & 0_{m \times s_1} & 0_{m \times s_2} \\
0_{s_1 \times m} & 0_{s_1 \times s_1} & 0_{s_1 \times s_2} \\
0_{s_2 \times m} & 0_{s_2 \times s_1} & 0_{s_2 \times s_2}
\end{pmatrix}
\begin{pmatrix}
y_{t-2} \\
\tilde{w}_{1t-2} \\
\tilde{w}_{2t-2}
\end{pmatrix}
+
\begin{pmatrix}
\mathcal{D}_t \\
v_{1t} \\
v_{2t}
\end{pmatrix}, \tag{3.77}
$$

or, in an obvious notation,

$$A_0X_t = A_1X_{t-1} + A_2X_{t-2} + U_t. \tag{3.78}$$

In this case, the number of cointegrating restrictions is determined by the rank of the matrix $A_0 - A_1 - A_2$. Analogous to (3.75), this rank is in general equal to $m + s_1$, and again the number of cointegrating restrictions is entirely determined by the specification of the stochastic processes generating the forcing variables.

We conclude this section by referring to a related result due to Broze, Gouriéroux, and Szafarz (1990). Suppose that we restrict our attention to solutions of (3.4) which are (time-independent) absolute-summable linear combinations of the stochastic processes fundamental for the forcing variables, namely solutions of the type

$$\mathbf{y}_t = \sum_{j=0}^{\infty} C_j \boldsymbol{\varepsilon}_{t-j} \equiv C(L)\boldsymbol{\varepsilon}_t. \tag{3.79}$$

If a solution exists, it has (as was shown in our discussion of the solution procedures of Whiteman, 1983 and Salemi, 1986) an autoregressive moving average representation of the form

$$\Phi(L)\mathbf{y}_t = \Theta(L)\boldsymbol{\varepsilon}_t, \tag{3.80}$$

where $\Phi(L)$ and $\Theta(L)$ are $m \times m$ matrix lag polynomials, and, depending on the dimensionality of the solution set, restrictions may have to be imposed on the elements of $\Theta(L)$. Broze, Gouriéroux, and Szafarz show that if $\Theta(1)$ is nonsingular, then all multiple bounded solutions satisfy the same long-run equilibrium in that they have the same cointegration properties. This in turn means that the selection of a particular from a set of possible covariance stationary solutions affects only the adjustment path toward the equilibrium, but not the long-run equilibrium itself.

3   Estimation of the Canonical Multivariate Rational Expectations Model

In this section we consider the problem of estimating the canonical multivariate rational expectations model (3.4). The discussion here in large part adapts the exposition in Pesaran (1987, chapter 7) to the multivariate context, and we refer to the latter for a more detailed account.[36] It is well known that one may in general estimate rational expectations models such as (3.4) in two different ways. So-called "limited information" estimators do not require the model to be solved explicitly and can be readily applied to equation system (3.4), assuming the unknown parameters are identified and that a sufficient set of instruments or moment conditions exists.[37] The main strength of this method lies in the fact that it does not necessarily require a complete characterization of the processes generating the forcing variables. More efficient estimators are, however, available using "full information" methods which require an explicit characterization of the processes generating the forcing variables $\mathbf{w}_t$ in (3.4).

3.1   Limited Information Estimation

Consider the canonical multivariate rational expectations model (3.4). Consistent estimation of this equation system is straightforward to accomplish, since the orthogonality of the forecast errors

$$\boldsymbol{\xi}_{t+1} = \mathbf{y}_{t+1} - E(\mathbf{y}_{t+1}|\Omega_t) \tag{3.81}$$

to the information set Ω_t implied by the rational expectations hypothesis allows upon substituting $\boldsymbol{\xi}_{t+1}$ back into (3.4) to rewrite (3.4) as

$$\mathbf{y}_t - A\mathbf{y}_{t-1} - B\mathbf{y}_{t+1} - \mathbf{w}_t = \boldsymbol{\xi}_t. \tag{3.83}$$

and thus

$$\tag{3.83}$$

Choosing a set of instruments $\mathbf{z}_t$ (where $\mathbf{z}_t$ is in the agents' information set at time t), one can readily apply Hansen's (1982) generalized method of moments (GMM) estimator to (3.83), which in turn nests the various instrumental variable procedures suggested in the literature and reviewed in Pesaran (1987).[38] Two issues should be mentioned in this context. First, recalling the definition of $\mathbf{y}_t$, it contains terms $E(\mathbf{x}_{t+1}|\Omega_t)$, $E(\mathbf{x}_{t+2}|\Omega_t)$, ..., $E(\mathbf{x}_{t+n_2}|\Omega_t)$, implying that some of the m expectations revision processes in $\boldsymbol{\xi}_t$ have a serial correlation pattern not exploited by the GMM estimator. These are exploited by the procedure of Hayashi and Sims (1983) which is an instrumental variable method conditional on a forward filtering, taking into account serial correlation structures in components of $\boldsymbol{\xi}_t$. Second, in the present context it is not clear whether the GMM estimates of the structural parameters in A and B are indeed consistent. This is because the cross-moment matrix of instruments and regressors in (3.83) cannot be established to be nonsingular without explicitly solving the model.[39]

3.2 Full Information Estimation

To estimate (3.4) by full information methods, one can readily use the quadratic determinantal equation method to construct the likelihood function.[40] For ease of exposition, let us focus in what follows on the regular case of m roots of (3.59) falling inside and m roots of (3.59) falling outside the unit circle. Let us also assume that the forcing variables are given by

$$\mathbf{w}_t = \Gamma\mathbf{z}_t + \boldsymbol{\varepsilon}_t, \tag{3.84}$$

in which

$$\mathbf{z}_t = R\mathbf{z}_{t-1} + \mathbf{v}_t, \tag{3.85}$$

where the fixed coefficient matrices Γ and R are of dimension $m \times s$ and $s \times s$, respectively, $\mathbf{v}_t \sim \text{iid}\,N(0_{s\times 1}, \Sigma_v)$, $\boldsymbol{\varepsilon}_t \sim \text{iid}\,N(0_{m\times 1}, \Sigma_\varepsilon)$, $E(\mathbf{v}_{it}\boldsymbol{\varepsilon}_{jt}) = 0$ for all entries i and j in $\mathbf{v}_t$ and $\boldsymbol{\varepsilon}_t$, and s is the dimension of the vector of the disturbance term, $\mathbf{v}_t$.

The unique stable solution (3.43) can then be written in the form

$$\mathbf{y}_t = C\mathbf{y}_{t-1} + \sum_{i=0}^{\infty} F^i(I_m - BC)^{-1}\Gamma R^i\mathbf{z}_t + (I_m - BC)^{-1}\boldsymbol{\varepsilon}_t, \tag{3.86}$$

which can be easily solved for $\boldsymbol{\varepsilon}_t$:

$$\boldsymbol{\varepsilon}_t = (I_m - BC)\left(\mathbf{y}_t - C\mathbf{y}_{t-1} - \sum_{i=0}^{\infty} F^i(I_m - BC)^{-1}\Gamma R^i\mathbf{z}_t\right). \tag{3.87}$$

The log-likelihood function $l(\theta)$, where θ contains all structural coefficients in A, B, Γ, R, Σ_v and Σ_ε, is then given by

$$l(\theta) = -\left(\frac{mT}{2} + \frac{sT}{2}\right)\ln(2\pi) - \frac{T}{2}\ln\left(\det\left(\Sigma_\varepsilon\right)\right) - \frac{T}{2}\ln\left(\det\left(\Sigma_v\right)\right), \qquad (3.88)$$

$$-\frac{1}{2}\sum_{t=1}^{T}\varepsilon_t'\,\Sigma_\varepsilon^{-1}\,\varepsilon_t - \frac{1}{2}\sum_{t=1}^{T}v_t'\,\Sigma_v^{-1}\,v_t,$$

where T denotes the sample size.

Maximum likelihood estimation is consequently achieved by maximizing (3.88) with respect to θ, assuming that the model is identified. Notice that the full maximum likelihood estimation method directly takes account of the cross-equation restrictions linking the coefficients of the decision rules to those of the forcing variables.

4   Applications and Some Numerical Examples

4.1   Real Business Cycle Models

This section shows how to solve a standard real business cycle model using the quadratic determinantal equation method of section 2.3. This solution is then compared with those obtained using the (log-) linear-quadratic approximation method of Kydland and Prescott (1982) and Hansen and Prescott (1995) and the undetermined coefficients procedure of Christiano (1991). The solution obtained by the quadratic determinantal equation method also allows one to directly approach the problem of evaluating real business cycle models without having to recourse to stochastic simulation. This section does not, however, aim to provide a comprehensive evaluation of real business cycle models.[41]

The model considered here is one of Christiano and Eichenbaum (1992), which augments a basic indivisible labor model by a demand shock in the form of innovations to government consumption and specifies the technological variation to be first-order integrated.[42] To formalize the setup, we employ the familiar insight that the aggregate laws of motion resulting from a Pareto-optimal competitive equilibrium correspond to those generated by a social planning problem. The social planner maximizes[43]

$$\max E\left\{\sum_{t=0}^{\infty}\beta^t[\ln(C_t) + \theta(N - N_t)]\,|\,\Omega_0\right\} \qquad (3.89)$$

subject to the aggregate resource constraint

$$C_t + K_{t+1} - (1 - \delta)K_t + G_t = Y_t, \qquad (3.90)$$

the technology constraint

$$Y_t = K_t^\alpha(X_t N_t)^{1-\alpha}, \qquad (3.91)$$

and the laws of motion for the forcing variables

$$\Delta \ln(X_t) \equiv \gamma_t = \gamma + \varepsilon_{tx}, \qquad \varepsilon_{tx} \sim \text{iid } N(0, \sigma_x^2), \qquad (3.92)$$

$$\ln(g_t) = \rho_0 + \rho_1 \ln(g_{t-1}) + \varepsilon_{tg}, \qquad \varepsilon_{tg} \sim \text{iid } N(0, \sigma_g^2), \qquad (3.93)$$

where $g_t = G_t/X_t$. Since the specification of labor-augmenting technological progress in (3.92) implies mean steady state growth at rate γ, it will be convenient to transform the economy into a covariance stationary one by defining the scaled variables $y_t = Y_t/X_t$, $k_t = K_t/X_{t-1}$, $c_t = C_t/X_t$, and $i_t = I_t/X_t$. Employing the maximum principle discussed, for example, in Whittle (1982), the social planner maximizes the Lagrangian for this transformed economy:

$$L_0 = E\left\{ \sum_{t=0}^{\infty} \beta^t (\ln(c_t) + \theta(N - N_t) + \ln(X_t)) \Big| \Omega_0 \right\}$$

$$\qquad (3.94)$$

$$+ E\left\{ \sum_{t=0}^{\infty} \lambda_t \beta^t (k_t^\alpha N_t^{1-\alpha} \exp(-\alpha\gamma_t) - c_t - k_{t+1} + (1-\delta)k_t \exp(-\gamma_t) - |\Omega_0 g_t) \right\},$$

with respect to $\{c_t\}$, $\{k_{t+1}\}$ and $\{N_t\}$. The first-order conditions for this optimization problem are nonlinear in the decision variables, c_t, k_{t+1}, and N_t, and in general do not lend themselves to an exact solution.[44] A standard approximate solution procedure is to compute the nonstochastic steady state values of the variables of the system, and then log-linearize the first-order conditions around the nonstochastic steady state values. Eliminating the shadow prices, λ_t, from these log-linearized first-order conditions, one then arrives at the following structural multivariate rational expectations equations:

$$M_{00} y_t = M_{10} y_{t-1} + M_{01} E(y_{t+1} | \Omega_t) + U_t, \qquad (3.95)$$

where

$$U_t = \begin{pmatrix} \tilde{s}_g \tilde{g}_t \\ \theta_1 \tilde{\gamma}_t \\ \alpha \tilde{\gamma}_t \\ \alpha \tilde{\gamma}_t \\ \phi \tilde{\gamma}_{t+1} \end{pmatrix}, \quad y_t = \begin{pmatrix} \tilde{k}_{t+1} \\ \tilde{N}_t \\ \tilde{c}_t \\ \tilde{y}_t \\ \tilde{i}_t \end{pmatrix}, \quad M_{00} = \begin{pmatrix} 0 & 0 & -\bar{s}_c & 1 & -\bar{s}_i \\ 1 & 0 & 0 & 0 & -(1-\theta_1) \\ 0 & -(1-\alpha) & 0 & 1 & 0 \\ 0 & \alpha & 1 & 0 & 0 \\ \theta_2 & 0 & -1 & 0 & 0 \end{pmatrix},$$

$$M_{10} = \begin{pmatrix} 0 & 0 & 0 & 0 \\ \theta_1 & 0 & 0 & 0 \\ \alpha & 0 & 0 & 0 \\ \alpha & 0 & 0 & 0 \\ 0 & 0 & 0 & 0 \end{pmatrix}, \quad M_{01} = \begin{pmatrix} 0 & 0 & 0 & 0 & 0 \\ 0 & 0 & 0 & 0 & 0 \\ 0 & 0 & 0 & 0 & 0 \\ 0 & 0 & 0 & 0 & 0 \\ 0 & \theta_2 & -1 & 0 & 0 \end{pmatrix},$$

where $\tilde{k}_t = \ln(k_t/\bar{k})$, $\tilde{N}_t = \ln(N_t/\bar{N})$, $\tilde{c}_t = \ln(c_t/\bar{c})$, $\tilde{y}_t = \ln(y_t/\bar{y})$, $\tilde{i}_t = \ln(i_t/\bar{i})$, $\tilde{g}_t = \ln(g_t/\bar{g})$, $\tilde{\gamma}_t = -(\gamma_t - \gamma)$, $\theta_1 = (1-\delta)\exp(-\gamma)$, $\theta_2 = \beta\alpha(1-\alpha)\bar{k}^{\alpha-1}\bar{N}^{1-\alpha} \exp(-\alpha\gamma)$, $\theta_3 = \bar{k}^{\alpha-1}\bar{N}^{1-\alpha}\exp(-\alpha\gamma)$, $\phi = \beta\alpha^2\theta_3 + \beta\theta_1$, $\bar{g}$ is the mean of g_t, and the nonstochastic steady state values $\bar{k}$, $\bar{N}$, $\bar{c}$, $\bar{y}$, and $\bar{i}$ satisfy the following nonlinear equations:

$$\bar{N} = \left[\frac{1-\alpha}{\theta} + \frac{\bar{g}}{\bar{s}_k^{\alpha/(1-\alpha)}\exp\left(-\frac{\alpha\gamma}{1-\alpha}\right)}\right]\Big/[(1-\delta)\exp(-\gamma))\bar{s}_k],$$

$$\bar{k} = (\exp(-\alpha\gamma)\bar{s}_k)^{1/(1-\alpha)}\bar{N},$$

$$\bar{y} = \bar{k}^\alpha\bar{N}^{1-\alpha}\exp(-\alpha\gamma),$$

$$\bar{i} = \bar{k} - (1-\delta)\exp(-\gamma)\bar{k},$$

$$\bar{c} = \bar{y} - \bar{i} - \bar{g},$$

$$\bar{s}_k = \frac{\alpha\beta}{1 - \beta(1-\delta)\exp(-\gamma)},$$

where $\bar{s}_k = \bar{k}/\bar{y}$, $\bar{s}_c = \bar{c}/\bar{y}$, $\bar{s}_i = \bar{i}/\bar{y}$, and $\bar{s}_g = \bar{g}/\bar{y}$.

The canonical form (3.4) for this problem is now obtained by premultiplying both sides of (3.95) by the inverse of M_{00}. This yields

$$A = M_{00}^{-1}M_{10}, \qquad B = M_{00}^{-1}M_{01}, \qquad \mathbf{w}_t = M_{00}^{-1}U_t.$$

It is now easily seen that A and B are singular with ranks at most equal to two, and do not commute. Notice also that $\mathbf{w}_t$ can be written more explicitly in terms of the forcing variables of the system as:

$$\mathbf{w}_t = M_{00}^{-1}D_0\mathbf{z}_t + M_{00}^{-1}D_1\mathbf{z}_{t+1}, \tag{3.96}$$

where

$$D_0 = \begin{pmatrix} \bar{s}_g & 0 \\ 0 & \theta_1 \\ 0 & \alpha \\ 0 & \alpha \\ 0 & 0 \end{pmatrix}, \qquad D_1 = \begin{pmatrix} 0 & 0 \\ 0 & 0 \\ 0 & 0 \\ 0 & 0 \\ 0 & \phi \end{pmatrix}, \qquad \mathbf{z}_t = \begin{pmatrix} \tilde{g}_t \\ \tilde{\gamma}_t \end{pmatrix}.$$

Using (3.92) and (3.93), the process for $\mathbf{z}_t$ can be (approximately) written compactly as a first-order Markov scheme:

$$\mathbf{z}_t = R\mathbf{z}_{t-1} + \boldsymbol{\varepsilon}_t, \qquad \boldsymbol{\varepsilon}_t \sim \text{iid}(0_{2\times1}, \Sigma) \tag{3.97}$$

where

$$\boldsymbol{\varepsilon}_t = \begin{pmatrix} \varepsilon_{tg} \\ -\varepsilon_{tx} \end{pmatrix}, \qquad R = \begin{pmatrix} \rho_1 & 0 \\ 0 & 0 \end{pmatrix}, \qquad \Sigma = \begin{pmatrix} \sigma_g^2 & 0 \\ 0 & \sigma_x^2 \end{pmatrix}.$$

The general solution for y_t in this example can now be readily obtained using the quadratic determinantal equation approach discussed above. The nature of the solution depends on the roots of the determinantal equation $\det(\lambda_b\lambda_c^2 - \lambda_c + \lambda_a) = 0$, and since A and B do not commute, can (within the framework of the quadratic determinantal equation) only be ascertained by considering a specific numerical application. For this purpose we first estimate the structural parameters by the generalized method of moments (GMM). The moment conditions are constructed using steady state relationships and some of the Euler equations for (3.94). As discussed in Christiano and Eichenbaum (1992), such GMM estimates in effect equate unconditional first moments in the sample data with those predicted by the model.[45] See appendix 1 for the detailed list of moment conditions and appendix 2 for the resulting parameter estimates.

Applying the quadratic determinantal equation method to (3.95) and using the parameter estimates in appendix 2, we find that the transformed model has a unique stable solution of the form of (3.43) in section 2.3. Indeed, the only non-zero eigenvalues of the matrices C and F are given by 0.9431 and 0.9361, respectively.

Before using the quadratic determinantal equation method framework to demonstrate possible ways of evaluating the above model, it should be useful to compare the above solution to those obtained using the (log-) linear-quadratic approximation methods of Kydland and Prescott (1982) and Hansen and Prescott (1995), and the Euler equation based approach of Christiano (1991). The former method considers a second-order Taylor-series approximation of the return function (around the (logs of the) nonstochastic steady state of the transformed stationary economy) and then solves the resulting dynamic programming problem using successive approximations, while the latter is based on the (log-) linearization of the Euler equation (derived from Bellman's equation) around the nonstochastic steady state. Christiano's method then proceeds by reducing the two log-linearized Euler equations to a single second-order difference equation in capital and the forcing variables, which is solved by a method of undetermined coefficients. While Christiano (1990) has shown that the linear-quadratic approximation method may be rather inaccurate for empirically reasonable values of the innovations in technology, the log-linear quadratic approximation and undetermined coefficients method based on the log-linearization of the Euler equation provide (given the uniqueness of the bounded solution) essentially equivalent numerical results.[46] We obtained the same results (up to four decimal digits) for the decision rules for $\tilde{k}_{t+1}$ and $\tilde{N}_t$ using the quadratic determinantal equation method, Christiano's (1991) method of undetermined coefficients (both based on the log-linearization of the Euler equations), and the log-linear quadratic approximation method. The decision rules are (using the estimated parameter values of appendix 2)[47]

$$\tilde{k}_{t+1} = 0.9431\tilde{k}_t - 0.9431(\Delta\ln(X_t) - \gamma) + 0.0021\tilde{g}_t, \tag{3.98}$$

$$\tilde{N}_t = -0.5898\tilde{k}_t + 0.5898(\Delta\ln(X_t) - \gamma) + 0.2328\tilde{g}_t. \tag{3.99}$$

While a detailed discussion of the evaluation of real business cycle models would be beyond the scope of this chapter,[48] it may be useful to indicate the ease with which the model's properties may be investigated once the solution has been derived in the framework of the quadratic determinantal equation method. Given the first-order Markovian structure of the forcing variables in

(3.92) and (3.93), and using the parameter values in appendix 2, the unique stable solution may be written as[49]

$$
\begin{pmatrix} \tilde{k}_{t+1} \\ \tilde{N}_t \\ \tilde{c}_t \\ \tilde{y}_t \\ \tilde{i}_t \end{pmatrix} = \begin{pmatrix} 0.9431 & 0 & 0 & 0 & 0 \\ -0.5898 & 0 & 0 & 0 & 0 \\ 0.5481 & 0 & 0 & 0 & 0 \\ -0.0417 & 0 & 0 & 0 & 0 \\ -1.3162 & 0 & 0 & 0 & 0 \end{pmatrix} \begin{pmatrix} \tilde{k}_t \\ \tilde{N}_{t-1} \\ \tilde{c}_{t-1} \\ \tilde{y}_{t-1} \\ \tilde{i}_{t-1} \end{pmatrix} + \begin{pmatrix} 0.9431 & 0.0021 \\ -0.5898 & 0.2328 \\ 0.5481 & -0.0803 \\ -0.0417 & 0.1526 \\ -1.3162 & 0.0840 \end{pmatrix} \begin{pmatrix} -(\gamma_t - \gamma) \\ \tilde{g}_t \end{pmatrix} . \quad (3.100)
$$

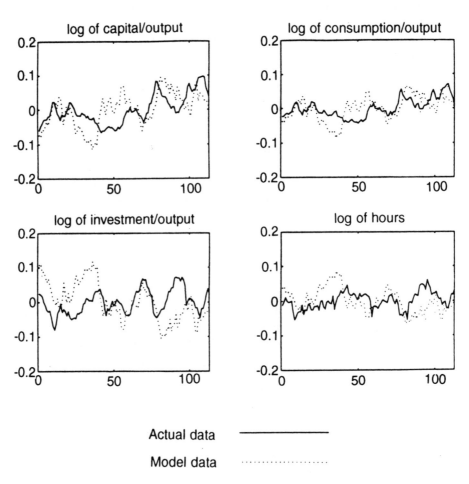

Actual data   ———

Model data   ················

Figure 3.1 Trajectories (log ratios) of actual and model data
Notes: *Definitions of the various trajectories:* The demeaned log of the capital output ratio is defined as $\ln(K_t/Y_t) - \Sigma_{t=1}^{T}(\ln(K_t/Y_t))/T$. Analogously, the demeaned log of the consumption output ratio is defined as $\ln(C_t/Y_t) - \Sigma_{t=1}^{T}(\ln(C_t/Y_t))/T$, and the demeaned log of the investment output ratio is given by $\ln(I_t/Y_t) - \Sigma_{t=1}^{T}(\ln(I_t/Y_t))/T$. The hours series is constructed as $\ln(N_t) - \Sigma_{t=1}^{T}\ln(N_t)/T$.

The unconditional and conditional moment properties of real business cycle models can consequently be derived directly and analytically using (3.100). In figures 3.1 to 3.3, we display actual observations and those simulated from the model.[50] The plots in figure 3.1 contrast the trajectories (measured as deviations from their respective sample means) of actual log ratios of capital, consumption, and investment to output with those simulated from the model over the period 1956/1 to 1984/1. Under the model, these trajectories should be stationary. Since hours are restricted by the model to evolve as a covariance stationary process, these are reported in log levels. Since the

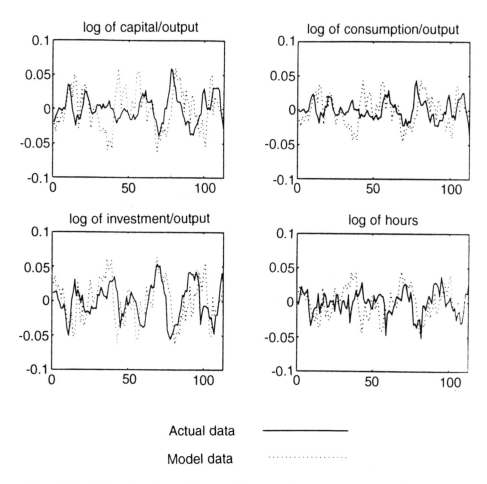

Actual data ————————

Model data · · · · · · · · · · · · · · ·

Figure 3.2 Trajectories (log ratios) of Hodrick-Prescott filtered actual and model data
Notes: *Definitions of the various trajectories:* The log of the capital output ratio is defined as $(\ln(K_t))^* - (\ln(Y_t))^*$, where $(\ )^*$ denotes a series transformed using the ·Hodrick-Prescott filter with $\lambda = 1,600$. The same filter is applied to the other log ratios and the log hours.

properties of simulated model time series are, as is well known,[51] substantially affected by the Hodrick-Prescott filter often applied in real business cycle investigations, we also present in figures 3.2 and 3.3 trajectories for model and corresponding actual data, after transforming both with the Hodrick-Prescott filter. Since this filter renders series which are first-order integrated stationary, we report levels (in figure 3.3) as well as log ratios of capital, consumption, and investment to output (in figure 3.2, to facilitate comparison with figure 3.1).

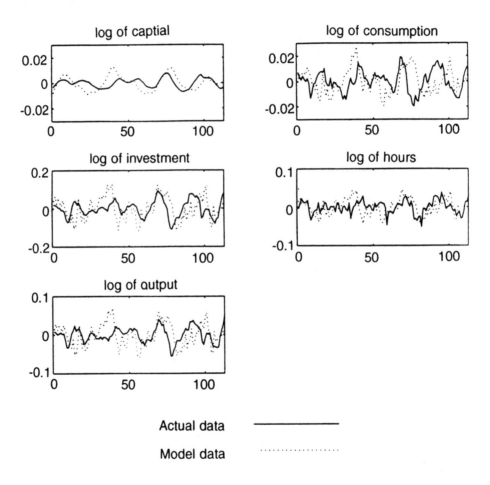

Figure 3.3　Trajectories (levels) of Hodrick-Prescott filtered actual and model data
Notes: *Definitions of the various trajectories:*　The log of capital is defined as $(\ln(K_t))^*$, where $(\ )^*$ denotes, as for figure 3.2, a series transformed using the Hodrick-Prescott filter with $\lambda = 1,600$. The same filter is applied to the logs of consumption, investment, hours, and output.

4.2 Adjustment Cost Models

Dynamic adjustment cost models were among the first (univariate, and later also multivariate) models to be studied applying the rational expectations methodology, and continue to be applied in a number of important areas in applied econometrics. The surveys of Nickell (1986) (focusing on models of labor demand), Bresson, Kramarz, and Sevestre (1992) (also discussing models of labor demand, with a particular emphasis on panel data), Blundell, Bond, and Meghir (1992) (studying capital investment, again with an emphasis on panel data), West (chapter 4 in this volume) (discussing inventory models), and Hansen and Sargent (1994) (providing an overview of linear-quadratic general equilibrium models with adjustment costs) illustrate this. The literature falling within this area may be distinguished as starting from an unrestricted nonlinear specification of the objective function (and linearizing the resultant first-order conditions) (for example Nickell, 1986), or, following the tradition of Holt et al. (1960) and Lucas and Prescott (1971), as starting directly with a quadratic objective function (as developed for the multivariate context in Hansen and Sargent, 1981a). The main concern of this section is to illustrate that a wide class of adjustment cost models imply a particular structure for the coefficient matrices of the resulting Euler equations. This discussion will therefore illustrate an important applied area where some of the special assumptions on the coefficient matrices A and B of equation system (3.4) made in section 2.3.4 may hold.

Consider the following quadratic optimization problem, which encompasses a broad class of dynamic adjustment cost problems:

$$\min_{\{\mathbf{x}_{t+s}\}} E\left\{\sum_{s=0}^{\infty} \beta^s\left[(\mathbf{x}_{t+s} - \mathbf{x}_{t+s}^*)'H(\mathbf{x}_{t+s} - \mathbf{x}_{t+s}^*) + \Delta\mathbf{x}_{t+s}'G\Delta\mathbf{x}_{t+s} + \Delta^2\mathbf{x}_{t+s}'K\Delta^2\mathbf{x}_{t+s}\right]\Big|\,\Omega_t\right\}$$

(3.101)

for given values of $\{\mathbf{x}_t^*, \mathbf{x}_{t+1}^*, \mathbf{x}_{t+2}^*, \ldots\}$, where $\mathbf{x}_t$ is the $p \times 1$ vector of decision variables, H, G, and K are symmetric $p \times p$ coefficient matrices of structural parameters, and β is a discount factor in $(0,1)$. $\mathbf{x}_t^*$ represents the corresponding vector of stochastically evolving targets whose evolution could be given, for example, by the vector ARMA specification

$$\Theta(L)\mathbf{x}_{t+s}^* \equiv \Phi(L)\boldsymbol{\varepsilon}_{t+s}, \qquad \boldsymbol{\varepsilon}_{t+s} \sim \text{iid}(0_{p \times 1}, \Sigma_\varepsilon), \qquad (3.102)$$

where $\Theta(L)$ and $\Phi(L)$ denote matrix lag polynomials of dimension $p \times p$, and ε_t is a $p \times 1$ vector of disturbances. The adjustment costs are quadratic and thus strictly convex and allow for two types of adjustments: one due to the cost of changing the level of $\mathbf{x}_t$, and another due to the cost of changing the speed with which changes in $\mathbf{x}_t$ are put into effect (see for example Pesaran, 1991a).[52] Differentiating (3.101) with respect to $\mathbf{x}_t$ and rearranging the resultant conditions yields the following stochastic Euler equation system:

$$\mathbf{x}_t = M^{-1}(G + 2(1 + \beta)K)\mathbf{x}_{t-1} - M^{-1}K\mathbf{x}_{t-2} \tag{3.103}$$

$$+ \beta M^{-1}(G + 2(1 + \beta)K)E(\mathbf{x}_{t+1}|\Omega_t) - \beta^2 M^{-1}KE(\mathbf{x}_{t+2}|\Omega_t) + M^{-1}H\mathbf{x}_t^*,$$

where $M = H + (1 + \beta)G + (1 + 4\beta + \beta^2)K$.

Consider first the case where adjustment costs are only of first order. It can be readily seen that (3.103) is then a first-order system in the canonical form of (3.4) for which $B = \beta A$, and furthermore, if H and G are nonsingular, so is B. Consequently, corollary 1 (in section 2.3.4) applies and the unique stable solution (if it exists) is given by (3.43).[53]

Hansen and Sargent (1981a) use the fact that $B = \beta A$ to develop z-transform based solution algorithms which are considerably easier to implement than that of Whiteman (1983) discussed in section 2.2. For the special case of $p = 2$ and there being only first-order adjustment costs, they provide analytical formulae based on a procedure described by Rozanov (1967) to factor the characteristic polynomial $-\beta A z^{-1} + I - Az$ associated with (3.4). Independent of the size of p and the order of the adjustment costs, they also describe a numerical algorithm to solve the stable roots backward and the unstable roots forward that does not require explicit factorization of this characteristic polynomial.

If second-order adjustment costs are allowed for, one may show that if (3.103) is transformed to the canonical form (3.4), the coefficient matrices A and B in general do not commute. While propositions 2 and 3 (in section 2.3.4) therefore do not apply any longer, one may of course still use the quadratic determinantal equation method to solve the resulting canonical form. It should also be noted that uniqueness of the resulting solution can still be proved easily if one restricts oneself to solutions which lie in the space spanned by (time-independent) absolute-summable combinations of the stochastic processes fundamental for the forcing variables, as Hansen and Sargent (1981a) and Whiteman (1983) do.[54]

Estimation of adjustment cost models can once more be accomplished either by the limited information methods (as done for example by Kennan, 1979; Pindyck and Rotemberg, 1983a; 1983b) or by the full information methods (for example Eichenbaum, 1984). We need not go into the details here again.

It is worth noting that the strict convexity of adjustment costs imposed in (3.101) seems, in a variety of contexts, to be quite implausible. As an example, there may be asymmetries between hiring and firing costs of firms' employment decisions. A particularly interesting generalized adjustment cost specification has been introduced by Pfann and Verspagen (1989): they describe the adjustment costs for the ith element in $\mathbf{x}_t$ as (neglecting interrelated costs of adjustment)

$$-1 + \exp(b_i \Delta \mathbf{x}_{it}) - b_i \Delta \mathbf{x}_{it} + \tfrac{1}{2} c_i (\Delta \mathbf{x}_{it})^2, \tag{3.104}$$

which nests the strictly convex case with $b_i = 0$; Pfann and Palm (1993) find evidence in manufacturing data that there indeed is asymmetry and thus provide some support in favor of (3.104). However, the model exhibiting a crucial nonlinearity, an exact solution cannot be provided anymore, and Pfann and Palm restrict themselves to estimating the model through a limited information procedure.

5 Conclusion

In this chapter we have been primarily concerned with the problems associated with the derivation and computation of solutions to multivariate linear rational expectations models. We have also briefly discussed the estimation of such models by the GMM and maximum likelihood methods. We have not, however, addressed the other three main areas in the rational expectations literature where important recent developments have taken place. Here we provide an overview of some of these developments in order to link them with our discussion and indicate areas of future research.

One important area not covered in this chapter is concerned with the problem of learning in rational expectations models. This literature may be motivated along two separate lines. A first line of reasoning is that the rational expectations postulate taken literally attributes to the agents formidable knowledge about their environment and computing capabilities. How do agents arrive – if at all – at such an equilibrium? Models of learning can therefore be viewed as trying to give the rational expectations hypothesis some operational content by studying the conditions under which learning processes may or may not converge to rational expectations equilibrium. Among the learning processes studied, one may particularly distinguish between models of linear (often least squares) learning, and models which adapt nonlinear learning algorithms originally developed in the literature concerned with artificial intelligence. The former, surveyed in Bullard (1990), Evans and Honkapohja (1995), Pesaran (1991b), and Sargent (1993), introduce the notion of agents being boundedly rational in that they either do not understand or are unable to take into account the full implications of their learning on the actual laws of motion generating the economy. Some remarkable convergence results have been proven (see for example Fourgeaud, Gouriéroux, and Pradel, 1986; Marcet and Sargent, 1989a; 1989b) and it has also been shown that such agents may not detect their misspecification of the actual laws of motion if they are equipped with simple econometric tools (Bray and Savin, 1986). Nevertheless, it is not entirely clear whether these models do give the rational expectations hypothesis operational content in that they still model agents as having enormous computing abilities and ignore the question of how they all agree to use the same learning rule in the first place. These models are therefore often motivated or used for different purposes. They may be viewed as a useful device to study – when a multiplicity of (stable) solutions in a model exists – which of the many solutions is the most likely for agents to settle on. Also, models of linear (least squares) learning actually may also provide a different way of computing rational expectations equilibria in certain settings (see for example Marcet, 1991; Sargent, 1991), a topic to which we shall return shortly. It is then likely that a more appropriate strategy to address agents' learning would be to study boundedly rational learning models which do not necessarily focus on convergence to rational expectations equilibrium and/or which establish a more satisfactory link with the issue of model selection in econometrics.[55] Models adapted from the literature in artificial intelligence appear particularly attractive to formalize the notion of learning in that they presume only limited computational sophistication on behalf of the decision makers. The emphasis consequently could be on achieving a more improved solution rather than actually attaining the optimum, thus reverting back to Herbert Simon's notion of "satisficing" rather than "optimizing" economic agents. Currently known results in this area suggest that the simulated behavior of model economies in which agents learn through some form of artificial intelligence seems to depend strongly on the complexity of the structure under investigation. In particular, if the behavior of artificially intelligent agents is not well described by the trajectories around global optima, this is *not* necessarily due to an inherent inconsistency in agents' learning rules.

A second circumstance (apart from agents being boundedly rational) in which the attainment of a standard rational expectations equilibrium may be questioned is when economic agents are differentially informed. As already noted by Keynes (1936) and Pigou (1927), and discussed more formally in Frydman and Phelps (1983), Townsend (1983), and Pesaran (1987), situations in which economic decision makers have private information and/or base their decisions on only a subset of the incalculable wealth of information possibly available and thus focus on signals which are most likely to minimize their forecast errors, often lead to the problem of infinite regress in expectations. Solution algorithms available to handle this problem are discussed in Binder and Pesaran (1994), which also introduces an alternative method to compute the equilibria of such models, based on a restriction about how economic agents update their mean beliefs and making use of the quadratic determinantal equation solution method. The solution method introduced in Binder and Pesaran (1994) is attractive particularly in that it provides an operational framework for the econometric analysis of rational expectations models under asymmetric or heterogeneous information. Models with differentially informed agents have been applied to asset markets (Hussman, 1992), wage bargaining (Lee and Pesaran, 1993), and real business cycles (Binder, 1994), and in each case appear to significantly augment the explanatory power of the models under consideration.

Finally, we should not conclude this chapter without sketching some of the developments which have taken place in the analysis of nonlinear multivariate rational expectations models and which are thought not to be well approximated by some form of linearization. The basic problem with such nonlinear models is that in general they cannot be solved exactly even by numerical methods. The solution methods proposed in the literature may be grouped under three headings.[56] An obvious first approach would be to employ certainty equivalence even though the model is nonlinear, a route taken up by Fair and Taylor (1983; 1990). The problem hereby is of course that such an approximation may, as with some variants of linearization techniques, be rather poor. A second, "brute force" approach is to discretize the state space and obtain an arbitrarily close approximation to the true solution by constructing an arbitrarily fine grid. Such methods have been used in different contexts for example by Deaton and Laroque (1992), Rust (1987), and Tauchen and Hussey (1991). Clearly, if the state space is larger than just a few variables, such an algorithm becomes numerically intractable, whatever the computer power available. Third, one may approximate (a subset of) the expectations of nonlinear functions appearing in a model by some general function, an approach followed by Judd (1992), Marcet (1991), and Sims (1989). This approximation procedure may take a variety of forms, being based, for example, on notions such as mimicking learning behavior or exploiting advances in the numerical analysis literature. Without going into a detailed discussion of the properties of these techniques, it is important to recognize that all these methods are subject to important shortcomings which have only begun to be addressed in the literature. First, most methods may or may not work in a specific context, that is, typically no general conditions for convergence are provided.[57] Second, one cannot judge the accuracy of a solution method in general if one has no information about the nature of the exact solution. Third and finally, the methods pick a specific solution which, as should be clear from our discussion in section 2, generally will not be unique. These are exciting questions to study, and will certainly be on macroeconometricians' research agenda for years to come.

Appendix 1   The Moment Restrictions Underlying the Parameter Estimates for the Real Business Cycle Model

The estimates of δ, α, θ, γ, σ_x, $\bar{g}$, ρ_1 and σ_g are obtained from the following conditions:

$$E\left(\delta - \left[1 + \frac{I_t}{K_t} - \frac{K_{t+1}}{K_t}\right]\right) = 0, \tag{3.105}$$

$$E\left(\beta^{-1} - \frac{C_t}{C_{t+1}}\left[\alpha\frac{Y_{t+1}}{K_{t+1}} + (1 - \delta)\right]\right) = 0, \tag{3.106}$$

$$E\left(\theta - (1 - \alpha)\frac{Y_t}{N_t C_t}\right) = 0, \tag{3.107}$$

$$E(\gamma - \Delta\ln(Y_t)) = 0, \tag{3.108}$$

$$E((\Delta\ln(X_t) - \gamma)^2 - \sigma_x^2) = 0, \tag{3.109}$$

$$E(\ln(g_t) - \rho_0 - \rho_1\ln(g_{t-1})) = 0, \tag{3.110}$$

$$E((\ln(g_t) - \rho_0 - \rho_1\ln(g_{t-1}))g_{t-1}) = 0, \tag{3.111}$$

$$E((\ln(g_t) - \rho_0 - \rho_1\ln(g_{t-1}))^2 - \sigma_g^2) = 0. \tag{3.112}$$

An estimate of $\bar{g}$ can then be obtained from (3.110) to (3.112) as follows. Recalling the specification of $\{\ln g_t\}$ given by (3.93), notice that this latter equation can be rewritten as

$$g_t = \exp\{\rho_0\} g_{t-1}^{\rho_1} \exp\{\varepsilon_{tg}\}, \tag{3.113}$$

where $\varepsilon_{tg} \sim$ iid $N(0, \sigma_g^2)$. Solving (3.113) forward, and assuming that $\rho_1 < 1$, one obtains[58]

$$\bar{g} = E(g_t) = \exp\left\{\rho_0/(1 - \rho_1) + \tfrac{1}{2}\sigma_g^2/(1 - \rho_1^2)\right\}. \tag{3.114}$$

Appendix 2   Estimates of the Parameters of the Real Business Cycle Model (Standard Errors in Parentheses)

δ	0.0209	(0.0003)
α	0.3447	(0.0059)
θ	0.0037	(<0.0001)
γ	0.0038	(0.0014)
σ_x	0.0183	(0.0015)
ρ_0	0.2249	(0.1534)
ρ_1	0.9572	(0.0291)
σ_g	0.0206	(0.0014)

The estimates for ρ_0, ρ_1, and σ_g imply an estimate of $\bar{g} = 191.16$. The parameters β and N were not estimated, but were set *a priori* to values of $\beta = [1/(1 + r)]^{0.25}$ per quarter with an annual real rate of $r = 0.03$, and $N = 1369$ (the time endowment per quarter, fixed here to the same value as in Christiano and Eichenbaum, 1992).

Data source   The data set used is the one described in Christiano and Eichenbaum (1992) (hours being based on the household survey). We are grateful to Larry Christiano for his permission to use this data set.

Notes

We are grateful to Mike Wickens for comments and suggestions on an earlier draft of this chapter.

1 Such a factorization method (developed for the univariate context in Pesaran, 1987 and used for the analysis of feedback by Timmermann, 1994) is, however, confined to the case where the forcing variables follow linear processes.

2 To keep the notation as simple as possible, we specify the vector $\mathbf{u}_t$ to have size p. Of course, the number of forcing variables will in general differ from the number of decision variables, in which case $\mathbf{u}_t$ should be understood to be the product of an appropriately dimensioned selector matrix and the vector of forcing variables.

3 A process $\{\mathbf{u}_t\}$ is said to be adapted to the increasing family $\{\Omega_t\}$ of sub-σ-algebras of Ω if, for each t, $\mathbf{u}_t$ is Ω_t measurable. For further details see for example Williams (1991).

4 While some of these models are nonlinear in the decision variables, they may be accommodated in the standard manner of linearizing the resultant first-order conditions around the steady state or long-run equilibrium. See also the discussion in sections 4 and 5.

5 See for example Broze, Gouriéroux, and Szafarz (1990).

6 There are also a number of contributions such as d'Autume (1990), Evans (1987), Gouriéroux, Laffont, and Monfort (1982), Hansen and Sargent (1980), Lucas (1972), and Pesaran (1981) (to cite only a few) that specifically consider the solution of univariate rational expectations models. Most of the univariate approaches, however, are rather specific and cannot be readily adapted to the analysis of multivariate rational expectations models.

7 One may include in this group also methods which solve quadratic dynamic programming problems as arising in many optimization models by some form of iteration on Bellman's equation directly, rather than working with the first-order conditions. An example of this group of methods is the linear-quadratic approximation of Kydland and Prescott (1982) applied to solving real business cycle models, discussed in section 4.1.

8 A solution method not reviewed here but also falling in the second group is Blanchard and Kahn (1980). See also Broze and Szafarz (1991) for a review of available solution methods.

9 While a more formal discussion of the z-transform technique would require usage of some more advanced concepts from functional analysis, our discussion here is meant to be heuristic to facilitate intuitive understanding. It is mainly for this reason also that we do not discuss Whiteman's (1985) contribution, which uses methods analog to the ones discussed here, but in the frequency domain. Even a heuristic discussion would require familiarity with functional analysis at a fairly advanced level.

10 See for example Kailath (1980) for a further discussion of the Smith normal form.

11 $\det(\cdot)$ stands for the determinant of the matrix inside the brackets.

12 We use $\mathrm{adj}(\cdot)$ to denote the adjoint matrix of the matrix inside the brackets.

13 Roughly, this martingale component may be viewed as an extraneous variable (different from $\mathbf{y}_t$, $\mathbf{w}_t$ and ε_t) which is believed by the agents to help forecast future realizations of $\mathbf{y}_t$. We will come back to this issue in full detail when discussing the quadratic determinantal equation method this chapter proposes in section 2.3.

14 A more formal argument is made by Hamilton and Whiteman (1985) who show that solutions with and without a martingale component are indistinguishable based on the econometrician having observations on $\mathbf{y}_t$ and $\mathbf{w}_t$ only.

15 See Salemi (1986) for the computational details when B is not of full rank.

16 A full account of martingale (difference) processes is for example given in Williams (1991).

17 See also section 2.3.5.

18 The conditions for $I_m - BC$ to be nonsingular will be discussed below. At this stage, however, it is worth noting that the nonsingularity of $I_m - BC$ does not necessarily require B to be nonsingular.

19 See Pesaran (1981; 1987, appendix C) for a detailed derivation in the univariate and multivariate contexts.

20 In going from the general solutions for y_t given in (3.39) to the general solution for x_t, the underlying variables in the structural model (3.1), it is important that special care is taken to allow for the fact that in addition to x_t, the composite vector y_t may also contain lagged values of x_t, which in turn would impose further restrictions on the martingale processes in (3.39). For an example of this in a simple context, see Pesaran (1987, appendix C.2).

21 It is important to note that the distinction between the general and a particular solution made in (3.39) is only partly analogous to a similar distinction which is present in the solution of perfect foresight difference equation systems. To determine the solution at t, more than knowledge of the past history of y_t and W_t is needed, in contrast to the opposite claim made by Whiteman (1983, p. 78).

22 Henceforth, we will call a solution stable if it is bounded in mean.

23 Note that if all eigenvalues of F fell inside the unit circle, but C had some eigenvalue on the unit circle, $y_t^0 = y_t^1$ would not need to hold almost surely.

24 For the exposition here, all eigenvalues of F are assumed real. However, complex eigenvalues of F can be easily accommodated by using the real Jordan form (see Lancaster and Tismenetsky, 1985) for (3.46).

25 A matrix Λ_{f_3} is nil-potent of order m_3 if $\Lambda_{f_3}^j = 0_{m_3}$ for $j \geqslant m_3$.

26 One such iterative procedure would be to start with an arbitrary estimate of C, say C_0 and then use the recursive relations $C_r = (I_m - BC_{r-1})^{-1}A$, where C_r is the value of C at the rth iteration $(r = 1, 2, \ldots)$.

27 See for example Bellman (1960).

28 The proper choice of eigenvalues depends on the number of roots of (3.59) falling inside and outside the unit circle. This will become clearer below when we discuss the links between these eigenvalues and those of F, which as described in detail above characterize the nature of the solution to (3.4).

29 In practice, though, this forecast horizon may be quite sensitive to the convergence criterion employed in computing the forward part of the solution, and interpretations of the forecast horizon should therefore be viewed with caution.

30 An alternative way of proving corollary 1 is given by Nickell (1984).

31 It is implicitly assumed here that there is at least one nonzero eigenvalue for both A and B.

32 This follows from the following theorem first proven by Frobenius, as restated in Motzkin and Taussky (1952): any function $f(A, B)$ of two commutative $m \times m$ matrices A and B has as eigenvalues the numbers $f(\lambda_a, \lambda_b)$, where λ_a and λ_b are the eigenvalues of A and B respectively, both taken in a special ordering independent of the function f. In fact, commutativity is a sufficient but not necessary condition. As discussed in Motzkin and Taussky, the weaker requirement that the two matrices A and B possess property P will do.

33 The model may, however, also have "endogenous" unit roots. A practically important example is real business cycle models exhibiting endogenous growth. In these models, even when all forcing variables are covariance stationary, the

decision variables are first-order integrated. In terms of (3.75) this may occur if some column of $I_m - C$ equals the zero vector. While the conditions for (3.43) to hold as derived above are not satisfied any more if C has eigenvalues on the unit circle, we may nevertheless find that (3.43) is the feasible (and unique stable) solution if the forcing variables work towards dampening an otherwise explosive system.

34 Using $F = (I_m - BC)^{-1}B$ and $BC^2 - C + A = 0_m$, it is easily seen that $(I_m - BC)(I_m - F)(I_m - C) = I_m - A - B$.

35 See for example Watson (1995) for a description of the transformations necessary to arrive at the common stochastic trend representation.

36 The estimation of rational expectations models is also discussed in depth by Blake (1991) and Hansen and Sargent (1991).

37 Notice that the existence of a sufficient number of moment conditions is a necessary condition for consistent estimation, and needs to be augmented with certain rank conditions on the correlation matrices of the instruments and the variables included in the model. For a demonstration of this point see example 7.1 in Pesaran (1987).

38 See for example West (chapter 4 in this volume) for a review of GMM estimation in an applied setting.

39 See again example 7.1 in Pesaran (1987).

40 A conceptually very different approach to maximum likelihood estimation is suggested by Watson (1989). He embeds solution and estimation within a single numerical framework using the Kalman filter. This idea was originally developed by Mehra (1970) in the literature on recursive state space estimation.

41 This section should therefore be viewed as complementary to Kim and Pagan (chapter 7 in this volume) who discuss a much broader range of issues arising in the evaluation of real business cycle models.

42 We thus consider their model with indivisible labor and with government. In the model, the process generating government consumption is assumed to be exogenous.

43 The notation is standard: Y_t denotes output, C_t consumption services, K_t the stock of capital, I_t investment in capital, N_t hours worked, N the time endowment of the representative worker, X_t labor-augmenting technological progress, G_t government consumption, β the discount factor ($0 < \beta < 1$), and δ the rate of depreciation of capital.

44 An exact solution can be obtained in the special case where $\delta = 1$, government consumption is a perfect substitute for private consumption, and the social planner maximizes $E\{\Sigma_{t=0}^{\infty}\beta^t[\ln(C_t) + \theta\ln(N - N_t)]\,|\,\Omega_0\}$ subject to (3.90) to (3.93). Note, however, that this result does not necessarily require the disturbance terms ε_{tx} and ε_{tg} to be normally distributed. All that is needed is a first-order Markovian structure for the processes generating the forcing variables. See Long and Plosser (1983) for further discussion of this point.

45 The issue of whether the model is identified and the GMM estimator well defined is not addressed here. For a discussion of which moment conditions one may most preferably use, we refer to Kim and Pagan (chapter 7 in this volume). It may also be noted that the estimation of the model may also be carried out by the maximum likelihood procedure discussed in section 3. Maximum likelihood estimation of real business cycle models has so far been explored by Altug (1989), Christiano (1988), and McGrattan (1994).

46   An important question that remains is, of course, the relative sizes of the approximation errors involved in the quadratic approximation of the return function or the linearization of the Euler equations. For a comparison of the above approximation methods with "exact" solutions, we refer the reader to Christiano (1990), Danthine, Donaldson, and Mehra (1989), and Dotsey and Mao (1992), who find that, for small fluctuations around stationary economies' nonstochastic steady state, the approximation appears to work quite well. See, however, also the "horse-race" of Taylor and Uhlig (1990) for a more cautioning point of view.

47   In our implementation of the quadratic determinantal equation method, for the computation of the forward part of the solution using the recursive procedure described in section 2.3.3, we set all components of $\bar{\mathbf{y}}_f$ equal to 5 initially, and then determined a forecast horizon of 160 periods if solutions are restricted to converge up to four decimal places. It should also be noted that $\mathbf{z}_{t+1}$ is not in the planner's information set at time t, and is consequently replaced by $\mathbf{R}\mathbf{z}_t$.

48   On this issue we again refer the reader to Kim and Pagan (chapter 7 in this volume).

49   The first two equations in the following system (which give the decision rules for $\tilde{k}_{t+1}$ and $\tilde{N}_t$) are of course the same as (3.98) and (3.99).

50   The trajectories for the simulated model data in figures 3.1 to 3.3 are generated as follows. The initial values of the variables in $\mathbf{y}_t$ are set equal to zero for $t = 1$ for each replication. Initial values for the variables in $\mathbf{z}_t$ are obtained using the estimates $\ln(X_t) = (\ln(Y_t) - \hat{\alpha}\ln(K_t) - (1 - \hat{\alpha})\ln(N_t))/(1 - \hat{\alpha})$ for $t = 0, 1$ (where $\hat{\alpha}$ is the GMM estimate of α reported in appendix 2). Initial values of $-(\eta - \gamma)$ and $\tilde{g}_t$ are then obtained as $-(\eta - \gamma) = -(\Delta\ln(X_1) - \hat{\gamma})$ and $\tilde{g}_1 = \ln(G_1/X_1) - \ln(\hat{\bar{g}})$, where $\hat{\gamma}$ and $\hat{\bar{g}}$ are the GMM estimates of γ and $\bar{g}$ reported in appendix 2. The model is then simulated forward up to $t = T$ (where T is the sample size adjusted for initial conditions, here 113). The trajectories in figures 3.1 to 3.3 are based on averages across 500 replications of time paths for the logs of the various ratios and levels. The value of the smoothing parameter, λ, in the Hodrick-Prescott filter is chosen to be $\lambda = 1600$.

51   See for example King and Rebelo (1993) for further discussion of this point.

52   Higher-order adjustment costs may also be viewed as being caused by aggregation problems: see for example Nickell (1986). We restrict ourselves here to first- and second-order adjustment costs, as they seem to be the most plausible types of quadratic adjustment costs to arise in practice. Mathematically, in terms of the relationships of the coefficient matrices in the Euler equations, this involves no loss of generality.

53   Again, while this result holds for a broad class of first-order dynamic adjustment cost models, it will not always be true. An example of models not exhibiting this property are interrelated factor demand models involving inventories of finished goods held for speculative purposes and/or technological considerations.

54   Such a proof may again use the Smith normal form factorization of section 2.2 and need therefore not be repeated here.

55   See again Sargent (1993) for a stimulating review and outline of how this line of reasoning may be further pursued.

56   See Marcet (1994) for a survey; a variety of methods are compared in the "horse race" of Taylor and Uhlig (1990). It should also be noted that recently an approach quite different from those listed in what follows has been suggested in Pesaran and

Samiei (1995), namely a backward recursive procedure which in principle is exact, but in general cannot be implemented in a numerically feasible manner. If economic agents are viewed as being boundedly rational, however, a limited forecasting horizon modification of the method, which is numerically tractable, is readily implementable.

57 See, however, Marcet and Marshall (1994) who provide conditions under which Marcet's (1991) method of parameterized expectations can provide an arbitrarily close approximation to the "true" solution.

58 Christiano and Eichenbaum (1992) implicitly postulate that $E(\ln g_t) = \ln(E(g_t))$, and thus arrive at $\bar{g} = \exp\{\rho_0/(1 - \rho_1)\}$, neglecting the second term in the exponential on the right-hand side of (3.114).

References

Altug, S. (1989): Time-to-Build and Aggregate Fluctuations: Some New Evidence, *International Economic Review*, 30, 889–920.

Bellman, R. (1960): *Introduction to Matrix Analysis*, New York: McGraw-Hill.

Binder, M. (1994): On the Quantitative Importance of Heterogeneous Information for the Business Cycle, Mimeo, University of Pennsylvania.

Binder, M. and M.H. Pesaran (1994): Multivariate Linear Rational Expectations Models under Asymmetric and Heterogeneous Information, Mimeo, University of Pennsylvania and University of Cambridge.

Blake, D. (1991): The Estimation of Rational Expectations Models: A Survey, *Journal of Economic Studies*, 18, 31–70.

Blanchard, O.J. and C.M. Kahn (1980): Solution of Linear Difference Models under Rational Expectations, *Econometrica*, 38, 1305–11.

Blundell, R., S. Bond and C. Meghir (1992): Econometric Models of Company Investment, in: L. Mátyás and P. Sevestre (eds): *The Econometrics of Panel Data*, Boston: Kluwer, 388–413.

Bray, M.M. and N.E. Savin (1986): Rational Expectations Equilibria, Learning, and Model Specification, *Econometrica*, 54, 1129–60.

Bresson, G., F. Kramarz and P. Sevestre (1992): Dynamic Labour Demand Models, in: L. Mátyás and P. Sevestre (eds): *The Econometrics of Panel Data*, Boston: Kluwer, 360–87.

Broze, L., C. Gouriéroux and A. Szafarz (1985): Solutions of Linear Rational Expectations Models, *Econometric Theory*, 1, 341–68.

Broze, L., C. Gouriéroux and A. Szafarz (1990): *Reduced Forms of Rational Expectations Models*, New York: Harwood Academic Publishers.

Broze, L. and A. Szafarz (1991): *The Econometric Analysis of Non-Uniqueness in Rational Expectations Models*, Amsterdam: North-Holland.

Bullard, J.B. (1990): Rethinking Rational Expectations, in: G.M. von Furstenberg (ed.): *Acting under Uncertainty: Multidisciplinary Conceptions*, Boston: Kluwer, 325–54.

Christiano, L.J. (1988): Why Does Inventory Investment Fluctuate So Much?, *Journal of Monetary Economics*, 21, 247–80.

Christiano, L.J. (1990): Linear-Quadratic Approximation and Value-Function Iteration: A Comparison, *Journal of Business & Economic Statistics*, 8, 99–113.

Christiano, L.J. (1991): Modeling the Liquidity Effect of a Money Shock, *Federal Reserve Bank of Minneapolis Quarterly Review*, 15, 3–34.

Christiano, L.J. and M.S. Eichenbaum (1992): Current Real-Business-Cycle Theories and Aggregate Labor-Market Fluctuations, *American Economic Review*, 82, 430–50.

Danthine, J.-P., J.B. Donaldson and R. Mehra (1989): On Some Computational Aspects of Equilibrium Business Cycle Theory, *Journal of Economic Dynamics and Control*, 13, 449–70.

D'Autume, A. (1990): On the Solution of Linear Difference Equations with Rational Expectations, *Review of Economic Studies*, 57, 677–88.

Deaton, A. and G. Laroque (1992): On the Behavior of Commodity Prices, *Review of Economic Studies*, 59, 1–23.

Dotsey, M. and C.S. Mao (1992): How Well Do Linear Approximation Methods Work? Results for Suboptimal Dynamic Equilibria, *Journal of Monetary Economics*, 29, 25–58.

Eichenbaum, M.S. (1984): Rational Expectations and the Smoothing Properties of Inventories of Finished Goods, *Journal of Monetary Economics*, 14, 71–96.

Emre, E. and Ö. Hüsseyin (1975): Generalization of Leverrier's Algorithm to Polynomial Matrices of Arbitrary Degree, *IEEE Transactions on Automatic Control*, 136.

Evans, G.W. (1987): The Structure of ARMA Solutions to a General Linear Model with Rational Expectations, *Journal of Economic Dynamics and Control*, 11, 79–91.

Evans, G.W. and S. Honkapohja (1995): Adaptive Learning and Expectational Stability: An Introduction, in: A.P. Kirman and M. Salmon (eds): *Learning and Rationality in Economics*, Oxford: Basil Blackwell (forthcoming).

Fair, R.C. and J.B. Taylor (1983): Solution and Maximum Likelihood Estimation of Dynamic Nonlinear Rational Expectations Models, *Econometrica*, 51, 1169–85.

Fair, R.C. and J.B. Taylor (1990): Full Information Estimation and Stochastic Simulation of Models with Rational Expectations, *Journal of Applied Econometrics*, 5, 381–92.

Fourgeaud, C., C. Gouriéroux and J. Pradel (1986): Learning Procedure and Convergence to Rationality, *Econometrica*, 54, 845–68.

Frydman, R. and E.S. Phelps (eds) (1983): *Individual Forecasting and Aggregate Outcomes: "Rational Expectations" Examined*, Cambridge: Cambridge University Press.

Gouriéroux, C., J.J. Laffont and A. Monfort (1982): Rational Expectations in Dynamic Linear Models: Analysis of the Solutions, *Econometrica*, 50, 409–25.

Hamilton, J.D. and C.H. Whiteman (1985): The Observable Implications of Self-Fulfilling Expectations, *Journal of Monetary Economics*, 16, 353–73.

Hansen, G.D. and E.C. Prescott (1995): Recursive Methods for Computing Equilibria of Business Cycle Models, in: T.F. Cooley (ed.): *Frontiers of Business Cycle Research*, Princeton: Princeton University Press, 39–64.

Hansen, L.P. (1982): Large Sample Properties of Generalized Method of Moments Estimators, *Econometrica*, 50, 1029–54.

Hansen, L.P. and T.J. Sargent (1980): Formulating and Estimating Dynamic Linear Rational Expectations Models, *Journal of Economic Dynamics and Control*, 2, 7–46.

Hansen, L.P. and T.J. Sargent (1981a): Linear Rational Expectations Models for Dynamically Interrelated Variables, in: R.E. Lucas Jr and T.J. Sargent (eds): *Rational Expectations and Econometric Practice*, Minneapolis: University of Minnesota Press, 127–56.

Hansen, L.P. and T.J. Sargent (1981b): A Note on Wiener- Kolmogorov Prediction Formulas for Rational Expectations Models, *Economics Letters*, 8, 255–60.

Hansen, L.P. and T.J. Sargent (1991): *Rational Expectations Econometrics*, Boulder: Westview Press.

Hansen, L.P. and T.J. Sargent (1994): Recursive Linear Models of Dynamic Economies, in: C.A. Sims (ed.): *Advances in Econometrics: Sixth World Congress*, vol. 1, Cambridge: Cambridge University Press, 97–139.

Hayashi, F. and C.A. Sims (1983): Nearly Efficient Estimation of Time Series Models with Predetermined, but not Exogenous Instruments, *Econometrica*, 51, 783–98.

Holt, C.C., F. Modigliani, J.F. Muth and H.A. Simon (1960): *Planning Production, Inventories and Work Force*, Englewood Cliffs: Prentice-Hall.

Hussman, J. (1992): Market Efficiency and Inefficiency in Rational Expectations Equilibria, *Journal of Economic Dynamics and Control*, 16, 655–80.

Judd, K.L. (1992): Projection Methods for Solving Aggregate Growth Models, *Journal of Economic Theory*, 58, 410–52.

Kailath, T. (1980): *Linear Systems*, Englewood Cliffs: Prentice-Hall.

Kennan, J. (1979): The Estimation of Partial Adjustment Models with Rational Expectations, *Econometrica*, 47, 1441–55.

Keynes, J.M. (1936): *The General Theory of Employment, Interest, and Money*, London: Macmillan.

King, R.G. and S.T. Rebelo (1993): Low Frequency Filtering and Real Business Cycles, *Journal of Economic Dynamics and Control*, 17, 207–31.

Kydland, F.E. and E.C. Prescott (1982): Time to Build and Aggregate Fluctuations, *Econometrica*, 50, 1345–70.

Lancaster, P. and M. Tismenetsky (1985): *The Theory of Matrices*, 2nd edn, New York: Academic Press.

Lee, K.C. and M.H. Pesaran (1993): The Role of Sectoral Interactions in Wage Determination in the U.K. Economy, *Economic Journal*, 103, 21–55.

Long, J.B. Jr and C.I. Plosser (1983): Real Business Cycles, *Journal of Political Economy*, 91, 39–69.

Lucas, R.E. Jr (1972): Expectations and the Neutrality of Money, *Journal of Economic Theory*, 4, 103–24.

Lucas, R.E. Jr and E.C. Prescott (1971): Investment under Uncertainty, *Econometrica*, 39, 659–81.

Marcet, A. (1991): Solving Non-Linear Stochastic Models by Parameterizing Expectations: An Application to Asset Pricing with Production, Mimeo, Universitat Pompeu Fabra.

Marcet, A. (1994): Simulation Analysis of Dynamic Stochastic Models: Applications to Theory and Estimation, in: C.A. Sims (ed.): *Advances in Econometrics: Sixth World Congress*, vol. 2, Cambridge: Cambridge University Press, 81–118.

Marcet, A. and D.A. Marshall (1994): Solving Nonlinear Rational Expectations Models by Parameterized Expectations: Convergence to Stationary Solutions, Mimeo, Universitat Pompeu Fabra and Northwestern University.

Marcet, A. and T.J. Sargent (1989a): Convergence of Least Squares Learning Mechanisms in Self Referential Linear Stochastic Models, *Journal of Economic Theory*, 48, 337–68.

Marcet, A. and T.J. Sargent (1989b): Convergence of Least Squares Learning in Environments with Hidden State Variables and Private Information, *Journal of Political Economy*, 97, 1306–22.

McGrattan, E.R. (1994): The Macroeconomic Effects of Distortionary Taxation, *Journal of Monetary Economics*, 33, 573–601.

Mehra, R.K. (1970): On the Identification of Variances and Adaptive Kalman Filtering, *IEEE Transactions on Automatic Control*, 15, 175–84.

Motzkin, T.S. and O. Taussky (1952): Pairs of Matrices with Property L, *Transactions of the American Mathematical Society*, 73, 108–14.

Muth, J.F. (1961): Rational Expectations and the Theory of Price Movements, *Econometrica*, 29, 315–35.

Nickell, S.J. (1984): An Investigation of the Determinants of Manufacturing Employment in the United Kingdom, *Review of Economic Studies*, 5, 529–57.

Nickell, S.J. (1986): Dynamic Models of Labor Demand, in: O. Ashenfelter and R. Layard (eds): *Handbook of Labor Economics*, vol. 1, Amsterdam: North-Holland, 473–522.

Pace, I.S. and S. Barnett (1974): Efficient Algorithms for Linear System Calculations, Part I – Smith Form and Common Divisor of Polynomial Matrices, *International Journal of Systems Science*, 5, 403–11.

Pesaran, M.H. (1981): Identification of Rational Expectations Models, *Journal of Econometrics*, 16, 375–98.

Pesaran, M.H. (1987): *The Limits of Rational Expectations*, Oxford: Basil Blackwell (reprinted with corrections in paperback, 1989).

Pesaran, M.H. (1991a): Costly Adjustment under Rational Expectations: A Generalization, *Review of Economics and Statistics*, 73, 353–8.

Pesaran, M.H. (1991b): Expectations in Economics, in: D. Greenaway, M. Bleaney and I. Stewart (eds): *Companion to Contemporary Economic Thought*, London: Routledge, 161–83.

Pesaran, M.H. and H. Samiei (1994): Limited-Dependent Rational Expectations Models with Future Expectations, *Journal of Economic Dynamics and Control* (forthcoming).

Pfann, G.A. and F.C. Palm (1993): Asymmetric Adjustment Costs in Non-Linear Labor Demand Models for the Netherlands and U.K. Manufacturing Sectors, *Review of Economic Studies*, 60, 397–412.

Pfann, G.A. and B. Verspagen (1989): The Structure of Adjustment Costs for Labor in the Dutch Manufacturing Sector, *Economics Letters*, 29, 365–71.

Pigou, A.C. (1927): *Industrial Fluctuations*, London: Macmillan.

Pindyck, R.S. and J.J. Rotemberg (1983a): Dynamic Factor Demands and the Effects of Energy Price Shocks, *American Economic Review*, 73, 1066–79.

Pindyck, R.S. and J.J. Rotemberg (1983b): Dynamic Factor Demand under Rational Expectations, *Scandinavian Journal of Economics*, 85, 223–38.

Rozanov, Y. (1967): *Stationary Random Processes*, San Francisco: Holden-Day.

Rust, J. (1987): Optimal Replacement of GMC Bus Engines: An Empirical Model of Harold Zurcher, *Econometrica*, 55, 999–1033.

Salemi, M.K. (1986): Solution and Estimation of Linear Rational Expectations Models, *Journal of Econometrics*, 31, 41–66.

Salemi, M.K. and J. Song (1992): Saddlepath Solutions for Multivariate Linear Rational Expectations Models, *Journal of Econometrics*, 53, 245–69.

Sargan, J.D. (1983): A Reformulation and Comparison of Alternative Methods of Estimating Models Containing Rational Expectations, Mimeo, London School of Economics.

Sargan, J.D. (1984): Alternative Models for Rational Expectations in Some Simple Irregular Cases, Mimeo, London School of Economics.

Sargent, T.J. (1991): Equilibrium with Signal Extraction from Endogenous Variables, *Journal of Economic Dynamics and Control*, 15, 245–73.

Sargent, T.J. (1993): *Bounded Rationality in Macroeconomics*, Oxford: Clarendon Press.

Sims, C.A. (1989): Solving Nonlinear Stochastic Optimization and Equilibrium Problems "Backwards," Mimeo, Institute for Empirical Macroeconomics, Minneapolis.

Tauchen, G. and R. Hussey (1991): Quadrature-Based Methods for Obtaining Approximate Solutions to Nonlinear Asset Pricing Models, *Econometrica*, 59, 371–96.

Taylor, J.B. and H. Uhlig (1990): Solving Nonlinear Stochastic Growth Models: A Comparison of Alternative Solution Methods, *Journal of Business & Economic Statistics*, 8, 1–17.

Timmermann, A. (1994): Present Value Models with Feedback: Solution, Stability, Bubbles and Some Empirical Evidence, *Journal of Economic Dynamics and Control*, 18, 1093–119.

Townsend, R.M. (1983): Forecasting the Forecasts of Others, *Journal of Political Economy*, 91, 546–88.

Watson, M.W. (1989): Recursive Solution Methods for Dynamic Linear Rational Expectations Models, *Journal of Econometrics*, 41, 65–89.

Watson, M.W. (1995): Vector Autoregressions and Cointegration, in: R.F. Engle and D. McFadden (eds): *Handbook of Econometrics*, vol. 4., Amsterdam: North-Holland.

Whiteman, C.H. (1983): *Linear Rational Expectations Models, A User's Guide*, Minneapolis: University of Minnesota Press.

Whiteman, C.H. (1985): Spectral Utility, Wiener-Hopf Techniques, and Rational Expectations, *Journal of Economic Dynamics and Control*, 9, 225–40.

Whittle, P. (1963): *Prediction and Regulation by Linear Least-Square Methods*, Princeton: Van Nostrand-Reinhold.

Whittle, P. (1982): *Optimization over Time*, vol. I and vol. II, New York: John Wiley.

Wickens, M.R. (1993): Rational Expectations and Integrated Variables, in: P.C.B. Phillips and V.B. Hall (eds): *Models, Methods, and Applications of Econometrics, Essays in Honor of Rex Bergstrom*, Oxford: Basil Blackwell, 317–36.

Williams, D. (1991): *Probability with Martingales*, Cambridge: Cambridge University Press.

4

Inventory Models: The Estimation of Euler Equations

Kenneth D. West

E 22

C 22, C 51

1 Introduction

After a period of dormancy in the 1960s and 1970s, empirical work on inventories has enjoyed a resurgence in the 1980s and 1990s. In this chapter, I discuss some of the econometric issues raised by this recent work, and survey results from some recent empirical papers. For reasons of comparative advantage, and to avoid overlap with other chapters in this volume, I focus on a rational expectations version of the linear quadratic inventory model of Holt et al. (1960).

My aim is to illustrate recent developments in time series econometrics by showing how such developments have or might be applied to this often used inventory model. Some of these developments, such as the optimal linear combination of a given vector of instruments in the presence of serial correlation, are relatively well known, and appear in standard regression packages such as RATS. Others are not as well known, and, as far as I know, do not appear in standard software packages. The intended reader is one who nonetheless is willing to consider use of these techniques, but finds it difficult or tedious to plow through theoretical papers. From a theoretical econometric point of view, the discussion is informal; the interested reader may consult the cited references for discussion of underlying technical considerations.

Because of space constraints, the discussion is by no means self-contained, in that some issues that are likely to be encountered in empirical work are not discussed. Prominent among these is the question of how to model trends (unit roots and all that). I simply take as given that the researcher has somehow decided whether or not a unit root is appropriate, without asking how the decision was made or whether the testing procedure (if any) used in making the decision should be taken into account when conducting subsequent inference. Other relevant econometric issues that are not discussed here include those raised by continuous time models (e.g. Mosser, 1988; Christiano and Eichenbaum, 1989) and by aggregation (e.g. Blinder, 1981; Lovell, 1993; Schuh, 1993). As well, economic models other than the linear quadratic model are given short shrift, with only passing discussion of the flexible accelerator model (Lovell, 1961), and not a single mention of, for example, models that put inventories in the production function (e.g. Christiano, 1988; Ramey, 1989). See Blinder and Maccini (1991a; 1991b) for fine reviews that discuss these models as well as a broader array of economic (as opposed to econometric) aspects of recent inventory research.

Section 2 presents the linear quadratic model. Sections 3 to 6 discuss instrumental variables estimation of a first order condition of this model, and section 7 provides the solution and estimation of a decision rule implied by the model. Section 8 compares the approach analyzed in sections 3 to 6 with that of section 7. Section 9 surveys some recent estimates of the model. Readers uninterested in the econometric discussion may proceed directly to section 9 after familiarizing themselves with the notation defined in section 2.

2 The Linear Quadratic Model

A number of papers have followed Holt et al. (1960) and used a model in which a representative firm maximizes the expected present discounted value of future cash flows, with a cost function that includes linear and quadratic costs of production and of holding inventories. In some papers, sales and revenue are exogenous, in which case an equivalent objective is to minimize the expected present discounted value of future costs.

To state the problem formally, let p_t be real price (say, ratio of output price to the wage), S_t real sales, Q_t real production, H_t real end of period inventories, C_t real period costs, b a discount factor, $0 \leqslant b < 1$, and E_t mathematical expectations conditional on information known at time t, assumed equivalent to linear projections. The objective function, then, is

$$\max \Pi_t \equiv \lim_{T \to \infty} E_t \sum_{j=0}^{\infty} b^j (p_{t+j} S_{t+j} - C_{t+j}) \tag{4.1}$$

subject to $\quad Q_t = S_t + H_t - H_{t-1}$,

$$C_t = 0.5 a_0 \Delta Q_t^2 + 0.5 a_1 Q_t^2 + 0.5 a_2 (H_{t-1} - a_3 S_t)^2 + u_{1t} Q_t + u_{2t} H_t.$$

For the moment, a_1 and a_2 are assumed positive, a_0 and a_3 nonnegative. The terms in a_0 and a_1 capture increasing costs of changing production and of production. The terms in a_2 and a_3 capture inventory holding and backlog costs. Section 9 discusses the role the a_is play in determining inventory behavior.

The scalars u_{1t} and u_{2t} are unobservable cost shocks that have zero mean and may be serially correlated, possibly with unit autoregressive roots. In this stripped down model, they capture any stochastic variation in costs. Some

richer models surveyed briefly below include observable cost variables such as
wages, raw materials prices, and interest rates.[1] Constant, trend, and seasonal
terms, which also typically are included in estimation, or are removed prior to
estimation, are omitted for simplicity.

An optimizing firm will not be able to cut costs by increasing production by
one unit this period, storing the unit in inventory, and producing one less unit
next period, holding revenue $p_t S_t$ unchanged throughout. Formally, differentiating costs with respect to H_t gives[2]

$$E_t\{a_0(\Delta Q_t - 2b\Delta Q_{t+1} + b^2\Delta Q_{t+2}) + a_1(Q_t - bQ_{t+1})$$
$$+ ba_2(H_t - a_3 S_{t+1}) + u_t\} = 0, \tag{4.2}$$

$$u_t = u_{1t} - bE_t u_{1t+1} + u_{2t}.$$

Note that a_0, a_1, and a_2 are identified only up to scale: doubling all of these
leaves the first order condition unchanged, apart from rescaling the unobservable disturbance u_t. Thus from this first order condition one can only aim to
estimate ratios of these parameters.[3]

There are four independent unknowns to be estimated: b, a_3 and the ratios
of (i) two of a_0, a_1, and a_2 to (ii) some linear combination of a_0, a_1, and a_2.
Estimation of the discount rate b is, however, problematical. Analytical
arguments, simulations, and empirical experience in estimating this and related
models (Blanchard, 1983; West, 1986b; Gregory et al., 1992) indicate that the
data are unlikely to yield sharp inferences about the value of b. Almost all the
relevant literature has therefore imposed rather than estimated a value for b,
which yields the additional benefit that the remaining three parameters (a_3 and
two of a_0, a_1 and a_2, the latter two identified only up to scale) may be estimated
linearly. A reasonable value of b comes from noting that with, say, monthly
data, values for b of about 0.995 to 0.998 imply annual rates of discount of
about 2% to 6%. In practice, estimates of the remaining parameters tend to be
insensitive to exact choice of b (Blanchard, 1983; West, 1986a). Through the
remainder of the discussion, therefore, I assume that a value of b is imposed,
and there are three parameters to be estimated.

Two approaches have been used in estimating and testing this model. A
limited information approach works off the first order condition (4.2), which,
it should be noted, was derived without making a parametric assumption
about the demand curve (e.g. does it depend on the price of competing
products?) or market structure (competitive, monopolist, etc.). Econometric
issues raised in this approach are discussed in sections 3 to 6. Section 3
discusses choice of instruments, section 4 covariance matrix estimation,
section 5 methods for testing, and section 6 implications of unit root nonstationarity.[4] In sections 3–5, I assume that S_t is I(0), possibly around a trend
that is not explicitly discussed, and that u_t is I(0) as well.

Section 7 discusses a second, *full information* approach, which makes a
parametric assumption about demand and then solves for the firm's equilib-

rium decision rule. Section 8 compares the limited and full information approaches.

3 Limited Information Estimation: Instrumental Variables

3.1 Introduction

This approach transforms (4.2) into an estimable equation and then uses instrumental variables to obtain parameter estimates and test statistics. As is standard in instrumental variables estimation, a choice of left hand side variable (a normalization) is required. Asymptotically, all normalizations are equivalent, provided the linear combination of a_0, a_1, and a_2 that multiplies the left hand side variable is nonzero.

For concreteness, put $-(\partial^2 \Pi_t / \partial H_t^2) H_t = [a_0(1 + 4b + b^2) + a_1(1 + b) + ba_2] H_t \equiv cH_t$ on the left hand side;[5] the Legendre-Clebsch condition (a dynamic analog of the usual second order necessary condition; Stengel, 1986, p. 213) states that $-\partial^2 \Pi_t / \partial H_t^2 > 0$ and thus that this particular linear combination is nonzero. Then (4.2) may be rewritten

$$H_t = (a_0/c)X_{0t+2} + (a_1/c)X_{1t+1} + (ba_2a_3/c)S_{t+1} + v_{t+2} \qquad (4.3)$$

$$\equiv X_t'\beta + v_{t+2},$$

$$X_{0t+2} \equiv -(\Delta S_t - 2H_{t-1} + H_{t-2}) + 2b(\Delta S_{t+1} + H_{t+1} + H_{t-1})$$
$$- b^2(\Delta S_{t+2} + H_{t+2} - 2H_{t+1}).$$

$$X_{1t+1} \equiv -S_t + H_{t-1} + b(S_{t+1} + H_{t+1}),$$

$$v_{t+2} \equiv u_t/c + e_{t+2},$$

$$e_{t+2} \equiv -(a_0/c)(X_{0t+2} - E_t X_{0t+2}) - (a_1/c)(X_{1t+1} - E_t X_{1t+1})$$
$$- (ba_2a_3/c)(S_{t+1} - E_t S_{t+1}),$$

$$X_t \equiv (X_{0t+2}, X_{1t+1}, S_{t+1})',$$

$$\beta \equiv (\beta_1, \beta_2, \beta_3)' \equiv (a_0/c, a_1/c, ba_2a_3/c)',$$

$$c \equiv a_0(1 + 4b + b^2) + a_1(1 + b) + ba_2.$$

From an estimate of β, one can recover estimates of a_0/c and a_1/c directly, and of a_2/c and a_3 using

$$a_2/c = [1 - \beta_1(1 + 4b + b^2) - \beta_2(1 + b)]/b, \qquad a_3 = \beta_3/(ba_2/c).$$

The idea is to use a vector of instruments that is uncorrelated with v_{t+2}, but correlated with X_t, taking account of serial correlation of v_{t+2}.

3.2   Optimal Linear Combination of Given Vector of Instruments

Suppose we are given a vector of instruments Z_t of finite dimension q; since three parameters are to be estimated, an order condition is that $q \geqslant 3$. Let Z_t satisfy $EZ_t v_{t+2} = 0$, $EX_t Z'_t$ of rank 3. In West (1986a), for example, Z_t consisted of lags of H_t and S_t; Kashyap and Wilcox (1993) included lags of stock prices as well. Which $(3 \times q)$ matrix selects the optimal linear combination of instruments? The answer depends on the serial correlation properties of $Z_t v_{t+2}$, the vector of cross-products of the instruments, and the unobserved disturbance. In particular, since, as illustrated below, $Z_t v_{t+2}$ is serially correlated, the conventional two stage least squares (2SLS) estimator is not the most efficient.[6]

Let $\hat{\Omega}$ be a consistent estimate of the $(q \times q)$ matrix

$$\hat{\Omega} \equiv \sum_{j=-\infty}^{\infty} EZ_t Z'_{t-j} v_{t+2} v_{t+2-j}$$

$$\equiv \Gamma_0 + \sum_{j=1}^{\infty} (\Gamma_j + \Gamma'_j), \qquad \Gamma_j \equiv EZ_t Z'_{t-j} v_{t+2} v_{t+2-j}. \tag{4.4}$$

Ω is sometimes called the "long run" covariance matrix of $Z_t v_{t+2}$; procedures to obtain $\hat{\Omega}$ are discussed in section 4.

Let Z be a $T \times q$ matrix whose tth row is Z'_t, and similarly let $X = [X'_t]$ be $T \times 3$, $H = [H_t]$ be $T \times 1$. Hansen (1982) shows that given the vector of instruments Z_t, the $3 \times q$ matrix that selects the optimal linear combination is $EX_t Z'_t \Omega^{-1}$, with finite sample counterpart $T^{-1} X' Z \hat{\Omega}^{-1}$. Once offsetting factors of T^{-1} and T are dropped to keep the algebra uncluttered, the resulting estimator is

$$\hat{\beta} = (X' Z \hat{\Omega}^{-1} Z' X)^{-1} X' Z \hat{\Omega}^{-1} Z' H, \qquad \hat{\beta} - \beta \approx N(0, \hat{V}), \qquad \hat{V} \equiv T(X' Z \hat{\Omega}^{-1} Z' X)^{-1}$$

$$\text{asymptotic } V = \text{plim } T\hat{V} = \text{plim } T^2 (X' Z \hat{\Omega}^{-1} Z' X)^{-1}. \tag{4.5}$$

Thus this estimator differs from the usual 2SLS one in that $\hat{\Omega}^{-1}$ replaces $(Z'Z)^{-1}$, although if $q = 3$, so that the equation is exactly identified and $X'Z$ is square and invertible, (4.5) and the 2SLS estimators are identical. Whether or not $q = 3$, 2SLS is consistent. But if $q > 3$, 2SLS is inefficient (larger asymptotic variance-covariance matrix), and, because of the serial correlation in $Z_t v_{t+2}$, the usual 2SLS variance-covariance matrix is inappropriate for inference whether or not $q > 3$.

The rather forbidding formula in (4.4) simplifies under assumptions often made in practice. If $u_t = 0$, so that there are no unobservable cost disturbances (e.g. Kashyap and Wilcox, 1993), $v_{t+2} = e_{t+2}$, and the regression disturbance is a sum of expectational errors. Now, as is well known, under rational expectations the expectational errors $X_{1t+1} - E_t X_{1t+1}$ and $S_{t+1} - E_t S_{t+1}$ are serially uncorrelated. But $X_{0t+2} - E_t X_{0t+2}$ depends on period $t+1$ and period $t+2$ information, and $X_{0t+3} - E_{t+1} X_{0t+3}$ on period $t+2$ and period $t+3$ information. This implies an MA(1) structure to $X_{0t+2} - E_t X_{0t+2}$ and thus to v_{t+2} as well. Since $E_t v_{t+2} = 0$, the vector $Z_t v_{t+2}$ is also MA(1): for $j > 1$,

$$E(Z_t v_{t+2} Z'_{t-j} v_{t+2-j}) = E[Z_t Z'_{t-j} v_{t+2-j} E(v_{t+2}|Z_t Z'_{t-j} v_{t+2-j})] = E[Z_t Z'_{t-j} v_{t+2-j} 0]$$

$= 0$. So in this case, $\Omega = \Sigma^1_{j=-1} E Z_t Z'_{t-j} v_{t+2} v_{t+2-j} = \Gamma_0 + (\Gamma_1 + \Gamma'_1)$.

If the unobservable cost shock u_t is present, Q_t, H_t and, in general, S_t will depend on that shock. But considerable simplification of (4.4) may nonetheless occur. If u_{1t} and u_{2t} and thus u_t are white noise (West and Wilcox, 1993b), $X_{0t+2} - E_t X_{0t+2}$ will depend in part on u_{t+1} and u_{t+2}, implying that v_{t+2}, which depends on u_t as well, will be MA(2). The vector $Z_t v_{t+2}$ will be MA(2) as well, so $\Omega = \Sigma^2_{j=-2} E Z_t Z'_{t-j} v_{t+2} v_{t+2-j} = \Gamma_0 + (\Gamma_1 + \Gamma'_1) + (\Gamma_2 + \Gamma'_2)$.

More generally, if u_t has an autoregressive component, so too will v_{t+2}. If u_t follows a particular parametric process, such as an AR(1), one can estimate the AR(1) parameter simultaneously with the cost parameters (Kollintzas, 1992).

3.3 Comparison with Two Stage Least Squares

What are the efficiency gains from using (4.5) rather than two stage least squares (2SLS)? Here, the 2SLS estimator $\dot{\beta}$ is

$$\dot{\beta} = [X'Z(Z'Z)^{-1}Z'X]^{-1}X'Z(Z'Z)^{-1}Z'H, \tag{4.6}$$

asymptotic $\dot{V} = \text{plim } T^2[X'Z(Z'Z)^{-1}Z'X]^{-1}X'Z(Z'Z)^{-1}\Omega(Z'Z)^{-1}$

$$Z'X[X'Z(Z'Z)^{-1}Z'X]^{-1}.$$

Plainly, the answer to this question depends on the data generating processes (DGPs) for the Z and X variables, as well as those of the unobservable shocks.

To illustrate what the gains might be, I have worked them out in a simple case. Sales are forecast from an exogenous AR(2), the cost shock u_t is serially uncorrelated, and two lags each of sales and inventories are used as instruments:

$$S_t = \phi_1 S_{t-1} + \phi_2 S_{t-2} + v_{2t},$$

$$Eu_t u_{t-j} = Eu_t v_{2t-j} = 0 \quad \text{for } j \neq 0, \tag{4.7}$$

$$Z_t = (H_{t-1}, H_{t-2}, S_{t-1}, S_{t-2})'.$$

Given ϕ_1, ϕ_2, a_0, a_1, a_2, a_3, b, and the variance-covariance matrix of (u_t, v_{2t}) one may then solve for the data generating process for inventories and sales, using methods outlined in section 7 on full information estimation.

I tried three data generating processes, each corresponding to a different set of cost parameters, but all using a common set of parameters for the sales processes and shocks. These sets of cost parameters are summarized in table 4.1. They are intended to correspond to parameters found in some studies of

Table 4.1 Cost parameters for data generating processes

Mnemonic	a_0	a_1	a_2	a_3
E	0.01	0.25	0.50	0.70
R	0.20	-1.00	2.00	0.35
W	0.10	0.40	0.01	2.00

(a) a_0, a_1, a_2 and a_3 are defined in (4.1).
(b) For all three data generating processes, the discount rate was set at $b = 0.995$. The sales process was assumed to follow an exogenous AR(2), $S_t = 0.7S_{t-1} + 0.25S_{t-2} + v_{2t}$, with var$(v_{2t}) = 0.128033$, corr$(u_t, v_{2t}) = -0.5$, var$(u_t) = 0.5$, with u_t the cost shock as defined in (4.1).

two digit manufacturing industries in the United States: Eichenbaum (1989, p. 862; top panel: mnemonic E), Ramey (1991, p. 323: R), and West (1986a, p. 393, top panel: W).[7] (The problem (4.1) is well posed for the R DGP despite the negative sign on a_1: see Killintzas, 1989; Ramey, 1991.)

I set the variance-covariance matrix of (u_t, v_{2t}) so that for the W DGP the unconditional variance-covariance matrix of (H_t, S_t) was approximately proportional to that of US monthly nondurables manufacturing, 1967–90; H_t are finished goods inventories, with var$(S_t) = 1$ (a harmless normalization). The exact parameters are given in the notes to table 4.1. It should be noted that the implied reduced forms for DGPs E and R (not given in the table) are implausible in that H_t displays little serial correlation; both Eichenbaum (1989) and Ramey (1991) implicitly accounted for the serial correlation that is empirically present in H_t by allowing for serially correlated cost shocks, which I omit for simplicity.

Table 4.2 compares some standard errors implied by the asymptotic variance-covariance matrices V (defined in (4.5)) and $\dot{V}$ (defined in (4.6)). Define

$$c_t \equiv \sum_{j=0}^{\infty} E_t C_{t+j}$$

as the expected present discounted value of costs. Then the quantity in column 2 of table 4.2, $(1 + b)a_0 + a_1 \equiv \partial^2 c_t / \partial Q_t^2$, is the slope of marginal production cost, which Ramey (1991) has argued is of central economic interest. To my surprise, the optimal estimator yields little efficiency gains, for any of the DGPs: column 4, for example, indicates that the asymptotic variance of $T^{1/2}(\hat{a}_3 - a_3)$ is at best $(0.998)^2$ times smaller for the optimal than for the 2SLS estimator. Similar ratios apply for $(1 + b)a_0 + a_1$ and a_3 (columns 2 and 3).

No doubt there are other data generating processes for which the gains from the optimal estimator are quite large. But even for the data generating processes assumed here, the small efficiency gains do not argue that it is a matter of indifference which estimator one uses, if one is interested in

Table 4.2 Comparison of asymptotic variance-covariance matrices resulting from optimal and 2SLS linear combinations of instruments

1 *DGP*	*2* *Ratio of SEs on* $[(1 + b)a_0 + a_1]/c$	*3* *Ratio of SEs* *on* a_2/c	*4* *Ratio of SEs* *on* a_3
E	0.990	0.982	0.976
R	0.999	0.999	0.998
W	0.992	0.962	1.000

(a) a_0, a_1, and a_2 are defined in (4.1); c is defined in (4.3).
(b) In the ratios referenced in columns 2–4, the numerator is the standard error computed from the variance-covariance matrix of the estimator (4,5), which optimally combines a given set of instruments; the denominator is the standard error from that of the two stage least squares estimator (4.6). Both estimators were assumed to use a (3×4) linear combination of a (4×1) instrument vector consisting of two lags each of H_t and S_t. The ratios must lie between 0 and 1, smaller numbers indicating a greater efficiency gain from using the optimal estimator.
(c) These asymptotic comparisons may not accurately predict the actual finite sample performance of the two estimators.

performing inference on the estimated parameters. If one estimates by 2SLS, the appropriate covariance matrix is given in (4.6). Suppose one instead uses the traditional (and, in the present example, incorrect) covariance matrix

$$\tilde{V} = E v_{t+2}^2 \operatorname{plim} T[X'Z(Z'Z)^{-1}Z'X]^{-1}. \tag{4.8}$$

How accurate are hypothesis tests?

Table 4.3 considers this question (asymptotically) for tests of three simple hypothesis tests. Interpretation of the tests is given at the foot of the table. By

Table 4.3 Asymptotic sizes of nominal 0.05 tests, when an inconsistent estimator of the 2SLS covariance matrix is used

DGP	$[(1 + b)a_0 + a_1]/c$	a_2/c	a_3
E	0.107	0.143	0.249
R	0.053	0.051	0.011
W	0.100	0.533	0.500

(a) This table presents the asymptotic size of a nominal 0.05 test of the null that the indicated parameter equals its population value, as given in table 4.2. For example, in the row E, column a_2/c, the null is that $a_2/c = 0.5$. It is assumed that the covariance matrix given in (4.8) is used in calculating the relevant standard error.
(b) These asymptotic calculations may not accurately predict the actual finite sample performance of such tests.

and large there are dramatic distortions. The a_3 entry for DGP W, for example, indicates that a test that should reject only 5% of the time in fact will reject 50% of the time. The implication is that it is important to use a consistent estimate of the covariance matrix. Since such a matrix requires estimation of Ω (see (4.7)), use of 2SLS in the end will be no simpler than use of the optimal estimator (4.5).

How accurately does the asymptotic theory underlying tables 4.2 and 4.3 apply in the finite samples used in practice? The answer to this question is not well known. Preliminary simulation results in West and Wilcox (1993a; 1993b) indicate that while the asymptotic theory often provides a good guide to finite sample performance, the estimator usually displays slightly more variability than is predicted by the asymptotic theory, and sometimes displays some bias as well; on occasion, test statistics are very poorly sized. In empirical work, the limited applicability of asymptotic theory is perhaps suggested by the sensitivity of estimates of the model to choice of left hand side variable (Krane and Braun, 1991; Ramey, 1991; Kashyap and Wilcox, 1993), a sensitivity not displayed by the asymptotic theory.

3.4   Alternative Instrumental Variables Techniques

What are the implications for empirical work of such inaccuracy in asymptotic approximations? For inference, one might want to use simulation or bootstrap techniques, although such techniques, which typically require specification of a data generating process for all the variables in the system, seem more natural in systems estimated by full rather than limited information techniques. See West (1992) for an illustration of the use of bootstrap techniques in a full information environment.

Alternatively, for estimation as well as inference one might want to consider estimators that have better asymptotic or finite sample properties. Full information estimators are discussed below. To motivate alternative limited information estimators, begin by considering how one chooses an instrument vector, a decision that so far has been taken as given. Obvious candidates for instruments include lags of S_t and H_t (equivalently, lags of H_t and Q_t, given the inventory identity $Q_t = S_t + \Delta H_t$). This is, indeed, done in many studies, with $Z_t = [H_t, S_t, H_{t-1}, S_{t-1}, \ldots]'$ if cost shocks are assumed absent, $Z_t = [H_{t-1}, S_{t-1}, H_{t-2}, S_{t-2}, \ldots]'$ if cost shocks are assumed present but serially uncorrelated. Hansen (1985) shows that given the serial correlation in $Z_t v_{t+2}$, an increased number of lags used (i.e. an increase in the dimension of Z_t) yields a strict increase in the asymptotic efficiency of the estimator. This applies even if, as in the example in section 7, there is a finite number of lags of H_t and S_t in the reduced form for $(H_t, S_t)'$. Since this result by itself gives little practical guidance on the number of lags to use, it is advisable to experiment with various lag lengths to see if results are sensitive to the exact number of lags used (e.g. Eichenbaum, 1989).

Alternatively, if one is willing to specify and estimate a finite parameter ARMA model for H_t, S_t, and v_{t+2}, one can apply the formulas in Hansen (1985) to obtain a 3×1 instrument vector Z_t^* (say) that is optimal in the space of instrument vectors that rely on lagged H_ts and S_ts. Suppose for concreteness that the environment is as in section 3.3: the cost shock u_t is iid, so that $v_{t+2} \sim MA(2)$ and $EH_{t-j}v_{t+2} = ES_{t-j}v_{t+2} = 0$ for $j \geq 1$. Then Z_t^* is a linear combination of past H_ts and S_ts, with nonzero weights on *all* lags: $H_1, S_1, \ldots, H_{t-1}$, and S_{t-1} are all used to construct Z_t^*. See West and Wilcox (1993a), who show how to make this estimator operational, and indicate that for some but not all plausible DGPs there are large asymptotic efficiency gains from using (a) Z_t^* rather than (b) section 3.2's conventional GMM estimator with Z_t the set of lags of H_t and S_t in the reduced form for $(H_t, S_t)'$.

Ramey (1991), however, notes that any lags of H_t will be correlated with the disturbance v_{t+2} if unobservable cost shocks have an autoregressive component, implicitly argues that we do not have *a priori* evidence about the parametric structure of such a component, and explicitly calls for using instruments that she describes as "truly exogenous." These include oil prices, military spending, and dummies for the political party of the president.

It is difficult to evaluate Ramey's suggested instruments. On the one hand, there is some Monte Carlo evidence that instruments that are only weakly correlated with the vector of right hand side variables may perform poorly in finite samples, even if they are uncorrelated with the disturbance (Nelson and Startz, 1990); on the other hand, it is well known that instruments that are correlated with the disturbance will perform poorly even in large samples, no matter how strongly correlated with the vector of right hand side variables. Monte Carlo evidence on what Shea (1993) calls the tradeoff between "exogeneity" and "relevance" would be very useful.

4 Limited Information Estimation: Covariance Matrix Estimation

As (4.5) indicates, one must compute $\hat{\Omega}$ for inference and (if the efficient estimator is used) estimation. To discuss how to do so, let $\dot{v}_t$ be the 2SLS residual, $\dot{v}_{t+2} = H_t - X_t'\dot{\beta}$, where $\dot{\beta}$ is defined in (4.6). Consider estimating Γ_j (defined in (4.4)) by

$$\hat{\Gamma}_j = T^{-1} \sum_{t=j+1}^{T} Z_t Z_{t-j}' \dot{v}_{t+2}\dot{v}_{t+2-j} \quad \text{for } j \geq 0. \tag{4.9}$$

For concreteness, focus initially on the case where the cost shock u_t is absent, so that $Z_t v_{t+2} \sim MA(1)$ and $\Omega = \Gamma_0 + (\Gamma_1 + \Gamma_1')$. The simplest technique used to estimate $\hat{\Omega}$ is the obvious one, $\hat{\Omega} = \hat{\Gamma}_0 + (\hat{\Gamma}_1 + \hat{\Gamma}_1')$. This is, indeed, consistent. But it is not guaranteed to be positive definite, and, indeed, in practice is not always positive definite (e.g. Cumby and Huizanga, 1990). In such a case, the variance-covariance matrix $\hat{V}$ (defined in (4.5)) will also fail to be positive definite, and there will be some linear combinations of parameters whose estimated standard errors will be negative.

While $\hat{\Gamma}_0 + (\hat{\Gamma}_1 + \hat{\Gamma}'_1)$ will be positive definite asymptotically, if the model is right, there is an evident need for an estimator that will be positive definite by construction. Early proposals include Cumby, Huizanga, and Obstfeld (1983) and Eichenbaum, Hansen, and Singleton (1988). Since Ω is proportional to the spectral density of $Z_t v_{t+2}$ at frequency zero (e.g. Granger and Newbold, 1977), recent research has built on the well developed literature on estimators of spectral densities.

One part of this literature suggests constructing $\hat{\Omega}$ as

$$\hat{\Omega} = \hat{\Gamma}_0 + \sum_{j=1}^{m} k_j (\hat{\Gamma}_j + \hat{\Gamma}'_j), \qquad (4.10)$$

for weights k_j chosen to insure that $\hat{\Omega}$ is positive definite, and a suitably chosen bound m. A simple choice of weights are what are called the "Bartlett" ones,

$$k_j = 1 - [j/(m+1)] \Rightarrow k_1 = m/(m+1), \ k_2 = (m-1)/(m+1), \ldots, k_m = 1/(m+1). \qquad (4.11)$$

The formal asymptotic theory underlying use of the estimator (4.10) requires that as the sample size T becomes arbitrarily large, then so too does m, but in such a fashion that $m/T^{1/2} \to 0$ (Newey and West, 1987a). This theory is applicable not only when the vector $Z_t v_{t+2}$ is MA(1), as in the simple case used to motivate the present discussion, but for any ARMA process for $Z_t v_{t+2}$, even when the order of the ARMA process is not known *a priori*.

It should be emphasized that even in the simple case that $Z_t v_{t+2}$ is known to be MA(1), the theory requires that m increase with T: even though one knows *a priori* that the population value of Γ_j is zero for $j > 1$, for sufficiently large T one will want to be using estimates of the form $\hat{\Omega} = \hat{\Gamma}_0 + [m/(m+1)] (\hat{\Gamma}_1 + \hat{\Gamma}'_1) + \ldots + [1/(m+1)](\hat{\Gamma}_m + \hat{\Gamma}'_m)$ for $m > 1$. The reason is that one wants $\hat{\Omega}$ to well approximate $\Gamma_0 + (\Gamma_1 + \Gamma'_1)$ in a large sample; if m is fixed at 1 independent of T, then $\hat{\Omega}$ will instead approximate $\Gamma_0 + (1/2)(\Gamma_1 + \Gamma'_1)$.

But just how large should m be for a given sized sample, in the simple MA(1) example or more generally? While it seems unlikely that a fully automatic rule for selecting m will be satisfactory in all attempts to estimate (4.3), Andrews (1991) and Andrews and Monahan (1992) have developed procedures that may be used to produce an initial choice of m that (i) is asymptotically optimal in a certain sense, and (ii) can be used as a starting point in subsequent experimentation.

I will illustrate this using Newey and West's (1993) extension of those procedures, since it is simpler to explain (in my totally unbiased opinion). Let [.] denote "integer part of." An asymptotically optimal choice of m satisfies

$$m = [\gamma T^{1/3}], \tag{4.12}$$

$$\gamma = 1.1447(\{s^{(1)}/s^{(0)}\}^2)^{1/3}, \qquad s^{(1)} = 2 \sum_{j=1}^{\infty} j\sigma_j, \qquad s^{(0)} = \sigma_0 + 2 \sum_{j=1}^{\infty} \sigma_j,$$

$$\sigma_j = w' \Gamma_j w, \qquad w = (1, 1, \ldots, 1, 1)',$$

where w is $(q \times 1)$.

Suppose first that cost shocks are absent, so that $Z_t v_{t+2} \sim \mathrm{MA}(1)$, $\sigma_j = \Gamma_j = 0$ for $j > 1$, $s^{(1)} = 2\sigma_1$ and $s^{(0)} = \sigma_0 + 2\sigma_1$. Then one could set

$$m = [\hat{\gamma} T^{1/3}], \tag{4.13}$$

$$\hat{\gamma} = 1.1447(\{\hat{s}^{(1)}/\hat{s}^{(0)}\}^2)^{1/3}, \qquad \hat{s}^{(1)} = 2\hat{\sigma}_1, \qquad \hat{s}^{(0)} = \hat{\sigma}_0 + 2\hat{\sigma}_1, \qquad \hat{\sigma}_j = w' \hat{\Gamma}_j w.$$

An alternative procedure for selecting m, applicable both when cost shocks are absent and when cost shocks follow any stationary process, is to choose m by

$$m = [\hat{\gamma} T^{1/3}], \tag{4.14}$$

$$\hat{\gamma} = 1.1447(\{\hat{s}^{(1)}/\hat{s}^{(0)}\}^2)^{1/3}, \qquad \hat{s}^{(1)} = 2 \sum_{j=1}^{n} j\hat{\sigma}_j, \qquad \hat{s}^{(0)} = \hat{\sigma}_0 + 2 \sum_{j=1}^{n} \hat{\sigma}_j,$$

$$n = [4(T/100)^{2/9}].$$

Thus, if $T = 100$, $n = 4$; if $T = 300$, $n = 5$.[8]

Andrews and Monahan (1992) emphasize the possible benefits of combining what is called "prewhitening" with a procedure such as that just described. To illustrate Newey and West's (1993) prewhitened estimator, let

$$\hat{g}_t = Z_t \hat{v}_{t+2}, \qquad \hat{A} = \sum_{t=2}^{T} \hat{g}_t \hat{g}'_{t-1} \left(\sum_{t=2}^{T} \hat{g}_{t-1} \hat{g}'_{t-1} \right)^{-1}, \qquad \tilde{g}_t \equiv \hat{g}_t - \hat{A} \hat{g}_{t-1}, \tag{4.15}$$

$$n = [4(T/100)^{2/9}],$$

$$\tilde{\sigma}_j = T^{-1} \sum_{t=j+1}^{T} \{(w' \tilde{g}_t)(w' \tilde{g}_{t-j})\}, \qquad j = 0, \ldots, n,$$

$$\hat{s}^{(1)} = 2 \sum_{j=1}^{n} j\tilde{\sigma}_j, \qquad \hat{s}^{(0)} = \tilde{\sigma}_0 + 2 \sum_{j=1}^{n} \tilde{\sigma}_j, \qquad \hat{\gamma} = 1.1447(\{\hat{s}^{(1)}/\hat{s}^{(0)}\}^2)^{1/3}.$$

Thus, $\hat{A}$ is the $(q \times q)$ matrix of VAR(1) regression coefficients obtained by regressing cross-products of instruments and residuals on their first lag, and $\tilde{g}_t$ is the resulting $(q \times 1)$ vector of period t residuals. The idea is to apply a procedure such as that just described to the VAR residuals $\tilde{g}_t$, and then use $\hat{A}$ to adjust the result. Specifically, one sets

$$\hat{\Omega} = (I - \hat{A})^{-1} \tilde{\Omega} (I - \hat{A})^{-1'}, \tag{4.16}$$

$$\tilde{\Omega} = \{\tilde{\Gamma}_0 + \sum_{j=1}^{m} \{1 - j/(m+1)\}(\tilde{\Gamma}_j + \tilde{\Gamma}_j')\}, \qquad \tilde{\Gamma}_j = T^{-1} \sum_{t=j+1}^{T} \tilde{g}_t \tilde{g}_{t-j}', \qquad j = 0, \ldots, m,$$

$$m = [\hat{\gamma} T^{1/3}].$$

When cost shocks are absent, (4.13) and (4.14) are asymptotically equivalent; whether the prewhitened estimator (4.16) is asymptotically preferable to (4.13) and (4.14) depends on the underlying data generating process. The argument for prewhitening is not so much that it yields great asymptotic gains as that it seems to work well in simulations.

But with or without cost shocks, (4.13), (4.14), and (4.16) might yield different values of m in a given application. This illustrates the general point that regardless of the process followed by cost shocks, there are a number of reasonable rules to choose m. For the data generating processes considered in Newey and West (1993), the rules (4.14) and (4.16) worked relatively well. But since asymptotic theory does not yield a single value of m for a given data set and sample size, it is advisable to do some experimentation with a range of values, computing at least some test statistics using different $\hat{V}$s, each $\hat{V}$ relying on a $\hat{\Omega}$ computed with a different m and/or n; the hope is that results will not be sensitive to the exact values of n chosen. Further theoretical and simulation evidence on alternative rules are of great interest.

How do the rules developed to date compare with longer established testing procedures? The Monte Carlo evidence in Andrews (1991), Andrews and Monahan (1992), and Newey and West (1993) indicates that their recommended procedures are preferable to more traditional ones. This evidence indicates as well, however, that when data are highly serially correlated, tests may suffer serious size distortions even in sample sizes larger than those typically used in inventory studies: nominal 0.05 tests may have actual sizes of 0.20 or higher.

5 Limited Information Estimation: Testing

Let $\hat{\beta}$ be defined as in (4.5). Given a hypothesis H_0: $g(\beta) = 0$, where $g(\beta)$ is $s \times 1$ and $\partial g / \partial \beta$ is of row rank $s \leq 3$, the usual Wald statistic is appropriate,

$$g(\hat{\beta})'[(\partial g/\partial \hat{\beta}) \hat{V} (\partial g/\partial \hat{\beta})']^{-1} g(\hat{\beta}) \overset{A}{\sim} \chi^2(s), \qquad (4.17)$$

where $\partial g/\partial \hat{\beta}$ denotes the $(s \times 3)$ matrix $\partial g/\partial \beta$ evaluated at $\hat{\beta}$. If the null is simply H_0: $\hat{\beta}_i = 0$, then (4.17) is of course just the square of the usual t-statistic.

Let $\hat{v}_{t+2} = H_t - X_t' \hat{\beta}$, $\hat{v} = [\hat{v}_{t+2}]$. If the number of instruments q exceeds the number of regressors 3, one can test the model by computing

$$T^{-1} \hat{v}' Z \hat{\Omega}^{-1} Z' \hat{v} \overset{A}{\sim} \chi^2(q - 3). \qquad (4.18)$$

This is sometimes referred to as Hansen's (1982) "*J*-test," or a test of instrument residual orthogonality. One interpretation of this is as a test of whether the coefficients of an arbitrarily chosen set of $q - 3$ instruments would all be zero if one added these instruments to the regression equation (4.3) (Newey and West, 1987b). In practice, it has been difficult to turn a rejection by (4.18) into a constructive suggestion about how the first order condition (4.3) or underlying model (4.1) should be modified, at least in my experience.

An easier to interpret, although perhaps less powerful, test was suggested by West (1986a), applied by Krane and Braun (1991) and Dimelis and Ghali (1992), and extended by Kollintzas (1992). It may be shown that the model (4.1) implies that certain weighted sums of the variances, auto- and cross-covariances of H_t, S_t, Q_t, and the cost shocks are nonnegative. If $u_t = 0$ as in West (1986a), for example, we have

$$a_0[\text{var}(\Delta S) - \text{var}(\Delta Q)] + a_1[\text{var}(S) - \text{var}(Q)] - a_2\text{var}(H) + 2a_2a_3\text{cov}(H, S_{+1}) \geqslant 0,$$
(4.19)

where "var" denotes variance and "cov" denotes covariance. To compute the left hand side of (4.19), one may use estimates of the a_is from the Euler equation and of the indicated second moments from the obvious sample counterparts. A standard error may be computed from the joint variance-covariance matrix of the estimated a_is and second moments. See West (1986a) for details.

The left hand side of (4.19) is the difference in average per period costs between the policy actually followed and that of an alternative feasible policy that leaves sales unchanged but sets $Q_t = S_t$ and H_t to zero. If $a_0 = a_3 = 0$, and a_1, $a_2 > 0$, for example, (4.19) reduces to $a_1[\text{var}(S) - \text{var}(Q)] - a_2\text{var}(H) \geqslant 0$: the average per period reduction in production costs allowed by inventory holdings had better be bigger than the average costs of holding inventories themselves – or why would a firm hold inventories? See West (1986a), Kollintzas (1992), and section 8 for further discussion and interpretation.

6 Limited Information Estimation: Unit Roots

6.1 H_t, S_t Cointegrated

Assume now that $S_t \sim I(1)$, but $u_t \sim I(0)$. Kashyap and Wilcox (1993) emphasize that H_t and S_t are then cointegrated. Specifically, with a little bit of algebra, the first order condition (4.2) can be rewritten as

$$E_t\{a_0[\Delta S_t + \Delta^2 H_t - 2b(\Delta S_{t+1} + \Delta^2 H_{t+1}) + b^2(\Delta S_{t+2} + \Delta^2 H_{t+2})]$$

$$- ba_1(\Delta H_{t+1} + \Delta S_{t+1}) + a_1\Delta H_t + ba_2(H_t - \gamma S_t)\} = - u_t, \quad (4.20)$$

$$\gamma \equiv a_3 - [a_1(1 - b)/a_2].$$

Let {.} denote the expression in braces. It may be shown that {.} − $I(0)$, and, since $\Delta S_t \sim I(0)$ by assumption, $H_t − \gamma_t \sim I(0)$: H_t and S_t are cointegrated with cointegrating parameter γ.[9]

Consider first the case where $E\Delta H_t \neq 0(\Rightarrow E\Delta S_t \neq 0)$, as is probably appropriate when one has a long time series from a growing industry. It follows from West (1988a) that the discussion in section 3 still applies: the optimal linear combination of instruments is as given in that discussion, and the resulting coefficient vector is asymptotically normal. The discussions in sections 4 and 5 are applicable as well: (4.18) is asymptotically chi-squared (West, 1988a) and certain variance bounds tests (not the one described in section 5) may be performed as well (West, 1988b; 1990). Andrews and Monahan (1992) indicate that data dependent procedures to select m (defined in (4.10)) still are appropriate.

It sometimes will be more reasonable to assume that $E\Delta H_t = 0$, however. There is little secular movement of the Depression era data in Kashyap and Wilcox (1993), for example. To my knowledge, no one has directly summarized the implications for estimation of equations such as (4.3) under such circumstances. Park and Phillips (1988) and Sims, Stock, and Watson (1990) emphasize that in the related contexts that they consider, the entire coefficient vector will not be asymptotically normal with a full rank variance-covariance matrix.

But as Kashyap and Wilcox (1993) illustrate, inference about many objects of interest may be done in a conventional fashion. Individual coefficients will be asymptotically normal, and inference about such coefficients may proceed as usual if procedures described in section 4 are used to estimate the variance-covariance matrix (Park and Phillips, 1988; West, 1988a; Sims, Stock, and Watson, 1990; Andrews and Monahan, 1992; Hansen, 1992); Kashyap and Wilcox (1993) conjecture that the equation (4.18) statistic will still be asymptotically chi-squared, which seems reasonable given that the statistic can be interpreted as testing the joint significance of $(q − 3)$ of the instruments.

For some other linear rational expectations models, Stock and West (1988) and West (1988a) present Monte Carlo evidence indicating that the asymptotic normal approximation is adequate in sample sizes typically encountered.

6.2 H_t, S_t Not Cointegrated

Now suppose that $u_t \sim I(1)$. Then H_t and S_t obviously may not be cointegrated. For inference to proceed along standard lines, one must difference equation (4.3). The discussion in sections 4 and 5 now applies, with some obvious modifications. Differences of H_t and S_t are now prominent candidates for instruments, for example. And if u_t is a pure random walk, the disturbance of the differenced equation is MA(2).

Lack of cointegration between H_t and S_t may at first blush seem surprising. But note that the model under consideration in fact rationalizes such an occurrence if cost shocks are I(1), as indeed is typically maintained in the literature on real business cycles. And standard tests applied to US data at the two digit SIC code and more aggregate levels generally do not reject the null of no cointegration (Granger and Lee, 1989; West, 1990; Rossana, 1992).

7 Full Information Estimation

7.1 Solution of the Model

For algebraic simplicity, assume that the firm views revenue $p_t S_t$ as exogenous, so that the objective function becomes one of cost minimization. (The assumption of exogenous revenue over an infinite horizon obviously is silly. But it makes discussion of the relevant econometric issues relatively straight-forward. Below I comment briefly on some implications of sales being endogenous: see Eichenbaum, 1984; Blanchard and Melino, 1986; Dimelis and Kollintzas, 1989; and West, 1990 for completely worked out examples of solution and estimation when sales are endogenous.) Also for simplicity, assume that both the firm and the econometrician forecast future sales from a univariate autoregression in S_t,

$$S_t = \phi_1 S_{t-1} + \ldots + \phi_p S_{t-p} + v_{2t},$$

$$\phi_p \neq 0, \qquad Ev_{2t} S_{t-j} = Ev_{2t} H_{t-j} = 0 \quad \text{for } j > 0,$$

$$1 - \phi_1 z - \ldots - \phi_p z^p = 0 \Rightarrow |z| \geq 1, \tag{4.21}$$

where $|z|$ denotes the modulus of a complex number z. Note that (4.21) allows S_t to have a unit autoregressive root. The innovation v_{2t} is assumed uncorrelated with lagged H_{t-j}, in accord with the assumption that sales are exogenous.

For the moment, assume $a_0 \neq 0$. Let L be the lag operator. Use the identity $Q_t = S_t + \Delta H_t$ to rewrite the Euler equation (4.2) as

$$E_t\{f(L)H_{t+2} = D_t\}, \tag{4.22}$$

$$f(L) \equiv 1 - b^{-2}a_0^{-1}[ba_1 + 2a_0b(1+b)]L + b^{-2}a_0^{-1}[a_0(1+4b+b^2) + a_1(1+b) + ba_2]L^2$$

$$- b^{-2}a_0^{-1}[a_1 + 2a_0(1+b)]L^3 + b^{-2}L^4,$$

$$D_t = -b^{-2}(\Delta S_t - 2b\Delta S_{t+1} + b^2\Delta S_{t+2}) - b^{-2}a_0^{-1}a_1(S_t - bS_{t+1}) + b^{-1}a_0^{-1}a_2a_3 S_{t+1}$$

$$- b^{-2}a_0^{-1}u_t.$$

Let λ_t be the roots of the fourth order lag polynomial $f(L)$, $|\lambda_1| \leq \ldots \leq |\lambda_4|$. It may be shown that $\lambda_4 = 1/(b\lambda_1)$ and $\lambda_3 = 1/(b\lambda_2)$, so that at $|\lambda_1|, |\lambda_2| < 1/b$. Suppose further that $|\lambda_1|, |\lambda_2| < 1$, and, for expositional convenience, that $\lambda_1 \neq \lambda_2$. (See Kollintzas, 1989 on the relationship between the cost parameters, the discount rate, and the modulus of these roots.) If we are to obtain a nonexplosive solution, we must solve the stable roots λ_1 and λ_2 backwards, and the unstable roots λ_3 and λ_4 forwards: indeed, a transversality condition forces the firm to do so (Kollintzas, 1989). One may verify that the following then satisfies the Euler equation (4.22):

$$H_t = (\lambda_1 + \lambda_2)H_{t-1} - \lambda_1\lambda_2 H_{t-2} + b^{-1}\lambda_1\lambda_2(\lambda_1 - \lambda_2)^{-1} \tag{4.23}$$

$$\times \sum_{j=0}^{\infty} \{[(b\lambda_1)^{j+1} - (b\lambda_2)^{j+1}]E_t D_{t+j}\}.$$

Note that if λ_1 and λ_2 are complex, they are complex conjugates, so that $\lambda_1 + \lambda_2$ and $\lambda_1\lambda_2$ are real.

Suppose finally, for simplicity, that the unobservable shock u_t is serially uncorrelated. Then one can use techniques such as those in Blanchard (1983) to solve for the reduced form, which expresses H_t in terms of lagged H_ts and S_ts and u_t, and for the decision rule, which expresses H_t in terms of lagged H_ts, current and lagged S_t, and current u_t. Define the scalars ρ_1, ρ_2, w_1, w_2, w_3, and w_4 the $(l \times p)$ vector e' and the $(p \times p)$ matrices Φ and D as

$$\rho_1 = \lambda_1 + \lambda_2, \qquad \rho_2 = -\lambda_1\lambda_2,$$

$$w_1 = b^2\rho_2, \qquad w_2 = -\rho_2[b^2 + 2b + b(a_1/a_0) + (ba_2a_3/a_0)], \tag{4.24}$$

$$w_3 = \rho_2[2b + 1 + (a_1/a_0)], \qquad w_4 = -\rho_2,$$

$$e' = (1 \ 0 \ \dots \ 0),$$

$$\Phi = \begin{matrix} (\phi_1 & \phi_2 & \dots & \phi_{p-1} & \phi_p) \\ (1 & 0 & \dots & 0 & 0) \\ & & \dots & & \\ (0 & 0 & \dots & 1 & 0), \end{matrix}$$

$$D = [I - b\rho_1\Phi - b^2\rho_2\Phi^2]^{-1}.$$

Then the reduced form is

$$H_t = \rho_1 H_{t-1} + \rho_2 H_{t-2} + \pi_1 S_{t-1} + \dots + \pi_p S_{t-p} + \upsilon_{1t}, \tag{4.25}$$

$$(\pi_1, \dots, \pi_p) = e'D(w_1\Phi^3 + w_2\Phi^2 + w_3\Phi + w_4 I),$$

$$\upsilon_{1t} = (\pi_p/\phi_p)\upsilon_{2t} + \upsilon_{Ht} \qquad (p \geq 2),$$

$$\upsilon_{1t} = [(\pi_1 + \rho_2)/\phi_1]\upsilon_{2t} + \upsilon_{Ht} \qquad (p = 1),$$

$$\upsilon_{Ht} = (\rho_2/a_0)u_t.$$

The underlying decision rule is

$$H_t = \rho_1 H_{t-1} + \rho_2 H_{t-2} + \delta_1 S_t + \dots + \delta_p S_{t-p+1} + \upsilon_{Ht} \qquad (p \geq 2), \tag{4.26}$$

$$H_t = \rho_1 H_{t-1} + \rho_2 H_{t-2} + \delta_1 S_t + \delta_2 S_{t-1} + \upsilon_{Ht} \qquad (p = 1),$$

where for $p \geqslant 2$,

$$\delta_1 = \pi_p/\phi_p, \qquad \delta_i = \pi_{i-1} - \delta_1 \phi_{i-1} \quad (i = 2, \ldots, p),$$

and for $p = 1$,

$$\delta_2 = -\rho_2, \qquad \delta_1 = (\pi_1 - \delta_2)/\phi_1.$$

7.2 Estimation and Inference

One aims to estimate the pair of equations (4.25) and (4.21) jointly. Given estimates of the coefficients of (4.25) and an imposed value of b, one can retrieve estimates of the underlying parameters of the cost function (the a_is) using (Blanchard, 1983)

$$a_1/a_0 = \rho_1(b - \rho_2^{-1}) - 2b - 2, \tag{4.27}$$

$$a_2/a_0 = -b^{-1}[\rho_2^{-1}(1 + b\rho_1^2) + b^2\rho_2 + (1 + b)(a_1/a_0) - (1 + 4b + b^2)].$$

Given estimates of the sales process (4.21) as well, estimates of a_3 can be disentangled from π_1 (or, for that matter, from any of the other π_is as well, if $p \geqslant 2$).

There are $p + 3$ parameters to be estimated: $\phi_1, \ldots, \phi_p$, a_3, and, relative to some linear combination of the a_is, the values of two of a_0, a_1, or a_2. There are $2p + 2$ right hand side variables in the bivariate system (4.21), (4.25). If (a) $p = 1$, the system is exactly identified. One can estimate by OLS. Inference may proceed in standard fashion even if S_t has a unit root, so that H_t and S_t are cointegrated (West, 1988a; Sims, Stock, and Watson, 1990), subject to caveats discussed in section 6.

If (b) $p > 1$, the system is overidentified. Consider first (b)(i) a stationary model ($S_t \sim I(0) \Rightarrow H_t \sim I(0)$). Estimation may proceed by maximum likelihood, imposing the nonlinear overidentifying restrictions (Blanchard, 1983). Since the variance-covariance matrix of the disturbances in (4.21), (4.25) is unrestricted, an asymptotically equivalent procedure is nonlinear three stage least squares, which may be computationally simpler (Amemiya, 1977).

To my knowledge, the formal asymptotic theory has not been completely worked out for restricted estimates of the model in the case that (b)(ii) $S_t \Rightarrow I(1)$ ($\Rightarrow H_t$, S_t cointegrated) and $p > 1$ so that the system is overidentified (the complication results from the nonlinear cross-equation restrictions). See Gregory, Pagan, and Smith (1992) for discussion of estimation in a related model.

For stationary models, Hansen and Sargent (1982) suggest another estimator that is applicable if there are variables observed by the firm but not the economist that help predict S_t (say, reports from sales representatives about deals likely to close the next period). The idea is to estimate simultaneously the first order condition (4.3), the time series process for predicting S_t (the analogue to (4.21)),[10] and the reduced form for H_t. (In the example above, in which there is no such private information, this appears to yield no gains relative to conventional full information estimation as just described.) As far as I know, this estimator has yet to be applied.

For the discussion of empirical work below, it is useful to note the decision rules implied by two other specifications. First, if we generalize the assumption maintained so far that u_t is serially uncorrelated in favor of the assumption that it follows an exogenous AR(1),

$$u_t = \theta u_{t-1} + \varepsilon_{ut}, \tag{4.28}$$

then the reduced form and decision rule are as above, but with

$$v_{Ht} = (\rho_2/a_0)(1 - b\theta\rho_1 - b^2\theta\rho_2)^{-1}u_t.$$

If $\theta = 1$, u_t is a random walk. If $S_t \sim I(1)$ as well, one can difference (4.21) and (4.26) and proceed as described above.

Second, if $a_0 = 0$, $a_1 \neq 0$, the reduced forms and decision rules are

$$H_t = \rho H_{t-1} + \pi_1 S_{t-1} + \ldots + \pi_p S_{t-p} + v_{1t}, \tag{4.29}$$

ρ is the smaller root of $ba_1 x^2 - (a_1 + ba_1 + ba_2)x + a_1 = 0$,

$$(\pi_1, \ldots, \pi_p) = e'(I - b\rho\Phi)^{-1}[b\rho(1 + a_1^{-1}a_2a_3)\Phi^2 - \rho\Phi],$$

$$v_{1t} = (\pi_p/\phi_p)v_{2t} + v_{Ht},$$

$$v_{Ht} = -(\rho/a_1)(1 - b\theta\rho)^{-1}u_t,$$

$$H_t = \rho H_{t-1} + \delta_1 S_t + \ldots + \delta_p S_{t-p+1} + v_{Ht} \tag{4.30}$$

$$\delta_1 = \pi_p/\phi_p, \qquad \delta_i = \pi_{i-1} - \delta_1\phi_{i-1} \quad (i = 2, \ldots, p).$$

8 Comparison of Full and Limited Information Estimation

The limited information techniques described in sections 3–6 are less efficient but more robust than are the techniques described in section 7. That they are more robust is illustrated by the following example. Suppose that sales are not exogenous but are determined by the intersection of a demand curve and supply. The demand curve might be

$$S_t = -(1/\alpha)p_t + \text{demand shock}, \tag{4.31}$$

where $\alpha > 0$ and p_t is defined in (4.1); a supply curve is obtained from a first order condition obtained by differentiating (4.1) with respect to S_t and/or p_t. The assumption maintained above that sales are exogenous is a special case of (4.31) resulting when $\alpha \to \infty$, so that $S_t = $ demand shock (Kollintzas, 1989).

We have seen in (4.25) and (4.26) that when $\alpha = \infty$, the reduced form of the model is a bivariate vector autoregression in S_t and H_t, and it may be shown that this holds even when $\alpha < \infty$. But if $\alpha < \infty$, S_t will be Granger-caused by H_t. The intuition in, say, a competitive market is that decisions about a firm's sales and inventories will be influenced by a comparison of this period's and next period's expected price, with the firm putting more in inventories the higher it expects next period's price to be (*ceteris paribus*). In equilibrium, then, industry wide H_t will help predict next period's price and thus next period's sales as well.

As a result, when the present value on the right hand side of (4.23) is projected onto past H_ts and S_ts, the H_ts will get nonzero coefficients. This means that the coefficients on the lagged H_ts in the reduced form or decision rule will not be related to the underlying cost parameters in the fashion given in (4.27), because these coefficients will reflect in part the ability of the H_t to predict future S_ts.[11] Thus, use of (4.27) will result in inconsistent estimates, while the instrumental variables estimation described in previous sections will still be consistent.

To see whether this might be a substantial problem in practice, I solved for the population values of ρ_1 and ρ_2 for a given set of values of a_0/c, a_1/c, a_2/c, and a_3, and for a range of αs; for each value of α, I then computed the values of a_0/c, a_1/c, and a_2/c that are implied by (4.27). Since use of (4.27) is

Table 4.4 Asymptotic bias of full information estimator, when sales are endogenous

1	2	3	4	5	6
			\multicolumn{3}{c}{*Value implied by (4.27) of:*}		
α	ρ_1	ρ_2	$a_0/2$	a_1/c	a_2/c
1 0.05	0.44	−0.09	0.07	0.11	0.36
2 0.19	0.73	−0.23	0.14	−0.01	0.16
3 0.32	0.81	−0.27	0.16	−0.02	0.12
True values:			0.17	−0.04	0.07

(a) a_0, a_1, and a_2 are defined in (4.1); c is defined in (4.3); α is defined in (4.31).
(b) Columns 2 and 3 present the coefficients in the decision rule for H_t when α is as indicated, a_0/c, a_1/c, and a_2/c are as given in the "True values" row, and $a_3 = -0.04$. These are the approximate values of the a_is estimated for aggregate inventories in West (1990, table III, row 1), when the demand shock in equation (4.31) follows a random walk. West's (1990) estimated value for α is that given in row 2, with the values in rows 1 and 3 being West's upper and lower bounds of the 95% confidence interval for α.
(c) Columns 4–6 give the values of a_0/c, a_1/c, and a_2/c that are implied by ρ_1 and ρ_2 under the incorrect presumption that $\alpha = \infty$ and sales are exogenous.
(d) To facilitate reading the table, only two digits are given. The values of α and the a_is actually used in the calculation are the three digit values given in West (1990).
(e) These asymptotic calculations may not accurately predict the actual finite sample performance of the full information estimator.

appropriate for $\alpha = \infty$, the question is whether plausible values of α are large enough that use of (4.27) results in little bias even though it is technically inappropriate.

I chose a data generating process consistent with one of the sets of estimates in West (1990).[12] Table 4.4 lists the values used. The table indicates that in this example, there is a plausible range of α for which one might be seriously misled by assuming that sales are exogenous ($\alpha = \infty$) when in fact sales are endogenous ($\alpha < \infty$). Row 1 of the table indicates that if $\alpha = 0.05$ (a value that is plausible in the sense that it falls within the 95% confidence interval for α given by West, 1990), use of estimates of H_i's reduced form would yield a value of a_1/c that not only is positive but is larger than that of a_0/c, at least in an arbitrarily large sample; in truth, however, a_1/c is negative and smaller in absolute value than a_0/c. Other values of α (rows 2 and 3) yield smaller biases.

Of course, full information estimation is still viable when $\alpha < \infty$; one must simply estimate α along with the cost function parameters (see West, 1990 for specifics). But then such information will yield inconsistent estimates if, say, there are costs of adjustment so that lags of S_t appear on the right hand side of (4.31), or if prices of competing products appear in the demand curve. The point is that limited information estimation is robust to possible misspecification of the demand curve, whereas full information estimation is not.

On the other hand, the full information technique will be more efficient, if the specification of demand is correct. For the three DGPs considered in tables 4.2 and 4.3, table 4.5 compares the full information technique with the limited information one that optimally uses two lags each of H_t and S_t as instruments

Table 4.5 Comparison of asymptotic variance-covariance matrices of limited and full information estimators

1 DGP	2 Ratio of SEs on $[(1 + b)a_0 + a_1]/c$	3 Ratio of SEs on a_2/c	4 Ratio of SEs on a_3
E	0.783	0.815	0.921
R	0.832	0.834	0.988
W	0.501	0.372	0.394

(a) In the ratios referenced in columns 2–4, the numerator is computed from the variance-covariance matrix of the full information estimator that estimates (4.21) and (4.25) jointly, and the denominator from that of the limited information estimator (4.5) that uses as instruments the set of variables appearing in the reduced form (4.21) and (4.25). The ratios must lie between 0 and 1, smaller numbers indicating a greater efficiency gain from using the full information estimator. Limited information use of lags of H_t and S_t beyond those in the reduced form would result in smaller efficiency gains.

(b) These asymptotic comparisons may not accurately predict the actual finite sample performance of the two estimators.

(i.e. estimates as in (4.5), with $Z_t = [H_{t-1}, S_{t-1}, H_{t-2}, S_{t-2}]')$. Table 4.5 indicates that the gains from using full information are modest for DGPs E and R, with standard errors typically falling by less than 20%. The gains for the W DGP are, however, dramatic. Recall that the W DGP is the only one that generates substantial serial correlation in H_t. These results are consistent with those of West (1986b), who, using a different linear rational expectations model, found that the gains for full information estimation were large only for highly serially correlated data. Recall that the efficiency gains would be smaller if the limited information estimator used more lags of H_t and S_t; preliminary calculations in West and Wilcox (1993a) indicate that the use of additional lags sometimes but not always results in an estimator nearly as efficient as full information.

In sum, there is a tradeoff familiar from the literature on the traditional linear simultaneous equations models. While the full information method can yield substantial efficiency gains, it requires specification of demand, and there is much less consensus on the form of demand than of the cost function. In contrast to the traditional literature, however, full information estimation is much more complex computationally, since it requires nonlinear estimation. Recent literature on the linear quadratic model has tended to emphasize use of limited information techniques.

9 Empirical Evidence

9.1 Decision Rules Implied by the Linear Quadratic Model

For the benefit of readers who skipped section 7, as well as those who tried but could not stay awake through that section, I begin by summarizing the decision rules implied by the model (4.1) when sales follow an exogenous AR(p), $p \geqslant 2$, and the cost shock u_t follows an AR(1) with parameter θ (possibly with $\theta = 0$, so that u_t is serially uncorrelated):

$$S_t = \phi_1 S_{t-1} + \ldots + \phi_p S_{t-p} + v_{2t}, \tag{4.21}$$

$$u_t = \theta u_{t-1} + \varepsilon_{ut}. \tag{4.28}$$

The equations are repeated from section 7, as are the following decision rules:

$$H_t = \rho_1 H_{t-1} + \rho_2 H_{t-2} + \delta_1 S_t + \ldots + \delta_p S_{t-p+1} + v_{Ht} \qquad (a_0 \neq 0), \tag{4.26}$$

$$H_t = \rho H_{t-1} + \delta_1 S_t + \ldots + \delta_p S_{t-p+1} + v_{Ht}, \qquad (a_0 = 0). \tag{4.30}$$

As detailed in section 7, the parameters ρ_1, ρ_2, and ρ are functions of b, a_0, a_1, and a_2; the δ_is are functions of b, the a_is, and the ϕ_is; the disturbance v_{Ht} is AR(1) with parameter $\theta(\theta = 0 \Rightarrow v_{Ht}$ is serially uncorrelated).

Note one implication of the cost shock being serially correlated (of $\theta \neq 0$). If one multiplies (4.30) by $(1 - \theta L)$ and rearranges, H_{t-2} appears on the right hand side (as does S_{t-p}, though that is not important): serially correlated cost shocks, as well as nonzero costs of adjustment ($a_0 \neq 0$, see (4.26)), put a second lag of H_t in the decision rule and reduced form.

9.2   Unrestricted Estimates of the Decision Rule

Since Lovell's (1961) pioneering research, empirical work in inventories has been dominated by unrestricted estimates of equations like (4.26) or (4.30) (that is, estimates that are not restricted to accord with estimates of an equation to forecast sales, such as (4.21)). For the sake of completeness, I briefly sketch the "flexible accelerator" model that Lovell and others have used to rationalize the equation estimated, and then note a couple of stylized facts about estimation results.

The model supposes that the representative firm balances costs of adjusting inventories against costs of having inventories deviate from their frictionless target level H_t^*:[13]

$$\min 0.5(H_t - H_t^*)^2 + 0.5w(H_t - H_{t-1})^2 + u_t H_t; \quad H_t^* = \alpha E_t S_{t+1}. \quad (4.32)$$

In (4.32), $w > 0$ is the weight of the second cost relative to the first, $\alpha > 0$ is a parameter, and u_t is an unobservable disturbance that follows an AR(1) with parameter θ, possibly with $\theta = 0$ (as in (4.28)). The first order condition is

$$H_t = \rho H_{t-1} + (1 - \rho)\alpha E_t S_{t+1} + v_{Ht}, \quad (4.33)$$

$$v_{Ht} \equiv -(1 - \rho)u_t; \quad 0 < \rho \equiv w/(1 + w) < 1.$$

If, as in (4.21), S_t is modeled as evolving according to an exogenous autoregression of order p, so that $E_t S_{t+1} = \phi_1 S_t + \ldots + \phi_p S_{t-p+1}$, (4.33) may be put in estimable form as

$$H_t = \rho H_{t-1} + \delta_1 S_t + \ldots + \delta_p S_{t-p+1} + v_{Ht}, \quad \delta_i = (1 - \rho)\alpha\phi_i. \quad (4.34)$$

It will be recognized that (4.34) is the same as (4.30), although the two models do predict different relationships between (1) the δ_is and the ϕ_is, and (2)ρ and underlying cost parameters.

Blinder and Maccini (1991a; 1991b) have discussed some stylized facts about unrestricted estimates of (4.34), two of which bear repeating here. First, even conditional on current and lagged S_t there is considerable serial correlation in H_t, in that estimates of ρ and/or θ (the serial correlation parameter of u_t) tend to be near one. Moreover, both ρ and θ tend to be significantly different from zero. Second, the estimate of δ_1 tends to be positive. This regression result reflects the business cycle fact that inventories move procyclically, tending to be accumulated during business cycle expansions as S_t and Q_t rise, and to be decumulated during recessions as S_t and Q_t fall. Given the inventory identity $Q_t = S_t + \Delta H_t$, the positive correlation between S_t and ΔH_t produces the well known result that Q_t is more variable than S_t.

The next two sections consider how such facts might be explained by the model (4.1), and briefly surveys the empirical evidence, focusing largely on papers that have explicitly used (4.1).

9.3 Explaining Extreme Serial Correlation

The extreme serial correlation of H_t that is typically observed can be rationalized in either of two ways. First, this fact will follow if u_t is highly serially correlated. Second, irrespective of the serial correlation of u_t, it will follow if ρ_1 and ρ_2 (see (4.26)) are such that the larger root of $x^2 - \rho_1 x - \rho_2$ is near unity, or, when $a_0 = 0$, if ρ (see (4.30)) is near unity.

The model will yield such a root, or yield $\rho \approx 1$ when $a_0 = 0$, when the marginal inventory holding cost a_2 is small relative to the slopes of marginal costs of production a_1 and of changing production a_0. For example, when $a_0 = 0$, $\rho \to 1$ as $a_2/a_1 \to 0$; more generally, the larger root of $x^2 - \rho_1 x - \rho_2$ approaches 1 as $a_2 \to 0$ for any fixed positive values of a_1 and a_0.

Recent empirical estimates of (4.1) have given some support to both the cost shock and cost parameter explanations. Using two digit US manufacturing data, and estimating a Euler equation such as (4.3), Eichenbaum (1989) and Ramey (1991) found a_is that by themselves implied little serial correlation, but very high serial correlation of an unobservable cost shock, while West (1986a) found a_is that implied high serial correlation (but did not test for serial correlated cost shocks). Blanchard's (1983) full information estimation, applied to automobile data, got results similar to West's.

Distinguishing between the two explanations may be difficult. Recall from the discussion in section 9.1 that if both ρ and θ are nonzero, when (4.30) is transformed to have a serially uncorrelated disturbance the resulting decision rule will have H_{t-2} on the right hand side. It will therefore look similar to the decision rule (4.26), which was derived assuming $a_0 \neq 0$ and a serially uncorrelated cost shock. What is involved, then, is distinguishing between costs of adjustment and serial correlation, which is not easily done (Blinder, 1986b; McManus, Nankervis, and Savin, 1992). Below I discuss these explanations further.

A final point to be made at present concerns the plausibility of explaining the serial correlation with a relatively flat curve describing marginal inventory holding costs. If a model such as (4.32) is used to interpret estimates of (4.30) or (4.34), $\rho \approx 1$ implies that the percentage of the gap between H_t and H_t^* that is closed each period is small (e.g. $\rho = 0.8 \Rightarrow 20\%$ closed). Following Carlson and Wehrs (1974) and Feldstein and Auerbach (1976), many find this implausible on the grounds that monthly and even quarterly changes in inventory stocks rarely amount to more than a few days production. But in the context of a model such as (4.1), a finding that $\rho \approx 1$, or that $x^2 - \rho_1 x - \rho_2$ has a large root, does not seem to me to be prima facie implausible, at least in the absence of any independent evidence about how fast marginal production costs increase relative to marginal inventory holding costs.

9.4 Explaining Procyclical Inventory Movements

The procyclical character of inventory movements may be rationalized by the model in at least three ways, which are not mutually exclusive.[14] Before discussing empirical evidence, I sketch the logic of the three explanations. Formal proofs using variance bounds inequalities such as (4.19) may be found in West (1986a; 1988b; 1990).

The simplest (and, peculiarly, sometimes overlooked) explanation is simply that this is a result of the accelerator term $a_2(H_{t-1} - a_3 S_t)^2$. This term captures a tradeoff between inventory holding costs on the one hand and stockout or backlog costs on the other. More inventories means higher holding costs but lower probability of stocking out, with the level of H_t that balances the two competing costs increasing in expected sales. In an extreme case in which there were no production costs $(a_0 = a_1 = u_t = 0)$, the firm would simply set $H_t = a_3 E_t S_{t+1}$: the more customers expected to walk in the door next period, the larger the inventory stock. In this case, positive serial correlation in S_t will cause H_t and ΔH_t to track actual as well as expected sales, and inventories clearly will move procyclically. And even if nonzero $a_0(\,)$, $a_1(\,)$, and u_t terms induce countercyclical movements (see below), as long as the influence of such terms is small enough relative to that of the accelerator term, H_t will move procyclically.

To understand the other two explanations, it is useful to first consider a set of circumstances under which H_t would *not* move procyclically. Suppose now that $a_0 = a_3 = u_t = 0$, $a_1, a_2 > 0$. Then with increasing marginal costs of production $(a_1 > 0)$, no accelerator motive $(a_3 = 0)$, and costs nonstochastic $(u_t = 0)$, firms use inventories to smooth production in the face of randomly fluctuating sales: they build up inventories when sales are low, draw them down when sales are high.

One of the two remaining explanations for procyclical inventory movements emphasizes the possible role of stochastic movements in costs. Now allow for $u_t \neq 0$, but, for clarity, continue to assume $a_0 = a_3 = 0$. Firms will intertemporally substitute production out of periods in which u_t is high into periods in which u_t is low, drawing down H_t when u_t is high, building them up when u_t is low.[15] This will produce a tendency for ΔH_t and Q_t to move in the same direction; if this tendency is strong enough relative to the one described in the preceding paragraph, inventories may move procyclically, and certainly will if movements in S_t are also driven by u_t (as is suggested by real business cycle models).

The third explanation is that marginal production cost slopes down. For simplicity, set $u_t = a_3 = 0$. Assume for the moment that $0 > \partial^2 c_t/\partial Q_t^2 = (1 + b)a_0 + a_1$. Then, in contrast to the previous paragraph but one, firms will use inventories not to smooth but to bunch production, producing high output in periods when sales are high to exploit the diminished costs that come from high output levels, and producing low output in periods when sales are low. As Ramey (1991) has emphasized, inventories will move procyclically. If one instead makes the milder assumption that $a_1 < 0$ but $(1 + b)a_0 + a_1 > 0$, so that marginal production cost slopes down only when one abstracts from costs of adjusting production, there will still be a tendency for inventories to move procyclically; whether they do or not depends on whether the motive to smooth $((1 + b)a_0 + a_1 > 0)$ or bunch $(a_1 < 0)$ is stronger.

In sum, the procyclical movement of inventories suggests a substantial role for the $a_2(H_{t-1} - a_3 S_t)^2$ term, or for cost shocks, or for downward sloping marginal costs, or indeed for more than one of these. The evidence on each of these is mixed. Blanchard (1983) and Ramey (1991) find estimates of a_3 that are positive and significant at conventional levels; West (1986a) and Krane and Braun (1991) find estimates that usually are positive but rarely are significant; Kashyap and Wilcox (1993) and West (1990) find estimates that are of mixed sign and usually are insignificant.[16] Perhaps an indirect indication of the importance of the stockout or backlog costs underlying $a_3 > 0$ is that measures of order backlogs often are significant in inventory regressions (e.g. Maccini and Rossana, 1984; Blinder, 1986a).

Consider now the possibility that marginal production costs slope down, in the sense that $(1 + b)a_0 + a_1 < 0$. Ramey (1991) vigorously argues that this is the case. Most others, including some who have used similar data (Eichenbaum,

Table 4.6 Statistical significance of cost variables

		Wage	Materials prices	Energy prices	Interest rate	Unobservable shock
1	Blinder (1986b)	?	?		n	?
2	Durlauf and Maccini (1992)	?	n	n		
3	Eichenbaum (1989)					y
4	Maccini and Rossana (1981)	y	?		n	?
5	Maccini and Rossana (1984)	n	y		n	y
6	Miron and Zeldes (1988)	n	?	n	n	
7	Ramey (1991)	n	?	n		y

(a) All the studies used two digit manufacturing data from the US. The exact data, sample period, specification, and estimation technique vary from paper to paper.
(b) A "y" entry indicates that the variable in a given column was significantly different from zero at the 5% level in at least three-fourths of the data sets in a given study; an "n" that it was significant in at most one-fourth of the data sets; and a "?" that it was significant in more than one-fourth but fewer than three-fourths of the data sets. A blank indicates that the variable was not examined.
(c) Line by line sources: (1) table 1 (pp. 360–1) (2) table 3, inst. set 4 (3) table 2 (p. 861) (4) table 1 (p. 20) (5) table 3 (p. 231) and discussion on p. 227 (6) table II (p. 892) (7) table 1 (p. 323).

1989; West, 1986a) have come to the opposite conclusion; a possible exception is Krane and Braun (1991, pp. 574–5), one of whose specifications yielded insignificant but negative slopes in about half their data sets. However, a number of authors have found the production cost a_1 insignificantly different from zero (Blanchard, 1983; West, 1990; Kashyap and Wilcox, 1993); in at least one study (West, 1990), the negative (but insignificant) point estimate of a_1 was large enough in absolute value to imply procyclical inventory movements.

Finally, with reference to unobservable cost shocks, there is a persistent tendency for unobservable cost shocks to be highly autocorrelated when one allows for such a possibility, as do Eichenbaum (1989), West (1990), and Ramey (1991) (but not, for example, Blanchard, 1983; or West, 1986b). One would hope that such shocks are crude proxies for observable measures of costs such as factor prices. Unfortunately, this seems not to be the case, since, in practice, such factor prices rarely are significant. See table 4.6, which summarizes some results from both flexible accelerator and linear quadratic models that have been applied to two digit manufacturing data from the US.

9.5   Summary

Highly serially correlated cost shocks rationalize both the considerable serial correlation in H_t and the procyclical nature of movements in H_t. But as Blinder and Maccini (1991b) note, one cannot be very confident that such disturbances in fact capture stochastic variation in costs rather than model misspecification, given that observable measures of costs do not seem to influence inventory movements very much.

Alternatively, both stylized facts fall out of demand driven models if the inventory holding cost a_0 is small relative to the production costs a_0 and/or a_1, and either (1) a_1 is slightly negative, or (2) the effects of the accelerator term $a_2(H_{t-1} - a_3 S_t)^2$ are large. Note that it is the *product* $a_2 a_3$ that determines the strength of the accelerator term (see (4.3), (4.19), and the definition of the w_2 in (4.24)). So there may be a tension between arguing that a_2 is small (to obtain extreme serial correlation) and that $a_2 a_3$ is large (to obtain procyclical movements), although given arbitrarily small a_2 there is an a_3 sufficiently large that the accelerator will yield arbitrarily strong effects. In any case, existing estimates do not come to a tight consensus about the magnitudes of these parameters. Perhaps microeconomic evidence from a more disaggregate level, such as in Bresnahan and Ramey (1991), will help narrow the range of plausible a_is, as well as help sharpen our understanding of the role of stochastic variation in costs in determining inventory movements.

Notes

I thank an anonymous referee, participants in a seminar at the Federal Reserve Board of Governors, Louis Maccini, Scott Schuh, and, especially, David Wilcox for helpful comments and discussions, and the National Science Foundation, the Sloan Foundation, and the Graduate School at the University of Wisconsin for financial support.

1 Formally, one adds to the cost function terms of the form $(1) c_1' w_t Q_t$, where c_1 is a parameter vector and w_t is a vector of input prices, and/or $(2) c_2 r_t H_t$, where r_t is the *ex ante* real interest rate.

2 An implicit assumption made is that one can parameterize the problem so that $\partial(p_{t+j} S_{t+j})/\partial H_t = 0$ for all j. Reasons why this might not be possible: (1) a nonnegativity constraint on inventories sometimes prevents the firm from holding revenue constant when it produces one fewer unit (Abel, 1985; Kahn, 1987); (2) in an imperfectly competitive industry, this period's level of inventories affects future revenues, for strategic reasons (Rotemberg and Saloner, 1989).

3 If data on output price p_t are available, an additional first order condition allows one to identify the $a_i s$ relative to the units in which p_t is measured (presumably, constant dollars, for US data) and not just relative to one another. But for simplicity of exposition, and for conformity with much empirical work, I focus on the case when such data are not used.

4 Hall (1992), Ogaki (1992), and Pesaran (1987) provide general discussions of the issues raised in these sections.

5 This implicitly assumes that $\partial(p_{t+j} S_{t+j})/\partial H_t = 0$ for all j and that Q_t is not a choice variable. This is a harmless assumption in that, in most of the literature, it is a matter of convenience as to whether one makes (1) H_t and S_t, or (2) H_t and Q_t the two choice variables. But see note 2 for some conditions under which one might not be able to set up the problem this way.

6 Nor is GLS correction for serial correlation generally desirable. The instruments generally (although not always) include lags of H_t and/or S_t, in which case application of a standard GLS transformation to eliminate serial correlation may yield inconsistent parameter estimates (Hayashi and Sims, 1983).

7 Eichenbaum sets $a_0 = 0$ and reports parameters that he denotes λ and α. I mapped his estimates into the present notation using $a_2/a_1 = \lambda + (1/\lambda) - 1 - (1/b)$, with $b = 0.995$, $a_3 = 2(1/\alpha)/(a_2/a_1)$. For computational convenience, I then set a_0 to a small nonzero number rather than zero. Eichenbaum also assumes that C_t includes a term of the form (in my notation) $(H_t - a_3 S_t)^2$ rather than $(H_{t-1} - a_3 S_t)^2$; I slur over this minor difference.

8 Just as $\tilde{\Gamma}_0 + (\tilde{\Gamma}_1 + \tilde{\Gamma}_1')$ might not be positive definite, $\hat{s}^{(0)}$ may be negative (as, of course, might $\hat{s}^{(1)}$ or even the underlying population quantity $s^{(1)}$ (but not $s^{(0)}$). But the fact that the ratio $\hat{s}^{(1)}/\hat{s}^{(0)}$ is squared in (4.13) means that m will be nonegative, and the resulting $\hat{\Omega}$ will be positive definite.

9 That $\{.\} \sim I(0)$ follows since $E_t\{.\} = -u_t \sim I(0)$ by assumption and $\{.\} - E_t\{.\} \sim I(0)$ as well. Further, $\{.\} \sim I(0) \Rightarrow H_t \sim I(1)$: if $H_t \sim I(d)$ for some $d > 1$, then the order of integration of H_t would be greater than that of any other variable and $\{.\}$ could not be $I(0)$, while if $H_t \sim I(0)$, $\{.\} \sim I(1)$. Incidentally, Q_t and S_t are "multicointegrated," in the terminology of Granger and Lee (1989; 1991).

10 Under these circumstances, equation (4.21) will not describe the time series process for S_t. For in this case H_t will Granger-cause S_t relative to an information set consisting of lagged $H_t s$ and $S_t s$, and lagged $H_t s$ will appear on the right hand side of S_t's time series process.

11 Let $E_t Y_t \equiv E_t \Sigma_{j=0}^{\infty} \{[(b\lambda_1)^{j+1} - (b\lambda_2)^{j+1}] D_{t+j}\}$ denote the present value on the right hand side of (4.23). Note that the problem described in the text is not trivially

circumvented by simply projecting Y_t onto past S_ts, and absorbing the difference between this projection and $E_t Y_t$ in the error term: the error term would then be correlated with the lagged H_ts.

12   In this example, the model is exactly identified, so full information estimation simply involves estimating the unrestricted reduced form. See West (1990). Over-identification would result if the demand curve were e.g. $S_t = -(1/\alpha)p_t + \phi_1 S_{t-1} + \phi_2 S_{t-2} + \text{demand shock}$, with ϕ_1, $\phi_2 \neq 0$.

13   As a rule, flexible accelerator studies measure inventories and sales in logs rather than levels. I ignore distinctions between logs and levels because results for the linear quadratic model do not change much when one rids the data of exponential growth before estimation (West, 1988b; 1990).

14   I consider here the *un*conditional relationship between inventories on the one hand and sales and production on the other; I will be deliberately vague about whether the analysis relates to levels or differences since I believe that neither the stylized facts nor their interpretation turns on how stationarity is induced. See Blinder (1986a) for discussion of a conditional relationship, specifically, an analysis of what makes the regression coefficient δ_1 positive; see Krane (1993) for evidence on the similar pattern that applies in the deterministic seasonal relationship between inventories and sales/production.

15   There is a sense in which inventories will move procyclically even if u_t follows a random walk and there are no possibilities for intertemporal substitution; see West (1990).

16   One interpretation of the disparity in estimates is that stockout or backlog costs indeed are central to explaining why inventories move procyclically, but are poorly modeled by a simple quadratic term like $a_2(H_{t-1} - a_3 S_t)^2$ (Krane, 1991). See Kahn (1987; 1992) for excellent work modeling such costs in a more sophisticated way.

References

Abel, Andrew B. (1985), "Inventories, Stock-Outs and Production Smoothing," *Review of Economic Studies* 52, 283–93.

Amemiya, Takeshi (1977), "The Maximum Likelihood and the Nonlinear Three Stage Least Squares Estimator in the General Nonlinear Simultaneous Equations Model," *Econometrica* 45, 955–68.

Andrews, Donald W.K. (1991), "Heteroskedasticity and Autocorrelation Consistent Covariance Matrix Estimation," *Econometrica* 59, 817–58.

Andrews, Donald W.K., and Christopher J. Monahan (1992), "An Improved Heteroskedasticity and Autocorrelation Consistent Covariance Matrix," *Econometrica* 60, 953–66.

Blanchard, Olivier J. (1983), "The Production and Inventory Behavior of the American Automobile Industry," *Journal of Political Economy* 91, 365–400.

Blanchard, Olivier J., and Angelo Melino (1986), "The Cyclical Behavior of Prices and Quantities: The Case of the Automobile Market," *Journal of Monetary Economics* 17, 379–408.

Blinder, Alan S. (1981), "Retail Inventory Behavior and Business Fluctuations," *Brookings Papers on Economic Activity* 2, 443–505.

Blinder, Alan S. (1986a), "Can the Production Smoothing Model of Inventories Be Saved?", *Quarterly Journal of Economics* CI, 431–53.

Blinder, Alan S. (1986b), "More on the Speed of Adjustment in Inventory Models," *Journal of Money Credit and Banking* 18, 355–65.

Blinder, Alan S. and Louis J. Maccini (1991a), "The Resurgence of Inventory Research: What Have We Learned?", *Journal of Economic Surveys* 5, 291–328.

Blinder, Alan S. and Louis J. Maccini (1991b), "Taking Stock: A Critical Assessment of Recent Research on Inventories," *Journal of Economic Perspectives* 5, 73–96.

Bresnahan, Timothy F. and Valerie A. Ramey (1991), "The Nature of Output Fluctuations: Evidence from Plant Level Data," manuscript, University of California at San Diego.

Carlson, John A. and William Wehrs (1974), "Aggregate Inventory Behavior," in G. Horwich and P. Samuelson (eds) *Trade, Stability and Growth: Essays in Honor of Lloyd A. Metzler*, New York: Academic Press.

Christiano, Lawrence J. (1988), "Why Does Inventory Investment Fluctuate So Much?", *Journal of Monetary Economics* 21, 247–80.

Christiano, Lawrence J., and Martin S. Eichenbaum (1989), "Temporal Aggregation and the Stock Adjustment Model of Inventories," 70–109 in T. Kollintzas (ed.) *The Rational Expectations Inventory Model*, New York: Springer Verlag.

Cumby, Robert E. and John Huizanga (1990), "Testing the Autocorrelation Structure of Disturbances in Ordinary Least Squares and Instrumental Variables Regressions," NBER Technical Working Paper no. 92.

Cumby, Robert E., John Huizanga and Maurice Obstfeld (1983), "Two Step, Two Stage Least Squares Estimation in Models with Rational Expectations," *Journal of Econometrics* 21, 333–55.

Dimelis, Sophia P., and Moheb A. Ghali (1992), "Classical and Variance Bounds Tests of Production and Inventory Behavior," manuscript, Athens University of Economics and Business.

Dimelis, Sophia P., and Tryphon Kollintzas (1989), "A Linear Rational Expectations Equilibrium Model for the American Petroleum Industry," 110–98 in T. Kollintzas (ed.) *The Rational Expectations Inventory Model*, New York: Springer Verlag.

Durlauf, Steven N. and Louis J. Maccini (1992), "Measuring Noise in Inventory Models," manuscript, The Johns Hopkins University.

Eichenbaum, Martin S. (1984), "Rational Expectations and the Smoothing Properties of Finished Goods," *Journal of Monetary Economics* 14, 71–96.

Eichenbaum, Martin S. (1989), "Some Empirical Evidence on the Production Level and Production Cost Smoothing Models of Inventory Investment," *American Economic Review* 79, 853–64.

Eichenbaum, Martin S., Lars Peter Hansen and Kenneth J. Singleton (1988), "A Time Series Analysis of A Representative Agent Model of Consumption and Leisure Choice under Uncertainty," *Quarterly Journal of Economics*, 51–78.

Feldstein, Martin S. and Alan J. Auerbach (1976), "Inventory Behavior in Durable Goods Manufacturing: The Target Adjustment Model," *Brookings Papers on Economic Activity* 351–96.

Granger, Clive W.J. and T.H. Lee (1989), "Investigation of Production, Sales and Inventory Relationships Using Multicointegration and Non-symmetric Error Correction Models," *Journal of Applied Econometrics* 4, S145–S159.

Granger, Clive W.J. and T.H. Lee (1991), "Multicointegration," 179–90 in R. F. Engle and C.W.J. Granger (eds) *Long Run Economic Relationships: Readings in Cointegration*, Oxford: Oxford University Press.

Granger, Clive W.J. and Paul Newbold (1977), *Forecasting Economic Time Series*, New York: Academic Press.

Gregory, Allan W., Adrian R. Pagan and Gregor W. Smith (1992), "Estimating Linear Quadratic Models with Integrated Processes," manuscript, Queens University.

Hall, Alistair (1992), "Some Aspects of Generalized Method of Moments Estimation," manuscript, North Carolina State University.

Hansen, Bruce (1992), "Consistent Covariance Matrix Estimation for Dependent Heterogeneous Processes," *Econometrica* 60, 967–72.

Hansen, Lars Peter (1982), "Asymptotic Properties of Generalized Method of Moments Estimators," *Econometrica* 50, 1029–54.

Hansen, Lars Peter (1985), "A Method for Calculating Bounds on the Asymptotic Covariance Matrices of Generalized Method of Moments Estimators," *Journal of Econometrics* 30, 203–38.

Hansen, Lars Peter, and Thomas J. Sargent (1982), "Instrumental Variables Procedures for Estimating Linear Rational Expectations Models,: *Journal of Monetary Economics* 9, 263–96.

Hayashi, Fumio, and Christopher A. Sims (1983), "Nearly Efficient Estimation of Time Series Models with Predetermined, but not Exogenous, Instruments," *Econometrica* 51, 783–98.

Holt, Charles C., Franco Modigliani, John F. Muth and Herbert A. Simon (1960), *Planning Production, Inventories and Work Force*, Englewood Cliffs, NJ: Prentice-Hall.

Kahn, James A. (1987), "Inventories and the Volatility of Production," *American Economic Review* 77, 667–80.

Kahn, James A. (1992), "Why is Production More Volatile than Sales? Theory and Evidence on the Stockout-Avoidance Motive for Inventory Holding," *Quarterly Journal of Economics* CVII, 481–510.

Kashyap, Anil K. and David W. Wilcox (1993), "Production and Inventory Control at the General Motors Corporation during the 1920s and 1930s," *American Economic Review* 83, 383–401.

Kollintzas, Tryphon A. (1989), "The Linear Rational Expectations Inventory Model: An Introduction," 1–33 in T. Kollintzas (ed.) *The Rational Expectations Inventory Model*, New York: Springer Verlag.

Kollintzas, Tryphon A. (1992), "A Generalized Variance Bounds Test, with an Application to the Holt et al. Inventory Model," manuscript, Athens University of Economics and Business.

Krane, Spencer D. (1991), "The Distinction between Inventory Holding and Stockout Costs: Implications for Target Inventories, Asymmetric Adjustment, and the Effect of Aggregation on Production Smoothing," manuscript, Federal Reserve Board of Governors.

Krane, Spencer D. (1993), "Induced Seasonality and Production Smoothing Models of Inventory Behavior," forthcoming, *Journal of Econometrics*.

Krane, Spencer D. and Steven N. Braun (1991), "Production Smoothing Evidence from Physical Product Data," *Journal of Political Economy* 99, 558–81.

Lovell, Michael C. (1961), "Manufacturers' Inventories, Sales Expectations, and the Acceleration Principle," *Econometrica* 29, 293–314.

Lovell, Michael C. (1993), "Simulating the Inventory Cycle," *Journal of Economic Behavior and Organization* 21, 147–79.

Maccini, Louis J. and Robert J. Rossana (1981), "Investment in Finished Goods Inventories: An Analysis of Adjustment Speeds," *American Economic Review* 71 (May), 17–22.

Maccini, Louis J. and Robert J. Rossana (1984), "Joint Production, Quasi-Fixed Factors of Production, and Investment in Finished Goods Inventories," *Journal of Money, Credit and Banking* XVI, 218–36.

McManus, Douglas A., John C. Nankervis and N.E. Savin (1992), "Multiple Optima and Asymptotic Approximations in the Partial Adjustment Model," University of Iowa Working Paper 92–10.

Miron, Jeffrey A. and Stephen P. Zeldes (1988), "Seasonality, Cost Shocks and the Production Smoothing Model of Inventories," *Econometrica* 56, 877–908.

Mosser, Patricia C. (1988), "Empirical Tests of the (S, s) Model for Merchant Wholesalers," 261–84 in A. Chikan and M. Lovell (eds) *The Economics of Inventory Management*, Amsterdam: Elsevier Science Publishers.

Nelson, Charles R. and Richard A. Startz (1990), "The Distribution of the Instrumental Variables Estimator and its *t*-ratio When the Instrument is a Poor One," *Journal of Business* 63, 125–40.

Newey, Whitney K., and Kenneth D. West (1987a), "A Simple, Positive Semidefinite. Heteroskedasticity and Autocorrelation Consistent Covariance Matrix," *Econometrica* 55 703–8.

Newey, Whitney K., and Kenneth D. West (1987b), "Hypothesis Testing with Efficient Method of Moments Estimation," *International Economic Review* 28, 777–86.

Newey, Whitney K., and Kenneth D. West (1993), "Automatic Lag Selection in Covariance Matrix Estimation," manuscript, University of Wisconsin.

Ogaki, Masao (1992), "An Introduction to Generalized Method of Moments," University of Rochester Center for Economic Research Working Paper no. 314.

Park, Joon Y. and Peter C.B. Phillips, (1988), "Statistical Inference in Regressions with Integrated Processes: I," *Econometric Theory* 4, 468–97.

Pesaran, M. Hashem, (1987), *The Limits to Rational Expectations*, New York: Basil Blackwell.

Ramey, Valerie A. (1989), "Inventories as Factors of Production and Economic Fluctuations," *American Economic Review* 79, 338–54.

Ramey, Valerie A. (1991), "Nonconvex Costs and the Behavior of Inventories," *Journal of Political Economy* 99, 306–34.

Rossana, Robert J. (1992), "The Long-Run Implications of the Production Smoothing Model of Inventories: An Empirical Test," manuscript, Wayne State University.

Rotemberg, Julio J., and Garth Saloner (1989), "The Cyclical Behavior of Strategic Inventories," *Quarterly Journal of Economics* CIV, 73–98.

Schuh, Scott (1993), "Linear-Quadratic Inventory Models and Aggregation," manuscript, Federal Reserve Board of Governors.

Shea, John (1993), "The Input–Output Approach to Demand-Shift Instrumental Variables Estimation," *Journal of Business and Economic Statistics*, 11, 145–55.

Sims, Christopher A., James H. Stock and Mark Watson (1990), "Inference in Linear Time Series Models with Some Unit Roots," *Econometrica* 58, 113–44.

Stengel, Robert F. (1986), *Stochastic Optimal Control: Theory and Application*, New York: Wiley.

Stock, James H. and Kenneth D. West (1988), "Integrated Regressors and Tests of the Permanent Income Hypothesis," *Journal of Monetary Economics* 21, 85–95.

West, Kenneth D. (1986a), "A Variance Bounds Test of the Linear Quadratic Inventory Model," *Journal of Political Economy* 94, 374–401.

West, Kenneth D. (1986b), "Full Versus Limited Information Estimation of a Rational Expectations Model: Some Numerical Comparisons," *Journal of Econometrics* 33, 367–86.

West, Kenneth D. (1988b), "Asymptotic Normality, When Regressors Have a Unit Root," *Econometrica* 56, 1397–418.

West, Kenneth D. (1988b), "Order Backlogs and Production Smoothing," 305–18 in Attila Chikan and Michael Lovell (eds) *The Economics of Inventory Management*, Amsterdam: Elsevier.

West, Kenneth D. (1990), "The Sources of Fluctuations in Aggregate Inventories and GNP," *Quarterly Journal of Economics* CV, 939–72.

West, Kenneth D. (1992), "Sources of Cycles in Japan, 1975–1987," *Journal of the Japanese and International Economies* 6, 71–98.

West, Kenneth D., and David W. Wilcox (1993a), "Finite Sample Behavior of Alternative Instrumental Variables Estimators of a Dynamic Linear Model," forthcoming, *Journal of Business and Economic Statistics*.

West, Kenneth D., and David W. Wilcox, (1993b), "Some Evidence on the Finite Sample Behavior of an Instrumental Variables Estimator of the Linear Quadratic Inventory Model," in R. Fiorito (ed.) *Inventory Cycles and Monetary Policy*, Berlin: Springer Verlag, 253–82.

5

The Consumption Function:
A Theoretical and Empirical Overview

John Muellbauer and Ralph Lattimore

£21

1 Introduction

Consumer expenditure accounts for between 50% and 70% of spending in most economies. Not surprisingly, the consumption function has been the most studied of the aggregate expenditure relationships and has been a key element of all the macroeconometric model building efforts since the seminal work of Klein and Goldberger (1955). The standard encyclopaedic reference work on economics, published in 1987, claimed that "the consumption function has faded as a topic of intense research because of the success of previous research in achieving a workable consensus" (see Darby, 1987 in the *New Palgrave*). The irony is that at the time, the US personal sector saving rate had recently undergone a considerable ten-year decline, the causes of which, ten years on, remain the subject of much controversy. In fact, savings ratios were declining in most industrial countries by the mid 1980s and this "savings shortage" was widely suspected of having been a cause of the high levels reached by real interest rates in the 1980s. Indeed, in some countries, for instance the UK and the Scandinavian countries, consumers embarked, in the second half of the 1980s, on the biggest spending spree, followed by probably the most dramatic rise in the savings rate, ever seen in these countries. Both the boom and its reversal were badly mispredicted by the pre-existing econometric models in these countries, accentuating the failures of macro policy makers in dealing with the consequent macroeconomic stresses.

By "the consumption function," the *New Palgrave* entry had in mind relationships between consumer spending, income, assets, interest rates,[1] and perhaps demography such as those which followed the pioneering work by Ando and Modigliani (1963), Ball and Drake (1964), Spiro (1962), and Stone (1964). At the micro level, such relationships were justified, at least loosely, as the solution to an optimization over an individual's life-cycle resulting in some version of the life-cycle (Modigliani and Brumberg, 1954; 1979) or permanent income (Friedman, 1957) hypotheses, in other words, a "solved out" or "structural" consumption function.[2]

The year 1978 proved to be a milestone for research on the aggregate consumption function. Empirical research of that time was, generally speaking, in a far from satisfactory state. The statistical problems of working with non-stationary time-series data (such as consumption, income, and assets) were not really understood. In many countries, time-series data on household asset holdings were not readily available. Consistency with economic theory was problematic. And the treatment of expectations remained fairly *ad hoc*. Two papers were published in 1978 that proved to be key pointers for subsequent research. One was Davidson, Hendry, Srba, and Yeo (1978) (DHSY), which effectively introduced the notion of an error correction model (though similar lag structures had earlier been used by Stone, 1964 and other researchers), setting the scene for subsequent work on cointegration[3] of non-stationary time series by Engle and Granger (1987).

The other paper of that year, Hall (1978), on the face of it eliminated all the other problems listed above in one fell swoop: by effectively analysing changes in consumption (at least in the version of his model popularized by his student Flavin, 1981), it made the series stationary; it eliminated the problem of paucity of asset data by making such data redundant; it claimed to solve the problem of theory consistency by estimating directly, from aggregate data, the first order condition, the "Euler equation," for an optimal intertemporal consumption decision by a "representative consumer;" and, building on the "rational expectations" revolution following Muth (1960), it adopted the rational expectations approach, assuming efficient information processing by consumers taken to be at least as well informed as the econometricians studying their behaviour. Hall showed that, under certain assumptions, this approach had the apparently revolutionary implication that the best forecast of next period's consumption was this period's. Many researchers, no doubt, asked themselves what the point was of laborious and difficult research on the traditional solved out consumption function, when supposedly it had no forecasting value beyond that obtainable from a simple regression on lagged consumption.

The burgeoning of research on Euler consumption equations was further stimulated by the relatively early discovery that empirical evidence did *not*, after all, accord with Hall's proposition that consumption could not be forecast better than by the previous period's level. One particular form of this forecastability is the empirical sensitivity of consumption changes to income changes predicted on the basis of lagged information. This is the "excess sensitivity" puzzle. Much of consumption research has been concerned with relaxing one or more of the key assumptions that underlie Hall's result to explain why the change in consumption is, in practice, forecastable. In the process, many important issues concerning consumer behaviour have been illuminated which have implications for the specification of solved out consumption functions and for developing better macroeconomics.

Partly because of the evidence from aggregate time-series data and partly because of gathering evidence from household survey data, some reinterpretation has been taking place of one of the cornerstones of post-war economics, the life-cycle model of Modigliani and Brumberg (1954; 1979). The basic idea, based on intertemporal utility maximization,[4] is that households try to smooth consumption over time so that workers save in order to spend in retirement. One useful macro prediction from the theory is its emphasis on the role of asset or wealth effects on consumption; another is the association of high aggregate savings rates with population and income growth. Note that the latter result is due to aggregation rather than being implied by the behaviour of some representative agent. An economy with population growth will have more savers relative to dissavers than one with a static population, and so will have a higher aggregate saving rate. This is essentially an age structure effect. Similarly, one with economic growth will have dissavers living on assets accumulated out of lower incomes than current workers are earning. On the face of it, this should result in a higher aggregate saving rate. However, higher *expected* real per capita income growth for given individuals will, if borrowing is possible for the young, result in higher consumption for them which could offset, for very high growth rates, the higher saving rate which comes from the bigger earning power of the working population.[5]

In practice, credit constraints will eliminate the latter possibility: the young without collateral typically cannot borrow. Indeed, cross-country empirical evidence does show a positive correlation of savings rates with income growth and with population growth or a young age structure[6] (Modigliani, 1990; Deaton, 1992a, chapter 2.1). This evidence is thus consistent with the life-cycle hypothesis holding for the majority but not for a young credit constrained minority.

Another puzzle concerning aggregate time-series consumption behaviour which has raised questions about the life-cycle/rational-expectations permanent income hypothesis is "excess smoothness" or the "Deaton paradox" (Deaton, 1987). This can be explained as follows: many time-series analysts believe that real per capita income is a non-stationary series which can be made stationary by taking differences of the data. In other words, statistical tests appear to accept the hypothesis that the aggregate income process has "a unit root." In the simplest case of a random walk, income innovations are permanent and, by the rational expectations permanent income hypothesis (REPIH), consumption should then vary at least as much as income. In fact, consumption is much smoother: on most seasonally adjusted aggregate data sets consumption growth has half or less of the variance of income growth.

Powerful support against the life-cycle theory, at least in its simplest form, has been building up from household survey data. Cross-section evidence suggests that consumption tends to follow the hump shape of income over the life-cycle more closely than life-cycle theory implies and that the old do not dissave on the scale one might have expected. This suggests that simple life-cycle theory needs considerable modification.

In this chapter, we will use a combination of theory and econometrics to illuminate these empirical micro and macro puzzles. We will also discuss the decline of the US savings rate and the dramatic oscillations the UK and Scandinavian countries experienced in the last decade. There are other puzzles too. One is the *lack* of a large fall in the Japanese savings rate in the 1980s despite the huge increase in real asset prices, particularly of land and housing. Further there is little empirical evidence of a strong and stable negative real interest rate effect on consumption which many economists expect. This can be explained relatively simply.

The structure of this chapter builds up the economic theory of consumer expenditure piece by piece, integrating each element with the relevant empirical evidence. The sequence begins by analysing consumption decisions under point (i.e. non-probabilistic) expectations in a two-period model, extending to the multi-period model. Probabilistic income expectations, in which households associate different probabilities with different possible future income levels, are introduced first in a linear rational expectations framework and then with precautionary behaviour. Credit constraints, interactions between consumption and leisure, and habits and durable goods are discussed next. The rationality of expectations is reconsidered and asset effects, including those of illiquid assets, on consumption are analysed. Aggregation, i.e. how one gets from micro theory to relationships that hold, at least approximately, for macro data is considered. Throughout, the implications of the analysis both for Euler equation and solved out forms of the consumption functions are discussed.

All the important elements of a general model having been considered, section 11 attempts an assembly of the pieces to build up an approximately theory-consistent solved out aggregate consumption function. The principle of general to specific modelling, i.e. beginning with a general maintained hypothesis and testing a series of simplifications to reduce it to a parsimonious model consistent with the data, is accepted by many though by no means all economists (see Gilbert, 1986) as ideal econometric practice. Therefore it is desirable, whether under the Euler approach or the solved out consumption function approach, to take a very general model as the starting point for empirical work. Theory consistency is also a necessity for model building: there are never enough data, and unless many possibilities are excluded by prior theoretical considerations, confusion reigns. However, precise theory consistency and theoretical generality are mutually exclusive, whether in the context of the Euler or of the solved out consumption function approach. Creative approximations or simulations of a theoretical model under a range of assumptions are essential to make progress.

The reasons for emphasizing the solved out consumption function in section 11 are several. One is that the Euler approach has been excellently covered in Angus Deaton's (1992a) book. Another is that the solved out approach has been excessively dominated in macroeconometric research in the last 15 years, particularly in North America, by the Euler approach and a small step is taken here to restore the balance. Each approach has merits and those claimed for the Euler approach have already been mentioned. Two important advantages of the solved out approach are as follows. First, the Euler approach involves quasi-differencing which eliminates from the data important long-run information, for example on the interrelation between consumption, income, and assets. DHSY (1978) and the cointegration literature have taught us that this is often unwise.[7] Second, consider the drawn out procedure needed to make the Euler approach useful for policy analysis, for example for simulating the medium-term impact on consumption of a change in tax policy: one needs to solve a set of intertemporal efficiency (i.e. Euler) conditions forward, combining them with the period-to-period budget constraints altered to take account of the change in tax policy and incorporating expectational assumptions. But this is just what the solved out consumption function is designed to do. For policy analysis, both need to make their expectational models explicit.

Each approach necessarily involves approximations, particularly dealing with aggregation, uncertainty, and credit constraints, or other non-linearities in budget constraints. Those usually made in the Euler approach are not necessarily superior, partly because, as we shall see, the aggregation problem has been neglected in much of the Euler literature.

To help readers who may be interested in particular topics, this introduction concludes by summarizing the content of the sections which follow.

Section 2.1 considers a simple two-period optimization problem with point expectations. Important conclusions can be drawn about the effects on spending of assets, income expectations, differing degrees of substitutability between consumption in different periods, and changes in real interest rates. Indeed, we show how theory can be consistent with weak and unstable real interest rate effects. Section 2.2 extends this analysis to many periods and discusses the effects of age and family circumstances on marginal propensities to spend out of income and assets. These effects will be of central importance in considering the aggregation of micro behaviour into macro behaviour. Potentially, they can also explain some of the survey evidence which shows consumption growing with age and income for younger households.

Section 3.1 introduces stochastic income and hence probabilistic expectations in the linear rational expectations framework made possible by the assumption of a quadratic utility function. Linear Euler equations and the connections between consumption and income innovations are discussed. Section 3.2 discusses the econometric issues entailed in testing the Hall model, with particular focus on "excess sensitivity." Section 3.3 considers the issue of persistence in the stochastic process for income for the solved out consumption function. The issue of income persistence gives rise to the debate about the "excess smoothness" or Deaton paradox.

These linear rational expectations approaches rest on the assumption that only the mathematical expectation (i.e. the first moment) of income matters, while its volatility and skewness are irrelevant. This necessarily precludes precautionary saving. The latter is the subject of section 4. Except in the case of constant absolute risk aversion, no analytical results appear to be available on the effect of uncertainty on saving, which means resorting to approximation or simulation. We follow the former approach and explain how, for a prudent individual, higher income uncertainty effectively means applying a bigger discount rate to future income.[8] The consequences for consumption of uncertainty about length of life and about the rate of return are also discussed. The approximate empirical implications of uncertainty both for Euler equations and for solved out consumption functions are derived.

Section 5 concerns credit constraints, a likely consequence of asymmetric information between borrowers and lenders and of government regulation of financial markets. The situations where credit constraints are most likely to arise are considered and the consequences of credit constraints both for Euler consumption equations and for solved out consumption functions are discussed. Credit constraints are the single most popular explanation of why consumption changes are forecastable and why the Hall consumption model fails. The literature is reviewed and it is shown how an "error correction form," linking consumption with income, lagged income, and lagged consumption, can be interpreted as a Euler equation modified by credit constraints. The interaction of credit constraints and income uncertainty is discussed.

Another potential reason why consumption changes are forecastable is discussed in section 6, which considers interactions between consumption and leisure. We consider what happens if intertemporal utility trade-offs between consumption levels in different periods are not independent of leisure in different periods. Yet further reasons arise in section 7 which introduces habits and durable goods and explains how these alter both Euler equations and solved out consumption functions.

Section 8 queries the assumption of "rational expectations," and considers less rational and rule of thumb behaviour when the utility gains from optimization may be small. The use of survey data on expectations is discussed.

The effects on consumption of assets and asset prices is the subject of section 9. Distinctions are drawn between more and less liquid assets and it is argued that lower spendability weights should be associated with less liquid assets. The special role of housing, which both represents a major component of household assets and enters the utility function directly, is discussed. The real price of owner-occupied houses has two effects on non-housing consumption: a positive wealth effect for owner-occupiers and a negative income/substitution effect for everyone whose price of housing services is affected by the market price of owner-occupied housing. Some evidence on the effect of real house prices on consumption is surveyed.

Section 10 considers problems of aggregation. Given that consumers have finite lives, it is quite likely that aggregate Euler equations are profoundly different from micro Euler equations. This problem, the subject of section 10.1, raises serious and, until quite recently, rather neglected difficulties for going from theory to empirical modelling. It also has implications for puzzles concerning excess sensitivity, excess smoothness, and the size of interest rate effects. Section 10.2 considers aggregation in the solved out consumption function.

Section 11, itself divided into subsections, builds up an aggregate solved out consumption function bringing to bear the material of the preceding sections. It considers some functional form issues in section 11.1 and the incorporation of interest rate and uncertainty effects, habits, and the liquid/illiquid asset distinction, and of rational income expectations by some households alongside the myopia of others, in section 11.2. Aggregation over credit constrained and unconstrained households is the subject of section 11.3 and the potential impact of financial liberalization is considered in section 11.4. Recent empirical literature on aggregate consumption functions with wealth effects is reviewed in section 11.5 and brought to bear on the empirical puzzles raised at the beginning of the introduction.

No survey of empirical work on consumption can be complete without a consideration of data issues. There are major measurement problems both in household surveys and at the macroeconomic level as illustrated by the scale of data revisions. This is the topic of section 12. Finally, section 13 draws conclusions, considers gaps in the literature, and suggests future research agendas.

2   The Consumption Function under Point Expectations

The context here is one of point expectations, i.e. the individual believes that next period's income will take a particular value rather than a range of values, each with an associated probability. The alternative of probabilistic or stochastic income expectations will be adopted in sections 3, 4, and beyond. Section 2.1 considers the simplest two-period consumption choice problem. We begin with the period-to-period budget constraint which, given lack of money illusion, can be expressed in real terms. We explain why conventionally defined savings rates are likely to rise with inflation even when the budget constraint in real terms is unaltered, an issue of some practical importance. The section then considers both "Euler equation" and "solved out" consumption functions resulting from utility maximization. The section concludes by considering why the effect of the real interest rate in the solved out consumption function is likely to be unstable and is even indeterminate in sign, an important issue for empirical work.

Section 2.2 considers the multi-period extension of the two-period model. We explain why the marginal propensity to consume (MPC) out of assets varies with the time horizon and so with age. Given the typical hump profile of income, the MPC out of income will be lowest just before income declines with retirement. Shifts in demography, as well as shifts in the distribution of income and assets over consumers of different ages, will then affect aggregate consumption, even where aggregate income and aggregate assets are held constant. We will also examine the spending implications of variations in needs over the life-cycle and of the bequest motive.

2.1 The Two-Period Case

We assume that consumers do not suffer from money illusion and are concerned with consumption, c, non-property income, y, and assets, A, all measured in constant prices, i.e. in real terms. To convert to current prices, we multiply by the price index p.[9] We can then write down the period-to-period budget constraints in nominal terms. These constraints require that the net change in assets, $(p_1 A_1 - p_0 A_0)$, is the difference between income (including property income arising from asset ownership), $p_1 y_1 + r_0^* p_0 A_0$, and consumption expenditure, $p_1 c_1$, where r_0^* is the nominal rate of return on assets held at the end of the previous period. This nominal rate of return includes any dividend or interest income from these assets as well as capital appreciation. Then

$$p_1 c_1 + p_1 A_1 = p_1 y_1 + p_0 A_0 (1 + r_0^*)$$
$$p_2^e c_2 + p_2^e A_2 = p_2^e y_2^e + p_1 A_1 (1 + r_1^*) \tag{5.1}$$

where the superscript "e" indicates expectations.

This pair of nominal, period-to-period budget constraints is easily converted to real terms by dividing throughout by p_1 and p_2^e respectively. We then find

$$c_1 + A_1 = y_1 + A_0 (1 + r_0),$$
$$c_2 + A_2 = y_2^e + A_1 (1 + r_1^e), \tag{5.2}$$

where r is the "real" interest rate. The period 1 real interest rate is thus defined by

$$1 + r_1^e = p_1 (1 + r_1^*) / p_2^e. \tag{5.3}$$

The well known conclusion that the real interest rate is approximately equal to the nominal rate minus expected inflation is easily established.[10]

At this stage it is worth making an important practical point concerning the national accounts definition of real disposable income which, under inflation or the presence of capital gains and losses, measures incorrectly the comprehensive real income in (5.2) $y_1 + r_0 A_0$. The latter measure, put forward by Haig (1921), Simons (1938), and Hicks (1946), is defined as the amount of consumption which maintains the level of real assets. Real disposable income under national accounting conventions is defined by real disposable non-property income y, plus a distorted measure of after-tax real property income:

$$yd_1 = y_1 + \frac{r_0^{**} p_0 A_0}{p_1},$$ (5.4)

where r_0^{**} is the nominal after-tax return excluding capital gains on illiquid assets (but including imputed rental income from owner-occupied housing). Higher inflation for a given real rate of return implies a higher nominal rate. Since the rise in r_0^{**} will be much sharper than the rise in the price level p, it is clear that $r_0^{**} p_0 A_0 / p_1$ will rise and so raise measured real disposable income even though, in real terms, nothing has altered. If indeed real consumption is unaltered, the conventional savings ratio defined as disposable income minus consumption divided by disposable income will rise. The practical implication is to take care in interpreting conventionally measured savings ratios and, wherever possible, to use real disposable non-property income in preference to conventional real disposable income in modelling consumption.

Having considered the budget constraints, let us now turn to consumption decisions. Most of the consumption literature assumes intertemporally additive preferences in which some increasing monotonic transformation (given an ordinal concept of utility) of life-time utility, U, is the sum of the subutilities of consumption in each period, discounted using the subjective discount rate δ.

$$U = u(c_1) + \frac{1}{1 + \delta} u(c_2),$$ (5.5)

where $u' > 0$, $u'' < 0$, and $\delta \geqslant 0$.

An especially convenient case of this is the homothetic[11] form of (5.5). The combination of additivity and homotheticity implies $u(c_i) = c_i^{-\rho}$ so that

$$U^{-\rho} = c_1^{-\rho} + \frac{1}{1 + \delta} c_2^{-\rho}$$ (5.6)

where the elasticity of substitution $\sigma = 1/(1 + \rho)$. The constant elasticity of substitution (hence the term CES to describe such preferences), σ, measures how responsive is the ratio of consumption in the two periods to relative prices, i.e. to $1/(1 + r_1^e)$.

Now we shall derive the Euler equation form of the consumption function. We can optimize by substituting the period-to-period budget constraints (5.2) into the utility function (5.5), optimizing with respect to A_1. At the optimum we find that

$$\frac{\partial U}{\partial A_1} = \frac{\partial u}{\partial c_1} \frac{\partial c_1}{\partial A_1} + \frac{1}{(1 + \delta)} \frac{\partial u}{\partial c_2} \frac{\partial c_2}{\partial A_1} = 0.$$

Thus we obtain a relationship between current marginal utility and next period's planned marginal utility:

$$\frac{\partial u}{\partial c_1} = \frac{(1 + r_1^e)}{(1 + \delta)} \frac{\partial u}{\partial c_2}. \tag{5.7}$$

This is the intertemporal efficiency condition and is the basis for the whole Euler equation literature following Hall (1978), the only difference being that probabilistic expectations are taken of (5.7) rather than point expectations as here. It says that the marginal utility of consumption in the first period equals the expected marginal utility in the second weighted by the ratio of the subjective discount factor $1/(1 + \delta)$ and the market discount factor $1/(1 + r_1^e)$.

In the Euler equation context under point expectations, planned consumption growth is higher at a higher real interest rate because of diminishing marginal utility. This is easy to see in the CES case where (5.7) takes the form

$$c_1^{-1/\sigma} = \left(\frac{1 + r_1^e}{1 + \delta}\right)(c_2^e)^{-1/\sigma},$$

so that $\ln c_2^e - \ln c_1 = \sigma[\ln(1 + r_1^e) - \ln(1 + \delta)]$. Effectively, one can think of the rise in the real interest rate raising the reward from saving and thus resulting in some substitution away from c_1 to c_2.

The solved out form of the consumption function can be obtained by combining the intertemporal efficiency condition (in the multi-period case there will be more than one) with the period-to-period budget constraints (5.2) and solving for the endogenous asset level A_1. This is then translated back into the consumption decision using the first part of (5.2).

The alternative method of obtaining the same solution for the consumption function is to combine the period-to-period budget constraints (5.2) into a single life-cycle budget constraint by eliminating A_1 between the two parts of (5.2). If the end of period 2 asset level is taken as zero (e.g. because the consumer desires to leave no bequest), the life-cycle budget constraint is:

$$c_1 + \frac{1}{1 + r_1^e} c_2 = A_0(1 + r_0) + y_1 + \frac{1}{1 + r_1^e} y_2^e \tag{5.8}$$

$$\equiv W.$$

Note that W is real life-cycle wealth: initial assets plus human capital, consisting of current non-property income plus discounted expected non-property income.

We then maximize life-cycle utility $U = U(c_1, c_2)$ subject to (5.8) using the Lagrangian method. If preferences are homothetic, the solved out consumption function takes the form

$$c_1 = \frac{W_1}{\kappa_1} = \frac{1}{\kappa_1}\left[A_0(1 + r_0) + y_1 + \frac{y_2^e}{1 + r_1^e}\right], \tag{5.9}$$

where κ_1 is the inverse of the marginal propensity to consume (MPC) out of assets. In general, κ_1 depends on the real interest rate and the subjective discount rate. In the context of CES preferences (5.6),

$$\kappa_1 = 1 + \left(\frac{1}{1+\delta}\right)^{\sigma}\left(\frac{1}{1+r_1^e}\right)^{1-\sigma} \tag{5.10}$$

For small values of δ and r_1^e,

$$\kappa_1 \approx 1 + \frac{1}{1 + \sigma\delta + (1-\sigma)r_1^e}. \tag{5.11}$$

Thus, the discount factor in (5.11) takes the weighted average of the subjective and market interest rates, the weights being the elasticity of substitution.[12] There are good reasons to believe that intertemporal substitutability is low: in other words, consumers prefer consumption to be steady over time, after accounting for needs variations due to seasonal and other external factors. This would suggest $0 < \sigma < 1$ and probably $\sigma < 0.5$, at least for annual data.

We can draw some interesting implications from (5.9) and (5.11). If the rate of expected income growth is g,

$$c_1 = \frac{A_0(1+r_0)}{\kappa_1} + y_1\left[1 + \frac{1+g}{1+r_1^e}\right]\bigg/\left[1 + \frac{1}{1+\sigma\delta+(1-\sigma)r_1^e}\right]. \tag{5.12}$$

Thus if the subjective discount rate δ equals the market interest rate and growth is zero,

$$c_1 = \frac{A_0(1+r_0)}{\kappa_1} + y_1. \tag{5.13}$$

Then the MPC out of income is unity. We return to the issue of income expectations and their implications in section 3.

Equation (5.12) tells us that the MPC out of income is above unity for positive growth and below unity for negative growth. But if y_2^e were a constant unrelated to y_1, then the MPC out of y_1 would be κ_1^{-1} and thus considerably below unity.

We can also draw interesting implications for the response of consumption to a higher real interest rate, taking different values for the elasticity of substitution, σ, initial assets, A_0, and expected income growth, g. Suppose income is expected to be constant. Then we have the following cases when r rises:

1 If $\sigma = 0$, $g = 0$, and $A_0 = 0$, then $c_1 = y_1$ and there is no interest rate effect. If, however, income growth is expected, this growth will be more discounted at a higher interest rate so that consumption falls at a higher real interest rate.

2 If $\sigma > 0$ and $A_0 = 0$, consumption will fall even with constant income. This is most obvious for Cobb-Douglas preferences (i.e. when $\sigma = 1$) because then κ_1 is independent of the interest rate.

3 If $\sigma = 0$ and $A_0 > 0$, and growth is zero, then (5.13) holds. Since κ_1 is lower at a higher interest rate, spending rises: effectively, initial assets yield higher returns and

consumption rises with the real interest rate. Note however that this result ignores any fall in real asset values associated with expectations of a higher real interest rate or rate of return.

4 If $\sigma > 0$ and $A_0 > 0$, the result is inconclusive, depending on how large are assets relative to income and on how small is the elasticity of substitution. Since the ratio of assets to income varies over the business cycle, one should not expect a stable aggregate real interest rate effect. An elasticity of 0.5 or less would be consistent with a relatively small and unstable real interest rate effect in aggregate consumption functions – which accords with most, though not all, empirical evidence (see Deaton, 1992a, section 2.2).

The relevance of positive asset effects on aggregate consumption, on the other hand, has been supported by most empirical work, ever since the early studies by Ando and Modigliani (1963) and Stone (1964).

2.2 Age and Consumption: the Multi-Period Case

In this section, we consider the multi-period extension of the two-period model. We explain why the marginal propensity to consume (MPC) out of assets varies with the time horizon and so with age. Given the typical hump profile of income, the MPC out of income will be lowest just before income declines with retirement. Shifts in demography, as well as shifts in the distribution of income and assets over consumers of different ages, will then affect aggregate consumption, even where aggregate income and aggregate assets are held constant. We will also examine the spending implications of variations in needs over the life-cycle and of the bequest motive.

Maintaining the assumption of point (i.e. not probabilistic) expectations, the multi-period extension of (5.9) and (5.10) is

$$c_1 = \frac{W_1}{\kappa_1} = \frac{1}{\kappa_1} \left[A_0(1 + r_0) + y_1 + \sum_{s=1}^{T} y_{1+s}^e / (1 + r)^s \right]. \tag{5.14}$$

We have also assumed that the same real interest rate will persist across periods. The inverse MPC out of assets, analogously to (5.10), is given by

$$\kappa_1 = 1 + \sum_{s=1}^{T} \left(\frac{1}{(1 + \delta)^\sigma (1 + r)^{1-\sigma}} \right)^s \approx 1 + \sum_{s=1}^{T} \left(\frac{1}{1 + \sigma\delta + (1 - \sigma)r} \right)^s \tag{5.15}$$

We can now illustrate the effects of age on the marginal propensity to consume out of assets. For simplicity, suppose the subjective and the market discount rate coincide. Then, with static real income expectations, equation (5.14) simplifies to (5.13). Under these assumptions, the effect of age on consumption will operate entirely through κ_1, the inverse MPC out of assets. To illustrate this, suppose

$$\sigma\delta + (1 - \sigma)r = 0.05.$$

The series $1 + a + a^2 + \ldots + a^{T-1}$, for $-1 < a < 1$, has the sum $(1 - a^T)/(1 - a)$. Here $a = (1.05)^{-1}$. Thus, making explicit the dependence of κ on the horizon T, $\kappa(10) = 8$, $\kappa(20) = 13.1$, $\kappa(30) = 16.1$, $\kappa(40) = 18$, and, for an infinitely lived consumer, $\kappa(\infty) = 21$.

This has the immediate implication that older people, with their shorter time horizons, have a larger MPC out of assets than younger people. Note that the difference between the old and young MPCs rises as the average discount rate falls. For the aggregate consumption function the old/young difference is important because the age distribution of assets will then affect consumption. This issue will be central to the question of the effects of per capita real income growth on aggregate savings behaviour. An economy with a higher growth rate will, generally speaking, have a bigger share of wealth held by the young – though there is the proviso discussed in the introduction that, if the young were free of credit constraints, then with optimistic expectations regarding their future income they would borrow to smooth life-cycle consumption. Another qualification arises if the old have heavily invested in illiquid assets such as equities and land that may appreciate with economic growth, especially if this growth is partly unexpected.

Let us now relax the assumption of static real income expectations and replace it by the hump profile of earnings which is widely observed. The smooth nature of the aggregate profile reflects, among other things, variations over individuals in the age of retirement. Someone at the earnings peak in middle age can only expect lower incomes ahead and, by equations (5.14) and (5.15), will have the lowest MPC out of current earnings. Deaton (1992a) notes that the age profile of saving varies a good deal across countries. The single common pattern appears to be raised savings rates in the years just before retirement. Thus, the expected drop in income at retirement clearly has important influences on saving in the immediately preceding years.

Based on the above conclusions, we might expect something like the following pattern for the MPCs out of assets and income over the age profile:

	MPC out of assets	*MPC out of non-property income*
Young	small	large
Pre-retirement	medium	small
Retired	large	medium

where, of course, the MPCs out of income exceed those out of assets.

Empirically, consumption follows income rather more closely over the life-cycle than predicted by the simplest life-cycle models where consumers try to keep planned consumption constant (see Carroll and Summers, 1991; Deaton, 1992a, section 2.1). As we saw in section 2.1, discounting future income provides part of the reason. As we will see in sections 4 and 5, credit constraints and uncertainty are important reasons for this empirical result. But there is another explanation which fits into the above model without incorporating either credit restrictions or uncertainty: the variation of needs over the life-cycle, especially related to child rearing. The reason why many young couples, who expect higher earning opportunities later, may not want to borrow (even if they could), is that they also expect higher expenses. This is particularly relevant if one of them stops or reduces work for several years to bring up children. Need variations can be readily introduced into the parents' CES utility function through the equivalence scale, m_s:

$$U^{-\rho} = \sum_1^T \left(\frac{1}{1 + \delta} \right)^{s-1} \left(\frac{c_s}{m_s} \right)^{-\rho} \tag{5.16}$$

where m_s increases with household needs such as the number and type of dependants present or expected to be present.[13] Given planned parenthood, these equivalence scales will reflect income expectations. Incidentally, for this specification in (5.16) to give the intuitively plausible results of higher needs at s, leading to higher consumption at s, the elasticity of substitution σ needs to be less than unity. Empirical estimates for a model of this kind have been obtained by Banks, Blundell, and Preston (1993).

Planned parenthood should thus have sharp consequences for the savings behaviour of households. There is strong empirical evidence for the effect of the presence of young children on labour force participation and hours of work by mothers. Lower income is typically associated with higher needs following the arrival of young children. One would therefore expect to see high savings rates associated with a high number of young childless couples, and low savings rates associated with large numbers of pre-school children as households run down assets in the expectation, in most cases, of work being resumed when the children reach school age. Brenner, Dagenais, and Montemarquette (1992) find evidence for the second effect.

Depending upon the system of finance for higher education, one may expect saving for the children's college education, followed by a certain amount of asset dissipation when children reach college age. For many households this may leave a relatively short gap before retirement age in which to top up saving for retirement. Over the individual life-cycle, this suggests quite sharp fluctuations in the savings rate. To pick up these effects in cross-section data, it would be necessary to condition quite carefully on the age and number of children as well as on the age and expected income profiles of the adults. On aggregate time-series data alone, the effects of such demographic variations are very difficult to estimate robustly.

There are bound to be economies of scale in operating a household. In most industrial countries the trend in recent decades has been towards a smaller number of people per household. With diseconomies of small scale, one might have thought that consumption needs would therefore be higher given per capita income. This does not necessarily reduce the saving rate if it affects consumption needs evenly at different ages. However, suppose that lower average household size is partly the consequence of later marriage or cohabitation by young people who can look forward to benefiting *in the future* from these economies of scale, but who currently suffer the diseconomies of being single. Then, in the absence of credit constraints, there would be a reduction in the aggregate savings rate.

The context of parenthood is the right one in which to raise the issue of bequests. A two-generation utility function from the viewpoint of the parents could look as follows:

$$U = \sum_{1}^{T_1} \left(\frac{1}{1+\delta}\right)^{s-1} u(c_s^1) + \alpha \sum_{1}^{T_2} \left(\frac{1}{1+\delta}\right)^{s-1} u(c_s^2), \qquad (5.17)$$

where $u'(c) > 0$, $u''(c) < 0$, and $0 < \alpha$. This sums the subutility $u(c_s^1)$ of the current generation, defined from the current period until their death at T_1, and the discounted subutility of the next generation (assumed already to be in existence) until their death at $T_2 > T_1$. α is a discount factor less than unity, reflecting some degree of selfishness in that a unit increase of subutility is valued more highly if it accrues directly to the parents rather than to the next generation.

As far as the budget constraint is concerned, the first generation household can only decide on its own assets. The marginal utility of the assets bequested can be low for two reasons: one is that $\alpha < 1$ and the other is that the receiving second generation household may have its own assets and income prospects. It would therefore be far from appropriate to treat the behaviour corresponding to equation (5.17) as that of an infinitely lived household with geometrically declining subjective discount factors as assumed by Barro (1974). Intuitively, behaviour will be somewhere between that of such a Barro household and one with no bequest motive. This is consistent with empirical evidence against Barro's proposition of Ricardian equivalence under which households do not respond to tax cuts now on the grounds that they or their descendants will have to pay higher taxes in the future. However, there are a number of other reasons to explain the failure of Ricardian equivalence, including uncertainty and credit constraints.

We examined above the effect of the size of the remaining horizon on the marginal propensity to consume out of wealth, κ_1^{-1}. The bequest motive is likely to reduce this MPC for retired households, narrowing the gap between retired and younger households.

3 The Consumption Function under Stochastic Income Expectations

The association of different probabilities with different income levels is more plausible than point expectations about future income. In the last two decades, the Muthian rational expectations assumption has been the most popular way of treating stochastic expectations about variables such as income. For tractability, this has been largely used in the framework of linear models. We develop the implications of linear rational expectations models both for Euler equation and for solved out consumption functions. In section 3.1, we explain the Hall (1978) Euler equation consumption model. This model, derived from a quadratic utility function, implies that consumption changes are not forecastable and that innovations in consumption relate to "news" in income (and other relevant variables). This section also discusses the relationship between news about income and the consumption innovation. Section 3.2 introduces the literature devoted to testing the Hall model and examines, in particular, the extent to which consumption responds to *anticipated* changes in income – the so-called "excess sensitivity" of consumption. Under the Hall hypothesis, consumption changes should be independent of any lagged information. Section 3.3 turns to the solved out consumption function, in which consumption depends on initial assets and on the mathematical expectation of permanent non-property income: hence the rational expectations permanent income hypothesis (REPIH). We consider the issue of the "persistence" of income. The more persistent is income, the more permanent are income innovations and the more responsive, other things being equal, is consumption to current income. If the stochastic process for income has a "unit root," first differencing is required to make the process stationary. Depending on the characterization of the I(1) process, the consumption innovation may well be as large as the income innovation, making the variance of consumption changes as large as that of income changes. Aggregate time-series evidence appears to support the unit root hypothesis. Yet the variance of consumption changes (on seasonally adjusted data) in most countries is one half or less of that of income changes: consumption is "excessively smooth." This is the excessive smoothness or Deaton paradox (see Deaton, 1987), and is the subject of section 3.4.

3.1   The Hall Euler Equation Model

Let us turn to the Hall (1978) result. Making expectations explicit in the Euler condition (5.7), which holds in the multi-period as well as the two-period case, gives

$$\frac{\partial u}{\partial c_1} = E\frac{(1 + r_1)\partial u}{(1 + \delta)\partial c_2} \tag{5.18}$$

where E is the expectations operator.

Two problems arise in deriving an analytical solution from equation (5.18) for consumption c_1. One is that r_1 is stochastic, and the expectation of the product of two stochastic variables is not the product of the expectations. The other one is that, in general, the marginal utility $\partial u/\partial c_2$ is non-linear in c_2, and then $Eu'(c_2) \neq u'(Ec_2)$.

One of the few cases where an easy solution is possible is when preferences are quadratic so that $u(c) = -\frac{1}{2}(\beta - c)^2$, which implies that marginal utility is linear in c. Note that β is the bliss point: $c < \beta$ for non-satiation. Then, given r is constant in equation (5.18),

$$\beta - c_1 = \frac{1 + r}{1 + \delta}(\beta - Ec_2) \tag{5.19}$$

If $r = \delta$ so that the market interest rate and the subjective discount rate coincide,

$$c_1 = E(c_2), \tag{5.20}$$

otherwise c_1 is a more general linear function of $E(c_2)$. Using t to denote the period, equation (5.20) implies that $c_t = E_t(c_{t+1})$, where E_t denotes expectations given the information set at t. Since $c_{t+1} = E_t(c_{t+1}) + \varepsilon_{t+1}$, where ε_{t+1} is an innovation error, i.e. non-forecastable, we obtain

$$c_{t+1} = c_t + \varepsilon_{t+1}. \tag{5.21}$$

This is the Hall (1978) type stochastic Euler equation. Equation (5.21) is an example of a "martingale process." If ε is independently and identically distributed (iid), (5.21) is called a "random walk." Hall himself argued for (5.21) as an approximation that holds if the market interest rate and the subjective discount rate are not far apart and if consumption shocks are small relative to the level of consumption (see Hall, 1978, p. 987).

Hall's result has the apparently revolutionary implication that, under certain assumptions, the best forecast of next period's consumption is this period's. No other currently available information is any use. The assumptions are:

   (i)   no credit restrictions or other non-linearities in the budget constraint
   (ii) a quadratic utility function additive over time
  (iii) no habits or adjustment costs
  (iv) non-durable goods
   (v) the subjective discount rate δ the same across consumers and, for (5.21), equal to the market real interest rate r
  (vi) no measurement errors or transitory shocks to consumption
 (vii) the coincidence of the frequency of consumers' decision making with the observation period of the data
(viii) a constant real interest rate
  (ix) rational expectations.

We now derive an important insight into the nature of the consumption innovation: we show that it is equal to the news about permanent non-property income. First, we derive the solved out form of the consumption function corresponding to (5.20) in which consumption is proportional to expected life-cycle wealth, $E_t W_t$, which can also be expressed in the "permanent income" form. We can then derive the result via a quasi-difference transform of expected permanent income or of life-cycle wealth.

In a multi-period model, the intertemporal efficiency condition (5.20) extends to all the periods in the planning horizon. By taking expectations of the period-to-period budget constraints (5.2),

$$E_t(c_s + A_s) = E_t(y_s + A_{s-1}(1 + r)),$$

we obtain the expectation of the standard life-cycle budget constraint,

$$\sum_{s=0}^{T} \left(\frac{1}{1+r}\right)^s E_t c_{t+s} = A_{t-1}(1+r) + \sum_{s=0}^{T} \left(\frac{1}{1+r}\right)^s E_t y_{t+s}, \tag{5.22}$$

$$\equiv E_t W_t$$

where $E_t c_t = c_t$ and $E_t y_t = y_t$. Since, $E_t c_{t+s} = c_t$, all $s \leqslant T$,

$$c_t = E_t W_t / \kappa_t, \tag{5.23}$$

where

$$\kappa_t = \sum_{s=0}^{T} \left(\frac{1}{1+r}\right)^s. \tag{5.24}$$

In the case $\delta \neq r$, c_t remains linear in $E_t W_t$ but there is also an intercept term. The solved out consumption function (5.23) can also be expressed in permanent income form, defining permanent non-property income y_t^p as that level which, if sustained over the life-cycle, has the same present value as the stream of non-property income actually expected by the household, i.e.

$$\sum_{s=0}^{T} \left(\frac{1}{1+r}\right)^s E_t y_t^p = \sum_{s=0}^{T} \left(\frac{1}{1+r}\right)^s E_t y_{t+s}, \tag{5.25}$$

where, of course, $E_t y_t = y_t$. Combining the previous four equations,

$$c_t = A_{t-1}(1+r)/\kappa_t + E_t y_t^p, \tag{5.26}$$

hence the terminology "rational expectations permanent income hypothesis" (REPIH).

The geometrically declining weights structure of (5.25) suggests considering the quasi-difference transformation

$$E_{t+1} \frac{W_{t+1}}{1+r} - E_t W_t = \left(A_t + E_{t+1} \sum_{s=1}^{T} \frac{y_{t+s}}{(1+r)^s}\right) - \left(A_{t-1}(1+r) + y_t + E_t \sum_{s=1}^{T} \frac{y_{t+s}}{(1+r)^s}\right)$$

$$= -c_t + \varepsilon_{t+1}^* \tag{5.27}$$

since $A_t - (1+r)A_{t-1} = y_t - c_t$, and where ε_{t+1}^* is the innovation in the disocunted present value of income from $t+1$ onwards. For quadratic utility and equality of the subjective and market discount rates, $\kappa_t c_t = E_t W_t$ (see (5.23)). Substituting for $E_t W_t$ and $E_{t+1} W_{t+1}$ in using (5.23), and the expression for κ in (5.24), gives[14]

$$\sum_{s=1}^{T}\left(\frac{1}{1+r}\right)^{s}(c_{t+1}-c_{t})=\varepsilon_{t+1}^{*}. \tag{5.28}$$

This is equivalent to (5.21) with

$$\varepsilon_{t+1}=\varepsilon_{t+1}^{*}\bigg/\sum_{s=1}^{T}\left(\frac{1}{1+r}\right)^{s}.$$

Clearly ε_{t+1} can be regarded as the innovation in discounted permanent non-property income y_t^p where y_t^p is defined by (5.25).

Thus the change in consumption is the news on permanent income.[15] The restriction imposed by rational expectations is the orthogonality condition on the disturbance term. Income revisions must be orthogonal to lagged available information with the implication that consumption should not respond to anticipated variables.

3.2 Testing the Hall Model and the Excess Sensitivity of Consumption

It was typical to test the orthogonality assumption by adding variables (dated $t-1$ and earlier) to a specification akin to (5.21) and testing for their significance. For example, Hall (1978) provided some empirical evidence that appeared to support the theory when he found that lagged income was insignificant in the regression of consumption on lagged consumption using standard significance levels,[16] but that lagged stock prices were not. Notwithstanding his formal rejection of the model, he noted that the additional information contained in stock prices contributed little to consumption growth and that therefore the REPIH was a reasonable approximation.

Most tests across different periods and various countries reveal violation of the orthogonality condition of the REPIH model. In the UK, Davidson and Hendry (1981) and Daly and Hadjimatheou (1981) found lagged income, consumption, and liquidity measures had significant explanatory power; Johnson (1983) found lagged unemployment significant in Australia. The Davidson and Hendry study is also interesting because it demonstrates via a Monte Carlo study that if the true data generating process (DGP) was a more traditional consumption function, then for certain parameterizations it mimics a random walk quite closely so that it is quite likely that a Hall test would fail to reject orthogonality. They take the DGP as an error correction model (ECM) of the form

$$\Delta c_t = \beta_0 + \beta_1 \Delta y_t + \beta_2(y_{t-1} - c_{t-1}) + \varepsilon_t. \tag{5.29}$$

This model, with slight modifications, has proved to be extremely useful as a characterization of aggregate consumption (e.g. DHSY, 1978 and Hendry, Muellbauer, and Murphy, 1990 for the UK; and Bladen-Hovell and Richards, 1983 and Dewhurst, 1989 for Australia).

Another strand in the testing of the Hall hypothesis (exemplified by the studies of Bilson, 1980; Flavin, 1981; Muellbauer, 1983; Blinder and Deaton, 1985) aimed to separately identify the consumer's reaction to anticipated and unanticipated income (and other) shocks by modelling both the income and the consumption processes. The theoretical link between consumption and income shocks is a close one, as we saw in section 3.1 under the admittedly strong assumptions leading to (5.21).

The link can be explained by modelling the joint income/consumption process. For example, let us specify an income process as in Muellbauer (1983):

$$y_t = \beta_0 + \beta_1 c_{t-1} + \sum_{i=2}^{k} \beta_i y_{t+1-i} + \varepsilon_t^y. \tag{5.30}$$

The feedback from lagged consumption to income could reflect the expenditure multiplier process and/or some expectational effect. A maintained hypothesis for the consumption process incorporating (5.21) as a special case is

$$c_t = \alpha_0 + \alpha_1 c_{t-1} + \sum_{i=2}^{k} \alpha_i y_{t+1-i} + \lambda \varepsilon_t^y + \eta_t. \tag{5.31}$$

Equation (5.30) models non-property income in terms of lagged non-property income and lagged consumption,[17] while (5.31) is a consumption function in which anticipated and unanticipated components appear separately. Note that the surprise term, ε_t^y, includes current income, so that the maintained model is the unrestricted version of the DHSY model, (5.27).[18] Muellbauer found that lagged income did have explanatory power once the regressions took account of a break in the series in the mid 1970s (thus reversing the findings of Bilson's earlier study). Flavin (1981) has also found that lagged income had explanatory power on US data.[19] Such findings led to the stylized fact that consumption appeared to exhibit excess sensitivity to anticipated income (and other variables) once account had been taken of the response to the innovation. It is important to emphasize that excess sensitivity is not to the innovation in income, but to the anticipated component of income, which should under RE have already been incorporated into lagged consumption.

The modelling of joint income/consumption processes and the growing interest in integrated processes led to two other major insights. First, as observed by Mankiw and Shapiro (1985; 1986) some tests of the REPIH (for example Flavin, 1981) assumed income was stationary around a deterministic trend. Consider the simplest possible form of the Flavin (1981, pp. 993–4) excess sensitivity test in order to explain these problems. Say that income follows an AR(1) process, i.e. $y_t = \beta_0 + \beta y_{t-1} + \varepsilon_t^y$. Flavin tested whether consumption exhibited excess sensitivity by augmenting (5.21) with the change in current income. Eliminating current income, using $E_{t-1}\Delta y_t = \beta_0 + (\beta - 1)y_{t-1}$, gives the unrestricted equation

$$\Delta c_t = \alpha + \phi y_{t-1} + u_t. \tag{5.32}$$

If, in fact, y is a non-stationary variable while Δc is stationary, the different sides of the equation have different orders of integration. Then the problems in making inferences about the excess sensitivity parameter ϕ are essentially the same as the problems that occur in discerning the existence of a unit root in a univariate time series, a point first noted by Mankiw and Shapiro (1985).[20] The Dickey-Fuller (Fuller, 1976; Dickey and Fuller, 1979) tests for the presence of a unit root are then appropriate. Use of the standard normal tables at usual significance levels would result in over-rejection of the null of a zero π. With a sample of 100, a researcher would need to find a t-value of around -3.45 to reject the null of a unit root at the 5% significance level. Of course, if y *were* trend stationary, these problems would not arise.

However, not all excess sensitivity tests have non-standard distributions. By augmenting the set of regressors it is possible to obtain combinations of variables which are stationary (for example $y_{t-1} - c_{t-1}$, Δy_{t-1} if c and y are cointegrated I(1) variables), so permitting inference. One example arises in the model given by (5.30) and (5.31). A related one is due to Campbell (1987), who showed that for an infinitely lived consumer with a quadratic utility function, equal and constant subjective and market discount rates, rational expectations, and no credit constraints, saving is the discounted value of expected declines in income. This is easy to see. With an infinite horizon, the consumption function (5.26) takes the form

$$c_t = r A_{t-1} + E_t y_t^p. \tag{5.33}$$

But consumption is also total income minus saving, i.e.

$$c_t = r A_{t-1} + y_t - s_t. \tag{5.34}$$

Subtracting (5.33) from (5.34) gives $s_t = y_t - E_t y_t^p$. This implies

$$s_t = -\sum_1^\infty \left(\frac{1}{1+r}\right)^s E_t \Delta y_{t+s},$$

which is the Campbell result.

The intuition is that consumers wish to avoid the utility costs of reductions in consumption, so that they smooth intertemporally, with savings as the mediator between the present and the future. Even if we move away from the extremely restrictive (and implausible) characterization of income as a pure random walk, and consider ARIMA(p, 1, q) processes, we still find that saving is stationary if the REPIH is true. Consider a test equation like:

$$\Delta c_t = \alpha_0 + \alpha_1 t + \pi_1 c_{t-1} + \pi_2 y_{t-1}^d + \eta_t$$
$$= \alpha_0 + \alpha_1 t + (\pi_1 + \pi_2)c_{t-1} + \pi_2 s_{t-1} + \eta_t, \tag{5.35}$$

where real disposable income y_t^d, in contrast to the conventional measure in (5.4), is defined as $rA_{t-1} + y_t$ so that $s_t = y_t^d - c_t$.

To test excess sensitivity we want to consider $\pi_1 = \pi_2 = 0$ or separately $\pi_1 = 0$, $\pi_2 = 0$. Under the null of the REPIH, consumption and disposable income are cointegrated (i.e. share a stochastic trend so that a certain linear combination is stationary). This means that inference (using (5.34)) can be made on s_{t-1} using standard normal tables, but the test of $\pi_1 + \pi_2 = 0$ remains non-standard. Empirical applications which augment the standard excess sensitivity equations find that the REPIH still fails the orthogonality requirement using US data (e.g. Stock and West, 1988; Campbell, 1987). We return to interpretations of these violations later.

3.3   The Solved Out Consumption Function and the Persistence of Income

Let us turn next to the implications for the solved out rational expectations consumption function of income processes with different degrees of persistence. This is critical for evaluating the size of the conventionally defined marginal propensity to consume out of current income. To introduce the issue of persistence, let us consider three simple alternative rational expectations models for income:

$$\begin{cases} (a) \; y_t = \bar{y} + \varepsilon_t \\ (b) \; y_t = \lambda_0 + \lambda y_{t-1} + \varepsilon_t, \quad 0 < \lambda < 1 \\ (c) \; y_t = y_{t-1} + \varepsilon_t, \end{cases} \tag{5.36}$$

where ε_t is a random error with mean zero. Note that time trends can be incorporated in (a) and (b), and a constant in (c), for trend growth.

Under (a), $y^p = \bar{y}$. The best estimate of y^p is a historical average in which current real income y has only a small weight. This seems to be the case Friedman had in mind in arguing for a small MPC out of current income.

Under (b), recursive substitution (e.g. $y_{t+2}^e = \lambda_0 + \lambda(\lambda_0 + \lambda y_t)$) implies with an infinite horizon, given the definition of permanent income in (5.25),

$$\left(\frac{1+r}{r}\right) y_t^p = \text{constant} + y_t \left(1 + \left(\frac{\lambda}{1+r}\right) + \left(\frac{\lambda}{1+r}\right)^2 + \cdots\right)$$

$$= \text{constant} + y_t \left(\frac{1+r}{1+r-\lambda}\right)$$

summing the geometric series. Thus the response of permanent income y_t^p, and hence, given the REPIH consumption function (5.26), also of consumption to current income y, is $r/(1 + r - \lambda)$. Taking a real interest rate of 3%, we can trace the response of y^p and hence c to current income y as in table 5.1.

This example illustrates the importance of *persistence* in the income process. In case (a), where persistence is zero, permanent income is only a little affected by changes in current real income. In case (c), where persistence is complete,

Table 5.1 Response of permanent to current income

Eqn (5.36)	λ	Response of y^P to y
Case (b)	0.8	0.13
	0.9	0.23
	0.95	0.38
	0.99	0.75
Case (c)	1	1

permanent real income is the *same* as current real income since the latter is the best estimate of all future incomes. Case (b) covers the spectrum of intermediate cases. Note that as λ tends to 1, small differences in λ make big differences to the weight of current income in y^P. The persistence issue was rather neglected by Friedman (1957) in favour of merely the randomness of income, which is a rather different matter. Farrell (1959) made rather more of the issue through the "elasticity of expectations" measuring the sensitivity of income expectations to current income.

Table 5.1, illustrating the response of permanent to current income, assumed an infinite horizon. For shorter horizons, e.g. ten years, there is greater responsiveness of y^P to y than shown in the table when λ is less then unity.

These simple insights generalize to more complicated stochastic processes for y. Consider the more general ARMA model

$$\alpha(L)(y_t - \lambda^*) = \lambda(L)\varepsilon_t, \tag{5.37}$$

where $\alpha(\ )$ and $\lambda(\ )$ are polynomials in the lag operator L. For an infinitely lived household, Hansen and Sargent (1981) have shown that the responsiveness of permanent to current income shocks in this case is given by

$$\frac{r}{1+r} \frac{\sum_0^\infty (1+r)^{-k}\lambda_k}{\sum_0^\infty (1+r)^{-k}\alpha_k}. \tag{5.38}$$

Under the permanent income hypothesis, this will also measure the response of consumption to current shocks.

Let us consider some examples of (5.37) with different persistence implications but all corresponding to "unit root" processes for income, i.e. where first differencing of income creates a stationary series.[21] First, take the case $y_t = y_{t-1} + \varepsilon_t - \lambda_1\varepsilon_{t-1}$. By (5.38), the responsiveness of permanent income to current income, which is a neat way of measuring persistence, is $1 - \lambda_1/(1 + r)$. When λ_1 is positive, the negatively autocorrelated moving average form of the income shock implies persistence less than unity, while for negative λ_1, persistence exceeds unity. Second, take the case $y_t = y_{t-1} + \alpha_1(y_{t-1} - y_{t-2}) + \varepsilon_t$. By (5.38), persistence equals $[1 - \alpha_1/(1 + r)]^{-1}$. If α_1 is positive, persistence exceeds unity, while if α_1 is negative, persistence is less than unity.

In the general unit root case,

$$\Delta y_t = \sum_{i=1}^{k} \alpha_i \Delta y_{t-i} + \varepsilon_t, \qquad (5.39)$$

where k is infinite if there is a moving average element. Persistence exceeds unity if $\Sigma \alpha_i / (1 + r)^i$ is positive and is less than unity if this term is negative. Thus, even when income follows a unit root, persistence and, by implication, the response of consumption to income shocks can vary widely.

3.4   The Excess Smoothness Debate

Tests of the Dickey-Fuller type appear to find it hard to reject the hypothesis that income has a unit root with a process of the type that implies a high degree of persistence.

Under the Euler equation (5.21), in the absence of transitory consumption shocks or measurement errors, the consumption surprise equals the surprise in permanent income (see section 3.1). So long as there are no significant negative moving average or autocorrelated components in the ARIMA $(p, 1, q)$ income process, then permanent income responds strongly to shocks in current income, and the variance of the consumption innovation should be at least as great as that of the current income innovation.

In fact, in the US (and other countries) seasonally adjusted[22] consumption growth has a variance of one-half or less of income. Consumption thus appears to be excessively smooth, i.e. insufficiently volatile for the assumption that income is generated by a standard difference stationary (DS) process. Since one of the stylized facts that the PIH was intended to explain was the smoothness of consumption, this gives rise to a paradox. This paradox was brought to light in Deaton (1987; also see 1992a) and Campbell and Deaton (1989).

However, Deaton's paradox is fragile to many amendments in the simple underlying model. It is far from trivial empirically to distinguish processes such as (5.36c) and its unit root generalizations in (5.39) from processes that are stationary about a deterministic trend (see Deaton, 1992a, pp. 110–17; Stock, 1990; 1993), or stationary about a smooth, but still stochastic trend. And either way, one may query the validity of the rational expectations hypothesis. We deal first with the issue of modelling income/output dynamics. Starting with Nelson and Plosser's (1982) seminal paper, the notion that many macroeconomic series could be described as random walks or variants of this difference stationary process has been extensively researched. Five basic approaches have been employed. First, and predominantly, traditional ARIMA techniques (combined with unit root tests) have been used.[23] Second, unobserved components ARIMA (UCARIMA) have been applied to directly estimate a particular decomposition into transitory and permanent components (e.g. Clark, 1987 finding lower persistence). An example of such a process is $y_t = y_{t-1} + \varepsilon_{1t} + \Delta\varepsilon_{2t}$, where ε_{1t} and ε_{2t} are independent white noise processes. The greater the relative variance of ε_{2t}, the lower the degree of persistence. Third, non-parametric estimates of the ratios of the variance of long- and short-run growth rates provide information at the zero frequency in the spectral density of the series (which is where TS and DS processes could be most easily distinguished).[24] Fourth, the more naturally interpretable structural time-series methods have also been applied (Harvey, 1985; 1989; Diebold and Nerlove, 1990; Diebold and Rudebusch, 1991; Harvey and Jaeger, 1993). Finally, multivariate models have been developed which separate transitory and permanent components in a less arbitrary way than the UCARIMA approach.

No consensus has been reached using these various methodologies. This is scarcely remarkable given the difficulties:

1 The findings are, in some cases, technique dependent. For example, the structure of UCARIMA models means that they must necessarily find measures of persistence less than unity (Lippi and Reichlin, 1992).

2 The results can be sensitive to whether data are seasonally adjusted or not (Ghysels, 1990).[25]

3 All the tests of the null hypothesis that the process is difference stationary (DS) with high persistence have low power relative to trend stationary (TS) alternatives which are non-local to the null in the economic sense, i.e. which have very different economic implications, for example, for the marginal propensity to consume. This applies to the variance ratio tests as well, which may reveal high persistence even when the underlying DGP is a TS process (Rudebusch, 1993; Christiano and Eichenbaum, 1990; Banerjee, Lumsdaine, and Stock, 1992; Faust, 1992).

4 In other cases, the results depend on the period of estimation (e.g. the break identified by Harvey, 1989 in US GDP).

5 Following on from the previous point, the notion that the income dynamics can be described by a single univariate process over many years is highly contestable. Ignoring structural breaks due to regime shifts in the series (such as floating exchange rates, different monetary regimes, and idiosyncratic shocks like the oil shock in 1973) biases tests towards finding higher orders of integration, and therefore greater persistence than may typically hold. This has spurred interest in segmented trends, where occasional large shocks perturb the slope and/or constant in what are otherwise deterministic trends (see Perron, 1989; and also Balke and Fomby, 1991; Banerjee, Lumsdaine, and Stock, 1992; Hamilton, 1989; Hall and Scott, 1990; Perron, 1990; Bai, Lumsdaine, and Stock, 1991; Rappoport and Reichlin, 1989; Demery and Duck, 1992).

With reference to the last point, let us take an empirical illustration on annual US data analysed in Muellbauer and Murphy (1993a), which suggests US income has fluctuated around a split trend. There is evidence of a slowdown in productivity growth throughout the industrial world after the oil price shock of 1973–4 which makes it the natural place to test for a break in trend. On US annual data for real per capita personal disposable non-property income one finds for 1956 to 1991:

$$\Delta \ln y(+1) = 0.54 - 0.365 \ln y(-1) + 0.0103\, t - 0.0064\, ts$$
$$ (4.0) \qquad (3.9) \qquad\qquad (4.0) \qquad\quad (3.9)$$

(5.40)

$$\bar{R}^2 = 0.307, \quad SE = 0.0153, \quad DW = 2.37, \quad t\text{-ratios is parentheses,}$$

where t is a time trend and ts is a trend shift which is 0 up to 1974, 1 in 1975, 2 in 1976, etc.[26] These results suggest that growth slowed by about 60% after 1974. The unexplained variation in next year's income growth has a standard error of 1.5% but the equation explains 31% of the variance. Note that next year's income growth will tend to be high if last year's log income was low relative to the path implied by the split trend, and low if the opposite is true. In other words, the reversion to the split time trend occurs via the lagged dependent variable $\ln y(-1)$: the long-run growth rate before 1975 was $0.0103/0.365 = 2.8\%$ p.a. and from 1975 was $(0.0103-0.0064)/0.365 = 1.1\%$. By the unit root hypothesis, $\ln y(-1)$ is I(1) so that the above regression should fail to give highly significant trend effects and feedback to the level of income. These results suggest income is stationary around a split time trend, thus rejecting the DS hypothesis. But if income is stationary then the smoothness of consumption follows immediately, so that the Deaton paradox vanishes.

The significance of these results is further improved by the inclusion of the unemployment rate un and the two-year change in the interest rate on three-month Treasury bills, $\Delta_2 rtb$ (for the US these are both stationary variables):

$$\Delta \ln y(+1) = 0.48 - 0.0051 un(-1) - 0.0055\, \Delta_2 rtb,$$
$$ (4.12) \qquad\quad (3.2) \qquad\qquad (5.7)$$

(5.41)

$$- 0.306 \ln y + 0.00930\, t - 0.00680\, ts$$
$$ (3.9) \qquad\qquad (4.1) \qquad\qquad (4.7)$$

$$\bar{R}^{-2} = 0.618, \quad SE = 0.0114, \quad DW = 2.13.$$

The same set of variables do remarkably well in forecasting the annual income change two years ahead. For several years beyond that, the trends and the lagged income term retain explanatory power.

An alternative view, which accords to the structural time series approach, is that there is a slowly evolving underlying trend in real income, say θ_t, that reflects primarily productivity growth and demography and perhaps long-term trends in the world economy. Such a trend would not be I(1) but I(2). Following Harvey (1990) and Harvey and Jaeger (1993), we represent such a trend θ_t by a varying coefficient model:

$$\Delta \theta_t = \beta_t + \beta_0,$$
$$\Delta \beta_t = \varepsilon_t,$$

(5.42)

where ε_t is white noise. As Harvey and Jaeger explain, such a model is close to the Hodrick-Prescott filter for generating a smooth but time varying underlying trend for income which, for US data, produces very similar results to (5.42). Using Koopman et al.'s (1995) STAMP program, the above models were re-estimated replacing the combination of effects of time trend and split time trend by θ_t. The estimated standard error of ε_t is 0.0035 in the model corresponding to (5.41), suggesting θ_t is very smooth. The graph of θ_t shows a fall-off in underlying growth from the late 1960s but some tendency for a resumption in the 1980s – a feature missed by the split trends model. The overall fit of the equation is marginally worse than (5.41).

These results suggest that income is not an I(1) variable at the macroeconomic level. This can be interpreted as follows. There are ceilings to output levels in the short run given by a slowly evolving supply side and there are forces for recovery if income drops far below trend. Macro policy makers change policy when unemployment reaches levels perceived to be too high. There are also spontaneous recovery forces via downward pressure on wages and commodity prices, and the wearing out of durable goods, which create private sector demands for replacement investment, helping the upturn. In such a world, rational consumers would become more pessimistic about growth prospects if growth had been very strong lately and more optimistic if growth had been weak for some time. Permanent income then would be smoother than current income: the largest part of income innovations would not be permanent and consumption would be smoother than income.

One of the chief difficulties in using the results of standard time-series analysis to infer excess smoothness is the hidden assumption that agents face only one type of shock. It seems more economically intuitive to suppose a range of different shocks, each having its own distribution and own persistence. As Quah (1990) and Christano and Eichenbaum (1990) point out, a given DS model can be decomposed into temporary and permanent components in an infinite number of ways. Thus even if the researcher was certain that the DS univariate representation was true, she would be ignorant of the particular decomposition on which agents conditioned their behaviour. This is crucial because there is always a decomposition which can make the permanent component arbitrarily small. So as long as consumers can distinguish these components, then univariate time-series representations observed by the econometricians will be uninformative. An extreme example illustrates the point. Suppose, following Christiano and Eichenbaum, that consumers know the entire future path of their labour income, so that there can be no surprises. Then under the REPIH their consumption is fixed. Suppose an econometrician does not share the information set of the consumers and finds a unit root and large persistence in the labour income series. She might infer incorrectly that consumption was excessively smooth.[27]

Campbell (1987) suggested an ingenious way of controlling for the superior information of private agents over econometricians. Campbell noted, as we saw in section 3.3 (the equation after (5.34)), that under the null of REPIH, saving should encapsulate the superior information of the agent: saving should

"Granger-cause" income (i.e. agents' forecasts of income should ring true on average under RE). Campbell set up a bivariate VAR for the US using differenced non-property income and saving (which we have already noted should be stationary under the null of the REPIH). He found that the weak implication of the REPIH that saving leads future income could not be rejected. However, the bulk of the evidence suggested that the restrictions required on the bivariate VAR for consistency with REPIH could be rejected: the change in consumption (expressed as $\Delta y + rs_{-1} - \Delta s$ from the identity $s = rA_{-1} + y - c$) was not orthogonal to lagged information.[28] These results have been replicated for the US (Campbell and Deaton, 1989, using a slightly different model); for the UK (Attfield, Demery, and Duck, 1990); Australia (MacDonald and Kearney, 1990); but not for Japan (Campbell and Mankiw, 1991), probably because of poor modelling of the income process which underwent a structural break in the 1970s.

However, Muellbauer and Murphy (1993a; 1993b) find in both the UK and the US (in the context of an only moderately sophisticated income forecasting process, such as (5.41)) that lagged saving does not have a significant negative effect on subsequent income. Alessie and Lusardi (1993) also find no evidence in favour of the Campbell effect on Dutch panel data for individual households (though their results may be sensitive to their treatment of fixed effects and measurement errors). This throws doubt at least on whether private agents have superior information about aggregate data. The issue of excess smoothness can be resolved in other ways. As we shall see, precautionary behaviour (section 4) and liquidity constraints (section 5) can explain the phenomenon, as can habits (section 7) or (less appealingly) varying real rates of return.[29]

We end this subsection with a note of caution which applies with equal force to the rest of section 3. While much of the literature referred to here claims to rest on rigorous microfoundations, their assumption of linear rational expectations in aggregate income, consumption, or saving is unappealing. Linearity requires a quadratic utility function. Working with linear aggregates requires that age is irrelevant for individual behaviour, i.e. that behaviour is equivalent to that of infinitely lived agents or at least of agents whose survival probability is independent of age (see Blanchard, 1985). Usually, the simplifying assumption is added that the market discount rate is constant and equal to the subjective discount rate. It is one thing to derive some stylized parables about behaviour, but it is quite another to take such assumptions literally, for they have quite absurd implications. If individuals can expect income to grow and are interested only in the expectation of income, i.e. are risk neutral, then aggregate saving would have to be negative since, as Campbell noted, it forecasts future income *declines*. Apart from the fact that, around the world, aggregate household saving tends to be positive, how could systematically negative saving be financed?

If one stays within the linear life-cycle and permanent income rational expectations framework, the fact of positive aggregate savings demands the assumption of finite lives, as discussed in section 3. This raises issues of aggregation over households varying by age and by demographic composition. These will be discussed in section 10, where we will see that aggregation could explain, at least in part, both the excess sensitivity of consumption growth to anticipated income and the excess smoothness phenomenon.

There are two further problems stemming from implications of quadratic utility. The first is the bounded bliss point in (5.19): eventually satiation is reached. The problem can be postponed by making the bliss point a function of time, or of past consumption, but is not removed unless extreme assumptions are made. More subtly, the linear-in-variables framework implied by quadratic utility does not handle well exponentially growing data, which is likely to lead to problems of heteroskedasticity.[30] The second, even more serious drawback is that income uncertainty is irrelevant for behaviour under quadratic utility. Amending this implausible implication is the concern of the next section.

4 Uncertainty and Precautionary Saving

It seems hard to believe that income uncertainty is irrelevant for consumption decisions. Given that consumers spend a great deal on other types of insurance, it seems almost incontrovertible that there is a precautionary element in the savings decision. As noted in Blanchard and Fischer (1989, pp. 288–90), under constant absolute risk aversion and normally distributed income, the effect of income uncertainty on saving can be derived analytically. Exact analytical results are otherwise rare, though the implications of uncertainty about length of life are straightforward. This section considers both types of uncertainty and uses an approximation argument to analyse the implications of income uncertainty. Two applications of risk-averse behaviour to explaining part of the decline in the US savings rate are also discussed.

One can retain the attractive features of the CES utility function and constant relative risk aversion to obtain approximate analytical results of great intuitive appeal. We can show that the savings decision under income uncertainty is, to a near approximation, equivalent to a certainty equivalent problem, in which expected income is reduced by a discount factor reflecting uncertainty. This can be explained, in a two-period context, as follows.[31] Let the consumer's objective be to maximize

$$u^* = u(c_1) + \frac{1}{1 + \delta} Eu(c_2)$$

$$(5.43)$$

where $c_1 = A_0(1 + r_0) + y_1 - A_1$, $c_2 = A_1(1 + r_1) + y_2$,

and, as in section 2, c_i is consumption in period i, y_i is real non-property income, A_i is the real end of period asset level, r_i is the real interest rate linking periods i and $i+1$, which is known with certainty, and δ is a positive parameter reflecting subjective discounting. Substituting the period-to-period budget constraints into the utility function:

$$\max u^* = u(A_0(1 + r_0) + y_1 - A_1) + \frac{1}{1 + \delta} Eu(A_1(1 + r_1) + y_2). \qquad (5.44)$$

w.r.t. A_1

The marginal condition, analogous to (5.7) in the context of point expectations, is

$$u'(A_0(1 + r_0) + y_1 - A_1) = \frac{1}{1 + \delta} (1 + r_1) Eu'(A_1(1 + r_1) + y_2). \qquad (5.45)$$

Certainty equivalent income y_2^* is defined by[32]

$$u'(A_1(1 + r_1) + y_2^*) \equiv Eu'(A_1(1 + r_1) + y_2). \qquad (5.46)$$

In the context of the CES utility function, where $u'(c) = c^{-1/\sigma}$, we can define z so that

$$A_1(1 + r_1) + y_2^* \equiv \left(\frac{1}{1 + z}\right)^\sigma [A_1(1 + r_1) + Ey_2]$$

$$\approx \left(\frac{1}{1 + \sigma z}\right)[A_1(1 + r_1) + Ey_2], \qquad (5.47)$$

where σ is the elasticity of substitution. z will help us find the relationship between certainty equivalent income y_2^* and expected income Ey_2. Formally speaking, $1 + z$ is the ratio of marginal utilities evaluated respectively at y_2^* and at Ey_2. By means of a second order Taylor expansion one can show that

$$z \approx \frac{(1 + \rho)(2 + \rho)}{2} \frac{\text{var } y_2}{(A_1(1 + r_1) + Ey_2)^2} \qquad (5.48)$$

where $\sigma = 1/(1 + \rho)$. When $A_1 = 0$, y_2^* is easily found since

$$y_2^* \approx \left(\frac{1}{1 + \sigma z}\right) Ey_2.$$

Then, with the coefficient of variation of income at 10% and $\sigma = 1/2$, $z = 3$ implying a $1\frac{1}{2}\%$ discount. With $\sigma = 1/3$, z rises to 6%, implying a 2% discount. An increase in the coefficient of variation to 20% then raises the discount to 8%. In the general cases where A_1 is not zero, the derivation of y_2^* from (5.47) is a little harder. The analogous discount factor is lower for those with assets and higher for net debtors.[33] Note further that uncertainty about consumption needs, where c_2 is replaced by $c_2 - \eta$ with η a random variable with mean zero, is similar to income uncertainty and gives an additional reason for discounting future income.

Lattimore (1993) has extended this analysis using third and fourth order Taylor expansions to incorporate skewness and kurtosis of the probability distribution of future income. When there is a small probability of a large income drop, for example because of the risk of unemployment, the second order Taylor expansion understates the discount factor.

Carroll (1992) shows that such a probability distribution of future income, and the assumption that consumers cannot hold net debt when they die, implies a buffer-stock theory of saving: as he says, "consumers hold assets so that they can shield their consumption against unpredictable fluctuations in income." Assuming that consumers are impatient (have a high enough subjective discount rate), Carroll simulates the optimal consumption rule, computed by dynamic programming methods, under plausible assumptions and derives implications for the target ratio of the asset buffer stock to income ratio. This is a good example of the simulation alternative to the approximation technique.

Returning to the latter approach, in the context of the two- period consumption functions implied by CES utility, (5.6), κ_1 given by (5.10) is unchanged, but in life-cycle wealth W_1, $y_2^e/(1 + r_1^e)$ is replaced by

$$\frac{Ey_2}{(1 + \sigma z^*)(1 + r_1^e)} \approx \frac{Ey_2}{1 + r_1^e + \sigma z^*} \tag{5.49}$$

for small z^*, where point expectations apply to r_1. In the many-period extension (5.14), uncertainty about future income may not widen geometrically as the horizon extends. But as an empirical approximation, the geometric widening assumption may not be so bad, and implies that (future) human capital is measured by

$$\sum_0^T E(y_{1+s})/(1 + r_1^e + \sigma z^*)^{s-1}. \tag{5.50}$$

One important implication of these considerations is that if future income is more heavily discounted because of uncertainty, then current income must necessarily play a bigger role in determining current consumption. And this must be particularly so for the young without a cushion of assets. This helps to explain why consumption follows income more closely over the life-cycle than simple life-cycle theory would suggest.

Hayashi (1982) used the approximation (5.50) for two purposes. The first was to make the point that if consumers are risk averse, then the standard Euler equation (5.21), based on quadratic preferences and thus risk neutrality, no longer holds. The second was to suggest an estimation method, incorporating a quasi-difference transformation, which avoids generating explicit income forecasts for (5.50). This method can be explained as follows. Let $1 + r_1^e + \sigma z^* = 1 + \mu$ where we take μ as constant. Then human capital

$$H_t = y_t + \frac{1}{1 + \mu} E_t y_{t+1} + \ldots + \frac{1}{(1 + \mu)^T} E_t y_{t+T}.$$

Since

$$\frac{H_{t+1}}{1+\mu} = \frac{1}{1+\mu} E_{t+1} y_{t+1} + \ldots + \frac{1}{(1+\mu)^T} E_{t+1} y_{t+T},$$

$$H_t - y_t - \frac{H_{t+1}}{1+\mu} = \varepsilon_{t+1}^*, \tag{5.51}$$

where ε_{t+1}^* is the innovation in the present value of expected non-property incomes.[34] Equation (5.51) is the basis of the quasi-difference transformation used to eliminate human capital H_t.

Thus, with a consumption function of the form

$$c_t = \alpha A_{t-1} + \beta H_t + v_t, \tag{5.52}$$

we subtract

$$\frac{1}{1+\mu} c_{t+1} = \frac{1}{1+\mu} \alpha A_t + \frac{1}{1+\mu} \beta H_{t+1} + \frac{1}{1+\mu} v_{t+1}$$

to obtain

$$c_t - \frac{1}{1+\mu} c_{t+1} = \alpha \left(A_{t-1} - \frac{1}{1+\mu} A_t \right) + \beta(y_t + \varepsilon_{t+1}^*) + v_t - \frac{1}{1+\mu} v_{t+1}. \tag{5.53}$$

Note that (5.53) has eliminated income expectations and can be estimated using non-linear instrumental variables or generalized method of moments (GMM) techniques. Hayashi (1982), with annual US data, finds the real interest rate $r \approx 3.4\%$ and $\mu \approx 13.2\%$ so that $\sigma z^* \approx 9.8\%$. He can reject the hypothesis $\mu = r$. In other words, the data suggest that indeed US households discount future income at a much higher rate than would be implied by the real interest rate. Such a possibility was already raised by Friedman (1957; 1963) who suggested μ might be as high as one-third. Similar results to Hayashi's for UK data are reported by Weale (1990) and Darby and Ireland (1994).

Equation (5.53) leads back to a standard Euler equation when $\mu = r$ and $\alpha/(1+r) = \beta$: using $A_t = (1+r)A_{t-1} + y_t - c_t$ we can eliminate the terms A_{t-1}, A_t, and y_t and amalgamate terms in c_t (see the argument leading to (5.28)). Except in this special case, we should not think of (5.53) as a Euler equation because it is not the first order condition for an intertemporal optimization. It shares all the characteristics of a solved out consumption function, except that income expectations are eliminated.[35]

To examine more directly the effects of uncertainty in the Euler equation when consumers are risk averse, let us analyse the two-period case, and follow the approximate certainty equivalent approach used above for the solved out consumption function (5.43). With the CES utility function and a non-stochastic real interest rate, the Euler equation (5.18) takes the form

$$c_1^{-1/\sigma} = \left(\frac{1+r}{1+\delta} \right) E(c_2^{-1/\sigma})$$

$$\approx \frac{(1+r)(1+z)}{(1+\delta)} (E(c_2))^{-1/\sigma}.$$

Thus

$$E(c_2) \simeq \left(\frac{(1 + r)(1 + z)}{(1 + \delta)} \right)^{\sigma} c_1, \tag{5.54}$$

where z is given by (5.48).[36] Higher uncertainty operates like a higher real interest rate here too: it depresses consumption in the first period, raising $E(c_2)/c_1$, other things being equal.[37]

Let us now turn to some of the general implications of precautionary behaviour in the face of uncertainty, first concerning consumption dynamics and then the aggregate savings rate. Precautionary behaviour may enhance the stability of consumption, thus helping to account for "excess smoothness." A large positive income shock is likely to be taken as an indicator that there is more uncertainty about the new, higher level of income and so lead to a smaller rise in consumption than in the absence of the precautionary motive.[38] As well, it can explain the significance of lagged information in the Hall model and "excess sensitivity." The Hayashi (1982) model (5.53) clearly implies that lagged information matters. So, in its way, does the approximate Euler equation (5.54) since z will depend upon lagged information.

The classic life-cycle model without uncertainty implies a relationship between the aggregate savings rate and pension and social security systems. Other things being equal, a higher level of pension provision lowers savings out of after-tax income (see Feldstein, 1977; 1980). Precautionary behaviour under uncertainty suggests additional reasons for such a relationship. Unemployment benefits insure against income shortfalls as does an income support floor present in the welfare states of advanced industrial countries. Also, progressive taxation reduces the upper tails of agents' uncertain future incomes. By making income less risky, they reduce precautionary saving. One reason for secular declines in savings rates in industrial countries may lie in improved income and health safety nets which have reduced uncertainty.

Recently, Hubbard, Skinner, and Zeldes (1994) have suggested that features of the US income support system additionally discourage saving and may help to account for the decline in the US saving rate in the 1970s and 1980s. The US system makes payment of most welfare benefits conditional on the household owning very little assets. For households with some probability of income falling below the support level, this strongly discourages the accumulation of assets. The expansion of the support system with inbuilt asset tests could help account for the savings decline in the US. Feldstein (1995) argues that asset tests associated with college scholarships have had similar consequences.

Brenner, Dagenais, and Montemarquette (1992) have suggested another aspect of risk-averse behaviour to help account for the US saving decline. They argue that liberalization of the divorce laws in the US in the 1960s and 1970s raised the probability of divorce and, indeed, divorce rates rose very strongly. They note that, on average, women do not obtain generous terms of income maintenance and asset splits on divorce. Hence, they argue, there was an increased incentive for women to accumulate human capital and enhance their personal earnings prospects.[39] Consistent with this, there was a sharp rise in the proportion of women attaining a college education and well paid professional women now account for a much higher fraction of the US labour force than was the case 30 years ago.

Since a woman's human capital is specific to her, it is much more secure on divorce than a household's collective financial or housing assets. Thus, this provides an incentive away from conventional saving. Moreover, increased participation in college education raises the demand for loans and runs down assets, where available. This implies a decline in the aggregate savings rate. Although the details of their empirical estimates are not convincing and they exaggerate the magnitude of the overall effect, the explanation of Brenner et al. has some plausibility as part of the explanation of a falling savings rate.

Another kind of uncertainty concerns the date of death. Even in the absence of a bequest motive this implies that many individuals die leaving substantial levels of assets. Let us take a simple case in which there is no uncertainty about income given survival: only survival itself is uncertain. The expected utility function takes the form

$$E(u) = u(c_1) + \sum_2^T \phi_s \left(\frac{1}{1+\sigma}\right)^{s-1} u(c_s), \tag{5.55}$$

where ϕ_s is the probability of surviving to the sth period. The period-to-period budget constraints, conditional on survival, are like (5.2) as before. T is the maximum possible horizon for survival. Then the expected time of survival is $1 + \sum_2^T \phi_s$. It would be risky to run down assets to zero for the *expected* time of survival: if one survived longer, consumption could then be very low. A simple special case is considered by Blanchard (1985) where the probability of surviving one more year is independent of age. Then the probability of surviving to year s is $\phi_s = \phi^{s-1}$ and the horizon is infinite. The probability of dying each period effectively increases the subjective discount rate. In this case, κ_1 is given by (5.15), with δ increased appropriately, and with an infinite horizon. On the other hand, the κ_1 that corresponds to the *expected* survival date is obviously a truncated form, and so smaller, and would result in consumption being too high early on.

Thus, uncertainty about date of death, as with the bequest motive, modifies the conclusions of section 3: the MPC out of assets for the retired will be rather smaller than the theory predicts when there is no uncertainty. Both considerations help to explain why, according to survey evidence,[40] the retired do not dissave on anything like the scale predicted by simple life-cycle theory. The uncertainty about consumption needs, discussed above, is likely to be particularly acute as individuals age into their 70s and 80s, when health becomes frail, and the risk of large medical or other support expenses looms. These considerations imply that the MPCs out of assets vary much less over age than implied by simple life-cycle theory. This result has several important practical implications. One is to reduce the importance of aggregation in explaining variations in savings rates across economies that differ in rates of population growth, and hence demographic structure, and that differ in rates of per capita income growth. One incidental benefit is to reduce the aggregation biases in aggregate time-series consumption functions conditioned on average incomes and average assets. Kotlikoff and Summers (1981) have argued, as against Modigliani, that most of US wealth is the result of bequests rather than life-cycle accumulation for later expenditure. An important implication of uncertainty in old age is that *unintentional* bequests may also be an important component of wealth. Meanwhile, the controversy continues (Modigliani, 1988; Kotlikoff, 1988).

Uncertainty affects not only income, consumption needs, and date of death but the rate of return on saving which is, in general, uncertain. Much of the Euler equation literature and the consumption asset pricing model (Lucas, 1978; Grossman and Shiller, 1981; Brock, 1982; Hansen and Singleton, 1983) assumes that a safe asset exists. In the UK this may not be a bad approximation given the indexed gilt market. But in most countries, inflation-indexed securities do not exist. If the rate of return is uncertain, the analysis of certainty equivalence which was applied to income can also be applied to analyse the implications of an increase in rate of return uncertainty. Realistically, rate of return uncertainty and income uncertainty have often risen together with inflation. Empirically, the effects are likely to be hard to distinguish from each other, especially as we have seen that, for aggregate consumption, interest rate effects are likely to be small and time varying.

5 Credit Restrictions

In the US and the UK about three-quarters of household debt is backed with housing collateral. A substantial fraction of the remaining debt finances purchases of cars and other consumer durables, which serve as collateral for the loans. Unsecured borrowing is only available in relatively small amounts and to a restricted set of people. The young, with current low incomes but good future prospects, are those, *a priori*, who would like to borrow but are denied credit. Credit restrictions seem an obvious reason for the tendency, observed in household surveys, for consumption to follow the hump-shaped profile of life-cycle income more closely than is predicted by the life-cycle model.

In this section, we ask under what conditions households are most likely to want to borrow and hence be most likely to run into credit restrictions. We go on to discuss the effects of credit constraints on aggregate solved out consumption functions and on aggregate Euler equations. As we shall see, credit constraints offer an explanation for the "excess sensitivity" of consumption changes to predictable income changes. We suggest that credit constraints also offer a potential explanation of an "error correction" form of the consumption function.

Let us re-examine the problem of maximizing CES utility (5.6) subject to the life-cycle budget constraint (5.8), but now include a borrowing restriction as in Tobin (1972) and Flemming (1973). The borrowing limit may be a function of income or some other characteristics which a lender can observe. But for simplicity, let us assume that no borrowing without collateral is possible, i.e. $A_1 \geq 0$. Let A_1^* be the optimally chosen asset level which ignores this constraint. With homothetic preferences,

$$c_1 = \kappa^{-1}(A_0(1 + r_0) + y_1 + y_2^*/(1 + r_1^e)), \tag{5.56}$$

where y_2^* is certainty equivalent expected income as discussed in section 4. Thus, solving for A_1^* in terms of c_1 from the period-to-period budget constraint (5.2) and substituting (5.56) we find that

$$A_1^* = A_0(1 + r_0) + y_1 - c_1 = (1 - \kappa^{-1})(A_0(1 + r_0) + y_1) - \kappa^{-1}y_2^*/(1 + r_1^e). \tag{5.57}$$

The borrowing limit bites if $A_1^* < 0$, i.e. if

$$A_0(1 + r_0) + y_1 < \frac{\kappa^{-1}y_2^*}{(1 - \kappa^{-1})(1 + r_1^e)}. \tag{5.58}$$

The right hand side of (5.58) equals

$$\left(\frac{1 + \sigma\delta + (1 - \sigma)r_1^e}{1 + r_1^e}\right)y_2^*$$

using (5.11). Therefore, the consumer is more likely to run into the credit constraint if initial income and assets are low (or debts are high) relative to expected income and if the real interest rate is low, assuming some intertemporal substitutability. Note that increased uncertainty about future income makes it less likely that the consumer would want to borrow and so run into the credit constraint.

If $A_1^* < 0$ then A_1 must be zero and (5.2) implies that consumption equals currently cashable resources:

$$c_1 = A_0(1 + r_0) + y_1. \tag{5.59}$$

In practice, for the majority of such households, consumption equals income, though some credit constrained households will have small levels of initial assets, and some may have debts. In the Euler equation literature, where credit constraints are considered, it is usually assumed that consumption is just equal to income for the credit constrained (see Hall and Mishkin, 1982; Campbell and Mankiw, 1989; 1991).

If the fraction of credit constrained households is π, then in per capita terms, aggregate consumption is given by

$$c = (1 - \pi)c^u + \pi c^c, \tag{5.60}$$

which, with c^u given by (5.56) and $c^c = y^c$, implies that

$$c = (1 - \pi)\kappa^{-1}[A_0(1 + r_0) + y_1^u + y_2^{u*}/(1 + r_1^c)] + \pi y_1^c, \qquad (5.61)$$

where superscripts "u" and "c" denote credit unconstrained and credit constrained households. To make this expression empirically tractable, one would typically assume that y_1^u and y_1^c move in parallel with observed aggregate non-property income, and that π is constant, as in the comparable Euler equation literature, which we discuss below. The implications of credit constraints for the solved out consumption function are, in aggregate, to reduce the MPC out of assets and to increase the MPC out of current income.

In the context of a three-period model, it is possible to examine the interaction of income uncertainty with the possibility of future credit constraints. The inequality (5.58) then applies to incomes y_2 and y_3^* and defines the probability of being credit rationed in period 2. For a household in period 1, this affects the expected utility in periods 2 and 3 and so enters the trade-off between consumption and saving in period 1. The consequence is to increase precautionary savings compared with the situation where no future possibility of credit rationing arises, and is roughly similar to extra discounting of future incomes. Deaton's (1992a, section 6.2) simulation results confirm the general tenor of these conclusions.

Let us return to the Euler equation literature. Much of the debate since Hall's famous 1978 paper has been about why the simple model (5.21) fails. Given the nine assumptions listed in section 3.1 for (5.21) to hold, there are nine reasons why the error term in (5.21) may not be an innovation but instead may be correlated with earlier information.[41] Papers have been written about all of them, but credit restrictions, suggested by Hall himself in Hall and Mishkin (1982), have proved the most popular.

The basic idea is very simple. The martingale condition (5.21) holds for the credit unconstrained, $c_t^u = c_{t-1}^u + \varepsilon_t$; while it is assumed that the credit constrained just consume income, $c_t^c = y_t^c$. If the latter holds without error, first differencing of (5.60) gives

$$\Delta c_t = (1 - \pi)\Delta c_t^u + \pi \Delta c_t^c = (1 - \pi)\varepsilon_t + \pi \Delta y_t^c. \qquad (5.62)$$

Generally speaking, the change in income for the credit constrained is proxied by the change in average non-property income, which is partly predictable – as we saw in section 3.4. Thus, taking expectations of (5.62) yields

$$E_{t-1}\Delta c_t = \pi E_{t-1}\Delta y_t, \qquad (5.63)$$

which is not zero and so provides an explanation of the excess sensitivity of consumption changes to anticipated income changes.

Deaton (1992a) suggests a direct link between excess sensitivity and excess smoothness, the latter being a direct result of the fact that changes in consumption are not unpredictable. Subtracting (5.63) from (5.62), assuming $\Delta y^c = \Delta y$,

$$\Delta c_t - E_{t-1}\Delta c_t = (1 - \pi)\varepsilon_t + \pi\varepsilon_t^y, \qquad (5.64)$$

where the income innovation is $\varepsilon_t^y = \Delta y_t - E_{t-1}\Delta y_t$ and ε_t is the innovation in permanent income for those whose consumption follows permanent income. Generally speaking, if ε_t and ε_t^y are not very highly correlated, and if the variance of ε_t is no bigger than the variance of ε_t^y, the variance of the weighted average, i.e. the consumption innovation in (5.64), is likely to be less than the variance of the income innovation ε_t^y (see Campbell and Mankiw, 1991, p. 729). This is by no means inevitable, particularly if income had a unit root, when the current income innovation and the permanent income innovation ε_t would be very highly correlated. However, Deaton's case would be enhanced if some other lagged information entered (5.62).

One such possibility can arise with the existence of transitory consumption, η_t^u for the unconstrained and η_t^c for the credit constrained:

$$\Delta c_t = (1 - \pi)(\varepsilon_t + \Delta\eta_t^u) + \pi(\Delta y_t^c + \Delta\eta_t^c). \qquad (5.65)$$

Taking expectations of (5.65) then, since $E_{t-1}\eta_t = 0$ for both household types (assuming no serial correlation of transitory consumption),

$$E_{t-1}\Delta c_t = \pi E_{t-1}\Delta y_t^c - (1 - \pi)\eta_{t-1}^u - \pi\eta_{t-1}^c. \qquad (5.66)$$

The transitory consumption shocks η_{t-1}^u and η_{t-1}^c are not directly observable but we can proxy them indirectly. Note that if y^P is permanent income including income from assets, then

$$c_{t-1}^u = E_{t-1}y_{t-1}^P + \eta_{t-1}^u \quad \text{and} \quad c_{t-1}^c = y_{t-1}^c + \eta_{t-1}^c.$$

Rearranging and substituting these two expressions into (5.66) yields

$$E_{t-1}\Delta c_t = \pi E_{t-1}\Delta y_t^c + [(1 - \pi)E_{t-1}y_{t-1}^P + \pi y_{t-1}^c - c_{t-1}]. \qquad (5.67)$$

We cannot observe y_{t-1}^P directly but the square bracketed term in (5.67) should at least be positively correlated with $(y_{t-1} - c_{t-1})$ and with A_{t-2}. This suggests an error correction form close to that of DHSY (1978) (see (5.29)) but in an expectational formulation. Given the negative correlation between real assets and inflation over the past 40 years, this helps to account for the negative inflation effect in DHSY.

An alternative way of expressing the link between DHSY and credit constraints was suggested in Muellbauer (1983) and Muellbauer and Bover (1986). They set up the intertemporal optimization problem subject to the credit constraint in Lagrangian form. The shadow price of the credit constraint then enters the Euler equation. But we know from (5.58) that the intensity of the credit constraint depends on the gap between initial assets and income and future income. Indeed, combining (5.58) and (5.59), we can see it depends on the gap between the consumption of the credit constrained and future income. Thus, the shadow price of the credit constraint at time $t-1$ depends on $E_{t-1}y_t - c_{t-1}$.

Since $E_{t-1}y_t - c_{t-1} = E_{t-1}\Delta y_t + y_{t-1} - c_{t-1}$, this gives an alternative rationalization of the DHSY form (5.29). Equation (5.67) is also consistent with another feature of the full version of DHSY: a negative inflation effect. We know that life-cycle wealth depends on assets as well as on current and expected non-property income. Empirically, inflation over the last 40 years has been associated with falling real asset values and thus declines in life-cycle wealth. Muellbauer and Bover (1986) found evidence for an expectational form of DHSY for the US:

$$E_{t-1}\Delta \ln c_t = -\underset{(2.2)}{0.017} + \underset{(1.9)}{0.18} E_{t-1}\Delta \ln yd_t + \underset{(2.7)}{0.11} (E_{t-1}\ln yd_t - \ln c_{t-1})$$

$$-\underset{(2.8)}{0.43} E_{t-1}\Delta \ln p_t,$$

where yd is per capita real personal disposable income as defined in the national accounts.[42] Estimation is on quarterly data for 1954/1 to 1981/4 and uses instruments dated $t-2$ or older: t-ratios are given in parentheses. For the UK, the parameters of such an equation fitted to data from 1957 to 1981 are even more significant.

Campbell and Mankiw (1989; 1991) deal with transitory errors by taking expectations at $t-2$: $E_{t-2}\eta_{t-1}^u = 0$ and $E_{t-2}\eta_{t-1}^c = 0$ assuming the ηs are not serially correlated. In their 1991 paper they forecast $\Delta \ln y_t$ using data on income and consumption and, in some specifications, interest rates, lagged two quarters or more. In a logarithmic formulation, they estimate

$$E_{t-2}\Delta \ln c_t = \pi E_{t-2}\Delta \ln yd_t,$$

where π is now the consumption share of credit constrained households. Implicitly it is assumed that observable per capital real disposable income growth is a good proxy for the income growth of households who are credit constrained, or who simply spend current income because of myopia. Estimates of π for six countries lie in a 0.2 to 0.6 range, except in Japan where the income forecasts are too poor. They suggest that the cross- country differences may be related to the depth and sophistication of credit markets: France has a relatively high value of π while Sweden, Canada, and the US have lower values.

They also examine whether there are trends in π which might be associated with financial liberalizations. Unfortunately, for the UK they find that π has a significant *upward* trend, implying, apparently, that credit rationing has tightened over the period 1957–88, a result also obtained by Jappelli and Pagano (1989). For the UK in much of the 1980s consumption growth exceeded income growth. If consumption growth is conditioned only on expected income growth, a rising value of π is the only way the Euler equation framework can cope. Explicitly incorporating uncertainty works in the wrong direction, since income uncertainty almost certainly fell in the 1980s and, by (5.54), lagged uncertainty has a *positive* effect on consumption growth. Introducing a variable real rate of return may partly explain the anomaly. However, the timing is not entirely plausible, since the consumption boom was at its strongest several years after the biggest rises in the real interest rate.[43] Apart from problems in measuring the real interest rate, the UK evidence raises doubts about the rational expectations assumptions in the Euler equation (see section 8).

Here we have focused on the macroeconometric literature on Euler equation with credit constraints. Many of the applications, following Hall and Mishkin (1982), have used micro panel data, raising additional problems such as income measurement errors. Hayashi (1987) and Deaton (1992a, chapter 5) survey this literature.

6   Saving and Leisure

So far, we have conditioned consumption decisions on non-property income. This is valid if consumption decisions are separable from leisure choices. If this is not so, consumption decisions depend also on leisure and leisure expectations. As we shall see, this gives yet another reason for the failure of the random walk consumption model.

For some households at least, income is a choice variable to the extent that their members can make unconstrained decisions on hours, labour participation, and human capital accumulation. For many others, hours of work, or even having a job, are constrained. If intertemporal consumption decisions are separable from leisure decisions, conditioning on labour income incurs only a potential endogeneity bias. If separability does not hold, and consumption and leisure are specific substitutes, one might expect high-earnings phases of the life-cycle to be associated with long hours of work and compensated by high consumption. On the other hand, if they were complements because leisure is needed for consumption of goods, consumption would tend to be lower in high-earnings phases of the life-cycle.[44] Browning, Deaton, and Irish (1985) argue that neither assumption can explain the way hours, wages, and consumption move together in the UK in terms of voluntary choice by households. Ando and Kennickell (1987) report similar negative results for the US.

This suggests that restrictions on hours and on whether employment is available or not affect significant proportions of households. With separability of intertemporal trade-offs in consumption from leisure in different periods, the standard approach as exploited in previous sections is valid. This implies a utility function of the following form, where ℓ_s is leisure in period s:

$$u(f(c_1, c_2, \ldots, c_T), \ell_1, \ell_2, \ldots, \ell_T). \tag{5.68}$$

Note that the marginal rate of substitution between consumption in any two periods, $(\partial u/\partial c_i)/(\partial u/\partial c_j)$, is independent of the ℓ's. With additivity in consumption, the life-cycle utility function is then

$$U\left(u(c_1) + \frac{1}{1+\delta}u(c_2) + \ldots + \frac{1}{(1+\delta)^{T-1}}u(c_T), \ell_1, \ell_2, \ldots, \ell_T\right).$$

If instead separability is violated, we would have, in the additive context,

$$u(c_1, \ell_1) + \frac{1}{1+\delta}u(c_2, \ell_2) + \ldots + \frac{1}{(1+\delta)^{T-1}}u(c_T, \ell_T). \tag{5.69}$$

With ℓ_s constrained to $\bar{\ell}_s$, this is like introducing a variable taste parameter into each of the period utility functions. If these remain homothetic in c_s, the generic form of the consumption function is as before, but with additional conditioning variables $\bar{\ell}_1$ and expectations of $\bar{\ell}_2, \ldots, \bar{\ell}_T$. In the aggregate, the unemployment rate, and changes in it, are likely to be reasonable proxies for the labour market opportunities and expectations of opportunities reflected in $\bar{\ell}_1, \bar{\ell}_2$, etc. Unfortunately the change in the unemployment rate is also likely to be a good proxy for uncertainty about labour income; while, among other things, the unemployment rate will be correlated with early retirement, and thus with shifts in the distribution of consumption between the retired and the pre-retirement population of households. This is bound to make unique interpretations difficult.

In the Euler equation context, the marginal utilities in (5.18) depend upon $\bar{\ell}_1$ and $\bar{\ell}_2$ respectively. Take a simple quadratic example, where

$$u(c, \bar{\ell}) = -\tfrac{1}{2}(\beta - c - \alpha\bar{\ell})^2 \tag{5.70}$$

and $\alpha > 0$. Then the relationships between the marginal utilities, in contrast to (5.19), become

$$\frac{\partial u}{\partial c_1} = (\beta - c_1 - \alpha\bar{\ell}_1) = \left(\frac{1+r}{1+\delta}\right)E\frac{\partial u}{\partial c_2} = \left(\frac{1+r}{1+\delta}\right)E(\beta - c_2 - \alpha\bar{\ell}_2).$$

In the case where $r = \delta$, in contrast to (5.20),

$$c_1 = E(c_2) - \alpha(\bar{\ell}_1 - E\bar{\ell}_2).$$

In the aggregate, in contrast to (5.21),

$$E_t(c_{t+1}) = c_t - \alpha^*(E_t un_{t+1} - un_t), \tag{5.71}$$

where $\alpha^* > 0$ since leisure $\bar{\ell}_t$ and the unemployment rate un_t are positively correlated.

Here we have a negative correlation between the expected consumption change and the expected change in the unemployment rate. Since the latter is forecastable to some degree, and also negatively correlated with the expected income change, we have an alternative interpretation of "excess sensitivity" of consumption. Note that credit constraints play no role in this story. Bean (1986) and Attanasio and Weber (1991; 1992) push an interpretation on these lines. It is not trivial to distinguish the two interpretations on empirical evidence. However, Bean's empirical results for the US are not robust to a slight alteration of his sample period, as Muellbauer and Bover (1986) showed.

As far as the solved out consumption function corresponding to (5.70) is concerned, consumption is a linear function of life- cycle wealth, as before, but can be shown to be *positively* related to the expected change in the unemployment rate. On the face of it, this appears to contradict empirical evidence. But given that the expected change in the unemployment rate is correlated with expected income, and given a role for the current change in the unemployment rate as a proxy for uncertainty, one cannot give a unique interpretation of unemployment effects in consumption functions.

7   The Role of Lagged Consumption and Durability

A classic conundrum in applied econometrics is whether lagged dependent variables represent agents' expectations or adjustment costs, habits, or the durability of goods. In the Hall (1978) type of Euler equation, lagged consumption has a pure expectational interpretation: it reflects the consumer's best prediction last period of future circumstances, particularly permanent income.

In this section we show that habits, like convex adjustment costs, imply partial adjustment of consumption to life-cycle wealth. This offers a partial explanation for "excess smoothness" and also gives an alternative link between aggregate savings rates and aggregate growth rates. In the Euler equation context, habits can explain why changes in consumption are not innovations.

Habits or convex costs of adjustment also imply partial adjustment in stocks of durables. If adjustment costs are non-convex, i.e. lumpy, there are discrete jumps in individual behaviour as economic conditions vary. Then the history of recent shocks to the economic environment matters in a way not allowed for by the usual partial adjustment story. Indeed, as we will see, there is empirical evidence against the latter.

The simplest treatment of habits, which have similar implications to convex adjustment costs, is to replace the c_{t+s} argument in the intertemporal utility function by $(c_{t+s} - ac_{t+s-1})/(1-a) = c_{t+s}^*$ say, where $0 < a < 1$. Note that if consumption was high last period, with diminishing marginal utility, the marginal utility of consumption will be high this period. The consumer is therefore more sensitive to variations in this period's consumption than she or he would be without habits. In the context of preferences that reflect the desire to stabilize the utility of consumption in each period, habits imply additional smoothing of consumption over time.

In the context of point expectations, one can reformulate the intertemporal budget constraint in terms of the c_{t+s}^* and c_{t-1}. It is then possible to show that the solved out consumption function has a simple partial adjustment form (see Muellbauer, 1988):

$$c_t = \beta \frac{W_t}{\kappa_t} + (1 - \beta)c_{t-1}. \tag{5.72}$$

This has several interesting implications. One is that it could be part of the explanation why aggregate consumption is smoother than aggregate income since only part of the adjustment to any shock in W_t occurs in any period. Thus it helps to account for "excess smoothness."

It also offers a potential alternative explanation to the Modigliani and Brumberg (1954) aggregation story for the connection between the aggregate savings rate and income growth. Equation (5.72) implies that consumption lags behind life-cycle wealth. At any one time, in a growing economy, consumption will be lower than in the zero-habits case (where $\beta = 1$). Thus the aggregate saving rate will be higher when habits are important. The argument can also be formalized in a logarithmic version of (5.72).

Over individual life-cycles, the presence of habits would give a reason for why the old, used to a certain level of consumption, would dissave. This adds force to the explanations offered earlier for the lower rates of dissaving observed in practice: uncertainty about time of death, uncertainty about health-related consumption needs, and the bequest motive.

Habits have been widely regarded as a possible explanation of the empirical failure of the random walk consumption model based on the Euler equation. With an additive intertemporal utility function defined on $(c_{t+s} - ac_{t-s-1})/(1 - a)$, the generalization of the Euler condition (5.18) (see Muellbauer, 1988, p. 57) is

$$u_t' - E_t \left\{ (1 + r + a) \frac{1}{1 + \delta} u_{t+1}' - \frac{a(1 + r)}{(1 + \delta)^2} u_{t+2}' \right\} = 0. \tag{5.73}$$

Since u_{t+s}' is a function of c_{t+s} and c_{t+s-1}, this looks like a non-linear fourth order difference equation in consumption. However, when r is constant, (5.73) factorizes into

$$E_t \left[\frac{1 + r}{1 + \delta} - L \right] \left[1 - \frac{a}{1 + \delta} L^{-1} \right] u_{t+1}' = 0, \tag{5.74}$$

where L is the lag operator so that L^{-1} is the lead operator. Provided the second term is non-zero (see also Hayashi, 1985, appendix A), then

$$E_t \left[\frac{1 + r}{1 + \delta} - L \right] u_{t+1}' = 0.$$

Since $Lu_{t+1}' = u_t'$, (5.18) remains valid:

$$u_t' = E_t \left(\frac{1 + r}{1 + \delta} u_{t+1}' \right).$$

In the context of quadratic preferences, where

$$u_t = -\frac{1}{2}\left[\beta - \frac{(c_t - ac_{t-1})}{1-a}\right]^2,$$

then, if $r = \delta$,

$$c_t - ac_{t-1} = E_t(c_{t+1} - ac_t). \tag{5.75}$$

Thus

$$\Delta c_{t+1} = a\Delta c_t + \varepsilon_{t+1} \tag{5.76}$$

is the generalization of the random walk Euler equation. The lagged term in the change of consumption clearly implies that $\Delta c_t + 1$ is not an innovation.

But the balance of empirical evidence does not favour (5.76) as the complete explanation for the failure of the random walk model. The empirical issues are not trivial. In high-frequency data, e.g. monthly, measurement errors are likely to be important, while in low-frequency data, time aggregation problems arise.[45] Also relative to a span of a month, many consumption items, e.g. a can of baked beans, appear as effectively durable when they would be classified as non-durable over the span of a year. For durable goods not subject to habits or adjustment costs, $a < 0$, in the absence of some other treatment of their durability since a purchase last period adds to current utility.

The conventional treatment of durable goods is to assume that consumption services are proportional to the stock S (see Deaton and Muellbauer, 1980, chapter 13):

$$S_t = (1 - d)S_{t-1} + cd_t,$$

where d is the rate at which the stock wears out or depreciates in real terms and cd is the flow of purchases. In the Euler equation framework, if there are no habits or adjustment costs, then, with a quadratic utility function, and given the market and subjective discount rates are equal, $S_{t+1} = S_t + \varepsilon_{t+1}$ (see for example Mankiw, 1982). In terms of purchases, since $\Delta cd_t = \Delta S_t - (1-d)\Delta S_{t-1}$, $\Delta cd_t = \varepsilon_t - (1-\delta)\varepsilon_{t-1}$. However, on quarterly data Mankiw finds no such first order correlation. This could be explained by habits or adjustment costs. If (5.76) held for stocks of durables, i.e. $\Delta S_{t+1} = a\Delta S_t + \varepsilon_{t+1}$, then $\Delta cd_t = \Delta S_t - (1-d)S_{t-1} = \varepsilon_t - (1-d-a)\Delta S_{t-1}$. If $1 - d > a$, as seems plausible, this would be consistent with negative autocorrelation in the residuals over longer periods as found by Caballero (1990), but only weak autocorrelation over one quarter.

Returning to the framework of the solved out consumption functions, the intertemporal budget constraint can be rewritten, substituting out for durable purchases in terms of stock. One can then derive the "user cost" price of durables (see Deaton and Muellbauer, 1980, p. 343):

$$pd_t^* \approx pd_t[r + d - \Delta \ln pd_{t+1}^e],$$

where pd is the relative price of durables, when r, d, and the expected appreciation in the real prices of durables are all small. This is the traditional user cost form as developed, for example, by Jorgenson (1963) for capital goods.

Abstracting from adjustment lags, the demand for the stock of durables as well as for purchases of non-durables is given as some function of life-cycle wealth, current and expected relative prices, and the interest rate:

$$S_t = f(W_t, r, pd_t^*, pd_{t+1}^*).$$

With habits or convex adjustment costs, this becomes

$$S_t = \beta f(W_t, \text{etc.}) + (1 - \beta) S_{t-1}. \tag{5.77}$$

In terms of purchases,

$$cd_t = S_t - (1 - d) S_{t-1}$$

$$= \beta f(W_t, \text{etc.}) - (\beta - d) S_{t-1}. \tag{5.78}$$

In practice, non-convex transactions costs are likely to be involved in the purchase of durables. The effective resale value of a new durable is likely to fall significantly upon acquisition. A potential buyer would be concerned because the seller has more information: a "lemon" might be on offer (see Akerlof, 1970). Also there are conventional search, advertising, and transport costs. Further, because durables are typically lumpy, these costs are liable to be lumpy.

Bertola and Caballero (1990) and Grossman and Laroque (1990) have considered such issues. One implication of fixed or more general non-convex adjustment costs is that, at the individual level, there are threshold effects: small shocks in the environment do not alter individual purchases of a durable good, but larger changes may do so. With heterogeneous agents, one observes smooth adjustment in the aggregate even if adjustment is discrete at the individual level. The history of shocks since the last purchase also matters in a way it does not with the habits or convex costs of adjustments model (5.78). For empirical work, this suggests that to (5.78) we need to add a richer lag structure – at the very least a role for lagged purchases – so that

$$cd_t = \beta_1 f(W_t, \text{etc.}) - \beta_2 S_{t-1} + \beta_3 cd_{t-1} \tag{5.79}$$

and $\beta_i > 0$, for all i. In recent unpublished empirical work, we find evidence that β_3 is significantly different from zero in the US, the UK, and Japan, thus rejecting the simple cost of adjustment model (5.78).

8 Alternatives to Rational Expectations

It is interesting to note that tests of the rational expectations permanent income hypothesis (REPIH) on aggregate consumption data were never quite such a lucid example of sharp scientific testing as sometimes perceived: see for example Summers' (1991) critique of Hansen and Singleton's (1982; 1983) path-breaking analysis of consumption and asset returns. After all, a rejection of the hypothesis leaves enormous scope for finding reasons for its failure other than any failing in the theory it was intended to appraise. On the other hand if it was not rejected, opponents of the theory could point either to statistical power problems or to violations in the auxiliary assumptions as potential explanations.

The principal focus of the last 15 years of US consumption research has been in finding out why the REPIH is typically rejected at the aggregate level. In all cases, rejections have been of the *joint hypotheses* of rational expectations and of the assumptions underlying the formulation of the intertemporal optimization problem. This has led to a reinterpretation of the basic Euler approach, relaxing its restrictive assumptions to examine the effects of variable interest rates and prices, finite life-times and retirement, temporal and cross-sectional aggregation bias, abandonment of certainty equivalence (i.e. relinquishing quadratic utility functions), credit constraints, relaxing intertemporal separability of preferences (i.e. habits allowed), and relaxing separability between consumption and leisure or other determinants of utility.

Remarkably, the strong prior that all consumers at all times form rational expectations has not been widely challenged (a notable exception being Cochrane, 1989). There are numerous alternatives to RE, of which two distinct subclasses can be distinguished. First, alternative myopic rules of thumb for forecasting can be asserted without providing any well defined theoretical basis for why agents might behave this way. Thus, in Friedman's original formulation of the PIH, income expectations were modelled as a distributed lag of past income. Alternatively, different micro theories about consumer behaviour can be used to infer expectations processes. For example, at its most prosaic, the optimizing problem for consumers can be reformulated to take account of the costs of information acquisition relative to the benefits of forecasting accuracy. One instance of this is Pischke's (1991) model in which consumers do not have the macro information to distinguish micro and macro elements in the shocks they observe. As Deaton (1992a, p. 174) observes, this has predictable consequences for aggregate behaviour quite similar to those of habits. Or, if more radical changes to the economic framework are visualized, some of the basic axioms of consumer behaviour may be discarded (see for example Simon, 1978; Tversky and Kahneman, 1974; Thaler and Shefrin, 1981; Shefrin and Thaler, 1988; Thaler, 1990; Kreps, 1988). Arguably, it would be preferable to call RE "Muthian expectations" (Pesaran, 1987), thus eliminating the value-based judgment that they are indeed in any sense especially rational.

If alternative behaviours have low utility costs relative to fully RE intertemporal optimizing behaviour, then completely different aggregate consumption patterns may be observed if agents make small, practically costless, systematic mistakes or if there are costs (hidden to the econometricians) to finding and processing relevant economic information. Simon (1978) argues that agents use heuristic decision rules, which may deviate from pure maximization strategies that economists ascribe to them. A relatively small literature has exploited the notion that deviations from pure maximization have small utility costs.[46] Using a model calibrated to the average US consumer, Cochrane (1989) found very small wealth costs from near-rational alternatives to full information intertemporal maximization. Cochrane demonstrates that if representative consumers simply consume in fixed proportion to current income, and if consumption growth is predictable with an R^2 of 0.25, then the utility costs are likely to be trivial. For example, with a coefficient of relative risk aversion set as high as 10, the costs of consuming income when $R^2 = 0.25$ (considerable excess sensitivity) is still only about 14 cents per quarter. Once information acquisition and processing costs are introduced, the benefits of full information intertemporal optimization may be too small to warrant the costs: simple rules of thumb are likely be optimal. In particular, the idea of optimizing agents using an error correction mechanism (ECM), such as (5.29), interpreted as a servomechanism, seems reasonable. A consumer following (5.29), with the βs between 0 and 1, would partially adjust consumption to current income changes but always, in the long run, aim to keep consumption approximately in line with income. If last period's consumption was higher than income, this year's would tend to be lower, other things being equal. A possible analogy to the (short-horizon) problem of a consumer might run as follows. Imagine a car travelling on the left hand side of a road with a line clearly marked in the centre. Heavy trucks are travelling in the opposite direction on the right hand side at high speed, so that a cautious driver might wish to avoid them. The verge on the left hand side is muddy and rocky: a car can only travel here very slowly without ruination. The windscreen has been smeared with dirt so that it is almost impossible to look forwards: the future direction of the road is therefore perilously uncertain. One thing is clear for the driver: the rear view. What should a driver wishing to get to her destination as quickly as possible do? The answer is to look backwards at the road, keeping the centre line well to the right, and correcting the steering as the car deviates from the line. In this metaphor for the consumer's dilemma, the heavy lorries are bad income states to be avoided because of convex marginal utility, the muddy verge is the cost of excess saving, while the dirt encrusted windscreen represents the difficulty of forecasting future states.

There is increasing evidence that consumers (1) do not optimize in the manner described by economists (e.g. Thaler and Shefrin, 1981; Jones and Stock, 1987; Kotlikoff, Samuelson, and Johnson, 1988) (2) do not have the information to form optimal plans (for example, Ricardian equivalence presumes that consumers know the value of outstanding government bonds, information which they do not appear to have: Gruen, 1988b). For consumers, the supposition of rationality is nowhere near so appealing as it is for firms. There is no obvious mechanism by which Darwinian survival of the fittest would eliminate suboptimizing consumers. Even in developing countries where starvation is possible if under-accumulation occurs, there is no such penalty for over-accumulation.

While near-rationality and non-rational expectations can generate results which explain failures of orthogonality, it would be useful if there were a test which could more clearly indicate whether consumers formed expectations in primarily a forward or a backward looking fashion. Lucas's (1976) criticism of traditional macroeconomic models indicated that when the marginal process for a forcing variable (say income) altered, then under RE the conditional expectation of the impact multiplier should also change. This provides a vehicle for testing whether expectations are primarily backward or forward looking:[47] see Hendry (1988) and Ericsson, Campos, and Tran (1990) for further exposition and empirical applications, including to consumption.

An alternative approach is to make use of consumer survey information on consumer sentiment, in particular responses to questions concerning future economic conditions. In the US such data are available back to the 1950s from the Michigan Survey Research Center. Evans (1969) reports somewhat negatively on the usefulness of such data in explaining consumption. More recently, Garner (1992) reports limited usefulness of consumer sentiment in forecasting durable expenditure in the US but only during war episodes, such as the Persian Gulf crisis of 1991, which were not quickly reflected in other macro data. Acemoglu and Scott (1994) suggest a link via uncertainty. Fuhrer (1993) and Carroll, Fuhrer, and Wilcox (1993) have found evidence of some usefulness of consumer sentiment for forecasting future US income or employment and hence consumption. Our own unpublished work with US annual data supports such findings. However, US evidence appears to suggest that one can forecast income about as well using only published macro data. Nevertheless, this is a promising line of inquiry where more research is needed.

9　The Role of Assets and Asset Prices

As we have seen, assets are accumulated to provide for retirement and bequests, and for rainy days that can arise earlier because of income falls resulting, for example, from unemployment, ill health, or consumption needs (e.g. paying for a child's education or medical bills). Assets are also accumulated to purchase "big ticket" durables such as a car or furniture.

In this section, we suggest that marginal propensities to spend are less for illiquid assets than for liquid ones. We also discuss the special role of house prices for expenditure decisions where a positive wealth effect is offset, in part, by a negative price effect.

Households typically hold a balance of liquid assets, which can easily be converted into expenditure when needed, and illiquid assets, which typically yield a higher rate of return. Illiquidity has the following dimensions:

1 Capital uncertainty: for example, equity or property prices might be low just as cash is needed for spending.
2 Transactions costs: stockbrokers charge commission; in some countries, transactions costs, including taxes, of selling a house can be over 10%.
3 Transactions restrictions: pensions are usually only accessible at retirement; tax benefits from many savings schemes are lost if they are cashed in early.
4 Indivisibilities: houses, yachts, or paintings can only be sold as units.

Different assets have different liquidity characteristics. Housing, pension funds, and life insurance funds are at the illiquid end of the spectrum. However, note that a general easing of credit relaxes these constraints to a degree: if housing or a painting can be used as collateral for a loan, the market value can, to a degree, be accessed. On the other hand, lenders, bearing in mind default risk and the volatility of asset prices, are unlikely to offer 100% collateral-backed loans – though the UK and Scandinavian housing markets seem to have been a temporary exception in this respect after financial deregulation in the 1980s.

As far as spending decisions are concerned, differences in liquidity suggest associating different spendability weights with different types of assets and debt. The characteristics of illiquidity are complex and multi-dimensional and it is no easy matter to formulate the budget constraint to reflect points 1 to 4 above. If one were to do so one could associate shadow prices or Lagrange multipliers with each of the constraints. One could then measure the marginal utility of increasing each asset by £1 relative to the marginal utility of increasing current income by £1. Cash then has a relative shadow price or spendability weight of 1 and less liquid assets would have lower spendability weights.[48] One would expect the assets with the highest long-term after-tax returns to have the lowest spendability weights. This is analogous to the index number approach to measuring monetary aggregates (see Barnett, 1981) where liquidity is indirectly measured by potential return for gone. However, one would expect spendability weights on illiquid assets to increase with financial deregulation – even though, in the short term, returns on such assets increased after deregulation. Potentially, as we shall see, the increased spendability of illiquid assets could be the most important consequence of financial liberalization.

It is important to note that owner-occupied housing wealth, which is the most important single asset for the majority of households, has spending consequences which differ from those of illiquid financial assets in one significant respect. This is because housing services also appear in the utility function. Housing is the consumer durable *par excellence*. It is distinguished by the low rate of physical depreciation and also by its different treatment in national accounts statistics compared with other durables. Purchases of houses are not regarded as spending to be included in total consumer expenditure. Instead, the imputed value of owner-occupied housing services is included both in consumption and in income in the national accounts. This recognizes the asset acquisition aspect of house purchase.

As we saw in section 7, the relative price of durables enters the consumption function for non-durables, as well as its own expenditure equation. Similarly, the demand for non-housing consumption will be affected by the price of housing. To see how, let us consider a permanent change in the price of housing after which the relative prices of non-housing consumption and housing are expected to remain fixed.[49] Let H be housing stock and p^* its relative price; h is the flow of services from housing and c is non-housing consumption. With a fixed real interest rate, relative prices through time of each good are fixed, so we can treat the vectors of housing and non-housing consumptions like single units of permanent consumption. Effectively, using the Hicks aggregation theorem (see Deaton and Muellbauer, 1980, pp. 120–2), we have reduced a $2T$ (two goods over T periods) dimensional optimization problem to a two-good problem with a budget constraint of the form

$$c + p^*h = \frac{r}{1+r}\,W \tag{5.80}$$

in the case of an infinitely lived household. We are interested in the effect of non-housing consumption of a permanent increase in the relative price of houses. Total differentiation gives

$$\mathrm{d}c + \mathrm{d}p^*h + p^*\mathrm{d}h = \frac{r}{1+r}\,\mathrm{d}W,$$

where $\mathrm{d}W = \mathrm{d}p^*H$. Thus

$$\frac{\partial c}{\partial p^*} = \frac{r}{1+r}\,H - h - \frac{p^*\partial h}{\partial p^*}, \tag{5.81}$$

$$= \frac{r}{1+r}\,H - h(1 + e_{hp}),$$

where e_{hp} is the own price elasticity of demand for housing services. On UK data, estimates suggest $e_{hp} \approx -0.6$ or -0.7.

The implication is that for those with housing wealth, the wealth effect $[r/(1+r)]H$ in (5.81) of a house price increase is likely to dominate the combined income and substitution effect $h(1 + e_{hp})$ from facing a higher house price. For those without housing wealth, there is no wealth effect, so that the negative effect remains. The smaller the proportion of people who are not owner-occupiers but have aspirations in that direction, the more the wealth effect dominates at the aggregate level.[50] One might expect non-owner-occupiers to save more when real house prices rise. Their saving would also depend on the size of the required deposit as a proportion of the price of a house when obtaining a mortgage. In the UK and in Scandinavia in the 1980s, financial deregulation reduced these deposit/value ratios. Further, those living in a deregulated private rented sector may anticipate having to pay higher rents in the future when they see real house prices rise and hence save more. In the UK, the deregulated private rented sector is under 7% of households.

It is important to note the difference between housing wealth increases and house price increases. The accumulation of owner-occupied housing capital through investment and the transfer of publicly owned housing into private hands at discounts of around 50%, experienced in the UK in the 1980s, are household wealth increases that do not rest on increases in real prices. Such increases have clearly positive expenditure implications.

Increases in real house prices tend to redistribute wealth between young households and older households since the young have typically accumulated less housing wealth. To the extent that older households may have higher MPC's to spend out of housing wealth, this redistribution adds to the aggregate spending effect.

Evidence is accumulating that house prices have these dual effects implied by theory: a positive wealth effect, which depends on the degree of liquidity of houses, and a negative relative price effect. Indeed, it is impossible to obtain sensible wealth effects for the aggregate Japanese consumption function without a negative relative price of land[51] effect (see Murata, 1994). Lattimore (1993) finds a similar effect for Australia. On the UK, it is hard to pin down a negative relative price effect on aggregate data, but on regional UK consumption data, where there is more price variation, Muellbauer and Murphy (1994) find a small negative relative price effect alongside a positive wealth effect. A recent survey on the consumption effects of house price increases in a range of OECD countries finds mixed effects,[52] consistent with the dual role of house price (Kennedy and Andersen, 1994).

The relative house price effect may also be expected to have different consequences for different types of goods. For example, the demand for household durables, which are probably complementary with housing, is likely to be particularly negatively affected when real house prices rise, *ceteris paribus*.

10   Some Aggregation Issues

One of the key insights of Modigliani and Brumberg's (1954) analysis of aggregate saving behaviour is that aggregate behaviour may be very different from that of any individual, even from that of a hypothetical "representative" consumer. For example, each individual household may plan to spend in retirement everything saved during its working life. Yet in the aggregate, with population growth or productivity growth, saving will be positive. Another example arises both for Euler equations and for the solved out consumption function in aggregation over households where some are credit constrained. As we saw in section 5, aggregate behaviour is unlike the behaviour of either type of household. The problem of aggregation – how one goes from models of individual behaviour to a model of aggregate behaviour – has been particularly neglected in the Euler equation literature. This may be partly because it calls into question the link between theory and modelling the data on which this approach has so prided itself. Section 10.1 discusses some aggregation problems in Euler equations. Paradoxically, these could explain some of the aggregate time-series evidence against the Hall Euler equation model. Section 10.2 discusses aggregation in the solved out consumption function, explaining, in the context of a stylized example, how demographic effects enter the aggregate consumption function.

10.1 Aggregation in Euler Equations

We begin by illustrating the lack of necessary connection between individual and aggregate behaviour. Consider the Euler equation for household h with quadratic preferences but where the real interest rate exceeds the subjective discount rate. By (5.19),

$$\beta - c_{ht} = \frac{1+r}{1+\delta}(\beta - Ec_{ht+1}), \tag{5.82}$$

where $\beta > c_{ht}$. Here planned consumption grows steadily over each household's life-cycle. Since (5.82) is linear and, by assumption, the parameters β, r and δ are the same across households,[53] it may seem that the linear aggregation theorem should hold so that the aggregate and micro equations have the same form. But, in general, (5.82) will not hold with $\bar{c}_t$, the average consumption level, replacing c_{ht}. Indeed, in the context of a stationary population in which each generation has the same permanent income and in which there are no bequests, average consumption will be constant.

What has gone wrong with the attempt to go from (5.82) to its equivalent for average consumption is the neglect of the distinctive behaviour of exiting households. In a stationary population, exiting households are replaced by entering households. At that point in the chain linking the household consumption level to that of the following year, there is a sudden drop from the high level in the last year of life to the low level in the first, compensating for the marginal growth implied by (5.82) for all the other years of the life-cycle, and leaving average consumption constant. Of course, with productivity growth, the permanent income of each cohort would be higher, resulting in growth of average consumption. But this has everything to do with the growth of average income and nothing to do with the amount by which the market interest rate r exceeds the discount rate δ in (5.82). In other words, the positive response of planned consumption growth to the real interest rate, which is a feature of intertemporal substitution, need not show up at all in aggregate data. Furthermore, note that at the point in the chain where exiting households are replaced by entering households, the change in consumption depends in particular on the income and expenditure history of the exiting households, thus violating the irrelevance of lagged information to explaining the period-to-period evolution of consumption. Gali (1990; 1991) and Clarida (1991) develop these points and also show how aggregation of households with finite lives can provide yet another explanation for the "excess smoothness" of consumption.[54]

The assumption of infinite lives or the equivalent through the assumption of dynastic behaviour by households circumvents these "problems." This helps account for its popularity in much of the literature on Euler equations for "representative consumers" applied to aggregate data, despite its lack of realism.

Demographic considerations enter the discussion of aggregation in Euler equations in two ways. One concerns systematic variations in parameters with age, for example the subjective discount rate as discussed in note 53. The other arises through the number as well as the different behaviour of entering and exiting households. The aggregate change in consumption is the weighted sum of the average consumption change for the surviving cohorts plus the consumption of new entrants minus the consumption of those exiting:

$$\Delta c_{t+1} = \sum_s \Delta c_{st+1} n_{st} + c_{ent+1} n_{ent+1} - c_{ext} n_{ext}, \qquad (5.83)$$

where c is aggregate consumption, c_s is the average consumption of the cohort of survivors aged s and n_s their number, c_{en} is the average consumption of entering households and n_{en} their number, and c_{ex} is the average consumption of exiting households and n_{ex} their number. For example, in the context of (5.82), each Δc_{st+1} component would be given by

$$\Delta c_{st+1} = \beta - \left(\frac{1 + \delta_s}{1 + r}\right)\beta + \left(\frac{\delta_s - r}{1 + r}\right)c_{st} + \varepsilon_{st} \qquad (5.84)$$

on the assumption of no credit constraints, or some average of (5.84) and expected growth of non-property income, as in (5.62), if some households are assumed credit constrained. The average consumption of entering and exiting households would have to be specified respectively using solved out consumption functions typical of young households with few assets and facing a long horizon, and of old households facing short horizons and, on average, high asset to income ratios. These functions, using proxies derived from available aggregate data, and weighted by estimated numbers of entering and departing households, would need to be estimated at the same time as the weighted averages of the parameters in (5.84).

We are not aware of any Euler equation studies which have actually implemented such a procedure. It is plain that, in reality, the parameters of Euler equations such as (5.84) cannot be systematically estimated from aggregate data without specifying and estimating solved out consumption functions for cohorts at the end and at the beginning of their life-cycles. This seems to us to destroy much of the supposed advantage of applying the Euler equation approach to aggregate data.

10.2 Aggregation in Solved Out Consumption Functions

We discuss the aggregation problem that arises because different age groups have different marginal propensities to spend. We work through an example with two age groups, young households and old households. This can be readily generalized to the case of more than two groups. Some illustrative calculations suggest that while demographic and distributional shifts are likely to be significant in explaining the long-term evolution of the savings ratio, these shifts are small relative to business cycle fluctuations. The aggregation "problem" may therefore not be as destructive of useful empirical work on aggregate data as might be feared.

Let's consider the aggregation problem in terms of two age groups and work with a simplified model. On a per capita basis,

$$c^0 = \alpha^0 A^0 + \beta^0 y^0 \quad \text{for the old} \tag{5.85}$$

$$c^1 = \alpha^1 A^1 + \beta^1 y^1 \quad \text{for the young.} \tag{5.86}$$

Differences in the marginal propensities to spend were justified in section 3 and reconsidered in the light of precautionary behaviour in section 6. Suppose *so* is the population share of the old, so that $1 - so$ is the share of the young. Let $ry = y^0/y^1$ be relative income and $ra = A^0/A^1$ be relative assets. In the aggregate, assets per capita are

$$A = so A^0 + (1 - so)A^1, \tag{5.87}$$

income per capita is

$$y = so y^0 + (1 - so)y^1, \tag{5.88}$$

and consumption per capita is

$$c = so c^0 + (1 - so)c^1.$$

Using these equations and the definitions of relative income *ry* and relative assets *ra*, we derive the following relationship between average consumption and average assets and income:

$$c = \left[\frac{so\,\alpha^0 ra + (1 - so)\alpha^1}{so\,ra + (1 - so)} \right] A + \left[\frac{so\,\beta^0 ry + (1 - so)\beta^1}{so\,ry + (1 - so)} \right] y \tag{5.89}$$

$$= \alpha A + \beta y, \tag{5.90}$$

where α and β are parameters that vary with the population share *so* and relative assets and incomes *ra* and *ry*.

It is obvious that if the MPCs did not differ between the old and the young, then α and β would be constant. Aggregation is both a "problem" for empirical work on macro data and a "phenomenon," e.g. the extent to which the aggregate savings rate is dependent on the demographic structure of the population *so* and on the income growth rate, which should manifest itself in relative asset holdings *ra* and relative incomes *ry*.

It is worth considering some numerical illustrations loosely based on Japan. Japan has experienced both a massive increase in the population share of the old and a massive decline in the 1970s in the rate of economic growth from the enormous levels experienced in the 1950s and 1960s. One would expect the result to be a decline in the aggregate savings rate. Indeed, the aggregate household savings rate did decline from a peak in the mid 1970s of around 23% to around 15% in the late 1980s, about the same as the average level for the 1960s. Regular annual surveys of income and assets for Japan suggest roughly the following changes between 1966 and 1991:

		1966	1991
Population share of the old	so	0.09	0.21
Ratio of assets	ra	1	1.5
Ratio of income	ry	0.7	0.5

Let us take some plausible values for the MPCs. Suppose $\alpha^1 = 0.06$, $\alpha^0 = 0.09$. These values reflect relatively small differences between age groups consistent with uncertainty about length of life, needs uncertainty, and the bequest motive (see sections 2 and 5). Suppose $\beta^1 = 0.8$, $\beta^0 = 0.9$. These are also relatively small differences roughly consistent with the observations that, on survey data, dissaving among the old is low and there is an aggregate savings ratio of around 15%.

Given these assumptions, the average MPC out of assets in 1966 was $\alpha = 0.0627$ which rose to 0.0686 in 1991. The average MPC out of income β was 0.8065 in 1966 and 0.8117 in 1991. These shifts are small relative to the typical standard errors one would find in estimating aggregate time-series models and would appear to suggest that aggregation biases may not distort the aggregate consumption functions greatly. However, this is a simplified example. It would be more realistic to give a separate role also to the middle-aged. It is possible that this would result in bigger behaviour shifts as the demographic structure and income and asset distribution altered.

Let us now discuss the implications of the above assumptions for the savings rate in Japan. If we make an assumption about the ratio of assets to non-property income, we can now compute the ratios of consumption to non-property income in 1966 and 1991. If we give illiquid assets a weight of around 1/3 of liquid assets, A/y in 1966 was of the order of 2. In 1966, $c/y = 2\alpha + \beta = 0.932$. With a rate of return on assets of 4%, disposable income would have been $1.08y$. Thus the implied conventional savings ratio was $1 - 0.863 = 0.137$ or 13.7%

By 1991, asset accumulation and rising real asset prices had raised the asset to income ratio to around 3.5, so that $c/y = 3.5\alpha + \beta = 1.052$. But disposable income would have been $1.14y$, so that the implied conventional savings ratio was $1 - 0.923 = 0.073$ or 7.3%. Note that if the asset to income ratio had stayed at 2, the savings ratio would have fallen from 13.7% in 1966 to 12.1% in 1991, a drop of only 1.6%. Thus, most of the change implied by this stylized model is due to the rise in the asset to income ratio rather than to demographic and distributional shifts. If we had assumed bigger differences between the MPCs of the old and the young, we would have obtained bigger demographic and distributional shifts. But given cross-section evidence on the low rates of dissaving of the old in Japan, differences in the MPCs *cannot* be very large. It seems unlikely that more than a 3% shift in the aggregate saving rate could have been implied even for relatively extreme assumptions. The lack of explicit attention given to the increasing numbers of the high-saving middle-aged is unlikely to alter this conclusion.

The fact that the savings ratio in Japan was actually fairly stable is explained by the rise in the real price of land and so of housing. As we saw in section 10, this has a negative effect on consumption, offsetting much of the rise, in Japan at any rate, in the value of land and housing wealth. The period of rapid economic growth in Japan up to the early 1970s was also associated with much bigger fluctuations in annual income changes. The Japanese consumption function estimated by Murata (1994) (see section 11.5 below) also attributes shifts in the savings ratio to the resulting decline in income uncertainty, which would have lowered the savings rate, and to a decline in the expected growth rate of income, which would have raised the savings rate.

Existing estimates of the effect of demography on the aggregate savings rate suggest they are quite small (see Bosworth, Burtless, and Sabelhaus, 1991). Kennickell (1990) obtains average savings rates for age groups from the US Surveys of Consumer Finances and the Consumer Expenditure Survey. If it is assumed that the distribution of income by age remains unchanged, but savings rates are reweighted to reflect the projected ageing of the population, then the implied change in the US savings ratio between 1990 and 2010 is less than 0.5%. However, these estimates do not build in the separate effects of assets and income. A more sophisticated approach would entail estimating the marginal propensities to spend out of assets and income by age and projecting forward the respective distribution of assets and income by age. However, outside Japan there appears to be a paucity of the relevant data on the asset distribution.

11   Towards an Aggregate Solved Out Consumption Function

We now draw together the practical implications for the solved out consumption function of stochastic income expectations (section 3), precautionary behaviour (section 4), credit constraints (section 5), lags (section 7), alternatives to rational expectations (section 8), the role of assets (section 9), and aggregation (section 10).

The material is arranged in the following subsections. Section 11.1 considers the functional form, arguing in favour of modelling log consumption, and derives implications for the inclusion of asset effects. Section 11.2 generalizes the basic model by introducing variable real interest rates, uncertainty, income expectations, and lags. Section 11.3 deals with aggregation over credit unconstrained and credit constrained households and shows that, with respect to income, the aggregate consumption function has an error correction form. Section 11.4 discusses how one might incorporate the parameter shifts arising from financial liberalization. Section 11.5 considers some empirical examples drawn from research on Japan, the UK and the US and reviews some of the debates about aggregate household saving behaviour in these countries, for example, concerning the decline in the US savings rate between the mid 1970s and the mid 1980s.

11.1 Functional Form

Let us consider functional forms for aggregate consumption functions. It seems very likely that the stochastic error term in a consumption function grows with the scale of consumption. If

$$c_t = f(W_t, \ldots)(1 + \varepsilon_t),$$

then, to a close approximation,

$$\ln c_t = \ln f(W_t, \ldots) + \varepsilon_t, \tag{5.91}$$

since, if ε is small, $\ln(1 + \varepsilon) \approx \varepsilon$. Incorporating a stochastic error ε in the stylized model (5.90) gives

$$c_t = (\alpha A_{t-1} + \beta y_t)(1 + \varepsilon_t), \tag{5.92}$$

where $\alpha \approx 0.065$, $\beta \approx 0.8$ in the hypothetical Japanese case considered in section 10.2. Equation (5.92) has important implications for the way assets enter a logarithmic consumption function. Most macro modellers[55] approximate (5.92) by

$$\ln c_t = \beta_1 \ln A_{t-1} + \beta_2 \ln y_t + \varepsilon_t, \tag{5.93}$$

sometimes imposing $\beta_1 + \beta_2 = 1$ to get long-run homogeneity implied by (5.92). Far better is to realize that (5.92) implies

$$c_t = \beta y_t[1 + (\alpha/\beta) A_{t-1}/y_t](1 + \varepsilon_t). \tag{5.94}$$

For the US and the UK, aggregate weighted asset to income ratios, which give illiquid assets a lower weight relative to liquid ones, rarely exceed 2. Thus the term $(\alpha/\beta) A_{t-1}/y_t$ is small and (5.94) is well approximated by

$$\ln c_t \approx \text{constant} + \ln y_t + \gamma A_{t-1}/y_t + \varepsilon_t. \tag{5.95}$$

The ratio form of assets/income also makes it much easier to disaggregate assets by liquidity which would be unsatisfactory in (5.93).

11.2 Introducing Variable Interest Rates, Uncertainty, and Lags

Let us now return to a more realistic specification which incorporates real interest rates, expectations uncertainty, and lags. In section 2, we considered a consumption function with CES preferences under non-probabilistic expectations (5.14):

$$c_t = \kappa_t^{-1} W_t,$$

where (5.15) defines κ. In the light of income and needs uncertainty, we modified (5.14) by discounting expected income by the real interest rate and an extra factor reflecting uncertainty, see section 4.

In practice, the real interest rate and income uncertainty have been negatively correlated in the last 40 years. The period of negative or low real interest rates after the 1973 oil shock and the inflation that followed was also a period of increased uncertainty. The 1980s on the other hand were a period of sustained recovery, especially in the UK, and of high real interest rates. This suggests that the sum of the real interest and the income uncertainty factor was closer to being constant than either component on its own. This suggests

$$\ln c_t \simeq \beta_0 - \beta_1 r_t - \beta_2 \theta_t + \ln y_t + \gamma A_{t-1}(1 + r_{t-1})/y_t + \sum_{s=1}^{T} \beta_{2+s} E_t \Delta_s \ln y_{t+s}, \quad (5.96)$$

where the weights on expected income growth decline as the horizon extends, $\beta_3 > \beta_4 > \beta_5$, etc. Here θ_t is a measure of income uncertainty. Equation (5.96) is an approximation[56] to (5.14) in which the effects of the real interest rate and income uncertainty θ_t are linearized and γ and $\beta_{2+s}(s \geq 1)$ are treated as constant parameters, when strictly speaking they are time varying since they depend on r_t and θ_t.[57] Moreover, the parameters in (5.96) depend upon demographic structure and the distribution of income and assets by age as exemplified in (5.89).

We now parameterize the expected growth term as

$$b(E_t \ln ym_{t+1} - \ln y_t), \quad (5.97)$$

where ym_{t+1} is a forward looking moving average of $\ln y_{t+1}$, $\ln y_{t+2}$, etc. whose weights sum to one, and where the weights are bigger for shorter forecasting horizons. Note that $b/(1 + r_t + \theta_t)$ can be taken as the relative weight of credit unconstrained households who have forward looking income expectations. For myopic households or those for whom income is a random walk plus a drift representing expected growth, (5.97) would be zero or a constant that would simply be absorbed in the overall intercept term of the equation. We also include a lagged dependent variable as in (5.72) to reflect habits[58] or convex costs of adjustment, and make transitory consumption η explicit. Then

$$\ln c_t^u = (1 - \beta) \ln c_{t-1}^u + \beta[\beta_0 - \beta_1 r_t - \beta_2 \theta_t + \ln y_t^u + \gamma A_{t-1}^u(1 + r_{t-1})/y_t^u$$
$$+ b(E_t \ln ym_{t+1}^u - \ln y_t^u)] + \eta_t^u. \quad (5.98)$$

Here we make explicit that (5.98) refers to credit unconstrained households.

It is worth recalling here that the quasi-difference transformation used by Hayashi (1982) (see (5.51) to (5.53) above) could be adopted to eliminate explicit expectations of future income. This could offer a useful check on the sensitivity of the parameter estimates to the particular income expectations generating model adopted.

We also need to find proxies for uncertainty, θ_t. In our empirical work (Muellbauer and Murphy (1993a; 1993b) we have found the change in unemployment Δun and ad, the absolute value of the deviation of current income growth from trend growth over the previous four or five years, to give sensible results for several countries. A negative coefficient on ad implies that the consumption to income ratio falls when there is both a sharp slump in growth and a sharp increase in growth. Both plausibly increase uncertainty that the current level of income will persist.

Our discussion of asset effects in section 9 suggested that assets be disaggregated into liquid and illiquid assets with different spendability weights. Further, positive housing wealth effects are partly offset by a negative real house price effect, interacted with a measure of the size of deposit relative to the value of a house required by mortgage lenders.

In practice, limited degrees of freedom prevent a high degree of disaggregation of different assets and debt. It makes sense to groups gross liquid assets minus debt into a single aggregate. Debt, like liquid assets, is not capital uncertain but is given in nominal terms. And in these days of deregulated financial markets, relatively low transactions costs are associated with taking on or repaying collateralized debt. In principle, life insurance and pension fund assets should have lower spendability weights than directly held bonds and equities and houses. But as values of directly and indirectly held assets tend to move together, aggregating them into a single group may not be a bad first cut.

11.3 Aggregation of Credit Unconstrained and Credit Constrained Households

We shall make the assumption that the non-property incomes of credit constrained and unconstrained households move in parallel. This is equivalent, in the context of (5.98), to replacing y_t^u by average non-property income y_t with a shift in the intercept β_0 and the asset coefficient γ. However, the lagged dependent variable in (5.98) is log consumption for unconstrained households, whereas we only observe aggregate consumption. We assume that for the credit constrained,

$$\ln c_t^c = \ln y_t^c + \eta_t^c. \tag{5.99}$$

Aggregate log consumption is approximately given by

$$\ln c_t^c = \pi \ln c_t^c + (1 - \pi) \ln c_t^c, \tag{5.100}$$

where π is now the consumption share of the credit constrained. This allows us to deduce $\ln c_{t-1}^u$ in terms of the observed aggregate in $\ln c_{t-1}$.

Then, weighting (5.99) by π and (5.98) by $(1 - \pi)$, and replacing y^c and y^u by y, we obtain an aggregate equation of the following form:

$$\varDelta \ln c_t = \beta(\ln y_t - \ln c_{t-1}) + \pi(1 - \beta)\varDelta \ln y_t$$

$$+ (1 - \pi)\beta[\beta_0 - \beta_1 r_t - \beta_2 \theta_t + \gamma A_{t-1}(1 + r_{t-1})/y_t] \qquad (5.101)$$

$$+ b(E_t \ln ym_{t+1} - \ln y_t)] + \eta_t,$$

where

$$\eta_t = (1 - \pi)\eta_t^u + \pi(\eta_t^c - (1 - \beta)\eta_{t-1}^c).$$

There is a moving average component in the error term η_t, but if the variance of transitory consumption for the credit constrained is small relative to that for the unconstrained, or if π is small or if $(1 - \beta)$ is small, the implied negative autocorrelation in the error term η_t can be ignored in practice.

Forecasts of $\ln ym_{t+1}$ can be obtained from equations of the kind exemplified by (5.41) which can also be augmented by incorporating expectations data generated from regular surveys of consumer opinion. For the US, Michigan Survey Research Center data are available back to the early 1950s. Equation (5.101) can then be estimated either by replacing $E_t \ln ym_{t+1}$ by its forecast value $\ln \widehat{ym}_{t+1}$ or by estimating a simultaneous system in which the parameters of the income forecasting equations such as (5.41) are estimated jointly with the parameters of (5.101).

11.4   Financial Liberalization

Financial deregulation has been an important phenomenon in many countries, particularly in the 1980s. Moves in this direction started a little earlier in the US with regulatory ceilings on interest rates paid by savings and loans institutions phased out after the mid 1970s. The move to targeting monetary aggregates made interest rates increasingly volatile at this time and interest rate regulation increasingly out of place in both the US and the UK. Furthermore, the UK abandoned exchange controls in 1979 which opened up its domestic credit markets to international capital movements.

To understand the financial deregulation that occurred in the UK and the Scandinavian countries in the 1980s, it is helpful to understand the preceding regime of credit controls. The UK and Scandinavian countries in the 1970s had very progressive income tax systems and tax deductibility by households of interest payments on debt, though in some cases, as in the UK, restricted to mortgage debt. After the first oil shock of 1973–4, inflation rose sharply in these countries while nominal interest rates rose only moderately. Real interest rates became negative, and hugely negative given tax deductibility of interest payments. To illustrate, with inflation at 15%, and the nominal borrowing rate at 13%, a marginal tax rate of 50% implies an after-tax real interest rate of $6.5 - 15 = -8.5\%$. At a marginal tax rate of 80%, common for higher incomes at this time, the real interest rate was $2.6 - 15 = -12.4\%$. This created strong incentives to borrow and a demand for credit which was held in check by rationing.

In the UK from 1979, nominal interest rates rose, and foreign exchange controls were abandoned. The "corset" which had restricted bank lending was removed in 1980 and the banks, suffering losses from Third World lending in the 1970s, were anxious to enter domestic mortgage markets. These became much more competitive. Restrictions on building societies were progressively relaxed, culminating in the 1986 Building Societies Act, and a new breed of mortgage lenders, often financed by overseas banks, entered the market. Credit become so easily available that, by 1986–8, many first time buyers were offered 100% loan to value ratios. From 1980 to 1989, household debt to income ratios in the UK more than doubled to one of the highest ratios in the world and there was a boom in house prices in which real prices in the UK doubled over the same period. These developments were not solely the result of financial deregulation since there was sustained economic growth and falling unemployment from 1986 to 1990. But it is hard to deny the connection.

Similar developments in Scandinavia, with Denmark followed by Norway, then Sweden, and finally Finland, occurred somewhat later: see Englund (1990), Lehmussaari (1990), Koskela and Viren (1992), and Berg (1994). In all countries, debt to income ratios grew strongly, real house prices boomed, and household savings ratios fell sharply – to negative levels in some cases.

As far as the consumption equation (5.101) is concerned, financial liberalization can have several effects on the parameters apart from effects on income or on asset values and debt. Most obviously, it could reduce π, the consumption share of the credit constrained. However, as noted in section 5, Euler equation evidence for the UK appears to suggest that π *rose* in the 1980s. This is circumstantial evidence that something else was going on. The most obvious candidate is a shift in the spendability coefficients associated with illiquid assets and debt. Financial liberalization, by making asset backed credit more easily available, made these illiquid assets more spendable. This makes good sense in the context of the shadow price interpretation of these weights in section 9. It is also plausible that it would have increased the negative spendability weight on debt, giving it a value close to -1 to correspond with a weight of 1 on liquid assets. During the credit rationing regime of the 1970s, a household with big debts could count itself lucky, even though, with *given* assets and income, lower expenditure would still be associated with a bigger debt.

There are other possible effects. During credit rationing, the intertemporal substitution which is partly represented by the real interest effect $-\beta_1 r_t$ is less likely to be operative.[59] Thus, we would expect more powerful real interest effects after financial liberalization. More subtly, since part of the uncertainty discount factor applied to future expected income growth via $b(E_t \ln ym_{t+1} - \ln y_t)$ rests on the possibility of future credit rationing, it is possible that b would increase with financial liberalization.

It is too much to ask aggregate time-series models to pick up all these possibilities, though there is some empirical support in the UK for both of the last two. Distinguishing such effects is especially hard because *international* financial liberalizations reduced the balance of payments constraints on UK and Scandinavian economic growth. In the UK this gave rise to the Burns-Lawson doctrine[60] which claimed that, as long as the government did not run a deficit, the balance of payments deficit was self-correcting as the private sector made the necessary adjustments. Indeed, in forecasting income growth in the UK, Muellbauer and Murphy (1993b) found that the coefficient on the lagged balance of payments deficit fell in the 1980s, reducing the balance of payments constraint on growth. Since the rise of the Burns-Lawson doctrine occurred at about the same time as domestic financial liberalization, it is hard to separate precisely the direct growth effect of international financial liberalization from the effect via the higher spendability of illiquid assets or a lower weight π on credit constrained households. The evidence we have so far is consistent with some effect on the spendability weights but not a very precisely determined one.[61]

11.5　Some Empirical Illustrations

The case of Japan offers a simple illustration of a specification of the type discussed above, drawing on Murata (1994). Because of Japanese survey data on the distribution of income and assets by age, it also has the merit of making a consistent treatment of aggregation possible. Consider equation (5.89). In principle, α^0, α^1, β^0 and β^1 can be estimated using non-linear methods. In practice, the trending nature of the data and other trend-like effects on consumption make this infeasible. An alternative is a mixture of estimation and "calibration." For reasons discussed in section 10.2, it seems reasonable to expect the MPC out of assets to be somewhat higher for the old than for the young: $\alpha^0 = 1.5\alpha^1$ seems plausible. Similarly we expect $\beta^0 > \beta^1$ but not much: $\beta^0 = (9/8)\beta^1$ seems plausible. With these restrictions, α and β defined in (5.90) are proportional to α^1 and β^1, where the factors of proportinality a^* and b^* are known numbers given by so, ra, and ry, so that $\alpha = a^*\alpha^1$, $\beta = b^*\beta^1$. Thus, in steady state,

$$c = a^*\alpha^1 A + b^*\beta^1 y = b^*\beta^1 y \left[1 + \frac{a^*a^1}{b^*\beta^1} \frac{A}{y} \right].$$

In logs,

$$\ln c = \ln b^* + \ln \beta^1 + \ln y + \frac{a^*}{b^*} \gamma \frac{A}{y}, \tag{5.102}$$

where $\gamma = \alpha^1/\beta^1$.

Murata (1994) estimates such an equation for non-durables with lagged adjustment, incorporating the relative price index of non-durables and durables, the relative price of land, and income uncertainty. Because the permanent income elasticity of demand for durables in the long run is greater than 1, that for non-durables must be less than 1 if total consumption is to have an elasticity of 1. Since durables make up around 10% of expenditure, an elasticity of 1.3 for durables implies an elasticity around 0.97 for non-durables, This is accepted by the data.

For 1967–91 the equation estimated on annual data is

$$\Delta \ln cn = \text{constant} + \underset{(0.057)}{0.662}(0.97 \ln y + \ln b^* - \ln cn_{-1}) + \underset{(0.066)}{0.385} \Delta \ln \hat{y}_{+1} \qquad (5.103)$$

$$+ \frac{a^*}{b^*} \underset{(0.010)}{0.038} \left(\frac{NLA_{-1}}{y} + 0.5 \frac{ILA_{-1}}{y} \right) - \underset{(0.12)}{0.27} ad - \underset{(0.055)}{0.14} \Delta^2 \ln y$$

$$- \underset{(0.012)}{0.029} \ln(pn/pd)_{-1} - \underset{(0.013)}{0.048} \ln (pland/pn)_{-1} + \underset{(0.090)}{0.49}r$$

$$R^2 = 0.978, \quad \sigma = 0.0045, \quad DW = 1.63, \quad \text{standard errors in parentheses.}$$

Here

cn	= per capita expenditure on non-durables at constant prices
y	= per capita disposable non-property income at constant prices
$\Delta \ln \hat{y}_{+1}$	= forecast value of income growth rate over next year
NLA	= liquid assets minus debt
ILA	= illiquid assets including land, housing, stocks and shares
ad	= "income uncertainty" = $\lvert \Delta \ln y -$ "trend"$\rvert$, where "trend" = trend growth over the previous five years
pn	= price index for non-durables
pd	= price index for durables
r	= real interest rate
$pland$	= land price index

Note that (5.103), in contrast to (5.102), makes explicit the disaggregation of assets, and relative price effects both of non-durables relative to durables and of land relative to non-durables. It also incorporates demographic effects via b^* and a^* at values which are imposed rather than estimated. The change in the unemployment rate, an indicator of income uncertainty, has a negative coefficient but, unlike in the US and the UK, is not significant. Given the very small levels and variation in the Japanese unemployment rate, this is not very surprising. The current rate of change of income $\Delta \ln y$ has a positive but insignificant coefficient of around 0.07. In (5.101) this is interpreted as $\pi(1 - \beta)$, where $1 - \beta$ is a measure of habit persistence. With $\beta = 0.66$, this suggests a point estimate of around 21% for the consumption share of credit constrained households in Japan. Though quite imprecisely determined, this is not implausible and is consistent with Hayashi (1985). The estimates of β are in the range 0.6 to 0.7 for all three countries, suggesting a similar degree of habit persistence measured by $1 - \beta$ (see (5.72)).

One of the most intriguing features of these estimates for Japan is the positive real interest rate effect which conflicts with negative effects estimated from similar models for the UK and the US. As we saw in section 2.1, when σ, the elasticity of intertemporal substitution, is low (or consumers are very risk averse, which is equivalent given a CES utility function), the asset to income ratio is high and the income growth rate is low, then consumption is likely to rise with the real interest rate. Since the early 1970s, when Japanese growth moderated, these conditions seem to apply in Japan. Asset to income ratios are higher than in the UK or the US yet, despite improvements in the welfare state, the Japanese savings rate remains high. This is at least consistent with a low value of σ, see Horioka (1990) and Hayashi (1986) for an exhaustive analysis of other potential reasons for the high Japanese savings rate. The positive real interest rate effect in Japan thus seems quite consistent with theory.[62]

Estimating (5.103) with the coefficients on the net liquid assets to income ratio and on the illiquid assets to income ratio freely estimated, the latter is fairly precisely estimated but the former is not. The point estimates suggest a relative weight of around one-half on illiquid assets, and 0.5 has been imposed in (5.103). Relative weights of 0.3 to 0.4 are indicated by US and UK evidence.

The parameter estimates of the model are quite stable for 1967 to 1985. The forecasting performance for the later 1980s is satisfactory relative to the estimated parameter uncertainty. For the US and the UK we have reasonably similar estimates, though the disadvantage of a less coherent treatment of aggregation. The asset effects have similar magnitudes to those estimated for Japan, though we did not include a relative price effect for land or housing. Incidentally, without the latter, it is impossible to find sensible wealth effects for Japan. For the US, the house price data are incomplete and for the UK too collinear to be significant. However, the negative real house effect is confirmed on UK regional consumption data by Muellbauer and Murphy (1994) and for Australia by Lattimore (1993).

The income uncertainty effect ad is quite interesting. Effectively, if current income growth is above the recent trend, it is discounted. But if current income growth is below trend, the effect of the negative income shock is accentuated. The negative effect of income acceleration in (5.103) can also be given an uncertainty interpretation, tending to offset the effect of a negative income shock but enhance those of a positive one. The income uncertainty effect ad has a marginally smaller coefficient in the US and the UK but, since the change in the unemployment rate is successful in those countries at picking up another aspect of income uncertainty, this is quite consistent with the Japanese evidence. Income expectations are somewhat less significant in the US and UK but this may be sensitive to the specification of the expectations generating model.

Estimates for π, the proportion of credit constrained households, are imprecisely determined both for the UK and for the US. Point estimates

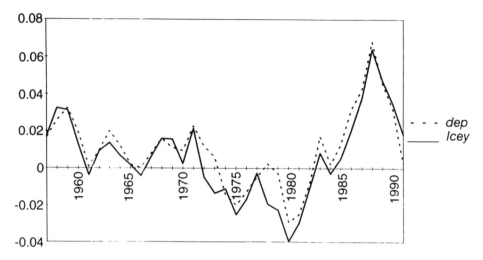

Figure 5.1 Log ratio of consumption to income *lcey* versus *dep*

suggest roughly 30%, broadly consistent with Euler equation estimates discussed in section 5.

As far as financial liberalization in the UK is concerned, interaction effects with illiquid wealth and debt are fairly imprecisely estimated. Some of the reasons were discussed in section 11.4. The implication is that an equation such as (5.101), of a relatively simple form, would have tracked quite well consumer expenditure in the 1980s without the massive breakdown experienced by all the UK macroeconometric models extant in the 1980s. For the UK, we have decomposed fluctuations in the consumer expenditure to non-property income ratio into the various estimated effects we are able to isolate. To simplify matters, we plot $(\ln c - 0.3 \ln y - 0.7 \ln c_{-1}) = dep$ say, given an estimate of $\beta = 0.7$, against the various estimated influences. Figure 5.1 shows that *dep* correlates closely with $\ln(c/y)$: note that, in a steady state, $dep = 0.3 \ln(c/y)$. The rise in the consumption to income ratio of around 10% between 1980 and 1988 was unprecedented in recorded UK history. Figure 5.2 shows the contribution of forecast income growth to this rise: it is just over 2% between 1980 and 1988. But the rise in the real interest rate reduced the consumption to income ratio by around 1% over the same period.

Figure 5.3 shows the estimated contribution of the fall in the change in the unemployment rate to be around 2.5% from 1980 to 1988, with a little over 0.5% from the fall in income volatility measured by *ad*. Altogether, this suggests reduced income uncertainty contributing around 3% to the upturn in *c/y*.

Figure 5.4 shows the contribution of two variables linked with credit rationing. Before 1979, the government used consumer credit controls to regulate consumer expenditure. These took the form of legal restrictions on down payments and length of contract when buying durable goods by "hire

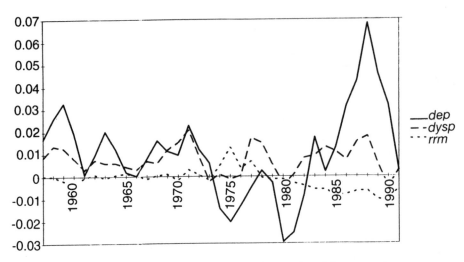

Figure 5.2   *dep* versus expected income growth *dysp* and real interest rate *rrm*

purchase." It is impossible to model the demand for durables in the UK before 1979 successfully without taking variations in these restrictions into account. Since their effect is only transitory and they were abolished in 1982 they have no effect on the 1980–8 comparison. The higher growth rate of current income, which enters (5.101) in the form $\pi(1 - \beta)\Delta \ln y$, explains around 0.5% of the rise in c/y. This seems small, but note that the effect of current income on consumption is already built in by taking the c/y ratio.

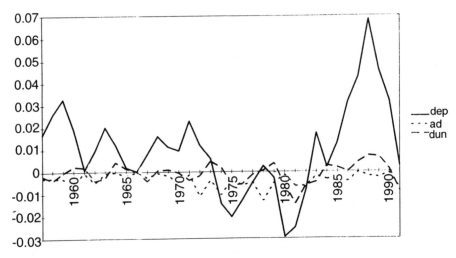

Figure 5.3   *dep* versus income volatility *ad* and unemployment change *dun*

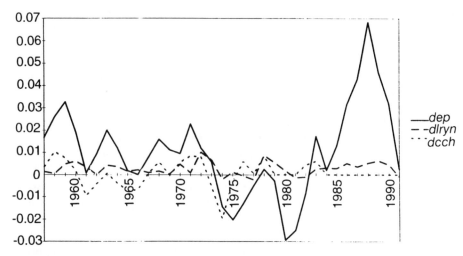

Figure 5.4 *dep* versus income growth *dlryn* and change in credit controls *dcch*

Figure 5.5 shows the biggest single contributor to the rise in the *c/y* ratio: the rise in the spendability weighted net asset to income ratio explains 5%, i.e. half, of the rise. The figure also shows an effect of around 1% from the fall in the proportion of middle-aged in the population, who tend to have higher savings rates.

Interestingly, the consumption to income ratio peaks before the asset to income ratio: the downturn in *c/y*, while assets to income are still rising, is

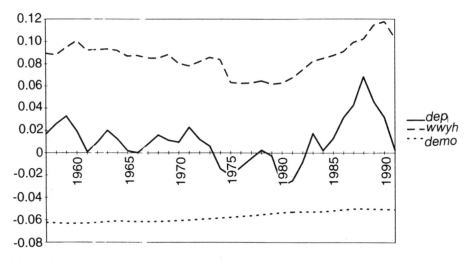

Figure 5.5 *dep* versus weighted wealth to income ratio *wwyh* and proportion of middle-aged *demom*

explained by a combination of factors. They include a sharp fall in expected income growth, a sharp rise in the rate of increase of unemployment, an increase in income volatility, a rise in the real interest rate, and the downturn in current income growth.

By 1991 the lagged asset to income ratio was falling too, mainly because of the direct and indirect consequences of the sharp increases in short-term interest rates which doubled between 1988 and 1990. This is all very consistent with the dramatic fall that occurred in the consumption to income ratio between 1989 and 1991 and beyond. The lower values of real share prices and later real house prices, and the high levels of debt – which has perhaps three times the spendability weight of illiquid assets, but a *negative* effect on consumption – help to explain the depth of the UK consumer recession in 1992 and the sluggishness of recovery in 1993 despite much lower interest rates.

Similar patterns of influences plausibly explain the analogous boom and bust experienced in consumer expenditure in Scandinavian economies in the 1980s and 1990s. For the US as a whole, fluctuations were much less pronounced though individual regions were as volatile as the UK and Scandinavia. Our estimates in Muellbauer and Murphy (1993a) show US asset effects of similar magnitude to those in the UK. But they explain less of the variation in c/y because they change by much less than in the UK. Undoubtedly, the debt overhang and employment insecurity contributed to the sluggish pace of recovery in the US until 1993, despite the very low levels reached by interest rates. The rapid increases in prices of financial assets experienced in 1993 together with falling unemployment and improved growth expectations explain much of the recovery in US consumption experienced from the vantage point of summer 1994.

At this stage the decline in the US savings rate from the mid 1970s to the mid 1980s remains only partly explained by wealth effects, a slowdown in growth, and other conventional macroeconomic variables. There is widespread agreement that changing demography can account for only very small changes (Kennickell, 1990; Bosworth, Burtless, and Sabelhaus, 1991).[63] In section 4 we reviewed hypotheses connected with aspects of risk-averse behaviour suggested by Hubbard, Skinner, and Zeldes (1994), who emphasize changes in the US welfare benefit system, and by Brenner, Dagenais, and Montmarquette (1992), who emphasize female human capital accumulation in place of asset accumulation in response to higher divorce probabilities. Bosworth, Burtless, and Sabelhaus (1991) and their discussants, Poterba and Summers, point to more widespread ownership of pension and insurance plans as well as improved regulation of pension schemes, which raised the probability that pension promises would be fulfilled. Poverty among the old fell in the 1970s and 1980s, suggesting that expected income security in old age improved, thus reducing saving. Participation rates for medical insurance rose too, thus reducing the need for precautionary saving.

The hypothesis advanced by Boskin and Lau (1988) of a cohort effect, whereby those born after 1930 have a lower savings propensity than those born in the Depression years, appears not to be strongly supported by the micro evidence discussed by Bosworth, Burtless, and Sabelhaus (1991) but may nevertheless have played a part.

Another hypothesis, advanced by Bernheim (1991) and Hatsopolous, Krugman, and Poterba (1989), is that corporate restructing, encouraged by the tax system, which retired much corporate equity and replaced it by debt, put a great deal of cash into the pockets of US owners of equity in the 1980s. Poterba (1991) argues that the marginal propensity to spend such cash receipts is around 50%, much higher than typical marginal propensities to spend out of wealth.

A final hypothesis is that financial liberalization improved access to credit, particularly for home loans, and reduced down payment to house price ratios for first time buyers. This has already been discussed in the UK context. Though there is considerable circumstantial evidence of changes in US credit markets, it is difficult to distinguish changes in credit market conditions that stem from changes in the supply side from those that result from changes in the demand side.

12 Data Issues

No discussion of the consumption function can be complete without mentioning data issues. Let us illustrate some of the measurement issues of consumer expenditure and the personal sector by examining some data revisions in the UK that are of particular concern. Table 5.2 shows figures for 1974 and 1975 seen from different standpoints. These figures show that consumer expenditure in current prices for 1974 was revised up from 1978 to 1992 by 3.3% and for 1975 by 3.9%. Thus, most of the downward revision in the saving ratios from 14.1% to 10% and from 15.3% to 10.6% is the result of revisions in consumer expenditure rather than in income. Similar revisions took place in figures for 1976 to 1980.

The sources of data for consumer expenditure include the Family Expenditure Survey (FES), the Food Survey, retail sales inquiries, and tax collection data from Customs and Excise. One of the major consistency checks in the national accounts is to compare expenditure and income based estimates of

Table 5.2 Revisions in UK data on consumer expenditure and saving

Data vintage	1978	1980	1983	1986	1989	1992
1974 nominal consumer exp. (£10^{10})	52.0	52.1	52.6	53.1	53.2	53.7
1975 nominal consumer exp. (£10^{10})	63.6	63.7	64.7	65.2	65.5	66.1
1974 savings ratio (%)	14.1	14.2	12.2	11.9	11.1	10.0
1975 savings ratio (%)	15.3	14.7	12.6	12.8	12.0	10.6

Source: Economic Trends Annual Supplement, table 5

output. In the 1960s and 1970s the income based estimates were typically 2% or 2.5% below the expenditure based estimates. This was thought reasonable in the light of the tendency to under-record income in data based on tax records. But in the late 1970s, the expenditure based figures for output began to be exceeded by the income based ones. This led to a search for ways in which expenditure might have been under-recorded. Upward revisions took place in consumer expenditure figures back to the early 1950s, though the biggest revisions of data occurred for the 1970s, particularly for 1974–75. As the table suggests, one of the biggest upward revisions took place as recently as after 1989. One of the areas known to be relatively badly measured is the service sector. However, it is puzzling that under-recording of expenditure on services was not accompanied by a similar under-recording of income from services. If both had been revised up, little change would have been recorded in the savings ratio.

These major revisions reduce the estimated increase in the savings ratio previously thought to have occurred in the great inflation that followed the 1973 oil and raw material price shock. If they are correct, they reduce estimated asset effects on consumption: the fall in real asset values in the 1970s *should* have led to a substantial increase in the savings rate. If it did not, asset effects must be weaker than would have been thought on the old data. This also reduces the negative inflation effect in the DHSY model of consumption which is probably capturing the same phenomenon (see Hendry, 1994). They must necessarily affect the stability of econometric models re-estimated over the same sample dates but taking a later vintage of data. Sefton and Weale (1994) have undertaken the major task of rebalancing the UK national accounts from 1920 to 1990 using a development of methods put forward by Stone, Champernowne, and Meade (1942). Their work suggests a substantial downward bias in official estimates of mid 1970s savings rates.

Slesnick (1992) discusses the consistency of the US National Income and Product Accounts with household survey data. He reports widening unexplained discrepancies between the two in the 1980s, a feature also of UK data (see below). Measurement problems from a US perspective are further discussed by Wilcox (1991) and Bosworth, Burtless, and Sabelhaus (1991).

Another significant source of revisions in data results from the rebasing of the national accounts in constant prices of different vintages. Price relativities can change considerably. Real energy and raw material prices have fluctuated a great deal. Technological advances have brought down quality-adjusted prices of anything applying micro-chip technology. Durable goods have tended to fall in price relative to non-durable goods. Thus, 1990 prices will give such goods a smaller weight than will 1980 and 1970 prices. Since volume increases in such goods have been greater than for, say, food, aggregate constant price consumption growth will be lower at 1990 prices than at 1970 prices. Economists have long known that Divisia or chain indices, which use annual reweighting, give a more sensible picture of the evolution of price and volume indices. In the US, they are gaining more widespread use in the national accounts, alongside the conventional fixed weight accounts.

In most national accounts, consumption and income data are classified as being measured with the smallest sampling error. Flow of funds of assets and liabilities and the corresponding stock data are regarded as rather less reliable. Pesaran and Evans (1984) argue that large errors of cumulation can occur in building up estimates of asset levels. This is a major reason for their (quasi-) differencing of a solved out consumption function: they argue that differencing reduces the errors in asset data to white noise. On the other hand, as originally argued in DHSY (1978), differencing can also remove valuable long-run information in the data. This is typical of the kind of trade-offs which must be faced in empirical work.

At the micro level, problems are no less serious. There is evidence that asset data are widely understated in surveys, especially by the wealthy. Such a conclusion comes from Ferber (1965; 1966) where information from bank and insurance companies on asset holdings was obtained first and these records compared with the subsequent survey responses.

Unless a household is observed over time, it is hard to take appropriate account of the effect of past on present behaviour and to model expectations. Variations in tastes affect not only consumption but, if they are long-lived differences, also asset holdings and income. A lower subjective discount rate will result in more thrifty behaviour and, other things being equal, higher accumulation of assets and human capital. Preferences between goods and leisure may affect labour supply and so income. Again, panel data on households are essential to properly control for such correlations. Synthetic panels of aggregate cohorts of households surveyed in repeated cross-sections such as the UK Family Expenditure Survey have been used as a partial substitute (see Deaton, 1985; Attanasio and Weber, 1991; 1992). Because the same households are not sampled repeatedly, population heterogeneity and the shifting response rate in the survey generate noise that, for example, would tend to underestimate the effect of lagged dependent variables. In the UK, major discrepancies developed in the 1980s between FES estimates of consumption and income growth and the national accounts estimates: for example, the national accounts show a big fall in the savings rate in 1986–8, absent in the FES. These discrepancies probably reflect some combination of shifts in the FES response rate; changes in the way some transactions, particularly involving credit and durable goods, were recorded in the FES; and continuing systematic biases such as the under-representation of purchasers of alcohol and tobacco and of the self-employed in the survey. In this period, there can be little doubt that the aggregates implied by the FES give a much less convincing picture of consumption and income trends then do the national accounts. Further, these surveys typically contain little direct asset information though some indirect inferences can be made from records of investment income received and mortgage payments made.

As we have seen, aggregation is potentially a serious issue for the aggregate time-series consumption function. The appropriate solution would be to pool micro and macro information. For example, the *diVerences* in the marginal propensities to spend out of assets and non-property income for different age and family compositions relative to some reference type could be estimated. They can then be used as outlined in sections 10.2 and 11.5 to build in aggregation effects, letting the marginal propensities for the reference household type be estimated from the macro data. One would not necessarily want to build in the restriction under which all the estimated micro propensities are assumed to hold also at the macro level. But one could test such a restriction. This is a fertile area for future research.

13   Conclusions

As we have seen, research on the Euler equation approach to aggregate consumption has burgeoned in the last 15 years, largely displacing work on the more traditional "solved out" consumption function. The Euler approach assumes rational expectations and focuses on the intertemporal efficiency condition linking consumption in adjacent periods. The solved out consumption function, in its most basic form, solves the full set of these efficiency conditions stretching to the horizon to derive a solution for consumption in terms of initial assets and human capital, i.e. ‚the present value of current and expected non-property income. There is a widespread belief that estimating an Euler equation corresponding to the optimization problem of a rational, infinitely lived representative agent operating in efficient financial markets without credit or transactions costs or restrictions is somehow more rigorous than trying to develop more comprehensive, realistic, but necessarily approximate models.

Apart from the desire to follow fashion, there are several reasons why a researcher might prefer modelling Euler equations to modelling solved out consumption functions. The first is that, for individual households under rational expectations, taking expectations of the intertemporal efficiency condition eliminates the need to model expectations explicitly and to introduce asset data, which may not always be accurate or easily available. The second is that under uncertainty, with risk-averse behaviour, the individual household Euler equation (5.18) can, in principle, be estimated directly using the generalized method of moments estimator (see Hansen and Singleton, 1981). In contrast, as we have seen in section 4, there does not exist an exact analytical expression for the solved out consumption function for this case, though there are convenient approximations.

However there are five significant reasons for questioning the alleged superiority of the Euler approach. First, except at the microeconomic level in the context of panel data, the advantage that there is a one-to-one connection under the Euler approach between theory and estimation is illusory. If (5.18) held at the micro level, it would not hold for aggregate data as we saw in section 10.1, except under incredible assumptions about households behaving as if life were infinite. Fundamentally, this is because when households die and are replaced (or more than replaced in a growing population) by new households, the information link connecting consumption in adjacent periods is broken. Further, non-linearities and household heterogeneity will complicate the mapping from micro to macro except under special restrictions.

Second, when some households are credit constrained, simplifying approximations for modelling aggregate behaviour are needed in both the Euler and the solved out approaches. This is because the fraction of credit constrained households is not observable and is unlikely to be constant and because not all the credit constrained just spend current income.

Third, knowledge of the parameters of a Euler equation consistent with precautionary behaviour, and hence non-linear in form, would be of limited usefulness for forecasting or policy analysis. To work out the effects of a tax cut or an increase in asset prices on consumption over the next few years necessitates obtaining an explicit solution for consumption of just the type that the solved out consumption function is designed to give. Inevitably, because no analytic solution exists, and because measures of uncertainty and expectations have to be given empirical content, this entails making the kinds of approximations discussed in sections 4 and 11.

Fourth, when a significant fraction of households do not have rational expectations, the martingale or "surprise" formulation of the Euler equation breaks down. Admittedly, in some of the Euler equation literature on excess sensitivity, e.g. Campbell and Mankiw (1989; 1991), the parameter π in (5.63) is interpreted as the proportion of credit constrained or myopic consumers. However, there is no reason why myopic consumers do not save or dissave out of accumulated assets and so no reason for their consumption to be constrained by income. We recognized this possibility in (5.101) in the context of the solved out consumption function.

Finally, because the Euler approach involved something close to first differencing of the data, it throws away long-run information on the levels of consumption, income, assets, and demography. As emphasized in the literature on cointegration and error correction, exploiting such information can convey substantial statistical advantages, providing that measurement errors in such data are stationary.

The usefulness of the solved out approach in decomposing cyclical and secular movements in the savings ratios into different elements such as income growth effects, asset effects, demographic effects, uncertainty effects, and financial liberalization effects was amply demonstrated in section 11.5, despite the inevitable empirical controversies surrounding such interpretations. A North American critic would be likely to accuse such solved out consumption functions of being over-parameterized (i.e. having more parameters than could robustly be estimated from the limited number of observations) and of suffering from simultaneity bias. A response to this is that such models become more credible if broadly similar estimates are obtained for a range of countries with broadly similar institutions; if the models hold up well in predictive tests; if quarterly models, where there is less scope for simultaneity bias, because of lower within-period feedback, give estimates similar to those from annual models; and finally, if the parameter estimates have plausible magnitudes, given both theory and a range of other evidence, e.g. from survey data.

Thus, we conclude that the enthusiasm for the Euler approach and the large-scale abandonment of the solved out approach, particularly in North America, for modelling aggregate consumption has gone too far. This is not to deny that many useful insights have been gleaned from the Euler equation controversies of the last 15 years – in conjunction with the analysis of a great deal of survey data. The latter have suggested that consumption follows income more closely over the life-cycle than the simple rational expectations permanent income hypothesis (REPIH) or its life-cycle equivalent would suggest. The explanation lies largely in a combination of credit constraints, precautionary behaviour under uncertainty, consumption habits depending on previous consumption levels, and, to some extent, in the variation of needs over the life-cycle being correlated with income. Survey data also suggest that the old do not dissave on the textbook scale. The explanation, again, is in terms of uncertainty about income and needs and, to some extent, the bequest motive.

There is some presumption in econometrics, though far from universal (see Gilbert, 1986), in favour of general to specific modelling, i.e. begin with a very general maintained hypothesis and apply a sequential testing procedure of simplifying restrictions to allow the data to speak in arriving at a more parsimonious model. As we have seen, both Euler equations and solved out consumption functions need to incorporate the effects of age (and perhaps other household characteristics), and a reasonable treatment of aggregation over households, precautionary behaviour in the face of uncertainty (which rules out the quadratic utility function and linear rational expectations approach popular in much of the literature), credit constraints, habits or costs of adjustment, and, where relevant, the durability of goods. To obtain tractable models, approximations are essential. We have demonstrated that there is scope for more imaginative use of theoretically based proxies, particularly for the solved out consumption function but also for Euler equations where consumption is modelled directly rather than indirectly via marginal utility (e.g. compare (5.54) with (5.18)).

Much remains to be done. The pooling of micro and macro information to get a better understanding of aggregation issues and hence of the effect of demographic and distributional changes on consumption is a high priority, despite the problems discussed in section 12. The development of good proxies for uncertainty and for income expectations, perhaps drawing on regular survey data, and comparative studies on regions or countries to test different measures on a wide set of sample information, are needed. More work is needed on the spendability of assets with different liquidity characteristics and on relating differences in the spendability of housing wealth across countries to the tax systems, transaction costs, and other institutional features. Potentially, the resulting weighted wealth aggregates could be of major importance in tuning monetary and fiscal policy and in macroeconomic forecasting.

One of the biggest holes, both at the level of theory and of data in the consumption literature and more generally in empirical macroeconomics, concerns variations in credit conditions. Particularly in the 1970s, when negative after-tax interest rates were common, credit rationing was rife, though not necessarily in the form of households wanting to spend more on current consumption than their income. Instead, borrowing at negative interest rates and investing in illiquid assets such as houses, paintings, or equities with more favourable after-tax return prospects than liquid assets was a highly desirable prospect. The freeing of interest rates, financial deregulation, the fall of inflation, and tax reform altered these conditions but asymmetric information between borrowers and lenders ensures that, generally, credit contracts depend not only on price. But few countries have regular surveys of credit conditions in which both financial institutions and households (and firms) are questioned about their perceptions of credit conditions, i.e. what credit contracts are on offer and whether, relative to the past, conditions are tighter or looser. This has made it very difficult to distinguish empirically the effects of financial liberalization on the fall in savings ratios which was such a feature of the 1980s.

Without data on the variation in credit market conditions, it is difficult to undertake the empirical integration of the consumption function with the modelling of portfolio decisions. This was one of the great hopes of the consumption capital asset pricing model (CAPM), a natural spin-off from the Euler equation (see Breeden, 1979; Singleton, 1990). The consumption CAPM examines the set of intertemporal efficiency conditions holding for each of a vector of assets. Unfortunately, realistic specifications of the budget constraints entail non-convex transactions costs and other trading restrictions on illiquid assets. These destroy the simple structure of the consumption CAPM and are not only difficult to articulate, particularly for aggregate data, but also likely to alter as credit conditions alter. This is an important area for research.

To conclude, progress is likely to come from an approach that eschews, at least on macro data, the two extremes of overly demanding theoretical rigour and pure empiricism. One needs to avoid, on the one hand, the theoretical rigour that demands analytical solutions which are precise but only derivable under extreme, unrealistic assumptions; and, on the other, simple empiricism which fails to take on board the many modelling insights which theory has to offer. It is possible to learn both from theory and from data in somewhat more flexible ways than have often been prevalent in the research of the last 15 years.

Notes

We are grateful to Robin Burgess, Gavin Cameron, Matthew Ellman, Lucy White, and especially to Janine Aron, Angus Deaton, and David Hendry, for helpful comments on earlier versions. This research was supported by the ESRC under grants R00023 1184 and R0023 4954.

1 Though real interest rate effects were often found insignificant and omitted.
2 Useful reviews of this literature on aggregate "solved out" consumption functions can be found in Evans (1969) and Modigliani (1975).
3 Cointegration refers to the existence of a stationary linear combination of two or more non-stationary variables: see Granger (1986) and Banerjee et al. (1993) for comprehensive reviews of the issues.
4 Intertemporal utility maximization also underlies Friedman's (1957) permanent income hypothesis (PIH). But Friedman focused not on wealth, retirement, and rate of growth effects but on the measurement links between current and permanent income which explained why, on short-run data, the marginal propensity to consume out of income could be substantially less than one. It is often forgotten that Friedman's consumers have much shorter horizons than do Modigliani and Brumberg's. Friedman (1963) claims that consumers behave in practice as if they applied 33% per annum discount rates to future expected income, giving an effective horizon of only around three years.
5 Note that growth which raises the incomes of cohorts born later, but does not affect income profiles in individual life-cycles, does not have such an expectations effect.
6 However, it is not clear that the causal mechanism is unique for income growth: a higher savings rate may also generate more investment via lower interest rates, if international capital markets are imperfect, and hence more growth, as suggested by some endogenous growth theories.
7 Though Pesaran and Evans (1984) have argued that asset data are riddled with systematic, cumulative errors which quasi-differencing can remove.
8 Skinner (1988), Carroll (1992), and Deaton (1992a, chapter 6) adopt the simulation approach, which has recently come into more widespread use.
9 See Deaton and Muellbauer (1980, chapters 5 and 7) for discussion of the index number and aggregation issues involved in treating a composite bundle of goods and the corresponding price vector as scalar indices.
10 Take logs of (5.3) so that $\ln(1 + r_1) = \ln(1 + r_1^*) - \ln(p_2^e/p_1)$. Then $r_1 \approx r_1^* - \Delta \ln p_2^e$, using the approximation $\ln(1 + x) \approx x$ for small x.
11 Homotheticity has the implication that the ratios of consumption in different periods are independent of income or wealth under linear budget constraints.
12 The approximation can be checked by considering $\ln(\kappa_1 - 1)$ in each of (5.10) and (5.11) and using the result that $\ln(1 + x) \approx x$ when x is small.
13 The equivalence scale thus says that, for higher needs, more consumption is needed to give the same utility (see Deaton and Muellbauer, 1980, chapter 8).
14 Note that $\kappa_{t+1}/(1 + r) = \kappa_t - 1$.
15 In this model consumption responds to news about current and future income. If income follows an ARMA process, then news about current income is also news about tomorrow's income. But it must be emphasized that there can be news about future income which has no influence on current income (e.g. a government announcement about future pension arrangements or tax rates). Accordingly, while

current income may contain much of the news for future income, it is unlikely to contain all of it.

16 Of course, there is no God-given threshold significance level enabling us to make definitive statements about closeness to orthogonality. Hall found that he could reject the joint hypothesis that the coefficients on four lagged income terms were equal to zero at the 10% level, but not at the 5% level. It should be noted that in most ordinary empirical work, a researcher has some theoretical prior about the empirical relevance of a variable, but wishes to eschew incorrect rejection of the null that a coefficient is zero by setting low probabilities of type 1 errors. The benefit of the doubt is therefore accorded to the null. In tests of orthogonality the benefit of the doubt is given to the null of orthogonality, though this is the theory whose "acceptance" we might wish to be conservative about. It is not, however, being suggested that we should establish some non-REPIH model as the null and then test the REPIH against it. The point to emphasize is that a non-rejection of the null of REPIH does not mean that the null is true: the confidence interval around the null must, by definition, include points under the alternative. For an exposition on these points concerning unit root testing see Rudebusch (1993), Christiano and Eichenbaum (1990), and the critical appraisal of Stock (1990).

17 Bilson (1980) models income in terms of lagged labour income, while Blinder and Deaton (1985) included lagged income and lagged stocks of durables among other variables.

18 It should be noted that estimation of (5.31) by OLS replacing ε_t^y by its fitted value produces correct inferences for λ but biases t-statistics for the α_i coefficients upwards (Pagan, 1984).

19 Blinder and Deaton (1985), who incorporate a richer suite of surprises from non-income variables (such as wealth, inflation, and relative prices), however, found no role for anticipated income in the US after all. But they find that anticipated relative prices and inflation matter for current consumption, which still violates the orthogonality assumption of the REPIH.

20 The asymptotic statistical theory underlying these problems of inference is described in detail in Phillips (1986; 1987) and Phillips and Durlauf (1986), while particularly lucid summary expositions are provided by Banerjee and Dolado (1988) and Stock and Watson (1988). Also see the critical papers of Nelson (1987) and Deaton (1987).

21 The first corresponds to an ARIMA (0,1,1) process and the second to an ARIMA(1, 1, 0) process. In an integrated autogressive moving average ARIMA $(p, 1, q)$ process, p is the order of polynomial $\alpha(L)$ in (5.37), 1 indicates the process is I(1), and q is the order of $\lambda(L)$.

22 In countries where non-seasonally adjusted data are routinely available (such as the UK and Australia) the variance of unadjusted consumption is greater than income. Quarterly time series in the US are seasonally adjusted, so that this stylized fact has received less notice than it might. However, in modelling the relative variance of consumption to income, it is valid to control for seasonal variations in tastes (e.g. Christmas, holidays) so that the fact that excess smoothness vanishes with unadjusted data is not by itself inimical to the truth of the observation.

23 Campbell and Mankiw (1987) and Deaton (1987) find high persistence in US output while Perron and Phillips (1987), using non-parametric adjustments for serial correlation, find ambiguous results.

24   Cogley (1990) using real per capita GDP data over the period 1871–1985 for nine
      OECD countries finds strong persistence in Italy, France, Norway, and Australia,
      and weaker persistence in Denmark, Sweden, the UK, Canada, and the US (in
      descending order of measures of persistence). Strong and Tan (1991) find strong
      persistence for Australia, while Cochrane (1988) finds low persistence for the US,
      as does Gagnon (1988) using a somewhat different test procedure.
25   He finds much lower persistence measures for the US if seasonally unadjusted data
      are employed and shows that the X11 filtering which is used to produce seasonal
      adjustment vitiates persistence measures.
26   An equation also incorporating $\ln y$ and $\Delta \ln y$ simplifies to the lag structure shown
      in (5.40).
27   In order to overcome the fact that univariate time-series analysis does not have
      enough information to disentangle transitory and permanent components of a
      series, some studies have used data on other variables. This growing literature has
      found lower measures of persistence than suggested by the univariate approach, but
      nevertheless finds that a large component of output fluctuations is permanent. For
      example, King et al. (1991) calculated the fraction of the variance of the three-
      to five-year-ahead forecast of output (and other variables) which could be traced to
      permanent innovations. They found that permanent components accounted for
      between about 45% and 66% of the forecast variance. Other studies in this vein are
      Lee, Pesaran, and Pierse (1992) for the UK; and Pesaran, Pierse, and Lee (1991),
      Blanchard and Quah (1989), and Cochrane and Sbordane (1988) for the US.
28   If there is transitory consumption, it is important to use information dated $t - 2$
      and before. Campbell finds he cannot reject the REPIH using a one-lag bivariate
      VAR, but can do so using a five-lag bivariate VAR. If transitory consumption is
      thought unimportant, all tests roundly reject the REPIH. Note also that a bivariate
      VAR is not essential to the test, though it is a convenient platform for testing both
      the Granger causality and the restrictions implied by the REPIH. An alternative is
      to simply regress Δc_t on lagged values of saving and differenced income (using data
      lagged two periods and before if the impact of transitory consumption is thought
      to be a concern). The t-tests on the coefficients suggest whether the null of
      orthogonality can be rejected.
29   Christiano (1987) notes that excess smoothness would be apparent even with
      perfectly optimizing forward looking agents if real rates of return and income
      changes were positively correlated. Consumers would then face an incentive to
      save, thus reducing the consumption response to the income innovation.
30   However, there may be other ways round this, for example by scaling the change
      in consumption by lagged income.
31   See Skinner (1988) and Kimball (1990) for a closely related analysis.
32   Kimball (1990) uses the same formulation to define a negative uncertainty pre-
      mium ψ so that $y_2^* = E(y_2) - \psi$. Kimball notes that this takes over the related
      analysis of Pratt (1964) but applies it not to the utility function but to the *marginal*
      utility function.
33   When $A_1 \neq 0$, the discount factor is obtained from

$$y_2^* \approx \left[1 - \frac{\dfrac{A_1(1 + r_1)\sigma z}{E(y_2)}}{1 + \sigma z} \right] \frac{E(y_2)}{(1 + \sigma z)} = \frac{1}{1 + \sigma z^*} E(y_2) \quad \text{say.}$$

The asset level A_1 is endogenous but practical computation involves a simple iteration in which a first estimate of A_0 is used for A_1. This gives a first round estimate of z with which a second estimate of A_1 and so of z can be found.

34 Note that this is the same as ε^*_{t+1} defined in the quasi-difference transformation (5.27), except that, in the latter, the discount factor involves only the interest rate r.

35 Blanchard (1985) derives the continuous time equivalent of (5.53) for aggregate data from a set of microeconomic assumptions without any approximation arguments. These include a survival probability independent of age and point expectations about income.

36 The same approximation technique can also be used to get a Euler equation in the form of the change in log consumption.

37 See Hansen and Singleton (1982) for an alternative approach leading to the same conclusion.

38 In the presence of some belief by households in trend reversion of income, a large negative shock of similar absolute size would result in a smaller consumption reaction in the opposite direction. This suggests some overall stabilization of consumption, though more for positive income shocks than for negative ones.

39 Since similar divorce risks apply to men, given some loss of assets on divorce, such incentives also apply to men.

40 See for example Börsch-Supan and Stahl (1991).

41 They include failure of rational expectations, credit restrictions, a variable and uncertain real interest rate, variable income uncertainty, presence of habits or costs of adjustments, durable goods, non-separability between consumption and other "goods" such as leisure or transactions balances, transitory consumption, and time aggregation.

42 See section 2.1 for a discussion of the limitations, in particular when inflation is high, of such a definition. This suggests an additional reason for a negative inflation effect.

43 Patterson and Pesaran (1992) incorporate a variable real interest rate in (5.63) following Wickens and Molana (1984). Testing parameter stability for the UK in the 1980s, they find π to be constant, but tendencies for lower coefficients on the real interest rate in the 1980s. As in many aggregate Euler equation studies, however, their results are quite sensitive to the instruments chosen.

44 See Deaton and Muellbauer (1980, pp. 310–13) for more discussion, and Blundell (1988) and Blundell, Browning, and Meghir (1994) for evidence on separability between consumption and leisure.

45 The problem of time aggregation refers to a situation in which decision times do not coincide with the units of time over which the data are measured. It arises not only in the attempt to distinguish hypotheses about habits and durability from simpler alternatives: see for example Muellbauer (1988), Heaton (1993), and Ermini (1994) for a more comprehensive discussion. Even in simpler contexts, time aggregation can be important: see for example Hall's (1988) discussion of time aggregation and the measurement of real interest rate effects in Euler equations.

46 Among these are Akerlof (1979) on the optimal holding of money; Akerlof and Yellen (1985; more generally, Gruen, 1988a) on the small costs of believing government bonds are net worth; Cochrane (1989) on the trivial costs of excess sensitivity in consumption; and Deaton (1992b) on simple rules for saving in uncertain environments when there are liquidity constraints. For a literature less grounded in traditional methods and which exploits some survey/experimental evidence see Shefrin and Thaler (1988) and Thaler (1990) on saving and fungibility.

It is interesting to compare Cochrane's approach via Taylor series approximations to those of Hall (1978) in his proof of corollary 5 (p. 987).

47 In Section 11 we consider a formulation which allows some consumers to be myopic and others forward looking.

48 There are previous studies which have allowed different weights on liquid and illiquid assets, e.g. Patterson (1984), and there are a number which have included liquid asset effects, e.g. Zellner, Huang, and Chau (1965), Hendry and von Ungern-Sternberg (1981).

49 Miles (1993) has considered this problem. The derivation that follows reaches the conclusion more simply.

50 For example, one should expect a lower wealth effect where transactions costs are high.

51 In the absence of good house price indices, the price of land is the best proxy.

52 However, not on the basis of formal econometric work or a comprehensive model of consumption.

53 As we saw in section 4, the subjective discount rate δ arguably incorporates the survival probability of households so that older households have higher δs and thus are less likely to plan for consumption growth.

54 Deaton (1992a, pp. 37–43, 65–75, 167–76) has an excellent discussion of these and other aspects of aggregation, such as non-linear functional forms, in the context of Euler equations. Deaton argues that another important reason for the failure of micro-Euler equations such as (5.82) to aggregate to their macro equivalents is that individuals are unlikely to possess the same information sets.

55 In the UK this includes modellers at the Bank of England, the Treasury, Oxford Economic Forecasting, the London Business School, and the National Institute (see Church, Smith, and Wallis, 1994 for a review and comparison of UK models); for Norway, see Brodin and Nymoen (1992); and for Sweden, see Berg and Bergström (1993).

56 The steps in the approximation are considered in Muellbauer and Murphy (1993a).

57 For example, the coefficient, γ, on the asset/income ratio is an increasing function of $r_t + \theta_t$, while the opposite is true of the coefficients, β_{2+s}, on future income growth prospects.

58 Where data are quarterly, habits motivate the inclusion also of a four-quarter lag in consumption in addition to a seasonably varying component of β_0. Seasonal effects are then a mixture of a fixed and an evolving component. Harvey and Scott (1994) find evidence for non-constant seasonality in UK consumption and discuss a stochastic seasonality specification.

59 However, when inflation and interest rates both rise and credit is rationed, a "front-end loading problem" arises for borrowers whose cash debt service payments rise as a bigger fraction of the long-term burden of interest charges and debt repayment is loaded onto the current period. This can give rise to a negative nominal interest rate effect on aggregate spending.

60 Named after the then Chief Economic Adviser and the Chancellor of the Exchequer, respectively (see Muellbauer and Murphy, 1990).

61 A further problem arises from the probable systematic measurement errors in the data discussed in section 12.

62 The evidence in Murata appears to contradict two other possible explanations. First, the positive real interest rate effect is not merely a disguised negative inflation

effect. The hypothesis of equal and opposite signs on the nominal interest rate and the inflation rate can be accepted. Second, this does not appear to be a case of reverse causation or endogeneity bias: if the authorities raise interest rates when consumption growth is too rapid, one might find a positive association between the real interest rate and consumption. However, Japanese short-term interest rates are driven mainly by inflation, US interest rates, and lagged growth. There remains one other possibility. The real interest rate, which was low in the 1970s and rose in the 1980s, may be a proxy for financial liberalization in Japan. This could induce a positive association with consumption.

63 Though it may be that conditioning on retirement status and not on whether someone is over or under 65 would yield somewhat bigger estimates. Earlier retirement and lower participation by the over 65s have been features of the 1970s and 1980s.

References

Acemoglu, D., and A. Scott (1994), "Consumer Confidence and Rational Expectations: Are Agents' Beliefs Consistent with the Theory?," *Economic Journal*, 104, 1–19.

Akerlof, G.A. (1970), "The Market for Lemons," *Quarterly Journal of Economics*, 84, 488–500.

Akerlof, G.A. (1979), "Irving Fisher on His Head: The Consequences of Constant Threshold Target Monitoring of Money Holdings," *Quarterly Journal of Economics*, 93, 169–87.

Akerlof, G.A. and J.L. Yellen (1985), "A Near Rational Model of the Business Cycle with Wage and Price Inertia," *Quarterly Journal of Economics*, Supplement, 100, 823–38.

Alessie, R., and A. Lusardi (1993), "Saving and Income Smoothing: Evidence from Panel Data," CentER, Tilburg University.

Ando, A., and F. Modigliani (1963), "The Life-Cycle Hypothesis of Saving: Aggregate Implications and Tests," *American Economic Review*, 53, 55–84.

Ando, A., and Arthur B. Kennickell (1987), "How Much (or Little) Life Cycle is there in Micro Data? The Cases of the United States and Japan," in Rudiger Dornbusch, Stanley Fischer, and John Bossons (eds), *Macroeconomics and Finance: Essays in Honor of Franco Modigliani*, Cambridge, Mass.: MIT Press, 159–223.

Attanasio, Orazio P., and Guglielmo Weber (1991), "Consumption Growth, the Interest Rate and Aggregation," *Review of Economic Studies*, 61, 19–30.

Attanasio, Orazio P., and Guglielmo Weber (1992), "Consumption Growth and Excess Sensitivity to Income: Evidence from US Micro Data," Stanford University and University College, London (Apr.), mimeo.

Attfield, C.L.F., D. Demery, and N.W. Duck (1990), "Saving and Rational Expectations: Evidence for the UK," *Economic Journal*, 100 (December), 1269–76.

Bai, Jushan, Robin L. Lumsdaine, and James H. Stock (1991), "Testing for and Dating Breaks in Integrated and Cointegrated Time Series," manuscript.

Balke, Nathan S., and Thomas B. Fomby (1991), "Shifting Trends, Segmented Trends and Infrequent Permanent Shocks," *Journal of Monetary Economics*, 28, 61–85.

Ball, R.J., and P.S. Drake (1964), "The Relationship between Aggregate Consumption and Wealth," *International Economic Review*, 5, 63–81.

Banerjee, Anindya, and Juan Dolado (1988), "Tests of the Life-Cycle Permanent Income Hypothesis in the Presence of Random Walks," *Oxford Economic Papers*, 40, 610–33.

Banerjee, Anindya, Robin L. Lumsdaine, and James H. Stock (1992), "Recursive and Sequential Tests of the Unit Root and Trend Break Hypothesis: Theory and International Evidence," *Journal of Business and Economic Statistics*, 10, 271–87.

Banerjee, Anindya, Juan Dolado, John W. Galbraith, and David F. Hendry (1993), *Cointegration, Error-Correction and the Econometric Analysis of Non-Stationary Data*, Oxford: Oxford University Press.

Banks, J., R. Blundell, and I. Preston (1993), "Life-Cycle Allocations and the Consumption Costs of Children," Institute for Fiscal Studies.

Barnett, W.A. (1981), *Consumer Demand and Labor Supply: Goods, Monetary Assets and Time*, Amsterdam: North-Holland.

Barro, Robert J., (1974), "Are Government Bonds Net Wealth?," *Journal of Political Economy*, 82, 1095–117.

Bean, Charles R. (1986), "The Estimation of 'Surprise' Models and the 'Surprise' Consumption Function," *Review of Economic Studies*, 49, 497–516.

Berg, L., and R. Bergström (1993), "Consumption, Income, Wealth and Household Debt: an Econometric Analysis of the Swedish Experience 1970–1992," Working Paper 1993.12, Dept. of Economics, Uppsala University.

Berg, L. (1994), "Household Savings and Debt – the Experience of the Nordic Countries," *Oxford Review of Economic Policy*, Summer.

Bernheim, B.D. (1991), *The Vanishing Nest Egg: ReXections on Saving in America*, New York: Twentieth Century Fund, Priority Press.

Bertola, Giuseppe, and Ricardo J. Caballero (1990), "Kinked Adjustment Costs and Aggregate Dynamics," in Olivier J. Blanchard and Stanley Fischer (eds), *NBER Macroeconomics Annual 1990*, Cambridge, Mass.: MIT Press, 237–95.

Bilson, J.F.O. (1980), "The Rational Expectations Approach to the Consumption Function", *European Economic Review*, 13, 273–99.

Bladen-Hovell, R.C., and G.M. Richards (1983), "Inflation and Australian Savings Behaviour," *Australian Economic Papers*, December, 290–301.

Blanchard, Olivier J. (1985), "Debts, Deficits, and Finite Horizons," *Journal of Political Economy*, 93, 1045–76.

Blanchard, Olivier J., and Danny Quah (1989), "The Dynamic Effects of Aggregate Demand and Supply Shocks," *American Economic Review*, 79 (4), 655–73.

Blanchard, Olivier J., and Stanley Fischer (1989), *Lectures on Macroeconomics*, Cambridge, Mass.: MIT Press.

Blinder, Alan S., and Angus S. Deaton (1985), "The Time Series Consumption Function Revisited," *Brookings Papers on Economic Activity*, 2, 456–521 (includes discussion).

Blundell, R. (1988), "Consumer Behaviour: Theory and Empirical Evidence – A Survey," *Economic Journal*, 98, 16–65.

Blundell, R., M. Browning, and C. Meghir (1994), "Consumer Demand and the Life-Cycle Allocation of Household Expenditures," *Review of Economic Studies*, 61, 57–80.

Börsch-Supan, Axel, and Konrad Stahl (1991), "Life-Cycle Savings and Consumption Constraints. Theory, Empirical Evidence, and Fiscal Implications," *Journal of Population Economics*, 4, 233–55.

Boskin, M.J., and L.J. Lau (1988), "An Analysis of Postwar US Consumption and Saving: Part 1 and Part 2, NBER Working Papers 2605, 2606.

Bosworth, B., G. Burtless, and J. Sabelhaus (1991), "The Decline in Saving: Evidence from Household Surveys," *Brookings Papers on Economic Activity*, 1, 183–256 (with discussion).

Breeden, D.T. (1979), "An Intertemporal Asset Pricing Model with Stochastic Consumption and Investment Opportunities," *Journal of Financial Economics*, 7, 265–96.

Brenner, R., M.G. Dagenais, and C. Montemarquette (1992), "The Declining Saving Rate: an Overlooked Explanation," CRDE Papers, 0792, University of Montreal, Centre of Research and Development in Economics, Montreal.

Brock, W.A. (1982), "Asset Prices in a Production Economy," in J. J. McCall (ed.), *The Economics of Information and Uncertainty*, Chicago: University of Chicago Press.

Brodin, P. Anders, and Ragnar Nymoen (1992), "Wealth Effects and Exogeneity: the Norwegian Consumption Function," *Oxford Bulletin of Economics and Statistics*, 54 (3), 431–54.

Browning, Martin J., Angus S. Deaton, and Margaret Irish (1985), "A Profitable Approach to Labor Supply and Commodity Demands over the Life-Cycle," *Econometrica*, 53, 503–44.

Caballero, R. (1990), "Expenditure on Durable Goods: a Case for Slow Adjustment," *Quarterly Journal of Economics*, 105, 727–43.

Campbell, John Y. (1987), "Does Saving Anticipate Declining Labour Income? An Alternative Test of the Permanent Income Hypothesis," *Econometrica*, 55, 1249–74.

Campbell, John Y., and Angus S. Deaton (1989) "Why is Consumption so Smooth?," *Review of Economic Studies*, 56, 357–74.

Campbell, John Y., and N. Gregory Mankiw (1989), "Consumption, Income and Interest Rates: Reinterpreting the Time Series Evidence," in Olivier J. Blanchard and Stanley Fischer (eds), *NBER Macroeconomic Annual 1989*, Cambridge, Mass.: MIT Press, 185–216.

Campbell, J.Y., and N. Gregory Mankiw (1989), "Are Output Fluctuations Transitory?", *Quarterly Journal of Economics*, 102, 857–80.

Campbell, John Y., and N. Gregory Mankiw (1990), "Permanent Income, Current Income and Consumption," *Journal of Business and Economic Statistics*, 8 (3), 265–79.

Campbell, John Y., and N. Gregory Mankiw (1991), "The Response of Consumption to Income: A Cross-Country Investigation," *European Economic Review*, 35, 715–21.

Carroll, Christopher D., and Lawrence J. Summers (1991), "Consumption Growth Parallels Income Growth: Some New Evidence," in B. Douglas Bernheim and John B. Shoven (eds), *National Saving and Economic Performance*, Chicago: Chicago University Press for NBER, 305–43.

Carroll, Christopher D. (1992), "The Buffer-Stock Theory of Saving: Some Macroeconomic Evidence," *Brookings Papers on Economic Activity*, 2, 61–156 (including discussion).

Carroll, Christopher D., Jeffrey C. Fuhrer, and W. Wilcox (1994), "Does Consumer Sentiment Forecast Household Spending," *American Economic Review*, 84, 1397–1408.

Christiano, Lawrence J. (1987), "Why is Consumption Less Volatile than Income?," *Federal Reserve Bank of Minneapolis*, Fall, 2–20.

Christiano, Lawrence J., and Martin Eichenbaum (1990), "Unit Roots in Real GNP: Do We Know, and Do We Care?," *Carnegie- Rochester Conference Series on Public Policy*, 32, 7–62.

Church, K.B., P.N. Smith, and K.F. Wallis (1994), "Econometric Evaluation of Consumers' Expenditure Equations," *Oxford Review of Economic Policy*, 10, Summer.

Clark, Peter K. (1987), "The Cyclical Component of US Economic Activity," *Quarterly Journal of Economics*, 102 (4), 797–814.

Clarida, Richard H. (1991), "Aggregate Stochastic Implications of the Life-Cycle Hypothesis," *Quarterly Journal of Economics*, 106, 851–67.

Cochrane, John H. (1988), "How Big is the Random Walk Component in GNP?," *Journal of Political Economy*, 96 (5), 893–920.

Cochrane, John H. (1989), "The Sensitivity of Tests of the Intertemporal Allocation of Consumption to Near-Rational Alternatives," *American Economic Review*, 79 (3), 319–37.

Cochrane, John H., and Argia M. Sbordane (1988), "Multivariate Estimates of the Permanent Components of GNP and Stock Prices," *Journal of Economic Dynamics and Control*, 12, 255–96.

Cogley, Timothy (1990), "International Evidence on the Size of the Random Walk in Output," *Journal of Political Economy*, 98 (3), 501–18.

Daly, V., and G. Hadjimatheou (1981), "Stochastic Implications of the Life Cycle–Permanent Income Hypothesis: Evidence for the UK Economy," *Journal of Political Economy*, 89, 596–99.

Darby, J., and I. Ireland (1994), "Consumption, Forward Looking Behaviour and Financial Deregulation," mimeo, University of Strathclyde.

Darby, Michael R. (1987), "The Consumption Function," in the *New Palgrave Dictionary of Economics*, London: Macmillan Press, 614–16.

Davidson, James E.H., and David F. Hendry (1981), "Interpreting Econometric Evidence: The Behaviour of Consumer Expenditure in the UK," *European Economic Review*, 16, 177–92.

Davidson, James E.H., David F. Hendry, Frank Srba, and Stephen Yeo (1978), "Econometric Modelling of the Aggregate Time-Series Relationship between Consumers' Expenditure and Income in the United Kingdom," *Economic Journal*, 88, 661–92.

Deaton, Angus, and John Muellbauer (1980), *Economics and Consumer Behaviour*, Cambridge: CUP.

Deaton, Angus (1985), "Panel Data from a Time-Series of Cross-Sections," *Journal of Econometrics*, 30, 109–26.

Deaton, Angus (1987), "Life-Cycle Models of Consumption: Is the Evidence Consistent with the Theory?" in Truman F. Bewley (ed.), *Advances in Econometrics, Fifth World Congress*, vol. 2, Cambridge and New York: Cambridge University Press, 121–48.

Deaton, Angus (1992a), *Understanding Consumption*, Oxford: Clarendon Press.

Deaton, Angus (1992b), "Household Saving in LDC's: Credit Markets, Insurance and Welfare," *Scandinavian Journal of Economics*, 94, 253–73.

Demery, D., and N.W. Duck (1992), "Are Economic Fluctuations Really Persistent? A Re-interpretation of some International Evidence," *Economic Journal*, 102 (September), 1094–11.

Dewhurst, J.H. (1989), "Australian State Consumption Functions," *Australian Economic Papers*, 28 (52), 112–21.

Dickey, D.A., and W.A. Fuller (1979), "Distribution of the Estimates for Autogressive Time Series with a Unit Root," *Journal of the American Statistical Association*, 74 (366), 427–31.

Diebold, Francis X., and Marc Nerlove (1990), "Unit Roots in Economic Time Series: a Selective Survey," in Thomas B. Fomby and George F. Rhodes (eds), *Advances in*

Econometrics: Cointegration, Spurious Regressions, and Unit Roots, Greenwich, Connecticut: JAI Press, 3–69.

Diebold, Francis X., and Glenn D. Rudebusch (1991), "Is Consumption too Smooth? Long Memory and the Deaton Paradox," *Review of Economics and Statistics*, 73, 1–17.

Engle, R.F., and C.W.J. Granger (1987), "Cointegration and Error Correction: Representation, Estimation and Testing," *Econometrica*, 55, 251–76.

Englund, P. (1990), "Financial Deregulation in Sweden," *European Economic Review*, 34.

Ericsson, Neil R., Julia Campos, and Hong-Anh Tran (1990), "PC-GIVE and David Hendry's Econometric Methodology," *Revista de Econometria*, 10, 7–117.

Ermini, L. (1994), "A Discrete-Time Consumption CAP Model under Durability of Goods, Habit Formation and Temporal Aggregation," mimeo, University of Hawaii, Manoa.

Evans, M.K. (1969), *Macroeconomic Activity*, New York: Harper and Row.

Farrell, M.J. (1959), "The New Theories of the Consumption Function," *Economic Journal*, 69, 678–96.

Faust, John (1992), "Near Observational Equivalence and Unit Root Processes: Formal Concepts and Implications," unpublished MS, Board of Governors of the Federal Reserve, Washington DC.

Feldstein, Martin S. (1977), "Social Security and Private Savings: International Evidence in an Extended Life Cycle Model," in M. Feldstein and R. P. Inman (eds), *The Economics of Public Services*, Macmillan: New York, 174–205.

Feldstein, Martin S. (1980), "International Differences in Social Security and Saving," *Journal of Public Economics*, 82 (5), 905–26.

Feldstein, Martin S. (1995), "College Scholarship Rules and Private Saving," *American Economic Review*, 85, forthcoming.

Ferber, Robert (1965), "The Relability of Consumer Surveys of Financial Holdings: Time Deposits," *Journal of the American Statistical Association*, 65, 148–63.

Ferber, Robert (1966), "The Relability of Consumer Surveys of Financial Holdings: Demand Deposits," *Journal of the American Statistical Association*, 91–103.

Flavin, Marjorie A. (1981), "The Adjustment of Consumption to Changing Expectations about Future Income," *Journal of Political Economy*, 89 (5), 974–1009.

Flemming, J.S. (1973), "The Consumption Function when Capital Markets are Imperfect," *Oxford Economic Papers*, 25, 160–72.

Friedman, Milton (1957), *A Theory of the Consumption Function*, Princeton: Princeton University Press.

Friedman, Milton (1963), "Windfalls, the 'Horizon' and Related Concepts," in Carl Christ et al. (eds), *Measurement in Economics: Studies in Mathematical Economics and Econometrics in Memory of Yeluda Grunfeld*, Stanford: Stanford University Press, 1–28.

Fuhrer, Jeffrey C. (1993), "What Role Does Consumer Sentiment Play in the US Macroeconomy?," *New England Economic Review*, Jan./Feb.

Fuller, Wayne A. (1976), *Introduction to Statistical Time Series*, New York: Wiley.

Gagnon, Joseph E. (1988), "Short Run Models and Long Run Forecasts: A Note on the Permanence of Output Fluctuations," *Quarterly Journal of Economics*, 103 (2), 415–24.

Gali, Jordi (1990), "Finite Horizons, Life-Cycle Savings and Time-Series Evidence on Consumption," *Journal of Monetary Economics*, 26, 433–52.

Gali, Jordi (1991), "Budget Constraints and Time-Series Evidence on Consumption," *American Economic Review*, 81, 1238–53.

Garner, C. Alan (1992), "Forecasting Consumer Spending: Should Economists Pay Attention to Consumer Confidence Surveys?," Federal Reserve Bank of Kansas City, *Economic Review*, May/June.

Ghysels, Eric (1990), "Unit-Root Tests and the Statistical Pitfalls of Seasonal Adjustment: The Case of US Postwar Real Gross National Product," *Journal of Business and Economic Statistics*, 8 (2), 145–51.

Gilbert, C. (1986), "Professor Hendry's Econometric Methodology," *Oxford Bulletin of Economics and Statistics*, 48, 283–307.

Granger, C.W.J. (1986), "Developments in the Study of Cointegrated Economic Variables," *Oxford Bulletin of Economics and Statistics*, 48, 213–28.

Grossman, S.J., and R. Shiller (1981), "The Determinants of the Variability of Stock Market Prices," *American Economic Review*, Papers and Proceedings, May, 222–7.

Grossman, S.J., and Guy Laroque (1990), "Asset Pricing and Optimal Portfolio Choice in the Presence of Illiquid Durable Consumption Goods," *Econometrica*, 58, 25–51.

Gruen, David W.R. (1988a), "Ignorance and Ricardian Equivalence (or Keynesians of the World Unite, You Have Nothing to Lose but your Bonds)," *Working Papers in Economics and Econometrics*, no. 165, Australian National University, Canberra.

Gruen, David W.R. (1988b), "What People Know and What Economists Think They Know: Surveys on Ricardian Equivalence," *Working Papers in Economics and Econometrics*, no. 164, Australian National University, Canberra.

Haig, R.M. (1921), "The Concept of Income: Economic and Legal Aspects," reprinted in R.A. Musgrove and C.S. Shoup (eds), *Readings in the Economics of Taxation*, Homewood, III.: Irwin, 54–76.

Hall, Robert E. (1978), "Stochastic Implications of the Life Cycle–Permanent Income Hypothesis: Theory and Evidence," *Journal of Political Economy*, 96, 971–87.

Hall, Robert E. (1988), "Intertemporal Substitution in Consumption," *Journal of Political Economy*, 96, 339–57.

Hall, Robert, E., and Federic S. Mishkin (1982), "The Sensitivity of Consumption to Transitory Income: Estimates from Panel Data on Households," *Econometrica*, 50, 461–81.

Hall, Stephen, and Andrew Scott (1990), "Seasonal Unit Roots, Structural Breaks and Cointegration," Discussion Paper, 24–90, Centre for Economic Forecasting, London Business School, London.

Hamilton, James D. (1989), "A New Approach to the Economic Analysis of Nonstationary Time Series and the Business Cycle," *Econometrica*, 57 (2), 357–84.

Hansen, Lars Peter, and Thomas J. Sargent (1981), "A Note on Wiener-Kolmogorov Forecasting Formulas for Rational Expectations Models," *Economics Letters*, 8, 253–60.

Hansen, Lars Peter, and Kenneth J. Singleton (1982), "Generalized Instrumental Variables Estimation of Non-Linear Rational Expectations Models," *Econometrica*, 50, 1269–86.

Hansen, Lars Peter, and Kenneth J. Singleton (1983), "Stochastic Consumption, Risk Aversion, and the Temporal Behavior of Asset Returns," *Journal of Political Economy*, 91 (2), 249–65.

Harvey, Andrew C. (1985), "Trends and Cycles in Macroeconomic Time Series," *Journal of Business and Economics Statistic*, 3, 216–27.

Harvey, Andrew C. (1989), *Forecasting, Structural Time Series Models and the Kalman Filter*, Cambridge: Cambridge University Press.

Harvey, Andrew C. (1990), *The Econometric Analysis of Time Series*, 2nd edn, New York: Philip Allan.

Harvey, Andrew C., and A. Jaeger (1993), "Detrending, Stylized Facts and the Business Cycle," *Journal of Applied Econometrics*, 8, 231–48.

Harvey, Andrew C., and Andrew Scott (1995), "Seasonality in Dynamic Regression Models," *Economic Journal*, 104, 1324–45.

Hatsopolous, G.N.P., R. Krugman, and J.M. Poterba (1989), *Overconsumption: The Challenge to US Policy*, Washington DC: American Business Conference.

Hayashi, Fumio (1982), "The Permanent Income Hypothesis: Estimation and Testing by Instrumental Variables," *Journal of Political Economy*, 90, 895–916.

Hayashi, Fumio (1985), "The Effect of Liquidity Constraints on Consumption: A Cross-Sectional Analysis," *Quarterly Journal of Economics*, 100, 183–206.

Hayashi, Fumio (1986), "Why is Japan's Saving Rate so Apparently High?," *NBER Macroeconomic Annual*.

Hayashi, Fumio (1987), "Tests for Liquidity Constraints: a Critical Survey and Some New Observations," in Truman F. Bewley (ed.), *Advances in Econometrics: Fifth World Congress*, 1–120.

Heaton, J. (1993), "The Interactions between Time-Non-Separable Preferences and Time Aggregation," *Econometrica*, 61, 353–85.

Hendry, David F., and Thomas von Ungern-Sternberg (1981), "Liquidity and Inflation Effects on Consumer's Expenditure," in A. S. Deaton (ed.), *Essays in Theory and Measurement of Consumers' Behaviour*, Cambridge: Cambridge University Press, 237–60.

Hendry, David F. (1988), "The Encompassing Implications of Feedback versus Feedforward Mechanisms in Econometrics," *Oxford Economic Papers*, 40, 132–49.

Hendry, David F., John N.J. Muellbauer, and Anthony Murphy (1990), "The Econometrics of DHSY," *A Century of Economics: 100 Years of the Royal Economic Society and the Economic Journal*, Oxford: Basil Blackwell, 298–334.

Henry, David F. (1994), "HUS Revisited," *Oxford Review of Economic Policy*, 10, Summer.

Hicks, J.R. (1946), *Value and Capital*, Oxford: Clarendon Press.

Horioka, Charles (1990), "Why is Japan's Saving Rate so High? A Literature Survey," *Journal of Japanese and International Economies*, 4, 49–92.

Hubbard, R.G., J. Skinner, and S.P. Zeldes (1994), "Precautionary Saving and Social Insurance," NBER Working Paper, 4884.

Jappelli, Tullio, and Marco Pagano (1989), "Consumption and Capital Market Imperfections: an International Comparison," *American Economic Review*, 79, 1088–105.

Johnson, Paul (1983), "Life-Cycle Consumption under Rational Expectations: Some Australian Evidence," *Economic Record*, 59 (167), 345–50.

Jones, Stephen R.J., and James H. Stock (1987), "Demand Disturbances and Aggregate Fluctuations: The Implication of Near-Rationality," *Economic Journal*, 97, 49–64.

Jorgenson, Dale W. (1963), "Capital Theory and Investment Behaviour," *American Economic Review*, Supplement, 53, 247–59.

Kennedy, Neale, and Palle Andersen (1994), "Household Saving and Real House Prices: An International Perspective," Basle: Bank for International Settlements.

Kennickell, A.B. (1990), "Demographics and Household Saving," Federal Reserve Board, Washington: Finance and Economics Discussion Series, Paper 123.

Kimball, Miles (1990), "Precautionary Saving in the Small and in the Large," *Econometrica*, 58, 53–73.

King, Robert G., Charles I. Plosser, James H. Stock, and Mark W. Watson (1991), "Stochastic Trends and Economic Fluctuations," *American Economic Review*, 81 (4), 819–40.

Klein, L.R., and A.S. Goldberger (1955), *An Econometric Model of the Unites States 1929–1952*, Amsterdam: North-Holland.

Koopman, S.J., A.C. Harvey, J.A. Doornick, and N. Shephard (1995), *STAMP 5.0: Structural Time Series Analyses and Predictor*, London: Chapman and Hall.

Koskela, Erkki, Heikki A. Loikkanen, and Matti Viren (1992), "House Prices, Household Savings and Financial Market Liberalisation in Finland," *European Economic Review*, 36 (2/3), 549–58.

Kotlikoff, Laurence J. (1988), "Integenerational Transfers and Savings," *Journal of Economic Perspectives*, 2, 41–58.

Kotlikoff, Laurence J., and Lawrence H. Summers (1981), "The Role of Intergenerational Transfers in Aggregate Capital Formation," *Journal of Political Economy*, 89, 706–32.

Kotlikoff, Laurence J., W. Samuelson, and S. Johnson (1988), "Consumption, Computation Mistakes and Fiscal Policy," *American Economic Association Papers and Proceedings*, 78 (2), 408–12.

Kreps, David M. (1988), *Notes on the Theory of Choice*, Boulder, Colorado: Westview Press.

Lattimore, R. (1993), *Consumption and Saving in Australia*, Oxford D Phil thesis.

Lattimore, R. (1994), "Australian Consumption and Saving," *Oxford Review of Economic Policy*, Summer.

Lee, Kevin C., M. Hashem Pesaran, and Richard G. Pierse (1992), "Persistence of Shocks and their Sources in a Multisectoral Model of UK Output Growth," *Economic Journal*, 102, 342–56.

Lehmussaari, O.P. (1990), "Deregulation and Consumption Saving Dynamics in the Nordic Countries," *IMF Stav Papers*, 37, no. 1.

Lippi, Marco, and Lucrezia Reichlin (1992), "On Persistence of Shocks to Economic Variables," *Journal of Monetary Economics*, 29 (1), 87–93.

Lucas, Robert E. (1976), "Econometric Policy Evaluation: a Critique," *Carnegie-Rochester Conference Series Supplement to the Journal of Monetary Economics*, 1, 19–46.

Lucas, Robert E. (1978), "Asset Prices in an Exchange Economy," *Econometrica*, 46, 1429–45.

MacDonald, Ronald, and Colm Kearney (1990), "Consumption, Cointegration and Rational Expectations: Some Australian Evidence," *Australian Economic Papers*, 29 (54), 40–52.

Mankiw, N.G. (1982), "Hall's Consumption Hypothesis and Durable Goods," *Journal of Monetary Economics*," 10, 417–25.

Mankiw, N.G., and M. Shapiro (1985), "Trends, Random Walks and Tests of the Permanent Income Hypothesis," *Journal of Monetary Economics*, 16, 165–74.

Mankiw, N.G., and M. Shapiro (1986), "Do We Reject Too Often? Small Sample Properties of Tests of Rational Expectations Models," *Economics Letters*, 20 (2), 139–45.

Miles, D. (1993), "House Price Shocks and Consumption with Forward Looking Households," mimeo, Birkbeck College, London.

Modigliani, Franco, and Richard Brumberg (1954), "Utility Analysis and the Consumption Function: an Interpretation of the Cross-Section Data," *Post-Keynesian Economics*, New Brunswick, New Jersey: Rutgers University Press.

Modigliani, Franco (1975), "The Life-Cycle Hypothesis of Saving Twenty Years Later," in M.J. Parkin and A.R. Nobay (eds), *Contemporary Issues in Economics: Proceedings of the AUTE Conference, 1973*, Manchester: Manchester University Press, 2–36.

Modigliani, Franco, and Richard Brumberg (1979), "Utility Analysis and the Consumption Function: an Attempt at Integration," in Andrew Abel (ed.), *The Collected Papers of Franco Modigliani*, vol. 2, Cambridge, Mass.: MIT Press, 128–97.

Modigliani, Franco (1988) "The Role of Integenerational Transfers and Life Cycle Saving in the Accumulation of Wealth," *Journal of Economic Perspectives*, 2 (2) 15–40.

Modigliani, Franco (1990), "Recent Declines in the Savings Rate: a Life Cycle Perspective," Frisch Lecture, Sixth World Congress of the Econometric Society, Barcelona (Aug.), mimeo.

Muellbauer, John (1983), "Surprises in the Consumption Function," *Economic Journal (Supplement)*, 93, 34–50.

Muellbauer, John, and Olympia Bover (1986), "Liquidity Constraints and Aggregation in the Consumption Function under Uncertainty," Discussion Paper, 12, Institute of Economics and Statistics, Oxford.

Muellbauer, John (1988), "Habits, Rationality and Myopia in the Life-Cycle Consumption Function," *Annales d'économie et de statistique*, 9, 47–70.

Muellbauer, John, and Anthony Murphy (1990), "Is the UK Balance of Payments Sustainable?," *Economic Policy*, 347–82.

Muellbauer, John, and Anthony Murphy (1993a), "Income Expectations, Wealth and Demography in the Aggregate US Consumption Function," Unpublished Paper Presented to the HM Treasury Academic Panel, Nuffield College, Oxford University, Oxford.

Muellbauer, John, and Anthony Murphy (1993b), "Income Expectations, Wealth and Demography in the Aggregate UK Consumption Function," Unpublished Paper Presented to the HM Treasury Academic Panel, Nuffield College, Oxford University, Oxford.

Muellbauer, John, and Anthony Murphy (1994), "Explaining Regional Consumption in the UK," mimeo, Nuffield College.

Murata, K. (1994), "The Consumption Function in Japan," Oxford MPhil Thesis.

Muth, John F. (1960), "Optimal Properties of Exponentially Weighted Forecasts," *Journal of the American Statistical Association*, 55, 299–306.

Nelson, Charles R., and Charles I. Plosser (1982), "Trends and Random Walks in Macroeconomic Time Series," *Journal of Monetary Economics*, 10, 139–62.

Nelson, Charles R. (1987), "A Re-appraisal of Recent Tests of the Permanent Income Hypothesis," *Journal of Political Economy*, 65, 641–6.

Pagan, Adrian R. (1984), "Econometric Issues in the Analysis of Regressions with Generated Regressors," *International Economic Review*, 25 (1), 221–45.

Patterson, K.D. (1984), "Net Liquid Assets and Net Illiquid Assets in the UK Consumption Function: Some Evidence for the UK," *Economics Letters*, 14 (4), 389–95.

Patterson, K.D., and B. Pesaran (1992), "The Intertemporal Elasticity of Substitution in the US and the UK," *Review of Economics and Statistics*, 74, 573–84.

Perron, Pierre (1989), "The Great Crash, the Oil Price Shock and the Unit Root Hypothesis," *Econometrica*, 57 (6), 1361–401.

Perron, Pierre, (1990), "Testing for a Unit Root in a Time Series with a Changing Mean," *Journal of Business and Economic Statistics*, 8 (2), 153–62.

Pesaran, M. Hashem, and R.A. Evans (1984), "Inflation, Capital Gains and UK Personal Savings: 1951–1981," *Economic Journal*, 94, 237–57.

Pesaran, M. Hashem (1987), *The Limits to Rational Expectations*, Oxford: Basil Blackwell.

Pesaran, M. Hashem R.G. Pierse, and K.C. Lee (1993), "Persistence, Cointegration and Aggregation: a Disaggregated Analysis of Output Fluctuations in the US Economy," *Journal of Econometrics*, 56, 57–88.

Phillips, P.C.B. (1986), "Understanding Spurious Regressions in Econometrics," *Journal of Econometrics*, 33, 311–40.

Phillips, P.C.B., and S.N. Durlauf (1986), "Multiple Time Series Regression with Integrated Regressors," *Review of Economic Studies*, 53, 473–95.

Phillips, P.C.B. (1987), "Time Series Regression with a Unit Root," *Econometrica*, 55, 277–301.

Pischke, Jörn-Steffen (1991), "Individual Income, Incomplete Information and Aggregate Consumption," Industrial Relations Section Working Paper no. 289, Princeton University, mimeo.

Poterba, J. (1991), "Dividends, Capital Gains, and the Corporate Veil: Evidence from OECD Nations", in B.D. Bernheim and J.B. Shoven (eds), *National Saving and Economic Performance*, Chicago: Chicago University Press for NBER.

Pratt, J.W. (1964), "Risk Aversion in the Small and the Large," *Econometrica*, 32, 122–36.

Quah, Danny (1990), "Permanent and Transitory Movements in Labour Income: an Explanation for 'Excess Smoothness' in Consumption," *Journal of Political Economy*, 98 (3), 449–74.

Rappoport, Peter, and Lucrezia Reichlin (1989), "Segmented Trends and Non-Stationary Time Series," *Economic Journal (Conference)*, 99, 168–77.

Rudebusch, Glenn D. (1993), "The Uncertain Unit Root in Real GNP," *American Economic Review*, 83 (1), 264–72.

Sefton, J.A., and M.R. Weale (1995), *Reconcilation of National Income and Expenditure: Balanced Estimates of National Income for the UK, 1920–1990*, Cambridge: Cambridge University Press.

Shefrin, H.M., and R.H. Thaler (1988), "The Behavioural Life- Cycle Hypothesis," *Economic Inquiry*, 26 (4), 609–43.

Simons, Henry (1938), *Personal Income Taxation*, Chicago: Chicago University Press.

Simon, Herbert A. (1978), "Rationality as Process and as Product of Thought," *American Economic Review*, 68 (May), 1–16.

Singleton, Kenneth (1990), "Specification and Estimation of Intertemporal Asset Pricing Models," in Benjamin M. Friedman and Frank H. Hahn (eds), *Handbook of Monetary Economics*, vol. I, Amsterdam: North-Holland, 583–626.

Skinner, Jonathan (1988), "Risky Income, Life-Cycle Consumption, and Precautionary Saving," *Journal of Monetary Economics*, 22, 237–55.

Slesnick, D.T. (1992), "Aggregate Consumption and Saving in the Post War US," *Review of Economics and Statistics*, 74, 585–97.

Spiro, A. (1962), "Wealth and the Consumption Function," *Journal of Political Economy*, 70, 339–54.

Stock, James H., and Mark W. Watson (1988), "Variable Trends in Economic Time Series," *Journal of Economic Perspectives*, 2 (3), 147–74.

Stock, James H., and Kenneth D. West (1988), "Integrated Regressors and Tests of the Permanent Income Hypothesis," *Journal of Monetary Economics*, 21, 85–96.

Stock, James H. (1990), "Unit Roots in Real GNP: Do We Know and Do We Care? A Comment," *Carnegie-Rochester Conference Series on Public Policy*, 32, 63–82.

Stock, James H. (1995), "Unit Root and Trend Breaks in Econometrics," to appear in M.H. Peseran and M. Wickens (eds), *The Handbook of Applied Econometrics*, vol. IV.

Stone, J.R.N., D.G. Champerowne, and J.E. Meade (1942), "The Precision of National Income Estimates," *Review of Economic Studies*, 9, 111–35.

Stone, Richard (1964), "Private Saving in Britain: Past, Present and Future," *Manchester School of Economic and Social Studies*, 32, 79–112.

Strong, Sam, and Stew Ping Tan (1991), "The Australian Business Cycle: its Definition and Existence." *Economic Record*, 67, 115–25.

Summers, Lawrence H. (1991), "The Scientific Illusion in Empirical Macroeconomics," *Scandinavian Journal of Economics*, 93 (2), 129–48.

Thaler, Richard H. and H.M. Shefrin (1981). "An Economic Theory of Self-Control," *Journal of Political Economy*, 89, 392–405.

Thaler, Richard H. (1990), "Anomalies: Saving, Fungibility, and Mental Accounts," *Journal of Economic Perspectives*, 4 (1), 193–205.

Tobin, J. (1972), "Wealth, Liquidity and the Propensity to Consume," in B. Strumpel, J. N. Morgan, and E. Zahn (eds), *Human Behaviour in Economic Affairs (Essays in Honor of George S. Katona)*, Amsterdam: Elsevier.

Tversky, Amos, and Daniel Kahneman (1974), "Judgment under Uncertainty: Heuristics and Biases," *Science*, 185, 1124–31.

Weale, M.R. (1990), "Wealth Constraints and Consumer Behaviour," *Economic Modelling*, 7, 165–75.

Wickens, M.R., and H. Molana (1984), "Stochastic Life-Cycle Theory with Varying Interest Rates and Prices," *Economic Journal*, 94, Supplement, 133–47.

Wilcox, David W., (1991), "The Construction of the US Consumption Data: Some Facts and their Implications for Empirical Work," Board of Governors of the Federal Reserve System, mimeo.

Zellner, A.D.S. Huang, and L.C. Chau (1965), "Further Analysis of the Short-run Consumption Function with Emphasis on the Role of Liquid Assets," *Econometrica*, 33, 571–81.

6

Large-Scale Macroeconometric Modeling

Kenneth F. Wallis

E17 C50

1 Introduction

Large-scale econometric models of national economies estimated from time series data have developed substantially since the pioneering work of Tinbergen (1937; 1939) and Klein (1947; 1950). They have benefited from advances in economic theory and econometric methods, improvements in the availability and quality of data, and a series of revolutions in computing. The resulting models are in regular use in forecasting and policy analysis in most of the Western economies, and several multi-country models have been constructed. Bodkin, Klein, and Marwah (1991) survey the history of macroeconometric model-building world-wide; Wallis (1994) reproduces, with an introduction, 40 of the key articles that have contributed to the development of macroeconometric modelling, interpreted more broadly to cover model formulation, analysis, and application. The experience of policy analyst-advisers is that macroeconometric models provide "a formal and quantified framework [that] is an irreplaceable adjunct to the processes of policy thought" (Higgins, 1988) and that there is no real alternative.

This chapter provides an account of some recent developments in this area of applied econometrics, restricting attention to the "systems of equations approach," contrasted with the "calibration approach" by Kim and Pagan (chapter 7 in this volume). First, by way of background, section 2 presents a brief review of developments in the economic structure of the models, drawing on reviews by Wallis and Whitley (1991a; 1991b). Although this has been a continuous development process, of particular importance are the changes that were prompted by the inability of existing models, with their overemphasis on effective demand, to deal with the supply-side shocks that became more prevalent in the 1970s.

The main focus of the chapter is then on some technical issues in macroeconometric modelling and the methods that have been developed to handle them. Three areas are considered. First, section 3 is concerned with the evaluation of forecasts, and the use of forecasts to evaluate models. Next, section 4 considers the use of stochastic simulation techniques, which apply to a range of problems which require a description of the probability distribution of possible outcomes that is more complete than a single point forecast. Finally, section 5 returns to a development in the structure of the models touched on in section 2, namely the incorporation of the rational expectations hypothesis or, to be more precise, the adoption of an explicit forward-looking treatment, using model-consistent solution procedures, of unobserved expectations variables. Extensions of standard methods to these new circumstances are considered, for a range of applications.

2   The Structure of Macroeconometric Models

The size and structure of economy-wide models reflect the different purposes for which they are built. In econometrics generally three purposes are typically distinguished, namely structural analysis, forecasting, and policy evaluation, in Intriligator's (1978) terms. In macroeconometric modelling these need to be further elaborated, in particular with respect to the level of aggregation, both sectoral and temporal. The latter is related to the time horizon over which forecasting and policy evaluation are conducted, short-term forecasting usually being based on a quarterly model, whereas an annual model may suffice for medium-term analysis. The attention given to structural analysis – the "scientific" purpose of econometrics – is reflected in differences across models and over time in the relative weights given to economic theory and empirical evidence in model specification.

Different purposes tend to be associated with the different institutions that construct and maintain models, although many of these pursue all three purposes, at least to some degree. Three categories can again be distinguished, namely government, academic, and corporate institutions. The size of models maintained by government agencies is often relatively large, reflecting the amount of detail their analysis requires. Thus a finance ministry needs a model with an elaborate fiscal sector, to track the economic response to the various tax and expenditure policy instruments available to it, while a central bank needs an elaborate monetary sector, to monitor stocks and flows of a range of monetary assets and the response of these and the economy more generally to such policy instruments as the interest rates it controls. The focus of other agencies on energy, housing, or transport questions, for example, may result in the development of "satellite" systems to be used alongside a "core" macroeconomic system whenever interactions between the two play an important part in the analysis. Questions of industrial policy and performance may require detailed sectoral analysis, with an input–output model being integrated into the macro system. Such questions also arise among the clients of commercial modellers, consultants, and so forth, who again require a model that supports disaggregate as well as aggregate analysis. Regional disaggregation may also be of importance, given an adequate database.

The scientific purpose of econometrics – the testing, elucidation, and development of economic theories – receives greater attention from academic modellers. These are groups based in universities and research institutes, or even individual modellers, Fair in the United States and Murphy in Australia being leading examples (see Fair, 1984 and other references below; and Murphy, 1988; 1992). Many academic groups nevertheless engage in forecasting and policy analysis too, and policy analyst-advisers in government may also base their thinking on academic models. Models designed around an underlying coherent theoretical structure are typically smaller than those described in the preceding paragraph – around 100 equations, say – and if used for forecasting are confined to broad macroeconomic aggregates. Procedures for reducing a large model to a smaller structural representation have also been devised (see for example Masson, 1988) with a similar objective, namely to make the theoretical structure more transparent and the core theoretical properties more tractable. In the remainder of this section we discuss some recent trends in the development of the core theoretical structure of macroeconometric models, leaving the question of the size of the model on one side.

As a baseline we consider the mainstream models of the early 1970s, overemphasizing effective demand, as noted above, that were about to be so rudely shocked by commodity price fluctuations and the 1974–5 recession, as described by Wallis (1989, section II). These models were developed around the national income–expenditure accounting framework, and had their origins in Keynesian IS–LM analysis – the "little apparatus" of Hicks (1937) – augmented to include dynamic adjustment processes and government and foreign sectors. Thus the level of output was determined through the components of the accounting identity: consumers' expenditure, fixed investment, stockbuilding, government current expenditure, and exports minus imports. With government expenditure predetermined, other components were largely demand-driven: consumers' expenditure as a function of real income, with an allowance for changes in credit conditions; fixed investment as an accelerator relationship; stockbuilding with reference to a target stock–output ratio; and exports and imports as functions of aggregate demand, foreign or domestic, and relative prices or costs. In this way the IS schedule was determined, in the face of a near perfectly elastic LM schedule. Monetary considerations were largely ignored, with interest rates virtually the only channel of influence of monetary policy. Moreover, the low interest elasticity of the expenditure components meant that the IS schedule was relatively steep, so considerable strength was imparted to fiscal policy. The implicit assumption was that the aggregate supply schedule was fairly elastic up to the "full employment" level of unemployment, but this was not explicitly modelled, being based on exogenous labour-force projections together with some judgement as to the level of structural and frictional unemployment. The potential supply of output was not part of the formal model either, but could be calculated from an assumed trend level of productivity growth and the exogenous labour-force growth. The resulting estimates of the degree of spare capacity could be used for demand-management considerations, but there was little role for excess demand in price or wage adjustment, with prices being largely a mark-up on costs, and wages being determined by Phillips curves in which the response of wage inflation to unemployment was often difficult to pin down. With output determined largely by demand the role of the production function was limited to the provision of a theoretical underpinning for the demand for labour, but even here a statement about the underlying production function was not always forthcoming. Factor prices were typically absent from factor demand equations. As more and more exchange rates floated following the collapse of Bretton Woods they could no longer be treated as exogenous variables, but exchange controls often remained and there were insufficient data on the new regimes for successful modelling.

Areas of subsequent development are indicated by several of the above statements about what the models did not include. An important stimulus for change was the inability of the models to cope with the coexistence, not previously experienced, of rapid inflation and high unemployment, leading into recession. Not only were the models' predictions "wildly incorrect," but Lucas and Sargent (1978) in their well-known polemic went on to argue "that the difficulties are fatal: that modern macroeconomic models are of no value in guiding policy and that this condition will not be remedied by modifications along any line which is currently being pursued." In their view the models should be replaced by equilibrium models which assume that prices and quantities continuously clear markets and that agents continuously optimize, which in turn leads to the imposition of the hypothesis of rational expectations. In such equilibrium or "new classical" models, fluctuations are caused by agents' reactions to unanticipated shocks. Mainstream modellers disagreed, and responded not by abandoning their models, but by amending and extending them, seeking to remedy the deficiencies to which the recent experience had drawn attention. And by the end of the decade the advice that they should be abandoned was itself amended, Lucas (1980) observing: "To what extent this forecast error should be interpreted as a 'fatal' error in models based on the neoclassical synthesis or simply as one suggesting some modifications is not so easy to determine." Nevertheless the theoretical criticism was itself an important stimulus for change, and modellers sought to achieve greater theoretical consistency: in respect of a better articulated macroeconomic framework incorporating both demand and supply; in respect of internal consistency, for example in the joint determination of output, prices, and the demand for factors of production; and more generally in respect of a stronger foundation in optimizing behaviour. Finally change was also stimulated by a shift in the emphasis of policy, in the face of the increased amplitude of short-term forecast errors in the mid 1970s, away from the fine tuning of demand and towards a more medium-term orientation.

All three forces worked in the same direction and resulted in greater attention to the supply side. (In France this had been somewhat anticipated by models built in the late 1960s to support the preparation of the "Plan," as described by Courbis, 1991.) As Nickell (1988) explains, the key parts of the supply side are represented by those equations that describe the behaviour of firms and those that reflect the determination of wages. Goods and labour markets are treated as imperfectly competitive; firms set output, prices, and factor demands consistently in this framework; and the most general form of wage equation is generated by the collective bargaining approach. Important questions are then whether a model possesses a non-accelerating inflation rate of unemployment (NAIRU), that is, whether the long-run aggregate supply schedule is vertical, and what causes it to shift. This leads to the testing and possible imposition of static homogeneity in wage and price equations. Whereas the NAIRU may itself depend on the steady-state rate of inflation if the wage and price equations do not in addition exhibit dynamic homogeneity or inflation neutrality, it is increasingly the case that this property does hold, so that the NAIRU is indeed the "natural" rate of unemployment, independent of the inflation rate but depending on supply-side "wage push" variables.

The supply side of a macroeconometric model determines its long-run properties, which means that one cannot be studied without the other. In model specification and model analysis, increased attention to the supply side has therefore called for increased attention to the long-run or steady-state implications of dynamic econometric models, from both a system perspective and a single-equation perspective. Greater emphasis on the underlying theoretical structure pushes in the same direction, since economic theory has most to say about the long run, and somewhat less to say about the process of short-run adjustment. From a system perspective this has led to the development of techniques to analyse the model's steady-state properties directly, rather than through numerical solution over an extended forecast horizon; see for example Malgrange (1989), Murphy (1992), and Wallis and Whitley (1987).

From a single-equation perspective considerable use has been made of the dynamic specification introduced by Sargan (1964), Marglin (1975), and Davidson et al. (1978), now known as the error correction model, following Phillips' (1957) use of this term in a control theory context. This model provides a convenient representation of the long-run implications of a dynamic model, together with a more data-based specification of the process of short-run adjustment. Of more recent importance is its direct connection with the statistical notion of cointegrated series, although care needs to be taken not to equate unthinkingly the statistician's cointegrating vector and the economist's long-run relationship. A different strand of the literature has used intertemporal optimizing theory to suggest suitable dynamic specifications –

the "Euler equation approach" – and so shift the basis of short-run dynamics from data back to theory. This requires the specification of the functional form of the underlying objective functions, and Nickell (1985) shows that a synthesis between the error correction approach and the Euler equation approach can be achieved if these are assumed to be quadratic. The interrelations between the two approaches, in the context of integrated series, are further explored by Dolado, Galbraith, and Banerjee (1991) and Gregory, Pagan, and Smith (1993).

Intertemporal optimizing models often incorporate the rational expectations hypothesis, which featured more generally in theoretical developments in the 1970s. In the United States it was associated in particular with new classical equilibrium business cycle models and the policy ineffectiveness proposition, although Barro and Fischer's (1976) survey drew a clear distinction between the rational expectations hypothesis as a theory of expectations and the type of equilibrium model in which it was typically embodied at the time. This distinction was blurred by leading US forecasters: in discussing the "rational expectations school" both Eckstein (1983) and Klein (1986) associate the rational expectations hypothesis with the policy ineffectiveness proposition, and Klein, Friedman, and Able (1983) describe the "many ways in which the thinking of monetarists and proponents of rational expectations are congruent." Given the opposition of the mainstream modellers to these positions it is perhaps not surprising that the rational expectations hypothesis was not widely embraced in US models, although Taylor (1979) presented a prototype model with rational expectations and staggered price and wage decisions, in which the Phillips curve is vertical in the long run, but not in the short run. Elsewhere the distinction between the theoretical stance of the model in which expectations variables appear and the theory of expectations adopted was more clearly appreciated. In the United Kingdom, despite its first appearance in the new classical Liverpool model, incorporation of the rational expectations hypothesis was part of the revision process of mainstream "sticky price" and quantity adjustment models (Wallis et al., 1986). Several multi-country models also incorporate this treatment of future expectations, notably of exchange rates and interest rates (Bryant et al., 1988). We return to this topic and deal with a range of the resulting technical issues in section 5.

3 Evaluating Macroeconometric Model-Based Forecasts

3.1 Introduction

Given one or more sets of economic forecasts over a period of time, we consider the question of how to assess forecasting performance *ex post*. There is an extensive literature on forecast evaluation exercises, in which an early landmark is Theil's classic *Economic Forecasts and Policy* (1958). Evaluations range from descriptive accounts of forecasts and forecast errors in specific periods, especially at business cycle turning points, which are of particular interest, to the statistical analysis of forecasts and forecast errors over a period of years, which is the approach considered here. The disadvantage of the former approach "lies in a natural tendency for the practitioner to explain away all ... errors in terms of events (strikes, dramatic shifts in government policy, and so on) that could not possibly have been anticipated at the time forecasts were prepared. Such an attitude is hardly likely to lead to improved performance in the future" (Granger and Newbold, 1977, p. 279).

Let y_t, $t = 1, \ldots, n$ be an observed time series and $\hat{y}_t$, $t = 1, \ldots, n$ be a series of forecasts of y_t made at time $t - l$, where l is the forecast lead time. In an alternative notation due to Theil (1958) that we shall also employ, the actual and predicted values are denoted respectively A_t and P_t. The forecast errors are then

$$e_t = y_t - \hat{y}_t = A_t - P_t, \quad t = 1, \ldots n.$$

Statistical analysis usually begins with the calculation of summary statistics such as the sample mean square error

$$\text{MSE} = \frac{1}{n} \sum_{t=1}^{n} e_t^2$$

or its square root (RMSE), which has the same units as the original series, or the sample mean absolute error

$$\text{MAE} = \frac{1}{n} \sum_{t=1}^{n} |e_t|.$$

The choice of summary measure should in principle be related to the cost function or loss function relevant to the decision problem at hand, the MSE measure being appropriate if the cost function is quadratic, and the MAE measure if the cost function is linear in the absolute value of the error. (Consideration of the impact of the choice of cost function on the computation of the forecast itself is deferred to section 4.2.) Statistical prediction theory predominantly adopts a least squares criterion of optimality, implicitly a quadratic cost function, and forecast evaluations predominantly follow suit. The optimal forecast is then the conditional expectation of y_t with respect to the given information set.

Practical forecast evaluations are typically addressed to one variable at a time, whereas econometric model-based forecasts are essentially multivariate. Hence a multivariate assessment may be more relevant, particularly if trade-offs between forecast errors in different variables have a bearing on the specific decision problem. In the multivariate context, defining e_t as a $g \times 1$ vector, the conditional expectation is the optimal forecast in the sense that it has the smallest MSE matrix $E(e_t e_t') = V_0$, say. That is, for a different forecast with MSE matrix V_j, we have that $V_j - V_0$ is positive definite. This comparison is invariant to selection or linear transformation of variables My_t, where M is $m \times g$, $m \leq g$, since the forecasts of the corresponding selected or transformed variables have MSE matrix MVM', and if $V_j - V_0$ is positive definite, then so is $M(V_j - V_0)M'$. In the decision theory approach, the standard quadratic loss function is $e_t' K e_t$, where K is symmetric and positive definite so that any nonzero error vector leads to a positive loss. The conditional expectation minimizes the expected loss $E(e_t' K e_t) = \text{tr}(KV)$, that is, as in the preceding comparison, we have $\text{tr}(KV_j) > \text{tr}(KV_0)$, whatever the choice of K. Nonzero off-diagonal elements of K indicate that a cost is incurred by forecast errors in particular variables in pairwise combination. On the other hand if K is diagonal, then only the individual forecasts' mean square errors, and not their cross-correlations, contribute to $\text{tr}(KV)$.

Macroeconomic forecasts are usually published for general use, and neither forecasters nor forecast evaluators can take account of the loss functions of all users of forecasts, even if users could make their loss functions explicit, which seldom happens, at least not in public. For practical reasons forecast evaluations usually focus on a small selection from the multitude of variables that appear in the output of a large-scale model. Typically the key macroeconomic aggregates that feature prominently in public discussion of economic policy are chosen, the objective being to present information that is useful to a wide range of users, who can then compute their own loss functions. However the summary statistics presented are almost invariably univariate, as noted above, rather than the complete sample MSE matrix; hence the users' K-matrices are implicitly assumed to be diagonal.

An immediate difficulty in forecast evaluation, whether univariate or multivariate, is that there is no absolute measure of the forecastability of a series, and hence there is no absolute standard against which to compare the summary statistics defined above. (The only exception to this statement is provided by Kolmogorov's expression for the minimum error variance attainable by a linear one-step-ahead forecast based on past values of the variable in question, in the case that this is a stationary variable: this has had little impact on practical forecast evaluations.) We consider several different approaches to forecast evaluation that have been developed in the absence of an absolute benchmark. The first is to test whether the forecast satisfies certain properties of an optimal forecast other than that of minimum MSE, such as unbiasedness and efficiency, in a sense to be defined. The second approach is to compare two or more sets of forecasts of the same quantity, which includes comparisons of competing econometric model-based forecasts and comparisons of such forecasts with those produced by different methods. Finally we consider the use of forecasts in the evaluation of macroeconometric models, which requires the different possible sources of error in a model-based forecast to be identified.

3.2   Testing Unbiasedness and Efficiency

An optimal forecast is unbiased and efficient. That is, the forecast error has an expected value of zero and cannot be predicted by – is uncorrelated with – any variable in the given information set. Full use of the available information has been made in constructing the forecast, to the extent that there remains no exploitable correlation that would improve the forecast.

A simple test of unbiasedness is to calculate the sample mean forecast error, $\bar{e}$, and compare it to its standard error. Many studies, instead or in addition, estimate the realization–forecast regression

$$A_t = \alpha + \beta P_t + u_t$$

and test the joint hypothesis $\alpha = 0$, $\beta = 1$. This has its origins in Theil's (1958) scatter diagrams of predicted and actual values, in which the 45° line $P_t = A_t$ represents "perfect" forecasts, although to test departures from this by regressing P_t on A_t has the regression the wrong way round. Ball (1962) uses the realization–forecast regression in an assessment of forecasts of UK wage rates, taking acceptance of the null hypothesis $\alpha = 0$, $\beta = 1$ to define an unbiased forecast, while "from the point of view of efficiency it is also desirable that the u_t should be non-autocorrelated." On the other hand Mincer and Zarnowitz (1969) consider a test of $\alpha = 0$, $\beta = 1$ to be a test of efficiency: since

$$A_t \equiv P_t + e_t$$

the estimate $\hat{\beta}$ differs from 1 only if P_t and e_t are correlated. Such a correlation indicates an inefficient forecast, since the correlation could be exploited to help predict the forecast error and hence improve the forecast. To reconcile these interpretations we note that the sample means satisfy

$$\bar{A} = \hat{\alpha} + \hat{\beta}\bar{P} = \bar{P} + \bar{e},$$

so that $\bar{e} = 0$ whenever $\hat{\alpha} = (1 - \hat{\beta})\bar{P}$. Thus $\hat{\alpha} = 0$, $\hat{\beta} = 1$ is sufficient but not necessary for unbiasedness, and the test is in fact a stricter test. Viewed as a test of efficiency, however, it is a relatively weak test, and the non-autocorrelation of forecast errors or their lack of correlation with the information set can be tested more directly.

Forecast evaluations commonly focus on variables expressed in a stationary form, as output growth rates and price inflation rates, for example, rather than output and price levels, which often appear to be trending or integrated series. Public discussion of economic performance also focuses on the former. If the variable under consideration is an integrated series, however, then the observation of Granger (1986) that it is cointegrated with the optimal forecast, provided that the information set includes the variable's own history, suggests a further test based on standard unit root testing procedures. Cointegration of forecast and realization is again a relatively weak requirement, however, amounting to stationarity, not non-autocorrelation, of the regression residual, without any requirement on the regression coefficients.

The validity of test procedures based on ordinary least squares calculations rests on the non-autocorrelation and homoskedasticity of the residuals in the realization – forecast regression. While a constant variance is typically assumed, two possible sources of autocorrelation can be distinguished. First, as noted above, a forecast that makes sub-optimal use of past information generally has an autocorrelated forecast error. Secondly, however, an optimal forecast with lead time greater than one period also has an autocorrelated error. Errors in forecasts more than one step ahead cumulate step by step, but the errors in an optimal l-step-ahead forecast exhibit autocorrelation of order $l-1$, not l, and so this cannot be exploited to improve the forecast. Its effect on standard inference procedures should nevertheless be taken into account whenever multi-step forecasts are being tested. One possibility is to use generalized least squares estimates of the realization – forecast regression, as in McNees' (1978) tests of two-, three-, and four-quarter-ahead forecasts. However, since the regressor is not strictly exogenous, the GLS transform is likely to yield inconsistent estimates (Hansen and Hodrick, 1980); an alternative possibility is to retain OLS estimates of α and β while using a corrected estimate of their asymptotic covariance matrix that accommodates the residual autocorrelation. This approach is followed by Holden and Peel (1985), who study model-based forecasts published by the National Institute of Economic and Social Research (NIESR). For forecasts of six variables, one to four quarters ahead, they find that the hypothesis $\alpha = 0$, $\beta = 1$, which they refer to as the unbiasedness hypothesis, is rejected at the 5% level in only one of the 24 cases, namely for forecasts of inflation four quarters ahead.

Stronger tests of efficiency can be conducted by rearranging and augmenting the realization – forecast regression in various ways. Usually it is first rewritten as

$$e_t = \alpha + (\beta - 1)P_t + u_t,$$

showing again that the basic test of efficiency is a test of the lack of correlation between forecast and forecast error. A further test (McNees, 1978) is to include preceding forecast errors on the right-hand side, significant coefficients indicating the existence of information that could have improved the forecasts. This is, in effect, a test for autocorrelation in the forecast errors, and with a forecast lead time $l > 1$ errors lagged less than l periods should not be included. More directly, the forecast's efficient use of the information set may be tested by replacing P_t by elements of that set. Holden and Peel (1985) consider an information set that comprises past values of the variable in question, and regress the forecast error on the four most recent values of the variable known when the forecast was made. Of the 24 cases considered, only the inflation forecasts over three and four quarters fail this test, and the remaining NIESR forecasts could not be improved by using "own-variable" information more efficiently.

Increased use of the rational expectations hypothesis has been associated with a further strengthening of the concept of efficiency, which in its most extreme form, "full rationality," requires that all available information be used in an optimal manner in constructing a forecast. Efficiency with respect to an information set containing other variables can be tested in the same way as above, by regressing the forecast error on lagged values of those variables known at the time the forecast was prepared. But the notion of "all available" information presents practical difficulties, and whereas a rejection of full rationality in such a test is convincing, a failure to reject does not dispel the thought that there might remain a relevant variable that has not been considered. On the other hand, if a pure search procedure among independent variables is employed, then a correct null hypothesis is expected to be rejected at the 5% level for one variable in 20. Brown and Maital (1981) assess one of the best-known anticipations surveys, namely the Livingston data, again using consistent inference procedures for their OLS regressions. Of the nine variables considered, only the wholesale price inflation expectations were found to be inefficient with respect to own-variable information, and the forecast errors in this variable and consumer price inflation could each be partly explained by past values of the other variable, indicating that their interrelationship was not properly appreciated by the forecasters. The more interesting finding, however, was that monetary growth helped to explain the forecast errors in both of the inflation variables, indicating that if monetary growth had been correctly understood and fully incorporated into expectations, then the forecasts would have been considerably improved.

3.3   Comparisons and Combinations of Forecasts

In the absence of an absolute standard against which to measure forecast performance, many evaluation exercises analyse the relative performance of several forecasts of the same quantity. Sometimes such forecasts are genuinely competitive, having been constructed by different groups using different models or methods; sometimes the competition is somewhat artificial, the competing forecasts having been constructed for comparative purposes by forecasters wishing to evaluate their own forecasts. In macroeconometrics there is a long tradition of using so-called "naïve" forecasts, constructed without reference to any economic theory and usually based on past values of the variable in question, to provide a yardstick for model-based forecasts. Gradually these have become less naïve, progressing from "no change" or "same change" forecasting rules, through the use of univariate autoregressive or ARIMA models, to the vector autoregressive (VAR) model discussed by Canova (chapter 2 in this volume).

Informal comparisons are often based on the same summary statistics considered above. Here the common finding is that there are no stable unambiguous rankings of competing forecasts independent of the forecast user's loss function. Whether tr(KV_i) is greater or smaller than tr(KV_j) depends on K, where V_i and V_j are the MSE matrices of the competing forecasts, and different weights on different variables or different forecast horizons would usually result in different overall rankings. Equivalently $V_i - V_j$ is an indefinite matrix, and neither forecast is optimal in the sense defined above. For example, using such measures as the MAE and the squared correlation between predicted and actual changes, Zarnowitz (1979) finds that rankings among six US forecasting groups show appreciable differences with respect to particular variables, subperiods, and forecast horizons. The differences in summary statistics are typically small, however: "the main lesson . . . is that the similarities greatly outweigh the differences between the forecasters' performance records." In the United Kingdom, Holden and Peel (1986) compare LBS (London Business School) and NIESR quarterly forecasts of growth and inflation, and find that for both variables NIESR is preferred to LBS in terms of RMSE and MAE over the period 1975–79, whereas the ranking is reversed in 1980–4.

Time series forecasts feature in the US comparisons of McNees (1986; 1990). While univariate forecasts of output and inflation are found to have greater RMSEs than model-based forecasts one to four quarters ahead (McNees, 1990), more serious competition is provided by the multivariate VAR model, with the Bayesian modification of Litterman (1986). The experience of forecasting with a six-variable BVAR model over the first half of the 1980s is described by Litterman (1986), and these forecasts are compared with model-based forecasts by McNees (1986), including the forecasts of a seventh variable – nominal GNP – that are implicit in the BVAR model's forecasts of real GNP and inflation. The remaining four variables are investment, the Treasury bill rate, the unemployment rate, and the money supply. McNees finds that the BVAR forecasts are generally the most accurate or among the most accurate for real GNP, unemployment, and investment, but least accurate for inflation. Curiously, for four of the seven variables, the RMSE of the BVAR forecast declines as the forecast horizon increases from one to eight quarters, in contrast to the usual expectation of an increase based on the properties of optimal forecasts. In an attempt to improve its poor inflation performance the six-variable BVAR model was expanded to nine variables (adding indices of stock prices, commodity prices, and the exchange rate), and the resulting forecasts are included in McNees' (1990) extended comparisons over the whole of the 1980s. The most striking finding, also remarked on by Canova (chapter 2 in this volume), is the change in the relative performance of the BVAR model between the first half and the second half of the 1980s. This is shown most clearly by the investment forecasts, the BVAR being the most accurate forecast in the early 1980s but the least accurate in the late 1980s, in both cases by sizeable margins. Moreover its relative performance on inflation deteriorates further in the extended comparison. With respect to two other variables for which the BVAR did relatively well in the early 1980s – real GNP and unemployment – the overall picture is mixed, the ranking varying with the forecast horizon. In contrast to several earlier studies in which time series forecasts performed relatively well at short horizons while forecasts based on structural models did better at longer horizons, here the model-based forecasts are preferred up to two or three quarters ahead but not subsequently. For real GNP the differences are nevertheless small, whereas for the unemployment rate seven quarters ahead, for example, one model-based forecast has an RMSE 50% greater than that of the BVAR forecast.

Formal tests of competing forecasts face the difficulty that their errors are not independent, given that their information sets overlap, at least to some degree. Hence a test based on a direct comparison of two forecast error variances, such as an F-test, is inapplicable. Granger and Newbold (1977) propose an indirect route. Given time series of errors, e_{1t} and e_{2t}, of two competing forecasts of the same variable, consider the constructed series $(e_{1t} + e_{2t})$ and $(e_{1t} - e_{2t})$. Since $\text{cov}(e_1 + e_2, e_1 - e_2) = \text{var}(e_1) - \text{var}(e_2)$ whatever the correlation between e_1 and e_2, the null hypothesis of forecast error variance equality can be tested by testing the significance of the correlation between the constructed series. Such a test requires the absence of autocorrelation, and hence is applicable only in the case of one-step-ahead forecasts. The restriction to pairwise comparisons may also be a practical limitation.

An alternative approach rests on the idea of combining forecasts (Bates and Granger, 1969; Nelson, 1972). Different forecasts based on different information sets, different models, or even different approaches to data analysis, as in econometric versus time series comparisons, in general may each be expected to contribute usefully to the forecasting problem, and so a composite forecast may be more accurate than any of the individual components. On the other hand if a combination of one forecast with a competitor has an error variance that is not significantly smaller than that of the first forecast then the competing forecast appears to offer no useful additional information. Various test formulations have been employed, all of which can be seen as extensions of the basic realization – forecast relation discussed above. Similar ideas recur in the literature on encompassing tests of one model against another (Hendry and Richard, 1982; Chong and Hendry, 1986).

For two forecasts P_{1t} and P_{2t}, each of which is unbiased either naturally or after a correction, the combined forecast

$$wP_{1t} + (1 - w)P_{2t}$$

is also unbiased, and Bates and Granger (1969) consider various choices of w, seeking to minimize the error variance of the combined forecast. If the two forecasts have uncorrelated errors with variance MSE_1 and MSE_2 respectively, then the appropriate choice of w is

$$w = \frac{\text{MSE}_2}{\text{MSE}_1 + \text{MSE}_2},$$

the standard pooled-estimator result. This also has a regression interpretation, and relaxing the above assumptions leads to consideration of the extended realization–forecast regression

$$A_t = \alpha + \beta_1 P_{1t} + \beta_2 P_{2t} + u_t,$$

applied by Nelson (1972). Subsequent discussion (Granger and Ramanathan, 1984; Clemen, 1986) has considered the general combination of k forecasts through the equation

$$A_t = \alpha + \beta_1 P_{1t} + \beta_2 P_{2t} + \ldots + \beta_k P_{kt} + u_t$$

and the question of whether or not the coefficient restrictions

$$\alpha = 0, \qquad \beta_1 + \beta_2 + \ldots + \beta_k = 1$$

should be imposed. The unconstrained regression clearly achieves a smaller residual sum of squares *ex post*, as Granger and Ramanathan indicate, but if the practical objective is to improve *ex ante* forecasting performance, then the imposition of the restrictions improves forecast efficiency, as Clemen shows. In Nelson's (1972) comparison of model-based and ARIMA forecasts of 14 variables, the hypothesis that $\beta_1 + \beta_2 = 1$ is rejected for only one variable, and tests of the null hypothesis $\beta_2 = 0$ are not influenced by the imposition of the restriction. This latter hypothesis is rejected for nine of the 14 variables, indicating that the ARIMA predictions do embody information which is omitted by the model-based predictions, in particular information from the history of the variables themselves.

On the question of the choice of weights or the estimation of coefficients, Lupoletti and Webb (1986) find that the pooling method (the "ratio technique," as they call it) produces the best results in post-sample testing of competing forecasts. They apply the idea of combining forecasts to the comparison of VAR and model-based forecasts and find that, in a clear majority of the cases considered, the VAR forecast adds information to the model-based forecasts in that the combined forecasts have smaller MSEs than the individual forecasts. (A special issue of the *Journal of Forecasting*, 1989 on combining forecasts contains a review by Granger and several other articles, with references to related literature.)

In the regression context Fair and Shiller (1989; 1990) interpret the extended realization–forecast relation as an assessment of the information content of competing forecasts and argue against the imposition of any restrictions. If both forecasts are just noise, then one would expect to find both β_1 and β_2 equal to zero; if each forecast makes efficient use of independent subsets of information, then one would expect to find both β_1 and β_2 equal to one (although it is the fact of life that competing forecasts are not independent that has led us down this route). In comparisons of real GNP growth forecasts from Fair's econometric model (see Fair, 1976; 1984) and various VAR models (P_{2t}), the estimate of β_1 is significantly different from zero but not from one for both one- and four-quarter-ahead forecasts, whereas the estimate of β_2 is in general small and is significantly different from zero only in the four-quarter-ahead case. Thus in this case there is some information in the VAR forecast that the Fair model is not using, perhaps indicating some dynamic misspecification, even though its RMSE is less than two-thirds of that of the VAR forecast (Fair and Shiller, 1990). In similar comparisons that also include several other model-based forecasts (Fair and Shiller, 1989) the VAR forecast always has the smaller coefficient, which is not always significant; hence it appears to contain "only a modest amount of information" not in the model-based forecasts. Comparing the Fair model with competing econometric models, each contains useful information not in the other, according to these tests; hence Fair and Shiller conclude that combinations of these forecasts may be useful in practice.

The conclusion that the results of comparisons with VAR models indicate dynamic misspecification in the structural models reflects the reaction to earlier comparisons with univariate ARIMA models such as those of Nelson (1972). Since the time series models emphasize dynamic and stochastic features of the data, their outperforming of econometric models simply suggests that the latter are deficient in these respects (Prothero and Wallis, 1976). Indeed, the equations of such models often exhibited substantial residual autocorrelation. Gilbert (1989) describes how these earlier findings prompted research on the relation between structural econometrics and time series analysis and their possible integration; in particular, a research programme at the London School of Economics combined the two approaches to result in "the LSE tradition in time series econometrics, which is now the dominant British tradition" (Gilbert, 1989, p. 128). This has had relatively little impact on the models and forecasts used in the comparisons discussed above, first owing to the obvious lags in an *ex post* exercise – for example, Lupoletti and Webb's forecast analysis covers the period 1970–83 – and secondly because keeping up to date in econometrics has not been a high priority for the proprietors of the US commercial forecasting models that feature in these comparisons (Klein, 1991; Wallis, 1993).

3.4 Sources of Forecast Error

Econometric model-based forecasts are a joint product of model and forecaster, and it is important to disentangle their different roles, particularly if forecasting performance is being used to evaluate the model. The forecaster's contribution has two distinct elements, although they may interact during the process of constructing a forecast. First, since the models are conditional models which cannot be solved without specifying the values of those variables that are treated as exogenous, the forecaster needs to provide projected future values of the exogenous variables: the more accurate are these projections, the more accurate the resulting forecasts of the endogenous variables might be expected to be. Secondly, forecasters make adjustments to pure model-based forecasts in an attempt to overcome perceived model inadequacies or to incorporate external information about future developments. These are variously termed residual adjustments, constant adjustments, add factors, and so forth, and represent a greater exercise of judgement on the part of the forecaster.

In order to undertake an *ex post* analysis of the respective contributions of model and forecaster to the observed error in an *ex ante* forecast, it is necessary first to have complete information about the assumptions and adjustments on which the forecast is based, and secondly to have access to the underlying model so that the forecast can be recomputed under a range of different assumptions – with actual values of exogenous variables replacing the *ex ante* projections, for example. Because such information and access are rarely available to independent researchers, the literature on this topic is relatively sparse, despite the importance of the subject. It begins with an NBER project in the early 1970s, which analysed the quarterly forecasts published by two US modelling groups over a two-and-a-half-year period, while refraining from systematic comparison of the two competing forecasts: see the monograph by Haitovsky, Treyz, and Su (1974) and other papers referenced therein, in particular Haitovsky, and Treyz (1972). Apart from an in-house analysis of the sources of error in two NIESR forecasts by Osborn and Teal (1979) a decade of silence then ensued until, beginning in 1983, the archiving of a sequence of models of the UK economy and the accompanying forecast calculations at the ESRC Macroeconomic Modelling Bureau allowed analysis to resume. An *ex post* comparative assessment of the 1983 forecasts is reported by Wallis et al. (1986, chapter 4), and the first four years' forecasts are analysed by Wallis and Whitley (1991c). Work on the US forecasts resumed with the reactivation of the US Model Comparison Seminar in 1985 (McNees, 1990; 1991), although McNees does not have access to the models and the individual inputs, and for forecasts under alternative assumptions he has to rely on calculations undertaken by the forecasters themselves.

Errors in projecting exogenous variables may make different contributions to the errors in *ex ante* forecasts if different models have different degrees of exogeneity. In an *ex post* assessment in which actual outcomes replace the projected values of exogenous variables, a model that treats as exogenous a variable that is difficult to forecast has an advantage over other models that try to explain its behaviour. To ensure comparability some researchers augment the model by adding autoregressive equations for exogenous variables. For example, in the work discussed above Fair and Shiller (1990) convert the Fair model to "a model with no exogenous variables" in this way, prior to comparing its performance to that of a VAR model, which treats all variables as endogenous. In the four UK models studied by Wallis and Whitley (1991c), however, the classification of variables is broadly similar. The variables treated as exogenous fall into three main groups: those describing economic conditions in the rest of the world; those concerned with domestic economic policy; and those relating to various natural resource or demographic trends, such as the growth of North Sea oil production and changes in the population of working age. Differences of detail may arise, for example, in the choice of the particular measure to be used or its level of aggregation, and within this broad agreement the responsiveness of the models may differ, but this is part of the reason why *ex post* forecasts differ, which is one of the questions being asked. With respect to the impact on forecast errors of replacing projected values by realized values of exogenous variables *ex post*, recent findings reflect those of Haitovsky and Treyz (1972), that this change, surprisingly, tends to increase forecast errors. Wallis and Whitley (1991c) find that in only 11 of 31 GDP forecasts considered and 13 of 31 inflation forecasts would substitution of the actual exogenous information have improved the published forecasts.

Residual adjustments often reflect recently observed errors in particular equations of the model. Whereas the optimal forecast of a non-autocorrelated disturbance term in a well-specified equation is its conditional expectation of zero, a sequence of recent residuals all of the same sign may suggest that an equation is not so well specified after all, and that some alteration is necessary to improve forecast performance. In the absence of a detailed scrutiny of the possible sources of misspecification, a simple adjustment is typically made, held constant over the forecast horizon, at a value equal to the average of a small number of the most recent observed residuals. Such adjustments are often described as "mechanical," since they require rather little judgement on the forecaster's part, but serve to bring the model on track at the start of the forecast period by zeroing out the recent errors. Greater judgement may be exercised by the forecaster in incorporating knowledge or anticipations of specific future developments not represented in the model's specification, or in determining the extent to which the model-based forecast should be brought into agreement with independent evidence such as that provided by surveys. Turner (1990) provides a detailed account of the residual adjustments made in the forecasts published in autumn 1988 by LBS and NIESR. In the LBS forecast, 113 out of 298 endogenous variables are subject to residual adjustment, and 68 out of 117 in the NIESR forecast. Coincidentally, the proportion of the adjustments that are held constant over the entire forecast is 57% in each case. Among the remaining 43% Turner identifies six specific instances where the adjustments involve an important element of judgement and, by recomputing the forecasts with these adjustments modified or removed, shows that they have a substantial influence on the overall forecast. He also finds, however, that there are few other examples in the remaining adjustments for which this is true. Thus genuine individual judgement, as opposed to mechanical adjustment rules, bears rather precisely on a few specific areas of the model, while nevertheless having a major impact on the published forecast.

The forecast error decomposition used by Wallis and Whitley (1991c) also identifies the contribution of residual adjustments. The basic accounting framework is as follows. The dependence of a forecast on the conditioning information about exogenous variables and the forecaster's adjustments is represented by writing the forecast function $\hat{y}(\cdot,\cdot)$ with two arguments. The published forecast is denoted $\hat{y}(\hat{x}, a)$, indicating its dependence on projections of exogenous variables, $\hat{x}$, and the forecaster's residual adjustments, a. After the event two variant forecasts are calculated. First, the projections $\hat{x}$ are replaced by the actual outcomes x to give an alternative forecast $\hat{y}(x, a)$: a comparison with the published forecast indicates the effect of incorrect assumptions about external developments, as discussed above. Second, all residual adjustments are set to zero to give a forecast variously described as a pure model-based or hands-off *ex post* forecast, denoted $\hat{y}(x, 0)$. The error in this forecast, termed "model error," includes the effect of model misspecification, parameter estimation, and random disturbances in the forecast period, together with the contribution of data errors not accounted for elsewhere. For a given variable (and, implicitly, a given model and time period), the observed error in the published forecast is then decomposed as follows:

	model error	$y - \hat{y}(x, 0)$
less	contribution of residual adjustments	$- \{\hat{y}(x, a) - \hat{y}(x, 0)\}$
plus	contribution of exogenous variable errors	$+ \{\hat{y}(x, a) - \hat{y}(\hat{x}, a)\}$
equals	error in published forecast	$= y - \hat{y}(\hat{x}, a).$

An alternative decomposition might measure the contribution of residual adjustments as $- \{\hat{y}(\hat{x}, a) - \hat{y}(\hat{x}, 0)\}$ and that of exogenous variable errors as $\{\hat{y}(x, 0) - \hat{y}(\hat{x}, 0)\}$: in a linear model this would give identical results, and in the nonlinear models considered by Wallis and Whitley (1991c) the differences are negligible. With the above definition, a residual adjustment that acts to offset the model error has a contribution of opposite sign to that of the model error, and this sign combination is observed in 20 out of 31 GDP forecasts and 25 out of 31 inflation forecasts. Thus the residual adjustments generally have a beneficial effect. However, in three of the GDP forecasts and three of the inflation forecasts the residual offset is overlarge, in that the absolute size of the forecast error is increased, while its sign is changed.

The contribution of residual adjustments can be broken down into mechanical and judgemental components by constructing an intermediate variant forecast $\hat{y}(x, \bar{a})$ based on a mechanical adjustment rule that sets the adjustment equal to the average of the last year's residuals. The mechanical adjustments are found to reduce model error in some two-thirds of the forecasts whereas the picture is less clear as far as the remaining "judgemental" component is concerned, as this has a beneficial effect on just over half of the GDP forecasts. McNees (1990) focuses on this distinction by analysing mechanical forecasts, $\hat{y}(\hat{x}, \bar{a})$ in present notation, supplied along with their published forecasts $\hat{y}(\hat{x}, a)$, by four anonymous US forecasters over a period of some three years. For a wide range of variables, and all four forecasters, the judgemental adjustments improve forecast performance in 62% of the one-quarter-ahead forecasts and 58% of the eight-quarter-ahead forecasts. By comparing the contribution of the judgemental adjustment to the error in the mechanical forecast McNees finds that adjustments are too large more often than they are too small: timidity is not a characteristic of these forecasters. However, the US and UK exercises both rest on a somewhat arbitrary distinction between mechanical and judgemental, or automatic and discretionary, adjustment. Fuller explanations by the forecasters of the reasons for their adjustments would contribute to progress in this area, as will a longer time series of forecasts available for such analysis.

4   Stochastic Simulation

4.1   Introduction

Forecasting and policy analysis with an econometric model usually rests on *deterministic* simulation of the model, in which a single point estimate of each of the variables of interest is calculated. The endogenous variables of an econometric model are random variables, however, and for various purposes it is useful to have more complete knowledge of their probability distributions. In the standard linear model of the textbooks, with random disturbances that are normally distributed, the endogenous variables have a multivariate normal distribution, whose properties can be readily evaluated. Practical large-scale models are typically nonlinear in variables, however. An analytic expression for the solution corresponding to the reduced form of the linear model does not exist, and numerical methods of solution must be employed. Nor are theoretical results about the probability distribution of the endogenous variables available, and this must be estimated by *stochastic* simulation, which is the subject of this section. (In this branch of the literature the words "solution" and "simulation" are used interchangeably.)

With respect to the deterministic solution itself, it has been known since the work of Howrey and Kelejian (1969) that this is generally a biased estimate of the conditional expectation of the endogenous variables in a non-linear model: stochastic simulation enables us to estimate this bias and assess its importance. Even if the deterministic solution is retained, perhaps because it approximates the median of the distribution of possible outcomes, stochastic simulation remains necessary to estimate its uncertainty. Stochastic simulation involves repeated drawings of artificial pseudo-random numbers to represent repeated samples of disturbances u_t, for each of which the model is solved, generating an empirical distribution of endogenous variable values whose mean, variance, and so forth can then be calculated. Measures of the dispersion of this distribution provide an indication of the uncertainty that surrounds the model's solutions and forecasts.

A second source of random variation in an empirical model is the estimation error in the model's coefficients. Stochastic simulation with respect to coefficients may be undertaken to assess the impact of the uncertainty arising from this source. When considering the uncertainty of a model-based forecast, the contribution of coefficient estimation error is an order of magnitude smaller than that of the model's random disturbance terms, and in our discussion we restrict attention to the latter. However when considering the uncertainty of policy responses and multipliers, the random disturbance terms make no contribution, since these quantities are themselves conditional expectations, and coefficient estimation error is the only remaining source of uncertainty in the model (see for example Fair, 1980; 1984, chapter 9).

We first consider the calculation of a model solution or forecast, and compare the deterministic solution with alternatives based on stochastic simulation. Next, some practical aspects of experimental design are discussed. Finally we describe some applications that study second moments or more general properties of the probability distribution of outcomes.

4.2   Deterministic versus Stochastic Simulation

A general nonlinear system may be written formally, in its structural form, as

$$f(y_t, z_t, \alpha) = u_t,$$

where f is a vector of functions having as many elements as the vector of endogenous variables y_t, and z_t, α, and u_t are vectors of predetermined variables, parameters, and random disturbances respectively. Although this notation is convenient, it is more general than is necessary, because the equations of empirical macroeconometric models are usually linear in simple instantaneous transformations (such as logarithms) or simple functions (such as products, ratios, or proportionate changes) of variables. Nonlinearity in parameters is relatively rare.

It is assumed that a unique solution for the endogenous variables exists. Whereas multiple solutions might exist from a mathematical point of view, typically only one makes economic sense with variables obeying known constraints – positivity, and so forth. In general the solution does not have an explicit analytic form, but it can be written implicitly as

$$y_t = g(u_t, z_t, \alpha),$$

analogous to the reduced form in the linear case. The solution can be approximated numerically to any desired degree of accuracy, and there is a large literature on numerical solution methods (see for example Fisher and Hughes Hallett, 1988a). The deterministic solution $\hat{y}_t$ is obtained as the numerical solution to the structural form, once the disturbance terms on the right-hand side have been set equal to their expected values of zero. It can thus be written implicitly as

$$\hat{y}_t = g(0, z_t, \alpha).$$

The common criticism of the deterministic solution is that it does not coincide with the *conditional expectation*

$$E(y_t|z_t, \alpha) = E[g(u_t, z_t, \alpha)] = h(z_t, \alpha),$$

say. Because the expected value of a nonlinear function of a random variable, such as $E[g(u_t)]$, is not in general equal to the nonlinear function of the expected value of the variable, namely $g[E(u_t)] = g(0)$, the deterministic solution has a *bias* $\hat{y}_t - h(z_t, \alpha) \neq 0$. Since g is not known, neither is h, and the conditional expectation cannot be calculated directly. It can be estimated as the mean of replicated stochastic simulations, as follows. First R vectors of pseudo-random numbers u_{tr}, $r = 1, \ldots, R$, are generated with properties corresponding to those assumed or estimated for the model disturbances. Then the model is solved for the corresponding values of the endogenous variables y_{tr}, say, where

$$f(y_{tr}, z_t, \alpha) = u_{tr}$$

to the desired degree of accuracy, or again implicitly

$$y_{tr} = g(u_{tr}, z_t, \alpha).$$

The estimate of the conditional expectation is the sample mean over the R replications, namely

$$\bar{y}_t = \frac{1}{R} \sum_{r=1}^{R} y_{tr},$$

and the difference $\hat{y}_t - \bar{y}_t$ is an estimate of the bias in the deterministic solution.

The bias due to the nonlinearity of practical large-scale models is of little importance, according to the popular view. For example, Fair (1984, p. 256) summarizes the empirical literature by reporting that "the bias that results from using deterministic simulation to solve nonlinear models appears to be small," although Fisher and Salmon (1986) criticize the experimental design of many studies, as discussed below, and find that in dynamic simulation or multi-period forecasting the bias can build up as the simulation period is extended. In such circumstances the solution may be moving far away from the initial conditions, which suggests a more general qualification to the popular view noted above, namely that the result that the bias is not a major concern is true only locally. In general the bias is *base dependent*, that is, it depends on the values of the variables z_t, and for larger perturbations it may assume greater importance.

Note that whether the bias matters or not should be assessed in the particular economic context, and that this is not a question of statistical significance. Whereas the estimate $\bar{y}_t$ is subject to sampling variation, its standard error can be made as small as we like simply by increasing the number of replications, R. For the ith endogenous variable the standard error of the mean is $s_i/\sqrt{R}$, where the variance estimates s_i^2, $i = 1, \ldots, g$, are obtained as the diagonal elements of the sample covariance matrix

$$\frac{1}{R-1} \sum_{r=1}^{R} (y_{tr} - \bar{y}_t)(y_{tr} - \bar{y}_t)'.$$

Thus there exists a value of R at which any nonzero bias will exceed two standard errors, but despite its statistical significance it may still be of no practical importance.

The emphasis on the conditional expectation derives from its optimality with respect to a quadratic loss function: it is the least squares forecast, as noted above. Consideration of alternative loss functions may lead to a preference for other solutions, and perhaps the most popular alternative is to assume that the loss is proportional to the *absolute* value of the forecast error. If this loss function is used, then the optimal point estimate or forecast is the *median* of the conditional probability distribution of outcomes. (Strictly speaking, this result applies only to the forecasting of a single variable, and there is no standard definition of the median of a multivariate distribution. Most commonly, however, this is taken to be the set of medians of the univariate marginal distributions, and the expected loss is evaluated in this distribution.) Since the random disturbances are usually assumed to have not only a zero mean but also a zero median, the deterministic solution coincides with the median provided that the transformation $g(\cdot)$ preserves the median, that is, provided that $[g(u)]^m = g(u^m)$, where superscript "m" denotes the median. This is satisfied if the transformation is bijective, a condition which is met by the most common example in practical models, namely the exponential function. This arises from the widespread use of log-linear behavioural equations, specified with an additive random error term: solution for the levels of the variables then requires the use of the exponential transformation. Under these conditions the deterministic forecast minimizes the absolute error, and hence it might be justified on these grounds. The practical question is whether the bijectivity condition is satisfied by large-scale models: Hall (1986a) presents evidence that the median of the distribution of stochastic simulations either coincides with the deterministic solution or is very close to it.

A further issue that influences the choice of solution is its internal coherency, by which is meant that the solution values should satisfy the identities and definitional equations of the model. This requirement is obviously met by the deterministic solution and by each individual replication in a stochastic simulation. But it is unlikely to be met by their average value, the estimate of the conditional expectation, if any of these equations are nonlinear. Particular examples arise through the use of quantity variables measured in both real and nominal terms, and the relation of one to the other via a price index. Neither the conditional expectation nor its mean stochastic simulation estimate is likely to satisfy such a relation, and imbalances and internal incoherencies in the forecast are the result. This feature, together with the view that nonlinearity is of little practical importance and the heavy computational burden of the stochastic simulation solution, explains why it is not in common use, despite its theoretical superiority under a quadratic cost function.

A measure of dispersion or a forecast interval can be associated with a model solution or point forecast. Whichever solution is chosen, it is subject to irreducible error due to the model's disturbance terms, and in a nonlinear model stochastic simulation is essential to evaluate this uncertainty. When an empirical distribution of endogenous variable values has been obtained by stochastic simulation, the variance of this distribution calculated as above might be reported if the conditional expectation is the preferred point estimate, or the inter-quartile range might be reported if the deterministic solution is used, approximating the median. In either case this measure of uncertainty might in due course be compared with actual observed forecast errors, as part of a model validation process, subject to the caveats discussed in section 3.4.

Policy multipliers too should theoretically be based on stochastic simulation, since these are defined as the partial derivatives of the conditional expectation of each endogenous variable with respect to each policy instrument. That is, adapting the conventional notation for the reduced form coefficients in a linear model,

$$\Pi_t = \partial h(z_t, \, \alpha)/\partial z_t$$

for relevant elements of the z_t vector. Since h is nonlinear, the multipliers are base dependent. Estimates of these quantities based on finite increments and stochastic simulation may be designated

$$\bar{\Pi}_t = \Delta \bar{y}_t / \Delta z_t$$

and could be computed as the difference between base and perturbed mean stochastic simulation estimates. To reduce the simulation variance of the multiplier estimate, the same pseudo-random disturbances u_{tr} should be used in a given replication of both solutions, whereupon the vector of estimated multipliers with respect to a perturbation δ_j in the jth z-variable is

$$\bar{\pi}_{jt} = \frac{1}{R} \sum_{r=1}^{R} [g(u_{tr}, \, z_t + \delta_j, \, \alpha) - g(u_{tr}, \, z_t, \, \alpha)]/\delta_j.$$

In practice, however, the deterministic solution is used, and the estimated multipliers

$$\hat{\pi}_{jt} = [g(0, \, z_t + \delta_j, \, \alpha) - g(0, \, z_t, \, \alpha)]/\delta_j$$

are computed as the difference between base and perturbed deterministic solutions. What little evidence we have (Bianchi, Calzolari, and Corsi, 1981; Fair, 1984, table 9–1) suggests that the difference between the two estimates is so small as to be of no practical significance.

4.3 Experimental Design

Under this heading we discuss three important practical aspects of stochastic simulation experiments with large-scale econometric models, namely variance reduction techniques, the generation of random disturbances, and the route by which these disturbances enter the model.

Like any real sampling experiment, artificial sampling experiments yield results that are subject to sampling variation. It is important not only to report the magnitude of this variation, but also to keep it as small as possible, within a given budget. As noted above, the simplest method of reducing the standard error of stochastic simulation estimates is to increase the number of replications, but repeated solution of a large-scale model, perhaps over an extended simulation base, remains a non-trivial computing task, and other methods of increasing the efficiency of the experiment are typically sought. First, and again as noted above, using the same set of pseudo-random disturbances in two situations generally reduces the variability of the difference between the estimates in the two situations.

Secondly, antithetic random numbers may be used to reduce the sampling variance of point estimates. For random variables x_i, $i = 1, \ldots, n$, with variance σ^2 and covariance σ_{ij}, the variance of their mean is

$$\text{var}(\bar{x}) = \left[n\sigma^2 + \sum_{i \neq j} \sigma_{ij} \right]/n^2.$$

Thus the objective is to make the covariance between individual replications as large and negative as possible, so that when these are averaged, the variance of the average is as small as possible. A common device is the use of pairs of antithetic random numbers, consisting of a given drawing u_{tr} and its negative $-u_{tr}$. Calzolari (1979) and Fisher and Salmon (1986) show that this can achieve "quite remarkable" efficiency gains.

Thirdly, control variates provide a further variance reduction method. Consider a linear approximation to the model solution in the neighbourhood of the deterministic solution, obtained as the first term of a Taylor series expansion of y_t around $u_t = 0$. This is

$$y_t^L = \hat{y}_t + u_t \left. \frac{\partial y_t}{\partial u_t'} \right|_{u_t = 0},$$

where $\hat{y}_t = g(0, z_t, \alpha)$ is the deterministic solution as above, and the Jacobian matrix of the derivatives of y_t with respect to u_t is computed once-and-for-all at $\hat{y}_t$. Thus, for a single replication u_{tr} the linear approximation is easily computed, and this is used as a control variate for the full nonlinear solution y_{tr}. Since $E(y_t^L) = \hat{y}_t$, the bias in the deterministic solution, $\hat{y}_t - E(y_t)$, is equal to $E(y_t^L - y_t)$. So an alternative estimate of the bias is obtained by calculating $y_{tr}^L - y_{tr}$ in each replication, and averaging across R replications. For a model which is not very nonlinear y_t^L is strongly correlated with y_t; hence $\text{var}(y_t^L - y_t) < \text{var}(y_t)$ and the control variate technique yields an improvement in the efficiency of estimation of the bias for a given number of replications, with relatively little increase in computational cost. Calzolari and Sterbenz (1986) consider the efficiency of estimation of the forecast variance, and present examples in which this control variate method increases the accuracy of estimation by a factor of 100 or more compared to the simple simulation method with the same number of replications.

Generation of the pseudo-random vector u_{tr} usually proceeds by generating a vector of pseudo-random independent standard normal random variables, ε_{tr} say, and then transforming these so that the resulting vector u_{tr} has a covariance structure which corresponds to that observed in the model's residuals. A common practical difficulty is that the estimate of the covariance matrix based on observed residuals is singular, because the number of observations is less than the number of estimated equations; hence the required transformation cannot be calculated as the standard Choleski decomposition of this matrix. An alternative procedure in widespread use, proposed by McCarthy (1972), is to generate a standard normal random vector of dimension equal to the number of observations, T say, and to transform this by the observed matrix of residuals: defining this last matrix as $\hat{U} = [\hat{u}_1 \ \hat{u}_2 \ \ldots \hat{u}_T]$, the transformation is

$$u_{tr} = \hat{U} \varepsilon_{tr}/\sqrt{T}.$$

The resulting vector has a covariance matrix which is a consistent estimate of the desired $E(u_t u_t')$, provided that the model is consistently estimated. McCarthy also gives an extension of this method which ensures that the pseudo-random disturbances are autocorrelated to the extent that the observed residuals are. A further extension is provided by Sterbenz and Calzolari (1990), whose method preserves the first *three* moments of the observed residuals. If a skewed distribution is reproduced in the pseudo-random disturbances in this way, note that it is no longer appropriate to obtain an antithetic pair by taking the negative of the random vector, since this would not have the correct distribution. Sterbenz and Calzolari show that their control variate method, discussed above, is particularly useful in this case.

Mariano and Brown (1984) propose using the observed residual vectors as simulation input, that is, $\hat{u}_1, \hat{u}_2, \ldots, \hat{u}_T$ are used as u_{tr}, $r = 1, \ldots, R$, for $R = T$. They show that the residual-based procedure gives better results than a standard stochastic simulation with $R = T$ replications, but as $R \to \infty$ this comparison is reversed; thus stochastic simulation is preferred if the cost of simulation is low. This analysis rests on the assumption of a correct distribution, whereas the residual-based procedure is more robust to departures from normality, since it duplicates the empirical distribution of the residuals. The difficulty of the limited sample size seems to be overriding, however, although antithetics could also be used.

The way in which the pseudo-random disturbances enter the behavioural equations of the model can influence the results, particularly on the question of the bias due to nonlinearity. Unlike the general representation of the nonlinear model given above, an empirical model is usually programmed for solution by normalizing each equation on a different endogenous variable, which corresponds to the assignment of a unit diagonal to the coefficient matrix in the linear case, and then by inverting any transformation applied to this variable, so that it appears as a "dependent" variable measured in its original units. To preserve the original stochastic specification, this same inverse transformation should be applied to the disturbance term, but this is not always done. For example, a log-linear behavioural equation of the form

$$\ln y_{it} = b \ln y_{jt} + c \ln z_{kt} + u_{it}$$

usually appears in the model code as

$$y_{it} = \exp(b \ln y_{jt} + c \ln z_{kt}) + a_{it},$$

so that a residual adjustment a_{it} measured in the same units as y_{it} may be applied. However, applying a normally distributed random error in this way changes the distributional assumptions, for if u_{it} is normally distributed then y_{it} has a conditional log-normal distribution, through the relation

$$y_{it} = \exp(b \ln y_{jt} + c \ln z_{kt})\exp(u_{it}).$$

Since $\exp(u_{it})$ has mean $\exp(\sigma_i^2/2) > 1$, in this example the conditional expectation exceeds the deterministic solution, but a stochastic simulation in which a normal random error was introduced as a_{it} would give no indication of this bias. Moving to the simultaneous-equation case no longer allows us to construct simple examples such as this one; in practical large-scale models Fisher and Salmon (1986) confirm the expected result, that applying random shocks as residual adjustments a_t rather than structural disturbances u_t understates the bias due to nonlinearity. Reviewing the empirical literature summarized above, they find that few authors specify how the random shocks were introduced into the model. Since the correct use of structural disturbances would typically require the model to be recoded rather than run in its standard forecasting and policy analysis mode, they suspect that random shocks were introduced as residual adjustments; hence the popular view that the bias is unimportant rests on unreliable evidence.

4.4   Second Moment and Event Probability Estimates

In a range of economic problems the variance of outcomes is of substantive interest for its own sake, rather than as an indicator of forecast uncertainty. These problems concern the ability of a system to accommodate random shocks in a variety of circumstances and the design of mechanisms or choice of policies to accomplish such accommodation. Attention usually focuses on the variability of key variables such as output and inflation, and stochastic simulation methods can be used to provide relevant model-based estimates.

The literature on the stability of alternative macroeconomic policy rules originates in Christ's (1968) examination of IS–LM models where it is argued that proper attention should be given to the role of the government budget constraint. Two distinct strands have subsequently emerged. One is concerned with dynamic instability and suggests, for example, that a fixed monetary rule, or equivalently the use of bond finance as the residual instrument, is likely to be destabilizing. The second considers stochastic models and suggests, for example, that output may have a higher variability when certain methods of financing the (random) government budget deficit are employed. Whether the theoretical propositions in this latter case are supported by empirical macroeconometric models is a question that is amenable to stochastic simulation methods. For example Fisher, Wallis, and Whitley (1986), using two large-scale models of the UK economy, find that pure bond financing is less stable than pure money finance in the sense that it results in a greater variance of output.

In a multi-country context the same approach can be used to evaluate the costs and benefits of policy coordination and cooperation. For example, Masson and Symansky (1992) appraise some previous studies of economic and monetary union (EMU) in Europe, and provide some new results using stochastic simulations of the International Monetary Fund's MULTIMOD model. The performance of monetary union relative to floating exchange rates or the exchange rate mechanism (ERM) of the European monetary system as it then operated is assessed on the basis of the variance of output and inflation in stochastic simulations under the various policy regimes. A new issue that arises in a multi-country context is whether policies should be evaluated in terms of the variance of (European) aggregates, irrespective of cross-country variability, or the variance of each country's output and inflation. Masson and Symansky use a hybrid set of measures, combining the different countries' variability measures for output into a single index, while focusing on the variability of aggregate European inflation, arguing that changes in relative prices should not matter if they have no harmful real effects but, on the contrary, are necessary for real adjustment.

Estimated variances or standard deviations are subject to sampling error, like any other stochastic simulation result. The variance of the second sample moment is $(\mu_4 - \mu_2^2)/n$, equal to $2\sigma^4/n$ in the case of the normal distribution, and using the approximation $\text{var}[g(x)] = (\partial g/\partial x)^2 \text{var}(x)$ for scalar nonlinear function g the standard error of the estimated standard deviation ($\hat{\sigma}$) is obtained as $\hat{\sigma}/\sqrt{(2n)}$ (Stuart and Ord, 1987, section 10.15). These quantities are reported by Fisher, Wallis, and Whitley (1986); Calzolari and Sterbenz (1986) report the results of similar calculations, with extensions to their control variate case.

Stochastic simulation can also be used to estimate the probability of occurrence of certain economic events. Although probability forecasts are much better established in meteorology than in economics, in recent years there has been considerable interest in methods of estimating the probability of a recession (Stock and Watson, 1989). Once such an event is defined in terms of the endogenous variables of a macroeconometric model, as at least two consecutive quarters of declining real GDP, for example, then the relative frequency of the event in R replications of a multi-step forecast can be observed, and this relative frequency is the required probability estimate. Fair (1993) applies this method to estimate the probability of a recession in 1989–90, as seen at the beginning of 1989. In stochastic simulation of his own model over an eight-quarter prediction period, Fair considers the randomness that arises not only from the model's disturbance terms but also from coefficient estimation error and exogenous variable uncertainty, the last being particularly relevant in a real-time forecasting context. The resulting estimate of the probability of a recession as defined above is 0.56, which Fair describes as "high;" the mean forecasts show no quarterly declines in output. With $R = 1000$, the usual expression for the standard error of a sample proportion gives 0.016.

5 Rational Expectations in Macroeconometric Models

5.1 Forward Expectations and Model-Consistent Solutions

Expectations of future values of endogenous variables, such as inflation or exchange rates, have long been recognized as important determinants of current behaviour, and modellers have long endeavoured to incorporate their influence in empirical models, using survey data on anticipations and expectations wherever possible. Reliable quantitative data on expectations are relatively rare, however, and auxiliary hypotheses about the expectation-formation process are commonly used instead.

A traditional way of dealing with unobserved expectations variables is to assume that they are functions of the current and lagged values of a few observed variables and then substitute them out, giving a conventional backward-looking dynamic or distributed lag model. This confounds the description of the expectation-formation process with the description of economic behaviour given expectations, and results in a model that is unlikely to remain invariant across policy regimes, as noted by Lucas (1976). Increasingly common, however, is the explicit treatment of expectations variables incorporating the hypothesis of rational expectations, namely that expectations coincide with the conditional expectations of the variables based on the model itself and "all available" information. Treating expectations variables explicitly, rather than substituting them by distributed lag functions, provides a practical response to the Lucas critique (Wallis, 1980), and appropriate estimation methods are available, surveyed for example by Pagan (1986). Then, in solving the model for the endogenous variable values over a forecast period, an internally consistent forward-looking solution is calculated, in which each period's future expectations variables coincide with the model's (deterministic) forecasts for the future period. This approach is more accurately and perhaps less controversially termed "model-consistent" expectations.

By adding the forward expectation y_{t+1}^e to the nonlinear model of the preceding section and distinguishing between lagged endogenous and exogenous variables, the first-order case may be written

$$f(y_t, y_{t+1}^e, y_{t-1}, x_t, \alpha) = u_t.$$

Again this notation is more general than is necessary, because typically only a few elements of the vector y appear as future expectations. An assumption about the dating of the information set on which y_{t+1}^e is based is necessary, and most commonly this is assumed to be $t-1$. In addition to inflation, exchange rates and interest rates noted above, future expectations of real quantities such as income or output may appear if the Euler equation approach is adopted in respect of the behaviour of households or firms: this typically results in a linear, scalar version of the above equation.

The rational expectations literature is usually assumed to start with Muth (1961), although Keuzenkamp (1991) has recently drawn attention to a remarkable early paper by Tinbergen (1932), published in German, which anticipates much of Muth's analysis. Also, following earlier discussions of the influence of forecasts on outcomes, Grunberg and Modigliani (1954) had already shown that where agents react to forecasts and thereby alter the course of events, this reaction can be taken into account to yield a correct, self-fulfilling forecast. This same kind of internal consistency is imposed by the rational expectations algorithms used to solve the model, and the dependence of the present on the future solution has sometimes led to the dynamic system being described as a "non-causal" system. In both forecasting and policy analysis, the explicit treatment of forward expectations allows such issues as the announcement effects of future policy changes, their credibility, and, indeed, the consequences of false expectations to be dealt with. In policy evaluation exercises, the use of consistent expectations allows policies to be tested under conditions in which their effects are understood, good performance in these conditions being a necessary condition for a satisfactory policy.

To solve a model with forward expectations variables in a consistent manner, it is necessary to ensure that the expectations variables coincide with the future solution values over a sequence of periods, as noted above. For the linear model Blanchard and Kahn (1980) give a closed form, analytic expression for the solution and consider its uniqueness and stability, a solution satisfying these conditions being referred to as a saddlepoint path. For the nonlinear model numerical techniques are again necessary to obtain a solution, to the desired degree of accuracy, of the equations

$$f(\hat{y}_t, \hat{y}_{t+1}, \hat{y}_{t-1}, x_t, \alpha) = 0, \quad t = 1, \ldots, n,$$

given initial conditions y_0. It is no longer possible to use period-by-period numerical solution techniques appropriate for nonlinear backward-looking dynamic models; at least conceptually it is necessary to iterate over the complete solution path, as in the method of Fair and Taylor (1983), although further research has led to improved methods (Fisher and Hughes Hallett, 1988b). Often there exists a multiplicity of consistent solution paths, of which only one is stable, and it is necessary to impose additional conditions to ensure that this stable path (saddlepoint) is selected. Typically this is done via terminal conditions $\hat{y}_{n+1}$ that specify the forecast values and expectations beyond the forecast horizon.

If the nature of the stable path is known *a priori*, from analysis of the steady-state properties of the model, for example, then the terminal conditions may explicitly incorporate this knowledge. This may require a relatively long solution period, however, to ensure that the model has reached an approximate equilibrium. In the absence of such information, or in a shorter solution period, terminal conditions should be specified that approximate the stable path after the end of the solution period, typically by requiring constant growth rates of relevant variables. In order to ascertain whether the time period is sufficiently long or whether appropriate terminal conditions have been used, so that the solution over the period of interest is unaffected, numerical sensitivity analysis may be undertaken. The sensitivity of the solution to variations in the terminal date indicates how much of the solution can be regarded as a genuine product of the model rather than a product of the assumed terminal conditions. Changes in the type of terminal condition, together with evidence from the different solution periods, can also suggest whether or not a unique stable solution exists. For examples of such sensitivity analysis, see Wallis et al. (1986, section 2.5).

5.2 Policy Analysis

Model-based policy analysis usually begins with the calculation of policy multipliers or ready reckoners, which describe the dynamic response of the endogenous variables (targets) to a unit shock in a policy instrument, treated as an exogenous variable. In a nonlinear model these are computed as the difference between two deterministic solutions, as noted in section 4.2. First a control solution or base run is obtained over some historical or forecast period for given values, actual or projected, of the exogenous variables. Then the relevant exogenous variable is perturbed and a second solution is obtained, and the difference between the two solutions is an estimate of the effect of this policy instrument. The perturbations are typically relatively small, and so represent examples of "normal policy-making," not "permanent shifts in policy regime" in Sims' (1982) terms. As such they can be realistically analysed in existing models without respecification. To the extent that a linear approximation is valid, such multipliers may be combined to describe the effect of a policy package. Alternatively several changes to exogenous variables may be implemented in a single solution, which is usually termed "scenario analysis."

Models with forward expectations allow a distinction to be drawn between anticipated and unanticipated policy changes: this distinction does not arise in conventional backward-looking models. If a shock is anticipated in a model with forward consistent expectations, then some response prior to the actual shock might be expected. Simulation of the effects of such anticipations can be achieved by introducing the perturbation at an intermediate point of the solution period, while solving over the whole period under model-consistent expectations. If a shock is unanticipated, no such prior response occurs, and the perturbed solution under model-consistent expectations begins in the period that the shock is introduced. Intermediate possibilities that can be studied by simulation methods include questions of credibility, where a policy might be believed to be one thing when it is in fact another, and recognition, where a policy change is not announced but in public perception has a probability that increases from zero to one over a period.

Similar anticipations or announcement effects arise in the treatment of temporary shocks in forward-looking models. In conventional backward-looking models permanent and temporary shocks have the same effect during the period they are in force, and once a temporary shock is removed, the model tends back to the original base run (in the absence of hysteresis effects). The same long-run response occurs in models with forward expectations, but whether a shock is believed to be permanent or temporary may lead to a different response during the period in which it applies. Forward-looking economic agents may anticipate the future removal of a temporary intervention, with effects on their current behaviour. Different reactions to permanent or temporary stimuli are seldom represented in the specification of individual behavioural equations, and can only be studied via a complete model solution with model-consistent expectations. Although the permanent income hypothesis might provide the theoretical foundation of an empirical consumption function, for example, income is itself an endogenous variable, and its permanent and transitory components are not separately distinguished.

Some research has sought to contrast directly the rational expectations and extrapolative expectations approaches in policy experiments of this kind. In an early example Fair (1979) showed that estimated fiscal and monetary policy responses in his model were sensitive to the imposition of an assumption of rational expectations in the bond and stock markets, in place of the model's estimated backward-looking equations. This implies that (at least) one view must be incorrect, and it would be interesting to determine which one. Subsequently, as methods of estimating rational expectations models have been incorporated into large-scale macroeconometric modelling practice, it has become clear that various important long-run model properties do not depend on the choice between forward-looking and backward-looking dynamic equations; rather, this choice principally affects the model's short-run properties. In models of small open economies operating under a floating exchange-rate regime the exchange rate itself is an important expectational variable. Fisher, Turner, and Wallis (1992) consider an equation of the form

$$e_t = \alpha e_{t-1} + (1 - \alpha)\hat{e}_{t+1} + r_t + x_t, \quad 0 \leqslant \alpha \leqslant 1,$$

which nests a number of the exchange-rate equations of models of the UK economy (r_t is the difference between domestic and foreign interest rates and x_t is a risk premium proxy, depending on the current balance). Three cases of particular interest are: (i) $\alpha = 1$, when the dependent variable is the first difference of the exchange rate, as in the error correction equation of one model; (ii) $\alpha = 0$, which gives the forward-looking modified uncovered interest parity condition which Fisher et al. (1990) find is data-admissible and which is used in another model; and (iii) $\alpha = 0.5$, which weights the forward and backward terms equally, as in a third model. Fisher, Turner, and Wallis (1992) show that, although the models' responses to shocks have different patterns of adjustment, the long-run response is not affected by the choice of α. This is in contrast to the results of Melliss et al. (1989), who appear to show that, for one of the present models, long-run simulation properties are changed substantially by using forward consistent expectations rather than adaptive expectations in the exchange-rate equation. However the two exchange-rate equations that are compared differ not only in their expectational assumptions but also in other respects, in particular their sensitivity to the current balance, and this is the source of the difference in long-run properties. Bikker, van Els, and Hemerijck (1993) show that, for a Dutch model, the switch from adaptive to rational expectations affects only short-run properties.

The application of control theory to problems of macroeconomic policy-making has a long history, and two distinct approaches can be found in the literature. The first is "classical" control theory, which is concerned with stabilization policy or, more generally, the dynamic implications of augmenting the model with a control rule describing the setting of the policy instrument. One focus of attention is the design of linear feedback rules for policy instruments that yield acceptable behaviour of the controlled system, correcting errors caused by unanticipated shocks as quickly and smoothly as possible, for example. This leads to the proportional, integral, and derivative (PID) controller introduced into economics by Phillips (1954; 1957). In contrast to the classical approach, in which the policy objective is formulated relatively informally, an alternative approach seeks the formal optimization of an explicit objective function, as first applied to problems of macroeconomic policy-making by Theil (1958). The objective function is typically a scalar function of the values of targets and instruments over the planning period, including terms in the deviations of actual values of target variables from their desired values and the trajectories of the policy instruments. Relative weights attached to terms of the first kind reflect the policy-maker's priorities, as between inflation and unemployment, for example, or between consumption now and consumption later. Terms of the second kind may reflect institutional constraints on the extent to which certain policy instruments can be used, or the desirability of relatively smooth changes in instruments. In a linear model, with a quadratic objective function, optimal control theory gives a control policy in the form of a linear feedback rule for the instruments; in the nonlinear case, a time series of policy instrument settings is obtained by numerical methods, conditional on exogenous variable trajectories.

Some recent research – see, for example, papers in Britton (1989) and references therein – attempts to link the two strands of the control-theory literature by seeking explicit feedback rules that approximate the fully optimized solution in large nonlinear models. One way of doing this is to linearize the nonlinear model, then apply linear techniques to the resulting approximation, and finally apply the optimal feedback rule so obtained to the original nonlinear model. A particular motivation is the desire to obtain simple policy rules whose ease of understanding and verification helps overcome the credibility problem, discussed below. Since the optimal rule involves feedback on the whole state vector, however, which moreover is difficult to interpret in the linear approximation case, these requirements are in conflict, and simplicity is often achieved by arbitrary selection of a small number of indicator variables; the PID approach suggests that these should include target variables. Similarly the choice of target values is often treated in an arbitrary fashion, although in principle these should be obtained as the fully optimized solution of the nonlinear model, which at least ensures that the targets are attainable.

The incorporation of explicit future expectations variables treated in a rational or model-consistent manner breaks the analogy with engineering systems on which the early work on control theory in economics rested. "Economic systems, like all systems of social interaction, are intelligent in a way that engineering systems are not. In economics, we are concerned with the control of intelligent systems that think about what policy-makers do to them and act accordingly" (Currie, 1985). In an influential paper, Kydland and Prescott (1977) argued that "there is *no* way control theory can be made applicable to economic theory when expectations are rational;" in particular the application of optimal control methods results in policies that are time inconsistent, in that it is not optimal to continue with an initial policy in subsequent periods. There is an incentive for the policy-maker to renege on previously announced policies, but this in turn can be anticipated; hence the announcement, or more generally the time-inconsistent optimal policy, lacks credibility in the absence of an enforcement or pre-commitment mechanism. Blackburn (1987) surveys the substantial literature inspired by this "fundamental dilemma." In much of the work surveyed the policy problem is formulated as a dynamic game between intelligent players – policy-maker and private sector – and different possibilities arise according to the assumed information structure and the types of strategic behaviour considered. In an important strand of this literature, namely that concerned with international policy coordination, the players are separate national policy-makers; see, for example, the papers and commentaries in the volume edited by Buiter and Marston (1985).

The single-economy policy game typically assumes non-cooperative behaviour, with the two players interacting according to Nash or Stackelberg assumptions. In the former each player takes the other's actions as given, and an equilibrium position is one that provides no incentive for either player to move, again taking the other player's (optimal) policy as given. In the latter one player acts as a leader, anticipating the reactions of the follower to announced policies and optimizing accordingly. For practical implementation in large-scale empirical models the Stackelberg assumption presents fewer difficulties, since the econometric model describes the behaviour of economic agents who form expectations on the basis of announced policy, which they treat as given, and the policy-maker proceeds to optimize this. Under Nash assumptions, however, the policy-maker must optimize taking agents' expectations as given, and an additional level of iterations is necessary to ensure that the expectations are consistent with the optimized policy. Nevertheless it might be argued that this is more in keeping with the rational expectations hypothesis – that economic agents understand and hence correctly anticipate the policy-maker's actions – and the resulting policy is time consistent.

Empirical applications are relatively few to date, as a result of the computational difficulties presented by the foregoing complications. Optimization algorithms usually require a Jacobian matrix of first derivatives of targets with respect to instruments in all time periods, constructed by numerical differences. To minimize the required number of model solutions, some structure is usually imposed on this matrix, and in conventional backward-looking models it is assumed first that target variables respond only to current and lagged instruments, and secondly that this response is invariant to the timing of the perturbation – a kind of stationarity assumption. In models with forward expectations, the derivatives must reflect the nature of the Nash or Stackelberg game. Each derivative evaluation requires a model-consistent forward expectations solution, and the first of the above assumptions is therefore no longer valid. Furthermore the second assumption becomes less reliable, particularly in the neighbourhood of the initial and terminal conditions. Hence additional derivative evaluations are necessary. Hall (1986b) presents a Nash-type exercise in a model with a single forward expectations variable, and Wallis et al. (1987, chapter 3) use the Stackelberg approach in calculating an inflation–unemployment trade-off by optimal control in a model with three forward expectations variables. Fisher (1992, chapter 7) appraises the performance of these and other methods in such exercises. In the face of these difficulties, it is perhaps not surprising that none of the exercises reported in Britton (1989) use a full optimization approach, those based on forward-looking models restricting attention to policy simulations and the derivation of feedback control rules; on the latter topic see also Weale et al. (1989) and Christodoulakis, Gaines, and Levine (1991).

5.3 Historical Tracking, Forecast Evaluation, and Stochastic Simulation Exercises

In this section we reconsider three further areas of model application, to see how the techniques developed for conventional backward-looking models can be adapted and extended for forward-looking models. The rational expectations hypothesis focuses attention on information – the question of who knows what and when, and what do they do with the information – and different responses are appropriate in each case.

Historical tracking exercises with conventional models have been based on both static and dynamic simulation. In a static solution for the endogenous variables of the model, all lagged variables and current exogenous variables take their known values: thus this form of solution represents a one-step-ahead *ex post* forecast from the model. In contrast, in a dynamic simulation, starting from given initial conditions, one period's solution provides the values of the lagged endogenous variables in the calculation of the next period's solution, and so on: this is the standard mode of operating the model in policy analysis and real-time forecasting exercises. In a historical tracking exercise, either solution is then compared with the historical data record, as a model validation procedure. However Howrey and Kelejian (1969) show that the errors in a dynamic simulation are both autocorrelated and heteroskedastic and hence difficult to interpret or analyse; moreover, within-sample dynamic simulation errors contain no information about the validity of the model additional to that contained in the single-equation residuals. Pagan (1989) extends these results and in particular shows that, for most estimation methods, running a simulation over the estimation period results in errors whose sample means tend to zero irrespective of the degree of misspecification of the model. Thus the unbiasedness of an in-sample dynamic simulation holds automatically; it is therefore not a good criterion for judging the adequacy of a model as a representation of the data, contrary to the way in which such exercises have often been interpreted. Although these formal results apply to linear models, they should nevertheless be treated with respect in the nonlinear case, as Pagan argues, because nonlinearities have not been found to be of great importance in normal operating circumstances, as noted above, and because it would be unreasonable to propose methods for nonlinear models that are ineffective in linear models, at least without an argument showing why the changed environment should improve matters.

Static simulation is therefore adopted as the appropriate method of analysis by Fisher and Wallis (1990), whose historical tracking study includes several rational expectations models. It is thus concerned with the fitted values, period by period, of equations of the form of

$$f(y_t, y_{t+1}^e, y_{t-1}, x_t, \alpha) = u_t,$$

as above. The question is what values to use for the forward expectations variable, assuming that this is equal to the conditional expectation given an information set dated $t - 1$, say, that comprises the values of all relevant variables known at that time, together with the model that describes their interrelationships. Note that two simple, but extreme, possibilities should be ruled out straight away. First, the actual outcome, y_{t+1}, might be considered, bearing in mind that this is sometimes used as a proxy variable in estimation. However the rational expectation differs from this by an error which depends on the random shocks that hit the system between expectation formation and outcome, so that the "perfect foresight" proxy implicitly adds to the information set the values of these future random disturbances, which is unrealistic. Secondly, y_{t+1}^e might be replaced by a linear combination of past ys, as is often done in the derivation of a backward-looking model. But this neglects all of the information set except the past values of the variable in question, which is again unrealistic.

The rational expectation y_{t+1}^e depends on forecasts of exogenous variables through the model solution, so the first step in Fisher and Wallis' procedure is to construct these from time series models for the exogenous variables. Next, given the forecasts $\hat{x}_t, \hat{x}_{t+1}, \ldots, \hat{x}_{t+n}$ based on $x_{t-1}, x_{t-2}, \ldots$ and an initial condition y_{t-1}, an $(n+1)$-period model-consistent solution for the endogenous variables is obtained. Finally, the value $\hat{y}_{t+1}$ from this solution is used as data in solving the model for the fitted value of y_t, conditioned on observed x_t in the usual way. Thus two rounds of model solution are required in each period, although only one of them is a model-consistent forward expectations solution. The horizon, n, for this solution should be chosen sufficiently large, in conjunction with the terminal conditions, that $\hat{y}_{t+1}$ is not affected by remote future expectations. If the information set is dated t, not $t - 1$, then only the first round is required: in this case the relevant fitted value is the first value, $\hat{y}_t$, from the model-consistent solution conditional on $x_t, \hat{x}_{t+1}, \ldots, \hat{x}_{t+n}$, where projections $\hat{x}_{t+1}, \hat{x}_{t+2}, \ldots$ are based on $x_t, x_{t-1}, \ldots$. In their study Fisher and Wallis (1990) find that the former, more realistic dating assumption produces better historical tracking results.

In evaluating forecasts based on rational expectations models the contribution of errors in exogenous projections, written as $\hat{y}(x, a) - \hat{y}(\hat{x}, a)$ in section 3.4, can be further disaggregated, as two separate influences of exogenous variables can now be identified. One is a contemporaneous influence as a direct result of the appearance of x_t in the model; the other works through the future expectation variable which, in turn, depends on expectations of future exogenous variables. To fix ideas Wallis and Whitley (1991c) use the example of a simple linear regression equation

$$y_t = \beta y_{t+1}^e + \gamma x_t + u_t.$$

The one- and two-step-ahead forecasts published at time t are obtained from a model-consistent solution and so satisfy

$$\hat{y}_{t+1} = \beta \hat{y}_{t+2} + \gamma \hat{x}_{t+1} + a_{t+1}$$
$$\hat{y}_{t+2} = \beta \hat{y}_{t+3} + \gamma \hat{x}_{t+2} + a_{t+2},$$

where future expectations depend on further projections $\hat{x}_{t+3}$, $\hat{x}_{t+4}$, ... The variant forecasts using actual data on x_{t+1} and x_{t+2}, *ex post*, satisfy

$$\tilde{y}_{t+1} = \beta \tilde{y}_{t+2} + \gamma x_{t+1} + a_{t+1}$$
$$\tilde{y}_{t+2} = \beta \tilde{y}_{t+3} + \gamma x_{t+2} + a_{t+2},$$

where these first two and the future model-consistent expectations depend on projections $\tilde{x}_{t+3}$, $\tilde{x}_{t+4}$, ... which utilize the observed x_{t+1} and x_{t+2}. The direct and expectational influences of exogenous variables can now be distinguished by calculating an intermediate variant in which future expectations are held fixed, but actual exogenous data are used, as follows:

$$y^0_{t+1} = \beta \hat{y}_{t+2} + \gamma x_{t+1} + a_{t+1}$$
$$y^0_{t+2} = \beta \hat{y}_{t+3} + \gamma x_{t+2} + a_{t+2}.$$

Of course this is not an internally consistent sequence, since the two-step-ahead forecasts in the first and second equations differ. Nevertheless it permits a further decomposition of the contribution of exogenous variable errors, reflecting the relative importance of contemporaneous and forward-looking effects. Wallis and Whitley (1991c) find that, for the LBS and NIESR forecasts of GDP and inflation, where the total contribution of exogenous variable error is small, the expectational effects are generally greater in absolute size than the contemporaneous effects, and the two effects are generally of opposite sign. These two models introduced rational expectations half-way through the period of study, whereas all the Liverpool model forecasts analysed were based on the rational expectations hypothesis: here the relative magnitudes are greater, and no generalization about the relative size of the contemporaneous and expectational effects is possible, although the same offsetting pattern is almost invariably observed.

Note that there is no role in this analysis for what might appear, at first sight, to be an interesting variant forecast, namely one in which actual outcomes are substituted, *ex post*, for future expectations of endogenous variables. In the context of our simple example, the best one-step-ahead forecast requires the best estimate of current expectations of y_{t+2}, that is, y^e_{t+2}. Such expectations are unobserved, and the model-consistent expectations framework represents one approach to their modelling, in particular substituting the *ex ante* forecast $\hat{y}_{t+2}$ to obtain $\hat{y}_{t+1}$. In some cases survey data on anticipations are available and are used, either directly, or indirectly to suggest residual adjustments if an initial forecast is out of line with anticipations data.

But the key question in forecast evaluation is not whether forward expectations were accurate, but whether they were accurately estimated at the time, which in the absence of direct observations is not answerable. Hence there is no role in analysing the error in $\hat{y}_{t+1}$ for substituting the actual y_{t+2} on the right-hand side: this value is in any event an estimate of previously held expectations that is subject to error, which in the context of model-consistent forecasts is the two-step-ahead forecast error that is itself a subject of the decomposition analysis.

Finally we consider stochastic simulation of rational expectations models, a subject which is in its infancy, because it compounds the computational complications of the two separate extensions to standard procedures discussed above – those concerned with stochastic simulation (section 4) and those concerned with model-consistent forward expectations (section 5.1). The simplest case to consider is that of the impact of the random disturbance term on the solution of the model in static simulation with the information set dated $t - 1$. First the model is solved forward to obtain the model-consistent solution sequence $\hat{y}_t$, $\hat{y}_{t+1}$, ... Then, with the future expectations variables $\hat{y}_{t+1}$, $\hat{y}_{t+2}$, . . . held fixed at these values, the model is subjected to artificial random shocks u_{tr}, $r = 1, \ldots, R$, and an empirical distribution of endogenous variable values, y_{tr}, is obtained as in the conventional case. Restricting attention to static simulation, and assuming that the random disturbances are unanticipated and so do not influence the formation of expectations, allows the future expectations to be treated as predetermined variables in the stochastic simulation. An application of this approach is presented by Fisher (1992, section 5.8), who extends the results of Fisher, Wallis, and Whitley (1986) cited in section 4.4 to the rational expectations versions of the two large-scale models considered there.

The deterministic solution for the future expectations is typically used in such exercises, although a strict interpretation of the rational expectations hypothesis might suggest that an estimate of the conditional expectation should be used instead; in a dynamic solution, however, the complications of stochastic simulation increase considerably. The solution of the model in the next time period, $t + 1$, depends on future expectations conditioned on information available at time t, and this conditioning information includes the influence of the first set of random shocks. Thus for each replication at time t, a new forward consistent solution is required, then these expectations are held fixed while the next random shock is inserted at $t + 1$, and so on. Hence an experiment comprising R replications of an n-period dynamic simulation requires nR pairs of solutions, the first a model-consistent forward solution for the expectational variables, and the second a conventional solution treating the expectations as predetermined. Fair and Taylor (1990) present an example of a four-period dynamic stochastic simulation of an illustrative six-equation model containing forward expectations of two endogenous variables.

References

Ball, R.J. (1962). The prediction of wage-rate changes in the United Kingdom economy 1957–60. *Economic Journal*, 72, 27–44.

Barro, R.J. and Fischer, S. (1976). Recent developments in monetary theory. *Journal of Monetary Economics*, 2, 133–67.

Bates, J.M. and Granger, C.W.J. (1969). The combination of forecasts. *Operational Research Quarterly*, 20, 451–68.

Bianchi, C., Calzolari, G. and Corsi, P. (1981). Estimating asymptotic standard errors and inconsistencies of impact multipliers in nonlinear econometric models. *Journal of Econometrics*, 16, 277–94.

Bikker, J.A., van Els, P.J.A. and Hemerijck, M.E. (1993). Rational expectation variables in macroeconomic models: empirical evidence for the Netherlands and other countries. *Economic Modelling*, 10, 301–14.

Blackburn, K. (1987). Macroeconomic policy evaluation and optimal control theory: a critical review of some recent developments. *Journal of Economic Surveys*, 1, 111–48.

Blanchard, O.J. and Kahn, C.M. (1980). The solution of linear difference models under rational expectations. *Econometrica*, 48, 1305–11.

Bodkin, R.G., Klein, L.R. and Marwah, K. (eds) (1991). *A History of Macroeconometric Model-Building*. Aldershot: Edward Elgar.

Britton, A.J.C. (ed.) (1989). *Policymaking with Macroeconomic Models*. Aldershot: Gower.

Brown, B.W. and Maital, S. (1981). What do economists know? An empirical study of experts' expectations. *Econometrica*, 69, 491–504.

Buiter, W.H. and Marston, R.C. (eds) (1985). *International Economic Policy Coordination*. Cambridge: Cambridge University Press.

Bryant, R.C., Henderson, D.W., Holtham, G., Hooper, P. and Symansky, S.A. (eds) (1988). *Empirical Macroeconomics for Interdependent Economies*. Washington DC: Brookings Institution.

Calzolari, G. (1979). Antithetic variates to estimate the simulation bias in non-linear models. *Economics Letters*, 4, 323–8.

Calzolari, G. and Sterbenz, F.P. (1986). Control variates to estimate the reduced form variances in econometric models. *Econometrica*, 54, 1483–90.

Chong, Y.Y. and Hendry, D.F. (1986). Econometric evaluation of linear macro-economic models. *Review of Economic Studies*, 53, 671–90.

Christ, C.F. (1968). A simple macroeconomic model with a government budget restraint. *Journal of Political Economy*, 76, 53–67. Reprinted in Wallis (1994).

Christodoulakis, N.M., Gaines, J. and Levine, P. (1991). Macroeconomic policy using large econometric rational expectations models: methodology and application. *Oxford Economic Papers*, 43, 25–58.

Clemen, R.T. (1986). Linear constraints and the efficiency of combined forecasts. *Journal of Forecasting*, 5, 31–8.

Courbis, R. (1991). Macroeconomic modelling in France. In Bodkin, Klein, and Marwah (1991), pp. 231–66.

Currie, D.A. (1985). Macroeconomic policy design and control theory – a failed partnership? *Economic Journal*, 95, 285–306.

Davidson, J.E.H., Hendry, D.F., Srba, F. and Yeo, S. (1978). Econometric modelling of the aggregate time-series relationship between consumers' expenditure and income in the United Kingdom. *Economic Journal*, 88, 661–92.

Dolado, J.J., Galbraith, J.W. and Banerjee, A. (1991). Estimating intertemporal quadratic adjustment models with integrated series. *International Economic Review*, 32, 919–36.

Eckstein, O. (1983). *The DRI Model of the U.S. Economy*. New York: McGraw-Hill.

Fair, R.C. (1976). *A Model of Macroeconomic Activity, Vol. 2, The Empirical Model*. Cambridge, Mass.: Ballinger.

Fair, R.C. (1979). An analysis of a macro-econometric model with rational expectations in the bond and stock markets. *American Economic Review*, 69, 539–52.

Fair, R.C. (1980). Estimating the uncertainty of policy effects in nonlinear models. *Econometrica*, 48, 1381–91. Reprinted in Wallis (1994).

Fair, R.C. (1984). *Specification, Estimation, and Analysis of Macroeconometric Models*. Cambridge, Mass.: Harvard University Press.

Fair, R.C. (1993). Estimating event probabilities from macroeconometric models using stochastic simulation. In *New Research on Business Cycles, Indicators, and Forecasting* (J. H. Stock and M. W. Watson, eds), pp. 157–76. Chicago: University of Chicago Press.

Fair, R.C. and Shiller, R.J. (1989). The informational content of ex ante forecasts. *Review of Economics and Statistics*, 71, 325–31.

Fair, R.C. and Shiller, R.J. (1990). Comparing information in forecasts from econometric models. *American Economic Review*, 80, 375–89.

Fair, R.C. and Taylor, J.B. (1983). Solution and maximum likelihood estimation of dynamic nonlinear rational expectations models. *Econometrica*, 51, 1169–86.

Fair, R.C. and Taylor, J.B. (1990). Full information estimation and stochastic simulation of models with rational expectations. *Journal of Applied Econometrics*, 5, 381–92.

Fisher, P.G. (1992). *Rational Expectations in Macroeconomic Models*. Dordrecht: Kluwer Academic Publishers.

Fisher, P.G. and Hughes Hallett, A.J. (1988a). Iterative techniques for solving simultaneous equation systems: a view from the economics literature. *Journal of Computational and Applied Mathematics*, 24, 241–55.

Fisher, P.G. and Hughes Hallett, A.J. (1988b). Efficient solution techniques for linear and non-linear rational expectations models. *Journal of Economic Dynamics and Control*, 12, 635–57.

Fisher, P.G. and Salmon, M.H. (1986). On evaluating the importance of nonlinearity in large macroeconometric models. *International Economic Review*, 27, 625–46.

Fisher, P.G. and Wallis, K.F. (1990). The historical tracking performance of UK macroeconometric models 1978–85. *Economic Modelling*, 7, 179–97.

Fisher, P.G., Turner, D.S. and Wallis, K.F. (1992). Forward unit root exchange-rate dynamics and the properties of large-scale macroeconometric models. In *Macroeconomic Modelling of the Long Run* (C.P. Hargreaves, ed.), pp. 207–28. Aldershot: Edward Elgar.

Fisher, P.G., Wallis, K.F. and Whitley, J.D. (1986). Financing rules and output variability: evidence from UK macroeconomic models. ESRC Macroeconomic Modelling Bureau Discussion Paper no. 7.

Fisher, P.G., Tanna, S.K., Turner, D.S., Wallis, K.F. and Whitley, J.D. (1990). Econometric evaluation of the exchange rate in models of the U.K. economy. *Economic Journal*, 100, 1230–44.

Gilbert, C.L. (1989). LSE and the British approach to time series econometrics. *Oxford Economic Papers*, 41, 108–28.

Granger, C.W.J. (1986). Developments in the study of cointegrated economic variables. *Oxford Bulletin of Economics and Statistics*, 48, 213–28.

Granger, C.W.J. (1989). Combining forecasts – twenty years later. *Journal of Forecasting*, 8, 167–73.

Granger, C.W.J. and Newbold, P. (1977). *Forecasting Economic Time Series* (2nd edn 1986). New York: Academic Press.

Granger, C.W.J. and Ramanathan, R. (1984). Improved methods of combining forecasts. *Journal of Forecasting*, 3, 197–204.

Gregory, A.W., Pagan, A.R. and Smith, G.W. (1993). Estimating linear quadratic models with integrated processes. In *Models, Methods, and Applications of Econometrics* (P.C.B. Phillips, ed.), pp. 220–39. Oxford: Basil Blackwell.

Grunberg, E. and Modigliani, F. (1954). The predictability of social events. *Journal of Political Economy*, 62, 465–78.

Haitovsky, Y. and Treyz, G. (1972). Forecasts with quarterly macroeconometric models, equation adjustments, and benchmark predictions: the U.S. experience. *Review of Economics and Statistics*, 54, 317–25. Reprinted in Wallis (1994).

Haitovsky, Y., Treyz, G. and Su, V. (1974). *Forecasts with Quarterly Macroeconometric Models*. NBER Studies in Business Cycles no. 23. New York: National Bureau of Economic Research.

Hall, S.G. (1986a). The importance of non-linearities in large forecasting models with stochastic error processes. *Journal of Forecasting*, 5, 205–15.

Hall, S.G. (1986b). Time inconsistency and optimal policy formulation in the presence of rational expectations. *Journal of Economic Dynamics and Control*, 10, 323–6. (Revised and abridged version of National Institute of Economic and Social Research Discussion Paper no. 71, 1984).

Hansen, L.P. and Hodrick, R.J. (1980). Forward exchange rates as optimal predictors of future spot rates: an econometric analysis. *Journal of Political Economy*, 88, 829–53.

Hendry, D.F. and Richard, J.F. (1982). On the formulation of empirical models in dynamic econometrics. *Journal of Econometrics*, 20, 3–33.

Hicks, J.R. (1937). Mr Keynes and the "classics"; a suggested interpretation. *Econometrica*, 5, 147–59. Reprinted in Wallis (1994).

Higgins, C.I. (1988). Empirical analysis and intergovernmental policy consultation. In Bryant et al. (1988), pp. 183–201.

Holden, K. and Peel, D.A. (1985). An evaluation of quarterly National Institute forecasts. *Journal of Forecasting*, 4, 227–34.

Holden, K. and Peel, D.A. (1986). An empirical investigation of combinations of economic forecasts. *Journal of Forecasting*, 5, 229–42.

Howrey, E.P. and Kelejian, H.H. (1969). Simulation versus analytical solutions. In *The Design of Computer Simulation Experiments* (T.H. Naylor, ed.), pp. 207–31. Durham, NC: Duke University Press. Reprinted in Wallis (1994).

Intriligator, M.D. (1978). *Econometric Models, Techniques, and Applications*. Amsterdam: North-Holland.

Keuzenkamp, H.A. (1991). A precursor to Muth: Tinbergen's 1932 model of rational expectations. *Economic Journal*, 101, 1245–53.

Klein, L.R. (1947). The use of econometric models as a guide to economic policy. *Econometrica*, 15, 111–51. Reprinted in Wallis (1994).

Klein, L.R. (1950). *Economic Fluctuations in the United States 1921–1941*. Cowles Commission Monograph 11. New York: Wiley.

Klein, L.R. (1986). Economic policy formation: theory and implementation (applied econometrics in the public sector). In *Handbook of Econometrics*, vol. 3 (Z. Griliches and M.D. Intriligator, eds), pp. 2057–93. Amsterdam: North-Holland.

Klein, L.R. (ed.) (1991). *Comparative Performance of U.S. Econometric Models*. Oxford: Oxford University Press.

Klein, L.R., Friedman, E. and Able, S. (1983). Money in the Wharton quarterly model. *Journal of Money, Credit and Banking*, 15, 237–59.

Kydland, F.E. and Prescott, E.C. (1977). Rules rather than discretion: the inconsistency of optimal plans. *Journal of Political Economy*, 85, 473–91.

Litterman, R.B. (1986). Forecasting with Bayesian vector autoregressions – five years of experience. *Journal of Business and Economic Statistics*, 4, 25–38.

Lucas, R.E. (1976). Econometric policy evaluation: a critique. In *The Phillips Curve and Labor Markets* (K. Brunner and A.H. Meltzer, eds), pp. 19–46. (Carnegie-Rochester Conference Series on Public Policy no. 1, supplement to the *Journal of Monetary Economics*, January 1976.)

Lucas, R.E. (1980). Methods and problems in business cycle theory. *Journal of Money, Credit and Banking*, 12, 696–715.

Lucas, R.E. and Sargent, T.J. (1978). After Keynesian macroeconomics. In *After the Phillips Curve: Persistence of High Inflation and High Unemployment*. Conference Series no. 19, Federal Reserve Bank of Boston, 44–72.

Lupoletti, W.M. and Webb, R.H. (1986). Defining and improving the accuracy of macroeconomic forecasts: contributions from a VAR model. *Journal of Business*, 59, 263–85.

McCarthy, M.D. (1972). Some notes on the generation of pseudo-structural errors for use in stochastic simulation studies. In *Econometric Models of Cyclical Behavior* (B.G. Hickman, ed.), pp. 185–91. New York: Columbia University Press. Reprinted in Wallis (1994).

McNees, S.K. (1978). The "rationality" of economic forecasts. *American Economic Review (Papers and Proceedings)*, 68, 301–5.

McNees, S.K. (1986). Forecasting accuracy of alternative techniques: a comparison of U.S. macroeconomic forecasts (with discussion). *Journal of Business and Economic Statistics*, 4, 5–23.

McNees, S.K. (1990). The role of judgment in macroeconomic forecasting accuracy. *International Journal of Forecasting*, 6, 287–99.

McNees, S.K. (1991). Comparing macroeconomic model forecasts under common assumptions. In Klein (1991), pp. 69–85.

Malgrange, P. (1989). The structure of dynamic macroeconometric models. In *Contributions to Operations Research and Econometrics: The Twentieth Anniversary of CORE* (B. Cornet and H. Tulkens, eds), pp. 521–50. Cambridge, Mass.: MIT Press.

Marglin, S.A. (1975). What do bosses do? Part II. *Review of Radical Political Economics*, 7, 20–37.

Mariano, R.S. and Brown, B.W. (1984). Residual based procedures for prediction and estimation in a nonlinear simultaneous system. *Econometrica*, 52, 321–43.

Masson, P.R. (1988). Deriving small models from large models. In Bryant et al. (1988), pp. 322–7.

Masson, P.R. and Symansky, S. (1992). Evaluating the EMS and EMU using stochastic simulations: some issues. In *Macroeconomic Policy Coordination in Europe* (R.J. Barrell and J. D. Whitley, eds), pp. 12–34. London: Sage Publications.

Melliss, C.L., Meen, G.P., Pain, N. and Whittaker, R. (1989). The new Treasury model project. Government Economic Service Working Paper no. 106.

Mincer, J. and Zarnowitz, V. (1969). The evaluation of economic forecasts. In *Economic Forecasts and Expectations*, NBER Studies in Business Cycles no. 19 (J. Mincer, ed.), pp. 3–46. New York: Columbia University Press.

Murphy, C.W. (1988). An overview of the Murphy model. *Australian Economic Papers*, 27 (supplement), 175–99.

Murphy, C.W. (1992). The steady-state properties of a macroeconometric model. In *Macroeconomic Modelling of the Long Run* (C.P. Hargreaves, ed.), pp. 159–205. Aldershot: Edward Elgar.

Muth, J.F. (1961). Rational expectations and the theory of price movements. *Econometrica*, 29, 315–35.

Nelson, C.R. (1972). The prediction performance of the FRB-MIT-PENN model of the U.S. economy. *American Economic Review*, 62, 902–17. Reprinted in Wallis (1994).

Nickell, S.J. (1985). Error correction, partial adjustment and all that: an expository note. *Oxford Bulletin of Economics and Statistics*, 47, 119–29.

Nickell, S.J. (1988). The supply side and macroeconomic modeling. In Bryant et al. (1988), pp. 202–21.

Osborn, D.R. and Teal, F. (1979). An assessment and comparison of two NIESR econometric model forecasts. *National Institute Economic Review*, no. 88, 50–62.

Pagan, A.R. (1986). Two stage and related estimators and their applications. *Review of Economic Studies*, 53, 517–38.

Pagan, A.R. (1989). On the role of simulation in the statistical evaluation of econometric models. *Journal of Econometrics*, 40, 125–39.

Phillips, A.W. (1954). Stabilisation policy in a closed economy. *Economic Journal*, 64, 290–323. Reprinted in Wallis (1994).

Phillips, A.W. (1957). Stabilisation policy and the time-forms of lagged responses. *Economic Journal*, 67, 265–77.

Prothero, D.L. and Wallis, K.F. (1976). Modelling macroeconomic time series (with discussion). *Journal of the Royal Statistical Society*, A, 139, 468–500.

Sargan, J.D. (1964). Wages and prices in the United Kingdom: a study in econometric methodology. In *Econometric Analysis for National Economic Planning* (P.E. Hart, G. Mills and J.K. Whitaker, eds), pp. 22–54. London: Butterworth. Reprinted in *Econometrics and Quantitative Economics* (D.F. Hendry and K.F. Wallis, eds), pp. 275–314. Oxford: Basil Blackwell, 1984.

Sims, C.A. (1982). Policy analysis with econometric models. *Brookings Papers on Economic Activity*, no.1, 107–52.

Sterbenz, F.P. and Calzolari, G. (1990). Alternative specifications of the error process in the stochastic simulation of econometric models. *Journal of Applied Econometrics*, 5, 137–50.

Stock, J.H. and Watson, M.W. (1989). New indexes of coincident and leading economic indicators. In *NBER Macroeconomics Annual 1989* (O.J. Blanchard and S. Fischer, eds), pp. 351–94. Cambridge, Mass.: MIT Press.

Stuart, A. and Ord, J.K. (1987). *Kendall's Advanced Theory of Statistics. Vol. 1, Distribution Theory*. London: Charles Griffin.

Taylor, J.B. (1979). Estimation and control of a macroeconomic model with rational expectations. *Econometrica*, 47, 1267–86. Reprinted in Wallis (1994).

Theil, H. (1958). *Economic Forecasts and Policy* (2nd edn 1961). Amsterdam: North–Holland.

Tinbergen, J. (1932). Ein problem der dynamik. *Zeitschrift fur Nationalokonomie*, 3, 169–84.

Tinbergen, J. (1937). *An Econometric Approach to Business Cycle Problems*. Paris: Hermann & Cie. Reprinted in Wallis (1994).

Tinbergen, J. (1939). *Statistical Testing of Business–Cycle Theories, Vol. II: Business Cycles in the United States of America, 1919–1932*. Geneva: League of Nations.

Turner, D.S. (1990). The role of judgement in macroeconomic forecasting. *Journal of Forecasting*, 9, 315–45.

Wallis, K.F. (1980). Econometric implications of the rational expectations hypothesis. *Econometrica*, 48, 49–73.

Wallis, K.F. (1989). Macroeconomic forecasting: a survey. *Economic Journal*, 99, 28–61.

Wallis, K.F. (1993). Comparing macroeconometric models: a review article. *Economica*, 60, 225–37.

Wallis, K.F. (ed.) (1994). *Macroeconometric Modelling*. International Library of Critical Writings in Econometrics, 2. Aldershot: Edward Elgar.

Wallis, K.F. and Whitley, J.D. (1987). Long-run properties of large-scale macroeconometric models. *Annales d'Economie et de Statistique*, 6/7, 207–24.

Wallis, K.F. and Whitley, J.D. (1991a). Large-scale econometric models of national economies: Part 1, Some current developments; Part 2, Comparative properties of models of the Nordic economies. *Scandinavian Journal of Economics*, 93, 283–314. Reprinted in *New Approaches to Empirical Macroeconomics* (S. Hylleberg and M. Paldam, eds), pp. 155–86. Oxford: Basil Blackwell, 1991.

Wallis, K.F. and Whitley, J.D. (1991b). Macro models and macro policy in the 1980s. *Oxford Review of Economic Policy*, 7, no. 3, 118–27.

Wallis, K.F. and Whitley, J.D. (1991c). Sources of error in forecasts and expectations: U.K. economic models, 1984–8. *Journal of Forecasting*, 10, 231–353.

Wallis, K.F. (ed.), Andrews, M.J., Fisher, P.G., Longbottom, J.A. and Whitley, J.D. (1986). *Models of the UK Economy: A Third Review by the ESRC Macroeconomic Modelling Bureau*. Oxford: Oxford University Press.

Wallis, K.F. (ed.), Fisher, P.G., Longbottom, J.A., Turner, D.S. and Whitley, J.D. (1987). *Models of the UK Economy: A Fourth Review by the ESRC Macroeconomic Modelling Bureau*. Oxford: Oxford University Press.

Weale, M.R., Blake, A.P., Christodoulakis, N.M., Meade, J.E. and Vines, D.A. (1989). *Macroeconomic Policy: Inflation, Wealth and the Exchange Rate*. London: Unwin Hyman.

Zarnowitz, V. (1979). An analysis of annual and multiperiod quarterly forecasts of aggregate income, output and the price level. *Journal of Business*, 52, 1–33.

7

The Econometric Analysis of Calibrated Macroeconomic Models

K. Kim and A.R. Pagan

1 Introduction

A recent assessment of the state of the discipline of psychology in Australia, Siddle (1993), began with the observation that

> psychology has a range of methodologies, and the methodology of choice depends upon the questions posed. What most of these methodologies have in common is a commitment to psychology as an empirical science. (p. 10)

One would hope to be able to make a similar claim for economics, and, although there may be some dissent over applying this description to all economic investigation, there is nevertheless a deep sense in which economics must eventually become an empirical science. As Hansen and Prescott (1991) observe,

> Theory alone imposes almost no restrictions; theory has content only when quantitative restrictions are imposed on preferences and technologies.

What has frequently stood in the way of this objective has been the complexity of computational algorithms needed to capture economic decisions, particularly intertemporal ones. In the past decade however this constraint has been greatly relaxed, and the simulation of complex decision processes has become a routine part of analysis. The ability to numerically simulate very complex systems has the potential for changing the face of economics a great deal. "Quantitative theory" or "theoretical simulation" – both terms having been applied to these developments at different points in the past – may well become the dominant perspective in much economic research in the next 20 years, and this feature forces a consideration of what the appropriate way to do quantitative research within such a framework might be.[1]

Just as for psychology, there are different methods of quantitative research in economics. Kydland and Prescott (1991) highlight two that are designed for the analysis of aggregate phenomena: what they term the "systems of equations approach" (SEA) and the "calibration approach" (CA). Although this is not an exhaustive taxonomy, it is probably the case that the majority of research does fit under these appellations. Formal definitions of the two approaches are rare, although Kydland and Prescott do attempt one for the CA, implicitly adopting the stance that the SEA is synonymous with the type of macroeconomic model building popular in the 1960s. These approaches are best thought of as two dimensional: one involves a "research style" reflecting an attitude towards the best strategy for constructing models, while the other consists of a set of techniques to be adopted in making the models "operational." To emphasize this point, section 2 of the chapter begins by contrasting the ways in which SEA and CA adherents would proceed to construct a model to explain macroeconomic outcomes. We concentrate upon macroeconomic models even though "quantitative theory" has been invoked in many other areas, e.g. asset pricing, industry studies. This outline serves to emphasize that there are many common aspects to the way in which the different methodologies proceed, especially when "modern" versions of the SEA are investigated rather than the caricature used by Kydland and Prescott. Much that has been written on the subject aims to highlight the differences and, consequently, these have been greatly exaggerated. There certainly are differences, but little is gained in over-stressing them.

Section 3 of the chapter provides a more intensive analysis of the techniques of "calibration," surveying the diversity of procedures that have been grouped under this heading, and considering some of the difficulties that are likely to be faced in attempting to implement particular methods. Section 4 turns to what many see as a fundamental difference between the more "traditional" methodologies of quantitative research and that adhered to by "calibrationists", namely the question of how one "assesses" a calibrated model. Once again, the differences can be narrowed a good deal. How to use a calibrated model occupies section 5, with the central theme being methods to assess the sensitivity of model solutions to the calibration performed. Finally, section 6 provides a brief summary of the principal points made in the chapter.

2 Two Styles of Quantitative Research

For the purpose of discussing the different approaches to quantitative analysis it is useful to begin with a simple macroeconomic model. Let C_t = consumption, Y_t = output, I_t = investment, K_t = capital stock, L_t = labour services, G_t = government expenditure, and D_t = depreciation (all aggregates in real terms). Identities provide two relationships between these series:

$$Y_t = C_t + I_t + G_t \qquad (7.1)$$

$$\Delta K_{t+1} = I_t - D_t. \tag{7.2}$$

By themselves the identities are not sufficient to determine all variables, i.e. the system needs to be "completed." Some of the decisions needed to do this recur in other modelling strategies. Thus, making depreciation proportional to the existing (beginning-of-period) capital stock, $D_t = \delta K_t$, and setting output by a constant returns to scale production function (say Cobb-Douglas), $Y_t = A_t K_t^\alpha L_t^{1-\alpha}$, are conventional ways of accounting for these variables. These equations then augment (7.1) to produce a three equation system of (7.1), (7.3), and (7.4):

$$\Delta K_{t+1} = I_t - \delta K_t \tag{7.3}$$

$$Y_t = A_t K_t^\alpha L_t^{1-\alpha}. \tag{7.4}$$

Another common characteristic, deriving from the framework established by the Cowles Commission, is to split the variables into those that are endogenous and those that are exogenous. At least for a simple model, the nature of such a division is probably not contentious, with G_t and A_t, the latter being total factor productivity (TFP), taken as exogenous, while the remaining variables are declared endogenous. With such an endogenous/exogenous split, the remaining task left was to describe how the endogenous variables C_t, I_t (or K_t) and L_t are determined. Detailing the mechanism for the determination of such variables is far more controversial, and we have witnessed considerable divergence over how to proceed. The original Cowles Commission researchers provided a very vague recommendation, Koopmans and Hood (1953, p. 115) saying:

> Let an economic theory specify the existence of a set of functional relations, each expressing an aspect of the economic behavior of a group of individuals, firms or authorities.

It was left to practitioners to be more precise about how the translation from theory to practice was to be effected. Much early work produced specifications for C_t and I_t that were, at best, "soft theory," for example borrowing Keynesian ideas that consumption was determined by current income, or Clark's observation that investment had an accelerator form in its relation to output. To some extent the past three decades can be seen as a retreat from this position, towards one where a greater degree of formal optimization is used to isolate specifications for C_t and I_t. Thus the development of the life cycle theory of consumption by Modigliani and Brumberg (1954) had consumers optimizing in the face of a given future income stream, while the "neoclassical investment function" of Jorgenson (1963) had the firm optimizing in the face of given profits.

In general it is possible to distinguish four crucial ways in which research styles differ when it comes to the specification of models:

1 whether a model is designed to possess a steady state
2 the extent of information available to agents
3 the specification of the dynamic structure for a model
4 the nature of exogenous variables.

Whether a model possesses a steady state has become an issue of some importance in recent years. Much early work in the SEA tradition did not insist upon this requirement, with the result that simulations and multipliers failed to converge as the period of time over which such exercises were conducted was lengthened. However, starting with the monetary models of Bergstrom and Wymer (1976), more attention was paid to designing models which incorporated ideas such as the long-run neutrality of monetary and fiscal policy, e.g. Jonson, Moses, and Wymer (1977), Murphy (1988), and McKibbin (1988). Nevertheless, the steady state solution in SEA inspired models is frequently implicit rather than explicit, stemming from the desire to impose such requirements as the constancy of the "great ratios" involving consumption to income or investment to income, without stating what value these ratios should be. Although the trend to implementation of these ideas is recent, awareness of them is not. Phillips (1957), for example, was sensitive to this need, and argued that agents' decision rules should be constructed so as to ensure such outcomes. The "proportional, integral, derivative" control philosophy in his work was seen as a good way of imposing steady state relations, and this philosophy found its expression in his "error correction mechanism" (ECM) models. Selecting an ECM of the form $\Delta \log C_t = \delta \Delta \log Y_t + \alpha(\log C_{t-1} - \log Y_{t-1})$ obviously ensures that C_t/Y_t is constant in the steady state. Notice that it is not necessary to know what this ratio is to set up the ECM or to ensure that convergence to a steady state occurs.

Calibrated models are much more explicit, placing great emphasis upon the construction of a steady state. To see how this is done consider a planner maximizing expected utility

$$E_t \left\{ \sum_{j=0}^{\infty} \beta^j U(C_t, (1 - L_t)) \right\} = E_t \{ \Sigma \beta^j [(1 - \sigma)^{-1} C_t^{\theta(1 - \sigma)} (1 - L_t)^{(1 - \theta)(1 - \sigma)}] \},$$

where $(1 - L_t)$ is the amount of leisure available to a consumer, subject to the constraints from the production side of the economy,

$$Y_t = A_t K_t^\alpha L_t^{1 - \alpha} = A_t F(K_t, L_t) \quad \text{and} \quad K_{t+1} = (1 - \delta) K_t + I_t.$$

Forming a Lagrangian

$$\mathcal{L} = E_t \sum \beta^j \{ [(1 - \sigma)^{-1} C_t^{\theta(1 - \sigma)} (1 - L_t)^{(1 - \theta)(1 - \sigma)}] + \lambda_t [A_t F(K_t, L_t) - C_t - K_{t+1}$$

$$+ (1 - \delta) K_t - G_t] \}$$

with multiplier λ_t for the resource constraint, the first order conditions for choosing C_t, L_t, K_{t+1}, and λ_t are

$$E_t\{U_C - \lambda_t\} = 0 \tag{7.5}$$

$$E_t\{U_L + \lambda_t A_t F_L\} = 0 \tag{7.6}$$

$$E_t\{\beta\lambda_{t+1}[A_{t+1}F_K + (1 - \delta)] - \lambda_t\} = 0 \tag{7.7}$$

$$A_t F(K_t, L_t) + (1 - \delta)K_t - C_t - G_t - K_{t+1} = 0, \tag{7.8}$$

where the subscripts C, L, K indicate derivatives with respect to that argument, i.e. $U_L = \partial U/\partial L$. The deterministic steady state versions of these quantities can now be solved to get the unknown values of K, L, etc. As an example of the procedure, equation (7.7) can be used to give $AF_K + (1 - \delta) = \beta^{-1}$ and, substituting $F_K = \alpha A^{-1}(Y/K)$, it is clear that $s_k = K/Y = \alpha\beta/(1 - \beta(1 - \delta))$. Continuing in this way, $s_c = C/Y = 1 - \delta s_k - s_g$, $L = \theta(1 - \alpha)/[(1 - \theta)s_c + \theta(1 - \alpha)]$, $K = (As_k)^{1/(1-\alpha)}L$, and $s_g = G/Y$. Hence, the steady state solution is intimately bound up with the "deep parameters" δ, α, s_g, and A.

After the steady state is found it may be desirable (or necessary) to linearize around the steady state values. To discuss this it is useful to consider linear approximations to (7.1), (7.3), (7.4) and to (7.5)–(7.7) around the steady state values using small letters to represent proportional deviations, and capitals for the steady state values, i.e. $a_t = (A_t - A)/A$, $g_t = (G_t - G)/G$, etc. ($\hat{\lambda}_t$ for λ_t being an exception to the rule). This gives[2]

$$y_t = s_c c_t + s_i i_t + s_s g_t \tag{7.9}$$

$$k_{t+1} = (1 - \delta)k_t + \phi i_t \tag{7.10}$$

$$y_t = a_t + \alpha k_t + (1 - \alpha)l_t \tag{7.11}$$

$$c_t = \gamma_{12}l_t + \gamma_{13}E_t(\hat{\lambda}_t) \tag{7.12}$$

$$l_t = \gamma_{21}c_t + \gamma_{23}E_t(\hat{\lambda}_t) + \gamma_{25}k_t + f_1 a_t \tag{7.13}$$

$$E_t(\hat{\lambda}_t) = E_t\{f_3\hat{\lambda}_{t+1} + \gamma_{32}l_{t+1} + \gamma_{35}k_{t+1} + f_2 a_{t+1}\}, \tag{7.14}$$

where $\phi = I/K$, and the parameters γ_{ij}, f_i depend on the steady state solutions and the "deep parameters" of the model, i.e. the production and utility function parameters α, θ, etc.[3] It is useful to contrast the nature of the equations (7.9)–(7.14) with analogous ones found by linearizing a model constructed under the SEA philosophy. Because the SEA is not explicit about the steady state values, equations such as (7.9) would be formed by replacing s_c, s_i, etc. by sample values, whereas in the CA the same quantities are functions of the "deep parameters" and cannot be set independently of them. The way in which a steady state equilibrium is enforced therefore differs between the two methodologies; the SEA implicitly seeks to avoid a very close association between the different decisions whereas the CA avidly embraces such a notion. Nevertheless, these differences may not be as marked in practice, since it is not uncommon in implementations of the CA to see quantities such as s_c being replaced by values found from a data set that has been constructed to represent a steady state solution, a theme that we will return to in the next section.

It is clear from (7.12) and (7.13) that the solution for c_t depends upon $E_t(\hat{\lambda}_t)$. As Pesaran and Smith (1995) observe, one might therefore think of different modelling strategies as different ways of proxying for the unknown variable $E_t(\hat{\lambda}_t)$. The simplest specification of consumption, $c_t = ky_t$, can therefore be viewed as replacing "the future," as represented by $E_t(\hat{\lambda}_t)$, with a linear function of current income, although most macroeconometric models use a wider range of variables than current income. Most of these solutions reflect the belief that consumers operate with limited information or are constrained in some fashion to focus simply on the present. The growth of the "new classical" and RBC schools took the opposite point of view, insisting that agents use all information when making decisions. Solving for $E_t(\hat{\lambda}_t)$ from (7.9)–(7.14), it can be shown to depend upon a linear combination of k_t, $E_t(a_{t+j})$, and $E_t(g_{t+j})$, and, when a_t and g_t are AR(1) processes,

$$a_t = \rho_a a_{t-1} + e_{at} \tag{7.15}$$

$$g_t = \rho_g g_{t-1} + e_{gt}, \tag{7.16}$$

the optimal decision rule is to set $c_t = \psi_1 k_1 + \psi_2 g_t + \psi_3 a_t$.[4] How different the perspectives are therefore depends a lot upon the utility of the extra information, in this instance as measured by the correlation between $E_t(\hat{\lambda}_t)$ and y_t. For the standard RBC model with no government expenditure, $\alpha = 0.3$, $\beta = 0.96$, $\theta = 0.3$, $\delta = 0.1$, $\rho_a = 0.9$ this correlation is -0.96, so that a simple consumption function emphasizing current income would produce a good representation of observed consumption outcomes.[5] It does not seem profitable to conclude that one of the views is "true" and the other "false." Choices made about the availability of information are frequently related to modelling strategy. It is quite likely that those devising models which incorporate limited information may well believe that consumers use a wider range of information, but that the advantages of incorporating that refinement into the model is outweighed by the disadvantages created by a more complex model or the need to gather a wider range of data. In summary, the first difference one sees in modelling styles is the extent to which one views agents as making decisions in a restricted or in a holistic fashion.

It has long been recognized that economic models must incorporate some dynamics. In the SEA these have been captured in a variety of ways but, because of its ability to ensure a steady state solution, the ECM has steadily become the favoured procedure. Mostly the type of ECM utilized, i.e. its order, is determined from the data, and is not derived from any formal optimizing exercise, although, as Nickell (1985) pointed out, one can always construct an intertemporal optimization problem with adjustment costs that would rationalize any given ECM. The attitude taken by proponents of the SEA is that there is very little theory about dynamics, in contrast to steady state properties, and therefore one might wish to be as flexible as possible. Turning to CA inspired models, the dynamics come from two sources: the fact of intertemporal optimization with resource constraints on capital accumulation alone introduces dynamics of the "intrinsic" variety, i.e. those originating from the solution for $E_t(\hat{\lambda}_t)$; while the incorporation of elements such as inertia into utility functions, and "time to build" into investment outcomes, results in "extrinsic" dynamics. Accordingly, CA models are inherently dynamic. To illustrate this point, for the standard RBC model described in (7.9)–(7.14), the states $z_t' = [k_t \; a_t \; g_t]$ evolve under the optimal solution as

$$z_t = \Phi z_{t-1} + \Gamma e_t, \tag{7.17}$$

where

$$\Phi = \begin{pmatrix} \phi_{11} & \phi_{12} & \phi_{13} \\ 0 & \phi_{22} & 0 \\ 0 & 0 & \phi_{33} \end{pmatrix},$$

ϕ_{1j} are functions of the unknown parameters δ, α, etc., $\phi_{22} = \rho_a$, $\phi_{33} = \rho_g$,

$$\Gamma = \begin{pmatrix} 0 & 0 \\ 1 & 0 \\ 0 & 1 \end{pmatrix}, \quad \text{and} \quad e_t = \begin{pmatrix} e_{at} \\ e_{gt} \end{pmatrix}.$$

Notice that the relation for k_{t+1}, i.e. the first element in z_{t+1}, is a *deterministic* function of the available information k_t, a_t, and g_t. Because variables such as c_t, i_t, etc. are related in a linear way to z_t, i.e. $c_t = \psi' z_t = \psi' \Phi z_{t-1} + \psi' \Gamma e_t$, defining the variables c_t, i_t, etc. as $\tilde{w}_t$, and

$$w_t = \begin{pmatrix} z_t \\ \tilde{w}_t \end{pmatrix},$$

it is apparent that w_t follows a VAR,

$$w_t = \begin{pmatrix} \Phi & 0 \\ \psi' \Phi & 0 \end{pmatrix} w_{t-1} + \begin{pmatrix} \Gamma \\ \psi' \Gamma \end{pmatrix} e_t, \tag{7.18}$$

or

$$w_t = \Phi_1 w_{t-1} + G e_t. \tag{7.19}$$

Thus there are substantial dynamics in such models and these stem solely from the fact of intertemporal optimization and the capital stock equation.

It is worth looking at the fact that CA oriented models can be regarded as VARs in greater depth. Clearly the VARs that result are *restricted*, since the only lagged variables entering are those of the states, whereas a proper VAR would have the lagged values of *all* variables entering each equation, unless some exogeneity assumption was being made, e.g. that g_t depended only on its own past history. Consequently, the fact that c_{t-1}, i_{t-1}, etc. fail to enter the VAR shows that the CA produces restrictions upon the dynamics of the process that are potentially testable.

Difficulties in working with the VAR (7.19) are either that not all the variables w_t are observable, or that perhaps it is felt that the measurements of them are poor. Examples of the first would be total factor productivity, and of the second the capital stock. Consequently, it might be desirable to find the implied VAR in the set of $(n \times 1)$ "observable" variables x_t alone. If $\dim(x_t) > \dim(z_t)$, Ingram and Whiteman (1994) point out that $x_t = Bz_t$ can be inverted to get $z_t = (B'B)^{-1}B'x_t$, thereby allowing the VAR in z_t (7.17) to induce a VAR in x_t,

$$x_t = B\Phi(B'B)^{-1}B'x_{t-1} + B\Gamma e_t \tag{7.20}$$

or

$$x_t = Dx_{t-1} + \bar{D}e_t. \tag{7.21}$$

Once the "deep parameters" are specified, D may be determined. As an example, with the numerical parameter values specified earlier for the basic RBC model (7.21) would be

$$
\begin{aligned}
c_t &= \quad 0.556c_{t-1} - 0.089l_{t-1} - 0.040i_{t-1} + 0.467y_{t-1} + 0.562e_{at} \\
l_t &= -0.096c_{t-1} + 0.034l_{t-1} + 0.134i_{t-1} - 0.062y_{t-1} + 1.042e_{at} \\
i_t &= -0.088c_{t-1} + 0.141l_{t-1} + 0.858i_{t-1} + 0.053y_{t-1} + 7.564e_{at} \\
y_t &= \quad 0.460c_{t-1} - 0.055l_{t-1} + 0.094i_{t-1} + 0.405y_{t-1} + 1.604e_{at}.
\end{aligned}
\tag{7.22}
$$

Exactly how a_t and g_t are to be rendered exogenous is likely to vary. In traditional Keynesian models, and in most large scale macroeconomic models, $\log A_t$ is made a deterministic time trend, perhaps breaking at some point. In contrast, real business cycle (RBC) models treat it as also having a stochastic component, generally represented by an autoregression. Actually, this difference may not be as striking as it appears. The substantial correlation in the residuals of the production function equation in many macroeconometric models was frequently accounted for by "constant term adjustments" that effectively made the intercepts of such equations evolve as AR processes. Since the log of TFP is essentially an intercept in an output equation it was therefore being implicitly endowed with some stochastic component.

Table 7.1 summarizes the way in which models constructed under the SEA and CA research styles would differ. There have clearly been differences in the past, and some of these are likely to remain, e.g. the treatment of information and dynamics. But the similarities are striking, and the fact that each approach ultimately asserts that a particular type of VAR can be used to describe the data highlights the fact that they may be contrasted within a common framework. The connection also points to the fact that it is not very productive to treat the two approaches as wildly different, which seems to be the attitude of Kydland and Prescott (1991); rather they end up with the same set of qualitative implications even if on the quantitative dimension they are different.[6]

Table 7.1 Differences between SEA and CA

	SEA	CA
Steady state	Not in old models Yes, in modern small scale models	Yes, by design
Information	Partial Full in financial sectors	Full
Dynamics	From data ECMs	From intertemporal optimization
Exogenous	Conditioned on current value or deterministic trend	Treated as autoregressive

3   Calibrating a Model

As mentioned in the introduction, the second dimension to methodologies for quantitative analysis is the way in which unknown parameters are accounted for. "Calibration" originally arose in the computable general equilibrium (CGE) model area, with possibly the earliest and most influential study being Johansen (1960). Johansen studied an economy in general equilibrium, but evolving along an underlying deterministic balanced growth path, and his aim was to find the vector of prices and quantities that would clear all markets. In his case the equations of the system were the demand and supply relations derivative from the optimizing behaviour of producers and consumers faced with specified production and utility functions; the endogenous variables were the prices and quantities of commodities and factors; and the exogenous variables depended upon how the model was to be "closed." Johansen solved the system by *linearizing* in the variable space around a *hypothetical equilibrium* (y^*, x^*), just as was done in section 2 for the RBC model. Since the linearized model will depend upon the point of linearization, the resulting set of linear equations involves *coefficients* such as factor shares, and it therefore becomes important that the equilibrium values be measured. Johansen did not wish to claim that an equilibrium existed in any specific economy, so that actual data could not be identified with (y^*, x^*). Instead a "benchmark data set" was constructed which was intended to make (y^*, x^*) a general equilibrium pair. Finding such a data set called for experience as well as good applied modelling skills and it was frequently the most time consuming task of an applied general equilibrium modelling exercise. Even after this was done there were still unknown values for parameters θ, largely derivative from the specified production and utility functions, and these were replaced by values found from a combination of assignment and "literature search," i.e. although estimated from data, these were rarely of the economy for which the model was being constructed. One reason for such a stance was the multisectoral nature of these

models, meaning that information was rarely available on production possibilities at the sectoral level. Such methods of selecting θ, even though subject
to the obvious criticism that the assumption of homogeneity in production and
consumption possibilities is a strong one, are nevertheless quite consistent with
the philosophy of these models, in which it is the deviation from a hypothetical
equilibrium which is being studied rather than an economy in "real time."

In the CGE model literature, "calibration" emerged as the short-hand way
of describing both steps above, while in the stochastic GE literature it has
generally been identified simply with the second step, in that a benchmark data
set is rarely constructed. An exception to this situation is Hansen and Prescott
(1993) who benchmark to the first quarter of 1987 in their study of whether
the recent US recession was due to a productivity slump. The difference in
attitude has two sources. Firstly, stochastic GE modellers view the economy
as always being in equilibrium, albeit a stochastic rather than a deterministic
one, and so actual observations may be taken as descriptive of equilibrium
positions. Secondly, the "hypothetical equilibrium" is internally generated as
the steady state of their model: see below (7.8).

Quantification of unknown parameters θ is therefore a key issue in the CA.
Exactly how this is to be done is unclear. A study of papers written by
"calibrationists" shows no unity of thought on the matter. Gregory and Smith
(1993) have an excellent survey of the range of approaches, in which they note
that θ may be set by:

1   reference to prior studies
2   matching of sample and model moments either formally or informally
3   GMM estimation using the moment conditions underlying intertemporal optimization.
4   maximum likelihood estimation.

We will only discuss the final three alternatives as one of these was probably
the way in which the chain of "prior studies" was initiated.

3.1   Matching of Moments

Some early work determined parameter values by choosing those values that
set selected sample moments equal to the corresponding population moments.
It is still employed when there are intrinsic dynamics within the model, e.g. if
there are adjustment costs to investment, the adjustment cost parameter is
found by matching the variance of investment in the data to that predicted by
the model (e.g. Cardia, 1991; Greenwood, Hercowitz, and Krusell, 1992).
Singleton (1988) addressed such methods, pointing out that one should
formally treat this as a method of moments estimation problem, since then one
would be able to attach a standard error to the estimated parameter. Perhaps
the main objection to this procedure concerns the choice of which moments
should be matched. For example, because a parameter such as an adjustment
cost term affects the complete dynamics of the system, it will impact on many

characteristics other than the variance of investment. Hence choosing a particular moment as the way of effecting a calibration may result in a failure to capture the dynamics elsewhere. In systems which are as interdependent as stochastic GE models are, it seems to make more sense to estimate a parameter using all the information from the system and not just a sub-set of it.

3.2 GMM Estimation

As pointed out by Singleton (1988), unknown parameters might be estimated by applying the GMM estimator with the moment conditions implied by the model. Recently Christiano and Eichenbaum (1992) have argued that this is the appropriate way to calibrate and have applied the method to their RBC model. To do so one has to find suitable moment conditions. There are two general approaches to this endeavour that have been advocated in the literature. First, moment conditions can be determined from the steady state relations. Second, the restrictions stemming from the Euler equations describing the optimal choices might be exploited. To illustrate the differences, consider the estimation of the parameter θ in the utility function

$$U(C_t, (1 - L_t)) = (1 - \sigma)^{-1} C_t^{\theta(1 - \sigma)}(1 - L_t)^{(1 - \theta)(1 - \sigma)}$$

used in section 2. Combining (7.5) and (7.6) to give

$$E_t[- (U_C/U_L) - MPP_L] = 0,$$

where MPP_L is the marginal product of labour, yields

$$E_t[\theta(1 - \theta)^{-1}(1 - L_t) - MPP_{L,t}^{-1} C_t] = 0. \tag{7.23}$$

Burnside, Eichenbaum, and Rebelo (BER) (1993) utilize this moment condition to estimate θ, producing $\hat{\theta}_S$. Obviously, (7.23) involves an unknown parameter α through MPP_L, necessitating the introduction of another moment condition to tie it down. The simplest of these would be[7]

$$E_t[(1 - \alpha) A_t K_t^\alpha L_t^{-\alpha} - W_t] = 0, \tag{7.24}$$

where W_t is the observed real wage. The second strategy is to work from the Euler equations for an intertemporally optimizing consumer,

$$E_t[U_{C,t} - BU_{C,t+1}(1 - \delta + r_{t+1})] = 0, \tag{7.25}$$

where r_t is the rental return to capital. Setting $MPP_{L,t} = W_t$ and combining (7.5), (7.6), and (7.25), we get the moment conditions used by Mao (1990) to find the Euler equation based estimator of θ, $\hat{\theta}_T$:

$$E_t[\beta(C_{t+1}/C_t)^{-\sigma}(1 - \delta + r_{t+1})(W_{t+1}/W_t)^{(1 - \theta)(\sigma - 1)} - 1] = 0. \tag{7.26}$$

From BER's derivations the moment conditions (7.23) and (7.26) involve different informational demands: (7.23) would be compatible with myopic consumers whereas (7.26) would not be. Prima facie it would seem to be advantageous to adopt the moments associated with intertemporal optimization, as the use of extra information should result in greater efficiency but, seemingly paradoxically, it has emerged from the literature that $\hat{\theta}_S$ is a far better behaved estimator than $\hat{\theta}_T$. Evidence in favour of this proposition is BER's report that θ is very precisely determined using $\hat{\theta}_S$, whereas Mao's simulation studies show that $\hat{\theta}_T$ has very poor sampling performance.

Table 7.2 illustrates Mao's results, recording the bias in estimating σ^{-1} and θ by GMM for different sample sizes,[8] when data have been generated from the RBC model of section 2 by an algorithm due to Mao (1990), except that government expenditure is excluded. Parameter values were $\beta = 0.96$, $\sigma^{-1} = 0.5$, $\theta = 0.3$, $\delta = 0.1$, $\alpha = 0.3$, and $\rho_a = 0.9$. GMM estimation uses the moment conditions in (7.26) with the same instruments as chosen by Mao: unity and $\{[C_{t-j}/C_{t-j-1}], (1 - \delta + r_{t-j}), W_{t-j}/W_{t-j-1}\}_{j=0}^1$. A total of 1000 replications were performed, with a replication being discarded if convergence was not achieved after 200 iterations (the maximum number of deletions was 30). Clearly the GMM estimator is strongly biased in small samples, and even with large numbers of observations a bias of the order of 10% is possible.

There is a simple explanation of this feature, coming from the properties of the GMM estimator in finite samples. BER replace the conditional expectation in (7.23) by the unconditional expectation, and so effectively perform OLS, which is a well behaved estimator. Because (7.26) involves three unknown coefficients Mao has to perform GMM with at least three instruments chosen from the past history of c_t, r_t, and w_t. Now the GMM estimator is an instrumental variables (IV) estimator exploiting the moment conditions $E[z_t \phi_t] = 0$, where $\phi_t = \beta(C_{t+1}/C_t)^{-\sigma}(1 - \delta + r_{t+1})(W_{t+1}/W_t)^{(1-\theta)(\sigma-1)} - 1$, and z_t are the instruments. It is known that the properties of the IV estimator in finite samples depend critically upon the correlation between z_t and $(\partial \phi_t/\partial \theta)$. Indeed, as Phillips (1989) shows in the context of a linear simultaneous model, when this correlation is zero the moments of the sampling distribution of $\hat{\theta}_{GMM}$ may well not exist in any sample size; for correlations that are small one would therefore expect considerable departures from the asymptotic distributions unless the sample size is extremely large: see for example Kocherlakota

Table 7.2 Bias in estimators of RBC model parameters

Estimator	σ^{-1}	θ
GMM ($T = 100$)	-0.053	-0.376
GMM ($T = 100$)	-0.006	-0.043
GMM ($T = 100$)		-0.349

The true values of σ^{-1} and θ are 0.5 and 0.3 respectively: σ is set to its true value for the third line.

(1990). Canova, Finn, and Pagan (1991), using data generated from Mao's simulation experiments, show that the correlation depends upon the value of σ when $\sigma = 1$ it is zero and, even: when $\sigma = 0.5$, the correlation is only 0.09. Hence it is likely that this is the source of the bias in table 7.2. To verify that it is due to a poor correlation of instruments and regressors, rather than the problem of estimating a number of parameters, the third line of table 7.2 gives the bias when σ and β are set to their true values, so that only σ is being estimated. As expected, the bias remains. Hence, although it would be true that in very large samples one would get good estimates of θ from $\hat{\theta}_T$, in the samples typically available to investigators working with time series data poor estimates are much more likely.[9]

3.3 Maximum Likelihood Estimation

Maximum likelihood estimation (MLE) has also been performed as part of calibration: see Altug (1989) and McGrattan (1991) *inter alia*. Invariably this work has linearized the model around the steady state solutions and then worked with the resulting VAR, (7.19), imposing the cross-equation restrictions arising from the fact that the VAR parameters in Φ_1 are functions of a much smaller number of parameters, namely δ, α, etc. Two complications arise. The first is that not all variables need be observed, e.g. productivity may be regarded as unobservable. Therefore the $(n \times 1)$ vector of observed variables would need to be related to the model variables as $x_t = Cw_t$, where C is known and the implied VAR would need to be derived as was done earlier in (7.21). Secondly, even if all variables are observed, the vector of errors e_t is of smaller dimension than n, being derivative solely from the forcing processes describing the exogenous shocks which drive the model.

When the number of errors e_t is less than n, the covariance matrix of x_t, V_x, will be singular and the log-likelihood

$$- T/2 \log| V_x| - \frac{1}{2} \sum_{t=1}^{T} (x_t - E_{t-1}(x_t))' V_x^{-1}(x_t - E_{t-1}(x_t))$$

cannot be evaluated. Three solutions to this difficulty have been proposed in the literature:

1. A minimum distance estimator minimizing $\Sigma_{t=1}^{T}(x_t - E_{t-1}(x_t))D^{-1}(x_t - E_{t-1}(x_t))$, where D is a matrix that is pre-specified, e.g. D might be the matrix consisting of the diagonal elements of V_x.
2. Canova, Finn, and Pagan (1994) point out it is always possible to consider reducing the VAR (7.19) to a smaller VAR involving the same number of variables as the forcing processes, e.g. if there are only two shocks one could consider a bivariate VAR in c_t and y_t and then perform MLE on this smaller system. There is a possible indeterminacy coming from the fact there are many possible ways of selecting such sub-sets of variables of the requisite dimension and this may result in a variety of estimates of the parameters of interest. Moreover, because it is clearly the case that

the covariance matrix of the data x_t is unlikely to be singular, there seems little point in proceeding along this route.

3 The addition of enough "errors of observation" to make the observables vector non-singular.

Authors proceeding with the last of these three solutions think of model variables corresponding to an observation x_t as latent, and these will be designated by x_t^*, with the relation between the observable and the latent variables being

$$x_t \equiv x_t^* + \zeta_t. \tag{7.27}$$

If $C = I_n$, i.e. all variables are observed, (7.19) becomes

$$x_t = \Phi_1 x_{t-1} + Ge_t + \zeta_t - \Phi_1 \zeta_{t-1}, \tag{7.28}$$

and the properties of the composite error term in (7.28) will depend upon what is assumed about ζ_t. In existing studies ζ_t is taken to be n.i.d and independent of e_t, so that the error term is the sum of two independent MA(1)s, making the process for x_t an ARMA(1,1). If $C \neq I_n$ the unobserved states such as productivity need to be eliminated first and this may make the relation in terms of observables an even higher order ARMA process. Estimation of the unknown parameters in all cases is probably best done using the predictive error likelihood decomposition due to Schweppe (1965), which takes as inputs the Kalman filter estimates of the mean and variance of x_t conditional upon the past, because x_t is generated by the state space form (7.19) and (7.27).

There are three potential problems. First, since the ARMA(1,1) process is only a linear approximation to an underlying non- linear process it may be that the implied autocovariances of the ARMA process deviate from the autocovariances of the original model. If so, one would get biased estimates of the underlying parameters, as the scores of the ARMA process would not have a zero expectation. Whether this is a problem is something that has been little investigated. Nevertheless, simulations we have run suggest that this is a minor problem. A second issue is the need to make auxiliary assumptions such as normality and independence for ζ_t and e_t which do not feature in the theoretical model. Proceeding as if the errors possess a normal density is benign, as it is well known that the resulting estimator of the parameters of ARMA models remains consistent and asymptotically normally distributed for a wide class of alternative densities. However, this is not true of a failure of the independence assumption for ζ_t, especially if it is reflected in a correlation with x_{t-1}. If the RBC model is regarded as being only a skeletal framework, many factors that determine macroeconomic variables will have been omitted, and, by default, these end up in ζ_t. Standard mis specification analysis then points to the potential for bias in estimates of the ARMA parameters. Apart from a brief comment in section 4.3, there is little of a constructive nature that can be said about this phenomenon, except to note that it is present in all small models, and to emphasize the need, when constructing such models, to capture the major elements at work. Finally, the likelihood may be extremely flat in certain directions. Cogley and Nason (1993) show that there are near common factors in the MA and AR polynomials of the ARMA process and that the processes are very close to being just those describing a_t and g_t, i.e. it may be that the forcing process parameters are the only parameters that can be identified with any precision in small samples.

Should the MLE be preferred to the GMM estimator? The MLE estimator finds the $(p \times 1)$ vector $\hat{\theta}_{MLE}$ that solves $\Sigma_{t=1}^{T} d_{\theta t}(x_t; \hat{\theta}_{MLE}) = 0$, where the $d_{\theta t} = \partial f_{t-1}(x_t)/\partial \theta$ is the score based on the density of x_t conditional upon the past history of x_t, $f_{t-1}(x_t)$. The GMM estimator is based on the moment conditions $E[m_t(x_{t+1}, x_t; \theta)] = 0$, where the presence of x_{t+1} and x_t in m_t follows from (7.26). Then the GMM estimator $\hat{\theta}_{GMM}$ is such that $\Sigma_{t=1}^{T} Q m_t(x_{t+1}, x_t; \hat{\theta}_{GMM}) = 0$ and $Q = - [E(\partial m_t/\partial \theta)][var(m_t)]^{-1}$ is the weighting matrix that optimally combines together the elements of the $(q \times 1)$ vector m_t into $(p \times 1)$ "normal equations" (see Hansen, 1982). By the generalized information equality,[10] $[E_t(\partial m_t/\partial \theta)] = - E_t[d_{\theta t+1} m'(x_{t+1}, x_t)]$ and this allows us to replace the population quantities $[var(m_t)]$ and $[E(\partial m_t/\partial \theta)]$ in Q by their sample equivalents $T^{-1} M' M$ and $- T^{-1} D' M$, where D and M are $(T \times p)$ and $(T \times q)$ matrices containing $d'_{\theta t+1}$ and $m'(x_{t+1}, x_t)$ as tth row. With Q being replaced by $- (D' M)(M' M)^{-1}$, the GMM estimator can be regarded as solving $\Sigma_{t=1}^{T}(D' M)(M' M)^{-1} m_t(\hat{\theta}_{GMM}) = \Sigma_{t=1}^{T} \tilde{m}_t(\hat{\theta}_{GMM}) = 0$. Comparing this to the MLE estimating equations it is clear that, if $\tilde{m}_t$ are perfectly correlated with the conditional scores $d_{\theta t}$, then the GMM and MLE estimators will coincide. Hence, the only reason for a difference in the two estimators must be either that the number and type of moments employed by GMM are insufficient to span the space of the scores, or that the sample of observations is not large enough to give a good estimate of Q. Indeed the correlations between the moments and scores for the simulations underlying table 7.2 are 0.05 (for θ) and 0.04 (for σ^{-1}).[11]

4   Assessing a Calibrated Model

Regardless of how calibration has been carried out there has always been great interest in discovering how well a calibrated model performs as a representation of actual outcomes. But, just as for quantification, there is no consensus on how this is best done, with three distinct suggestions in the literature:

1   comparison with stylized facts
2   application of formal model evaluation techniques under the assumption that there are no "errors in observations" ζ_t, or that they are independent of x_{t-1}
3   construction of criteria for measuring the correspondence of model and data when ζ_t is not independently distributed of x_{t-1}.

4.1 Stylized Facts

The majority of work done when assessing calibrated models has been in this vein. Undoubtedly, the most important issue has been the selection of features of the data which it is important for the model to emulate. Moments and some cross-correlations have been the items favoured by RBC modellers, but those working with calibrated financial models have also looked at characteristics such as the presence of ARCH in data (Backus, Gregory, and Zin 1989) or the estimated coefficients obtained by regressing volatility upon the level of transactions (Fisher, 1990). The range of possible features should not be too restrictive if one is to grasp the suitability of these models for understanding reality. Asset prices, for example, should be tested to see if they are integrated, while asset returns should exhibit ARCH and high leptokurtosis, and should behave as if higher order moments do not exist: see Pagan (1995) for documentation of some of these features. Very few calibrated financial models have ever addressed such a range, an exception being Kearns (1992) when studying the utility of various models of the term structure. Accordingly, one can be justifiably sceptical about any claims that these models are capable of capturing the determinants of asset returns.

There are a number of issues that arise in the use of stylized facts to evaluate models. One that is rarely canvassed is exactly how to interpret such a comparison. Most of those favouring this approach seem to be proponents of the "latent variable" view mentioned in connection with maximum likelihood estimation, i.e. the attitude that the models cannot be expected to exactly duplicate reality. Hence, we can distinguish between the model variable x_t^* and its observed counterpart x_t, making the equation $x_t = x_t^* + \xi_t$. This equation has important implications for "stylized facts" comparisons. Suppose that one follows most of the RBC literature and compares var(x_t) with var(x_t^*). Clearly, var(x_t) = var(x_t^*) + 2 cov(x_t^*, ζ_t) + var(ζ_t). Now, in some sense the discrepancy between var(x_t) and *var*(x_t^*) is interpreted by most calibration enthusiasts as a statement about var(ζ_t), but that would require cov(x_t^*, ζ_t) = 0, which would not seem to be a restriction they would be very comfortable with, since it would mean that the calibrated model could be evaluated in traditional ways (as discussed in section 4.2). But, once one allows for potential correlation between x_t^* and ζ_t, it is even possible that var(x_t) = var(x_t^*) yet the var(ζ_t) could be large. Hence, the method of stylized facts really fails to come to grips with what is the fundamental problem in evaluating all small models, namely the assumptions that need to be made about the nature of the errors ζ_t.

Even if we ignore the errors of measurement problem by setting ζ_t equal to zero, technical difficulties can also arise when converting the data into a form whereby they can be reasonably compared with the predictions of a model. RBC models, for example, construct the moments of variables that are deviations from a steady state, and therefore data need to be adjusted to correspond to such a concept. In most RBC models it is assumed that there is a deterministic steady state growth path, and this can be easily removed from the data. However, such "detrended" data generally still possess a *stochastic trend*, i.e. they are integrated, and hence the variance of the detrended data does not exist. As the debate over excess volatility in stock prices showed, it can be highly misleading to compute a "variance" for an integrated process (Kleidon, 1986). Because of this fact, RBC modellers have removed the stochastic trend with somewhat arbitrary filters, almost invariably the Hodrick-Prescott (HP) filter (Hodrick and Prescott, 1980), and then compared the HP filtered data with the moments produced by the RBC model.

This strategy involves a serious inconsistency. If it is maintained that the forcing processes are not integrated then the RBC model cannot produce a stochastic trend, yet there is one in the data. This alone would seem to be sufficient grounds for doubting the validity of the calibrations performed on many RBC models. Leaving this point aside, one might ask what are the consequences of removing a stochastic trend from the data. To answer this one needs to know what type of process one expects the data to follow and what type of process the filter being applied assumes. Unless the two coincide we would expect that the answers provided by the filter are likely to be incorrect. Consequently, it is important to realize that the HP filter is an optimal signal extractor for y_t^* in the uncorrelated components model

$$y_t = y_t^* + \varpi_t,$$
$$(1 - L)^2 y_t^* = \eta_t,$$

(7.29)

where $\lambda = \text{var}(\eta_t)/\text{var}(\varpi_t)$ is set by Hodrick and Prescott (1980) to 1,600 for quarterly data (see Harvey and Jaeger, 1993; King and Rebelo, 1993). This model is not a reasonable one for most macroeconomic time series as it implies that y_t would be an I(2) process.[12] The importance of this observation is that existing RBC models predict that the log of output would be at most an I(1) process, and so the HP filter removes too much as trend. Most arguments for the HP filter concentrate upon the fact that its response function is close to unity at the "business cycle frequencies" and so it passes through such cycles. However, as shown in Watson (1993), and as can be seen from the eigenvalues of RBC models, these models do not possess a peak in the spectral density at business cycle frequencies, so that this argument is quite misleading. An RBC model may produce business cycles, but its output spectral density has no peaks except near the origin. It is no wonder then that the HP filter has unfortunate consequences for the construction of stylized facts: for example, as Soderlind (1994) and Cogley and Nason (1991) point out, if y_t is an AR(1) process with AR parameter 0.95, the HP filtered y_t has a spectral density with a peak at the business cycle frequency, i.e. the filtering operation itself induces a business cycle where there was not one originally.

One way to ensure consistency of operations is to stochastically detrend both model and data by their respective implicit stochastic trends.[13] This strategy enables a sharp distinction to be made about deficiencies in the model due to trend behaviour and those applying to deviations around trend. It seems sensible to evaluate the model on these two dimensions separately. Writing the VAR for either the model or the data as $A(L)x_t = \varepsilon_t$, the innovations representation is[14]

$$\Delta x_t = (B_0 + B_1 L + \ldots)\varepsilon_t, \tag{7.30}$$

and, when x_t is $I(1)$, has the Beveridge and Nelson (1981) decomposition,

$$x_t = x_0 + B(1)\xi_t + B^*(L)\varepsilon_t$$
$$\xi_t = \xi_{t-1} + \varepsilon_t, \tag{7.31}$$

where $B^*(L) = \Sigma_{i=0}^{\infty} B_i^* L_i$, $B_i^* = -\Sigma_{j=t+1}^{\infty} B_j$, and $B(1)\xi_t$ is the permanent component. It is also the case that the presence of r cointegrating vectors among the n variables in x_t implies the existence of $n-1$ stochastic trends, τ_t, driving the system, allowing one to express x_t in the Stock and Watson (1988) common trends representation

$$x_t = x_0 + J\tau_t + N(L)v_t \tag{7.32}$$
$$\tau_t = \tau_{t-1} + \phi_t.$$

Stochastically detrended values of x_t are then defined as $x_t - J\tau_t$, leaving the task as one of computing $J\tau_t$. This is easily done for the model. Using the RBC model of section 2 as an example,

$$\tau_t = \begin{bmatrix} a_t \\ g_t \end{bmatrix}$$

as $\rho_a = \rho_g = 1$ are needed to make the system have stochastic trends. Because variables such as consumption are linear combinations of the states, $c_t = \psi_1' z_t$, it is only necessary to express the states in terms of τ_t, $z_t = D\tau_t + v_t$, where v_t is an $I(0)$ process, since then $J = \psi_1' D$. But

$$z_t = \begin{bmatrix} k_t \\ a_t \\ g_t \end{bmatrix}$$

and therefore k_t must be made a function of τ_t and an $I(0)$ process. The state dynamics equation (7.17) shows that $(1 - \phi_{11}L)k_t = \phi_{12}a_{t-1} + \phi_{13}g_{t-1}$, and so $k_t = (1 - \phi_{11}L)^{-1}[\phi_{12}a_t + \phi_{13}g_t] + v_{kt}$, where $v_{kt} = -(1 - \phi_{11}L)^{-1}\phi_{12}\Delta a_t - (1 - \phi_{11}L)^{-1}\phi_{13}\Delta g_t$ is $I(0)$. Drawing together these features gives

$$D = \begin{bmatrix} (1 - \phi_{11})^{-1}\phi_{12} & (1 - \phi_{11})^{-1}\phi_{13} \\ 1 & 0 \\ 0 & 1 \end{bmatrix}.$$

Probably the simplest way to do the detrending is to stochastically simulate τ_t and x_t and then to compute the moments of the detrended variables $x_t - J\tau_t$ rather than attempting to find these moments analytically.

For the data a different strategy is needed. Comparing (7.31) and (7.32) reveals that

$$J\tau_t = J\tau_0 + B(1) \sum_{k=1}^{t} \varepsilon_t,$$

reducing the task to that of quantifying $J\tau_0$, $B(1)$, and ε_t. All of these items may be estimated: $B(1)$ and ε_t can be found after estimating the VAR (from data), while $J\tau_0$ is constructed from $B(1)\xi_0$, with Beveridge and Nelson's technique used to get an estimate of $B(1)\xi_0$.[15] By using this approach, $\text{var}(x_t - J\tau_t)$ can be computed for both model and data on a consistent basis, as output from both has now been detrended by the filter that is appropriate for each. Of course, it might be interesting to compare the two stochastic trends, but such a comparison may not be desirable if only business cycle phenomena are of interest. In essence this is the test advocated by Rotemberg and Woodford (1993). They compare the variance of prediction errors k periods into the future from the data and model based VARs. When $k = \infty$ and the cointegration restrictions are imposed, these quantities would just be $\text{var}(x_t - J\tau_t)$. Rotemberg and Woodford find cointegration between their data series, and specify an I(1) process for a_t in their RBC model, but do not impose this restriction upon the VAR estimated from the data.

Sometimes the question being studied can suggest the most appropriate set of stylized facts, i.e. rather than being "general purpose" as moments tend to be, they are specific to the endeavour. A good example of this is the "Adelmans' test" used in King and Plosser (1994) to assess an RBC model. This test asks whether the RBC model is capable of replicating selected characteristics of business cycles such as the number, length, and duration of expansions and contractions seen in the data. To perform such a comparison, data were simulated from the RBC model and the Bry and Boschan (1971) business cycle dating algorithm was applied to record the model characteristics. Table 7.3 shows the outcome for output when the method is applied to an RBC model. Also included in this table are cases where output has been generated by various univariate processes for output: white noise, an AR(1) with coefficient $\rho = 0.8$, an I(1) process with normally distributed white noise errors, and the same I(1) process with drift. These simple processes are constructed to show that output needs to be close to an I(1) process with drift if it is to successfully capture the chosen stylized facts, and that any RBC model would therefore need to be constructed in such a way as to ensure that outcome. They also support the earlier contention that the "business cycle" generated by an RBC model does not require that there be a peak in the spectral density of output at the business cycle frequency. Inevitably the requirement that output be I(1) means that the processes driving it must be either I(1) or very close to it. Hence, in this instance, a use of stylized facts can be very informative about the nature of models needed to faithfully reproduce a business cycle.

4.2 Evaluation with Either No or Independent Errors in Variables

If it is assumed that there are no errors in variables, it is possible to test whether the restrictions that the theoretical model places upon the VAR are valid or not. That is, for any given values of the "deep parameters," there are a specific set of values for ψ and Φ in (7.18) which become the null hypothesis in a test using the estimated *unrestricted* VAR coefficients. An example is the VAR in (7.22) which is implied by the basic RBC model set out in section 2. If the deep parameter values are assigned, this test becomes one of testing a set of linear restrictions on estimated parameters, a task easily performed with existing computer packages. If the parameters were estimated by MLE a likelihood ratio test can be performed. For other ways of estimating the parameters however special computations need to be made to obtain the correct test statistics. Smith (1993), Canova, Finn, and Pagan (1994), and Chow (1992) all operate with this idea when testing whether particular RBC models are compatible with the data. Canova Finn, and Pagan also point out that the presence of a stochastic trend in the model implies strong cointegrating restrictions, and such restrictions might also be tested. In this situation separate tests need to be applied to investigate both the relations between the trend behaviour of variables in the system and those that are connected with the dynamic behaviour around this trend. Canova, Finn, and Pagan apply these tests to the Burnside, Eichenbaum, and Rebelo (1993) model, finding that it is rejected along both dimensions.

King and Watson (1992) advocate a comparison between the theoretical and estimated impulse response functions rather than the respective VARs, i.e. one should utilize the unrestricted estimated B_j in (7.30). A difficulty with this suggestion is that the joint distribution of the B_j is singular, since they are functions of the finite number of estimated parameters in $A(L)$. For this reason

Table 7.3 Business cycle characteristics of selected processes

Process	No. peaks, troughs	Average duration (months) of:	
		expansion	*contraction*
Data	6	40	18
RBC model	6	36	16
White noise	10	18	14
AR(1), $\rho = 0.8$	10	15	15
I(1)	8	23	21
I(1) with drift	6	38	16

Results for the simulated processes are averages over 50 replications. The standard deviation of the innovations in the AR models is taken as that of the data. The drift term is put at 0.0137% per month to agree with the quarterly growth rate of 0.41% used by BER.

they are reduced to implementing the comparisons through measures such as $\Sigma_{j=1}^{M} B_j' B_j$. For the purpose of *testing* a model there is little to be gained by working with the impulse responses rather than the VARs; the two representations are isomorphic in respect to the information they contain, but the latter is much easier to work with when engaging in statistical testing. For the purpose of gaining an *economic understanding*, however, the impulse responses may well be the better way of organizing the information contained in both model and data.

Instead of assessing the model as a complete system it might be desirable to compare the univariate representation of variables such as output provided by the model with that found in the data. Zellner and Palm (1974) advocated this procedure as the bridge between structural econometric models and time series analysis. As they pointed out, a VAR(1) in n variables implies that each individual variable potentially follows an ARMA(n, $n-1$) process, although whether the maximum orders are attained or not depends upon whether there is any cancellation due to common factors in the lag polynomials. Cogley and Nason (1992; 1993) have applied this idea to the assessment of RBC models. In the latter paper they demonstrate that the Christiano and Eichenbaum (1992) RBC model implies an ARMA(3,2) process in the percentage deviation of output from a deterministic linear trend ($\tilde{y}_t$) of the form

$$\tilde{y}_t = 1.89 \left(\frac{1 - 0.944L}{1 - 0.942L} \right) \frac{e_{at}}{1 - 0.95L} + 0.152 \left(\frac{1 - 0.943L}{1 - 0.942L} \right) \frac{e_{gt}}{1 - 0.96L},$$

where e_{at} and e_{gt} are the innovations into the productivity and fiscal variables. Clearly this is approximately an AR(1), $(1 - 0.95L)\tilde{y}_t = \varepsilon_t$. Data however follow an AR(2), $(1 - 0.944L)(1 - 0.379L)\tilde{y}_t = \varepsilon_t$, so that the RBC model does not generate sufficient dynamics. Comparison may also be made with a VAR reduced to (say) two variables rather than one. Canova, Finn, and Pagan (1994) follow the latter strategy, concentrating upon pairs such as consumption/output and investment/output in order to determine how the BER model might be respecified.

Although it is important to have some idea of the extent to which the chosen model corresponds to the data, in many instances such an absolute standard is too harsh for models that are designed as severe abstractions. Rather than a comparison with an unrestricted VAR, it may be more relevant to investigate the relative performance of different simple models. As emphasized in section 2, provided attention is restricted to linear models, these are all capable of being absorbed into the VAR framework, with each being regarded as imposing a set of restrictions upon the VAR parameters. Contrasting two models therefore normally involves making a selection of one of the two sets of restrictions or, more formally, of comparing two non-nested models. This task falls under the purview of the encompassing literature set out in Mizon and Richard (1986) and Gouriéroux, Monfort, and Trognon (1983). A decision has to be made about what dimension the models are to encompass, but once that is done it is straightforward to pit one model against another. Suppose for example that the chosen criterion was the trace of the covariance matrix of the errors in each model. Then the difference between these may be taken as a test of the superiority of one model over another and this forms the basis of the encompassing test statistic. Asymptotic theory may be used to place a standard error upon this quantity: see Mizon and Richard (1986) and Gouriéroux, Monfort, and Trognon (1983). However, it is probably easiest to bootstrap the test statistics. Here the unrestricted VAR becomes a crucial element as it may be estimated and its residuals taken as the random numbers used by the bootstrap. The idea of comparing the two models through the VAR has been suggested by Hoover (1991) and by Canova, Finn, and Pagan (1994). The latter implemented a comparison of an RBC and a multiplier-accelerator model using the relative variances of output, consumption, and investment as the basis of the comparison.

All of the above discussion has assumed that there are no errors in variables. If there are, but they are restricted to exhibiting a correlation with only the contemporaneous errors, e_t, the analysis changes in so far as the model now implies that the data should have been generated by a vector ARMA rather than a VAR process. This makes estimation and testing harder owing to the non-linearities in parameters that arise, but there are no new conceptual difficulties.

There is another tradition for assessing the relation of the model to data that holds the data as fixed and asks how likely it is that the statistics computed from the data could have come from the model. To summarize this strategy, suppose the variable of interest is output, and that the variance of output data is s_D^2. For any given sequence $\{e_t\}$, one could compute an estimator of the same quantity, $\hat{\sigma}_M^2$, with x_t^*, the latent variable in the model. Gregory and Smith (1991) and Canova (1994) propose simulating many sequences for e_t so as to find the distribution of the estimator $\hat{\sigma}_M^2$. They then locate the estimate s_D^2 in this distribution; if it lies too far out in the tails it is regarded as unlikely that the model is a good representation of the data (or at least the data as summarized by s_D^2).

This approach is not as straightforward as it appears. Many realizations of the latent variable x_t^* are being generated, but the observations x_t remain fixed. By definition $x_t = x_t^* + \zeta_t$, and the fixity of the LHS here means that $var(x_t)$ is effectively being set to zero (the variance here is across the replications of the simulation being performed). Accordingly, this equation demands that x_t^* be negatively related to ζ_t, a restriction that is hard to justify. Expressed differently, since the model's latent variables are related to the real world outcomes, it is illegitimate to assume that we can generate different states of the hypothetical (model) world without recognizing that this also requires us to consider that the real world outcomes would also change. Perhaps the simplest way to see this point is to consider the actual data generating process to be $x_t = b_1 x_{t-1} + b_2 x_{t-2} + e_t$, whereas the model has the form

$x_t^* = b_1 x_{t-1}^* + e_t$, so that $\zeta_t = b_1 \zeta_{t-1} + b_2 x_{t-2}$, and this is clearly correlated with x_{t-1}^* unless $b_2 = 0$, in which case it is zero. If one simulated x_t^* by choosing different sequences for e_t, of necessity these imply different sequences for x_t.

Now, suppose that x_t is taken to be identical to x_t^* in the simulations. Then ζ_t is zero and the question naturally arises of why one would want to do this exercise rather than the formal model evaluation programme described earlier. To investigate this question it is important to understand what each technique does. In the standard mode of analysis $\hat{\sigma}_D^2$ is regarded as being asymptotically $N(\sigma_M^2, V_D)$, under the null hypothesis that the model is correct. In the simulation approach $\hat{\sigma}_M^2$ has a distribution determined by the sample size and the distribution of e_t; in large samples $\hat{\sigma}_M^2$ is $N(\sigma_M^2, V_M)$. Hence, in large samples the conclusions we would reach using either method would be identical if V_D and V_M are the same. Now the variances will be identical if the regressors and errors in their respective VARs are the same. But that requires ζ_t to be zero. Obviously, the two procedures are closely related; one concentrates upon the small sample distribution of $\hat{\sigma}_M^2$ rather than asserting asymptotic normality, while the other allows for slightly more flexibility when addressing the nature of ζ_t. It is clearly not true, as the proponents of the simulation approach tend to imply, that there is anything radically different in the attitudes registered by each technique towards how models should be assessed.

4.3   Evaluation with Non-Independent Errors in Variables

Underlying much work with calibrated models is the view that the specification errors being committed are of sufficient magnitude as to make conventional estimation and testing procedures of dubious value. For example, Kydland and Prescott (1991, p. 170) say

> Unlike the SEA, no attempt is made to determine the true model. All model economies are abstractions and are by definition false.

Canova (1994) says that

> Roughly speaking, the SEA asks the question "Given that the model is true, how true is it?," while the CA asks "Given the model is false, how false is it?"

Both of these statements evidence some misconceptions about the SEA. Traditional model building never proceeded under the assumption that any model was true.[16] Instead, the *modus operandi* of the SEA was to study the discrepancy, ζ_t, between model and data by reference to its ability to satisfy a set of desirable features, examples of which would be that it possess a zero correlation with its own past history and with the past history of variables in the model etc.: see Hendry and Richard (1982) for a statement of these. A model was regarded as inadequate if it failed to satisfy these demands, although, in practice, the magnitude of the failure was very important to one's attitude towards how inadequate the model had been revealed to be. For example, a large amount of serial correlation was regarded as evidence of a major deficiency, whereas a small amount would be tolerated. Hence, despite the belief of calibrators, the difference between the SEA and the CA cannot reside in questions of truth or falsity of a model but rather must reside in what characteristics ζ_t would have to possess to make one regard the formulated model with suspicion. By and large these are clearly set out in the SEA, but very murky for the CA. Nevertheless, one would hope that similar criteria would apply to both approaches; for example, large amounts of serial correlation in a calibrated model should throw a lot of doubt upon whether it has managed to capture the forces at work in an economy and should lead to a respecification of it. If calibrators do not share this philosophy it is hard to see how one could ever take the CA seriously.

Although one might agree upon what ζ_t should look like, it is difficult to extract a series of observations upon this quantity from some calibrated models, such as those of the RBC variety. The problem can be seen from (7.28); unless e_t is known, ζ_t cannot be recovered. Even a knowledge of the autocorrelation function for e_t does not suffice, as the autocorrelation function for ζ_t can only be recovered if the cross-covariances between e_t and ζ_{t-j} are known. Watson (1993) represents an ingenious attempt to place some bounds upon certain quantities that might be used for model evaluation and which depend upon this covariance. Suppose that one wanted to measure the $\mathrm{var}(\zeta_t)/\mathrm{var}(x_t)$, i.e. to develop an R^2 measure for the calibrated model. Watson observes that

$$\mathrm{var}(\zeta_t) = \mathrm{var}(x_t - x_t^*) = \sigma_x^2 + \sigma_{x^*}^2 - 2\mathrm{cov}(x_t, x_t^*) = \sigma_x^2 + \sigma_{x^*}^2 - 2\rho_{x,x^*}\sigma_x\sigma_{x^*},$$

where ρ_{x,x^*} is the correlation coefficient between x_t and x_t^*, and, given the non-negativity of σ_x and σ_{x^*}, the $\mathrm{var}(\zeta_t)$ reaches a minimum when ρ_{x,x^*} is unity. Accordingly, an upper bound on the R^2 of the model can be found that is independent of the correlation of ζ_t and $\{e_{t-j}\}_{j=0}^{\infty}$.

To isolate the time series attributes of the resulting ζ_t one observes that $\mathrm{var}(\zeta_t) = \int_{-\pi}^{\pi} f_\zeta(\omega)\,d\omega$, where $f_\zeta(\omega)$ is the spectrum of ζ_t at the frequency ω. For each frequency ω between 0 and π, $f_\zeta(\omega) = f_x(\omega) + f_{x^*}(\omega) - 2f_{x,x^*}(\omega)$ where $f_{x,x^*}(\omega)$ is the cross-spectrum at ω. The $\mathrm{var}(\zeta_t)$ is minimized by minimizing each of the $f_\zeta(\omega)$, and this is achieved by setting the cross-spectrum to $f_x^{1/2}(\omega)f_{x^*}^{1/2}(\omega)$. The value of $f_\zeta(\omega)$ then shows how much needs to be added to the model to reproduce the spectrum of the data at this frequency. Generalization of the idea to vector x_t requires that some weights be assigned to the different variances in order to set up an appropriate quantity to be minimized.

Even though Watson's idea is striking, one has to have some reservations about its utility. By and large its ultimate worth derives from the nature of the negative information it conveys: a low R^2 must be taken as evidence that the calibrated model is performing very poorly, but a high R^2 does not validate the model, owing to the fact that it could be a consequence of the assumption of a perfect correlation between the predictions from the model and the data. As this correlation is not part of the model itself, it would be inappropriate to be sanguine about the model's performance based on its influence. Some insight into the relative contributions of the model and the zero-correlation assumption is available by studying how the R^2 changes as ρ_{x,x^*} varies from zero to unity (assuming it is plausible to rule out negative correlations). Similar comments can be made about the lessons to be drawn from the spectrum of ζ_t found by maximizing the R^2. If a lot has to be added to the spectrum at frequencies of interest, then the model must be poor indeed, but it could be that only a little has to be added owing to the assumption of a coherence of unity between the model output and data. Watson's discovery that substantial augmentation was necessary around the business cycle frequencies for King, Plosser, and Rebelo's (1988a) model is a good illustration of the power of the method to provide evidence against a calibrated RBC model. It also points to the inability of the measures to provide much insight into the possible respecifications that might improve the model. Despite all of these qualms, however, Watson's measures are always worth computing, simply because they are the only sources of information available about the nature of the errors in variables when there is correlation with model output.[17]

5   Using a Calibrated Model

Calibrated models are generally constructed to shed light upon some effect. For example, within the RBC tradition a perennial question has been the relative contributions of supply and demand side shocks to the variation in output, and this has been examined by comparing the predicted variance from an RBC model emphasizing productivity shocks to the actual variance of output data. Such quantities can be regarded as functions, $g(\theta)$, of the $(p \times 1)$ vector of fundamental parameters, θ, and therefore the magnitude of g will depend upon the values assigned to the parameters θ. Because θ is never known exactly, any usage of a calibrated model inevitably involves some sensitivity analysis to determine how conclusions would be modified under alternative configurations for θ.

How to perform sensitivity analysis was a question investigated in some depth in the computable general equilibrium literature over the past decade, with two types of sensitivity analysis being distinguished:

1   local sensitivity analysis
2   global sensitivity analysis.

5.1   Local Sensitivity Analysis

Pagan and Shannon (1985) proposed that $g(\theta)$ be expanded in a Taylor series around the point θ^* featured in the calibrated model. To a linear approximation

$$g(\theta) = g(\theta^*) + [\partial g/\partial \theta]_{\theta = \theta^*}(\theta - \theta^*),$$

which, transformed into proportionate changes, is

$$[g(\theta) - g(\theta^*)]/g(\theta^*) = \sum_{j=1}^{p} \eta_j[(\theta_j - \theta_j^*)]/\theta_j^*, \tag{7.33}$$

where $\eta_j = \{[\partial g/\partial \theta_j][\theta_j/g]\}_{\theta = \theta^*}$ is the "sensitivity elasticity" for the jth coefficient. Predictions can then be made about changes in g as θ is varied from θ^* using (7.33). The key items in local sensitivity analysis therefore are the elasticities η_j, and these may be computed numerically by perturbing the coefficients.[18] Table 7.4 gives an example of such elasticities for the BER model, where g is the ratio of model to sample variance of output and the parameters are those given in section 2.

Although the sensitivity elasticities show which are the important parameters of a model, to complete a sensitivity analysis one also needs to know what is a reasonable proportionate variation in them. In table 7.4 the output variance ratio responds very strongly to the AR(1) parameter describing productivity movements (ρ_a), but if only small changes in it are likely the magnitude of the impact may be small. If θ is estimated one might describe this uncertainty by confidence intervals. In fact, if θ is a scalar, defining the t-statistics for g and θ being zero as $t_g = \hat{g}/\text{std}(\hat{g})$ and $t_\theta = \hat{\theta}/\text{std}(\hat{\theta})$, and using the approximation $\text{var}(\hat{g}) = (\partial g/\partial \theta)^2 \text{var}(\hat{\theta})$, it follows that $t_g = [(\partial g/\partial \theta)(\hat{\theta}/\hat{g})]^{-1} t_\theta = \eta_\theta^{-1} t_\theta$. Thus, uncertainty regarding g depends upon the model, through the sensitivity elasticity, and the data, through the t- statistic for $\hat{\theta}$. Even though this formula is not applicable if there is more than one parameter, it constitutes a useful guide.[19] For example, from BER's estimation

Table 7.4 Sensitivity elasticities for output variance ratio in BER's model

Parameter	HP filtered	First difference filter
δ	0.0	0.54
α	0.98	1.11
θ	0.0	0.0
ρ_a	-20.3	-18.9
σ_a	2.0	3.33
ρ_g	1.0	2.22
σ_g	0.33	0.11

The sensitivity elasticities are computed with numerical estimates of $\partial g/\partial \theta_j$.
These are approximated by $[g(\theta^* + \Delta_j) - g(\theta^*)]/\Delta_j$, where $\Delta_j = 0.001\theta_j^*$.
Experimentation with $\Delta_j = 0.01$ gave no important differences.

results, $t_{\rho a} = 38$, and $t_{\sigma a} = 7$, making σ_s quantitatively the more important coefficient. It is interesting to pursue this result a little further. If the innovations driving the AR(1) process for productivity are $N(0, \sigma_a^2)$, then $\text{var}(\hat{\sigma}_a^2) = 2\sigma_a^2/T$, where T is the sample size. Estimating this variance by $2\hat{\sigma}_a^4/T$, the $t_{\sigma_a^2} = \sqrt{(T/2)}$, making $t_{\sigma_a} = 2\sqrt{(T/2)}$. Hence, $t_g \approx 1.4\eta_{\sigma_a}^{-1} T^{1/2}$ which, after substituting $\eta_{\sigma_a} = 3.33$, produces a t-statistic for $g(\hat{\theta})$ of approximately $0.42T^{1/2}$. From this computation it is apparent that the limiting factor which makes the predicted output variance from BER's model highly uncertain is the way productivity innovations are translated into output variations; even if $T = 500$, rather than the 115 used by BER, the model would still not be capable of a very accurate prediction about the output variance ratio. Hence, there seems little prospect of getting more precise results by better measurement techniques for θ.

5.2   Global Sensitivity Analysis

Local sensitivity analysis assumes that higher order terms in the Taylor series expansion can be ignored, either because the function is close to linear or because they are quantitatively negligible. Asymptotic theory is sometimes invoked to justify the last stance – (see Pagan and Shannon, 1985). Because the higher order terms involve $(\hat{\theta} - \theta)^k$ $(k > 1)$, consistency of the estimator $\hat{\theta}$ points to these terms being small. However, as the terms also depend upon the kth order derivatives of the function g, it is possible that the combined product may be large if these derivatives take large values. Normality of the estimator of θ, and consequently of g, could also be questioned if the sample size is not very large. Nevertheless, this approach has been used to engage in global sensitivity studies (see Eichenbaum, 1991).

To overcome problems about non-normality and potentially badly behaved functions, recourse has been had to simulation methods. The method involves drawing θ from some density, either found from data or a "prior," computing g for each such draw, and finally constructing the density of $\hat{g}$ from the empirical density of the estimated $\hat{g}$. Once the density of $\hat{g}$ is found it is possible to compute the p-value for any nominated value of g. Examples of this approach are Harrison and Kimbell (1985) with CGE models and Canova (1994) for RBC models. The latter is particularly interesting, as he uses a wide variety of distributions for θ in order to capture prior research or "conventional wisdom." Because the approach is simply a "brute force" one, most attention centres upon efficient experimental design, e.g. Harrison and Vinod (1989) and the alternatives such as Gibbs sampling mentioned in Canova (1994). Probably its biggest defects are the complications arising when there are a number of parameters, as now one needs to specify and simulate from multidimensional densities. Inevitably, compromises are likely, for example that the joint density can be expressed as the product of marginal densities, and these may cast doubt upon the whole exercise; in particular it seems unlikely that one would have a great deal of confidence in the *p*-values computed with the method.

Fundamentally, the difficulty with this perspective is that it is too ambitious, in that it attempts to perform global sensitivity analysis ignoring local information, while the latter seems closer to what modellers have in mind when they seek information on "sensitivity," i.e. the concern is not as much with the consequences of extreme values of θ as with the variation that might be expected as a consequence of moderate departures from the preferred parameter values used in the calibration. There are good reasons for this concentration on local information, most importantly that any global outcomes will be dependent upon how one specifies the range of possibilities. Thus, if the derivative of g with respect to θ is high, it will matter a good deal if the density for θ is normal or if it is uniform, whereas, if it is small, the specification of a density is of little concern. Perhaps one should see the approaches as complementary rather than competitive, and some cross-fertilization between the viewpoints is possible. For example, local information might be profitably exploited to reduce the number of parameters for which a prior is needed, simply by fixing those with low sensitivity elasticities. There is a cost if the local information is a bad predictor of global information, but there is also a cost in making invalid specification of priors.

6 Conclusion

This chapter has tried to set out a framework for the examination of calibrated macroeconomic models. Econometric analysis has traditionally focused upon five issues: specification, estimation, goodness of fit, quality, and usage of models. This five fold classification has inspired the structure of the chapter. Section 2 argued that calibration is frequently interpreted as a way of thought, culminating in specifications that are derivative from intertemporal optimization, stochastic driving forces, and full information upon the part of agents. The estimation of the parameters of such specifications has also been frequently done in standard ways that resemble much econometric work with macroeconomic models of the past, although in section 3 we have raised some questions about the ability to effectively estimate the parameters of many small stochastic general equilibrium models, given the sample sizes generally available for this purpose. Our intention in this section has been more to caution the investigator than to provide strategies that might be usefully applied. Section 4 considers the way in which one might try to grasp whether a calibrated model is a good one or not. In doing this our aim has been to be both destructive and constructive. It is important to know when a model is bad, but, unless the methods adopted have the potential to indicate where some suitable respecification of the calibrated model might be made, they have to be regarded as being of limited use. To this end we have suggested some methods that might be applied, and have canvassed their applicability in the special circumstances of a calibrated model. Finally, section 5 has looked at the confidence one might have in conclusions drawn from a calibrated model. Fundamentally, we view this as an exercise in the sensitivity of conclusions to the calibration performed, and methods are proposed that would enable a systematic analysis of this question.

Notes

We would like to record our appreciation of the efforts of Fabio Canova, Mark Watson, and Colin Hargreaves in locating errors in an earlier version of this chapter and in providing insights into the issues.

1   In this chapter we will not be concerned with that strand of "quantitative theory" in which the objective is to primarily learn about the workings of a complex model and only secondarily to attempt to discover how useful the model is as a representation of observed phenomena.

2   Although most theoretical models are non-linear, it appears that either the degree of non-linearity is low or the approximation is accurate (see Dotsey and Mao, 1992). Notice that it would also be possible to allow for a (deterministically) changing steady state, e.g. a constant growth path. In practice most applications do allow for this feature, in which case (7.9)–(7.14) should be interpreted as representing deviations from a deterministic growth path.

3   The variables are taken to be ordered as c_t, l_t, λ_t, y_t, and k_t, so that γ_{23} is the coefficient of the third variable (λ_t) in the equation describing the second variable (l_t).

4   There are different ways of getting this result: see Marcet (1994) or Taylor and Uhlig (1990). One is by solving the Euler equations (7.14) for λ_t, as in King, Plosser, and Rebelo (1988a). Another widely used procedure is that employed by Kydland and Prescott (1982), in which utility is expanded as a quadratic around the steady state values. Then one has a stochastic linear quadratic optimization problem to solve and the methods to do this are described in Chow (1973). Christiano (1989) and Hansen and Prescott (1991) are good descriptions of this method for finding the optimal decision rules in RBC models. Notice that it is assumed that agents have available to them information regarding the exogenous variables at time t.

5   It is important to note that the decision rule parameters in an RBC model are functions of the AR parameters driving the exogenous variables, and so these models are as much subject to the "Lucas critique" as the simple models that just assume relations such as $c_t = ky_t$.

6   An alternative to describing the models through their implied VARs is to form their innovations representations, $w_t = (I - \Phi_1 L)^{-1} Ge_t$, and to compare models by their impulse response functions. This position is advocated by King and Watson (1992). For understanding the differences in models it may well be the best option, in that it has more economic content than a VAR does, but for the purpose of assessing how well the models replicate a set of data, or for deciding how their faults might be rectified, this is unlikely to be true – a theme we return to in section 4.

7   If this moment is used for estimation it involves a variable A_t that is unknown, possibly requiring the use of the method of simulated moments in which A_t is simulated from the process (7.15) and then the expectation is estimated by averaging over these replications. Gregory and Smith (1990) give an account of the literature on simulated method of moments and some of its difficulties.

8   β is also estimated but its bias is always extremely small.

9   The sampling distribution of the J-statistic for the validity of (7.26) is also affected by this phenomenon. When $T = 100$ the true sizes of the $\chi^2(4)$ statistic referred to the asymptotic 0.01 and 0.05 critical values are 0.32 and 0.39. When β and σ are fixed the sizes of the $\chi^2(6)$ statistic become 0.40 and 0.47 respectively.

10 See Tauchen (1985). Tauchen assumes independent observations so that his result involves the unconditional density, but it is a simple matter to make it apply to conditional expectations. The connection between the MLE and GMM exploited here is due to Newey (1989).

11 The GMM estimator replaces quantities such as var(m_t) by the sample quantities rather than those implied by the model. If the latter was used var(m_t) would be singular if dim(e_t) < n. Hence the GMM estimator manages to avoid the major difficulty facing the MLE essentially by ignoring the complete model.

12 King and Rebelo (1993) give another filter, the ES filter, that implies the series are I(1) and this would seem to be the better option. The 13-point Henderson filter used by many official statistics bureaux also seems a superior choice as it results in less distortion of business cycle phenomena.

13 King, Plosser, and Rebelo (1988b) effectively do this by detrending with the log of productivity which is treated as an I(1) variable. There is only a single stochastic trend in their model.

14 If there is cointegration among the x_t, (7.30) is derived by enforcing the cointegration constraints when deriving B_i. If this is not done the dependent variable would be x_t and not Δx_t. Mellander, Vredin, and Wane (1992) give a simple algorithm for doing this once one has determined the cointegrating vector in some way.

15 Writing (7.31) as $x_t = B(1)\xi_t + c_t$, they suggested that $\hat{c}_0 = \lim_{k \to \infty}\{[\Delta \hat{x}_t + \Delta \hat{x}_{t+1} + \ldots + \Delta \hat{x}_{t+k}] - k\mu\}$, where $\mu = E(\Delta x_t)$ and $\Delta \hat{x}_{t+j}$ is the prediction of Δx_{t+j} given information at time t. Then $B(1)\xi_0 = x_0 - \hat{c}_0$.

16 It is important to distinguish actual model building from textbook presentations, where a true model was hypothesized and estimators were analysed under idealized conditions in order to understand what difficulties might be encountered in their application.

17 Watson's idea might also be used to correct for the fact that the MLE of the deep parameters is incorrectly centred if the errors in variables are correlated with x_{t-1}. The asymptotic expected value of $(\sqrt{T})(\hat{\theta} - \theta)$ depends on the unknown covariances, but these can be replaced by the "maximal" values as done in deriving the R^2. Perhaps the simplest way to work out this expectation is to generate normally distributed sequences for x_t and x_t^* with joint covariance matrix determined by the data, the model, and the maximal covariances. The normality assumption is unimportant as the asymptotic results do not depend upon the distribution of the errors.

18 Since most RBC models are solved in either GAUSS or MATLAB the numerical derivatives $[\partial g / \partial \theta_j]$ are easily found.

19 There are other ways of using information about the uncertainty in θ that take account of more than one parameter. Suppose that θ is known to be $N(\theta^*, V_\theta)$, so that $(\theta - \theta^*)'V_\theta^{-1}(\theta - \theta^*)$ is a χ_p^2 random variable. Defining the proportionate deviations in g and θ as $d \log g$ and $d \log \theta$, (7.33) may be written as $d \log g = \eta'd \log \theta$, and we could maximize this linear objective subject to (say) the quadratic constraint that the θ lie in the 95% confidence ellipsoid, i.e. $(d \log \theta)'(D_\theta V_\theta D'_\theta)^{-1}(d \log \theta) = \chi_p^2(0.05)$ where $D_\theta = \mathrm{diag}\{\theta_j\}$.

References

Altug, S. (1989). Time-to-build and aggregate fluctuations: some new evidence. *International Economic Review* 30, 889–920.

Backus, D.K., A.W. Gregory and S.E. Zin (1989). Risk premiums in the term structure: evidence from aritifical economies. *Journal of Monetary Economics*, 24, 371–99.

Bergstrom, A.R. and C.R. Wymer (1976). A Model of Disequilibrium Neoclassical Growth and its Application to the United Kingdom. In A.R. Bergstrom (ed.), *Statistical Inference in Continuous Time Econometric Models*. Amsterdam: North-Holland.

Beveridge, S. and C.R. Nelson (1981). A new approach to the decomposition of economic time sereis into permanent and transitory components with particular attention to measurement of the business cycle. *Journal of Monetary Economics* 7, 151–74.

Bry, G. and C. Boschan (1971). Cyclical analysis of time series: selected procedures and computer programs. Technical Paper no. 20, National Bureau of Economic Research.

Burnside, C., M. Eichenbaum and S. Rebelo (1993). Labor hoarding and the business cycle. *Journal of Political Economy* 101, 245–73.

Canova, F. (1994). Statistical inference in calibrated models. *Journal of Applied Econometrics*, 9, S123–44.

Canova, F., M. Finn and A.R. Pagan (1991). Econometric issues in the analysis of equilibrium models. Paper given at the Canadian Econometric Study Group Meeting, Quebec City.

Canova, F., M. Finn and A.R. Pagan (1994). Evaluating a real business cycle model. In C. Hargreaves (ed.) *Nonstationary Time Series Analyses and Co-integration*. Oxford: Oxford University Press, 225–55.

Cardia, E. (1991). The dynamics of a small open economy in response to monetary, fiscal and productivity shocks. *Journal of Monetary Economics* 28, 411–34.

Chow, G.C. (1973). Problems of economic policy from the viewpoint of optimal control. *American Economic Review* 43, 825–37.

Chow, G.C. (1992). Statistical optimization and testing of a real business cycle model. Econometric Program Research Memorandum no. 365, Princeton University.

Christiano, L.J. (1989). Solving a particular growth model by linear quadratic approximation and by value function iteration. Discussion Paper no. 9, Institute for Empirical Macroeconomics, Federal Reserve Bank of Minneapolis.

Christiano, L. and M. Eichenbaum (1992). Current real business cycle theories and aggregate labor market fluctuations. *American Economic Review* 82, 430–50.

Cogley, T. and J.M. Nason (1991). Real business cycle models and the HP filter. Mimeo, University of British Columbia.

Cogley, T. and J.M. Nason (1992). Do real business cycle models pass the Nelson-Plosser test? Discussion Paper no. 92–24, University of British Columbia.

Cogley, T. and J.M. Nason (1993). Impulse dynamics and propagation mechanisms in a real business cycle model. *Economics Letters* 43, 77–81.

Dotsey, M. and C.S. Mao (1992). How well do linear approximation methods work? Results for suboptimal dynamic equilibria. *Journal of Monetary Economics* 29, 25–58.

Eichenbaum, M. (1991). Real business cycle theory: wisdom or whimsy? *Journal of Economic Dynamics and Control* 15, 607–21.

Fisher, S. (1990). Trading frictions, volume and asset returns. Mimeo, Simon School of Business, University of Rochester.

Gouriéroux, C., A. Monfort, and A. Trognon (1983). Testing nested or non-nested hypotheses. *Journal of Econometrics* 21, 83–115.

Greenwood, J., Z. Hercowitz and P. Krusell (1992). Macroeconomic implications of investment-specific technological change. Discussion Paper no. 76, Institute for Empirical Economics, Federal Reserve Bank of Minneapolis.

Gregory, A.W. and G.W. Smith (1990). Calibration as estimation. *Econometric Reviews* 9, 57–89.

Gregory, A.W. and G.W. Smith (1991). Calibration as testing: inference in simulated macroeconomic models. *Journal of Business and Economic Statistics* 9, 297–303.

Gregory, A.W. and G.W. Smith (1993). Statistical aspects of calibration in macroeconomics. In G. S. Maddala, C. R. Rao and H. D. Vinod (eds), *Handbook of Statistics*, vol. 11. Elsevier Science Publishers, 703–19.

Hansen, G.D. and E.C. Prescott (1991). Recursive methods for computing equilibria of business cycle models. Discussion Paper no. 36, Institute for Empirical Macroeconomics, Federal Reserve Bank of Minneapolis.

Hansen, G.D. and E.C. Prescott (1993). Did technology shocks cause the 1990–1991 recession? *American Economic Review, Papers and Proceedings* 83, 280–6.

Hansen, L.P. (1982). Large sample properties of generalized method of moments estimators. *Econometrica* 1029–54.

Harrison, G.W. and L.J. Kimbell (1985). Economic interdependence in the Pacific Basin: a general equilibrium approach. In J. Piggott and J. Whalley (eds), *New Developments in Applied General Equilibrium Analysis*. Cambridge University Press.

Harrison, G.W. and H.D. Vinod (1989). The sensitivity analysis of applied general equilibrium models: completely randomized factorial sampling designs. Mimeo, University of New Mexico.

Harvey, A.C. and A. Jaeger (1993). Detrending, stylized facts and the business cycle. *Journal of Applied Econometrics* 8, 231–47.

Hendry, D.F. and J.F. Richard (1982). On the formulation of empirical models in dynamic econometrics. *Journal of Econometrics* 20, 3–33.

Hodrick, R.J. and E.C. Prescott (1980). Post-war U.S. business cycles: an empirical investigation. Discussion Paper no. 451, Carnegie-Mellon University.

Hoover, K.D. (1991). Calibration and the econometrics of the macroeconomy. Mimeo, University of California at Davis.

Ingram, B.F. and C.H. Whiteman (1993). Toward a new Minnesota prior: forecasting macroeconomic series using real business cycle model priors. *Journal of Monetary Economics* 34, 497–510.

Johansen, L. (1960). *A Multi-Sectoral Study of Economic Growth*. Amsterdam: North Holland.

Jonson, P.D., E.R. Moses and C.R. Wymer (1977). The RBA model of the Australian economy. In *Conference in Applied Economic Research*, Reserve Bank of Australia.

Jorgenson, D.W. (1963). Capital theory and investment behaviour. *American Economic Review, Papers and Proceedings* 53, 247–59.

Kearns, P. (1992). Pricing interest rate derivative securities when volatility is stochastic. Mimeo, University of Rochester.

King, R.G., C. Plosser and S. Rebelo (1988a). Production, growth and business cycles I: the basic neoclassical model. *Journal of Monetary Economics* 21 195–232.

King, R.G., C. Plosser and S. Rebelo (1988b). Production, growth and business cycles II: new directions. *Journal of Monetary Economics* 21, 309–41.

King, R.G. and C. Plosser (1994). Real business cycles and the test of the Adelmans. *Journal of Monetary Economics* 33, 405–38.

King, R.G. and M. Watson (1992). On the econometrics of comparative dynamics. Mimeo, Northwestern University.

King, R.G. and S. Rebelo (1993). Low frequency filtering and real business cycles. *Journal of Economic Dynamics and Control* 17, 207–31.

Kleidon, A.W. (1986). Variance bounds tests and stock price valuation models. *Journal of Political Economy* 96, 953–1001.

Kocherlakota, N. (1990). On tests of representative consumer asset pricing models. *Journal of Monetary Economics* 26, 285–304.

Koopmans, T.C. and W.C. Hood (1953). The estimation of simultaneous linear economic relationships. In W.C. Hood and T.C. Koopmans (eds), *Studies in Econometric Method*. Cowles Foundation Monograph 14, Yale University Press.

Kydland, F. and E. Prescott (1982). Time to build and aggregate fluctuations. *Econometrica* 50, 1345–70.

Kydland, F. and F. Prescott (1990). The econometrics of the general equilibrium approach to business cycles. *Scandinavian Journal of Economics* 93, 161–78.

Mao, C.S. (1990). Hypothesis testing and finite sample properties of generalized method of moments estimators: a Monte Carlo study. Mimeo, Federal Reserve Bank of Richmond.

Marcet, A. (1994). Simulation analysis of dynamic stochastic models: application to theory and estimation. In C.A. Sims (ed.), *Advances in Econometrics*, Sixth World Congress, Cambridge University Press, 81–118.

McGrattan, E.B. (1991). The macroeconomic effects of distortionary taxation. Discussion Paper no. 37, Institute for Empirical Macroeconomics, Federal Reserve Bank of Minneapolis.

McKibbin, W.J. (1988). Policy analysis with the MSG2 model. In M. E. Burns and C. W. Murphy (eds), *Macroeconomic Modelling in Australia*. Supplementary conference issue of *Australian Economic Papers*, 61–88.

Mellander, E., A. Vredin and A. Warne (1992). Stochastic trends and economic fluctuations in a small open economy. *Journal of Applied Econometrics* 7, 369–94.

Mizon, G.E. and J.F. Richard (1986). The encompassing principle and its application to non-nested hypotheses. *Econometrica* 54, 657–78.

Modigliani, F. and R. Brumberg (1954). Utility analysis and the consumption function: an interpretation of cross-section data. In K. Kurihara (ed.), *Post-Keynesian Economics*. New Brunswick: Rutgers University Press.

Monfort, A. and R. Rabemananjara (1990). From a VAR to a structural model, with an application to the wage price spiral. *Journal of Applied Econometrics* 5, 203–27.

Murphy, C.W. (1988). An overview of the Murphy model. In M. E. Burns and C.W. Murphy (eds) *Macroeconomic Modelling in Australia*. Supplementary conference issue of *Australian Economic Papers*, 61–8.

Newey, W.K. (1989). Efficient estimation of semiparametric models via moment restrictions. Mimeo. Princeton University.

Nickell, S. (1985). Error correction, partial adjustment and all that. *Oxford Bulletin of Economics and Statistics* 47, 119–30.

Pagan, A.R. and J.H. Shannon (1985). Sensitivity analysis for linearized computable general equilibrium models. In J. Piggott and J. Whalley (eds), *New Developments in Applied General Equilibrium Analysis*. Cambridge University Press.

Pagan, A.R. (1995). The econometrics of financial markets. Mimeo, Australian National University.

Pesaran, M.H. and R. Smith (1995). Theory and evidence in economics. *Journal of Econometrics*, 67, 61–79.

Phillips, A.W. (1957). Stabilisation policy and the time-forms of lagged responses. *Economic Journal* LXVII, 265–77.

Phillips, P.C.B. (1989). Partially identified models. *Econometric Theory* 5, 181–240.

Rotemberg, J.J. and M. Woodford (1993). Can the real business cycle model explain forecastable movements in GNP? Mimeo, Massachussetts Institute of Technology.

Schweppe, F.C. (1965). Evaluation of likelihood for Gaussian signals. *I.E.E.E. Transactions on Information Theory* 11, 61–70.

Singleton, K.J. (1988). Economic issues in the analysis of equilibrium business cycle models. *Journal of Monetary Economics* 21, 361–86.

Smith, A.A. (1993). Estimating non-linear time series models using simulated vector autoregressions. *Journal of Applied Econometrics* 8, S63–84.

Soderlind, P. (1994). Cyclical properties of a real business cycle model. *Journal of Applied Econometrics* 9, S113–22.

Stock, J.H. and M.W. Watson (1988). Testing for common trends. *Journal of the American Statistical Association* 83, 1097–1107.

Tauchen, G. (1985). Diagnostic testing and evaluation of maximum likelihood models. *Journal of Econometrics*, 30, 415–43.

Taylor, J. and H. Uhlig (1990). Solving nonlinear stochastic growth models: a comparison of alternative solution methods. *Journal of Business and Economic Statistics* 8, 1–18.

Watson, M.W. (1993). Measures of fit for calibrated models. *Journal of Political Economy*, 101, 1011–41.
Zellner, A. and F. Palm (1974). Time series analysis and simultaneous equation econometric models. *Journal of Econometrics* 2, 17–54.

8

Macroeconometric Disequilibrium Models

Guy Laroque and Bernard Salanié

1 Introduction

Since the beginning of the 1980s, there has been a continuing research effort in the specification and estimation of macroeconometric models where prices and wages are not assumed to clear instantaneously all markets. The theoretical challenge in such a framework is to provide a consistent description of the allocation of resources at noncompetitive prices that offers a substitute for general competitive equilibrium theory. Such a theory has been available for *static* economies, since the work of Clower (1965) on the dual decision hypothesis, and its embedding in a multi-market setup by Barro and Grossman (1971), Bénassy (1975), and Drèze (1975). However, modeling the dynamics of such an economy has proved much more difficult. In theory, the behavior of the economic agents depends on the expected evolution of prices and wages, as well as on the expected evolution of rationing. There are a number of competing theories that try to explain price rigidities and to relate the dynamics of prices to excess demands and the fundamentals in the economy, but unfortunately no consensus exists in the profession. Furthermore, there are very few models where the expectation of rationing is related (rationally) to the price and wage changes. Therefore, most, if not all, of the literature has proceeded under the assumption of predetermined prices, with a simple (often implicit) *ad hoc* model of the agents' expectation formation and forward looking behavior.

This literature has been reviewed from a variety of viewpoints in the past ten years. Quandt (1988) gives a thorough account of the problems of specification and estimation of disequilibrium models. Laffont and Monfort (1976) and Gouriéroux, Laffont and Monfort (1984) describe statistical issues related to estimation. The present chapter is more empirically oriented; it aims at presenting the main advances of the applied literature since the early survey of the first generation of macroeconometric disequilibrium-based models by Laffont (1985), which compared pioneering studies by Artus, Laroque, and Michel (1984), Kooiman and Kloek (1985), and Sneessens (1981).

The scope of the current study is limited to econometric models of market economies. We therefore do not attempt to review the number of works that have used the disequilibrium paradigm to model the behavior of planned economies (see, for instance, Portes et al. 1987; and the volume edited by Davis and Charemza, 1989). The chapter focuses on what we believe to be the two major problems that the literature has tried to tackle in the past ten years. The first issue is aggregation. Early macroeconometric disequilibrium models relied on the "minimum condition," which states that the minimum of supply and demand is traded in the aggregate. It has been recognized very early on that this condition lacks realism. Furthermore, it makes it difficult to consistently integrate into the framework the data on business surveys and other disequilibrium macroeconomic indicators which are widely used by observers of the economy. A large part of the literature has therefore undertaken to generalize the models of the first generation based on the minimum condition; this effort led to the so-called micromarkets formulation. Section 2 describes the aggregation problem and the micromarkets approach and discusses the econometric techniques that have been proposed to handle these models. The second problem that has received attention, albeit to a lesser degree, is the modeling of prices. This gives rise to a difficult econometric problem. A natural price adjustment model would involve lagged latent (unobserved) variables, such as excess demand, which enter into a complex dynamic structure that includes stochastic trends, lagged prices and wages, etc. Standard estimation techniques do not apply in this setup. Section 3 reviews the state of the art on this issue.

2 Aggregation of Micromarkets and Disequilibrium Indicators

Fixed-price models have mostly been developed with macroeconomic applications in mind; one basic aim was to give a consistent setup that accounts for spillovers from the labor market to the commodity market, yielding a Keynesian consumption function. However, the simple canonical model has a *theoretical* drawback, which was pointed out early on by Muellbauer (1978). This model is built on the efficiency condition, which says that, at the current price, the minimum of supply and demand is traded on a market. While it is suitable for small homogeneous markets, it should not be applied to the whole economy without an explicit aggregation procedure: typically one expects to see some markets in excess demand, and others in excess supply. This specification issue also turns up in *empirical* applications. Day-to-day analysts of the state of the economy follow various indicators of disequilibrium: unemployment and vacancies, degree of capacity utilization, etc. The interpretation of these indicators requires that some parts of the economy be supply constrained while others are demand constrained. More importantly, these indicators should give valuable information for estimation and testing of disequilibrium models, provided that they appear in the specification of the model. A number of authors, e.g. Malinvaud (1982), Lambert (1988), Sneessens and Drèze (1986), and Gouriéroux and Laroque (1985), have proposed alternative ways to deal with this specification problem, sometimes with associated estimation procedures. In this section, we describe the present state of the art in this still unsettled domain, making use of results in our Laroque and Salanié (1989) paper.

2.1   Theoretical Models with Micromarkets

We take as our primitive model an economy where there are N different commodities, indexed by $n = 1, \ldots, N$. We have in mind here a typical reinterpretation of the Arrow-Debreu model, where these different commodities are in fact the same physical product, available on separate markets in N different locations. For each of these commodities, there are suppliers and demanders, whose behavior at predetermined prices is summarized through supply and demand functions which depend on the quantities traded on the other markets q^{-n}, on a vector of exogenous variables x, on some vector of parameters θ, and on random shocks ε. We let:

$$d^n = D^n(q^{-n}, x, \theta, \varepsilon) \tag{8.1}$$

$$s^n = S^n(q^{-n}, x, \theta, \varepsilon), \tag{8.2}$$

where d and D (respectively s and S) stand for demand (respectively supply). To interpret the above demand and supply functions, note that the vectors of exogenous variables x, of parameters θ, and of disturbances, ε, which are not indexed by n, can be taken to be of very large dimension, with for instance some parameters or some random shocks specific to markets other than n appearing as dummy arguments of the functions D^n and S^n. The minimum rule is assumed to hold on each micromarket, so that the traded quantity on market n must satisfy:

$$q^n = \min(d^n, s^n). \tag{8.3}$$

Equations (8.1), (8.2), and (8.3) form a system of $3N$ equations in the $3N$ unknowns (d^n, s^n, q^n), $n = 1, \ldots, N$. Drèze (1975) gives sufficient conditions for the existence of a solution to this system when the supply and demand functions are derived from utility and profit maximizations in a microeconomic setup. Sufficient conditions for uniqueness appear in Laroque (1981a) and Schultz (1983), as well as, in the linear case, in Gouriéroux, Laffont, and Monfort (1980) and Ito (1980).

The econometrician usually does not have data on the N different markets, and the object of study is a macroeconomic relationship linking, say, aggregate output to some aggregate exogenous variables, using some fixed-weights aggregation formula. This is an instance of the general aggregation problem, and there is obviously no hope of obtaining any results without restricting the model to a very specific formulation. Our general aim therefore is to find some examples where the aggregation exercise can be carried out fruitfully, and which yield formulations suitable for empirical research.

The above theoretical specification allows for *spillover effects*. The traded quantities on markets other than n, q^{-n}, appear as a potential argument of the demand and supply on market n in (8.1) and (8.2). For instance, if there is excess demand for skilled workers, rationed firms will substitute unskilled for skilled labor, and the level of skilled employment will be an argument of the demand (but not of the supply) for unskilled labor. What becomes of spillovers in the aggregate? The few models that have studied in depth the issue (Gouriéroux and Laroque, 1985; 1990) yield aggregate specifications that do not differ very much from the models without spillover effects, and have not led to empirical applications. As a consequence, most of the research effort has so far been concentrated on a model without spillover effects, and where the aggregate quantity is simply the arithmetic sum of the quantities traded on the elementary markets. The structure of this basic model is as follows. The supply and demand functions are assumed to be the same on all markets, so that for all n, $n = 1, \ldots, N$,

$$D^n(q^{-n}, x, \theta, \varepsilon) = D(x, \theta, \varepsilon_d^a, \varepsilon_d^n)/N$$

$$S^n(q^{-n}, x, \theta, \varepsilon) = S(x, \theta, \varepsilon_s^a, \varepsilon_s^n)/N.$$

On each side of each market, the disturbance term has two components: a common aggregate shock, indexed by a, and an idiosyncratic shock, indexed by the market index n. These equations imply in particular that the deterministic components of supply and demand, obtained by letting $\varepsilon_d^a = \varepsilon_s^a = \varepsilon_d^n = \varepsilon_s^n = 0$, are equal on all micromarkets. The aggregate quantity Q becomes:

$$Q = \frac{1}{N} \sum_{n=1}^{N} \min[D(x, \theta, \varepsilon_d^a, \varepsilon_d^n), S(x, \theta, \varepsilon_s^a, \varepsilon_s^n)]. \tag{8.4}$$

Typically, the aggregate quantity traded is smaller than the minimum of aggregate demand $\sum_{n=1}^{N} D(x, \theta, \varepsilon_d^a, \varepsilon_d^n)/N$ and aggregate supply $\sum_{n=1}^{N} S(x, \theta, \varepsilon_s^a, \varepsilon_s^n)/N$, since some micromarkets are in excess demand while some others are in excess supply. Indeed, the proportion of markets in excess demand, $p_{D>S}$, is easily computed:

$$p_{D>S} = \frac{1}{N} \sum_{n=1}^{N} 1[D(x, \theta, \varepsilon_d^a, \varepsilon_d^n) > S(x, \theta, \varepsilon_s^a, \varepsilon_s^n)], \tag{8.5}$$

where 1[A] denotes the indicator function of the set A.

In empirical applications, it is further assumed that the idiosyncratic shocks $(\varepsilon_d^n, \varepsilon_s^n)$ are independent from the aggregate shocks, as well as across markets, an assumption which is consistent with our previous ruling out of spillover effects. Finally, conditionally on the exogenous variables x and on the aggregate shocks $(\varepsilon_d^a, \varepsilon_s^a)$, the $(\varepsilon_d^n, \varepsilon_s^n)$s are assumed to be identically distributed across markets. Then, when N goes to infinity, by the law of large numbers which applies under mild regularity conditions,[1] we obtain the popular formulation:

$$Q = E\{\min[D(x, \theta, \varepsilon_d^a, \varepsilon_d^n), S(x, \theta, \varepsilon_s^a, \varepsilon_s^n)] \,|\, x, \varepsilon_d^a, \varepsilon_s^a\}. \tag{8.6}$$

Similarly, the proportion of markets in excess demand becomes equal to the probability:

$$p_{D>S} = \Pr\{[D(x, \theta, \varepsilon_d^a, \varepsilon_d^n) > S(x, \theta, \varepsilon_s^a, \varepsilon_s^n)] \,|\, x, \varepsilon_d^a, \varepsilon_s^a\}. \tag{8.7}$$

2.1.1   A particular case: the CES formulation   A number of empirical applications have specialized this specification further, in order to get an analytical closed form of the model. Following Broeder (1983), write in multiplicative form:

$$D(x, \theta, \varepsilon_d^a, \varepsilon_d^n) = D(x, \theta, \varepsilon_d^a) \times \varepsilon_d^n$$

$$S(x, \theta, \varepsilon_s^a, \varepsilon_s^n) = S(x, \theta, \varepsilon_s^a) \times \varepsilon_s^n,$$

and assume that ε_d^n and ε_s^n are independent and identically distributed with a Weibull distribution of mean 1. Then for some $\rho > -1$:[2]

$$Q = [D(x, \theta, \varepsilon_d^a)^{-\rho} + S(x, \varepsilon, \varepsilon_s^a)^{-\rho}]^{-1/\rho}. \tag{8.8}$$

Furthermore, the proportion of markets in excess demand also takes a simple form:

$$p_{D>S} = \left(\frac{Q}{S(x, \theta, \varepsilon_s^a)}\right)^{\rho}. \tag{8.9}$$

The parameter ρ decreases with the variance of the idiosyncratic shocks; when the variance of the micromarket shocks goes to zero, ρ goes to ∞, and the minimum condition applies in the aggregate.

2.2   Econometric Issues

The literature on disequilibrium models with micromarkets has mainly studied two econometric issues. The first question is common to all the empirical disequilibrium literature, and deals with the difficulties of estimation in the absence of direct information on the prevailing regimes. The second, more specific, issue deals with the use of disequilibrium indicators to get information on the proportion of micromarkets in a given regime; is it possible to write a tractable model that does not assume too much on the quality and adequacy of these indicators? We now briefly review each of these points in turn.

2.2.1 Estimation without regime classification information Two estimation strategies appear in the literature. First, there are the standard estimation techniques, either limited information or full information maximum likelihood (FIML), which can only be carried out under very specific assumptions. Second, there are the more recent simulated pseudo-maximum likelihood techniques (SPML), which allow for very flexible specifications.

In order to use the standard estimation techniques, researchers have postulated, explicitly or implicitly, a micromarket structure which yields a CES expression for the traded quantity. Indeed, a well-known study in the field is Sneessens and Drèze (1986), who write:

$$Q = [D(x, \theta)^{-\rho} + S(x, \theta)^{-\rho}]^{-1/\rho} \times \varepsilon^a, \qquad (8.10)$$

with $\log(\varepsilon^a)$ centered normal. Note that such a model can be derived from our premises, if we assume Weibull-distributed multiplicative idiosyncratic shocks and multiplicative aggregate shocks in (8.8), with furthermore $\varepsilon_d^a = \varepsilon_s^a = \varepsilon^a$.

The FIML estimator of the parameters under (8.10) has the usual asymptotic properties for finite ρ. When ρ is infinite, the traded quantity becomes equal to the minimum of demand and supply, and one obtains the usual macromarket formulation, albeit with equal shocks on demand and supply:

$$Q = \min(D(x, \theta), S(x, \theta)) \times \varepsilon^a.$$

This particular formulation was popular in early disequilibrium models. While the FIML estimator is still consistent in this model, its speed of convergence does not follow from standard asymptotic theory, since the likelihood function is *not* differentiable with respect to the parameters.[3]

In order to avoid resorting to a very specific formulation, Laroque and Salanié (1989) propose a new, simulation-based estimation method. While it is *a priori* less efficient than FIML, it is much more flexible, since it can be applied to any identifiable micromarkets-based model. The new (SPML) method is based on pseudo-maximum likelihood (PML), which relies on the analytical expressions of the mathematical expectation and of the variance of the endogenous variable, say respectively $m_1(x, \theta)$ and $v(x, \theta)$, conditional on the exogenous and predetermined variables. Then the PML estimators of θ maximize the likelihood function of the pseudo-model:

$$Q_t = m_1(x_t, \theta) + \eta_t,$$

where the residuals η_t are assumed to be normally distributed. First-order-based PML (PML1) assumes a variance independent of the parameters for η_t, while the second-order technique (PML2) postulates that the variance of η_t is equal to $v(x_t, \theta)$. In multi-market disequilibrium models, the moments of the endogenous variables typically do not have analytical expressions. However, these moments can be approximated through Monte Carlo simulations, provided one can simulate the model – a very minimal requirement. For instance, if we want to estimate the model defined by (8.1), (8.2), and (8.3) with micromarkets, where Q is the sum of the productions on the individual micromarkets, we get with, say, $h = 1, \ldots, H$ the drawings:

$$d^n(h) = D^n(x, \theta, \varepsilon(h))$$

$$s^n(h) = S^n(x, \theta, \varepsilon(h))$$

$$m_1^H = \frac{1}{H} \sum_{h=1}^{H} \left(\frac{1}{N} \sum_{n=1}^{N} \min(d^n(h), s^n(h)) \right)$$

$$v^H = \frac{1}{H-1} \sum_{h=1}^{H} \left(\frac{1}{N} \sum_{n=1}^{N} \min(d^n(h), s^n(h)) \right)^2 - (m_1^H)^2,$$

where the $\varepsilon(h)$ are independent drawings from the assumed[4] distribution of ε, and the superscript H indicates the number of drawings used to compute the simulated moments. Replacing the exact moments with their simulated counterparts in the PML objective functions yields the SPML (SPML1 and SPML2) estimators.

Looking at the moments of the traded quantities draws attention to an important identification issue. It is easily seen that the expectation of the traded quantity, EQ, only depends on the parameters of the disturbances through the parameters of the distribution of $(\varepsilon_d^a + \varepsilon_d^n, \varepsilon_s^a + \varepsilon_s^n)$. If the specifications of the idiosyncratic shocks and of the aggregate shocks are similar, knowing the first moment of the endogenous variable will not suffice to identify one from the other. Indeed, if we make the assumption that all random terms are centered normals in (8.6), EQ only depends on the variance of $\varepsilon_d^a + \varepsilon_d^n - \varepsilon_s^a - \varepsilon_s^n$! The difference between a model with or without micromarkets can only show up at the second order, in the expression of the variance. This property implies that first-order-based estimation methods are robust with respect to micromarkets; it also suggests that for some purposes, "minimum condition" models may not be severely misspecified.

Both the theoretical asymptotics and the finite distance properties of the PML and SPML estimators have been investigated in some detail (see Laroque and Salanié, 1989; 1994; Gouriéroux and Monfort, 1991). First, it is natural to wonder about the loss of efficiency associated with the use of these limited information estimators, as compared with FIML. In a Monte Carlo experiment on the canonical single-market disequilibrium model, Laroque and Salanié (1994) find that the exact PML2 method is very close to reaching the Cramer-Rao efficiency bound: the information in the first two moments seems to be almost exhaustive for the purpose of recovering the parameters of the model. On the other hand, PML1, or equivalently nonlinear least squares, turns out to be very inefficient; it also has poor finite distance properties, which result in particular in multiple local maxima of the objective function. Second, if exact PML2 seems satisfactory, what of SPML2, in which the exact moments are replaced with simulators? Since the pseudo-likelihood function is *not* a linear function of the simulated moments, the simulation procedure biases the estimators. These biases seem to be small for the parameters that are identified at the first order; they can be larger when one tries to recover parameters that are only identified at the second order. In the Monte Carlo experiment under review, computing the moments with 20 drawings yields satisfactory estimators. Going to 50 should often be quite sufficient in practice.

2.2.2 *The use of regime classification information*

As is well known from the canonical minimum macromodel, the main difficulty in estimating a disequilibrium model when only the traded quantity is observed stems from the latent variable problem. Getting supply and demand estimates is easy when the prevailing regime is known at each date: one must just be careful and beware of the fact that the distribution of the residuals of the supply and demand equations, conditional on the observed regime, differs from the unconditional one. Estimation is much more difficult when the information on the regime is not directly available but has to be inferred from the traded quantity. The main advantage of the micromarkets specification is therefore not theoretical, but empirical, since it may allow the use of various disequilibrium indicators and thus alleviate the latent variable problem.[5] (As discussed in section 3.3, another way to proceed is to specify a relationship between price changes and excess demand on the market, and to use the (indirect) information on the regimes provided by this equation together with data on prices.)

Following most studies in the field, assume the micro shocks are multiplicative and have Weibull distributions, leading to the CES formulation (8.8). Furthermore, assume that perfect data are available on the proportion of markets in excess demand $p_{D > S}$. Following Lambert (1988, p. 55), it is easy to compute S from (8.9) and to get a system of two equations in the observables, each with a single random term:

$$\log Q = \log(D(x, \theta, \varepsilon_d^a)) + \frac{1}{\rho} \log(p_{S > D}) \tag{8.11}$$

$$\log Q = \log(S(x, \theta, \varepsilon_s^a)) + \frac{1}{\rho} \log(p_{D > S}). \tag{8.12}$$

This system then can be estimated by standard methods, e.g. nonlinear two-stage least squares.

There are two difficulties in the implementation of this idea in macroeconomic modeling, which it is appropriate to discuss briefly at this stage. The first one is a further specification issue. The models under study are models with two macromarkets, the commodity market and the labor market, with spillovers from one market onto the other (typically the Keynesian consumption function). There are therefore potentially four regimes, depending on whether supply or demand is constrained on each market. However, the simple CES formulation has been derived for a single macromarket; it is in fact easily seen that allowing for spillovers between macromarkets at the micro level yields intractable specifications at the aggregate level. The two-market model must be very specific if the simplicity of the CES formulation is to be preserved. In practice, the description of the model, which goes back to Sneessens (1981), runs as follows. For the short-run determination of equilibrium, the technology is assumed to be Leontief up to capacity, the latter being determined by the available capital stock. Each firm therefore has a notional demand for labor l_p, corresponding to profitable capacity. This notional labor demand compares with the amount of labor l_k necessary to meet the demand addressed to the firm, and with the available supply of labor l_s. In a macromodel without micromarkets, the fixed-price equilibrium employment level is the minimum of these three quantities. This property is assumed to hold for each firm with the disturbances being conveniently written (see e.g. Lambert, 1988, p. 60):

$$l = \min(l_s \varepsilon_s^n, \min(l_p \varepsilon_p^n, l_k \varepsilon_k^n) \varepsilon_d^n).$$

Further, let ε_s^n, ε_d^n, ε_p^n and ε_k^n be distributed as independent Weibull with expectations equal to 1, the variance of ε_s^n being equal to that of ε_d^n, the variance of ε_p^n to that of ε_k^n. Then:

$$El = [l_s^{-\rho 1} + (l_p^{-\rho 2} + l_k^{-\rho 2})^{\rho 1/\rho 2}]^{-1/\rho 1}.$$

The price to pay to keep a simple closed form seems to be rather high, in terms of *ad hoc* assumptions.

The second difficulty is related to the data themselves. The notion of excess demand is a highly theoretical construct, and has no immediate counterpart in the accounts of the firms, contrary to effectively traded quantities. Furthermore, the various disequilibrium indicators were designed before anyone talked of equilibria with quantity rationing, and it requires some faith to assimilate the reported statistics to the proportions of demand- or supply-constrained micromarkets of the theory. On the labor market, the data on vacancies[6] are of poor quality. The main indicators in use therefore are taken from opinion surveys. While they do shed some light on the bottlenecks experienced by the productive units in the economy, they are only collected from firms, and not from households. This leads one to assimilate a firm with a micromarket, each firm being weighted by its sales, which corresponds to the size of the market. When a firm reports difficulties in recruiting workers, it is assumed that $l = l_s$. When a firm states that it is unable to produce more because of insufficient production capacities, l is taken to be l_p. The other firms are supposed to produce to meet demand. These assumptions yield proportions of micromarkets in each regime, which can be plugged into the equivalent of (8.11) and (8.12) for estimation. There are a host of reasons why these proportions of regimes may be affected by measurement errors, and/or do not fit in the theoretical model. First, labor being a quasi-fixed factor, at least in European countries, the decision to hire is a long-run decision, whereas the determination of employment has a decidedly short-run flavor in the model described above. Second, there is no reference whatsoever in opinion surveys to the monopolistic power of firms and to the predeterminedness of prices; in short, the conceptual framework of the model is far from the vocabulary used in the questionnaire. Finally, the available surveys concentrate on the manufacturing sector, but they have sometimes been used in models of the whole economy.

These remarks should not be taken as a dismissal of the use of disequilibrium indicators, but as a warning sign regarding many empirical studies that *a priori* assume that the indicators give the proportion of markets in excess demand *without any measurement error*. This assumption, forced upon econometricians by the intractability of the alternative, should be relaxed. It is unclear to us whether the current practice (a micromarkets-based model with supposedly a perfect measure of the regime probabilities) should be preferred to the more traditional methods. An example of these is provided by Quandt and Rosen's (1986) study of the labor market. They model the official unemployment statistics U as an endogenous *noisy* indicator of excess supply for labor in a minimum-based model. Their study clearly shows that using the official unemployment figures U considerably helps in getting reasonable estimates. The treatment of switching regression models with imperfect regime classification information by Lee and Porter (1984) could also be applied to noisy regime observation at the micro level. Simulated estimation methods should be very fruitful in this area, since they can handle micromarket-based specifications with error-prone regime indicators.

2.3   Empirical Results

We give here a brief summary of the empirical results that have been obtained in the models described previously, without going into details. We focus mainly on two questions. Does the introduction of micromarkets in the specification bring major changes in the results? Is the use of survey data a big help in the estimation of macro disequilibrium models?

2.3.1   On the relevance of micromarkets   The available studies, which have only explored a small number of the possible specifications, give a clear answer to the first question. Using the minimum condition at the aggregate level does not change much the estimation results, or most of the diagnoses that can be drawn from the model, provided that the interpretation of the results is not pushed too far.

First consider the CES specification.[7] Lambert, Lubrano, and Sneessens (1985) compare the results from the CES with those from a minimum specification, on the French economy, using annual data from 1955 until 1982. They find very similar estimators. The amount of frictional unemployment, associated with the fact that some micromarkets are in excess supply while others are in excess demand, is allowed to exhibit a trend. These authors find frictional unemployment to be rather small: it is 1.39% at the beginning of the period,[8] and increases slowly to 2.56% at the end of the estimation period. Gagey, Lambert and Ottenwaelter (1990), working on a similar specification on French quarterly data from 1964 to 1986, but using opinion surveys as in (8.11)–(8.12), also get rather small estimates for frictional unemployment; the other parameters of the model are little affected. Mehta and Sneessens (1990), studying the Belgian economy, find a larger rate of frictional unemployment, rising slightly from 3.3% in 1955 to 4.7% in 1985.

Laroque and Salanié (1989) compare a two-macromarkets specification with its corresponding micromarkets extension, estimated by SPML using second-order moments.[9] Again, the differences in the results turn out to be very small. The estimated variance of the micro disturbances is significantly different from zero on the goods market, but the labor market is found to behave as if it were a single efficient market.

The main differences between the results of, say, the Sneessens and Drèze (1986) study and those of Artus, Laroque, and Michel (1984) seem to be associated not with the micromarkets specification, but rather with the host of other auxiliary assumptions. In this respect, were it not for its making possible the use of opinion surveys, the small (mainly theoretical) advantages associated with the CES specification would not seem to justify the constraints that come with it in the literature.

2.3.2 The use of opinion surveys

The use of opinion surveys brings precious information to the econometricians, indeed information that cannot be dispensed with when one works with yearly data and short samples. The use of survey data in disequilibrium studies[10] on yearly data was therefore the rule even before the formal introduction of micromarkets. Following a practice initiated in macro production function studies, Sneessens (1983) estimates the long-run production function after correcting the output series for the degree of capacity utilization. A similar device is used in the other previously mentioned studies (e.g. Lambert, Lubrano, and Sneessens, 1985). This correction is not justified by the theoretical analysis, but it should not be hard to incorporate in a fully consistent model.

Even with long samples, for instance with quarterly data, information on regime separation is very useful: it simplifies the estimation process and therefore allows the routine estimation of complicated models, as exemplified by Gagey, Lambert, and Ottenwaelter (1990) for France, Toyohara (1991) for Japan, Stalder (1989) for Switzerland, and by the studies collected in Drèze and Bean (1990). For the US, Rudebusch (1987) was able to estimate a model with three macromarkets.

While we do not doubt the usefulness of information on the regime probabilities to estimate disequilibrium models, this information has up to now been incorporated in a highly constrained fashion, without allowing for the many possible measurement errors in the data. Other information bearing directly on the diversity of the micromarkets should also help to go beyond the rather mechanical distributional assumptions described above. In particular, multi-sector models that model explicitly the differences between the production technologies, tastes, etc., of various sectors seem to be worth exploring. For instance, Morissette and Salvas-Bronsard (1992) use the intersector variance of the growth rates as an indicator of sectorial misadjustments between supply and demand for labor, following the lead of Lilien (1982). Artus (1984) and Artus, Avouyi-Dovi, and Laffargue (1991) are first steps towards the specification and estimation of multi-sector disequilibrium models. The SPML estimation techniques, by allowing more flexibility in the specification as well as estimation with or without such information on the regimes, may be an interesting tool to explore these new topics. Its application should be the subject of further research.

3   Dynamic Disequilibrium Models

As mentioned in the introduction, the literature has not made much progress towards the specification of dynamic disequilibrium models. Most of the work has dealt with models where the allocation at date t is determined as an equilibrium with quantity rationing, without much regard for expectation formation, and prices are revised from t to $t + 1$ according to the state of excess demand. Our aim in this section is to review the estimation techniques for dynamic models with lagged latent variables and to present their applications to price adjustment. While price adjustment clearly does not exhaust the topic of dynamic disequilibrium models, it is a first step towards a truly dynamic application of the theory, and it has therefore figured prominently in the literature.

We show in section 3.1 that introducing lagged latent variables in limited dependent variables (LDV) models both is desirable and implies that the likelihood function involves integrals of order T (if T is the number of periods), so that traditional estimation methods cannot be used. We describe there a new simulation-based method that may allow the estimation of a wide class of dynamic LDV models. We discuss in section 3.2 the specification of price adjustment equations in disequilibrium models. Finally, section 3.3 presents a few applications.

One shortcoming of the literature should be mentioned here. The macroeconomic variables studied in disequilibrium models, such as production, GDP, or prices, exhibit varying degrees of nonstationarity. While there has been a huge literature on the treatment of nonstationarity in linear models, the nonlinear case has received very little attention. It is not even clear what modeling strategy should be adopted in nonlinear models with nonstationary variables; in particular, there does not appear to exist any simple generalization of the cointegration concept to nonlinear situations. Most authors have therefore chosen to pretend that the presence of nonstationary variables did not invalidate their estimators, or (an even less palatable assumption) their test statistics. We unfortunately have nothing better to propose at this stage.

3.1 Estimation Methods

It is of course not difficult to estimate models with lagged exogenous variables and/or lagged *observable* endogenous variables, provided that the disturbances are serially uncorrelated. As is well known, OLS estimators remain consistent in linear models when the disturbances are serially correlated, even though they neglect the dynamic character of the model. Gouriéroux, Monfort and Trognon (1985)[11] show that this result extends to a large class of nonlinear models that includes the usual limited dependent variables (LDV) models: the FIML (or PML) estimators computed under the hypothesis that the model is not dynamic remain consistent if the errors are serially correlated and no lagged endogenous variables appear in the model. They moreover provide an estimator of the parameters of the error process that can be used to correct the estimated standard errors of the parameters. They also show how to test for the presence of serial correlation on the basis of the "generalized residuals," i.e. the estimated conditional expectations of the disturbances, given the observed endogenous variables.[12] Their test statistic is similar to the usual Durbin-Watson statistic. It has been extended by Bera and Robinson (1989) so as to test for $AR(p)$ or $MA(p)$ structural errors in a disequilibrium model; the resulting test statistic looks very much like the portmanteau statistic, again replacing the unobserved residuals with the generalized residuals. Hall, Henry, and Pemberton (1992) apply this test to a model of the UK labor market, with a correction for the presence of lagged dependent variables.

The situation is less favorable for LDV models with lagged *latent* variables. There are many reasons why including lagged latent variables in a disequilibrium model may be desirable. If for instance one wants to take into account adjustment costs in the supply function, then it may be more reasonable to measure these costs starting from installed capacity S_{t-1}, rather than from the actual production level Q_{t-1}, as is usually done. On another plane, buyers that are rationed in $(t - 1)$ may increase their demand in t, giving rise to intertemporal spillovers and to a dependence of D_t on $(D_{t-1} - Q_{t-1})$. Unfortunately, Gouriéroux, Monfort, and Trognon (1985) prove that if errors are serially uncorrelated but the true model contains lagged latent variables, then the estimators obtained under the false assumption that the coefficients of the lagged latent variables are zero are inconsistent, except in some very special cases. There is thus no solution but to resort to estimators that take into account the presence of these lagged latent variables. But since these variables are not observed, it is not possible to condition on their lagged values for estimation. Therefore the resulting objective functions are integrals of order

T, if *T* is the sample size. FIML or PML estimation thus is unfeasible, except in some special cases where it is possible to eliminate the lagged dependent variables from the equations.[13]

It is however easy to modify the simulation-based estimation methods so as to obtain estimates of all (second-order identifiable) parameters of the model, even if both lagged dependent variables and serially correlated errors are present. It suffices to replace the static simulations used in the previous section with *dynamic* simulations, provided that the exogenous variables are strongly exogenous. Consider for instance the following model:

$$\begin{cases} Q_t = \min(D_t, S_t) \\ D_t = x_{1t}\theta_1 + a_1 Q_{t-1} + a_2 D_{t-1} + \sigma_1 \varepsilon_{1t} \\ S_t = x_{2t}\theta_2 + b_1 Q_{t-1} + b_2 S_{t-1} + \sigma_2 \varepsilon_{2t}, \end{cases}$$

where the errors are serially uncorrelated, and x_1 and x_2 are strongly exogenous. Assume[14] a given (D_1, S_1) and choose a number of simulations H. For $h = 1, \ldots, H$, draw

$$((\varepsilon_{12}^h, \varepsilon_{22}^h, \ldots, (\varepsilon_{1T}^h, \varepsilon_{2T}^h))$$

independently in the distribution of $(\varepsilon_{1t}, \varepsilon_{2t})$ and compute recursively for each parameter value $\theta = (\theta_1, \theta_2, a_1, a_2, b_1, b_2, \sigma_1, \sigma_2)$,

$$\begin{cases} Q_t^h(\theta) = \min(D_t^h(\theta), S_t^h(\theta)) \\ D_t^h(\theta) = x_{1t}\theta_1 + a_1 Q_{t-1}^h(\theta) + a_2 D_{t-1}^h(\theta) + \sigma_1 \varepsilon_{1t}^h \\ S_t^h(\theta) = x_{2t}\theta_2 + b_1 Q_{t-1}^h(\theta) + b_2 S_{t-1}^h(\theta) + \sigma_2 \varepsilon_{2t}^h, \end{cases}$$

starting the recursion at $t = 2$ with

$$\begin{cases} Q_1^h(\theta) = \min(D_1, S_1) \\ D_1^h(\theta) = D_1 \\ S_1^h(\theta) = S_1. \end{cases}$$

The quantity

$$m_t^H(\theta) = \frac{1}{H} \sum_{h=1}^{H} Q_t^h(\theta)$$

then provides an unbiased estimator[15] of

$$E(Q_t | (x_{12}, x_{22}), \ldots, (x_{1t}, x_{2t})),$$

and the estimator obtained by minimizing

$$\frac{1}{T-1} \sum_{t=2}^{T} (Q_t - m_t^H(\theta))^2$$

can be shown to converge to the true parameter value when both H and T go to infinity. The second-order simulated pseudo-maximum likelihood method obtains in the same manner, by taking

$$v_t^H(\theta) = \frac{1}{H-1} \sum_{h=1}^{H} (Q_t^h(\theta) - m_t^H(\theta))^2$$

as an unbiased estimator of

$$V(Q_t | (x_{12}, x_{22}), \ldots, (x_{1t}, x_{2t})).$$

Two remarks are in order here. First, identification must be checked with care in dynamic models. All parameters are second-order identifiable in model P_d unless all variables in x_{1t} or x_{2t} are constant. This will not be true if errors are serially correlated;[16] however, the method will still provide consistent and asymptotically normal estimators of θ_1 and θ_2 under any identification constraint. Second, the estimation of the variance-covariance matrix of the estimators involves an estimate of the expectation of the outer products of the scores. Since, under the null, the vectors of the scores are correlated from date to date, corrections *à la* Newey and West (1987) must be made to get consistent standard errors.

The dynamic simulation amounts to a Monte Carlo simulation of a *T*-dimensional integral. It may seem strange that such a procedure leads to reliable estimates. However, the integral has a rather specific structure: past simulation errors are weighted by decreasing coefficients if the model is stationary, which amounts to reducing the order of the integral. We present in Laroque and Salanié (1993) some Monte Carlo experiments we have run on artificial data for a one-market disequilibrium model where demand follows a stationary $AR(1)$ process. The results show that the second-order dynamic simulated pseudo-maximum likelihood method performs rather well. This may open the way to the estimation of general dynamic LDV models.

3.2 Price Adjustment

While the allocation of resources at predetermined prices has been thoroughly investigated and gives solid foundations for empirical analysis and testing, models of price determination are the subject of much controversy, and a number of possible modeling strategies coexist. There is of course the classical theory, according to which prices clear the market at each date. Neo-Keynesian theories introduce monopolistic competition: the current prices are fixed at the outset of the period before resources are allocated, and agents in the economy revise the prices of their products from one period to the next (see e.g. Grandmont and Laroque, 1976 for an early model along these lines). Of course, a recurrent theme in this literature is the idea of rigidities and adjustment costs in price-setting. This type of consideration appears to be hard to mix with the traditional approaches; it yields formulations that assume an implausible amount of planning on the agents' part. Indeed, when fixing a price for several periods ahead, a rational economic agent must anticipate the consequences of his decision on his trade, taking into account the other agents' price decisions and the complexities of the allocation of resources at predetermined prices; the task appears rather daunting. The literature presents a number of possible short cuts: a *tâtonnement*-like process, where prices vary from one period to the next depending on the level of excess demand[17] (Veendorp, 1975; Laroque, 1981b); staggered contracts whose lengths are exogenous (Taylor, 1979); or endogenous with exogenous menu costs of changing prices (e.g. Benabou, 1988). The newer developments typically focus on price determination and are not very explicit on the allocation of resources. The empirical work has therefore mostly built on *tâtonnement*-like specifications, using excess demands as a natural tension variable. This is in line with traditional macroeconometric models, whose price adjustment equations rest on indicators of excess demand (unemployment in the Phillips curve, and the degree of capacity utilization in the price equation). Let us therefore complement the canonical disequilibrium model with the following equation:

$$p_t - p_{t-1} = \sum_{i=0}^{n} a_i(D_{t-i} - S_{t-i}) + \sigma_p u_t. \tag{P}$$

In empirical work, this equation should obviously include additional explanatory variables and a more flexible dynamic specification. We will concentrate in the following on models where σ_p is *a priori* strictly positive and where u_t is iid, independent of the demand and supply disturbances. This simple equation will however be quite sufficient for our purpose, which is to stress the feedback from disequilibria to price changes.[18]

A nonzero a_0 in model P implies that price reacts to current excess demand.[19] The model then becomes formally equivalent to a partial adjustment model. Take for instance the simpler case when only a_0 is nonzero, and assume that p_t enters linearly as an explanatory variable in D_t and S_t, so that $(D_t - S_t)$ is proportional to $(p_t - p_t^e)$, where the price p_t^e equilibrates demand and supply. As shown by Bowden (1978), model P can then be rewritten as

$$p_t - p_t^e = \mu(p_{t-1} - p_t^e) + v_t \tag{P$_0$}$$

so that it describes an adaptive adjustment of price to its (changing) equilibrium value.[20]

On the other hand, when a_0 is zero, price is predetermined at each period: it only reacts to excess demand with a lag (see e.g. Laffont and Garcia, 1977). This specification is in the spirit of the fixed-price method. The choice between these two specifications must however rest on an empirical basis, with the length of the observation period as an important factor.[21]

Finally, all empirical papers in the field until Laroque and Salanié (1993) have severely restricted the lag structure in model P by assuming that a_i is zero for all $i \geq 2$ and that only one of the coefficients a_0 and a_1 is nonzero. This hypothesis precludes that price be a moving average of past excess demands; it clearly is unsatisfactory. Its adoption by the literature stems from the difficulties related to estimation of dynamic models with lagged latent variables which we detailed in section 3.1.[22]

3.3 Empirical Results

While price adjustment equations are interesting *per se*, they also serve a specific function in disequilibrium models. In so far as excess demand does contribute to current or future price increases, its estimated coefficient should be positive. Observed price increases then provide very useful information that can keep the estimates of the demand and supply parameters from going too much astray. For instance, generalized excess supply predominates in macro-models estimated on recent European data, so that supply functions are estimated on very few points. Any information that bears on supply therefore is very valuable.

This benefit appears clearly in Hall, Henry, Markandya, and Pemberton (1989) (hereafter HHMP). They study a model of the UK labor market with an adjustment equation for the real wage. In their preferred specification, labor demand depends on the gross real wage, on a measure of expected output generated by a small VAR model, on lagged employment, and on an index of raw materials and energy prices. Labor supply depends on the net real wage, the level of unemployment benefits, the working population, and a measure of union strength. Finally, the adjustment equation is a Phillips curve; it links the yearly growth rate of the real wage, the excess supply for labor, an income policy variable, and the change in employer's tax.

The model is estimated on quarterly data from 1964/4 to 1982/4. Because the dynamic specification of the Phillips curve only allows for one nonzero coefficient (a_0 in our earlier notation), the model can be estimated by the maximum likelihood method. Most estimated coefficients have the expected sign. The elasticity of labor demand with respect to the real wage is fairly small, while that of labor supply is somewhat larger. There appears to be a unit root in the labor demand equation; this probably reflects the fact that labor is a quasi-fixed factor in European countries.

HHMP compare their estimated disequilibrium model with an equilibrium model based on the same explanatory variables. They show that the estimated labor supply for the equilibrium model has a very poor fit. Since unemployment is very high in the last years of the sample and the estimated labor supply must attempt to track observed employment on the whole period in the equilibrium model, it is no surprise that the resulting estimates make little sense. The disequilibrium model, on the other hand, yields an estimated excess labor supply that tracks the UK unemployment series very well.

A feature of interest in HHMP is the strength of the Phillips effect. According to their estimates, a sustained increase of one point in excess labor supply lowers the yearly rate of growth of the real wage by about one point. This seems to be somewhat on the lower side of most evaluations of the short-term inflation–unemployment trade-off in Europe.

HHMP take output[23] to be exogenous in their model of the labor market. The natural next step is to consider a two-market model with both price and wage adjustment. This is done in Salanié (1991). His model consists of two blocks: a "real block" that takes current wage w_t and current price p_t as predetermined and determines employment L_t and GNP Q_t (with its break-down into consumption C_t, imports M_t, and exports X_t);[24] and a "nominal block" that yields the rates of growth of price and wage between t and $(t + 1)$ as a function of the excess effective demands on both markets at t. The model therefore describes nominal adjustment with a one-period lag; in the terminology of the preceding sections, only a_1 is nonzero, and the resulting structure is recursive.

The nominal block has two equations, one for the wage w, and one for the GDP deflator p. The price equation links the rate of growth of price to those of unit labor costs and of foreign prices, with lagged excess demand for goods as a tension variable. The wage equation is a standard expectations-augmented Phillips curve, with the rate of growth of wage responding to that of the consumption deflator[25] and to lagged excess demand for labor.

The model comprising the real block and the nominal block was estimated by Salanié (1991) on quarterly French data from 1964/1 to 1984/4. The complex structure of the joint model clearly makes it impossible to write the likelihood function in closed form, and second-order simulated pseudo-maximum likelihood estimation was used. The parameter estimates for the real block do not change much when it is reestimated jointly with the nominal block; this is consistent with the view that effective excess demands provide good tension variables in the wage and price adjustment block. On the other hand, the precision of these real block estimates increases slightly when the nominal adjustment process is taken into account, so that the nominal equations seem to bring in useful information.

The most interesting coefficients are those that measure the effect of excess supply in each market on the corresponding price. Excess supply for the good appears to have no effect on its price: the corresponding estimate is small and is not robust to changes in the specification. The observed price changes do not seem to provide any information on the size of excess supply on the goods market, and this market presents an implausibly large excess supply at the end of the estimation period. On the other hand, the "Phillips effect" estimate is very significant and robust. Its value implies that the estimated excess supply of labor of 14% in 1984/4 depressed wage growth in the following quarter by 3.2% at an annual rate.[26] These findings are consistent with those of various authors who have studied the dynamics of price and wage on French data, even though the methodology used is rather different.

Much work remains to be done in this area. In particular, it is noteworthy that these models have no mechanism anchoring prices in the long run, such as a money demand equation or a purchasing power parity relation. The price equation on the goods market has very fragile theoretical foundations and does not perform very well. More generally, the "Walrasian *tâtonnement*" approach is only a point of departure; models that integrate price adjustment into the optimizing framework of price-setting individuals while not assuming too much on their capacities for planning are clearly called for.

4 Concluding Remarks

The topic of nonstationarity is perhaps the most glaring *terra incognita* in this survey. While no econometrician would now dare present test statistics in a linear model without justifying them by a careful scrutiny of the non-stationarities in the variables, researchers in nonlinear econometrics still have to content themselves with using the standard (and probably in-adequate) formulae. Further theoretical research is very badly needed in this area.

While we have tried to do justice to the topics we covered, there are quite a few research fields which we deliberately omitted. The most prominent one has to do with the modeling of variables that crucially involve expectations: investment and inventories come to mind here.

When a firm chooses its investment demand, it needs to have expectations not only of future prices and wages, as in market-clearing models, but also of future regimes, as the firm will certainly reduce its investment demand if it expects to be constrained by the demand for goods in the future. This makes for an extremely complicated planning problem; indeed, no full theoretical model of the behavior of the firm exists in fixed-price economics. Empirical studies have so far bypassed this difficulty. Sneessens and Maillard (1988) postulate that investment tends to close the gap between the actual capital–labor ratio and its optimal value; the latter is a long-term concept that corresponds to the equilibrium level of the degree of capacity utilization. Rudebusch (1989) has an investment demand equation in the same vein, but actual investment is the minimum of investment demand and the supply of investment goods. Artus and Muet (1984) take this approach further by considering possible constraints on demand, on labor supply, and on financing.

There have been even fewer disequilibrium studies on inventories, even though they certainly take their part of the rationing on the goods market. Stalder (1989) indeed uses the proportion of firms who report that their inventories are "too large" as an indicator of excess supply for goods. In his monograph (Stalder, 1991), inventories act as buffer stocks: they adjust to close the gap between supply and demand within each period, and firms plan to take inventories back to their "desired" level after a demand shock. However, there is no consensus on the production-smoothing role of inven-tories, especially in view of the speculative motives in inventory holding. All this should be the subject of further research.

Notes

1 It may also hold if the idiosyncratic shocks are correlated across markets, for instance if there is a notion of "proximity" of markets and the correlation structure is "local."

2 The derivation of (8.8) can be found in Gouriéroux, Laffont, and Monfort (1984).

3 Indeed, to avoid the numerical difficulties associated with this non-differentiability, Ginsburgh, Tishler, and Zang (1980) long ago suggested approximating the minimum function with a CES formulation, without specific reference to micromarkets. Recent theoretical results of Laroque and Salanié (1994) show that the usual asymptotic results carry forward to the non- differentiable case provided that the (full) expectation of the score (which exists almost everywhere) is smooth enough.

4 Assuming that the unknown parameters in the distribution of the disturbance are included in θ.

5 The pioneering monograph of Rudebusch (1987) should be mentioned at this stage. Although Rudebusch uses the aggregate minimum condition, he introduces (exact) information on the regime classification using unemployment and vacancies or business surveys data, which are endogenized in his model in a somewhat *ad hoc* way since there are no micromarkets. His experiments (Rudebusch, 1987, pp. 64–70) give convincing evidence on the informational value of regime indicators.

6 Sometimes measured as the length of the job offers advertising section in newspapers. . . .

7 One of the main practical problems faced by Lambert, Lubrano, and Sneessens (1985, p. 54) is the fact that the maximum seems to correspond to a large value of ρ (creating numerical difficulties in the computation of the expected traded quantity), as if the preferred specification was that of a single macromarket, at least at the beginning of the estimation period. The other studies do not mention this issue.

8 This is a lower bound imposed by the accuracy of their computer.

9 Recall from section 2.2.1 that the models cannot be distinguished on the basis of the first moments only.

10 And, more generally, in large macroeconometric models.

11 Following a lead by Robinson (1982).

12 The computation of these generalized residuals may require simulations in LDV models.

13 Dagenais (1980) has a model where D_{t-1} enters D_t but S_{t-1} does not enter S_t. Using a well-chosen price adjustment equation, the D_{t-1} term can be written as a (stochastic) function of past price increases and the lagged explanatory variables of S_t, all of which are observed. Orsi (1986) has lagged dependent variables in both demand and supply, but wage increases are a perfect indicator of excess labor demand in his model, which eliminates the latent variable problem altogether.

14 We abstract here from the difficulties linked with the choice of initial values for the latent variables, which may be important in finite samples.

15 If the x were not strongly exogenous, then the current value of x would bring information on the past values of ε, whose distribution would depend on the conditioning variables.

16 The dynamic simulation method trivially extends to that case: if $\varepsilon_t = \rho \varepsilon_{t-1} + v_t$, then draw (v_t^h) instead of (ε_t^h) and proceed as above, with ρ as an additional parameter to be estimated.

17 For countries with regulated markets, it is sometimes assumed that prices are set by a central authority, given adjustment costs (see e.g., the work of Portes et al., 1987 on pre-1989 Poland).

18 When $\sigma_p = 0$, price increases are an exact indicator of demand, as in the earliest (and somewhat misguided) example of Fair and Jaffee (1972). The resulting price adjustment equations are often written as $p_t - p_{t-1} = a_0(D_t - S_t)$ or $p_t - p_{t-1} = a_0(D_{t-1} - S_{t-1})$, so that a rise in prices exactly indicates the presence and magnitude of current or past excess demand. These restricted models are appealing in that they can be estimated by two-stage least squares (see Rudebusch, 1987), as argued here in section 2. However, this comes at a large cost, since the additional information they use stems from a very restrictive assumption.

19 We should note at this point that the existence and uniqueness of the reduced form then becomes a complicated matter, especially in multi-market models. A general theoretical approach can be found in Myerson (1980).

20 Note that the disturbance v_t in model P_0 is correlated with the demand and supply disturbances.

21 Tests for price exogeneity are available (see e.g. Gouriéroux and Laroque, 1987) but they have rarely been used in practice.

22 When only a_0 is nonzero, the estimation of the partial adjustment model does not present any new problem: by substituting the implied reduced form for p_t in the demand and supply equations, one obtains a model where all right-hand side variables are predetermined, and whose likelihood function is much like that of the canonical disequilibrium model.

Such is also the case for the models where only a_1 is nonzero. Since p_t then is predetermined at t, the trick is to define $p'_t = p_{t+1}$ to be the endogenous price variable at t. The demand and supply equations then contain lagged values of p'_t, which creates no particular difficulty for estimation since p_t is observed. The price equation itself only has the current excess demand $(D_t - S_t)$ on the right-hand side, so that the model has a recursive structure, with p'_{t-1} and the other predetermined variables determining D_t and S_t, which in turn yield p'_t.

23 More precisely, "expected output."

24 The other terms in the accounting identity are taken to be exogenous.

25 The ratio of the consumption deflator p^c to the GNP deflator p is assumed to be exogenous and fixed at its historic value.

26 The excess supply of labor, as estimated in the model, is very highly correlated with the official unemployment figures, but it is somewhat higher.

References

Artus, P. (1984), "Analyse du marché des biens dans les secteurs industriels," *Annales de l'INSEE*, 55–6, 77–107.

Artus, P., S. Avouyi-Dovi and J.P. Laffargue (1991), "Déséquilibre, investissement et désagrégation sectorielle: une application au cas français," *Annales d'Economie et de Statistique*, 23, 137–58.

Artus, P., G. Laroque and G. Michel (1984), "Estimation of a Quarterly Macroeconomic Model with Quantity Rationing," *Econometrica*, 52, 1384–1414.

Artus, P. and P.A. Muet (1984), "Investment, Output and Labor Constraints and Financial Constraints: The Estimation of a Model with Several Regimes," *Recherches Economiques de Louvain*, 50, 25–44.

Barro, R.J. and H.I. Grossman (1971), "A General Disequilibrium Model of Income and Employment," *American Economic Review*, 61, 82–93.

Benabou, R. (1988), "Search, Price Setting and Inflation," *Review of Economic Studies*, 55, 353–76.

Bénassy, J.-P. (1975), "Neo-Keynesian Disequilibrium Theory in a Monetary Economy," *Review of Economic Studies*, 42, 503–23.

Bera, A.K. and P.M. Robinson (1989), "Tests of Serial Dependence and Other Specification Analysis in Models of Markets in Disequilibrium," *Journal of Business and Economic Statistics*, 7, 343–52.

Bowden, R.J. (1978), *The Econometrics of Disequilibrium*, Amsterdam: North-Holland.

Broeder, G. (1983), "A Family of Market Transaction Functions," Working Paper, Erasmus University, Rotterdam.

Clower, R.W. (1965), "The Keynesian Counterrevolution: a Theoretical Appraisal," in F.H. Hahn and F. Brechling (eds), *The Theory of Interest Rates*, London: Macmillan.

Dagenais, M.G. (1980), "Specification and Estimation of a Dynamic Disequilibrium Model," *Economics Letters*, 5, 323–8.

Davis, C. and W. Charemza, eds (1989), *Models of Disequilibrium and Shortage in Centrally Planned Economies*, Chapman and Hall.

Drèze, J. (1975), "Existence of an Equilibrium under Price Rigidity and Quantity Rationing," *International Economic Review*, 16, 301–20.

Drèze, J. and C.H. Bean, eds (1990), *Europe's Unemployment Problem*, Cambridge, MA: MIT Press.

Fair, R.C. and D.M. Jaffee (1972), "Methods of Estimation for Markets in Disequilibrium," *Econometrica*, 40, 497–514.

Gagey, F., J.P. Lambert and B. Ottenwaelter (1990), "Disequilibrium in the Labor Market: An Estimation Relying on Survey Data," in P. Champsaur et al. (eds), *Essays in Honor of Edmond Malinvaud*, vol. 3, MIT Press.

Ginsburgh, V., A. Tishler and I. Zang (1980), "Alternative Estimation Methods for Two-regime Models: a Mathematical Programming Approach," *European Economic Review*, 13, 207–28.

Gouriéroux, C., J.J. Laffont and A. Monfort (1980), "Coherency Conditions in Simultaneous Linear Equations Models with Endogenous Switching Regimes," *Econometrica*, 48, 675–95.

Gouriéroux, C., J.J. Laffont and A. Monfort (1984), "Econométrie des modèles d'équilibre avec rationnement: une mise à jour," *Annales de l'INSEE*, 55–6, 5–37.

Gouriéroux, C. and G. Laroque (1985), "The aggregation of commodities in a quantity rationing model," *International Economic Review*, 26–3, 681–99.

Gouriéroux, C. and G. Laroque (1987), "Testing Price Exogeneity in the Canonical Disequilibrium Model," INSEE DP no. 8713.

Gouriéroux, C. and G. Laroque (1990), "Search and Aggregation in a Fixed-Price Equilibrium Model," in P. Champsaur et al. (eds), *Essays in Honor of Edmond Malinvaud*, vol. 2, MIT Press.

Gouriéroux, C. and A. Monfort (1991), "Simulation Based Inference in Models with Heterogeneity," *Annales d'Economie et de Statistique*, 20/21, 69–107.

Gouriéroux, C., A. Monfort and A. Trognon (1985), "A General Approach to Serial Correlation," *Econometric Theory*, 1, 315–40.

Grandmont, J.-M. and G. Laroque (1976), "On Keynesian Temporary Equilibria," *Review of Economic Studies*, 43, 53–67.

Hall, S.G., S.G.B. Henry, A. Markandya and M. Pemberton (1989), "The UK Labour Market; Expectations and Disequilibrium," *Applied Economics*, 21, 1509–23.

Hall, S.G., S.G.B. Henry and M. Pemberton (1992), "Testing a Discrete Switching Disequilibrium Model of the UK Labour Market," *Journal of Applied Econometrics*, 7, 83–91.

Ito, T. (1980), "Methods of Estimation for Multimarket Disequilibrium Models," *Econometrica*, 48, 97–126.

Kooiman, P. and T. Kloek (1985), "An Empirical Two-Market Disequilibrium Model for Dutch Manufacturing," *European Economic Review*, 29, 323–54.

Laffont, J.J. (1985), "Fixed-Price Models: a Survey of Recent Empirical Work," in K.J. Arrow and S. Honkapohja (eds), *Frontiers of Economics*, Oxford: Basil Blackwell.

Laffont, J.J. and R. Garcia (1977), "Disequilibrium Econometrics for Business Loans," *Econometrica*, 45, 1187–204.

Laffont, J.J. and A. Monfort (1976), "Econométrie des modèles d'équilibre avec rationnements," *Annales de l'INSEE*, 24, 3–40.

Lambert, J.P. (1988), *Disequilibrium Macroeconomic Models: Theory and Estimation of Rationing Models using Business Survey Data*, Cambridge University Press.

Lambert, J.P., M. Lubrano and H.R. Sneessens (1985), "Emploi et chômage en France de 1955 à 1982: un modèle macroéconomique annuel de rationnement," *Annales de l'INSEE*, 55–6, 39–75.

Laroque, G. (1981a), "On the local uniqueness of the fixed price equilibria," *The Review of Economic Studies*, 48, 113–29.

Laroque, G. (1981b), "A Comment on 'Stable Spillovers among Substitutes'," *Review of Economic Studies*, 48, 355–61.

Laroque, G. and B. Salanié (1989), "Estimation of Multi-Market Fix-Price Models: An Application of Pseudo Maximum Likelihood Methods," *Econometrica*, 57, 4, 831–60.

Laroque, G. and B. Salanié (1993), "Simulation-Based Estimation of Models with Lagged Latent Variables," *Journal of Applied Econometrics*, 8, S119–33.

Laroque, G. and B. Salanié (1994), "Estimating the Canonical Disequilibrium Model: Asymptotic Theory and Finite Sample Properties," *Journal of Econometrics*, 62, 165–210.

Lee, L.F. and R.H. Porter (1984), "Switching Regression Models with Imperfect Sample Separation Information – With an Application on Cartel Stability," *Econometrica*, 52, 391–418.

Lilien, D.M. (1982), "Sectoral Shifts and Cyclical Unemployment," *Journal of Political Economy*, 90, 777–93.

Malinvaud, E. (1982), "An Econometric Model for Macrodisequilibrium Analysis," in M. Hazewinkel and A. H. G. Rinnooy Kan (eds), *Current Developments in the Interface: Economics, Econometrics, Mathematics*, Reidel: Dordrecht.

Mehta, F. and H.R. Sneessens (1990), "Belgian Unemployment: The Story of a Small Open Economy Caught in a Worldwide Recession," chapter 4 in J. Drèze et al. (eds), *Europe's Unemployment Problem*, MIT Press.

Morissette, R. and L. Salvas-Bronsard (1992), "Structural Unemployment and Disequilibrium," mimeo, Université de Montréal.

Muellbauer, J. (1978), "Macrotheory vs Macroeconometrics: The Treatment of Disequilibrium in Macromodels," Discussion Paper no. 29, Birkbeck College.

Myerson, R.B. (1980), "Prix et indicateurs de tension dans un modèle d'équilibre général," *Cahiers du Séminaire d'Économétrie du C.N.R.S.*, 22, 51–69.

Newey, W. and K. West (1987), "A Simple, Positive, Semi- definite, Heteroskedasticity and Autocorrelation Consistent Covariance Matrix," *Econometrica*, 55, 703–8.

Orsi, R. (1986), "On the Dynamic Specification of Disequilibrium Econometrics: An Analysis of the Italian Labour Market," *Statistica*, 46–3, 305–23.

Portes, R., R. Quandt, D. Winter and S. Yeo (1987), "Macroeconomic Planning and Disequilibrium: Estimates for Poland, 1955–1980," *Econometrica*, 55, 19–41.

Quandt, R. (1988), *The Econometrics of Disequilibrium*, Basil Blackwell.

Quandt, R. and H. Rosen (1986), "Unemployment, Disequilibrium and the Short-Run Phillips Curve: An Econometric Approach," *Journal of Applied Econometrics*, 1, 235–53.

Robinson, P. (1982), "On the Asymptotic Properties of Estimates of Models Containing Limited Dependent Variables," *Econometrica*, 50, 27–41.

Rudebusch, G.D. (1987), *The Estimation of Macroeconomic Disequilibrium Models with Regime Classification Information*, Lecture Notes in Economics and Mathematical Systems no. 288, Springer Verlag.

Rudebusch, G.D. (1989), "An Empirical Disequilibrium Model of Labor, Consumption, and Investment," *International Economic Review*, 30, 633–54.

Salanié, B. (1991), "Wage and Price Adjustment in a Multimarket Disequilibrium Model," *Journal of Applied Econometrics*, 6, 1–15.

Schultz, N. (1983), "On the Global Uniqueness of Fix-Price Equilibria," *Econometrica*, 51, 47–68.

Sneessens, H.R. (1981), *Theory and Estimation of Macroeconomic Rationing Models*, Berlin: Springer Verlag.

Sneessens, H.R. (1983), "A Macroeconomic Rationing Model of the Belgian Economy," *European Economic Review*, 20, 193–215.

Sneessens, H.R. and J.H. Drèze (1986), "A Discussion of Belgian Unemployment, Combining Traditional Concepts and Disequilibrium Econometrics," *Economica*, 53, 89–119.

Sneessens, H.R. and B. Maillard (1988), "Investment, Sales Constraints and Profitability in France, 1957–1985," *Recherches Economiques de Louvain*, 54, 151–67.

Stalder, P. (1989), "An Empirical Disequilibrium Model of Switzerland's Labour Market with a Keynesian Spillover and Smooth Regime Transitions," *European Economic Review*, 33, 863–93.

Stalder, P. (1991), *Regime Transitions, Spillovers and Buffer Stocks*, Springer Verlag.

Taylor, J. (1979), "Staggered Wage Setting in a Macro Model." *American Economic Review*, 69, 108–13.

Toyohara, N. (1991), "Estimation of a Macro Disequilibrium Model with Survey Data," Faculty of Business Administration, Ritsumeikan University, Kyoto.

Veendorp, E. (1975), "Stable Spillovers among Substitutes," *Review of Economic Studies*, 42, 445–56.

9

Financial Market Efficiency Tests

Tim Bollerslev and Robert J. Hodrick

1   Introduction

Testing for the efficiency of financial markets has generated enormous attention. In this chapter we provide a selective survey of the econometric tests and
estimation procedures that have been employed in this literature. Throughout
the chapter we illustrate the different ideas using monthly data on the New
York Stock Exchange (NYSE) value-weighted price index and divided
series. Many of the results and techniques apply equally well to other financial
markets, however.

As emphasized by Fama (1970; 1991), any test for market efficiency necessarily involves a joint hypothesis regarding the equilibrium expected rate of
return and market rationality. The earliest tests for market efficiency were
primarily concerned with short-horizon returns, where by "short horizon" we
refer to holding periods within one year. These tests typically assumed that the
expected rate of return was constant through time. It follows that if markets
are efficient, the realized returns should be serially uncorrelated. Statistically
significant own temporal dependencies at daily, weekly, and monthly frequencies have been documented for a wide variety of different asset categories, but
the estimated autocorrelations are typically found to be numerically small. It
has been argued that the autocorrelations are spurious or economically
insignificant.

At the same time, however, most high frequency financial asset returns
cannot be considered independently distributed over time since most returns
are characterized by periods of relative tranquility followed by periods of
turbulence. Since most modern asset pricing theories involve a direct mean–
variance tradeoff, at least at the level of the market return, the explicit
modeling of time variation in the conditional second-order moments of the
returns and the underlying fundamentals process is potentially very important
in tests for market efficiency. Of particular importance in these developments

have been the autoregressive conditional heteroskedastic (ARCH) and generalized ARCH (GARCH) time series models. In the absence of any structural model explaining the time-varying second-order moments, simple ARCH models have provided a convenient statistical description of the conditional heteroskedasticity. Bollerslev, Chou, and Kroner (1992) provide a recent survey of this literature.

While the short-horizon tests generally suggest only minor violations of market efficiency, defined as constant expected returns, more recent evidence in Fama and French (1988a) and Poterba and Summers (1988), using multiperiod regressions and variance ratio statistics, suggests that for longer return horizons a large proportion of the return variance is explainable from the history of past returns alone.[1] Of course, the finding of a large predictable component in long-horizon returns does not necessarily imply market inefficiency, as the variation in expected returns could be due to a time-varying risk premium. Indeed, consistent with the idea of a slowly moving equilibrium risk premium, Fama and French (1988b) find that the variation in dividend yields explains a large proportion of multi-year return predictability. Poterba and Summers (1988), though, argue that the magnitude and variability of the implied risk premium are too large to be explained by appeal to any rational asset pricing theory, and they suggest that asset prices are characterized by speculative fads in which market prices experience long systematic swings away from rational fundamentals prices. These highly serially correlated fads are difficult to distinguish from a martingale model on the basis of the earlier short-horizon tests for market efficiency, but their existence is more evident in long-horizon autocorrelations of returns.

Subsequent work has illustrated that the apparent predictability of the long-horizon returns should be interpreted very carefully. There are very few degrees of freedom, and the overlapping nature of the data in the multi-year return regressions gives rise to non-standard small sample distributions of the test statistics. Better approximations to the small sample distributions appear to be provided by the alternative asymptotic distribution discussed in Richardson and Stock (1989). The overlapping data problem may also be overcome by using the vector autoregressive techniques discussed in Baillie (1989) and Hodrick (1992).[2] Interestingly, while the own long-horizon return predictability may be spurious, the statistically more reliable return forecasting specifications employed in Campbell (1991), Hodrick (1992), and Bekaert and Hodrick (1992) suggest a statistically and economically significant long-horizon return predictability on the basis of fundamental variables including dividend yields and interest rates.

The variance bounds or volatility tests pioneered by Shiller (1979; 1981a) and LeRoy and Porter (1981) constitute another important class of tests for market efficiency. In the first generation of volatility tests the null hypothesis was taken to be the standard present value model with a constant discount rate. In the vast majority of these tests, the point estimates implied apparent clear rejections of market efficiency, with actual asset prices being excessively volatile compared to the implied price series calculated from the discounted value of the expected or actual future fundamentals. One possible explanation of excess volatility was the idea that asset prices may be characterized by self-fulfilling speculative bubbles that earn the fair rate of return, but cause prices to differ from their rational fundamentals. Flood and Hodrick (1990) provide a survey of this literature.

Although volatility tests appear different from traditional autocorrelation-based tests of market efficiency, they are equivalent to standard Euler-equation-based tests in the sense that each involves a joint hypothesis regarding the return generation process and the first-order condition for economic agents. Of course, as noted by Shiller (1981b), the power of the different approaches depends on the alternative hypothesis, and the volatility tests may have superior power against certain interesting alternatives.

Relaxing the null hypothesis of a constant discount rate results in much more mixed conclusions regarding excess volatility and market inefficiency. Additionally, many of the early volatility tests did not take seriously the non-stationarity of prices and fundamentals in calculating and interpreting the test statistics. At the same time, the non- stationarity gives rise to a robust testable cointegrating relationship based on the present value model that remains valid in the presence of stationary stochastic discount rates.

In summary, the current challenges for asset pricing theories can be expressed as the search for a model of expected return variability that is consistent with the empirical findings pertaining to the predictability of returns and that provides an explanation for the pronounced volatility clustering in returns. In this survey, we illustrate how a present value model for the NYSE price index that accounts for the time-varying uncertainty in dividend growth rates can actually explain most of the rejections of market efficiency on the basis of the different tests discussed above. In particular, the conditional mean and variance of monthly NYSE dividend growth rates both have a distinct seasonal pattern, whereas annual dividend growth rates show little serial correlation and appear homoskedastic. Using simulation methods, we demonstrate how incorporating this predictable monthly time variation into a model with stochastic discount rates provides a reconciliation of the actual empirical findings in tests for market efficiency with the present value relationship.[3] In addition to this new fundamental price process, we also report simulations for the conventional constant discount rate present value model, together with fads and bubble alternatives.

The plan for the rest of the chapter is as follows. The next section presents the different simulated models used throughout the chapter along with a discussion of the seasonal ARCH model for the fundamental dividend process. Section 3 reports a number of short-horizon summary statistics for the NYSE return series and illustrates how the volatility clustering in the returns may be conveniently modeled with a GARCH formulation for the conditional variance. Section 4 examines the long-horizon return tests. While the multi-period regression test statistics may be severely biased in small samples, we show how to develop tests based on an iterated version of the null hypothesis using Hansen's (1982) generalized method of moments (GMM). We find some improvement in the small sample performance of the test statistics using this method. In section 5, tests for market efficiency based on the ideas underlying cointegration are briefly analyzed. Section 6 considers a recent class of volatility tests derived by Mankiw, Romer, and Shapiro (1991) and examines the relation of excess volatility to expected return variability. Section 7 provides some concluding remarks.

2   Data Generation Mechanisms

In this section we describe the different data generation mechanisms used below in the Monte Carlo experiments. According to the standard present value relationship, the fundamental real price of an asset at time t is

$$P_t^f \equiv E_t \left[\sum_{j=1}^{\infty} \left(\prod_{i=1}^{j} \rho_{t+i} \right) D_{t+i} \right],$$
(9.1)

where $E_t[\cdot]$ denotes the mathematical expectation conditional on all information available at time t, and D_t refers to the accumulated real dividend or other payoff on the asset from time $t - 1$ through t.[4] Finally, the discount factor is

$$\rho_t \equiv \exp(-r_t),$$
(9.2)

where r_t is the continuously compounded required rate of return. Derivation of equation (9.1) imposes a transversality condition that the market fundamental price does not grow faster than the expected value of the product of the discount factors. If the present value model is true and markets are efficient, the observed price process should equal the fundamental price in equation (9.1) with the required rate of return being driven by a risk premium. This fundamental price relationship, coupled with an explicit formulation for the discount rate, r_t, forms the basis for three of our simulated models, considered below. Two alternative simulations involve explicit deviations of the actual price process, P_t, from the fundamentals price, P_t^f.

Of course, simulation of any of these price processes requires a characterization of the stochastic process governing dividends. All of the simulations are based on a model for an annualized dividend series, defined as the current value of the monthly dividends over the previous year,

$$D_t = \sum_{j=0}^{11} (ND_{t-j}/CPI_t) \prod_{h=1}^{j} (1 + i_{t-h+1}), \tag{9.3}$$

where the product from $h = 1$ to 0 is defined to be one. In equation (9.3) i_t denotes the monthly US Treasury bill rate at the beginning of month t, ND_t is the nominal value-weighted NYSE dividend series during month t, and CPI_t is the corresponding monthly US consumer price deflator. With monthly data from January 1926 through December 1987, there are 733 observations on D_t starting in December 1926. We chose to work with monthly observations on the annualized dividend series in equation (9.3), in contrast to modeling ND_t/CPI_t directly, because of the reduced seasonality and the consequent ease in computational burden. We note that most previous studies in this literature use annual data and are implicitly subject to similar problems of time aggregation. The same annualized dividend series is used in Hodrick (1992). Plots of the logarithmic dividend series, $d_t \equiv \ln(D_t)$, together with the logarithmic value-weighted, *CPI*-deflated, NYSE price index, $p_t \equiv \ln(P_t)$, are given in figure 9.1.

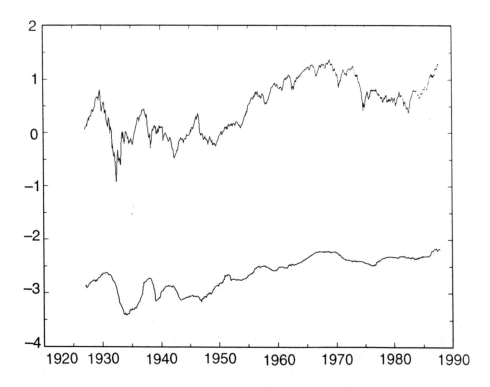

Figure 9.1 Log price and log dividend

It is apparent from figure 9.1 that both dividends and prices experienced growth in real terms during the sample period. In the subsequent analysis we therefore concentrate on modeling the growth rate in the dividend process, i.e. $\Delta d_t \equiv d_t - d_{t-1}$. Formal augmented Dickey and Fuller (1981) tests for a unit root in the autoregressive polynomial in the univariate time series representation for d_t are generally consistent with the idea that Δd_t is stationary. In particular, we consider the following regression:

$$\Delta d_t = \mu + \delta(t/T) + \gamma d_{t-1} + \phi_1 \Delta d_{t-1} + \ldots + \phi_{12} \Delta d_{t-12} + \varepsilon_t. \tag{9.4}$$

Note that this specification of the unit root test includes a linear deterministic trend under the alternative that $\gamma < 0$ in which case d_t is stationary around a linear time trend. Not including the time trend results in an inconsistent test against trend stationarity, as noted by West (1987a). We fail to reject the null hypothesis of no deterministic trend and a unit root in the autoregressive polynomial by the F-test of $\delta = 0$ and $\gamma = 0$ which equals 6.19. This value is slightly below the 5% critical value of 6.25. The t-statistic for $\gamma = 0$ equals -3.46. This value is also close to the 5% critical value of -3.41 and above the 1% critical value of -3.96 in the asymptotic unit root distribution given $\delta = 0$ tabulated in Dickey and Fuller (1981). We shall return to this and other tests for unit roots in both dividends and prices in our discussion of cointegration-based tests for market efficiency in section 5.

Examination of the correlation structure for Δd_t indicates a distinct seasonal pattern with highly significant autocorrelations at the seasonal frequencies and a clear cutoff in the partial autocorrelation function at lag 12.[5] This is consistent with the well-known observation that dividends are lumpy with payoffs concentrated at certain times of each quarter. To capture the seasonal dependence in the annual dividend series we estimate an unrestricted AR(12) model for Δd_t as in equation (9.4) with $\delta = 0$ and $\gamma = 0$. It is certainly possible that a seasonal ARMA model might provide a more parsimonious representation, but as a data generating process the unrestricted AR(12) model conveniently captures the own temporal dependencies in the conditional mean of the dividend series.

The residuals from this AR(12) model are uncorrelated, but they are clearly not independently distributed through time. Strong seasonality remains in the uncertainty associated with dividend growth, as manifest by highly significant autocorrelations of the squared residuals at the seasonal lags.[6] To account for this feature of the dividend process, we estimated a restricted ARCH(12) model for the conditional variance. ARCH models were first introduced by Engle (1982) and have subsequently found very wide use in the modeling of volatility clustering in high frequency financial data. This is discussed further in section 3. The maximum likelihood estimates for the AR(12)-ARCH(12) model for Δd_t obtained under the assumption of conditional normality for the sample period January 1928 through December 1987 are

$$\Delta d_t = 0.00033 - 0.035\ \Delta d_{t-1} + 0.053\ \Delta d_{t-2} + 0.337\ \Delta d_{t-3} + 0.065\ \Delta d_{t-4}$$
$$\ _{(0.00038)}\qquad _{(0.048)}\qquad\qquad _{(0.027)}\qquad\qquad _{(0.062)}\qquad\qquad _{(0.032)}$$

$$+\ 0.018\ \Delta d_{t-5} + 0.121\ \Delta d_{t-6} + 0.010\ \Delta d_{t-7} - 0.019\ \Delta d_{t-8} + 0.182\ \Delta d_{t-9}$$
$$\ _{(0.023)}\qquad\qquad _{(0.061)}\qquad\qquad _{(0.026)}\qquad\qquad _{(0.021)}\qquad\qquad _{(0.036)}$$

$$-\ 0.009\ \Delta d_{t-10} + 0.012\ \Delta d_{t-11} - 0.238\ \Delta d_{t-12} + \varepsilon_t \qquad\qquad (9.5)$$
$$\ _{(0.026)}\qquad\qquad\ _{(0.021)}\qquad\qquad\ _{(0.058)}$$

$$\varepsilon_t | I_{t-1} \sim N(0, \sigma_t^2)$$

$$\sigma_t^2 = 0.000042 + 0.0105\ \varepsilon_{t-1}^2 + 0.289\ \varepsilon_{t-3}^2 + 0.164\ \varepsilon_{t-6}^2 + 0.287\ \varepsilon_{t-12}^2$$
$$\ _{(0.000008)}\qquad _{(0.078)}\qquad\quad _{(0.075)}\qquad\quad _{(0.085)}\qquad\quad _{(0.113)}$$

The notation I_{t-1} refers to the information set consisting of the past history of the dividend process. Robust asymptotic standard errors as in Bollerslev and Wooldridge (1992), which are discussed in section 3, are reported in parentheses. Notice that the seasonal AR and ARCH coefficients are all statistically important. Also, standard summary statistics, available upon request, indicate that this relatively simple time series model provides a good description of the own temporal dependencies in Δd_t.[7] We use this model throughout the chapter to forecast future dividends. Of course, agents may have a much richer information structure underlying their forecasts. This will generally lead to a more variable fundamental price series for a particular model of the return generating process as documented in LeRoy and Parke (1992).

The fundamental price series defined in equation (9.1) depends on forecasts of the levels of the future dividends, D_t, as opposed to the growth rates modeled in equation (9.5). Using a first-order Taylor series expansion, it follows that

$$E_t(D_{t+j}) \simeq \exp[E_t(d_{t+j}) + 0.5\text{var}_t(d_{t+j})], \quad j = 1, 2, \ldots . \qquad (9.6)$$

Equation (9.6) is satisfied exactly if the dividend growth rate is conditionally normally distributed. Closed-form expressions for $E_t(d_{t+j})$ and $\text{var}_t(d_{t+j})$ are available by expressing the AR(12)-ARCH(12) model in first-order companion form, as in Baillie and Bollerslev (1992). These expressions are presented in the appendix.

In practice, the infinite sum in equation (9.1) is necessarily truncated at some value J.[8] Since the process for dividends is difference stationary, it follows that for large values of j,

$$E_t(d_{t+j+1}) \simeq E_t(d_{t+j}) + \eta,$$
$$\phantom{E_t(d_{t+j+1})}\qquad\qquad\qquad j = J, J+1, \ldots, \qquad\qquad (9.7)$$
$$\text{var}_t(d_{t+j+1}) \simeq \text{var}_t(d_{t+j}) + \xi,$$

where $\eta = E(\Delta d_t)$ denotes the unconditional expected real growth rate, and ξ denotes the unconditional increase in the prediction error uncertainty at long horizons. For the model estimates reported in equation (9.5), $\eta = 0.00066$ and $\xi = 0.00106$.[9] Also, suppose that the expected future discount rate associated with distant dividends is approximately constant,

$$E_t(\rho_{t+j+1}) \simeq \rho = \exp(-r), \quad j = J, J+1, \ldots, \tag{9.8}$$

In the implementation, we took $J = 120$, corresponding to a forecast horizon of ten years. Some informal sensitivity analysis revealed almost no change in the results with a longer truncation lag. Combining equations (9.1), (9.6), (9.7), and (9.8), the fundamental price may be approximated by

$$
\begin{aligned}
P_t^f &\simeq \sum_{j=1}^{J-1} \left(\prod_{i=1}^{j} E_t(\rho_{t+i}) \right) \exp(E_t(d_{t+j}) + 0.5\mathrm{var}_t(d_{t+j})) \\
&\quad + \sum_{j=J}^{\infty} \left(\rho^{j-J} \prod_{i=1}^{J} E_t(\rho_{t+i}) \right) \exp(E_t(d_{t+J}) + 0.5\mathrm{var}_t(d_{t+J}))\exp((\eta+0.5\xi)(j-J)) \\
&= \sum_{j=1}^{J-1} \left(\prod_{i=1}^{j} E_t(\rho_{t+i}) \right) \exp(E_t(d_{t+j}) + 0.5\mathrm{var}_t(d_{t+j})) \\
&\quad + \left(\prod_{i=1}^{J} E_t(\rho_{t+i}) \right) \exp(E_t(d_{t+J}) + 0.5\mathrm{var}_t(d_{t+J})) \sum_{j=0}^{\infty} (\rho \exp(\eta + 0.5\xi))^j \quad (9.9) \\
&= \sum_{i=1}^{J-1} \left(\prod_{j=1}^{j} E_t(\rho_{t+i}) \right) \exp(E_t(d_{t+j}) + 0.5\,\mathrm{var}_t(d_{t+j})) \\
&\quad + \left(\prod_{i=1}^{J} E_t(\rho_{t+i}) \right) \exp(E_t(d_{t+J}) + 0.5\,\mathrm{var}_t(d_{t+J}))(1 - \rho\exp(\eta + 0.5\xi))^{-1}
\end{aligned}
$$

where for the last equality to hold true it is assumed that $\rho^{-1} = \exp(r) > \exp(\eta + 0.5\xi)$. Note that a sufficient condition for the validity of the approximation in equation (9.9) is that the expected future discount rates and dividend growth rates are conditionally uncorrelated, which is trivially satisfied with a constant discount rate.

We simulate five different price series using the present value relationship in equation (9.9) and the estimated model for the dividend growth rate in equation (9.5). Each of the models is simulated 1,000 times. The Null1 prices are calculated under the assumption of a constant discount rate,

$$E_t(\rho_{t+j}) = \rho = \exp(-r), \quad j = 1, 2, \ldots, \tag{9.10}$$

and no ARCH effects in the dividend series, i.e. ε_t iid normally distributed with a variance equal to the implied unconditional variance from equation (9.5). The discount rate is set at $r = 0.00635$, corresponding to the 7.9% real annual return on the NYSE value-weighted index over the sample period underlying the estimation results for the dividend model in equation (9.5). The Null1 model is the standard present value relationship typically employed in volatility tests, most of which use annual data. The use of monthly data provides a richer representation of the data generation process and possibly avoids serious temporal aggregation bias.

Following Shiller (1981b; 1984), Summers (1986), and Poterba and Summers (1988) we also consider a fads model as a possible explanation for the actual empirical findings. According to the Fads alternative, the market price differs from the fundamental price by a highly serially correlated fad. More formally, let P_t^f denote the fundamental price under Null1 as described above. The Fads price series is then generated according to

$$P_t = \exp\left(\ln(P_t^f) + \ln(F_t)\right), \tag{9.11}$$

where $\ln(F_t)$ follows the AR(1) process,

$$\ln(F_t) = \phi \ln(F_{t-1}) + u_t, \tag{9.12}$$

with u_t iid normally distributed. In the simulations, $\phi = 0.98$, and σ_u^2 equals 0.330 times the unconditional variance of $\Delta\ln(P_t^f)$ for the particular sample realization. With these parameter choices the process for the fad accounts for 25% of the unconditional variance in the change in logarithmic price.[10]

This particular parametric specification was chosen following Poterba and Summers (1988). The parameter choices differ from other studies such as West (1988) who uses annual S&P data from 1871 to 1985 to estimate the parameters of a fads model analogous to equations (9.11) and (9.12). West (1988) assumes that d_t follows a random walk with drift and that the fundamental rate of return is a constant. Thus, the fundamental price/dividend ratio would be constant. In order to match the sample means and variances of Δd_t and $p_t - d_t$ as well as the first-order autocorrelation of $p_t - d_t$ over this longer period of annual data, the fad must account for 57% of the variance of Δp_t.

In the Bubble alternative, the price differs from the Null1 present value relationship by a self-fulfilling speculative bubble. That is,

$$P_t = P_t^f + B_t, \tag{9.13}$$

where B_t earns the required real rate of return, r,

$$E_{t-1}(B_t) = B_{t-1}\exp(r). \tag{9.14}$$

Notice that the existence of such bubbles violates the transversality condition underlying the fundamental pricing condition in equation (9.1). Stochastic collapsing bubbles were introduced by Blanchard and Watson (1982). The bubble continues with a certain conditional probability and collapses otherwise, where the probability-weighted average of these two events must satisfy equation (9.14). The bubble simulated here takes the form

$$B_t = I_{z_t \leq \pi_{t-1}}(\pi_{t-1})^{-1}[\exp(r)B_{t-1} - (1 - \pi_{t-1})(0.1P_{t-1}^f)]\exp(v_t - 0.5\sigma_v^2)$$

$$+ I_{z_t > \pi_{t-1}}(0.1P_{t-1}^f). \tag{9.15}$$

In equation (9.15) the probability of the bubble continuing is denoted π_{t-1}. If the bubble bursts, it does not collapse to zero but begins again at a value of 0.1 times the fundamental price, P_t^f.[11] To generate stochastic bubbles we drew an iid random variable z_t from the uniform distribution on the unit interval. The indicator variable $I_{z_t \leqslant \pi_{t-1}}$ signifies whether $z_t \leqslant \pi_{t-1}$. If the bubble continues, an innovation in the bubble is generated from v_t. By assumption, v_t is iid normally distributed with mean zero and variance σ_v^2, so that $E_{t-1}[\exp(v_t - 0.5\sigma_v^2)] = 1$. We allow the probability that the bubble will collapse to depend explicitly on the current deviation from the fundamental price,

$$1 - \pi_t = 2[1 - \Phi(P_t^f/B_t)], \tag{9.16}$$

where $\Phi(\cdot)$ refers to the cumulative standard normal distribution function. The larger the bubble relative to the fundamental price, the greater the chance of a collapse. In the simulations we set $\sigma_v^2 = 0.0009$. This parameterization of the bubble process led to an average of eight collapsing bubbles, a minimum of two and a maximum of 16, across the 1,000 simulations of 720 months of data.[12]

The Null2 model incorporates the serial dependence in the conditional variances into the optimal forecasts for the levels of future dividends using the forecast formula for the conditional variances based on model (9.5). Details of these calculations are in the appendix. Given the strong conditional heteroskedasticity in the data, we think it is important in simulations to explicitly account for higher-order moment dependencies in the fundamentals in a pricing relationship as illustrated in equation (9.9). In accordance with the Null1, Fads and Bubble series, the Null2 alternative maintains the assumption of a constant discount rate, $r = 0.00635$.

The final model develops a crude time-varying risk premium or TVRP, price series. It extends the Null2 alternative by allowing for a variable discount rate. In order to keep things relatively simple and to avoid the use of additional data series, we do not work directly with any formal structural model of the variable discount rate. Instead, we simply postulate that the discount rate is a linearly increasing function of the change in the prediction error uncertainty associated with future values of the fundamental dividend process. Specifically, in equation (9.2) we set

$$r_{t+i} = \lambda[\text{var}_t(d_{t+i}) - \text{var}_t(d_{t+i-1})], \quad i = 1, 2, \ldots, \tag{9.17}$$

where $\lambda = 6.017$. This choice of λ ensures that the unconditional discount rate associated with long-horizon predictions converges to the sample real returns employed in the other simulations.

3   Short-Horizon Returns

In this section we review some of the time series techniques and test statistics used to examine the short-run temporal dependencies in asset returns and their relation to the market efficiency hypothesis. It is generally accepted that most high frequency returns are approximately linearly unpredictable, although this is not a requirement of an efficient market. It is also well recognized that returns are characterized by volatility clustering and leptokurtic unconditional distributions. The documentation of these facts dates back to at least Mandelbrot (1963) and Fama (1965).

The first column in table 9.1 reports a number of summary statistics for the real monthly value-weighted NYSE percentage rates of return for the sample period January 1928 through December 1987. These returns are denoted by R_t throughout the chapter. As noted in the previous section, the average real monthly return on the index over this period was 0.635%, or 7.9% on an annual basis. The realized return is very variable around this mean return, however, with a monthly variance of 33.5. Multiplying this monthly variance by 12, as if the returns are serially uncorrelated, produces an annualized

Table 9.1 Real monthly percentage returns, short-horizon summary statistics

	Data	Asymp.	Null1	Fads	Bubble	Null2	TVRP
μ	0.635	–	0.636	0.654	0.624	0.634	0.694
	(0.216)		[0.503]	[0.567]	[0.458]	[0.496]	[0.670]
σ^2	33.5	–	10.5	14.0	14.2	9.12	22.8
	(1.77)		[0.000]	[0.000]	[0.047]	[0.025]	[0.282]
b_3	0.389	0.000	0.097	0.112	−5.35	0.818	−1.32
	(0.091)	[0.000]	[0.000]	[0.000]	[0.003]	[0.893]	[0.126]
b_4	10.6	3.00	2.99	2.99	75.2	6.76	16.1
	(0.182)	[0.000]	[0.000]	[0.000]	[0.897]	[0.259]	[0.832]
ρ_1	0.116	0.000	−0.002	−0.004	−0.018	−0.003	−0.012
	(0.037)	[0.001]	[0.000]	[0.001]	[0.023]	[0.012]	[0.020]
Q_{12}	32.3	11.3	11.6	11.1	10.4	19.4	32.2
	(4.90)	[0.001]	[0.002]	[0.001]	[0.023]	[0.199]	[0.499]
$\rho_1^{(2)}$	0.289	0.000	−0.001	−0.003	0.005	0.077	0.045
	(0.037)	[0.000]	[0.000]	[0.000]	[0.007]	[0.023]	[0.013]
$Q_{12}^{(2)}$	398.4	11.3	11.3	11.1	0.896	172.1	190.2
	(4.90)	[0.000]	[0.000]	[0.000]	[0.002]	[0.064]	[0.139]

The sample statistics are the mean, μ, the variance, σ^2, the skewness, b_3, the kurtosis, b_4, the first-order autocorrelations for returns, ρ_1, and for squared returns, $\rho_1^{(2)}$. The Ljung-Box portmanteau tests for up to 12th-order serial correlation in the levels of returns and the squared returns are denoted Q_{12} and $Q_{12}^{(2)}$, respectively. The "Data" column gives the sample statistics with asymptotic standard errors constructed under the null hypothesis of iid normally distributed constant expected returns in parentheses. The column labeled "Asymp." reports the medians and the p-values for this null hypothesis. The last five columns give the small sample or empirical medians of the sample statistics from the five Monte Carlo experiments with the corresponding p-values of the sample test statistic reported in square brackets.

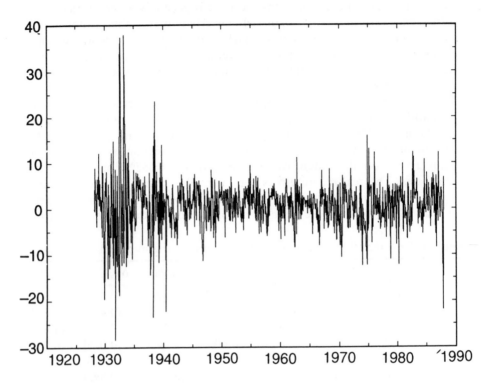

Figure 9.2 Value-weighted monthly real returns

standard deviation of 20.1%. This high degree of return variability is also obvious from the plot in figure 9.2.

The sample skewness and kurtosis coefficients are reported in the next two rows of table 9.1.[13] The column labeled "Asymp." provides the medians under the null hypothesis of iid normally distributed returns, i.e. $b_3 = 0$ and $b_4 = 3$. The p- values in the asymptotic distributions are reported in square brackets.[14] The results indicate positive skewness and very pronounced leptokurtosis in the sample unconditional distribution of returns.

The first-order sample autocorrelation coefficient is denoted by ρ_1. Although statistically significant, the estimated value implies that only 1.3% of the total variation in the return is explainable from last month's return alone. Furthermore, the predictability of this index return may, in part, be attributed to a non-synchronous trading phenomenon, as discussed in Lo and MacKinlay (1988) and Fama (1991). The next row in table 9.1 reports the Ljung and Box (1978) portmanteau test for up to 12th- order serial correlation, Q_{12}.[15] The second column indicates that this test statistic is highly significant at conventional levels in the asymptotic chi-square distribution under the null hypothesis of iid observations. As noted by Diebold (1986) and Cumby and

Huizinga (1992), however, the presence of conditional heteroskedasticity or excess kurtosis will bias the portmanteau test towards over-rejection of the less restrictive null hypothesis of uncorrelated returns. Also, excluding the first lag, the test for the joint significance of lags 2 through 12 equals only 22.6.

Recently, a number of authors have employed variance ratio statistics,

$$v(k) \equiv \text{var}(R_{t+k-1} + R_{t+k-2} + \ldots + R_t)/[k \ \text{var}(R_t)], \qquad (9.18)$$

as an alternative way of summarizing own temporal dependencies, particularly at horizons longer than one year. If the returns at horizon k are dominated by positive autocorrelation, the variance ratio will be greater than one, whereas predominantly negative autocorrelation results in a variance ratio below one.[16] Consistent with the results reported in Lo and MacKinlay (1988), the variance ratio at the one-year horizon for the real value-weighted NYSE returns equals 1.151. This indicates only minor and statistically insignificant positive short-run own dependencies in returns. We defer discussion of longer-run dependencies to section 4.

In contrast to the weak evidence for autocorrelation in returns, the last two rows in table 9.1 highlight the importance of conditional heteroskedasticity. The first-order autocorrelation coefficient for the squared returns, $\rho_1^{(2)}$, and the portmanteau test for up to 12th-order serial correlation in the squared returns, $Q_{12}^{(2)}$, are highly significant at any reasonable level. The variance ratio statistic for the squared returns equals 3.027 at the one-year horizon, indicating very strong positive dependence. This pronounced dependence in the second-order moments is immediately evident from figure 9.2. It is worth noting that this finding of strong dependence in the even-ordered moments does not necessarily imply market inefficiency. The presence of high frequency volatility clustering is perfectly consistent with a martingale hypothesis for stock prices which is implied by the assumption of a constant short-run expected rate of return.[17] In addition, though, modern asset pricing theories rely crucially on time variation in the second-order moments of returns and market fundamentals as sources of rational time-varying risk premiums, e.g. Abel (1988), Hodrick (1989), and Bekaert (1992). We return to this issue in more detail below.

We next consider the simulation results for the various price processes discussed in section 2 as possible explanations of these empirical findings. The last five columns of table 9.1 report the medians for the sample statistics under the different data generating mechanisms along with the p-values of the statistics in the simulated distributions over the 1,000 replications. If the sample statistic does not fall within the empirical distribution generated by a particular model, we will judge the model as being inconsistent with the data along that dimension. We note that this interpretation of the test statistics does not incorporate parameter estimation uncertainty for the simulated models. It is possible that inclusion of this additional source of variation could overturn our assessment regarding the shortcomings of a model.

The Null1 constant discount rate model with no ARCH effects and the Fads alternative are both unable to explain the magnitude of the unconditional variance of returns. The medians of the Null2 and Bubble distributions are also considerably lower than the sample statistic of 33.5, although the distributions from these models are more dispersed.[18] Only for the TVRP alternative is the *p*-value relatively large, 0.282, and the median of the simulated distribution close to the sample unconditional one-month return variance. Similarly, neither the Null1 nor the Fads alternative with normally distributed errors is able to explain the non-normality of returns. In contrast, the Bubble specification results in a considerably higher median kurtosis coefficient than the sample analog. The simulated Null2 and TVRP alternatives are both consistent with the actual data regarding the unconditional sample kurtosis.

None of the five models produces any positive first-order autocorrelation in the medians of the test statistics. Both the Null2 and TVRP alternatives, however, lead to test statistics for the joint significance of the first 12 autocorrelations, Q_{12}, that are broadly consistent with the actual data.

As noted above, a striking feature of the monthly returns is volatility clustering. Although the portmanteau statistic for the 12 autocorrelations of the squared returns is inconsistent with the null hypothesis of iid observations in the asymptotic distribution and with the simulated Null1, Fads, and Bubbles models, the Null2 and TVRP price series yield test statistics that exceed the sample value of 398.4 in 6.4% and 13.9% of the replications, respectively.

In order to better understand the nature of this volatility clustering, we follow Bollerslev (1986; 1987) and estimate an MA(1)-GARCH(1,1) model for the monthly real percentage rates of return:

$$R_t = \mu + \theta \varepsilon_{t-1} + \varepsilon_t$$

$$E_{t-1}(\varepsilon_t) = 0,$$

$$E_{t-1}(\varepsilon_t^2) \equiv \sigma_t^2 = \omega + \alpha \varepsilon_{t-1}^2 + \beta \sigma_{t-1}^2. \tag{9.19}$$

This relatively simple non-linear time series model provides a useful characterization of the temporal variation in the second-order moments of returns for a wide variety of financial assets.

A number of alternative estimation schemes are available for the model in equation (9.19). The estimation results reported below are all obtained under the auxiliary distributional assumption of conditional normality; i.e. $\varepsilon_t | I_{t-1} \sim N(0, \sigma_t^2)$, where I_{t-1} refers to the information set at time $t-1$. In particular, if $\Xi' \equiv (\mu, \theta, \omega, \alpha, \beta)$ denotes the vector of unknown parameters, it follows by a standard prediction error decomposition argument that conditional on the initial observations, the quasi-log-likelihood function for the sample realizations $\{R_1, R_2, \ldots R_T\}$ takes the form

$$L_T(\Xi) = \sum_{t=1}^{T} l_t(\Xi) = \sum_{t=1}^{T} -0.5(\ln(\pi) + \ln(\sigma_t^2) + \varepsilon_t^2 \sigma_t^{-2}). \tag{9.20}$$

While standard maximum likelihood theory requires the correct distributional assumptions, asymptotic standard errors that remain valid in the presence of conditional non-normality may be calculated from the matrix of the outer products of the gradients post-and pre-multiplied by an estimate of the hessian; see e.g. Domowitz and White (1982) and Weiss (1986). A simple expression for this estimator in the context of dynamic models with conditional heteroskedasticity that involves only first derivatives is given in Bollerslev and Wooldridge (1992).[19] The quasi-maximum-likelihood estimates obtained by maximizing equation (9.20) are given in the first column of table 9.2, with robust standard errors in parenthesis.

The significant MA(1) term in the conditional mean captures most of the autocorrelation in the returns. The Q_{12} portmanteau test for significant

Table 9.2 Real monthly returns, MA(1)-GARCH(1,1) quasi-maximum-likelihood estimates:

$$R_t = \mu + \theta\varepsilon_{t-1} + \varepsilon_t, \quad \sigma_t^2 = \omega + \alpha\varepsilon_{t-1}^2 + \beta\sigma_{t-1}^2, \quad \varepsilon_t|I_{t-1} \sim N(0, \sigma_t^2)$$

	Data	Asymp.	Null2	TVRP
μ	0.778	–	0.643	0.431
	(0.184)		[0.092]	[0.002]
θ	0.101	–	−0.004	−0.002
	(0.044)		[0.006]	[0.030]
ω	0.668	–	0.233	0.563
	(0.328)		[0.008]	[0.383]
α	0.123	–	0.108	0.127
	(0.023)		[0.357]	[0.523]
β	0.861	–	0.865	0.853
	(0.026)		[0.554]	[0.435]
b_3	−0.547	0.000	0.555	−1.89
	(0.091)	[1.00]	[1.00]	[0.000]
b_4	4.39	3.00	4.39	10.5
	(0.182)	[0.000]	[0.499]	[1.00]
Q_{12}	14.2	11.3	11.0	12.6
	(4.90)	[0.288]	[0.263]	[0.396]
$Q_{12}^{(2)}$	11.8	11.3	64.9	22.5
	(4.90)	[0.462]	[0.984]	[0.804]

The "Data" column reports the quasi-maximum-likelihood estimates for the actual returns with robust asymptotic standard errors in parentheses. The summary statistics for the standardized residuals, $\hat{\varepsilon}_t\hat{\sigma}_t^{-1}$, are denoted as in table 9.1. The "Asymp." column reports the medians and the *p*-values in the asymptotic distribution under the null hypothesis of iid normally distributed standardized innovations. The Null2 and TVRP columns provide the medians and the *p*-values from the quasi-maximum-likelihood estimates for the data generated under the two hypotheses. The *p*-values are reported in square brackets.

autocorrelations within a year drops from 32.3 for the raw data to 14.2 for the standardized residuals, $\hat{\varepsilon}_t \hat{\sigma}_t^{-1}$, from the model in (9.19). The estimate for $\alpha + \beta$ indicates a very long memory in the conditional variance. The implied half-life of a shock to the conditional variance equals $\ln(1/2)/\ln(\hat{\alpha} + \hat{\beta}) = 43.0$ months. This high degree of persistence corresponds to the findings for a large number of other financial assets as noted by Bollerslev and Engle (1993). The parameterization for the conditional variance in equation (9.19) does a very good job of tracking the strong temporal dependence in the variance.[20] The $Q_{12}^{(2)}$ portmanteau test statistic for the squared standardized residuals, $\hat{\varepsilon}_t^2 \hat{\sigma}_t^{-2}$, equals 11.8 compared to 398.4 for the raw squared returns.

The negative skewness coefficient for $\hat{\varepsilon}_t \hat{\sigma}_t^{-1}$ in table 9.2 contrasts sharply with the positive value for b_3 reported in table 9.1. Negative skewness is consistent with the so-called leverage effect in which volatility increases with bad news but decreases with good news, as analyzed by Black (1976) and Christie (1982). This observation also provides one of the primary motivations behind the exponential GARCH model in Nelson (1991) that allows both the sign and the magnitude of past shocks to influence the conditional variance.[21]

Even though the GARCH(1,1) model does a very good job of capturing the dependence in the second-order moments, the temporal variation in the conditional variance does not explain all of the leptokurtosis in the data, necessitating the use of robust inference procedures. Again, this is not unique to the present return series. As an alternative to the robust quasi-maximum-likelihood procedures, the conditional distribution for $\varepsilon_t \sigma_t^{-1}$ could be parameterized directly or estimated by non-parametric methods, as discussed by Bollerslev (1987), Gallant and Tauchen (1989), and Engle and Gonzalez-Rivera (1991).

The last two columns of table 9.2 report the results of estimating the same MA(1)-GARCH(1,1) model in (9.19) for each of the 1,000 realizations of the 720 monthly simulated Null2 and TVRP returns. These are the only two models that exhibit significant heteroskedasticity as evidenced by the $Q_{12}^{(2)}$ statistic in table 9.1. The similarity between the estimated GARCH coefficients for the artificially generated returns and the actual data is striking. The median values of the quasi-maximum-likelihood estimates for α over the 1,000 replications for the Null2 and TVRP alternatives are 0.108 and 0.127, respectively, compared to 0.123 for the real data. Similarly, the median values for the estimates of β are 0.865 and 0.853, respectively, compared to 0.861 for the actual returns. Note also that although the Null2 alternative is unable to explain the negative skewness in the standardized returns, the TVRP hypothesis results in excess negative skewness and excess leptokurtosis compared to the real data.

In summary, the results in table 9.2 illustrate how explicitly allowing for time-varying uncertainty in the fundamental real dividend growth process within the context of a simple present value relationship may endogenously account for the observed ARCH effects in the data. Reconciliation of a fundamental model and the volatility of short-horizon real returns appears to require time variation in the discount factor.

4 Long-Horizon Tests

The previous section documents that the evidence in autocorrelations of short-horizon returns against the hypothesis of a constant conditional mean return is not very strong. At the same time, the results indicate that returns appear to be too volatile relative to the models with a constant discount factor. Shiller (1981b; 1984) and Summers (1986) argued that fads would make returns more volatile. However, it would be difficult to detect a fads alternative hypothesis, as developed above, with short-horizon autocorrelation tests because of their low power when transitory components are very highly serially correlated. As noted by Poterba and Summers (1988) and Fama and French (1988a; 1988b), the negative serial correlation in returns implied by such a model would manifest itself more transparently at longer horizons. Consequently, Poterba and Summers (1988) investigated long-horizon vari-ance ratios as in equation (9.18), while Fama and French (1988a) analyzed regressions of long-horizon returns on lagged long-horizon returns. Of course, if the researcher has a specific alternative hypothesis in mind, such as the parametric Fads model in equations (9.11) and (9.12), the asymptotically most powerful procedure would be to estimate the resulting parametric model for one-period returns by maximum likelihood using the full data set. Nothing can be gained by lengthening the return horizon.

The statistical properties of the Fama and French (1988a) analysis have generated much controversy in the literature. For example, Jegadeesh (1990), Kim, Nelson, and Startz (1991), Mankiw, Romer, and Shapiro (1991), Ri-chardson (1993), and Richardson and Stock (1989) all argue that the case for predictability of long-horizon stock returns is weak when one corrects for the small sample biases in the test statistics. Our simulations demonstrate these biases. We then present two additional ways that hypotheses regarding the long-horizon predictability of returns can be investigated which are not as severely biased. These techniques apply generally in other long-horizon fore-casting situations.

To begin, let $\ln(R_{t+k,k}) = \ln(R_{t+1}) + \ldots + \ln(R_{t+k})$ denote the continuously compounded k-period rate of return. Then, a typical OLS specification of Fama and French (1988b) is the following:

$$\ln(R_{t+k,k}) = \alpha_{k,k} + \beta_{k,k}\ln(R_{t,k}) + u_{t+k,k}. \tag{9.21}$$

Note that the k-period error term $u_{t+k,k}$ is not realized until time $t+k$. Therefore, if the data are sampled more finely than the compound return interval, $u_{t+k,k}$ is serially correlated, even under the null hypothesis of constant expected returns. If all of the data are employed, $u_{t+k,k}$ is correlated with

$k-1$ previous error terms as discussed in Hansen and Hodrick (1980).[22] Under alternative hypotheses in which returns have a variable conditional mean, however, $u_{t+k,k}$ can be arbitrarily serially correlated if lagged returns do not capture all of the variation in the conditional mean.

Since lagged returns are predetermined but not strictly exogenous, asymptotic distribution theory must be used to determine the properties of an estimator for $\kappa_{k,k} = (\alpha_{k,k}, \beta_{k,k})'$. Ordinary least squares provides consistent estimates, but traditional OLS standard errors are not appropriate asymptotically since the error term is serially correlated when forecasting more than one period ahead. Furthermore, the variability of the conditional variance of returns, documented in section 3, makes it inappropriate to assume homoskedasticity which underlies the derivation of the conventional OLS standard errors.

Nevertheless, the OLS coefficient estimator from equation (9.21), $\hat{\kappa}_{k,k}$, is readily interpreted as a generalized method of moments (GMM) estimator based on the instruments $x_t = (1, R_{t,k})'$. Hence, it is straightforward to derive appropriate asymptotic standard errors. Following Hansen (1982), it can be demonstrated that $(\sqrt{T})(\hat{\kappa}_{k,k} - \kappa_{k,k}) \sim N(0, \Omega)$, where $\Omega = Z_0^{-1} S_0 Z_0^{-1}$, $Z_0 = E(x_t x_t')$, and S_0 denotes the spectral density evaluated at frequency zero of $w_{t+k,k} = u_{t+k,k} x_t$. Under the null hypothesis that the returns are not predictable,

$$S_0 = \sum_{j=-k+1}^{k-1} E(w'_{t+k,k} w_{t+k-j,k}). \tag{9.22}$$

This matrix is consistently estimated by

$$S_T^a = C_T(0) + \sum_{j=1}^{k-1} [C_T(j) + C_T(j)'], \tag{9.23}$$

where $C_T(j) = (1/T)\Sigma_{t=j+1}^{T}(\hat{w}_{t+k,k} \hat{w}'_{t+k-j,k})$, and $\hat{w}_{t,k}$ denotes $w_{t,k}$ evaluated at the estimated residuals. It is important to note that the estimator in equation (9.23) is not guaranteed to be positive definite in finite samples. Various weighting schemes may be imposed on the terms in equation (9.23) to guarantee that the estimator is positive definite; see Newey and West (1987; 1994) and Andrews (1991). In all of the simulations reported below, we employed the unweighted estimator, and in no case was the estimated covariance matrix negative semi-definite. A consistent estimator for Z_0 is given by $Z_T = (1/T)\Sigma_{t=1}^{T} x_t x_t'$.

We present the results for this estimation of equation (9.21) for five horizons in table 9.3a. The first column indicates the horizon k equal to 1, 12, 24, 36, and 48 months. As in the previous tables, the second column labeled "Data" provides the sample statistics, which in this case are the OLS estimates of the slope coefficients, $\beta_{k,k}$, with asymptotic standard errors in parentheses. The medians of the t-tests for the hypothesis $\beta_{k,k} = 0$ from the asymptotic distribution and the five simulated economies are presented in the next six columns. The p-values of the test statistics are in square brackets.

Notice that at the 24-month horizon, the asymptotic p-value is effectively zero, while the one-month and 36-month values both equal 0.162. Richardson (1993) notes that considerable care must be exercised when examining the individual test statistics since they are highly correlated. Hence, we also report the $\chi^2(5)$ statistic that examines the joint test that all five slope coefficients are zero. It has a value of 15.8, which corresponds to an asymptotic p-value of 0.007. Clearly, if the asymptotic distributions are validated by the simulations, this would be strong evidence of long-horizon return predictability.

Examination of the columns for Null1 and Null2 indicates that the asymptotic distribution is a poor approximation to the distribution of the test

Table 9.3 Real monthly returns, multi-period regressions:

$$\ln(R_{t+k,k}) = \alpha_{k,k} + \beta_{k,k}\ln(R_{t,k}) + u_{t+k,k}$$

(a) Traditional GMM standard errors

k	Data	Asymp.	Null1	Fads	Bubble	Null2	TVRP
Slope coefficients							
1	0.095	0.000	−0.064	−0.127	−0.359	−0.098	−0.251
	(0.068)	[0.162]	[0.145]	[0.158]	[0.108]	[0.175]	[0.217]
12	−0.068	0.000	−0.244	−0.511	−0.801	−0.324	−0.713
	(0.140)	[0.626]	[0.649]	[0.690]	[0.741]	[0.680]	[0.730]
24	−0.200	0.000	−0.363	−0.637	−0.768	−0.507	−1.14
	(0.044)	[0.000]	[0.006]	[0.014]	[0.008]	[0.012]	[0.018]
36	−0.205	0.000	−0.448	−0.738	−0.785	−0.553	−1.31
	(0.146)	[0.162]	[0.327]	[0.368]	[0.371]	[0.362]	[0.516]
48	−0.187	0.000	−0.611	−0.704	−0.884	−0.664	−1.40
	(0.227)	[0.408]	[0.577]	[0.610]	[0.612]	[0.590]	[0.737]
$\chi^2(5)$ *statistics*							
	15.8	4.35	8.61	9.77	10.6	11.1	14.3
		[0.007]	[0.237]	[0.278]	[0.311]	[0.324]	[0.460]
Coefficients of multiple correlation, R^2							
1	0.009		0.001	0.001	0.001	0.001	0.002
			[0.014]	[0.017]	[0.049]	[0.061]	[0.102]
12	0.005		0.006	0.006	0.011	0.008	0.014
			[0.535]	[0.554]	[0.661]	[0.606]	[0.712]
24	0.045		0.012	0.013	0.014	0.015	0.031
			[0.169]	[0.204]	[0.217]	[0.226]	[0.378]
36	0.058		0.018	0.021	0.020	0.021	0.042
			[0.228]	[0.270]	[0.235]	[0.245]	[0.410]
48	0.046		0.026	0.032	0.028	0.024	0.048
			[0.353]	[0.422]	[0.385]	[0.368]	[0.512]

Table 9.3   (*Cont.*)

(b) GMM standard errors calculated under the null hypothesis

k	Data	Asymp.	Null1	Fads	Bubble	Null2	TVRP
Slope coefficients							
1	0.095	0.000	−0.064	−0.127	−0.360	−0.098	−0.250
	(0.069)	[0.171]	[0.152]	[0.166]	[0.110]	[0.172]	[0.208]
12	−0.068	0.000	−0.232	−0.446	−0.481	−0.253	−0.587
	(0.170)	[0.688]	[0.691]	[0.717]	[0.675]	[0.678]	[0.748]
24	−0.200	0.000	−0.309	−0.472	−0.433	−0.345	−0.834
	(0.244)	[0.411]	[0.410]	[0.443]	[0.372]	[0.414]	[0.578]
36	−0.205	0.000	−0.331	−0.538	−0.487	−0.372	−0.836
	(0.223)	[0.357]	[0.380]	[0.397]	[0.344]	[0.368]	[0.504]
48	−0.187	0.000	−0.423	−0.600	−0.518	−0.449	−0.857
	(0.172)	[0.276]	[0.291]	[0.335]	[0.255]	[0.289]	[0.414]
$\chi^2(5)$ *Statistics*							
	3.37	4.35	1.48	1.68	1.50	1.30	1.84
		[0.644]	[0.373]	[0.380]	[0.382]	[0.341]	[0.396]

The "Data" column provides the sample statistics with asymptotic standard errors in parentheses. The "Asymp." column reports the medians and the *p*-values in the asymptotic distributions for testing the null hypothesis $\beta_{k,k} = 0$. The remaining five columns provide the medians from the empirical distributions for the sample statistics together with the *p*-values in square brackets.

statistics in small samples. The median values of the sample $\chi^2(5)$ statistics for these two simulated economies are 8.61 and 11.1, respectively, compared to the median of a true $\chi^2(5)$ of 4.35. The corresponding *p*-values from the two distributions are 0.237 and 0.324. Hence, there is actually little evidence against the null hypothesis. The deterioration of the *t*-tests is apparent as the horizon is increased, with the median values becoming increasingly negative.[23]

Notice also that the median and the *p*-value of the $\chi^2(5)$ statistic for the Bubble model are close to those of the Null1 and Null2 simulations. This is not surprising, as the Bubble model maintains a constant expected return. More surprisingly, perhaps, are the medians and *p*-values for the Fads alternative which are only slightly larger than those under the Null1 hypothesis. This latter finding illustrates the low power of these tests when type I error rates are fixed at the traditional levels. Given the large overlap in the distributions of the test statistics under the null and the alternative hypotheses, the probability of failing to reject the null hypothesis when it is actually false is quite high. Finally, notice that the *p*-value for the $\chi^2(5)$ statistic for the TVRP model is 0.460 which is the largest of any of the models.

The bottom part of table 9.3a reports the coefficients of multiple correlation, R^2 statistics, for the five horizons. Although the sample values increase from 0.009 at the one-month horizon to 0.058 at the 36-month horizon, the smallest p-values of the simulated economies are actually at the one-month horizon. The serial correlation of the residuals induced by using overlapping forecasting intervals causes a spurious regression phenomenon as in Granger and Newbold (1974).

We next develop an alternative estimator of S_0 that is valid only under the null hypothesis. This estimator utilizes the fact that the values of unconditional expectations of covariance stationary time series depend only on the time intervals between the observations.[24] In particular, notice that under the null hypothesis, $u_{t+k,k} = (e_{t+1} + \ldots + e_{t+k})$, where e_{t+1} is the serially uncorrelated one-step-ahead forecast error of returns. Estimates of e_{t+1} can be obtained from the residuals of a regression of $\ln(R_{t+1})$ on a constant because under the null hypothesis $e_{t+1} = u_{t+1,1}$. To derive the alternative estimator, examine a typical term, $E(w_{t+k,k}w'_{t+k-j,k})$, where $k > j > 0$. Substituting $(e_{t+1} + \ldots + e_{t+k})$ for $u_{t+k,k}$,

$$E(u_{t+k,k}x_t u_{t+k-j,k}x'_{t-j}) = E\left[\left(\sum_{i=1}^{k} e_{t+i}\right) x_t \left(\sum_{h=1-j}^{k-j} e_{t+h}\right) x'_{t-j}\right] = E\left[\left(\sum_{i=1}^{k-j} e_{t+i}^2\right) x_t x'_{t-j}\right]$$

(9.24)

With stationary time series, the unconditional expectation of each of the $(k-j)$ terms on the right-hand side of equation (9.24) depends only upon the time interval between the variables. Hence, rather than summing e_{t+j} into the future, one can sum $x_t x'_{t-j}$ into the past:

$$E\left[\left(\sum_{i=1}^{k-j} e_{t+i}^2\right) x_t x'_{t-j}\right] = E\left[e_{t+1}^2 \left(\sum_{i=0}^{k-j-1} x_{t-i} x'_{t-j-i}\right)\right].$$

(9.25)

Applying the same logic to all of the terms in equation (9.22) implies that

$$S_0 = E\left[e_{t+1}^2 \left(\sum_{i=0}^{k-1} x_{t-i}\right)\left(\sum_{i=0}^{k-1} x_{t-i}\right)'\right] = E(v_{t+1,k}v'_{t+1,k})$$

(9.26)

where

$$v_{t+1,k} \equiv e_{t+1}\left(\sum_{i=0}^{k-1} x_{t-j}\right).$$

(9.27)

Let $\hat{v}_{t+1,k}$ denote $v_{t+1,k}$ evaluated at the estimated residual, $\hat{e}_{t+1}$. An alternative estimator for S_0 from equation (9.26) is then

$$S_T^b = \frac{1}{T}\sum_{t=k}^{T} \hat{v}_{t+1,k}\hat{v}'_{t+1,k}.$$

(9.28)

Two aspects of the estimator S_T^b are important, and both are induced by the fact that it avoids the summation of autocovariance matrices as in equation (9.23). First, the estimator is guaranteed to be positive definite. Second, if it is the summation of the autocovariance matrices that causes the poor small sample properties of the test statistics in table 9.3a, the finite sample behavior of test statistics constructed with S_T^b might be better.

The properties of this estimator are investigated in table 9.3b. The point estimates of the slope coefficients reported in the "Data" column are identical, but the standard errors are different from these in table 9.3a. In particular, the test statistic at the 24-month horizon now has an asymptotic p-value of 0.411 and the $\chi^2(5)$ statistic is only 3.37, below the median value of 4.35 in the asymptotic distribution. However, 3.37 is actually larger than the median values of the small sample distributions for the test statistics from the Null1 and Null2 simulations. Also, notice that the deterioration of the median values of the t-test statistics as the horizon increases is mitigated only slightly.

The last part of this section demonstrates how inference about the statistical significance of lagged returns as predictors of long-horizon returns can be conducted by considering the regression of one-period returns on the weighted sum of the lagged returns.[25] This specification also avoids the summation of autocovariance matrices and may therefore have better small sample properties under the null hypothesis than the estimates based on equation (9.21).

Since the compound k-period return is the sum of k one-period returns, the numerator of the regression coefficient $\beta_{k,k}$ in equation (9.21) is an estimate of $\text{cov}[\sum_{j=1}^{k}\ln(R_{t+j}); \sum_{j=0}^{k-1}\ln(R_{t-j})]$. This covariance is the weighted sum of $(2k-1)$ autocovariances of returns separated by between one and $(2k-1)$ periods. With covariance stationary time series it follows that

$$\text{cov}\left[\sum_{j=1}^{k}\ln(R_{t+j}); \sum_{j=0}^{k-1}\ln(R_{t-j})\right] = \text{cov}\left[\ln(R_{t+1}); \sum_{j=1}^{2k-1}\omega_j\ln(R_{t+1-j})\right], \quad (9.29)$$

where $\omega_j = j$ for $1 \leq j \leq k$, and $\omega_j = 2k - j$ for $(k+1) \leq j \leq (2k-1)$. The sum of the covariances on the right-hand side of equation (9.29) is equal to the numerator of the slope coefficient in the following regression:

$$\ln(R_{t+t}) = \alpha_{1,2k-1} + \beta_{1,2k-1}\left[\sum_{j=1}^{2k-1}\omega_j\ln(R_{t+1-j})\right] + u_{t+1}. \quad (9.30)$$

Under the null hypothesis of constant expected returns, the error term in equation (9.30) is serially uncorrelated in contrast to $u_{t+k,k}$ in equation (9.21). The asymptotic distribution of the OLS estimator for $\kappa_{1,h} = (\alpha_{1,h}, \beta_{1,h})'$ can be derived as above. Since only the term corresponding to $j = 0$ is different from zero in equation (9.22), this specification might have better small sample properties under the null hypothesis.

The results of estimating $\beta_{1,2k-1}$ in equation (9.30) are presented in table 9.4. The small sample properties of the test statistics are better than the results of the tests in table 9.3a and are comparable to those in table 9.3b. The deterioration in the medians of the individual test statistics is again quite evident, even though the p-values for the asymptotic distribution and for the Null1 and Null2 models are quite close. There is little evidence for predictability of returns. Again, notice from the closeness of the medians for the Fads

Table 9.4 Real monthly returns, one-period regressions:

$$\ln(R_{t+1}) = \alpha_{1,2k-1} + \beta_{1,2k-1}\left(\sum_{j=1}^{2k-1} \omega_j \ln(R_{t+1-j})\right) + u_{t+1}$$

$$\omega_j = j, \ 1 \leqslant j \leqslant k; \quad \omega_j = 2k - j, \ k + 1 \leqslant j \leqslant 2k - 1$$

k	Data	Asymp.	Null1	Fads	Bubble	Null2	TVRP
Slope coefficients							
1	0.034	0.000	−0.065	−0.100	−0.340	−0.072	−0.250
	(0.052)	[0.504]	[0.491]	[0.512]	[0.436]	[0.523]	[0.552]
12	−0.201	0.000	−0.249	−0.402	−0.465	−0.287	−0.593
	(0.171)	[0.239]	[0.260]	[0.242]	[0.187]	[0.236]	[0.319]
24	−0.279	0.000	−0.294	−0.459	−0.448	−0.343	−0.789
	(0.260)	[0.283]	[0.282]	[0.311]	[0.239]	[0.251]	[0.435]
36	−0.153	0.000	−0.349	−0.510	−0.464	−0.359	−0.819
	(0.321)	[0.633]	[0.641]	[0.649]	[0.605]	[0.637]	[0.760]
48	−0.161	0.000	−0.407	−0.580	−0.489	−0.407	−0.875
	(0.336)	[0.631]	[0.648]	[0.667]	[0.618]	[0.638]	[0.753]
$\chi^2(5)$ *statistics*							
	2.85	4.35	4.57	4.79	4.58	4.58	5.74
		[0.723]	[0.731]	[0.762]	[0.732]	[0.737]	[0.851]
Coefficients of multiple correlation, R^2							
1	0.001		0.001	0.001	0.001	0.001	0.001
			[0.403]	[0.427]	[0.495]	[0.533]	[0.586]
12	0.005		0.001	0.001	0.001	0.001	0.002
			[0.183]	[0.172]	[0.269]	[0.262]	[0.369]
24	0.003		0.001	0.001	0.001	0.001	0.002
			[0.258]	[0.277]	[0.271]	[0.289]	[0.462]
36	0.001		0.001	0.001	0.001	0.001	0.001
			[0.587]	[0.596]	[0.572]	[0.590]	[0.712]
48	0.000		0.001	0.001	0.001	0.001	0.001
			[0.634]	[0.649]	[0.589]	[0.634]	[0.733]

For additional notes see table 9.3.

model and the TVRP model that these tests are likely to have very low power. We note here that the results in this section only provide evidence regarding the own predictability of returns and do not demonstrate that returns are unpredictable when additional information is used. We return to this issue in section 6.

5   Cointegration Tests

Recently, a number of authors have proposed various tests for the presence of speculative bubbles and market efficiency that are based on the idea of cointegration. In light of space constraints and related coverage elsewhere in this volume, our discussion of these techniques is brief.[26] Intuitively, two time series are defined to be cointegrated if each of the individual series is non-stationary, yet a linear combination of the two series is stationary.

According to the present value model, the fundamental price must equal the expected discounted value of next period's fundamental price plus any dividend payouts. In particular, after deflating by D_t, we have

$$\frac{P_t^f}{D_t} = E_t\left(\rho_{t+1}\left(\frac{P_{t+1}^f}{D_{t+1}} + 1\right)\frac{D_{t+1}}{D_t}\right). \tag{9.31}$$

Assuming the transversality condition is satisfied, and using the approximation $D_{t+1}/D_t \simeq 1 + \Delta d_{t+1}$, it follows that

$$\frac{P_t^f}{D_t} \simeq E_t\left(\sum_{j=1}^{\infty}\prod_{i=1}^{j}\rho_{t+i}(1 + \Delta d_{t+i})\right). \tag{9.32}$$

If the dividend growth rate, Δd_t, and the discount factor, ρ_t, are jointly covariance stationary, $p_t^f \equiv \log(P_t^f)$ and d_t will be cointegrated with cointegrating vector $(1, -1)$; see Cochrane (1991a) for a formal proof. If the actual price contains a rational speculative bubble as in equation (9.13), the transversality condition underlying equation (9.32), would be violated for $P_t = P_t^f + B_t$. In that situation, $p_t - d_t$ would be non-stationary. It is worth noting that this argument does not depend on any particular model for the equilibrium rate of return but only requires that the implied discount factor and the dividend growth rate are jointly covariance stationary.

The augmented Dickey-Fuller tests reported in table 9.5a are consistent with the hypothesis that the logarithms of real prices and real dividends are non-stationary or integrated of order one. The evidence for a unit root in d_t on the basis of the asymptotic distribution was discussed above. With p_t substituted for d_t in equation (9.4), the F-test for $\delta = 0$ and $\gamma = 0$ equals 4.34, corresponding to a p-value in the asymptotic unit root distribution of 0.795. The t-statistic for $\gamma = 0$ equals -3.01, which has an asymptotic p-value of 0.869.

Table 9.5 Real monthly stock prices and dividends

(a) Unit root tests:

$$\Delta u_t = \mu + \delta(t/T) + \rho u_{t-1} + \phi_1 \Delta u_{t-1} + \ldots + \phi_{12}\Delta u_{t-12} + e_t$$

u_t	Data	Asymp.	Null1	Fads	Bubble	Null2	TVRP
$p_t : t_{\rho=0}$	−3.01	−2.17	−2.19	−2.31	−1.31	−2.11	−2.33
		[0.869]	[0.862]	[0.827]	[0.960]	[0.892]	[0.795]
$p_t : \Phi_3$	4.34	2.87	2.93	3.08	3.49	2.98	4.08
		[0.795]	[0.779]	[0.755]	[0.653]	[0.765]	[0.538]
$d_t : t_{\rho=0}$	−3.46	−2.17	−2.19	−2.19	−2.19	−2.11	−2.11
		[0.953]	[0.947]	[0.947]	[0.947]	[0.958]	[0.954]
$d_t : \Phi_3$	6.19	2.87	2.90	2.90	2.90	2.95	2.99
		[0.949]	[0.933]	[0.933]	[0.933]	[0.909]	[0.923]

(b) Cointegration tests:

$$p_t = a + bd_t + u_t$$

	Data	Asymp.	Null1	Fads	Bubble	Null2	TVRP
a	3.94	−	5.26	5.25	5.21	5.26	5.28
			[1.00]	[0.991]	[0.962]	[1.00]	[0.947]
b	1.31	−	1.00	1.00	0.954	1.00	0.994
			[0.000]	[0.001]	[0.002]	[0.001]	[0.024]
$t_{\rho=0}$	−4.57	−2.21	−7.25	−3.39	−3.55	− 6.51	−4.06
$\mu = 0$		[0.999]	[0.000]	[0.954]	[0.952]	[0.054]	[0.718]
$t_{\rho=0,\,\mu \neq 0}$	−3.87	−1.56	−7.23	−3.17	−3.40	−6.42	−3.95
$a = 0, b = 1$		[0.999]	[0.000]	[0.848]	[0.794]	[0.029]	[0.499]

Augmented Dickey-Fuller tests for a unit root. In (a), $t_{e=0}$ refers to the t-test for $\rho = 0$, given $\delta = 0$. The joint F-test for $\rho = 0$ and $\delta = 0$ is denoted Φ_3. In (b), the coefficients a and b denote the OLS estimates from the cointegrating regression. The statistics $t_{e=0}$ give the t-tests for a unit root in the regression residuals, i.e. the null hypothesis of no cointegration. The row labelled $t_{\rho=0,\,u\neq0}$ denotes the t-test for a unit root in $p_t - d_t$, i.e. imposing $a = 0$ and $b = 1$. The "Data" column provides the sample statistics. The "Asymp." column reports the medians and p-values in the simulated asymptotic distributions. The last five columns provide the medians from the Monte Carlo experiments under the different hypotheses with the p-values reported in square brackets.

The conformity among the p-values for the Null1 and Null2 models illustrates the robustness of the standard unit root tests to the presence of conditional heteroskedasticity as shown by Phillips (1987).

The tests for cointegration of p_t and d_t are presented in table 9.5b. Following Engle and Granger (1987), if p_t and d_t are not cointegrated, the residuals from the cointegrating regression of p_t on a constant and d_t will contain a unit root. Note that under the null hypothesis of no cointegration the regression of p_t on d_t is spurious in the sense of Granger and Newbold (1974). The asymptotic distribution of this residual- based unit root test has been formally derived by Phillips and Ouliaris (1990).[27] The 1% and 5% critical values are -3.96 and -3.37, respectively. Consistent with the predictions of the present value model and the absence of speculative bubbles, the null hypothesis of a unit root in the mean-zero residuals from the cointegrating regression is easily rejected since the test statistic is -4.57.

When we impose the cointegrating vector $(1, -1)$, the null hypothesis of a unit root in the logarithmic price/dividend ratio is also firmly rejected. Note that, when imposing the cointegrating vector, the corresponding, t-statistic should be evaluated in the standard asymptotic unit root distribution for $\rho = 0$ given $\mu = 0$. From Fuller (1976), the 1% and 5% critical values in this distribution are -3.43 and -2.86, respectively. A time series plot of the logarithmic price/dividend ratio is given in figure 9.3.

These results are counter to related findings reported in the literature, which fail to reject the null of no cointegration using annual data. The findings in

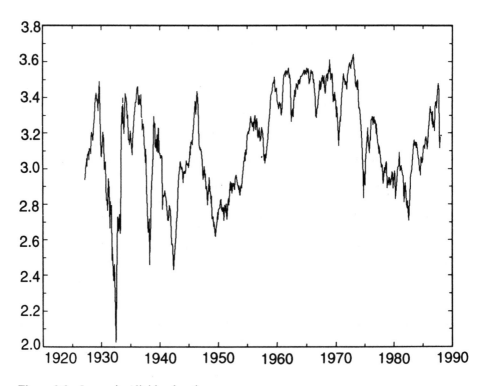

Figure 9.3 Log price/dividend ratio

table 9.5 for monthly data suggest that these results may be due to a lack of power in the tests using time-aggregated annual data, even though the annual span of the data is comparable. Note that while the *p*-values for the Null1 model suggest much more powerful rejections than the sample statistics, the medians and the *p*-values for the TVRP model are broadly consistent with the actual empirical findings. At the same time, the median values of the test statistics in the empirical distributions from the Bubble model suggest that the nominal sizes of the cointegration test are misleading for the collapsing bubble analyzed here. In fact, the medians for the Fads model, in which p_t and d_t are cointegrated, are closer to the asymptotic counterparts under the null of no cointegration than are the same statistics for the Bubble model. Additional evidence on this issue is provided in Evans (1991).

Even though the estimate of *b* from the cointegrating regression is significantly different from the implied value of unity in the TVRP model at the 0.024 level, it is interesting to note that all of the other alternatives, including the Bubble specification, result in even lower *p*-values for the estimated coefficient $\hat{b} = 1.31$.[28] It follows also that $\hat{a} = 3.94$ is too small compared to the results for the five simulated price processes.

To better understand the results from the simulations, suppose that real monthly dividends followed a logarithmic random walk with drift μ and normal innovations with a variance of σ^2. It follows then from equation (9.1) that if the required rate of return were constant and equal to *r*,

$$p_t^f - d_t = -\ln[\exp(r - \mu - 0.5\sigma^2) - 1]. \qquad (9.33)$$

When evaluated at the sample analogues of $\mu = 0.00086$, $\sigma^2 = 0.000311$, and $r = 0.00635$, the right-hand side of equation (9.33) equals 5.23. The median values of the intercept in the cointegrating regression under each of the alternatives are all close to this value.

6 Volatility Tests

In the late 1970s researchers interested in the efficiency of asset markets shifted their focus from the predictability of returns to the volatility of prices. As always, the hypothesis of market efficiency could not be tested directly but was part of a joint hypothesis. Researchers were still required to specify a particular model of expected returns. Additionally, the predictions of price volatility from a particular model depended on the assumed time series properties of the dividend process and the information set of economic agents.

The first volatility tests were conducted by Shiller (1979; 1981a) and LeRoy and Porter (1981) using the constant expected rate of return model as the null hypothesis. The point estimates from these studies implied overwhelming rejections of market efficiency, although LeRoy and Porter's (1981) calculation of standard errors suggested that the sampling variation of the estimates implied only marginal statistical significance. Subsequent research, particularly by Flavin (1983) and Kleidon (1986a; 1986b), questioned the small sample statistical properties of these analysis. For recent surveys of this literature see West (1988), Pesaran (1991), Gilles and LeRoy (1991), and Cochrane (1991a).

In order to illustrate the issues, we focus here on a volatility test developed by Mankiw, Romer, and Shapiro (1991), which we denote the MRS test. This class of tests is designed to avoid some of the biases that plagued previous studies and to provide for more reliable statistical inference. Like many volatility tests, the MRS test recognizes that in an efficient market the price of an asset must equal the discounted conditional expected payoff from holding the asset for k periods and reselling it. That is,

$$P_t = E_t(P_t^{*k}), \tag{9.34}$$

where

$$P_t^{*k} \equiv \sum_{j=1}^{k} \left(\prod_{i=1}^{j} p_{t+1} \right) D_{t+j} + \left(\prod_{i=1}^{k} p_{t+1} \right) P_{t+k}. \tag{9.35}$$

Note that the *ex post* rational price defined in equation (9.35) is only observable at time $t + k$.[29]

Equation (9.34) implies that $P_t^{*k} - P_t$ is uncorrelated with any information available at time t. In particular, let P_t^0 denote any "naïve forecast" of the *ex post* rational price. Then, the following second-order moment condition must hold:

$$E_t[(P_t^{*k} - P_t)(P_t - P_t^0)] = 0. \tag{9.36}$$

This, in turn, implies the following condition for the corresponding uncentered second-order moments:

$$E_t[(P_t^{*k} - P_t^0)^2] = E_t[(P_t^{*k} - P_t)^2] + E_t[(P_t - P_t^0)^2]. \tag{9.37}$$

Equation (9.37) remains valid when the price constructs are deflated by any variable in the time t information set. As the results in table 9.5 indicate, such a transformation is necessary to ensure stationarity and the existence of unconditional expectations required in deriving the test statistics. In our implementation of the MRS volatility test we follow their lead and divide by P_t. Hence, from equation (9.37),

$$E_t\left[\left(\frac{P_t^{*k}}{P_t} - \frac{P_t^0}{P_t}\right)^2\right] - E_t\left[\left(\frac{P_t^{*k}}{P_t} - 1\right)^2\right] - E_t\left[\left(1 - \frac{P_t^0}{P_t}\right)^2\right] = 0. \tag{9.38}$$

Let q_{t+k} denote the corresponding sample realizations of equation (9.38):

$$q_{t+k} \equiv \left(\frac{P_t^{*k}}{P_t} - \frac{P_t^0}{P_t}\right)^2 - \left(\frac{P_t^{*k}}{P_t} - 1\right)^2 - \left(1 - \frac{P_t^0}{P_t}\right)^2. \tag{9.39}$$

The null hypothesis from equation (9.38) is then conveniently stated as $E_t(q_{t+k}) = 0$.

By the law of iterated expectations, $E(q_t) = 0$, and the sample mean of q_t, denoted $\bar{q}$, should be close to zero under the null hypothesis. The asymptotic distribution of $\bar{q}$ may be derived, as in section 4, by use of the GMM distribution theory for stationary but serially correlated and conditionally heteroskedastic processes. That is,

$$(\sqrt{T})\bar{q} \sim N(0, V_0),\tag{9.40}$$

where

$$V_0 = \sum_{j=-k+1}^{k-1} E(q_{t+k}q_{t+k-j}).\tag{9.41}$$

The sample variance may be estimated by

$$V_T = C_T(0) + \sum_{j=1}^{k-1} 2C_T(j),\tag{9.42}$$

where $C_T(j) = (1/T)\Sigma_{t=j+1}^{T}(q_{t+k}q'_{t+k-j})$. Following Mankiw, Romer, and Shapiro, the jth-order autocovariance is weighted by $(k-j)/k$ as in Newey and West (1987) in order to guarantee a positive estimate of the variance in equation (9.42). This weighting scheme is derived under the assumption that both k and T are going to infinity. Since the order of the autocorrelation is known to be k under the null hypothesis, a more appropriate truncation point with this weighting scheme might include terms of higher order than k. To circumvent this problem, the actual truncation lag could be based on the automatic lag selection procedures discussed in Andrews (1991) and Newey and West (1994).

As our measure of a naïve price prediction, we use a version of the Gordon (1962) model assuming a constant rate of return, r, and a constant dividend growth rate, μ:

$$P_t^0 = \frac{D_t}{r - \mu}.\tag{9.43}$$

The tests are reported in table 9.6a for the same five horizons as in table 3 and 4. Notice in the "Data" column that $\bar{q}$ is negative at all five horizons.[30] The asymptotic p-values are also quite small with the largest being 0.023 at the 24-month horizon. Given the strong significance for each of the individual MRS test statistics at all horizons, we did not calculate a joint test.

Several features of the MRS test are noteworthy in the simulated data. First, for both the Null1 and Null2 models, there is no bias in the test statistics in the sense that the median values of the test statistics are essentially zero. This desirable feature of the MRS volatility test arises because of its use of uncentered second moments rather than sample variances which are biased because of the necessity of estimating the sample mean. Next, notice that the p-values for the Null1, Null2, Fads, and Bubble models are all quite small. It is unlikely that any of these models could generate the sample volatility statistics. Only for the TVRP model are the *p*-values reasonable. Here we find values ranging from 0.142 to 0.346.

The orthogonality condition in equation (9.36) also forms the basis for Scott's (1985) regression test of the present value model. If equation (9.34) is true, a regression of $(P_t^{*k} - P_t)$ on anything in the time *t* information set should have insignificant coefficients. Note, again, that deflation of the price series by some trending variable W_t in the time *t* information set does not formally change this null hypothesis but is desirable to ensure stationarity. In particular, consider the regression specified without a constant term as

$$\frac{P_t^{*k} - P_t}{W_t} = \beta \left(\frac{P_t - P_t^0}{W_t} \right) + e_t. \tag{9.44}$$

The OLS estimate for β is

$$\hat{\beta} = \frac{\dfrac{1}{T} \sum_{t=1}^{T} [(P_t^{*k} - P_t)/W_t][(P_t - P_t^0)/W_t]}{\dfrac{1}{T} \sum_{t=1}^{T} [(P_t - P_t^0)/W_t]^2}. \tag{9.45}$$

For $W_t = P_t$ the numerator of $\hat{\beta}$ equals $(1/2)\bar{q}$. Mankiw, Romer, and Shapiro (1991) note that their volatility test has an advantage and a disadvantage relative to the regression test. The disadvantage is that regression coefficients

Table 9.6 Volatility tests

(a) Second-moment volatility tests:

$$q_{t+k} \equiv \left(\frac{P_t^{*k}}{P_t} - \frac{P_t^0}{P_t} \right)^2 - \left(\frac{P_t^{*k}}{P_t} - 1 \right)^2 - \left(1 - \frac{P_t^0}{P_t} \right)^2$$

k	Data	Asymp.	Null1	Fads	Bubble	Null2	TVRP
1	-0.007	0.000	-0.001	-0.002	-0.002	-0.001	-0.005
	(0.002)	[0.001]	[0.000]	[0.000]	[0.041]	[0.008]	[0.346]
12	-0.032	0.000	-0.002	-0.003	-0.006	-0.001	-0.009
	(0.003)	[0.000]	[0.000]	[0.000]	[0.173]	[0.013]	[0.142]
24	-0.059	0.000	-0.001	-0.007	-0.010	-0.001	-0.034
	(0.026)	[0.023]	[0.000]	[0.000]	[0.009]	[0.000]	[0.331]
36	-0.082	0.000	-0.001	-0.010	-0.014	-0.001	-0.041
	(0.031)	[0.008]	[0.000]	[0.000]	[0.012]	[0.000]	[0.307]
48	-0.112	0.000	-0.001	-0.012	-0.018	-0.001	-0.046
	(0.041)	[0.006]	[0.000]	[0.000]	[0.021]	[0.003]	[0.266]

(b) Diagnostics on *ex post* rational prices and dividend yields

Horizon	Data	Null1	Fads	Bubble	Null2	TVRP
Second moment of ex post *rational price relative to naïve price*						
1	0.142	0.005	0.016	0.030	0.004	0.047
	(0.023)	[0.000]	[0.000]	[0.093]	[0.008]	[0.180]
12	0.117	0.004	0.013	0.024	0.003	0.041
	(0.020)	[0.000]	[0.000]	[0.017]	[0.003]	[0.187]
24	0.155	0.023	0.036	0.049	0.022	0.056
	(0.028)	[0.000]	[0.000]	[0.114]	[0.015]	[0.140]
36	0.144	0.033	0.042	0.055	0.028	0.061
	(0.028)	[0.000]	[0.000]	[0.118]	[0.017]	[0.153]
48	0.141	0.040	0.048	0.061	0.033	0.063
	(0.029)	[0.000]	[0.000]	[0.115]	[0.030]	[0.155]
Second moment of ex post *rational price relative to unity*						
1	0.003	0.001	0.001	0.001	0.001	0.002
	(0.001)	[0.000]	[0.000]	[0.045]	[0.027]	[0.274]
12	0.003	0.001	0.001	0.001	0.001	0.001
	(0.001)	[0.000]	[0.000]	[0.197]	[0.021]	[0.166]
24	0.069	0.021	0.027	0.027	0.018	0.042
	(0.016)	[0.000]	[0.000]	[0.083]	[0.023]	[0.295]
36	0.080	0.029	0.036	0.038	0.024	0.052
	(0.018)	[0.000]	[0.000]	[0.085]	[0.035]	[0.316]
48	0.107	0.035	0.044	0.047	0.030	0.061
	(0.028)	[0.000]	[0.000]	[0.074]	[0.033]	[0.269]
Second moment of naïve price relative to unity						
	0.146	0.005	0.016	0.031	0.004	0.049
	(0.023)	[0.000]	[0.000]	[0.092]	[0.008]	[0.184]

Mankiw, Romer, and Shapiro (1991) volatility tests. The *ex post* rational price is denoted P_t^{*k}, and the naïve price is P_t^0. The results reported in (a) test the mean of q_{t+k} equal to zero. The three second-moment components of q_{t+k} are reported in (b). The columns report the medians for the sample statistics with the *p*-values in square brackets.

and the coefficient of multiple correlation, R^2, have natural interpretations in terms of the predictability of returns. The advantage is that regression tests may be more systematically biased.

Equation (9.38) implies two volatility inequalities which serve as diagnostics for the models:

$$ E\left[\left(\frac{P_t^{*k}}{P_t} - \frac{P_t^0}{P_t}\right)^2\right] \ge E\left[\left(\frac{P_t^{*k}}{P_t} - 1\right)^2\right], \qquad (9.46) $$

$$E\left[\left(\frac{P_t^{*k}}{P_t} - \frac{P_t^0}{P_t}\right)^2\right] \geq E\left[\left(1 - \frac{P_t^0}{P_t}\right)^2\right]. \tag{9.47}$$

Table 9.6b reports the sample analogue for the left-hand side of equations (9.46) and (9.47) as *ex post* rational price relative to naïve price. The realization of the right-hand side of equation (9.46) is denoted *ex post* rational price relative to unity, while the sample realization of the right-hand side of equation (9.47) is referred to as naïve price relative to unity. Interestingly, it is the latter quantity that is the primary source of evidence for excess volatility in the data. From inspection of the *p*-values for the various models, it follows that only the TVRP model is consistent with the data at a 10% significance level.

The right-hand side of equation (9.47) is a measure of the variability in the dividend/price ratio. The naive Gordon (1962) model predicts that the dividend/price ratio should be a constant. There are three sources of movement in the TVRP model that improve on this counterfactual prediction. First, information other than the current level of dividends is useful for predicting future dividends, which is true for all the models. Second, the time variation in the conditional variance of dividends matters to investors who are forecasting the levels of dividends, which is true for Null2 as well. The third feature is that the required rate of return is not a constant.[31]

As noted above, there is also a direct relation between the volatility of prices and the predictability of returns. To further understand this relation consider the following argument. Assuming a constant discount factor ρ, and $W_t = P_t$, it follows from equation (9.35) that for $k = 2$,

$$\frac{P_t^{*2}}{P_t} - 1 = \rho \frac{D_{t+1}}{P_t} - 1 + \rho^2 \left(\frac{D_{t+2} + P_{t+2}}{P_t}\right). \tag{9.48}$$

Add and subtract $\rho(P_{t+1}/P_t)$ to the right-hand side of equation (9.48) and multiply the second term on the right-hand side by (P_{t+1}/P_{t+1}). The result is

$$\frac{P_t^{*2}}{P_t} - 1 = \rho\left(\frac{D_{t+1} + P_{t+1}}{P_t}\right) - 1 + \rho^2\left(\frac{P_{t+1}}{P_t}\right)\left(\frac{D_{t+2} + P_{t+2}}{P_{t+1}}\right) - \rho\frac{P_{t+1}}{P_t}.$$
$$\tag{9.49}$$

$$= (\rho R_{t+1} - 1) + \rho\left(\frac{P_{t+1}}{P_t}\right)(\rho R_{t+2} - 1).$$

Clearly, if the null hypothesis is true and expected returns have a constant mean equal to ρ^{-1}, $(P_t^{*2}/P_t - 1)$ is not predictable.

Let $x_t \equiv (1 - P_t^0/P_t)$, and let $u_{t+1} \equiv (\rho R_{t+1} - 1)$. Substituting these definitions into equation (9.49) and the results into equation (9.36) with its variables deflated by P_t yields

$$E_t[(u_{t+1} + \rho(P_{t+1}/P_t)u_{t+2})x_t] = 0. \tag{9.50}$$

It is apparent that both the MRS volatility test and Scott's regression test examine the null hypothesis that a variable in the time t information set cannot predict returns at various horizons.

As in section 4, stationarity of the variables in equation (9.50) allows us to reorganize the equation and express its unconditional expectation as

$$E[u_{t+1}(x_t + \rho(P_t/P_{t-1})x_{t-1})] = 0. \tag{9.51}$$

This formulation of the volatility test makes it transparent that it is predictability of one-period returns that is being tested, and from the definition of x_t, any predictability of returns is due to a filtered measure of dividend yields. The sample counterparts to the unconditional expectation of equation (9.50) and equation (9.51) only differ by the first and last observations. Of course, estimates of the variance of the sample mean might be very different in small samples. The variance for the estimator based on equation (9.50) may be calculated as in equation (9.42). However, the variance for the estimator based on equation (9.51) avoids the overlapping data problem and the summation of the autocovariances and may be calculated analogously to equation (9.28). The small sample properties of the resulting test statistics will therefore differ. We conjecture that reorganizing the test statistics as in equation (9.51) to avoid the overlapping data problem will result in superior small sample behavior.

7 Conclusion

The analysis in this chapter provides a partial survey of the econometric methods employed in testing for own temporal dependencies in the distribution of asset returns. It also addresses the relationship of these dependencies to the concept of market efficiency. We intentionally worked only with price, dividend, and return data, and avoided the use of other macroeconomic variables that might help explain the evolution of returns over time. We focused the discussion on tests that have been primarily designed for broadly defined asset categories. A large literature in finance analyzes cross-sectional differences in returns. Fama and French (1992) and Ferson (1995) provide recent contributions to this literature. Our somewhat narrow focus was motivated in part by space considerations and by the relevance of expected return variability for issues in macroeconomics.

Much of the literature on testing for market efficiency has proceeded under the convenient assumption that rational asset pricing requires a constant rate of return. While simple short-horizon serial correlation tests often cannot reject this hypothesis, the idea that equilibrium required rates of returns may vary through time has been in the literature since the early discussions of LeRoy (1973) and Merton (1973) and the general equilibrium models of Lucas (1978) and Breeden (1979). The latter models are often referred to as consumption-based capital asset pricing models.

Although the time-varying risk premium model postulated in our simulations was not rigorously derived from a rational expectations model, its performance in the simulations was broadly consistent with the empirical findings pertaining to US stock returns. In contrast, the alternative models assuming a constant discount factor or modifications to incorporate fads or bubbles in asset prices were grossly inconsistent with some aspects of the data. These results illustrate the importance of explicitly recognizing the presence of a time-varying risk premium in tests for market efficiency.

The particular functional form for our time-varying risk premium model related the expected return on the market to the change in the conditional variance of future dividends. This formulation was motivated by the analysis in Abel (1988) and Hodrick (1989). Such an approach is radically different from much of the empirical literature that has been devoted to testing restrictions implied by the consumption-based capital asset pricing model. In spite of its theoretical appeal, the consumption-based CAPM does not perform well empirically, as exemplified by the many tests following the approach of Hansen and Singleton (1982; 1983). The basic problem stems from the fact that consumption is much too smooth compared to the variability of most financial asset returns. This is formally documented in Hansen and Jagannathan (1991) who derive bounds on intertemporal marginal rates of substitution using asset market data. In a related context, Pesaran and Potter (1991) argue that predictability of negative excess returns is inconsistent with most equilibrium consumption-based asset pricing models. While the consumption-based asset pricing models generally fail specification tests, the more recent developments in Cochrane (1991b) and Braun (1991) suggest that alternative dynamic asset pricing models based on the investment decisions of firms may provide a better explanation for the observed time-varying risk premiums.

The ready availability of data on asset returns and the declining cost of computing have generated a large literature documenting the stylized facts of financial markets. The current challenge facing financial economists is to develop models that are consistent with the observed variability in the distributions of returns. Variability of expected returns appears to be a necessary aspect of rational explanations of these phenomena. We also conjecture that understanding the link between conditional volatility of market fundamentals and variation in required expected returns that arises from risk aversion of economic agents will be critical to success in this endeavor.

Appendix

Forecast expressions for $E_t(d_{t+j})$ and $\text{var}_t(d_{t+j})$ from the estimated AR(12)-ARCH(12) model for the dividend growth rate in equation (9.5) are most easily evaluated by expressing the model in first-order companion form in the logarithmic levels. That is,

$$\begin{bmatrix} d_t \\ d_{t-1} \\ \vdots \\ d_{t-12} \end{bmatrix} = \begin{bmatrix} \mu \\ 0 \\ \vdots \\ 0 \end{bmatrix} + \begin{bmatrix} \phi_1 + 1 & \phi_2 - \phi_1 & \cdots & \phi_{12} - \phi_{11} & -\phi_{12} \\ 1 & 0 & \cdots & 0 & 0 \\ \vdots & & & & \\ 0 & 0 & \cdots & 0 & 0 \end{bmatrix} \begin{bmatrix} d_{t-1} \\ d_{t-2} \\ \vdots \\ d_{t-13} \end{bmatrix} + \begin{bmatrix} \varepsilon_t \\ 0 \\ \vdots \\ 0 \end{bmatrix},$$

or more compactly,

$$\mathbf{d}_t = \boldsymbol{\mu} + \boldsymbol{\Phi}\mathbf{d}_{t-1} + \boldsymbol{\epsilon}_t, \tag{9.52}$$

where μ denotes the constant, and ϕ_i the ith autoregressive parameter for Δd_t in equation (9.5). By repeated substitution in equation (9.52),

$$\mathbf{d}_{t+j} = \sum_{i=0}^{j-1} \boldsymbol{\Phi}^i \boldsymbol{\mu} + \sum_{i=0}^{j-1} \boldsymbol{\Phi}^i \boldsymbol{\epsilon}_{t+j-i} + \boldsymbol{\Phi}^j \mathbf{d}_t.$$

Define $\mathbf{e}_i$ to be a 13×1 basis vector of zeros except for unity in the ith element. Also, define $\psi_i \equiv \mathbf{e}'_1 \boldsymbol{\Phi}^i \mathbf{e}_1$. Then,

$$d_{t+j} = \mu \sum_{i=0}^{j-1} \mathbf{e}'_1 \boldsymbol{\Phi}^i \mathbf{e}_1 + \sum_{i=0}^{j-1} \mathbf{e}'_1 \boldsymbol{\Phi}^i \mathbf{e}_1 \varepsilon_{t+j-i} + \mathbf{e}'_1 \boldsymbol{\Phi}^j \sum_{i=1}^{13} \mathbf{e}_i d_{t+1-i} \tag{9.53}$$

$$= \mu \sum_{i=0}^{j-1} \psi_i + \sum_{i=0}^{j-1} \psi_i \varepsilon_{t+j-i} + \mathbf{e}'_1 \boldsymbol{\Phi}^j \sum_{i=1}^{13} \mathbf{e}_i d_{t+1-i}.$$

It follows now directly from equation (9.53) that

$$E_t(d_{t+j}) = \mu \sum_{i=0}^{j-1} \psi_i + \mathbf{e}'_1 \boldsymbol{\Phi}^j \sum_{i=1}^{13} \mathbf{e}_i d_{t+1-i}, \tag{9.54}$$

and

$$\text{var}_t(d_{t+j}) = \sum_{i=0}^{j-1} \psi_i^2 E_t(\varepsilon_{t+j-i}^2). \tag{9.55}$$

Evaluation of the expression for the conditional variance of d_{t+j} requires forecasts from the ARCH(12) conditional variance process for ε_j. Following Baillie and Bollerslev (1992), the ARCH(12) model is conveniently expressed in first-order companion form as

$$\begin{bmatrix} \varepsilon_t^2 \\ \varepsilon_{t-1}^2 \\ \vdots \\ \varepsilon_{t-11}^2 \end{bmatrix} = \begin{bmatrix} \omega \\ 0 \\ \vdots \\ 0 \end{bmatrix} + \begin{bmatrix} \alpha_1 & \alpha_2 & \cdots & \alpha_{12} \\ 0 & 0 & \cdots & 0 \\ \vdots & & & \\ 0 & 0 & \cdots & 0 \end{bmatrix} \begin{bmatrix} \varepsilon_{t-1}^2 \\ \varepsilon_{t-2}^2 \\ \vdots \\ \varepsilon_{t-12}^2 \end{bmatrix} + \begin{bmatrix} v_t \\ 0 \\ \vdots \\ 0 \end{bmatrix}$$

or compactly as

$$\boldsymbol{\epsilon}_t^2 = \boldsymbol{\omega} + \boldsymbol{\Gamma}\boldsymbol{\epsilon}_{t-1}^2 + \boldsymbol{v}_t, \tag{9.56}$$

where $v_t \equiv \varepsilon_t^2 - \sigma_t^2$. Note that $E_{t-1}(v_t) = 0$, and v_t is readily interpreted as the innovation to the conditional variance for ε_t. Analogous to the expression for d_{t+j} in equation (9.53), it follows by repeated substitution in equation (9.56) and post-multiplication with the 12×1 basis vector e_1 that

$$\varepsilon_{t+j}^2 = \omega \sum_{i=0}^{j-1} e_1' \Gamma^i e_1 + \sum_{i=0}^{j-1} e_1' \Gamma^i e_1 v_{t+j-i} + e_1' \Gamma^j \sum_{i=1}^{12} e_i \varepsilon_{t+1-i}^2 . \tag{9.57}$$

By the law of iterated expectations $E_t(v_{t+j}) = 0$ for all $j > 0$, and

$$E_t(\varepsilon_{t+j}^2) = \omega \sum_{i=0}^{j-1} e_1' \Gamma^i e_1 + e_1' \Gamma^j \sum_{i=1}^{12} e_i \varepsilon_{t+1-i}^2 . \tag{9.58}$$

Combining equations (9.55) and (9.58) we get

$$\mathrm{var}_t(d_{t+j}) = \sum_{i=0}^{j-1} \psi_i^2 \left[\omega \sum_{h=0}^{j-i-1} (e_1' \Gamma^h e_1) + \sum_{h=1}^{12} (e_1' \Gamma^{j-i} e_h) \varepsilon_{t+1-h}^2 \right]. \tag{9.59}$$

This completes the derivation of the forecast formula used in the evaluation of equation (9.9) for $j \leqslant J$.

Notes

We thank Geert Bekaert, John Cochrane, Martin D. Evans, Stephen F. LeRoy, Robert J. Shiller, Kenneth D. West, and seminar participants at the Australasian Meetings of the Econometric Society, Monash University, the NBER Asset Pricing Group, the University of Kentucky, and the University of North Carolina for helpful comments.

1 The estimates in Fama and French (1988a) for monthly US stock returns imply that for three to five year returns up to 40% of the variability is predictable. The evidence in Kim, Nelson, and Startz (1991) suggests that much of this predictability may be driven by data around the time of the Great Depression.
2 We do not discuss these techniques here because of related coverage in this volume.
3 The simulation approach employed in this chapter was inspired by the earlier work of Mattey and Meese (1986) which could be usefully read in conjunction with the present study.
4 Although we illustrate the tests for market efficiency using stock market data, the same ideas apply equally well to tests of other present value relations such as the rational expectations theory of the term structure of interest rates; see Campbell and Shiller (1987), for example. We also note that dividends are not the only way of distributing value to shareholders, as documented by Bagwell and Shoven (1989). Dividends are also a decision variable of management which may choose to smooth them or to have a liquidating dividend. Marsh and Merton (1986) note that such behaviour can cause serious problems with econometric analysis of present value relations.
5 Even though the annualized dividend series exhibit seasonality, it is worth noting that the degree of own temporal dependence is substantially reduced when com-

pared to the real monthly growth rate in the raw dividend series. For instance, the Ljung and Box (1978) portmanteau test statistic, defined formally below, for up to 12th-order serial correlation in Δd_t equals 342.7 compared to 4042.7 for $\Delta \ln(ND_t)$.

6 The autocorrelations for the squared residuals at lags 1, 3, 6, and 12 equal 0.066, 0.245, 0.120, and 0.164 respectively, and all but lag 1 exceed the 5% critical value of $1.96/\sqrt{T} = 0.073$ under the null of $\hat{\varepsilon}_t^2$ iid through time.

7 The maximized value of the conditional normal log-likelihood function for the model in equation (9.5) equals -4472.4 compared to -4644.8 for the homoskedastic normal AR(12) model restricting the four ARCH coefficients to be zero. The resulting likelihood ratio test statistic for no ARCH equals 344.8, which is highly significant.

8 While a closed-form expression for the infinite discounted sum in equation (9.1) may be derived using the methods of Hansen and Sargent (1980; 1981) in the case of a constant discount rate (see e.g. West, 1987b), the presence of time-varying discount rates coupled with time-varying conditional variances renders a closed-form solution infeasible.

9 Let $\zeta(L) = \phi(L)^{-1}$ denote the lag polynomial in the infinite moving average representation for the AR(12) model with parameters ζ_i, where $\phi(L)\Delta d_t = \mu + \varepsilon_t$. It follows that

$$\text{var}_t(d_{t+j+1}) = \text{var}_t(d_{t+j}) + \sum_{h=0}^{j} \sum_{i=0}^{h} \zeta_h \zeta_{h-i} E_t(\varepsilon_{t+j+1-h}^2).$$

Thus, in the limit,

$$\xi = \sigma^2 \sum_{h=0}^{\infty} \sum_{i=0}^{h} \zeta_h \zeta_{h-i},$$

where σ^2 equals the unconditional variance of ε_t. Also, $\eta = \mu\phi(1)^{-1}$.

10 From equations (9.11) and (9.12) it follows that $\text{var}[\Delta \ln(P_t)] = \text{var}[\Delta \ln(P_t^f)] + \text{var}[\Delta \ln(F_t)] = \text{var}[\Delta \ln(P_t^f)] + 2\sigma_u^2(1 + \phi)^{-1}$. Setting $\phi = 0.98$ and requiring that $2\sigma_u^2(1 + \phi)^{-1}$ equals 25% of $\text{var}[\Delta \ln(P_t)]$ implies $\sigma_u^2 = 0.330\text{var}[\Delta \ln(P_t^f)]$.

11 Our stochastic bubbles do not collapse to zero because, as Diba and Grossman (1988) note, the theoretical impossibility of a rational negative bubble rules out a zero-mean innovation in a bubble starting at zero.

12 We also imposed two other restrictions on the bubble process. We required that the bubble continue with probability one if its current value is less than the reversion value under a collapse, and we set the maximum probability of collapse at 0.99. Flood and Hodrick (1986; 1990) provide a discussion of tests for bubbles.

13 Let $\hat{\mu}_i$ denote the ith centered sample moment. Then $b_3 \equiv \hat{\mu}_3/(\hat{\mu}_2)^{3/2}$ and $b_4 \equiv \hat{\mu}_4/(\hat{\mu}_2)^2$.

14 Under the null of iid the standardized test statistics, $[\sqrt{(T/6)}]b_3$ and $[\sqrt{(T/24)}]$ $(b_4 - 3)$, should both be the realization of a standard normal distribution; see e.g. Jarque and Bera (1980).

15 Let ρ_i denote the ith sample autocorrelation. The Ljung and Box (1978) test for up to Nth-order serial dependence is then given by $Q_N = (T + 2)T[\rho_1^2/(T - 1) + \rho_2^2/(T - 2) + \ldots + \rho_N^2/(T - N)]$, where T denotes the sample size. Under the null hypothesis of iid observations, Q_N has an asymptotic chi-squared distribution with N degrees of freedom.

16 The variance ratio statistic in equation (9.18) is consistently estimated by $\hat{v}(k) = \{1 + 2[(k - 1)\rho_1 + (k - 2)\rho_2 + \ldots + \rho_{k-1}]\}/k$. Under the null hypothesis of iid observations, with $k = 12$ and $T = 720$, the standard error for the variance ratio statistic in the asymptotic normal distribution with mean one equals 0.140. A heteroskedasticity consistent standard error may be calculated from White's (1980) covariance matrix estimator for the sample autocorrelations; see Lo and MacKinlay (1988) for further details.

17 The martingale model is sometimes incorrectly referred to as the random walk model. Whereas the random walk model assumes iid innovations, a martingale difference sequence only stipulates that the innovations be serially uncorrelated, or white noise.

18 Clearly, increasing the importance of the fad from our *a priori* specification of 25% would help explain the variability of returns, but it may cause problems for the model along other dimensions. Similarly, by increasing the innovation variance of the bubble, it would be possible to match the sample variance of returns.

19 Let μ_t and σ_t^2 denote the conditional mean and variance functions, with gradients $\nabla\mu_t$ and $\nabla\sigma_t^2$, respectively. The asymptotic covariance matrix for the quasi-maximum-likelihood estimator, $\hat{\Xi}_T$, is then consistently estimated by $A_T B_T^{-1} A_T$, where

$$A_T = \sum_{t=1}^{T} \nabla\mu_t(\nabla\mu_t)'\sigma_t^{-2} + 0.5\nabla\sigma_t^2(\nabla\sigma_t^2)'\sigma_t^{-4},$$

$$B_T = \sum_{t=1}^{T} \nabla l_t(\Xi)\nabla l_t(\Xi)',$$

$$\nabla l_t(\Xi) = \nabla\mu_t\sigma_t^{-2}\varepsilon_t + 0.5\nabla\sigma_t^2\sigma_t^{-4}(\varepsilon_t^2 - \sigma_t^2),$$

all evaluated at $\hat{\Xi}_T$.

20 A possible explanation for this phenomenon and the estimate of $\alpha + \beta$ close to one is provided by the continuous time approximation arguments given in Nelson (1992) and Nelson and Foster (1994). The apparent strong persistence in the conditional variance could also be a result of stochastic regime changes as in the analysis of Cai (1994).

21 In the EGARCH(1,1) model the conditional variance is given by

$$\ln(\sigma_t^2) = \omega + \theta z_{t-1} + \gamma(|z_{t-1}| - E(|z_{t-1}|)) + \beta\ln(\sigma_{t-1}^2),$$

where $z_t \equiv \varepsilon_t\sigma_t^{-1}$ denotes the standardized innovations. Alternative asymmetric conditional variance formulations include the model in Glosten, Jagannathan, and Runkle (1993) and the specifications in Engle and Ng (1993). Recent evidence in Gallant, Rossi, and Tauchen (1992) and Andersen (1992) explores structural links between conditional volatility and volume. Space considerations prevent us from pursuing these specifications here.

22 If the one-period returns are serially uncorrelated, it is possible to solve explicitly for the parameters in the corresponding moving average representation for $u_{t+k,k}$ as a function of the overlap, as in Baillie and Bollerslev (1990) and Richardson and Smith (1991).

23 Richardson and Stock (1989) develop an alternative asymptotic distribution theory based on a functional central limit theorem. They argue that if T is the sample size

and k is the forecast horizon, a better asymptotic approximation to the finite sample distribution is obtained by letting (k/T) go to a non-zero constant rather than to zero as in the conventional asymptotic distribution theory. Inference under this alternative distribution theory provides little support for the hypothesis that lagged long-horizon returns predict future long-horizon returns. Nelson and Kim (1993) and Hodrick (1992) use Monte Carlo simulations and Goetzmann and Jorion (1992) use bootstrap techniques to investigate the regressions of dividend yields as predictors of long-horizon returns. These authors also find that the small sample properties of estimators are not well approximated by conventional asymptotic distribution theory.

24 Lars Hansen suggested this estimator, which is a heteroskedastic counterpart to the covariance matrix in Richardson and Smith (1991). This section draws heavily from Hodrick (1992).

25 Jegadeesh (1990) uses this logic and the fads alternative hypothesis to derive the test with the largest asymptotic slope for investigating long-horizon predictability of returns on the basis of lagged returns. He argues that using the one-period return as the dependent variable and the sum of k lagged returns as the regressor is a superior way to conduct inference. The choice of k depends on the share of the variance of returns attributed to the transitory components in prices.

26 See Campbell and Shiller (1987; 1988a; 1988b), Cochrane (1991a; 1992), Craine (1991), Evans (1991), and Froot and Obstfeld (1991) for more complete discussions and applications.

27 The likelihood ratio test in Johansen (1988; 1991) provides an alternative non-residual-based testing procedure for cointegration.

28 As noted in note 4, if the importance of dividends as a means of distributing cash to shareholders has declined systematically, one would expect that the slope coefficient in the cointegrating regression would exceed one. Asymptotically valid standard errors for the estimated cointegrating vector that would allow a standard t-test of the hypothesis $b = 1$ could be calculated as in Stock and Watson (1993) by including leads and lags of Δd_t on the right-hand side of the cointegrating regression of p_t on d_t.

29 This contrasts with Shiller's (1981a) definition of *ex post* rational price in which $k = \infty$ in equation (9.34). Shiller develops a measurable counterpart by substitution of $k_t = T - t$ for k in equation (9.35), where T is the end of the sample observed by the econometrician. Flood and Hodrick (1990) refer to equation (9.34) as an interated Euler equation.

30 We use the sample mean return for r and the sample mean of the dividend growth rate for μ, rather than preselected values, in the construction of the naïve prices.

31 Several authors including Campbell (1991), Cochrane (1992), and LeRoy and Parke (1992) have reformulated volatility tests to examine the variance of the price/dividend ratio.

References

Abel, A.B. (1988), "Stock Prices under Time-Varying Dividend Risk: An Exact Solution in an Infinite Horizon General Equilibrium Model," *Journal of Monetary Economics*, 22, 375–93.

Andersen, T.G. (1992), "Return Volatility and Trading Volume in Financial Markets: An Information Flow Interpretation of Stochastic Volatility," manuscript, Department of Finance, J. L. Kellogg Graduate School of Management, Northwestern University.

Andrews, D.W.K. (1991), "Heteroskedasticity and Autocorrelation Consistent Covariance Matrix Estimation," *Econometrica*, 59, 817–58.

Bagwell, L.S. and J.B. Shoven (1989), "Cash Distributions to Shareholders," *Journal of Economic Perspectives*, 3, 129–40.

Baillie, R.T. (1989), "Econometric Tests of Rationality and Market Efficiency," *Econometric Reviews*, 8, 151–86.

Baillie, R.T. and T. Bollerslev (1990), "A Multivariate Generalized ARCH Approach to Modeling Risk Premia in Forward Foreign Exchange," *Journal of International Money and Finance*, 9, 309–24.

Baillie, R.T. and T. Bollerslev (1992), "Prediction in Dynamic Models with Time Dependent Conditional Variances," *Journal of Econometrics*, 52, 91–113.

Bekaert, G. (1992), "Empirical Analyses of Foreign Exchange Markets: General Equilibrium Perspectives," PhD dissertation, Department of Economics, Northwestern University.

Bekaert, G. and R.J. Hodrick (1992), "Characterizing Predictable Components in Equity and Foreign Exchange Rates of Return," *Journal of Finance*, 47, 467–509.

Black, F. (1976), "Studies of Stock Market Volatility Changes," *Proceedings of the American Statistical Association, Business and Economic Statistics Section*, 177–81.

Blanchard, O.J. and M.W. Watson (1982), "Bubbles, Rational Expectations and Financial Crises," in P. Wachtel (ed.), *Crises in the Economic and Financial Structure: Bubbles, Bursts and Shocks*, Lexington, Mass.

Bollerslev, T. (1986), "Generalized Autoregressive Conditional Heteroskedasticity," *Journal of Econometrics*, 31, 307–27.

Bollerslev, T. (1987), "A Conditionally Heteroskedastic Time Series Model for Speculation Prices and Rates of Return," *Review of Economics and Statistics*, 69, 542–7.

Bollerslev, T., R.Y. Chou and K.F. Kroner (1992), "ARCH Modeling in Finance: A Review of the Theory and Empirical Evidence," *Journal of Econometrics*, 52, 5–59.

Bollerslev, T. and R.F. Engle (1993), "Common Persistence in Conditional Variances," *Econometrica*, 61, 167–86.

Bollerslev, T. and J.M. Wooldridge (1992), "Quasi-Maximum Likelihood Estimation and Inference in Dynamic Models with Time Varying Covariances," *Econometric Reviews*, 11, 143–72.

Braun, P. (1991), "Asset Pricing and Capital Investment: Theory and Evidence," manuscript, Department of Finance, J. L. Kellogg Graduate School of Management, Northwestern University.

Breeden, D.T. (1979), "An Intertemporal Asset Pricing Model with Stochastic Consumption and Investment Opportunities," *Journal of Financial Economics*, 7, 265–96.

Cai, J. (1994), "A Markov Model of Switching-Regime ARCH," *Journal of Business and Economic Statistics*, 12, 309–16.

Campbell, J.Y. (1991), "A Variance Decomposition of Stock Returns," *Economic Journal*, 101, 152–79.

Campbell, J.Y. and R.J. Shiller (1987), "Cointegration and Tests of Present Value Models," *Journal of Political Economy*, 95, 1062–88.

Campbell, J.Y. and R.J. Shiller (1988a), "The Dividend–Price Ratio and Expectations of Future Dividends and Discount Factors," *Review of Financial Studies*, 1, 195–228.

Campbell, J.Y. and R.J. Shiller (1988b), "Stock Prices, Earnings, and Expected Dividends," *Journal of Finance*, 43, 661–76.

Christie, A.A. (1982), "The Stochastic Behavior of Common Stock Variances: Value, Leverage and Interest Rate Effects," *Journal of Financial Economics*, 10, 407–32.

Cochrane, J.H. (1991a), "Volatility Tests and Efficient Markets: A Review Essay," *Journal of Monetary Economics*, 27, 463–85.

Cochrane, J.H. (1991b), "Production-Based Asset Pricing and the Link between Stock Returns and Economic Fluctuations," *Journal of Finance*, 46, 207–34.

Cochrane, J.H. (1992), "Explaining the Variance of Price Dividend Ratios," *Review of Financial Studies*, 5, 243–80.

Craine, R. (1991), "Rational Bubbles: A Test," manuscript, Department of Economics, University of California, Berkeley.

Cumby, R.E. and J. Huizinga (1992), "Testing the Autocorrelation Structure of Disturbances in Ordinary Least Squares and Instrumental Variables Regressions," *Econometrica*, 60, 185–95.

Diba, B.T. and H.I. Grossman (1988), "The Theory of Rational Bubbles in Stock Prices," *Economic Journal* 98, 746–54.

Dickey, D.A. and W.A. Fuller (1981), "Likelihood Ratio Statistics for Autoregressive Time Series with a Unit Root," *Econometrica*, 49, 1057–72.

Diebold, F.X. (1986), "Testing for Serial Correlation in the Presence of ARCH," *Proceedings of the American Statistical Association, Business and Economic Statistics Section*, 323–8.

Domowitz, I. and H. White (1982), "Misspecified Models with Dependent Observations," *Journal of Econometrics*, 20, 35–58.

Engle, R.F. (1982), "Autoregressive Conditional Heteroskedasticity with Estimates of the Variance of U.K. Inflation," *Econometrica*, 50, 987–1008.

Engle, R.F. and G. Gonzalez-Rivera (1991), "Semiparametric ARCH Models," *Journal of Business and Economic Statistics*, 9, 345–59.

Engle, R.F. and C.W.J. Granger (1987), "Cointegration and Error Correction: Representation, Estimation and Testing," *Econometrica*, 55, 251–76.

Engle, R.F. and V.K. Ng (1993), "Measuring and Testing the Impact of News on Volatility," *Journal of Finance*, 48, 1749–78.

Evans, G.W. (1991), "Pitfalls in Testing for Explosive Bubbles in Asset Prices," *American Economic Review*, 81, 922–30.

Fama, E.F. (1965), "The Behavior of Stock Market Prices," *Journal of Business*, 38, 34–105.

Fama, E.F. (1970), "Efficient Capital Markets: A Review of Theory and Empirical Work," *Journal of Finance*, 25, 383–417.

Fama, E.F. (1991), "Efficient Capital Markets: II," *Journal of Finance*, 46, 1575–617.

Fama, E.F. and K.R. French (1988a), "Permanent and Temporary Components of Stock Prices," *Journal of Political Economy*, 96, 246–73.

Fama, E.F. and K.R. French (1988b), "Dividend Yields and Expected Stock Returns," *Journal of Financial Economics*, 22, 3–25.

Fama, E.F. and K.R. French (1992), "The Cross-Section of Expected Stock Returns," *Journal of Finance*, 47, 427–65.

Ferson, W.E. (1995), "Theory and Empirical Testing of Asset Pricing Models," in R.A. Jarrow, W.T. Ziemba and V. Maksimovic (eds), *The Handbook of Finance*, North-Holland, Amsterdam, forthcoming.

Flavin, M. (1983), "Excess Volatility in Financial Markets: A Reassessment of the Empirical Evidence," *Journal of Political Economy*, 91, 929–56.

Flood, R.P. and R.J. Hodrick (1986), "Asset Price Volatility, Bubbles, and Process Switching," *Journal of Finance*, 41, 831–42.

Flood, R.P. and R.J. Hodrick (1990), "On Testing for Speculative Indeterminacies in Models with Rational Expectations," *Journal of Economic Perspective*, 4, 85–101.

Froot, K.A. and M. Obstfeld (1991), "Intrinsic Bubbles: The Case of Stock Prices," *American Economic Review*, 81, 1189–214.

Fuller, W.A. (1976), *Introduction to Statistical Time Series*, New York: John Wiley and Sons.

Gallant, A.R., P.E. Rossi and G. Tauchen (1992), "Stock Prices and Volume," *Review of Financial Studies*, 5, 199–242.

Gallant, A.R. and G. Tauchen (1989), "Seminonparametric Estimation of Conditionally Constrained Heterogeneous Processes: Asset Pricing Applications," *Econometrica*, 57, 1091–120.

Goetzmann, W.N. and P. Jorion (1992), "Testing the Predictive Power of Dividend Yields," manuscript, Graduate School of Business, Columbia University.

Gilles, C. and S.F. LeRoy (1991), "Econometric Aspects of the Variance-Bounds Tests: A Survey," *Review of Financial Studies*, 4, 753–91.

Glosten, L.R., R. Jagannathan and D. Runkle (1993), "On the Relation between the Expected Value and the Volatility of the Nominal Excess Return on Stocks," *Journal of Finance*, 48, 1779–1801.

Gordon, M.J. (1962), *The Investment, Financing and Valuation of the Corporation*, Irwin, Homewood, IL.

Granger, C.W.J. and P. Newbold (1974), "Spurious Regressions in Econometrics," *Journal of Econometrics*, 2, 111–20.

Hansen, L.P. (1982), "Large Sample Properties of Generalized Method of Moments Estimators," *Econometrica*, 50, 1029–54.

Hansen, L.P. and R.J. Hodrick (1980), "Forward Rates as Optimal Predictors of Future Spot Rates: An Econometric Analysis," *Journal of Political Economy*, 88, 829–53.

Hansen, L.P. and R. Jagannathan (1991), "Implications of Security Market Date for Models of Dynamic Economies," *Journal of Political Economy*, 99, 225–62.

Hansen, L.P. and T.J. Sargent (1980), "Formulating and Estimating Dynamic Linear Rational Expectations Models," *Journal of Economic Dynamics and Control*, 2, 7–46.

Hansen, L.P. and T.J. Sargent (1981), "Linear Rational Expectations Models for Dynamically Interrelated Variables," chapter 8 in R.E. Lucas and T.J. Sargent (eds), *Rational Expectations and Econometric Practice*, University of Minnesota Press, Minneapolis.

Hansen, L.P. and K.J. Singleton (1982), "Generalized Instrumental Variables Estimation in Nonlinear Rational Expectations Models," *Econometrica*, 50, 1269–86.

Hansen, L.P. and K.J. Singleton (1983), "Stochastic Consumption, Risk Aversion, and the Temporal Behavior of Asset Returns," *Journal of Political Economy*, 91, 249–65.

Hodrick, R.J. (1989), "Risk, Uncertainty and Exchange Rates," *Journal of Monetary Economics*, 23, 433–59.

Hodrick, R.J. (1992), "Dividend Yields and Expected Stock Returns: Alternative Procedures for Inference and Measurement," *Review of Financial Studies*, 5, 357–86.

Jarque, C.M. and A.K. Bera (1980), "Efficient Tests for Normality, Homoskedasticity and Serial Independence of Regression Residuals," *Economics Letters*, 6, 255–9.

Jegadeesh, N. (1990), "Evidence of Predictable Behavior of Security Returns," *Journal of Finance*, 45, 881–98.

Johansen, S. (1988), "Statistical Analysis of Cointegration Vectors," *Journal of Economic Dynamics and Control*, 12, 231–54.

Johansen, S. (1991), "Estimation and Hypothesis Testing of Cointegration Vectors in Gaussian Vector Autoregressive Models," *Econometrica*, 59, 1551–80.

Kim, M.J., C.R. Nelson and R. Startz (1991), "Mean Reversion in Stock Prices? A Reappraisal of the Empirical Evidence," *Review of Economic Studies*, 58, 515–28.

Kleidon, A.W. (1986a), "Variance Bounds Tests and Stock Price Valuation Models," *Journal of Political Economy*, 94, 953–1001.

Kleidon, A.W. (1986b), "Bias in Small Sample Tests of Stock Price Rationality," *Journal of Business*, 59, no. 2, part 1, 237–62.

LeRoy, S.F. (1973), "Risk Aversion and the Martingale Property of Stock Prices," *International Economic Review*, 14, 436–46.

LeRoy, S.F. and W.R. Parke (1992), "Stock Price Volatility: Tests Based on the Geometric Random Walk," *American Economic Review*, 82, 981–92.

LeRoy, S.F. and R.D. Porter (1981), "The Present-Value Relation: Tests Based on Implied Variance Bounds," *Econometrica*, 49, 555–74.

Ljung, G.M. and G.E.P. Box (1978), "On a Measure of Lack of Fit in Time Series Models," *Biometrika*, 65, 297–303.

Lo, A.W. and A.C. MacKinlay (1988), "Stock Market Prices Do Not Follow Random Walks: Evidence from a Simple Specification Test," *Review of Financial Studies*, 1, 41–66.

Lucas, R.E. (1978), "Asset Prices in an Exchange Economy," *Econometrica*, 46, 1429–45.

Mandelbrot, B. (1963), "The Variation of Certain Speculative Prices," *Journal of Business*, 36, 394–419.

Mankiw, N.G., D. Romer and M.D. Shapiro (1991), "Stock Market Forecastability and Volatility: A Statistical Appraisal," *Review of Economic Studies*, 58, 455–77.

Marsh, T.A. and R.C. Merton (1986), "Dividend Variability and Variance Bounds Tests for the Rationality of Stock Market Prices," *American Economic Review*, 76, 483–503.

Mattey, J. and R. Meese (1986), "Empirical Assessment of Present Value Relations," *Econometric Reviews*, 5, 171–233.

Merton, R.C. (1973), "An Intertemporal Capital Asset Pricing Model," *Econometrica*, 41, 867–87.

Nelson, C. and M.J. Kim (1993), "Predictable Stock Returns: The Role of Small Sample Bias," *Journal of Finance*, 48, 641–61.

Nelson, D.B. (1991), "Conditional Heteroskedasticity in Asset Returns: A New Approach," *Econometrica*, 59, 347–70.

Nelson, D.B. (1992), "Filtering and Forecasting with Misspecified ARCH Models I: Getting the Right Variance with the Wrong Model," *Journal of Econometrics*, 52, 61–90.

Nelson, D.B. and D.P. Foster (1994), "Asymptotic Filtering Theory for Univariate ARCH Models," *Econometrica*, 62, 1–41.

Newey, W.K. and K.D. West (1987), "A Simple Positive Semi-Definite Heteroskedasticity and Autocorrelation Consistent Covariance Matrix," *Econometrica*, 55, 703–8.

Newey, W.K. and K.D. West (1994), "Automatic Lag Selection in Covariance Matrix Estimation," *Review of Economic Studies*, 61, 631–53.

Pesaran, M.H. (1991), "On the Volatility and Efficiency of Stock Prices," *Cuadernos Economicos de ICE*, 49.

Pesaran, M.H. and S.M. Potter (1991), "Equilibrium Asset Pricing Models and Predictability of Excess Returns: Theory and Evidence," manuscript, Department of Applied Economics, University of Cambridge.

Phillips, P.C.B. (1987), "Time Series Regression with Unit Roots," *Econometrica*, 55, 277–302.

Phillips, P.C.B. and S. Ouliaris (1990), "Asymptotic Properties of Residual Based Tests for Cointegration," *Econometrica*, 58, 165–93.

Poterba, J. and L.H. Summers (1988), "Mean Reversion in Stock Prices: Evidence and Implications," *Journal of Financial Economics*, 22, 27–59.

Richardson, M. (1993), "Temporary Components of Stock Prices: A Skeptic's View," *Journal of Business and Economic Statistics*, 11, 199–207.

Richardson, M. and T. Smith (1991), "Test of Financial Models in the Presence of Overlapping Observations," *Review of Financial Studies*, 4, 227–54.

Richardson, M. and J.H. Stock (1989), "Drawing Inferences from Statistics Based on Multi-Year Asset Returns," *Journal of Financial Economics*, 25, 323–48.

Scott, L.O. (1985), "The Present Value Model of Stock Prices: Regression Tests and Monte Carlo Results," *Review of Economics and Statistics*, 67, 599–605.

Shiller, R.J. (1979), "The Volatility of Long-Term Interest Rates and Expectations Models of the Term Structure," *Journal of Political Economy*, 87, 1190–1219.

Shiller, R.J. (1981a), "Do Stock Prices Move Too Much to be Justified by Subsequent Changes in Dividends?," *American Economic Review*, 71, 421–36.

Shiller, R.J. (1981b), "The Use of Volatility Measures in Assessing Market Efficiency," *Journal of Finance*, 36, 291–304.

Shiller, R.J. (1984), "Stock Prices and Social Dynamics," *Brookings Papers on Economic Activity*, 2, 457–510.

Stock, J.H. and M. Watson (1993), "A Simple Estimator of Cointegrating Vectors in Higher Order Integrated Systems," *Econometrica*, 61, 783–820.

Summers, L.H. (1986), "Does the Stock Market Rationally Reflect Fundamental Values?," *Journal of Finance*, 41, 591–601.

Weiss, A.A. (1986), "Asymptotic Theory for ARCH Models: Estimation and Testing," *Econometric Theory*, 2, 107–31.

West, K.D. (1987a), "A Note on the Power of Least Squares Tests for a Unit Root," *Economics Letters*, 24, 249–52.

West, K.D. (1987b), "A Specification Test for Speculative Bubbles," *Quarterly Journal of Economics*, 102, 553–80.

West, K.D. (1988), "Bubbles, Fads and Stock Price Volatility Tests: A Partial Evaluation," *Journal of Finance*, 43, 639–56.

White, H. (1980), "A Heteroskedasticity Consistent Covariance Matrix Estimator and a Direct Test for Heteroskedasticity," *Econometrica*, 48, 817–38.

INDEX